INSIDE

3D STUDIO

MAX

VOLUME III:
ANIMATION

GEORGE MAESTRI
SANFORD KENNEDY
RALPH FRANTZ
STEVE BURKE
JASON GREENE
ERIC GREENLEIF
JEREMY HUBBELL
PAUL KAKERT
RANDY KREITZMAN
BOB LAMB
DAN O'LEARY
ANDREW VERNON
AND ADAM SILVERTHORNE

COVER ART BY RAYMOND BINTZ

New Riders

New Riders Publishing, Indianapolis, Indiana

Contributions from , a Division of Autodesk

Inside 3D Studio MAX Volume III: Animation

By George Maestri, Sanford Kennedy, Ralph Frantz, Steve Burke, Jason Greene, Eric Greenleif, Jeremy Hubbell, Paul Kakert, Randy Kreitzman, Bob Lamb, Dan O'Leary, Andrew Vernon, and Adam Silverthorne

Published by:
New Riders Publishing
201 West 103rd Street
Indianapolis, IN 46290 USA

Printed in the United States of America 2 3 4 5 6 7 8 9 0

Library of Congress Cataloging-in-Publication Data
Inside 3D Studio MAX / Steve D. Elliott … [et al.].
    p.   cm.
    Includes index.
    ISBN 1-56205-699-9 (v. 3)
    1. Computer animation. 2. 3D Studio.
    1960-
    TR897.7.I56   1997   96-38753
    006.6-dc20   CIP

Warning and Disclaimer

PUBLISHER	Don Fowley
ASSOCIATE PUBLISHER	David Dwyer
MARKETING MANAGER	Mary Foote
MANAGING EDITOR	Carla Hall
DIRECTOR OF DEVELOPMENT	Kezia Endsley

PRODUCT DIRECTOR
Alicia Buckley

DEVELOPMENT EDITOR
Laura Frey

ACQUISITIONS EDITOR
Dustin Sullivan

SENIOR EDITORS
Sarah Kearns
Suzanne Snyder

SERIES EDITOR
Phillip Miller

PROJECT EDITOR
Cliff Shubs

COPY EDITORS
Keith Cline, Gina Brown, Wendy Garrison, Cricket Harrison, and Michelle Warren

TECHNICAL EDITORS
Mark Gerhard, Larry Minton

SOFTWARE SPECIALIST
Steve Flatt

ASSISTANT MARKETING MANAGER
Gretchen Schlesinger

ACQUISITIONS COORDINATOR
Stacey Beheler

ADMINISTRATIVE COORDINATOR
Karen Opal

MANUFACTURING COORDINATOR
Brook Farling

COVER DESIGNER
Karen Ruggles

COVER PRODUCTION
Aren Howell

BOOK DESIGNER
Anne Jones

DIRECTOR OF PRODUCTION
Larry Klein

PRODUCTION TEAM SUPERVISORS
Laurie Casey, Joe Millay

GRAPHICS IMAGE SPECIALISTS
Kevin Cliburn, Sadie Crawford, Wil Cruz, Tammy Graham

PRODUCTION ANALYSTS
Dan Harris, Erich J. Richter

PRODUCTION TEAM
Kim Cofer, Tricia Flodder, Laure Robinson, Elizabeth San Miguel, Scott Tullis

INDEXER
Chris Barrick

About the Authors

George Maestri is a Los Angeles-based writer and animator with experience in both traditional and computer animation. He has written for a number of animated shows, including the Cable Ace-nominated series, *Rocko's Modern Life*. George has developed original shows for several major networks and studios, including Nickelodeon, Fox, ABC, MGM, Film Roman, and Carlton UK. He has also written numerous articles about computer animation for magazines such as *Digital Video*, *Computer Graphics World*, *Publish*, *New Media*, and *Animation Magazine*.

Sanford Kennedy left a career as a Design Engineer working on guided missiles and communication satellites in the aerospace industry to work in special effects after he saw *Star Wars*. He met Special Effects Director John Dykstra, winner of the Academy Award for the visual effects on *Star Wars* and was hired to design and build computer motion-controlled camera systems. He later established Sanford Kennedy Design in Los Angeles and over the next 20 years expanded into movie props, special makeup effects, and mechanical effects for commercials. He has worked on 48 motion pictures, ranging from *The Empire Strikes Back* to *Batman* and *Starship Troopers*. He began writing about computer graphics in 1988, and when 3D Studio came out, he added computer

animation to his activities. He now works full-time as an animator, writer, multimedia content producer, and beta tester. Sanford has three Bachelor's degrees in the fields of Fine Art, History, and Industrial Technology. Recently, he taught 3D Studio classes at the American Film Institute in Hollywood.

Ralph Frantz is a successful freelance animator working out of Southern California. He keeps busy by working on a wide variety of 3D animation projects, including work on the film *Virtuosity*, as well as work for broadcast network television and local TV commercials. He has worked on game projects, commercial 3D screen savers, industrial videos, corporate presentations, and technical animation for a CD-ROM–based training program for Nissan sales and service personnel. He spent Siggraph 96 in the Kinetix plug-in partners booth giving demos of the softbody dynamics system plug-in HyperMatter by Second Nature Industries. He helps out with MAX demos at the local 3D users groups and is often called upon to supplement in-house animators at the local animation houses.

Danny J. O'Leary is vice president of n-Space, Incorporated, of Orlando, FL, where he helps oversee product and concept development. He co-founded n-Space in November 1994 as a premiere developer of games for advanced console and PC platforms. Danny was a beta tester for 3D Studio MAX and remains and active member in

CompuServe's Kinetix forum. He holds a Bachelor's degree in Mechanical Engineering from Auburn University.

Adam Silverthorne studied Electronic Visualization in the Department of Architecture at UC Berkeley. His education included 2D Drafting CAD/CAM, 3D Modeling, and Lighting Techniques. Adam has also studied traditional animation and sculpting, and he holds a degree in Twentieth Century Literature, with a focus on Narrative Fiction. Currently, Adam works in television, where he helps coordinate the production of an animated children's show. Adam also created and maintains the San Francisco 3D Studio MAX User's Group Web Page, and helps coordinate monthly meetings.

Larry Minton is the owner of Avguard Animations near Columbus, OH. He has been a 3D Studio hobbiest since 1991, but recently decided to turn his hobby into his career. Larry was a 3D Studio MAX beta tester, as well as the technical editor of New Riders' *3D Studio MAX Fundamentals*. Larry is an active participant in CompuServe's Kinetix and AMMEDIA forums.

Jeremey Hubbell is a senior technical instructor for Kinetix. His primary responsibilities range from developing multimedia course curriculum to worldwide training and product development. His current project is the development of all training for 3D Studio MAX and the implementation of that training within the U.S., Canada, and Latin America. Since joining Autodesk in 1994, Jeremy has been involved in many projects—from the complete reengineering of Kinetix training materials and curriculum to the development and publishing of all Autodesk training materials on an interactive CD.

Eric Greenlief is co-owner of Image Production Company, of Salt Lake City, Utah, which specializes in architectural walkthroughs and product presentations using 3D Studio and 3D Studio MAX. Eric teaches and develops curriculum for Computer-Aided Industrial Design at ITT Technical Institute in Murray, UT. Other courses he has taught since 1992 include AutoCAD Modeling and AutoCAD Customization. He has a degree in CAD and a Bachelor's degree in Industrial Design. Eric has been using 3D Studio since version 1 and is an active participant in the 3D Studio mailing list on the Internet. He also has close ties with the film industry in Salt Lake City and Los Angeles.

Randy Kreitzman is employed with Kinetix as a Quality Engineering Analyst, working exclusively with 3D Studio MAX. He has been animating since 1991, starting out with 3DSr1, working his way through Alias/Wavefront, and finally coming back to Kinetix to work with MAX. Randy lives in Northern California's Sonoma County with his loving partner, three sled dogs, and two horses. He wishes to thank Kimberlie and the girls for their never-ending inspiration and support, and the Yost Group for making some of the best software on the planet.

Paul Kakert is founder and president of Forensic Media, an Iowa-based corporation that specializes in producing animations for use in the courtroom. He has used 3D Studio since Release 1 and has published articles regarding the use of 3D Studio, MAX, and numerous plug-ins for *3D Artist* magazine. He has developed state bar-accredited seminars on forensic animation for attorneys, investigators, and reconstructionists. His animations have been used by attorneys throughout the U.S. and featured in TV specials and training videos for accident investigators and animators. He may be reached at (319) 391-8289 or by e-mail at pk@forensicmedia.com.

Steve Burke is a graduate of the Business Entrepreneurship program at the University of Southern California. In addition to running his own art company, Steve has worked as an artist in the game industry for six years. He currently is the Art Director at Strategic Simulations, Incorporated, makers of some of the best strategy, fantasy, and war games on the planet. Steve also has a beautiful wife, a baby girl, a wacky brother, and a passion for creating happy, friendly artwork with a smattering of sarcasm.

Andrew Vernon is an animator specializing in Character Studio. He operates Moving Figure Animation & Multimedia of San Rafeal, CA. For more information about Moving Figure, visit their web site at www.movingfigure.com.

Bob Lamm is a manager at the CYNC Corporation, a video/multimedia equipment dealership that also sells Kinetix products. He graduated from MIT in 1978 and spent most of his career in facility design. He can be reached at (617) 277-4317 and lamm@cync.com.

Trademark Acknowledgments

Contents at a Glance

Introduction   1

Part I: Animation—State of the Art   7

   Chapter 1: Computer Animation Industry Overview 9

   Chapter 2: Using 3D Studio MAX in Production 45

Part II: Animation Techniques   65

   Chapter 3: Advanced Transformation Animation 67

   Chapter 4: Animating with Controllers 107

   Chapter 5: Animating with Expressions 149

   Chapter 6: Animating with Multiple Modifiers 175

   Chapter 7: Animating Accuracy for Forensics 207

Part III: Character Animation   251

   Chapter 8: Setting Up Characters for Animation 253

   Chapter 9: Animating Walking 289

   Chapter 10: Animating with Biped 329

   Chapter 11: Mesh Deformation 373

   Chapter 12: Animating with Physique 407

   Chapter 13: Facial Animation and Lip Sync 435

Part IV: Animating the Environment   471

    Chapter 14:   **Animating Cameras**   473

    Chapter 15:   **Animating Lights and Atmospheres**   519

    Chapter 16:   **Particles, Space Warps, and Physics**   565

    Chapter 17:   **HyperMatter**   617

Part V: Video Post   663

    Chapter 18:   **Compositing and Editing**   665

    Chapter 19:   **Video Post Effects**   699

    Chapter 20:   **Sound in MAX**   741

    Appendix A: **Marketing Your Animations—**
                  Ins and Outs of the Business   CD

    Appendix B: **Rendering Animation**   CD

                  Index   767

Table of Contents

Introduction   **1**

Organization of the Book   2

How to Read the Exercises   3

Exercises and the CD-ROM   4

Using the *Inside 3D Studio MAX Volume III* CD-ROM   4

Installing the Exercise Files   4

Registering Shareware   5

Using CompuServe and the Web   5

New Riders Publishing   6

Part I   Animation—State of the Art   **7**

1   Computer Animation Industry Overview   **9**

The State of the Art in 3D Animation   10

The Genesis of 3D Studio MAX   12

Building the Team   13

Creating the "Virtual" Yost Group   16

MAX Meets the Public   17

MAX in the Future   19

How 3D Studio MAX Is Being Used   19

3D Studio History at Sony Pictures Imageworks   20

3D Studio Has Strength in Computer Games   23

DreamWorks Interactive   24

Westwood Studios   27

SoftImage and 3D Studio MAX: Respectful Competitors   28

An Interview with SoftImage's David Morin   29

3D Studio MAX in Visual Effects   33

Blur Studio   33

Digital Phenomena   36

A Wide Variety of Media for MAX   38

Pyros Pictures   39

Evolution of MAX in 3D Animation   42

Summary   42

2   Using 3D Studio MAX in Production   **45**

Computer Graphics Production Studio   46

MAX in the Working Environment   49

Finding Your Strengths   52

Importance of Specialization   52

Concept to Delivery   53
   Estimating Time of Completion   *54*
   Deadlines Written in Stone   *57*
Working with Producers   58
   Dealing with Client's Source Materials   *58*
   Visualizing the Flow of Work   *60*
   Learning to See Through the Camera   *61*
Networking Windows NT and Unix   61
MAX in Production with Other Software   61
   File Translation Programs   *62*
   MAX with Matador and Flame   *62*
   MAX and SoftImage   *63*
   MAX and Alias   *63*
   MAX and Wavefront   *63*
   Working with a Service Bureau   *64*
In Practice: Using 3D Studio MAX in Production   64

Part II   Animation Techniques   65

3   Advanced Transformation Animation   67
Using Combinations of Basic Tools   68
   The R.E.A. Exterminators Script   *69*
Transform Animation with Out-of-Range Type Curves   70
Using Helper Objects to Link Complex Objects   74
Using Grouped Objects to Create Complex Animations   79
   Using the Transform Type-In   *80*
   Animating Rocky's Legs for the Run Cycle   *83*
Use Nested Groups of Objects to Create
  Complex Animations   86
   Transforming Groups by Using Offset Dummies   *87*
Using XForm and Linked XForm Modifiers   91
   Distorting Objects with XForm   *91*
   Use XForm to Animate Portions of Objects   *94*
   Use Linked XForm to Modify a Lofted Object   *96*
Perform Pick Transformations Along Surfaces   98
   Using Tape Measure Objects as a Motion Axis   *99*
   Using Grid Objects as Transform Paths   *101*
Animating Multiple Object Instances   102
   Transforming Lights   *103*
   Finishing the R.E.A. Exterminators Animation   *103*
In Practice: Advanced Transformation Animation   104

4 Animating with Controllers   **107**
   Project: WWII Air Combat   108
   Animating with Path Controllers   110
      Background Cloud Motion   *110*
      Fighter Attack   *112*
      Relative Velocities   *114*
   Animating with Euler XYZ Rotation Controllers   115
      Bomber Wobble   *116*
   Animating with the Look-At Controller   119
      Tracking Turrets   *119*
   Animating with Noise and List Controllers   122
      Gunfire Effects   *122*
   Expression Controllers   126
      Project: Making Crepes   *126*
      Controlling the Crepe's Roll with the
         Bend(Main) Modifier   *127*
      Using Expressions to Control the Angle and
         Upper Limit Values   *130*
      Controlling the Crepe's Outer Radius   *138*
      Controlling the Filling's Transforms with
         the Crepe's Bend Modifiers   *140*
   In Practice: Animating with Controllers   147

5 Animating with Expressions   **149**
   Expression Controllers Overview   150
   Transform Animation with Expression Controllers   151
      Tornado Project   *151*
   Control Objects and Modifier Animation   163
      The Whirlygig Project   *164*
   In Practice: Animating with Expressions   173

6 Animating with Multiple Modifiers   **175**
   Animating Object Modifier Parameters   176
      Air Pump Project   *176*
      Magnetic Boots Project   *191*
   In Practice: Modifier Animation   205

7 Animating Accuracy for Forensics   **207**
   Forensic Animation Industry Overview   208
      Accuracy—Make It Obvious in Your Animation   *209*
      Animation Proves Nothing   *211*

Accurate Timing 212

Advanced Character Studio Motion 219

Details 230

Human Models 231

Vehicle Models 232

Skid Marks, Tracks, and Trails 232

In Practice: Animating Accuracy for Forensics 249

Part III Character Animation 251

8 Setting Up Characters for Animation 253

Types of Characters 254

Object Level Animation—Segmented Characters 254

Solid Mesh Characters 256

Metaball Characters 260

Hybrid Characters 261

Creating Skeletons that Deform Meshes 262

MAX Bones 263

Boxes as Bones 265

Building a Skeleton from Scratch 266

Creating Bones 266

Creating a Skeleton 268

Methods for Linking the Bones Together 272

Setting Up and Controlling IK 275

Skeletons for Hands 282

Construction of the Skeleton 282

Attaching a Hand to the Arm 283

Using Reference Objects to Animate a Hand 284

In Practice: Setting Up Characters for Animation 285

9 Animating Walking 289

The Mechanics of Walking 290

The Feet and Legs 290

The Hips, Spine, and Shoulders 294

The Arms 295

The Head 295

Body Posture and Emotion 295

Walk Cycles 297

Animating a Walk   298
   An Animated Walk Cycle   298
   Animating the Legs   302
   Animating the Arms   306
Moving the Cycled Character   307
   Calculating the Stride Length   308
   Duplicating the Cycle in Track View   308
   Moving the Ground to Match   309
Creating Four-Legged Walks   310
   Creating a Quadruped Skeleton   312
   Analysis of a Four-Legged Walk   313
   Animating a Four-Legged Walk Cycle   315
Animating Six-Legged Walks   316
   Body   317
   The Legs   318
   Using Expressions to Automate an Insect Walk 321
In Practice: Animating Walking   325

10 Animating with Biped   **329**
Creating a Biped   330
Manipulating a Biped   332
   Other Biped Selection and Manipulation Tools 334
Animating a Biped   336
   Animating with Footsteps   336
   Dynamics of Motion   344
   Bipeds in Track View   348
   Directly Animating a Biped   355
   Free-Form Animation   359
   Attaching the Hands and Feet to MAX Objects 362
   Saving and Loading Canned Motions   368
In Practice: Biped   371

11 Mesh Deformation   **373**
Getting Meshes to Behave   374
   Patches over Polygons   374
   Arms Outstretched   375
   Extra Detail at the Bends   376
Fitting a Skeleton to a Mesh   377
   The Elbow and Knee Areas   378
   The Hip and Pelvis Area   378
   The Shoulder Areas   378

Basic Mesh Deformation   380
    Deforming a Cylinder with Linked XForms   380
    Deforming a Cylinder with Bones Pro   383
    Deforming a Cylinder with Physique   385
    Differences Between Bones Pro and Physique   386
Deformations Using FFD Lattices   386
    Creating a Bulging Muscle by Using FFDs   387
Bones Pro   388
    Bones Pro Rollout   388
    Influence Editor   390
    Deforming a Body with Bones Pro   392
MetaReyes   396
    Metaball Concepts   396
    Using MetaReyes   398
In Practice: Mesh Deformation   404

12 Animating with Physique   **407**
Using Physique   408
    Hierarchies and Physique   409
    Creating Realistic Bulges   410
    The Cross Section Editor   411
    Physique Link Parameters   413
    Physique Joint Intersections   416
Physique and Biped   416
    Fitting a Biped to a Mesh   417
    Applying Physique to a Biped   419
    Refining How Physique Affects the Mesh   420
    Vertex Control   420
Tendons   426
    How Tendons Work   428
    Creating Tendons   429
    Modifying Tendons   430
In Practice: Physique   433

13 Facial Animation and Lip Sync   **435**
Anatomy of the Face   436
    How Muscles Move the Face   437
    Modeling and Setting Up Faces for Animation   438
Surface Tools   438
    Modeling a Simple Face with Surface Tools   438
    Setting Up a Surface Tools Face for Animation 442

Morphing   445
    Single Target Morphing   445
    Modeling Morph Targets   446
Multiple Target Morphing   447
    Morph Magic Interface   448
    Weighted Channel Morphing   449
Setting Up a Face with Bones   449
Setting Up Eyes and Other Facial Features   452
    Internal Eyes   453
    External Eyes   454
    Cartoon Eyes   455
    Eyebrows   457
    Tongues   458
Animation and Lip Sync   458
    Creating a Library of Poses   458
The Eight Basic Mouth Positions   460
Loading Sound into MAX   463
Using an Audio Controller for Automatic Lip Sync   464
Using a Third-Party Sound Editor   466
Reading the Track   467
In Practice: Facial Animation and Lip Sync   470

Part IV   Animating the Environment   471

14   Animating Cameras   473
Traditional Film Cameras   474
    Field of View   476
    Transitions   479
    Camera Angle   480
    Camera Moves   481
    Zoom Lenses   485
The "Vertigo" Effect   485
Architectural Walkthrough   487
    Creating the Establishing Shot   489
    Exterior Detail Shot   492
    Creating the Interior Shot   494
    Closing Shot   499

Previews   500
Camera Animation for Characters   501
   Preview and Video Post   *508*
"MTV" Camera Style   509
Shaky Cam   509
Earthquake Cam   510
Depth of Field   513
In Practice: Animating Cameras   517

15 Animating Lights and Atmospheres   519
Using Candlelight to Create Ambience   520
   Examining the Lighting   *521*
   Creating the Flame Material   *529*
   Animating the Scene   *535*
Using Moonlight for Effect   544
   Realistic Moonlight   *544*
   Casting the Tree Shadow   *548*
Creating a Lightning Storm Effect   552
   Examining the Basic Lightning Effect   *552*
Animating Volumetric Light   555
In Practice: Animating Lights and Atmospheres   561

16 Particles, Space Warps, and Physics   565
Particles and Their Space Warps   566
   The Snow Particle System with
     Deflector Space Warp   *567*
   All Purpose Particles Plug-In   *573*
   Sand Blaster Particle Plug-In   *578*
   Spray Particle System with Wind Space Warps   *582*
   Spray with Deflector and Gravity Space Warps *589*
Object Space Warps   596
   The Displace Space Warp   *597*
   Path Deform Space Warp   *605*
   The Bomb Space Warp   *610*
In Practice: Particles, Space Warps, and Physics   615

17 HyperMatter   617
Doing Its Own Thing   618
   Processing and Time Stepping   *620*
   Substances   *620*

Rigid Objects, Dynamics, and One-Way Collisions   621
   Using the HyperMatter Velocity Constraint   *626*
Fully Deformable Collision Detection
   Between Two Objects   631
   Examine the Fix Constraint   *633*
Inheriting the Keyframed Momentum   636
Sub-Object Solidification of a HyperMatter
   Control Object   643
Animating Substance Parameters and the
   Follow Constraint   651
In Practice: HyperMatter   661

Part V   Video Post   663

18   Compositing and Editing   665

Compositing Basics   666
   System Performance   *666*
   Modular Design Approach   *667*
Using the Alpha Compositor   668
   Image Setup Parameters   *669*
   The Virtual Frame Buffer Window   *670*
   The G-Buffer   *671*
   The Image File List   *672*
   Multi-Layer Compositing   *677*
Understanding Shadows and Compositing   679
   Screen Mapping and Compositing   *679*
   Camera Mapping   *683*
   Shadow/Matte and Matte/Shadow   *684*
Masking   687
Bluescreening   689
Other Methods of Compositing   692
   Pseudo Alpha   *693*
   Simple Additive Composite   *693*
Editing Your Animations   694
   Video Post Event Transitions   *694*
   Video Post Masking Transitions   *696*
In Practice: Compositing and Editing   697

19   Video Post Effects   **699**

Glows   700
   Glow (Frame Only)   *701*
   Animated Glow   *704*
   Waveform Controller   *705*
   Super Glow   *707*
   Real Lens Glow   *708*
   LensFX Glow   *709*
   Glow Tips   *709*
Lens Flares   713
   RealLensFlare (RLF)   *714*
   LensFX MAX   *718*
Blurs   721
   Blur (Frame Only)   *722*
   Fields Of Depth   *723*
   RealLensFlare: Distance Blur   *726*
   LensFX Focus   *727*
Adobe Photoshop Plug-In Filters   727
Fractal Flow MAX   731
Miscellaneous Effect Plug-Ins   734
   Negative   *734*
   Outline   *735*
   Stamper   *735*
   Starfield Generator   *736*
In Practice: Video Post Effects   738

20   Sound in MAX   **741**

The Basics   742
   Digitizing   *742*
   Sampling Rates   *743*
   Bit Depth   *744*
PC Sound Technologies   745
   MIDI   *745*
   FM Sound Chips   *746*
   Wavetable Synthesis   *746*
   Digital Signal Processing (DSP) and 3D Sound   *747*
Speakers   747
   Traditional Desktop Speakers   *748*
   Other Speaker Types   *751*

Windows NT and Sound   752
   Volume Control   753
   The Windows NT Mixer   753
Animating to Recorded Sounds   755
   Using WAV Files in Track View   755
   Using the Metronome   757
The Audio Controller Plug-In   758
   Setting Up the Audio Controller   758
   Audio Controller Parameters   759
   Making an Alarm Clock Ring with Audio Controller 762
In Practice: Sound   766

Index   **767**

Introduction

Inside 3D Studio MAX, Volume III: Animation *is the third book in a three-volume set. Due to the robust nature of 3DS MAX, New Riders is dedicated to bringing users detailed, top-quality information on all the features and functions of the software.* Inside 3D Studio MAX, Volume III *is a complete tutorial and reference on animation. It includes coverage of the many different animation techniques used in the industry, from animating with transforms to character animation to animating the environment. Also included is expert coverage of MAX's powerful Video Post module. Learn how to use the Video Post module for compositing and editing animations as well as for creating special effects.*

The previous volume in the *Inside 3D Studio MAX* set is *Volume II: Advanced Modeling and Materials*. Like this book, it is presented in the *Inside* style, packed full of detailed tutorials, and valuable tips and techniques from industry experts. Look for *Inside 3D Studio MAX, Volume II: Advanced Modeling and Materials* in your bookstore.

Organization of the Book

Inside 3D Studio MAX, Volume III: Animation is organized around six sections. These sections are as follows:

- Part I, "Animation—State of the Art," Chapters 1 and 2
- Part II, "Animation Techniques," Chapters 3 through 7
- Part III, "Character Animation," Chapters 8 through 13
- Part IV, "Animating the Environment," Chapters 14 through 17
- Part V, "Video Post," Chapters 18 through 20
- Bonus CD chapters!

Part I is an overview of the computer animation industry. Learn the story behind the creation of MAX. Hear what major production houses have to say about MAX's power. Also learn how you can more effectively use MAX in your own productions.

Part II covers animation techniques in MAX. The tools are not explained, rather the techniques that are best served by MAX's tools and plug-ins are described. Animation tutorials take you through the steps needed to animate with transforms, controllers, expressions, and multiple modifiers. Also covered is accurate animation for forensics.

Part III takes you through the unique world of character animation. From creating a character to animating it with MAX tools and plug-ins, this section teaches the best methods of animating for a variety of situations.

Part IV explores animating the environment. These chapters cover how to animate cameras, lights, and atmospheres to get just the feel your are looking for in your animations. Also covered is how to animate with particles and space warps to generate snow, confetti, a windtunnel effect and more. The expert advice doesn't stop there, however; HyperMatter is also covered in this section.

Part V covers the powerful Video Post module within MAX. This section extends your knowledge of Video Post by teaching you how to create special effects and how to compose and edit your animations within Video Post.

The bonus CD chapters include information on how to market yourself and your animations. It tells the secrets of how to network, create a demo reel, and get your animations noticed! The bonus CD chapters also provide animation rendering information.

How to Read the Exercises

Unlike most tutorials that you read, the *Inside 3DS MAX* exercises do not rigidly dictate every step you perform to achieve the desired result. These exercises are designed to be flexible and to work with a wide range of situations. The benefits you receive from this approach include:

- A better understanding of the concepts because you must think through the example rather than blindly follow the minutiae of many steps

- A stronger ability to apply the examples to your own work

Most exercises begin with some explanatory text as shown in the following sample exercise. The text tells you what the exercise should accomplish and sets the context for the exercise.

SAMPLE EXERCISE FORMAT

You may encounter text such as this at the beginning of or in the middle of an exercise when one or more actions require an extended explanation.

1. Numbered steps identify your actions to complete the excercise.

   Indented text adds extra explanation about the previous step when it is needed.

The word *choose* in an example always indicates a menu selection. If the selection involves a pull-down menu, you will be told explicitly where to find the menu item. If the selection is from another part of the user interface, you will be told which component to click and the location of the interface. Setting the Hemisphere option for a Sphere object, for example, requires clicking the Hemisphere check box in the Creation Parameters rollout (you would have been told previously whether you were accessing the rollout from the Create panel or the Modify panel). The word *select* always refers to selecting one or more objects, elements, faces, or vertices. Select never refers to menus or other user interface components.

Because this book is designed for people who already have some experience with 3DS MAX, some exercise steps are implied rather than explicitly stated. You may, for example, find yourself instructed to "Create a smooth, 20-segment Sphere with a radius of 100 units," rather than reading all of the steps required to create the sphere.

Exercises and the CD-ROM

Most of the examples and exercises use files that are either included on the *Inside 3D Studio MAX Volume III* CD-ROM or shipped with 3D Studio, or they show you how to create the necessary geometry. Example files are located on the accompanying CD. Instructions on how to use the CD-ROM files or to install them on your hard drive are described in the following section.

Using the *Inside 3D Studio MAX Volume III* CD-ROM

Inside 3D Studio MAX Volume III comes with a CD-ROM packed with many megabytes of plug-ins, scenes, maps, and other sample software. The example files can be used directly from the *Inside 3D Studio MAX, Volume III* CD-ROM, so "installing" them is not necessary. You may want to copy files from the CD-ROM to your hard drive or another storage device. In that case, you can use the install routines found with some of the sample programs or copy the files directly to a directory on your hard disk.

Installing the Exercise Files

All exercise files not included with 3D Studio MAX are contained in a single subdirectory on the *Inside 3D Studio MAX Volume III* CD-ROM: \I3DSMAX. You can access these files directly from the CD-ROM when you execute the examples, or you can create a directory called \I3DSMAX on your hard drive and copy the files there. Some of the example files require maps from the

CD-ROM that ships with 3D Studio MAX. You will need to copy these files to a subdirectory that is referenced in the 3DS MAX Map-Paths parameter.

3D Studio MAX automatically looks for map files in the directory from which a scene file was loaded. If you copy the example files to your hard drive, make sure you keep the mesh files and map files together or at least put the map files in a directory where 3D Studio can find them at rendering time.

A number of sample scenes, animation files, and maps are provided on the *Inside 3D Studio MAX, Volume III* CD-ROM for your use. These are licensed free for your use. You cannot, however, resell or otherwise distribute the files.

Registering Shareware

Most of the sample programs on the accompanying CD are either demonstration programs or shareware programs. Shareware programs are fully functioning products that you can try out prior to purchasing—they are not free. If you find a shareware program useful, you must pay a registration fee to the program's author. Each shareware program provides information about how to contact the author and register the program.

Using CompuServe and the Web

The CompuServe Information Service is an online, interactive network that you can access with a modem and special access software. The most important feature of this service (at least as far as this book is concerned) is the Kinetix forum.

The Kinetix forum is an area of CompuServe that is maintained by Kinetix for the direct support of 3D Studio MAX and other Kinetix software. Hundreds of people from all over the world visit this forum daily to share ideas, ask and answer questions, and generally promote the use of 3D Studio MAX. If you ask a question on the forum, you are as likely to receive an answer from one of the original programmers as you are to receive an answer from any number of other 3D Studio MAX artists. And every question, from the most basic to the most mind-bending puzzler, receives the same quick and courteous treatment.

Kinetix also maintains a site on the World Wide Web where you can get the latest information about 3DS MAX, future software releases, and plug-in development. You can also send questions and feedback direct to Kinetix and download software. The Kinetix web site is www.ktx.com.

New Riders Publishing

The staff of New Riders Publishing is committed to bringing you the very best in computer reference material. Each New Riders book is the result of months of work by authors and staff who research and refine the information contained within its covers.

As part of this commitment to you, New Riders invites your input. Please let us know if you enjoy this book, if you have trouble with the information and examples presented, or if you have a suggestion for the next edition.

Please note, however: New Riders staff cannot serve as a technical resource for 3D Studio MAX or for questions about software- or hardware-related problems. Please refer to the documentation that accompanies your software or to the applications' Help systems.

If you have a question or comment about any New Riders book, there are several ways to contact New Riders Publishing. We will respond to as many readers as we can. Your name, address, or phone number will never become part of a mailing list or be used for any purpose other than to help us continue to bring you the best books possible.

You can write us at the following address:

New Riders Publishing
Attn: Publisher
201 W. 103rd Street
Indianapolis, IN 46290

If you prefer, you can fax New Riders Publishing at:

317-817-7448

You can also send electronic mail to New Riders at the following Internet address:

abuckley@newriders.mcp.com

New Riders Publishing is an imprint of Macmillan Computer Publishing. To obtain a catalog or information, or to purchase any Macmillan Computer Publishing book, call 800-428-5331 or visit our web site at http://www.mcp.com.

Thank you for selecting *Inside 3D Studio MAX Volume III: Animation*!

Part I

ANIMATION—STATE OF THE ART

IMAGE CREATED BY MECHADEUS

Chapter 1

by Sanford Kennedy

COMPUTER ANIMATION INDUSTRY OVERVIEW

Three-dimensional computer animation has revolutionized the way motion picture special effects, computer games, television, multimedia, and even architectural presentations are created. But the traditional 2D animation industry still remains firmly entrenched in its own market: 2D animation dominates Saturday morning and children's cartoon programming. Disney-style 2D animated motion pictures are blockbuster hits, and a sizable portion of television commercials use 2D animated characters. So where is 3D computer animation today? 3D animation has moved solidly into computer and arcade video games, taken over all visual effects for television, grabbed a big share of television commercial production, dominates forensic animation, has run away with theme park motion rides and flight simulations, made major inroads into multimedia, and completely eliminated traditional optical film methods in all forms of visual effects and post production for motion pictures.

Both 2D and 3D animation are vying for the available dollars in the media industries. The lion's share of new investment and new technology, however, is being poured into 3D computer animation. 3D animation has generated continuous growth and made a great leap forward in the 1990s.

This chapter introduces you to some of the companies in the 3D computer animation industry through actual interviews, providing insight into the following topics:

- The state of the art in 3D animation

- Who created 3D Studio MAX

- A history of 3D Studio in motion pictures

- Who are the leading game creators using MAX

- What Softimage says about being MAX's competitor

- Who is using MAX in visual effects

- The wide variety of projects currently using MAX

The State of the Art in 3D Animation

The motion picture industry has taken the lead in generating spectacular, groundbreaking 3D computer animation. In the last five years, a series of blockbuster special effects movies have broken all the rules about what is possible with 3D computer graphics. In the early '90s, the first major films with computer animated sequences were released with startling success. First in 1989 came the marvelous computer-animated water snake in Jim Cameron's *The Abyss*, for 20th Century Fox, followed closely in 1991 by the fantastic computer animated liquid metal Terminator 1000 in Cameron's production of *Terminator 2*, for Carolco. Then in 1993, Steven Spielberg and George Lucas's Industrial Light and Magic visual effects studio stunned the world again with *Jurassic Park*, for Universal Studios.

The unbelievable quality of the 3D computer-animated dinosaurs astounded the public worldwide. Even for those who worked every day in the visual effects industry, it was an amazing revelation to see a photorealistic computer generated Tyrannosaurus Rex rampaging through the rain in the darkness, chasing three helpless victims in a jeep. These images of primal fear were so well done that the film reaped unprecedented profit and caused a ripple of surprise to move through the entire media industry. 3D computer animation had arrived.

Until the mid-'90s, the capability to create photorealistic animation had been the exclusive domain of high-end software such as Alias/Wavefront, SoftImage, Prisms, and Renderman. But Intel changed the rules with its Pentium processor. Around this time, the technology of Intel-based workstations took a giant leap forward. The PC, and the available software such as 3D Studio, improved to the point where the so-called "low-end" PC platform was beginning to be used to generate animation and visual effects for broadcast television and motion pictures.

3D Studio for DOS scored a major breakthrough into high-resolution motion picture visual effects with scenes in the films *Johnny Mnemonic*, *The Craft*, and the titles for the movie *Speed*, all features produced at Sony Pictures. Despite this early success, all off-the-shelf software that ran on the DOS operating system on Intel PCs had serious limitations in color bit depth, memory, and rendering speed. During this period, another "low-end" software package found success in television production—LightWave. It originally ran on the Amiga and was later ported to the PC. Its potential was tapped by Steven Spielberg to create underwater visual effects for his television show *Seaquest*, by Amblin Entertainment. That led to later success in creating special effects for *Hercules* and *Babylon 5*, which are still in production.

By 1994, nearly every major Hollywood motion picture contained at least some computer-manipulated scenes. Digitally generated content ranged from digital compositing using high-end software such as Flame or Wavefront Composer, to special effects such as 3D computer-animated space ships, animated creatures, digitally created environments, or atmospheric visual effects. The majority of these visual effects were done using Alias/Wavefront, Prisms, or Softimage and rendered using Renderman Pro on Silicon Graphics workstations.

When Microsoft purchased SoftImage in 1994 and ported it to Windows NT on the Intel platform (by the end of 1995), the Silicon Graphics–based high-end 3D computer graphics industry got an abrupt wake-up call. To add to their consternation, the new version of 3D Studio MAX for Windows NT was released a few months later. At about the same time, Lightwave, Animation Master, Photoshop, Digital Fusion, and Razor Pro released versions for Windows NT. Suddenly—by the summer of 1996—enough tools were available running on NT on the PC platform to do serious production work. When combined with the new real-time Open GL video display cards and the dual and quad processor Intel PC workstations from Intergraph, the Windows NT platform was finally a force to be taken seriously as a high-end production tool.

The Genesis of 3D Studio MAX

The sudden appearance of all this software for Windows NT was not as miraculous or coincidental as it may seem. Many of these companies had been working on versions for Windows NT for years, and it was generally recognized that Windows NT was the software platform of the future.

Gary Yost realized the possibilities of the Windows NT platform for 3D animation. (Image done in 3D Studio MAX created by Gene Bodio.)

The development of 3D Studio MAX for Windows NT was special because it was not a port of an existing product to a different software platform. MAX was all-new from the ground up.

The story of the creation of 3D Studio MAX is remarkable in both its ground-breaking new technology, and for the way the program was written by a small group of specialists in different parts of the country. Gary Yost was able to gather around him a group of individuals who shared a common vision of creating the first object-oriented 3D animation program for Windows NT.

The birth of MAX took three years and three months. The Yost Group started working on the code in January of 1993. The main problem they had was that they had to "re-invent the wheel." The existing version of 3D Studio ran in DOS and was one of the most un-object–oriented programs available for 3D animation. In writing MAX, they were trying to create the most object-oriented animation program ever written and make it run in Windows NT on regular PC compatibles. They had no prior work on which they could base their new software. Twenty months was spent just working on prototypes.

At the time the 3D Studio MAX project began, the Yost Group was still working to finish 3DS Release 3, so they could not spend full time on MAX's development. They knew that if they didn't get to Windows with an object-oriented program by 1996, however, 3D Studio would be considered archaic.

Gary recalls thinking, "You know, if you are a market leader and you don't obsolete yourself, someone's going to do it for you."

They knew they had a big challenge, and they knew they could not get it all in one jump, so they started writing prototypes.

Building the Team

Gary brought Don Brittain into the Yost Group to begin work on the core code for MAX. Don had been the vice-president of Research and Development at Wavefront. He left because Wavefront decided it did not want to go into NT or Windows and preferred to stay in Unix. Don saw what was coming in the future. Gary explained, "Don was essential to our being able to get this project done because none of us were as deeply involved in Windows as Don was."

Assembling the MAX team. (Image from Westwood Studio's game Lands of Lore, Guardians of Destiny.*)*

Another essential member of the team, who had been working with Gary on 3D Studio since Release 1, was Dan Silva. He had a tremendous amount of object-oriented programming background from his experience at Xerox Park, where they basically invented object-oriented programming. Dan's dream, since he started working on 3D Studio R1 in 1989, was to one day make it object-oriented.

Dan and Don were able to form the nucleus of this new object-oriented seed that would become 3D Studio MAX. Gary described the early stages of the working method of the MAX team:

> They would all fly in to my home every six weeks through 1993 and the first half of 1994. We would have these big marathon sessions where we sat down for four days and looked at Don's prototypes and discussed them. Slowly we zeroed in on how to do something like this.

The Yost Group had a major breakthrough in January of 1994 when they were able to bring in Michael Girard, Susan Amkraut, and John Chadwick of Unreal Pictures. They were responsible for creating the Character Studio Biped plug-in, which was in development on another platform before work started on MAX. Gary recalled:

> They actually had a complete working Biped prototype running in early 1993. When I first saw it, Biped was running on a Silicon Graphics box, but there was nothing available on the SGI platform that they could plug their code into.

When the Unreal folks joined the MAX team, they became an instrumental factor in determining what was needed to make MAX capable of supporting such extensive plug-ins.

> They would come in on one of the days during each one of the marathon sessions, and we would spend the whole day talking to them about what they needed. Having that feedback during the course of the prototype stage gave us the knowledge of what was needed to make sure that the API was as robust as it had to be. They were the API challenge.

By early 1994, the Yost Group had shipped their last IPAS programs, disks 6 and 7, for the DOS version of 3D Studio. Rolf Berteig, who had written many of the most popular IPAS routines, was brought into the MAX team. At 27, he was the youngest member. Gary admitted:

> If it wasn't for his youthful exuberance along with his strong technical background, we couldn't have done the project. We needed that extra bit of energy and drive in the team to keep going with this brutally difficult project. At every critical juncture we'd add another essential person. If you took away any one of these folks, we couldn't have done it.

The last person added to the team who was really critical to the project was Mark Meier. Gary was impressed with the IPAS plug-ins that Meier had written and then given away in the 3D Studio forum. Gary remembered:

> He was a computer artist who got into IPAS programming to create the effects that he needed. He was the first person I discovered who was giving away free plug-ins for 3D Studio. The documentation for his plug-ins was very good, so I asked him if he would like to be a part of the team and develop the SDK.

Gary felt it would be pointless to develop a platform such as MAX and then put it out there without including very good documentation that would enable other people to develop plug-ins for it. He also did not want to farm out the SDK to someone outside the core group.

The third prototype of MAX was finished right before Siggraph of 1994 at Orlando, Florida—Release 4 was launched there as a plug-in upgrade. The reason it was just a plug-in release was that by that time almost all their attention was focused exclusively on developing MAX. Gary said that he was very frustrated at Siggraph because he could not tell anyone about MAX.

Creating the "Virtual" Yost Group

In October 1994, the MAX team actually started writing the shell that was to become MAX. By that point, they had Tom Hudson in Wisconsin, Rolf Berteig in Seattle, Dan Silva and Jack Powell in Marin County, California, Don Brittain in Santa Barbara, and Gary Yost in San Francisco; all were sending data back and forth to each other over modems. But the modems turned out to be a big problem. Gary related:

> We thought we were going to be able to work fast enough by exchanging data over 28.8 modems. We put together a server in Santa Barbara with four incoming lines with source code control software. Then we started sending in code, but we discovered that the source code control software would choke when the line was dropped, so we would get these line hits. The source code would get scrambled and Don had to spend entire days at a time recovering from the line hits.

The isolation of the team brought about data transfer problems. (Image of stingray done in 3D Studio MAX by Marcus Morgan, Kinetix.)

It got so bad that by mid-November they realized that they could not do the project. Because everyone lived in remote locations in different parts of the country, the project was not going to work. It was impossible to relocate everyone.

One day Gary was speaking to Gus Grubba about his frustrations and fears of having to end the project after all the work they had done, and Gus asked whether Gary had thought about using high-speed ISDN modems that are immune to line hits. Gary said:

> I didn't realize that ISDN could be brought into private homes virtually anywhere in the country, but as it turned out, ISDN had just recently become available from each of our regional phone companies.

Gus knew that there had been a recent ruling that said if you were within a few miles of a switch, the phone company was required to make ISDN available to you. In November, all the MAX team members called their local phone companies and requested ISDN. It took five weeks to get connected, but by January 1995 the "Virtual" Yost Group was online and running.

ISDN modems operate at 128 K baud compared with the 28.8 K baud of the consumer modem lines. This was the last key element that fell into place, enabling the creation of MAX to move forward. Gus Grubba then joined the team and took on responsibility for writing the Network Rendering software and the Video Post module.

MAX Meets the Public

By the time of Siggraph 1995 in August, Gary did the first presentation of MAX for the public. One of the greatest problems faced by the Yost Group was how to make a purely object-oriented program run on a regular PC P5-90, which was the target platform. It had to run without performance problems while interactively maintaining real time. The program interface appeared to be finished, and during the demonstrations everything worked well. Considering how far they had come in a relatively short time, this working demonstration was the most amazing feat that the Yost Group had ever accomplished. At that time, there was no renderer, and in terms of the total number of features that shipped with MAX when it was released, only about 20 percent of the total feature set was running. The MAX beta program was started a month later, and the team kept working seven days a week until the program was shipped in April of 1996.

*The Yost Group's
creation was first seen
by the public at
SIGGRAPH 1995.
(Flower image done in
3D Studio MAX
created by
Mechadeus.)*

After MAX was released, it was very well received, winning awards for its advanced technology and rich feature set. Within the 3D Studio community, a number of people wondered how so few people were able to create such a massive and groundbreaking program. Many rumors were heard that Gary and his cohorts were actually androids like Data on *Star Trek*. Gary smiled and said:

> I know there is that impression out there that we are not built like everyone else because we're so good at writing software. The reality is that we are just regular people working toward our potential. Everyone has that potential. The customers who use 3D Studio have sent back so much positive energy to us over the years that it has helped us achieve our goals.

When asked what made the Yost Group able to work so well together, he stated firmly:

> There are no junk food addicts among us at all. We are all very health-conscious. You can't sustain this kind of work pace unless you take very good care of yourself. The only thing that is perhaps unique about us is that as a team, we are all musicians. We all play at least one, and in many cases, two and three instruments.

The Yost Group functioned like a coalition of experts, with each member of the MAX team responsible for his or her own modules within MAX. The only exception was Dan Silva and Rolf Berteig, who together created the Modifier Stack object pipeline. There was a tremendous amount of specialization. Almost no crossover occurred because the program is so object-oriented and modular. Because of that, any programmer familiar with the SDK could write a plug-in and upload it to the web. Then when it is loaded into MAX, it will look and feel just like it was written by one of the core programmers.

MAX in the Future

When asked what his future goals are for MAX, Gary said:

> One of our goals is to create the biggest programming team that has ever been seen on the planet. Because the SDK is shipped for free, and because you are going to see more low-cost educational versions of MAX, you could potentially get 10,000 programmers working on plug-ins by the end of the century. The SDK is a new language and a new way of thinking about graphics and object-oriented programming. It can teach people who never thought they were interested how to do object-oriented programming in 3D graphics. We already have people working on MAX plug-ins all over Europe, in Russia, in Africa, Latin America, Australia, Canada, China, and Japan. In India there is a tremendous amount of work being done on plug-ins. The goal is to make MAX world-wide and to reflect the diversity of the human spirit.

How 3D Studio MAX Is Being Used

Some of the top visual effects and animation studios were interviewed to find out how they were using 3D Studio MAX in production. One of the pioneer users of 3D Studio in Hollywood is Sony Pictures Imageworks of Culver City, California. Sony Pictures is one of the "big seven" Hollywood movie studios, a group that includes Paramount Pictures, Universal Studios, Warner Brothers, 20th Century Fox, Walt Disney Studios, and the newest big studio—which has recently chosen 3D Studio MAX for its Interactive Division—Steven Spielberg's DreamWorks SKG. All these studios now have 3D animation and interactive media divisions employing hundreds of animators and multiple software and hardware platforms.

3D Studio History at Sony Pictures Imageworks

Frank Foster, head of the Multimedia Division of Sony Pictures Imageworks, has been using 3D Studio to create motion picture visual effects for a number of years. In a recent interview, Frank recalled the first time he took an interest in 3D Studio:

> In 1990, I was involved in an R & D project at Tri-Star Pictures (now a division of Sony Pictures). We were looking for a method for doing electronic storyboarding for our pre-visualization work. We looked into a number of different platforms and software applications. We selected 3D Studio to be our pre-visualization software primarily because of how quickly we could place the camera, and how quickly we could render a scene.

Tri-Star's R & D project was one of the first successful uses of 3D Studio in Hollywood. Their first major pre-visualization project was a film called *Striking Distance*. Frank explained how pre-visualization worked:

> We animated about a half hour of the movie in 3D Studio before any film was shot, including boat chases, car chases, train crashes, and some fight scenes. We constructed the location in the computer and then designed the sequence. The scene that got the most focus was a car chase sequence through downtown Pittsburgh. We built accurate models of the city streets based on data from the City Planning Department. We actually had 3D Studio running on computers on location. By doing that project, we learned a lot about what could be done with pre-visualization, and what could be done with 3D Studio and IBM PCs on the road.

During that time, Frank began to expand the activities of his department. It wasn't long before they took on motion picture title design. Frank explained:

> We started looking at doing motion picture title design by incorporating desktop publishing techniques and 3D Studio's ability to take in Adobe Illustrator file format. One of the first title projects we did was a relatively unknown film called *Wilder Napalm*, in 1993. After that, we did a whole string of movie title sequences, including *Manhattan Murder Mystery* and *Thief*. Probably the most well-known titles we have done were in the opening sequence of the movie *Speed*. The elevator sequence was pre-visualized in 3D Studio, and the title sequence itself was designed and rendered at high-resolution in 3D Studio.

Frank pushed the envelope still further by taking on the first actual 3D Studio special effects scene in a Michael Keaton film called *My Life*, for Columbia Pictures. The effects were very bright lighting tricks that created the illusion of going into the "after-life." The effects were rendered in 3D Studio and then handed off for compositing into the film on Wavefront Composer. The visual effects supervisor on that project was John Nelson, who became instrumental in getting further effects shots for 3D Studio.

The next breakthrough came when John Nelson took over as visual effects supervisor on the *Johnny Mnemonic* film project. After doing extensive tests, Frank was able to convince him that 3D Studio could do the cyberspace sequence for the picture. Frank is justifiably proud of his work on *Johnny Mnemonic*. He looked away for a moment, remembering what the project was like, and said:

> We created the telephone call sequence at the beginning of the picture where Keanu Reeves tries to track down the man who wanted to kill him. When the film was almost completed, and in post production, the producer came back to us because they were quite pleased with the work and asked us to do the entire opening of the film. It was a very long sequence that begins with the prologue and goes on for about two and a half minutes of film-resolution work. The prologue is a scene with a scroll moving upward, explaining the story. That is followed by a particle system explosion of the title *Johnny Mnemonic*, and then a trip through the cyberworld of the Internet 20 years in the future. The three scenes lead to the wake-up call scene in the hotel room. The entire sequence was a single render and was our first opportunity to use 3D Studio to create a full film-resolution motion picture effect.

The 3D Studio group moved on to create the stereoscopic 3D titles for the IMAX project *Wings of Courage*, which gave them experience in rendering high-resolution output to large film sizes. Then in 1995, staff graphic designer Brummbaer took on the project of doing the opening for the Siggraph electronic theater using 3D Studio. This was to be a large-format, 70mm Showscan presentation projected at 60 frames per second. Frank said:

> We rendered that out at high resolution. It involved a large number of elements and a sophisticated sound track. It was extremely well received and was shown for five nights at Siggraph.

The next 3D Studio project at Sony was for a film called *The Craft*. Frank explained, very seriously:

> This was a difficult sequence where photorealistic butterflies had to fly around and interact with two live actresses, exhibiting the behavior of real butterflies. Butterflies don't fly like a bird. They have a very erratic kind of floating and jumping movement. It was a key sequence in the film, and we worked very hard doing numerous tests to prove that 3D Studio was capable of doing this kind of high-end animation and rendering. Finally, it came down to a lot of hard work by Dave Schaub, who created the actual animation of the butterflies.

> *The Craft* was the first time that a project used 3D Studio's capability to render in full 16-bit linear colorspace for a motion picture. The way people had used 3D Studio in the past was to dither down the 64-bit 3D Studio colorspace to a TARGA file with 8 bits. Joe Munkaby, our staff plug-in programmer, wrote a custom IPAS that would allow us to input and output RLA file format images directly. Originally, the sequence was to be composited into the movie using the SGI systems, but we were able to get such good results within 3D Studio, that we did the actual final composite for the film and saved significant costs on the production.

Sony Imageworks moved to using 3D Studio MAX in 1996. Imagework's character animation relies heavily on MAX's Character Studio, with its capability to do IK blending. They are also very enthusiastic about the recent developments in using MAX for cartoon rendering. This is done using a plug-in that flattens the image, puts edge lines around the characters, and then does the inking and painting. Imageworks predicts that this will be a very important market area for 3D Studio MAX animation in the future.

The department where 3D Studio MAX is used at Sony is called the Multimedia Department. Frank explained that:

> Pre-visualization, title design, and animation for television and feature effects are just part of the work we do. Our multimedia department is based around both animation and Internet production, including VRML content for the Sony Internet web site is done here with MAX. In character animation, we have recently completed 158 shots using 3D Studio MAX for one of the last episodes in this season's *The Adventures of Johnny Quest*, the television series produced by Hanna-Barbera.

Matt Hausle and Frank Foster (on right) in the video editing suite at Sony Pictures Imageworks Multimedia Division, the facility for laying off MAX images to video.

When asked how they get images from MAX on to motion picture film, Frank replied:

> Sony Imageworks has an input/output department which does both film scanning and film printing. We have multiple cameras so we can do multiple projects at the same time. For any of the film resolution projects that we do, the files will be sent over to the server that supports the film recorders and then output directly to 35mm motion picture film.

3D Studio Has Strength in Computer Games

3D Studio and 3D Studio MAX have a substantial share of the interactive media market and are widely used in computer game production. 3D Studio has been used to create nearly 70 percent of all PC games including *7th Guest, 11th Hour, Area 51, Rebel Assault, Wing Commander II, Crash and Burn, Daedalus Encounter, SimCity 2000, F10-Strike Eagle III,* and *X-Wing.* Major users read like a who's who in Game producers: LucasArts, Turner Interactive, Mechadeus, Electronic Arts Sports, Westwood Studios, Sega, Virgin Interactive, Warner Interactive, Amazing Media, Activision, and DreamWorks Interactive.

DreamWorks Interactive

One of the newest users of 3D Studio MAX is DreamWorks Interactive, in Los Angeles. DreamWorks Interactive is a joint venture between Microsoft Corporation and DreamWorks SKG, owned by Steven Spielberg, Jeffrey Katsenberg, ex-head of production at Disney Studios, and David Geffen, owner of Geffen Records. MAX was chosen by DWI as the main production tool for modeling and animating their characters and building realistic three-dimensional environments for their games.

The DreamWorks Interactive logo.

Currently they are using MAX to produce four new interactive game titles. *Goosebumps II* is a sequel to their successful game *Goosebumps: Escape from Horrorland*, based on R.L. Stine's popular book. *The Lost World*, for the Sony PlayStation, about to be released in August 1997, is based on *The Lost World: Jurassic Park*, the sequel to the original film (released in May 1997). *Trespassers: Jurassic Park* is a whole new kind of game with built-in artificial intelligence, to be released by Christmas 1997. They are also working on *Chaos Island*, a real-time strategy game in which kids can guide expeditions into the heart of *The Lost World's* Dinosaur Island.

Hunter Deinonychus Raptors on the prowl in Jurassic Park: The Lost World.

The Lost World is being created under the guidance of Patrick Gilmore, executive producer. One of the game's five animators, Sunil Thankanushy, spoke about how they are using 3D Studio MAX to create the dinosaurs:

> I am building six different deinonychus variations for the game, each of which will attack the player in a slightly different way. They are modeled in MAX at low resolution so they can be moved quickly by the real-time game engine of the Sony PlayStation. Players can encounter deinonychus (which is a cousin to the velociraptor made famous in the first film) while playing one of three different dinosaurs, or two different human player characters. During the game, deinonychus can stalk and attack the player, who has to figure out a strategy to survive.

When Sunil finishes animating a model, it is not exported from MAX into the PlayStation as a MAX file. Instead, the model and its animation are exported as data only. The programming team takes the data and programs the PlayStation game engine to reconstruct and render the dinosaurs moving in real-time during game play. In this way, a library of different moves can be stored. The PlayStation game engine generates both the characters and the environment in real time from data exported from 3D Studio MAX.

When asked how he did the animation of the raptors, Sunil said:

> The models are animated with the Bones Pro plug-in from Digimation,
> using simple rotations to control the bone skeleton, which in turn deform
> the character mesh. Philosophically, we chose not to use inverse kine-
> matics because it doesn't accurately capture how creatures really move
> in nature (nature seems to have a preference for *forward* kinematics).
> We also experimented with Character Studio, but we ended up going
> back to using Bones Pro because we got better results.

A Deinonychus ready to attack. (Modeled by Sunil Thankamushy and textured by Matt Hall.)

DEINONYCHUS GAME MODEL — RUN

THE LOST WORLD: JURASSIC PARK FOR SONY PLAYSTATION
TM & C 1996 DREAMWORKS INTERACTIVE, L.L.C.
THE LOST WORLD: JURASSIC PARK
TM & C 1996 UNIVERSAL CITY STUDIOS, INC.
AND AMBLIN ENTERTAINMENT, INC.
ALL RIGHTS RESERVED
LICENSED BY MCA/UNIVERSAL MERCHANDISING, INC.

Another group at DreamWorks Interactive is working on *Trespassers: Jurassic Park*, using a completely different approach under the technical guidance of Executive Producer Seamus Blackley. This game should prove to be a groundbreaking improvement in interactivity with higher resolution models and bump-mapped surfaces. Its unique features will include a built-in artificial intelligence that helps the dinosaurs decide how to react in different situations and a physics engine that makes the animals and their environment react to impacts and move just like animals in real life. This game is due out by Christmas 1997 and is attracting considerable pre-release interest. All the dinosaurs and their environments are being built by an 11-man team working with 3D Studio MAX on Pentium Pro 200s running Windows NT. DWI has 35 3DS MAX seats at the present time.

A Rhamphorhynchus created with 3D Studio MAX at DWI. (Modeled by Scott Hyman and textured by Matt Hall.)

Westwood Studios

Westwood Studios, founded by Louis Castle in Las Vegas, Nevada, has over 65 3DS MAX workstations plus a render farm making it the largest MAX studio in the country. Mr. Castle was unavailable for an interview, but he did provide a number of exciting images, reprinted here, from Westwood's game *Lands of Lore, Guardians of Destiny.*

Westwood's chief character designer is Elie Arabian, and the creator of the environments is Frank Mendeola. This game contains some very fine examples of modeling and surface texturing done with MAX. Top titles include *Command & Conquer* and *Monopoly*, the world's first game with full Internet support for multiple players.

A gallery of characters and environments created with 3D Studio MAX for Westwood Studio's game Lands of Lore, Guardians of Destiny.

SoftImage and 3D Studio MAX: Respectful Competitors

SoftImage is considered to be the top high-end character animation and modeling software in the industry. When new software such as 3D Studio MAX comes out, it is only natural to make a feature-by-feature comparison with other packages considered the leaders in the industry. SoftImage and MAX both share the Windows NT platform and in many areas have surprisingly similar features. One of the main differences between the two is the fact that SoftImage has had many years in which to mature, adding features in response to market pressures. This author presents the following interview with the head of Special Projects at SoftImage as a way of informing MAX users what their top competitor has to offer, and to try to set up a kind of "reality check" for those of you who don't know what is out there in the marketplace. It is also hoped that some benefit will be derived for all through the cross-pollination of ideas that should occur between the users of the two packages. Remember that it is likely you will be sharing studio space with SoftImage users in the years to come. It is wise, therefore, to know what they can do.

An Interview with SoftImage's David Morin

David Morin is the Director of Special Projects at SoftImage. He regularly commutes between SoftImage in Montreal, Canada, and their movie industry research center near Hollywood in Santa Monica, California.

SoftImage has a strong development team focused on providing leadership in high-end 3D computer graphics and has also invested in creating strong development tools for the clients and third-party market. Through the Software Development Kit (SDK), their third-party developers can work directly with the software to do things like connecting any device to SoftImage, or developing shaders or plug-ins for the 3D interactive interface.

> As the field widens and more and more people do computer graphics, it will be impossible for us to do everything for everybody.

> At Siggraph in 1996 we had 19 third-party developers in our booth and this number is booming. We have worked very hard to open a rich development environment to our clients and third-party developers, and as a result we see more enhancements coming to SoftImage.

In the last six years SoftImage has accomplished a great deal in the motion picture industry. It is hoped that by understanding the high level of this accomplishment, everyone who used both MAX and SoftImage will be inspired to do better and greater works.

SoftImage has been essential to the creation of some of the finest 3D-animated special effects that have come out of the Film Industry. David explained their relationship with the top special effects houses in the business:

> ILM is one of our big customers. They have been instrumental in breaking new ground and making new special effects, continuously bringing new imagery to the movie screen. SoftImage has been their tool of choice for character animation. They started using SoftImage back in 1992. The first use of SoftImage at ILM was in the movie *Death Becomes Her*, for the "twisting neck" scene. Then they became involved in preparing for *Jurassic Park* where they had some articulated dinosaur figures to do. In the past they had done some figures with other software, such as the liquid man who walks very stiffly in *Terminator 2*. For this project they needed to go beyond that level and to achieve realistic movement. SoftImage 2.5 had just come out at the time which included the first implementation of Inverse Kinematics ever to be offered in any software.

ILM is always looking over the market to see if there is a new tool there to solve their problems and they chose SoftImage to animate the dinosaurs. During that project ILM also developed their own software that works with SoftImage.

After *Jurassic Park*, ILM used SoftImage to do the ghosts in *Casper*, the effects in *The Mask*, and the animals in *Jumanji*. Then they did *Twister*, *Mission Impossible*, and *Mars Attacks*. In all of those productions SoftImage formed a part of their tool set.

SoftImage was used at ILM to generate the 3D Animated tornado for the film Twister.

There are a large number of movie companies using Softimage like Digital Domain, DreamWorks, and Sony Pictures. All of them use it to a different extent for different things. David maintained that:

We have recently introduced a completely new renderer called Mental Ray, which is the best rendering technology available today. It is a fully open, distributed, and configurable raytracer. Developers can add their own effects into it by writing new shaders. Other renderers use shaders very successfully, but they are not ray tracers, and anything that you want to do in terms of reflection or refraction is faked. Over the years Renderman users (for instance) have become very good at developing realistic looking fakes for all their effects. But, it is an old technology. Mental Ray is based more directly on the laws of optics and physics. It reads the scene and allows you to do volumetric rendering like smoke effects and very smooth area lighting. It will even compute caustics for use in animating water.

David explains:

People buy SoftImage sometimes for the character animation, sometimes for rendering, but always because it is a well-rounded tool in all the other areas. In modeling SoftImage has full support for polygonal objects, three types of patches, and complete support of metaballs, and parametric nurbs (non-uniform rational B-splines). SoftImage's modeling attributes are the most complete on the market today.

Caught Their Eye *is an Oldsmobile-Aurora commercial done with SoftImage by R/Greenberg Associates* © 1996.

Characters created in SoftImage for the game Tekken 2.

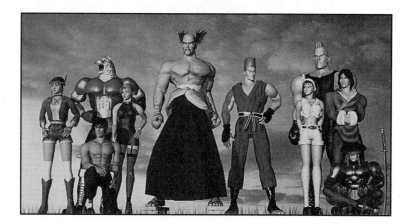

Said Morin:

The game industry is very important to us, as well as video, 2D animation, and post production. In games we have been very happy to help Sega who used SoftImage to do the animation for their *Virtua Fighter* games. These were the first fight games done with motion capture and were very demanding on the computer. Because of that, back then, they could only be played on an arcade machine. Today these types of games are running on home game consoles. In the meantime we have developed a whole set of tools for the game industry in general, including PSX converters, Sega Saturn converters, on-target viewing, and playback. We have color reduction and polygon reduction, and a number of polygon selection tools such as raycasting selection.

Sony's Pygnosis game division uses SoftImage to create its characters for its game Tenka.

One of the most visible examples of the ability of Softimage to do Character Animation is the popular Saturday morning television show *Reboot* produced in Vancouver, Canada. David pointed out that:

> The *Reboot* studio is turning out one episode with 22 minutes of full computer animation every two weeks, a very impressive throughput and quality of work done without motion capture, using only the classical animation approach to maintain the *Reboot* "look."

David's final comment was that:

> One of our ultimate goals at SoftImage is to enable professional artists to create great images and animations and to help them translate what they have in their heads in a way that can be shared by other people.

He encourages all animators to do the best work possible, express their own vision, and learn the tools of the trade.

3D Studio MAX in Visual Effects

Visual effects is the most demanding area of 3D computer animation, and pushes both the software and the hardware to the limits to get the great shots needed to create a special effects sequence for motion pictures or television. A number of independent studios have entered the visual effects field and are finding success by using 3D Studio MAX.

Blur Studio

Pushing MAX to the limit is the normal mode of operation at Blur Studio in Venice, California. Established in 1995 by animators Tim Miller and David Stinnett, with Cat Chapman producer, Blur is a compact, state-of-the-art facility based on Intergraph dual and quad processor workstations. Since they launched the Blur, they have been doing broadcast-quality work for commercials and high-resolution visual effects sequences for motion pictures.

Tom Dillon, a veteran 3D Studio user, was the first animator to join their staff. His background includes 2D animation background painting.

When asked about his use of MAX, he said:

> We have used 3D Studio MAX on movie effects projects, commercial
> effects projects, Saturday morning cartoon projects, and game work. For
> the movie *The Crow: City of Angels* we built simulated holographic
> visual effects that were composited into live action for the film's trailer.
> One shot was a holographic effect using a round screen with the holo-
> gram projected up on to it. It used particle systems and volume lights.
> Another effect was a morphing shadow of a figure looming up against a
> wall that morphed from a crow silhouette into a figure.

Blur also generated an intricate effects shot for the trailer for *Hellraiser:
Bloodline*, produced by Miramax/Dimension Films. MAX was used to model
a close-up section of the cracks in the evil character Pinhead's face. In the
sequence, his head explodes. Tom recalls:

> He had little cracks in his face. We built a camera that would fly into the
> cracks so it looked like a camera flying through a canyon. We added
> volume lights coming up through all the pinholes in his head. If you have
> seen any of the *Hellraiser* films, you know that Pinhead has these big
> nails driven into his head. In the sequence, you see giant nails coming up
> through the canyon as you are flying through it. When the camera pulls
> up out of the canyon, his head explodes, and then you cut to a live action
> shot of him reacting.

Commercials are another area of activity for Blur. For McDonalds, Blur used
MAX to create a holographic *Star Trek* transporter effect to animate a shot
of a Big Mac hamburger that lands on a space port. For Cadillac, they did a
spot called *The Car that Ziggs*. In that commercial, they had to match
animation to live action background footage. Tom describes the shot:

> *The Car that Ziggs* is a commercial advertising the new intelligent brake
> and handling controls. We used MAX's rotoscoping capability to create a
> line that follows behind the car as it moves along the road. I did the
> camera tracking in MAX for the shot.

Toy commercials are big business on weekday afternoons and Saturday
mornings. Blur did a 30 second 3D-animated *Fruity Pebbles* cereal commercial that involved the use of the Hanna-Barbera *Flintstones* characters. Tom
recalls:

> I had fun because I got to work with one of the 2D animators who does
> the *Flintstones*. We storyboarded out the entire commercial. The scene
> involved creating a virtual reality background environment where we

built and animated a number of characters like a dinosaur made out of fruit. When our animation was finished, Hanna-Barbera composited their 2D characters into our virtual 3D environment.

The scene of a missile being fired was created in MAX for the television show Pandora's Clock, courtesy of NBC.

Their most recent project is a long animation sequence for the 3D-animated version of *The Real Adventures of Johnny Quest*, produced by Hanna-Barbera, which includes 3D animated segments. One episode required the creation of $9^1/_2$ minutes of 3D character animation and many different environments at broadcast resolution. Eric Pinkel is one of the animators who worked on *Johnny Quest*. Eric talked about his work:

> We put MAX through its paces. I have worked with Electric Image and with Alias, and I find MAX far superior to work with. For me, the strongest points in MAX are its modeling and its texture mapping abilities. The modeling in *Johnny Quest* is very complicated. Patches are used extensively, as well as lofting. What is nice about MAX's lofter is that you can convert a loft into a patch. If you want to use Free Form Deformation to sculpt the model, you can. And when you are done, you can convert it back to an editable mesh, and then back again into a patch, and continue to modify it.

Blur is now working on two more *Johnny Quest* sequences that will be five minutes and three minutes long, respectively.

Blur uses an assortment of MAX's built-in tools and plug-ins. Because Blur is a beta tester for a number of the people who write plug-ins, they get to work with them before the general users do. The plug-ins add tremendously to their ability to create exactly the kind of effects needed for a particular look. Just like the high-end studios, Blur has their own in-house programmers writing plug-ins ranging from simple utilities that optimize MAX for the animator, to elaborate effects to create special explosions. Blur has recently put some of their in-house plug-ins up on the web as freeware plug-ins.

At Blur, they have the capability to do a full range of image output sizes from D1 all the way up to IMAX. They have 12 quad-processor Intergraph workstations in their render farm, and the animators use a mix of dual- and quad-processor Intergraph machines. The quad-processor machines can double the rendering speed when you have a scene with heavy calculations such as volume lighting and atmosphere. Intergraph is working on Render-GL that will enable a frame that normally renders in three minutes to be rendered in 30 seconds. When Intergraph moves from software to hardware-based rendering, they predict a very big increase in rendering speed that is going to give Silicon Graphics serious competition.

Eric Pinkel felt strongly about working at Blur:

> Blur is a really great studio to work in because all of us, including the owners, are animators. Blur was started by animators, so everyone here looks at the work from the viewpoint of an animator. All the way up the chain to Tim Miller, everyone knows what it takes to get the shot done. That makes the pressure go toward quality, instead of toward cranking it out as fast as you can.

Digital Phenomena

Digital Phenomena, located in Corte Madera, California, just north of San Francisco, uses 3D Studio MAX for commercials and film-resolution visual effects. They are the animators responsible for creating the first Character Studio demo animation of dancing figures for the Release 1.0 CD-ROM called *Character Conflict*. The studio is operated by Kevin Olin, who spent many years using AutoCAD, and Jamie Clay, who has been using 3D Studio since its beginnings.

Kevin explained how they got involved in the Character Studio CD:

> Kinetix contacted us mostly because we were a local studio that was familiar with 3D Studio MAX. They needed to produce a Character

Studio demo animation before the release deadline. We wrote the story and started animating. We had to utilize what tools were available in the still un-finished Character Studio beta version. The initial animation was done using pre-release software that was far from stable, but it was powerful enough for us to produce one minute of finished character animation in less than 12 days.

MAX's capability to "solve old problems in new ways," as well as its capability to display full-color, rotoscope-animated backgrounds enabled them to do their latest film project, *Dog's Best Friend*, for the Family Channel on HBO. The production was shot on film and converted to D1 video at 24 frames per second. They did motion tracking and 3D jaw replacement in 3D Studio MAX to make the dog talk.

Kevin explained:

We did 120 shots in about 75 days. MAX enabled us to build an "animation kit" for each of the five barnyard animals. The animation kit consisted of the geometry for the given jaw that was going to be replaced, and the jaw controls. The kits gave the animators high-level controls that enabled them to move a jaw, curl the lower lip, pull the tongue forward, or curl the tongue to simulate speech. They moved the controls and synchronized the jaw movements with MAX's sound track.

John Wainwright, creator of MaxScript, contributed to the project by writing software for tracking objects in MAX. Building the jaw and locating it in the correct position in a background plate is very time-consuming. Through John's plug-in for MAX, the animator could position the jaw automatically in each plate. When in the correct location, it was automatically tracked and maintained in position by the plug-in. Jamie Clay recalled, "With our network, we were able to render a large number of shots for *Dog's Best Friend* very quickly because we were only rendering the animal's jaw as it moved."

Jamie and Kevin did an interesting group of visual effects shots using MAX for the independent film called *Conceiving Ada*, produced by Hot Wire Productions of San Francisco. It was produced and directed by Lynn Hershman. Jamie explained:

It stars Tilda Swinton, Karen Black, and Timothy Leary. Leary's character dies in this movie. Coincidentally, Timothy Leary died about two weeks after he finished the film. 3D Studio MAX was used extensively to embellish his final scene as he passes on.

The exteriors were all shot on 35mm film. Then we came in and shot the interiors on a digital betacam. We stitched together scenes to create a

virtual set by combining modified photographs and actors. Using MAX
and our network rendering ability we were able to build animations on
the fly for use during the actual shoot. The director would ask for some
cloud effects, or maybe some rain to go on outside the windows, or maybe
some fire in the fireplace, and we would build those on the fly and cue
those up during the shooting. We stitched together many images in real
time using Digital Ultimatte.

With innovators such as Kevin and Jamie at Digital Phenomena, the
versatility of 3D Studio MAX is just beginning to be explored.

A Wide Variety of Media for MAX

Even though 3DS MAX is known as a 3D animation software package, it is
the MAX users who determine how it will be applied in the real world. The
range of imagery that can be created with MAX covers a broad spectrum from
flying logos for a television news hour, to photorealistic growing bacteria for
a science-fiction movie thriller. Even a 2D cartoon with lip sync sound, a
cover for a fashion magazine, or an industrial product presentation could
easily be done using only a portion of MAX's capabilities.

Part of what makes MAX a great software product is its flexibility. Part of
what makes 3D Studio MAX fun to work with is the community of creative
computer artists that make up the bulk of the MAX users. Unlike the high-
end software packages that cost thousands and thousands of dollars, MAX
is affordable even on a modest budget. This means that a much wider variety
of creative individuals can become MAX users. The major studios and the big
media corporations that insist on using Silicon Graphics-based mega-buck
software have little room for flexibility and even less imagination in their
headlong pursuit of profits at all costs. It is in the domain of the smaller
independent animation studios where you find the small groups of dedicated
animators with great depth of talent, adaptability, and creativity.

As a realistic but somewhat tongue-in-cheek example of the talent and
adaptability of a typical independent animation studio, the following anec-
dote describes the exotic kinds of job opportunities that are often presented
to the independent 3D Studio animation houses. This scene could take place
at any studio, anywhere from Hollywood to the Lower East Side of New York
City: A producer has just received a large sum of money from an eccentric
software billionaire, and he is searching frantically for a studio to do his
revolutionary multimedia film and graphics project. The producer meets

with the creative director of an independent 3D Studio MAX–based production company and proposes the following project that has never been done before.

Waving his arms he explains:

It will be the greatest multimedia project ever produced! It will be shot on 35mm film with a cast of hundreds, and then digitized as a background plate for computer animation. You will be expected to create fantastic visual effects, with two monsters that fight a battle. Then you will synchronize a sound track with a video screen that plays interactive cartoons during a love scene between the prince and the fair maiden in the castle tower, just before the explosion of the extinct volcano. During the explosion, the Castle will tumble down with lightning and flames belching up through the cracked earth, and the lovers will fall into the boiling lava. You will end the sequence as a tidal wave of water rushes in to drown the flames, and the lovers emerge as winged angels rising up with the steam that morphs into a stairway to heaven as the camera flies into the clouds and we fade to black! Can you do it?

The owner/animator of the studio glances at his partner, who is a programmer for MAX plug-ins. They smile at each other. The owner/animator says, "We can do *that*. That will only use a small part of 3D Studio MAX's capabilities."

Pyros Pictures

Greg Pyros is well known within the 3D Studio community for his ability to wear many hats. Like many independent studios in the field, Pyros Pictures has a small, but very talented staff of ten animators. With the programming expertise of his associate Gus Grubba, who was part of the team that wrote 3D Studio MAX, there are few tasks that Greg and his staff at Pyros Pictures could not take on. They have done a variety of work that covers the animation field from games, to commercials and visual effects for TV and feature films, to forensic animation.

When you enter the Pyros Pictures studio located high atop a modern glass and steel high rise edifice in Orange County, California, you are immediately impressed with the warm, yet businesslike atmosphere that resembles an architectect's office that suddenly discovered it was fun to do animation and play music. As a matter of fact, that is exactly what Pyros Pictures is. Greg

Pyros was destined from an early age to be an architect, following in his father's footsteps. But right in the middle of a budding career, he contracted the dreaded 3D Studio animator's bug and has never recovered.

Greg, who is still an architect, but prefers to animate, explains:

> I started out in 1981 as an architectural firm. I became a dealer for AutoCAD because there weren't any dealers who could answer my questions, and later for 3D Studio when I realized I could do fly-through animations of my buildings. My architectural firm was busy designing commercial industrial buildings, so our first 3D Studio projects were doing fly-through renderings first for ourselves, and then for other architects. The experiences we had there made me realize that once you have done a number of fly-through animations of entire buildings, it is relatively easy to do flying logos. About three years ago I sold the software dealership, and I have been doing nothing but computer animation since then.

Pyros Pictures is using 3D Studio MAX exclusively on a number of different kinds of jobs. Some of their animators are working on a game, another group is doing visual effects for a feature film, and two more are doing a television commercial. They have a forensic animation division called TrialVision that is booked solid with forensic animation work for lawyers. And finally, a programming group works on projects with Gus Grubba. Greg explained that his team:

> [H]as probably written and sold more IPAS plug-in routines for 3D Studio than any other group. The difference between us and other companies, who only distribute plug-ins written by other people, is that we write them and test them right here under production conditions. We are currently shipping a plug-in for MAX that allows you to output YUV images to the Abekas, Accom, and other digital disk recorders, in both PAL and NTSC. MAX ships with a YUV reader, which we wrote, but without this plug-in, there is no way to output files.

Their current feature film project is a sequel to *Oh God,* the hit film that starred George Burns back in the 1970s. Pyros is bringing him back for this one. They have scanned a portrait sculpture of George Burns and created a very detailed model in MAX. They also modeled George's famous El Producto cigar and his trademark round glasses. Rich Little is going to do the voice for the film. They are currently doing facial animation tests with dialogue. The animated model was shown on television on the first anniversary of George Burns' death.

Greg recalled a few more film projects they have worked on over the past three years:

On *Fair Game,* with William Baldwin and Cindy Crawford, we did the animated images for all of the computer monitors and the Sun laptop that they used. We also worked on a pilot for Francis Ford Coppola based on his film *The Conversation*, and we created visual effects for a film called *Lightspeed* that still is not finished.

Game work has kept Pyros Pictures busy, including a baseball game for Virgin Interactive called *Grand Slam* in which they modeled all 28 North American baseball stadiums for a real-time rendered game. The first large game project that Pyros Pictures did was *Zork Nemesis* for Activision. Greg's studio was chosen because Activision wanted to create a number of realistic architectural-animated interiors for their game. His expertise as an architect proved to be the deciding factor that got him the job.

The whole game was built around a number of interior environments with wrap-around walls. Activision wrote their own version of QuickTime VR. In the game, the players have the ability to spin completely around 360 degrees and look at any part of the environment or the room they are in. The spin is completely seamless.

We did 1,800 frame renderings of all the environments, and from those images, we took a one pixel wide strip out of the center of each one. When we put them all together, they formed a 360 degree circular image of the room. The game engine was programmed to paste the image strips on to the left or right side of the game viewport in real time if the player decided to spin left or right. You never notice a gap or a seam in the wall. Activision even figured out how to do animations during a spin. For example, they have flickering torches on the wall that are animated as the room spins. *Zork Nemesis* runs on Windows 95 and Macintosh.

The resourcefulness and flexibility of Pyros Pictures, and other independent production studios using 3D Studio MAX, is filling an important function in finding and developing new markets for 3D animation created with MAX. The size of the studio in no way limits the size of the project you can do. Greg would agree that the motto of his company could be "We can do that."

Evolution of MAX in 3D Animation

It has been a year since the first version of 3D Studio MAX was released, and many changes have taken place in both MAX and in the market for 3D Animation. A very significant number of 3D animation production studios have embraced 3DS MAX as one of their main production tools, and there are now over 25,000 licensed MAX systems out of 70,000 3D Studio systems now operating worldwide. With its open architecture and powerful new operating system, 3D Studio MAX is being accepted rapidly throughout the 3D Animation Industry, and is on its was toward becoming the most widely used, flexible, and feature-rich 3D animation software package in the industry.

Summary

The versatility of 3D Studio MAX is constantly being extended by third-party plug-ins. This has enabled a talented group of 3D animation studios to enter into new areas of high-end animation production. The improvements in MAX over 3D Studio R4 in the areas of character animation, modeling, lighting, and visual effects have established MAX as a professional-level production tool. Special effects animation for motion pictures was formerly the exclusive domain of expensive Unix-based software systems. But MAX, running on the Windows NT platform, has revolutionized the way motion picture special effects studios think about the most cost-effective ways to create their computer games, television commercials, and special effects. Softimage has recently ported its professional software from Unix to take advantage of the widely used Windows NT platform, and many studios now use both 3D Studio MAX and SoftImage in production.

Studios such as Sony Pictures Imageworks, Digital Phenomena, Blur, and Pyros Pictures have been instrumental in the development and testing of MAX under rigorous production conditions. Kinetix and the Yost Group development team have been extremely responsive to the needs of the 3D Studio animation community. It is their open and helpful relationship with the MAX users that has driven the rapid development of MAX into what could become the most versatile, powerful, and widely used 3D animation software available. The quality of the work presented in this chapter is just the tip of the iceberg, and a hint of what can be done with the advanced animation tools in 3D Studio MAX.

IMAGE CREATED BY SANFORD KENNEDY

Chapter 2

by Sanford Kennedy

USING 3D STUDIO MAX IN PRODUCTION

You are probably comfortable by now with 3D Studio MAX, and you have worked with all the tools. The next step is to integrate these tools into effective systems for solving a variety of advanced real-world animation problems. However, working effectively in the real world of production computer animation goes beyond simply knowing how to use software and computers. On a daily basis, you deal with clients, directors, producers, animation supervisors, network system administrators, your fellow animators, and the ever-present deadlines. In nearly every animation project, a similar sequence of events must be followed to bring the project to completion. As an animator using MAX in a production studio, you function as part of a team that may create hundreds of different visual elements over a period of months. At the end of the production, all these different elements must come together perfectly to integrate into the final product.

This chapter provides an overview of how a large production computer animation studio operates in the motion picture industry, and what kinds of opportunities and problems exist in this fast-paced, creative world. This chapter covers the following concepts:

- Organization of a production studio

- Production flow from concept to completion

- Working with producers and directors

- Windows NT and UNIX on one network

- MAX sharing files with other production software

Computer Graphics Production Studio

One of the most rewarding jobs in computer graphics is the creation of digital visual effects for film and video productions. The greatest benefit that digital effects can provide to movie production is the capability to manipulate the source imagery so that the digital effects fill in all the gaps between the different kinds of mechanical and practical special effects. Good digital effects can create a smoothly flowing visual experience, with transitions and elements otherwise impossible to obtain by using traditional sets, props, and miniature photography.

In the past ten years, it has been repeatedly predicted that computer graphics will take the place of traditional special effects and will make miniature photography obsolete. But, digital visual effects still comprise less than half of the special effects seen each year on the movie screen. It appears that a stable balance has been achieved in the struggle between digital and traditional special effects. Rather than taking over the effects industry, digital effects have joined with traditional special effects to enhance the director's ability to tell a story.

Many of the major motion picture studios have physical effects departments that work in concert with their digital effects departments. Digital effects directors now work with traditional special effects directors sharing storyboards and information, for example. Because much of the film effects footage is shot for use by the digital effects division, this kind of collaboration guarantees that the footage falls well within acceptable color, lighting, and camera steadiness parameters. This practice ensures that no unpleasant surprises arise when the digital and physical effects shots are composited together during the final stages of the production.

Figure 2.1 shows the physical organization of a typical high-end digital animation studio. All large computer graphics studios have similar equipment and departmental divisions. Until recently, if you walked into any of the well-established computer animation studios in Hollywood, you would find nothing but rows of Silicon Graphics workstations running extremely expensive 2D and 3D software packages. But, since the introduction of Adobe Photoshop running on the Macintosh computer, studios have gradually opened their doors to other software and hardware combinations, including 3D Studio MAX running on the IBM Pentium Pro.

FIGURE 2.1

The physical layout of a large computer animation studio in the motion picture industry.

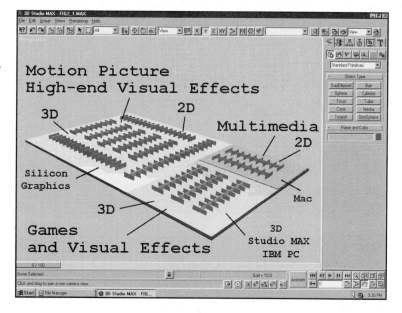

Figure 2.1 shows how a large computer animation studio in the motion picture industry is divided into different areas of activity. The upper half is the high-resolution motion picture visual effects division. The lower half is the game and multimedia division. In practice, both divisions share the workload, passing parts of projects back and forth according to what needs

to be done. At any time, a studio may be working on one or more motion pictures, a game, a multimedia CD-ROM, and a music video. The digital effects business is diversified, always with a wide variety of projects in production.

The top half of figure 2.1 is a large area labeled High-end Visual Effects. It is split into two sections, 3D Animation and 2D Compositing.

The following list identifies the departments in the 3D Animation section:

- Modeling
- Animation
- Character Animation
- Color and Lighting
- Particle and Atmospheric Effects
- Character Animation
- Textures and 3D Paint
- Programming (which includes Renderman)

This next list identifies the departments in the 2D and Compositing section:

- Compositing
- Rotoscope
- 2D Paintbox and Stunt Wire Removal
- Flame Compositing and Image Stabilization
- Image Processing and 2D Morphing

These department titles may vary in different studios, but the division of work is generally the same everywhere. A number of the studios in Hollywood also use the Silicon Graphics machines for games, commercials, television station logos, music videos, and motion capture. The separation of all these different functions into departments is necessary because it helps divvy up the massive workload and frees the individual animator from the tedium and stress of having to do every process on every shot by himself.

The lower half of figure 2.1 is labeled Games and Visual Effects. 3D Studio MAX can usually be found here. The "Games" label does not mean that MAX is only used in Hollywood for game production. Substantial work overlap occurs between divisions in the visual effects, game, and multimedia production studios. 3DS MAX is used for a wide variety of animation work, including animation and special effects for commercials, special effects and character animation for television productions, station breaks and logos, music videos, motion picture pre-visualization, games, and some visual effects for motion pictures.

MAX in the Working Environment

As figure 2.1 shows, the Games and Multimedia division is smaller than the Silicon Graphics-based Visual Effects division.

The Games division is not so obviously divided into separate departments. But, during a project, the same functional divisions in labor will appear, as animators are assigned in groups to perform different jobs. One group of animators, for example, might be asked to do modeling, another group the Character Studio animation, and another the particle systems. The following list indicates how MAX animators are grouped by function. This list looks almost the same as the previous list of Visual Effects department names.

The division of labor in 3D Studio MAX productions follows here:

- Modeling
- Animation
- 3D Morphing
- Character Animation with Bones Pro
- Color and Lighting
- Camera Tracking
- Particle and Atmospheric Effects
- Character Studio Animation
- Texture Mapping and 3D Paint
- Image Processing and LenzFX
- Video Post Compositing
- Pre-visualization and Video Animatics

This list makes it clear that 3D Studio MAX has the capability to do many of the 3D functions performed by the Silicon Graphics Visual Effects division. Most large studios that have purchased 3DS MAX have set up their MAX workstations in an area separate from the main visual effects production area because MAX is still primarily perceived as a strong game and character animation software package.

3D Studio MAX has not taken over a larger part of the visual effects work in the motion picture industry for two important reasons. The first reason is its lack of file compatibility with UNIX-based 3D Animation software. Almost all motion picture visual effects are rendered using Renderman Pro, which requires a new type of RIB file format that can only be written based on a Nurbs surface model. A NURBS (non-uniform rational B-spline) surface model is built from curved splines. The surface that is generated behaves like a quad patch in MAX, but it is not converted to polygons before it is exported for rendering, so it is resolution independent and very smooth. You cannot output this kind of a RIB file from a polygon-based software package, and MAX is a polygon-based package.

The second reason is that 3D Studio MAX cannot run on anything but an IBM PC. The current version of MAX is limited to the processor speed and databus throughput of the Pentium Pro microprocessor. The dual and quad multiple processor machines will render atmospheric scenes faster, but a straight geometry animation renders the same speed no matter how many processors are used. Geometry rendering is not multithreaded. The SGI rendering driver that allowed 3DS R4 .3DS files to render on multiprocessor SGI machines was released in 1995, but has never been updated to work for MAX files. In production, 3DS MAX files cannot be rendered on any of the big production render servers. IBM PC desktop workstations do not have the data throughput to deal directly with the massive frame sizes typical of visual effects work on digitized film footage. Here are the typical digitized image memory requirements: in the 70mm format, one individual 4 K film frame, which is over 4,000 pixels wide, requires 40 MB to store. A shot of 2,400 frames, which is just over 1 1/2 minutes long at 24 frames per second film speed, would require 96 GB! Even a single digitized frame of 35mm film is 2,048 pixels wide and requires 10 to 12 MB of RAM per frame to store. It is known as 2 K image. With images this size, the currently available Pentium Pro workstations are not powerful enough to render the thousands of images needed in the production of a typical effects film with 150 to 200 effects shots. Even a large rendering farm built from IBM Dual Pentium Pro workstations would not have the massive file handling capability and multi-megabyte data throughput necessary to keep up with the Silicon Graphics Render Servers in motion picture production today. At the larger studios it is not uncommon to have image storage capacities of 250 GB or more.

So how does an animation studio use 3DS MAX to do visual effects for motion pictures? Even though you cannot display a 2,048-pixel-wide image in the MAX viewport, you can render your output at that size. MAX can output finished images in the RLA, Targa, and TIF file formats, which can be read by high-end compositing programs, such as Flame, after translation by a file conversion program. It is not necessary to work directly on the film images themselves. Instead, animated effects sequences are done in MAX at film resolution, and then later composited into the film as animated elements. Figure 2.2 shows a number of the film and animated elements composited together to create one frame of a motion picture visual effects shot.

FIGURE 2.2

Film and digital image elements are combined to create one frame of a typical visual effects shot for a motion picture.

Any of the computer-generated image elements shown in figure 2.2 could be created with MAX by translating MAX's output images to UNIX-compatible 24-bit color TIF or TGA files, and then loading them, along with their alpha channel files, into Flame for compositing. MAX cannot do some of the fine subtle vapor effects that Alias can, but many films don't need vapor effects. The real trick is to correctly match the perspective of the original image with the inserted image, and then get the resolution, color, and lighting to match.

After the images are color balanced and color matched, they can be composited seamlessly into the motion picture visual effects sequence, and will be undetectable from the images created by the SGI high-end software. As a result, MAX is being used increasingly for low- and medium-budget visual effects shots where economy, modeling, lighting, and animation capabilities are more important than the issues of brute strength rendering speed, subtle vapors, and file incompatibility with Renderman.

Finding Your Strengths

As you find yourself drawn to a particular area of interest in MAX, it is important to realize that after you are identified as having a special skill in a particular area, a studio is unlikely to move you to any other specialty. That particular skill may become what you do for your entire career as an animator. This is a common practice for people who are good at character animation, modeling, or compositing. Fitting yourself into a company usually means that you fit your skills to the needs of the team, and then everyone counts on you to continue doing that specific job.

But what do you do if you lose interest in modeling and are drawn toward compositing? Telling your supervisor that you no longer want to be a modeler and would like to switch jobs will very likely result in him telling you that the company thinks of you as a modeler only, and that the company cannot afford to retrain you. In simple terms, that means if you want to switch jobs, you must also switch studios.

If you are determined to make a change, you need to be able to present yourself as a compositor, not a model builder. To do this, you need a show reel that only contains examples of compositing you have done. The new company must see you as a compositing specialist, not a modeler. You can prepare a "compositing" show reel by using Video Post in MAX, and then look for a new job while continuing to build models for your present employer.

Importance of Specialization

The demand for specialists in the animation industry is very high, especially for people good at modeling, texture mapping, or lighting. A generalist animator who has learned a little about everything in MAX cannot compete on the same level as someone who has spent years on computers doing lighting only. The reality of the business is that specialists at every level fill the vast majority of the jobs.

Learning complicated animation procedures, such as the sequence of steps for setting up all the rotation limits on a skeleton, would be very useful if you wanted to specialize in character animation. Of course it is important to know all the tools in MAX, but after you are on the job, most of the work you are asked to do will be tailored to match your specialty. In this way, the company is best served, and your skills always remain in demand.

Concept to Delivery

The long journey from storyboard to finished visual effects can take anywhere from six weeks to more than a year. Even animated video game productions last for many months. No matter what kind of production you find yourself involved in, you still need to go through the same careful steps to turn a storyboard's line drawings into smooth, professional animations, filled with color, action, and excitement. In a production containing only computer animation, the storyboard depicts every important moment in the finished project. You can get a sense of the flow of the story, which helps you understand how everything fits together.

In motion picture visual effects or even in commercial work, however, rarely do the computer animators see the complete storyboards for the production. Instead, you are given a bundle of storyboard pages showing miscellaneous disconnected visual effects shots (which make little sense). You may never be given a script to read, so you may never know how those shots fit into the production until it is shown in the theater. You have to trust the art director's instructions and come as close to the storyboard images as you can.

At the initial production meeting, the producer and art director discuss the shots assigned to the individual animators. The animators hear about how the storyboards should be interpreted from the viewpoint of the client, and they ask questions to clarify what the final project should look like. The entire project is examined in detail and the final look of the project is agreed upon. At this point the storyboards become the guiding force behind the project. From then on, the animators refer to them as the final authority for how each shot should be done. But, even though they are the main reference that you go by, they are subject to constant revision, sometimes two or three times a day. A good assistant producer stays on top of all the changes and comes by your desk with new boards and the director's latest notes while you work.

Problems often arise, especially if the storyboards have been drawn incorrectly. Poor storyboards can be a constant source of damaging trouble to a project. Many times you will see wild distortions of perspective, impossible to re-create in the computer. The artists seem to have a subconscious need to cheat the laws of perspective to give their boards drama, and in their enthusiasm, they draw objects in impossible situations. This causes the client and the producer endless hours of discussion to try to work out a compromise between the dynamic appearance they see in the storyboards and what can be done in real life. Figure 2.3 shows a frame from an exciting storyboard, but one that violates the laws of perspective and scale to achieve an exciting image.

FIGURE 2.3

A storyboard with incorrect perspective, object scale, and in the angle at which the plane is approaching the ground, which in the real world would crash traveling at supersonic speeds.

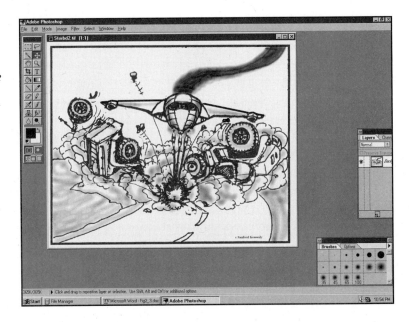

It is always important to point out any errors you see in the storyboards as early in the production as possible. This gives your producer time to get the boards corrected early, and protects the production from needless trouble as it nears completion.

Estimating Time of Completion

Time estimation in most industries is based on the tracking and measuring of repetitive tasks that are the same, year after year. In this way, most industries have compiled extensive lists of data about the costs of production and the length of time it takes to perform a specific task. If computer graphics were as simple and straightforward as traditional cel animation production, each action could be added up by a secretary who could prepare an accurate time estimate from years of previous data.

But you are working with 3D Studio MAX, which did not even exist as a production tool a short time ago. The process of animation can still be measured, but the tremendous increase in the number of variables associated with the computer animation production process makes it difficult to estimate the actual cost of production per frame.

Yet you will be asked to provide this information to your supervisor and producer at a moment's notice, even if you are doing something you have never done before. It makes business sense for them to want to know how long it will take, but it is very difficult to estimate something that has not been done before. In reality, this expectation is placed on every animator in the business, and they are often asked to meet a deadline set by making an educated guess.

The basic dilemma inherent in the business is that the people estimating the time and costs of a job are often not the ones doing the job. An interesting problem also occurs when producers used to working with Silicon Graphics machines come in to supervise a job in the PC/MAX department. They fail to ask what can and cannot be done in 3DS MAX and go ahead and start the job assuming that you can do anything an SGI machine can do. Even though MAX is tremendously powerful and versatile, it cannot do everything. They simply pass out the storyboards and start telling you when your part of the job has to be done. Because they do not understand MAX, it is important to tell them where the area of difficulty will be and then negotiate an adjusted deadline based on reality, not assumption. Remember, you are responsible for finishing the shot on their deadline, no matter how incorrect their time estimate might be.

Keeping a log book in a situation where the estimating of time and the capability of the system to do the job come into question helps you to cover your back. A log book is the best job insurance an animator can have. This proves especially true when problems with the machine or your work load prevent you from delivering your work by deadline. Toward the end of any project, the progress of the work undergoes constant re-examination, and the producer often calls so many meetings to ask for information on what you are doing, that you spend a great deal of time away from your machine, causing you to be later still.

Figure 2.4 shows a page from a dated sequential log book, with a list of every instruction change that you receive.

Animator's Log Book

Shot No.	Revision No.	Production:

Date of this page: Date Due:

Approved by?:

Storyboard Revision No.   Date.

Change Requested:

Notes:

By Who?:	Supervisor:	Director:

Problem:	Bad Machine:	Bad Art Work:	Bad Instructions:

Description:

Solution:

Fixed:?   Time Lost:

Witness: Person Notified:

It is simple to make up a notebook of these pages and then add more if needed. This effort is not wasted if you are working on many different shots or animation sequences at the same time. It is not unusual to be told to change something, and then be told to change it back to the way you were doing it originally, and then to be given slightly different directions by the art director, and then to have to change it again when the storyboard artist gives you a new version of her updated boards. The log helps you keep it all straight, which comes in handy when someone tells you, "that's not what I told you to do." It is impossible to try to keep track of all details in your head, especially when you run into problems. Record the exact time when you discovered the problems, what the problems were, and how they were resolved. Finally, note how much time you lost. It may not seem important until the producer asks you why you are late finishing your work and tells you that you are responsible for holding up production.

Deadlines Written in Stone

Deadlines can be a positive force in an animation studio. They can get everyone pulling together and help get your work organized quickly. Where deadlines cease working is when technical or artistic difficulties arise that stop you. Often you need more information or a *buy off*, which means that your work is approved and your progress is accepted. On most jobs, that can only come from one or two people (such as the director or the art director). On a motion picture, the art director is on the set, and you rarely get to see or talk to him because he is too busy. Many times during a project, you find yourself sitting at your computer for days trying to work on other parts of a project, without being able to go forward because the director is shooting on location and has not approved what you have done so far.

In every production studio, the deadline is treated by management as the most important event in your life. When a project gets close to the completion deadline, and shots are not yet finished, the producer goes into panic mode, which usually means that you don't go home until you have finished your work for the day and have it rendering on the network. Some companies expect you to camp out for 24 hours a day, seven days a week if necessary, and they compensate you by bringing in catered food and crackers.

Producer's assistants and animation supervisors have a tough job because they are the people in the middle. They are expected by management to get the work out by the deadline, but they can do little more than watch you work. Gung-ho assistant producers often slow the animation process by calling numerous pep-talk meetings where all the animators have to explain why their work is not yet finished. Big studios have two or three meetings a day with different people involved in supervising different portions of the project, and then the animators find themselves staying late to make up the time lost sitting in the meetings.

When production is behind, there is no best way to reduce the tension. The best strategy is to encourage everybody to be open about mistakes and problems as soon as they happen. Many animators become virtual hermits in their cubicles, buried under a pair of headphones and surrounded by trinkets they brought from home. Hiding under headphones is a mistake. An open, communicative group is always more efficient.

Working with Producers

The producer can be your best friend because he or she is directly responsible for keeping the animation studio running and keeping you employed. You can benefit by knowing as much as possible about the kinds of problems that can arise between producers, clients, and the animators who do the work.

The producer's main functions include searching for animation jobs, preparing estimated budgets, bidding against other companies to get the jobs, dealing with clients, and staying on top of every production problem and process along the way until the job is finished. They are the ones who take the final product of your labors to the client to ask them to sign off on the project. Half the time, the client does not approve the work on its first submission. The producer must then return to the studio for *re-dos*, which could mean anything from redoing a simple animation scene, to doing the entire job over again. Producers cope with a great deal of stress, but at the same time they get tremendous satisfaction from seeing a job they brought in turn out well.

Dealing with Client's Source Materials

One of the most critical contributing factors to problems in a production is the quality—or more often the lack of quality—of the source image materials. This one factor has been a major cause of losses for computer graphics companies for years. The image providers don't understand what level of quality must be maintained in the source material to make it usable for compositing and computer animation. Figure 2.5 shows the different types of source images that an animator must be expected to work with, and lists some of the problems that occur.

The animation supervisor is responsible for ensuring that the source images are placed on the network so that the animators can start reviewing the source material. It is important to familiarize yourself with what must be done and to check all the source material as soon as possible for image instability and color flaws.

In many cases, you must start the job before all your materials are available. Sometimes the digital scanning of the source material is delayed. Or, if you are working on a film or a commercial, the scene you are supposed to work on may not even be filmed yet (hence, no source images). This prevents you from checking the footage for omissions or bad frames.

FIGURE 2.5

Chart showing the different kinds of source imagery with associated problems.

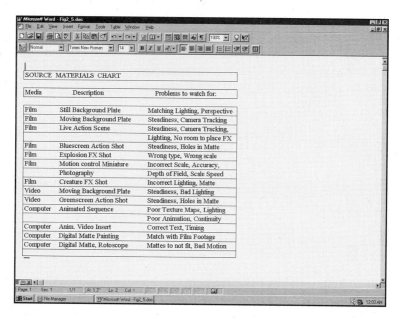

As soon as the visual effects job is awarded to the Digital Animation Studio, all the source images on film negative are delivered to the Digital Film Scanning department. They begin scanning the film immediately, testing for color matching and performing the necessary corrections to the digital files they are generating. In practice, studios often reject part or all of the source footage, usually because the developing process has badly modified the color, the source image is scratched, a shaking or wobbling image appears, or there are missing frames in a shot.

Normally, a motion picture is photographed with special curved lenses in the 35mm Anamorphic Wide Screen Format, which is a horizontally squeezed image. It appears distorted when you look at the film negative. Many digital effects companies can work with squeezed images just as easily as unsqueezed. It is not unusual to be asked to work directly with Anamorphic squeezed footage when doing digital effects. This request is popular with low-budget filmmakers who need to save the extra cost of getting an unsqueezed *dupe* or negative copy made. After working with squeezed images for a few days, you get used to it.

Bluescreen footage must also be tested to determine whether there are any blue areas on the actor, caused by *blue spill*—blue light that reflects back on to the actor from the blue background. Wherever there is blue spill, the matte is incomplete, and there is a hole that must be repaired before the image is acceptable.

If you work on any project that has elements shot on video or film, whether for commercials or an action movie, you are likely to have some of the previously mentioned problems.

Visualizing the Flow of Work

A production schedule bar chart is used by most studios to track the progress of each shot or animation sequence. Using the chart as a reference, the producer lets everyone involved see the flow of work. This works as a useful visual yardstick by which to measure your own progress and to remind yourself of forgotten details and upcoming deadlines. It is easy to get so bogged down in a barrage of details that a deadline seems to sneak up. Figure 2.6 shows a sample production schedule bar chart for one animator doing camera tracking.

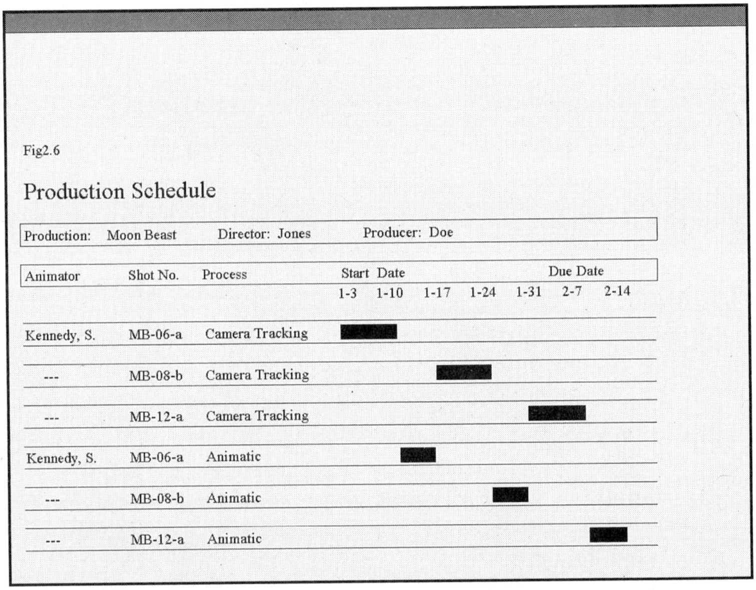

FIGURE 2.6

A typical production schedule bar chart.

Fig2.6

Production Schedule

Production:	Moon Beast		Director: Jones			Producer: Doe	

Animator	Shot No.	Process	Start Date				Due Date	
			1-3	1-10	1-17	1-24	1-31	2-7	2-14
Kennedy, S.	MB-06-a	Camera Tracking	▬▬▬						
---	MB-08-b	Camera Tracking			▬▬				
---	MB-12-a	Camera Tracking					▬▬		
Kennedy, S.	MB-06-a	Animatic			▬				
---	MB-08-b	Animatic				▬			
---	MB-12-a	Animatic						▬	

An updated, printed copy of the production schedule chart is handed out to each animator, usually every Monday morning as a reminder of how much time remains for the completion of each shot. Referring to this chart often makes it easy to plan your work.

Learning to See Through the Camera

Chapter 20 from *Inside 3D Studio MAX Volume I*, "Cameras and Setting the Shot," provides a conceptual overview of proper camera movement, but learning to see through the computer's camera is a skill that can best be perfected by shooting film or video. Physically moving around the room while peering through a camera viewfinder teaches you to see what the computer's camera should see and helps you understand lens angles. In this way, you soon accumulate and recall many different alternative kinds of camera moves. Sadly, exercise with a real camera does not free you from the awkwardness of having to use the computer's mouse interface to drag the camera icon around, but it gives you some great camera move ideas.

Networking Windows NT and Unix

On a studio network where Silicon Graphics machines are running Unix, IBM PCs are running Windows NT, and Macintosh Power PCs are running System 7.5, the machines are invisible to each other. Special software must be installed that enables all machines to be recognized and files to be read and stored on the main network file server. This can be accomplished by using a Silicon Graphics workstation as the Network File Server, and installing the KA Share software package. After installation, it enables the SGI server to recognize IBM and Mac machines on the network if they are NFS mounted. Each machine then shows up on the SGI Server as just another accessible hard drive.

For a detailed explanation of how to set up and run a rendering network with Windows NT and 3D Studio MAX, refer to Chapter 29, "Network Rendering," in *Inside 3D Studio MAX Volume I*.

MAX in Production with Other Software

Very few studios run only one software package or computer platform. Most studios combine many different programs to come up with a set of tools that best satisfies the demands of the work they do. Even game companies and architectural firms employ other software in addition to 3D Studio MAX to get work finished. The motion picture visual effects industry uses a tremendous variety of different software in the course of a motion picture production. No single package can do it all.

File Translation Programs

File Translation programs fall into two categories: consumer and professional. These programs convert both model and image files from one format to another to make them readable by different software platforms.

Many studios use Kodak's digital scanning services to scan their film footage. The patented Kodak Cineon digital image format is 10-bit color. It can be stored on DLT digital tape, on a large Metrum, or on an Exabite tape. The files can then be uploaded and read by most compositing software on a Silicon Graphics workstation, or it can be uploaded to a Macintosh Power PC and read by software packages such as DeBabelizer or Missing Link. No software is currently available on Windows NT that reads the Kodak Cineon format in the full 10 bits of color depth. To be used in MAX, the files must be converted to 8 bits per color channel TGA or TIF files. Then they can be loaded into 3D Studio MAX for use as background images for modeling or animation.

MAX with Matador and Flame

Matador and Flame are industry-standard, compositing and matte creation software packages that run on the Silicon Graphics Irix (UNIX) platform. 3D Studio MAX can output 24-bit TIF and TGA image files that can be read by both programs after translation. Matador is the real workhorse of the visual effects industry.

Matador is the software in which most of the matting, rotoscope, paintbox wire removal, and a major portion of the compositing is performed. Other packages, such as Prism's ICE and Wavefront Composer are used, but they are not quite as versatile. Flame is the high end of the compositing programs made for image stabilization and equipped with an extensive set of color and automated interactive compositing tools. Most of the final visual effects shots in a motion picture are finished in Flame. In Flame, images created by Alias, Wavefront, SoftImage, and Lightwave can be mixed together seamlessly with images generated by 3DS MAX.

MAX and SoftImage

The main competition for MAX in character animation is SoftImage running in Windows NT with its spline-based modeler, excellent inverse kinematics, and built-in motion capture data interface. It also has very advanced particle system capability and raytracing. SoftImage can read standard 3D Studio files, but at present it cannot read 3D Studio MAX files. It can be found in both large studio game divisions and in smaller, independent computer animation studios. SoftImage can output MAX-readable DXF files.

MAX and Alias

Alias is well-known as one of the best spline-based NURBS surface modeling programs available. It can also generate and work with polygonal models. This enables you to import models into Alias created in MAX as DXF files. This works well on models that are not too complex. If you try to import a model with a high number of faces, however, the resulting file in Alias can be very large, slowing redraw speed. Polygonal models cannot be converted to spline models, but MAX can read properly translated DXF output files from Alias.

MAX and Wavefront

An .OBJ file export plug-in now exists for MAX, which outputs a .MAX file and a polygonal .OBJ file with no spline or NURBS surface information. It can be read and animated in Wavefront Kinemation, but it cannot be output from Wavefront to Renderman Pro because it is not a NURBS surface model. Some game companies have written in-house conversion programs to change MAX triangular polygonal models to Wavefront-style quad polygonal models so that MAX models can be used in standard game authoring software that require quad polygons.

Working with a Service Bureau

Most studios must send all film scanning or film printing work out to a service bureau. Only the largest studios have their own digital film scanners and printers. The scanner stores digital output from a super high-resolution nitrogen-cooled LCD photo array, which converts light projected through the film into digital information. After the scanning is complete, the digital images are transferred to the studio on digital tape and then stored on the main network server's hard drive where all the animators have access to them.

Digital data to film image conversion, called *film printing*, is also available. A film printer is a combination of a motion picture camera and an enclosed high-resolution CRT (cathode ray tube) screen, which the camera photographs. One digital frame can be displayed on the unit's CRT screen at a time as a full-color image, or as three separate color separation images. The camera automatically photographs the CRT screen and then steps forward to the next frame.

Other services available at service bureaus include digital-to-video output, video editing, audio editing, and video tape duplication.

In Practice: Using 3D Studio MAX in Production

- **Model Building and Character Animation.** 3D Studio MAX workstations are proving to be very capable, powerful, and extremely cost-effective per investment dollar when compared with Alias/Wavefront UNIX-based workstations.

- **Game Production.** At the present time in the computer animation industry, the game and multimedia departments are where most of the 3D Studio MAX animators can be found.

- **Visual Effects.** Producers and directors in the motion picture and television production studios are beginning to recognize that real savings can be obtained by using 3D Studio MAX for music videos, television commercials, and motion picture visual effects.

- **Animation.** MAX is fully capable of creating high-end, professional quality animation for any media.

Part II

ANIMATION TECHNIQUES

IMAGE CREATED BY SANFORD KENNEDY

Chapter 3

by Sanford Kennedy

ADVANCED TRANSFORMATION ANIMATION

Since doing your first MAX tutorial, you have been building and animating objects by using move, rotate, and scale transforms. In almost all animation projects, you will find constant uses for transform animation. In this chapter, you work with transformations to solve advanced animation problems in a real-world project. Transformation techniques are applicable to all forms of animation, including games, multimedia, television commercials, and animation for motion pictures.

This chapter demonstrates the following advanced transformation methods:

- Transform animation with Out-of-Range Type Curves

- Using Helper objects to link complex objects for transform animation

- Using grouped objects and linked dummies to create complex animations

- Using XForm and Linked XForm modifiers to animate selected portions of objects at the sub-object vertex level

- Performing pick transformations along surfaces by using Grid objects

- Transform instances

Using Combinations of Basic Tools

Advanced transform animation is actually a collection of strategies for combining a wide variety of animation tools and tricks, which enables you to use basic tools in complex ways. Transform animations are the most commonly used techniques in 3D Studio MAX's set of animation tools. With them, you can open the power of MAX's modifiers and controllers and create nested layers of motion. The challenge is to figure out new ways to do sophisticated types of motions with the existing set of tools. Every animator's goal is to bring objects and characters to life and to create the kind of entertaining professional animations driving the current success of the animation industry.

In this chapter, you use advanced transform animation techniques to animate a television commercial about one of mankind's most familiar and constant companions: the cockroach.

Before you begin a real-world project such as this television commercial, you need to study the action needed for the characters. In most cases, you will be given a storyboard that illustrates the important actions in the animation. If you are handling the art direction yourself, however, you start with a script and then generate your own storyboards. In this chapter, the script for the R.E.A. Exterminators animation project is reprinted to give you an idea of the sequence of events and what the characters should be doing. The following tutorials are based on the script in which a sophisticated voice-over narrator speaks the dialogue in the pompous manner of an English lord. All the action you will animate is timed to synchronize to the words as the narrator speaks them.

The R.E.A. Exterminators Script

Opening Scene: An interior shot of a small table on which is a plate with a slice of cheese. The camera begins with a close-up of a cockroach sitting on the plate quietly eating the corner of the cheese. A "sophisticated" British voice begins speaking:

Voice-over Narration:

Narrator:

Since the Garden of Eden, mankind has tried to rid himself of the cockroach. In the beginning, there were primitive implements such as:

Cut to: Wide shot of the kitchen table.

Narrator:

A rock...

A huge rock falls on the table, hitting the edge of the plate and sending Rocky and the cheese flying into the air and onto the floor.

Cut to: Close-up dolly shot that follows the action closely for the rest of the commercial as Rocky falls to the floor, flips over, and runs across the floor trying to escape a series of weapons. Each one narrowly misses him.

Voice-over continues along with the action as Rocky runs:

Narrator:

A club...

A club swings in from the side causing Rocky to veer to one side.

Darts...

Three feathered darts sock into the floor around him and he jinks left.

Narrator:

When mankind became civilized, he turned to more advanced weapons, such as:

Traps...

A box "roach hotel" looms up ahead and Rocky leaps through it and out the other side without being caught.

Spray...

A spray can of poison appears over his head, and the stream of poison just misses him as he runs by.

Shoe...

A big shoe stomps down on him, and it looks like he is crushed, but miraculously he runs, unhurt, out from under the instep.

Magic charms...

A crude cloth cockroach voodoo doll looms up in his path stuck with long pins and he runs between its legs.

Demons...

An irregular ball of dirt suddenly unfolds into a spiny demon with two big angry eyes. Rocky veers around it.

And brooms...

A broom slaps the floor right behind him as Rocky reaches the wall and dives into a hole in the baseboard before the broom can smash him.

End Dolly Shot in Close-Up: Hole in the baseboard. The camera stops moving and zooms into the hole in the baseboard. Rocky's head peeks out for a moment and then ducks back out of sight.

Narrator (still serious):

Wouldn't it be easier to call R.E.A. Exterminators? Pick up the phone now and call: ROACH EATERS ANONYMOUS, the exterminators with an appetite.

Fade to Black

In this script, an undertone of ironic humor must be translated to the screen through your animation. In all comedic animations, the timing, the pace, and the follow-through of the action are very important. First, however, you must prepare your cockroach model and set the scene.

Transform Animation with Out-of-Range Type Curves

To establish a foundation of related techniques used in advanced transform animation, you will begin with a simple example of a series of boxes linked together with dummies similar in shape to an insect's leg. The boxes are arranged to resemble the leg segments with Dummy helper objects placed at every joint. After the leg is constructed and animated, you will learn to create a looping animation that simulates the walking motion of an insect's leg by setting the Parameter Curve Out-of-Range Type to Ping Pong in Track View. Figure 3.1 shows the simple chain of boxes that will simulate the motion of a cockroach's leg.

NOTE

For a detailed explanation of Parameter Curve Out-of-Range Types, review Chapter 23 of *Inside 3D Studio MAX, Volume I*, "Animation Control Tools."

FIGURE 3.1

View of the box leg with the Helpers rollout menu open.

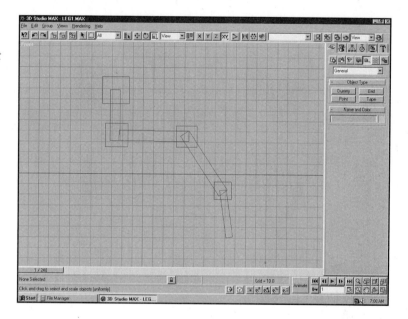

To set up the box leg for animation, you will use the leg1.max file from the book's accompanying CD. The boxes have already been created. You will create and place the dummies and link the leg together.

PLACING THE DUMMIES AND LINKING THE LEG TOGETHER

1. Load leg1.max from the accompanying CD.

2. In the Create command panel, click on the Helpers icon to display the Helper object types. In the Object Type rollout, click on Dummy.

3. Create four dummies in the Front view, starting at the upper-left end of the upper-left box (refer to fig. 3.1).

4. Click on the Select and Link icon and then click and drag a link from the lower-right box, Box04, to the lower-right dummy, Dummy04.

5. Click and drag a link from Dummy04 to the next higher box, Box03. Move up the leg and link Box03 to Dummy03, then link Dummy 03 to Box 02, and so on. Repeat this process, linking all the boxes and their dummies together in a hierarchy to the parent Dummy01.

6. Save the scene as **cleg01.max**.

You have now established a parent-child hierarchical relationship between the leg segments. The nature of hierarchies dictates that the parent will pass on its transformations to the child. The child adds its transformation to the parent's and passes the total on to the next child in the chain. To simulate the motion of an insect's leg, each box in the chain will be rotated slightly farther than the box higher up in the hierarchical chain. The last box, called the Leaf, will rotate the farthest. In the next exercise, you apply a rotation transform to each dummy to create the motion of the leg. The boxes will be moved as passive objects controlled by the transformations of the linked dummies.

APPLYING A ROTATION TRANSFORM

1. Click on the Time Configuration icon and in the dialog, set the Animation Frame Range to 30.

2. Close the dialog and click on the Go To End icon to move the Time Slider to frame 30.

3. Click on the Animate button to turn on Animation mode.

4. Click on the Select and Rotate icon. To apply the first rotate transform, click on Dummy01 and drag upward so that the entire leg rotates clockwise 15 degrees.

5. Click on Dummy02 and rotate it counterclockwise 20 degrees.

6. Click on Dummy03 and rotate it clockwise 30 degrees.

7. Click on Dummy04 and rotate it clockwise 40 degrees, and then turn off Animate.

8. Play the animation. The leg pulls in and moves like an insect's leg.

9. Save the scene as **cleg02.max**.

This animation does not cycle correctly. If played in a loop, it would jerk each time it made the transition from frame 30 back to frame 0 as the animation repeats. To create a smooth repeating cycle of motion, you can change the Out-of-Range Type Curve to Ping Pong to make the leg move in and out smoothly.

CHANGING THE OUT OF RANGE CURVE

1. Click on the Min/Max Toggle icon and then click on the Track View icon.

2. In the Track View window, click on the Filter icon. In the menu, click on Animated Tracks and then click on OK.

3. All the Dummy animation tracks will be displayed with their range bars. Now change the length of the animation by opening the Time Configuration dialog and changing the animation length to 240.

4. In the lower toolbar of the Track View, click on the Zoom Horizontal Extents icon. This enables you to see the new length of the animation.

5. In the Hierarchy window of the Track View, click on the name of the Rotation track for Dummy01. It will be surrounded by a blue box.

6. In the upper Track View toolbar, click on the Parameter Curve Out-of-Range Types icon. A Param Curve dialog opens (see fig. 3.2).

7. In the Param Curve dialog, click on Ping Pong. This causes MAX to smoothly cycle the motion of the leg over the length of the animation.

8. Repeat step steps 5–8 to change to a Ping Pong curve for each of the four Rotation tracks.

9. Minimize the Track View and play the animation. The leg will move in and out smoothly four times.

10. Save the scene as **cleg03.max**.

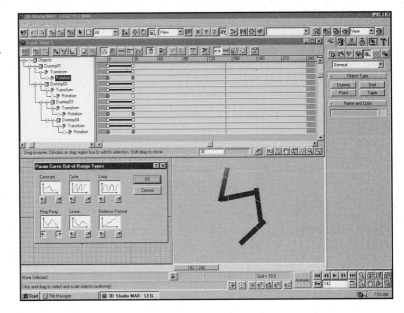

FIGURE 3.2

View of the Track View showing the Parameter Curve Out-of-Range Types menu.

To examine a finished version of this animation load legcyc2.max from the Ch03 directory on the accompanying CD. The looping animation you have just created is identical to the way you will set up and animate the run cycle motion of the legs of the cockroach. This is one of many ways to apply advanced transforms to complex models for character animation without the need for Inverse Kinematics.

Of course, you can use IK because the hierarchy is already set up. You can try to animate the leg with IK by clicking on the Inverse Kinematics On-Off toggle, turning on Select and Move, and then dragging Dummy04 around. But without going through the process of applying axis constraints, the leg will twist on every axis and be totally uncontrollable in the IK interactive mode. IK is not needed for transform animation, therefore no further discussion of it appears in this chapter.

Using Helper Objects to Link Complex Objects

In the first tutorial of this section, you prepare the main character, Rocky the Roach, for animation by setting up the linkages in his head and legs. You use Rotate transformations to animate Rocky's frantic run through the gauntlet of weapons that rain down on him during the commercial. You use helper objects to aid in the animation of his head movements in the opening eating scene and his leg movements for his running scenes.

Helper objects in 3DS MAX are extremely flexible and useful in transformation animations. By using dummy and grid objects, simple transformations can be made to produce complicated multiple motions.

Note

For a general discussion of Grid and dummy helper objects, see Chapter 6, "Selections, Transforms, and Precision," of Inside 3D Studio MAX Volume I.

You will begin the tutorial by using a grid object to quickly place Dummy objects in the correct location for linking together the different parts of the insect's head. In animating any model, you can find axes that are not in the correct location or orientation. Moving the pivot point with the Place Pivot command can be effective for your current transformations, but does not permanently fix the problem. The use of Dummy objects will permanently solve these problems by enabling you to build the parts in any orientation you want. Then you place a dummy where you want the object's pivot located, and link the object to the dummy. This enables you to place the axis exactly where you want it.

The use of a Grid Object as a temporary construction plane speeds up the process of adding dummies to a complex model. Normally, you would create a dummy in a front or side view. It will look correct, but in fact it is only correct in two of the three axes because the dummy's origin is always on the active construction plane for the viewport in which it was created. In a 3D model, the joints are seldom located on the same flat construction plane. That means that if the dummy is placed correctly in the front view, the X and Y axes, you must then go to the side or top view to select and move the dummy in the Z axis. If the model has a dense overlapping mesh structure, or has many overlapping dummies, you may have difficulty selecting and placing it correctly. It is important to give a logical name to each of the dummies as you create them. That way, when you want to translate a particular dummy, you can quickly select it in the Select By Name dialog.

You will create and position six dummies in the cockroach's head to act as pivots for the feelers, palps (mouth appendages), and the jaws (see the following exercise). After the dummies are placed on the head, you link the parts to the dummies and then the dummies to the head. Then you link the head to the forward body shell. To prepare the model correctly, you need to place dummies at all the joints and link all the leg parts to the abdomen. The reason for using so many dummies is twofold. The first reason is to correct any of the X, Y, and Z axes orientations that are incorrectly located or flipped in the wrong direction on one side of the model. Many times the axes are rotated at the wrong angle for correct leg movement. The second reason to use dummies is that each joint should have its own specific name so that they can be easily located and selected for translation. Figure 3.3 shows the Grid Object creation rollout in the Helpers menu. Figure 3.4 shows how to position the grid object.

FIGURE 3.3

The Grid Object rollout menu in the Create/ Helper Object panel.

FIGURE 3.4

View of the model cockroach's head showing a Grid object temporary construction plane bisecting the head of the cockroach with dummies in place to link to feelers, palps (mouth appendages), and jaws.

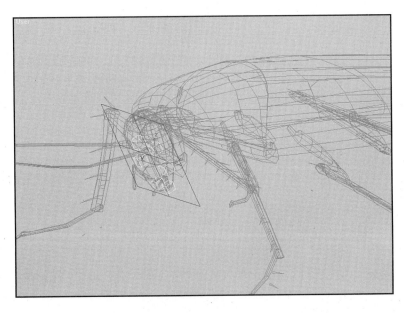

Note

All of the following exercise files can be found in the CHAP03 directory on the accompanying CD. You will also need the roach.mat material library file, and the bitmaps found on the CD-ROM in the Chap03\Maps directory. You can temporarily add the CD-ROM to MAX's Bitmap file path so MAX can find all the bitmaps for the materials. For example, if your CD-ROM is drive E:, the entry in the Configure Paths/Bitmaps dialog would look like this: E:\CHAP03\Maps. The room.tif background image for the rendering screen background is also in the Maps directory. If you need to review how to set up the bitmap in background for rendering, review Chapters 26 and 27 in *Inside 3D Studio MAX, Volume I*, or your 3D Studio MAX manual.

CREATING A GRID OBJECT AND PLACING DUMMY HELPER OBJECTS

1. Load croach01.max from the accompanying CD. The scene includes a cockroach, a kitchen table, and a plate with a piece of cheese sitting in the middle of it.

2. In the toolbar, click on the Select By Name icon, and in the Select Object menu that opens up, select the Head, Antennas, Palps, and Jaws, and then click on Select. When the menu closes, click on the Zoom Extents All Selected button.

3. It is important to freeze all the parts except the Head, Antennas, Palps, and Jaws to prevent incorrect linkages from being made. Click on Display, and then click on the Freeze by Selection bar to open the rollout. Click on Freeze Unselected.

4. To create a Grid helper object, click on the Create tab and then click on the Helpers icon. In the Object Type rollout menu, select Grid.

5. In the Left viewport, click and drag a rectangle around the Head object to create a grid object (refer to fig. 3.4 for the approximate size).

6. In the Front viewport, zoom out until you can see the new grid and the head of the cockroach. The grid is currently located on the Home construction plane, but the roach's head is some distance away.

7. Select and move the grid in the Front viewport in the X axis until it is centered in the head, and then rotate it until it passes through the base of the feelers and the palps as shown in figure 3.4.

8. With the Grid selected you will Activate the Grid object by clicking Views in the menu bar, and from the pull-down menu, click on Grids. From the pop-out menu select Activate Grid Object.

9. Again in the Helpers, Object Type rollout menu, click on Dummy. In the Left viewport, click and drag to create a small dummy at the base of the feeler on the right.

10. In the Name and Color window in the Command panel, rename the dummy **DummyLFeel** for Dummy Left Feeler. This enables you to identify exactly which dummy is linked to which feeler. Repeat the process to create identical dummies for the feelers, palps, and jaws as shown in figure 3.4. Be certain to give them all names that identify them, such as **DummyRJaw**.

11. Now you link all the parts to their respective dummies. Click on the Select and Link icon and select the first feeler. Click and drag from the feeler to DummyLFeel to link the feeler to its dummy. Then click on that same dummy, and drag a link from the dummy to the head.

12. Repeat the process with the right feeler and its DummyRFeel, and then do the left and right jaw, and the left and right palp.

13. To link the head to the cockroach shell and place the pivot under the shell behind the head, you create another dummy. But first you must unfreeze the body of the roach. Click on the Display tab, and in the Freeze by Selection rollout, click on Unfreeze by Name. Select RoachBody and click on Unfreeze.

14. Before creating the neck dummy, turn off the Grid Object by clicking on Views, and then in the drop-down menu, click on grid, then on Activate Home Grid.

15. To create the dummy for the neck as shown in figure 3.5, click on the Create/Helpers icon, and then click on Dummy. Click and drag in the front view to create a neck dummy at the back of the roach's head.

16. Click on the Name and Color window in the Command panel, and then change the name of the dummy to **DummyNeck**. Lock the selection and use Select and Move to position the dummy near the top of the head, under the front lip of the forward body shell.

17. Activate the top viewport, click Zoom Extents and drag the dummy downward until it is centered on the centerline of the roach's head. Click on the spacebar to unlock the selection.

18. In the right, link the roach's head to the DummyNeck object and link the DummyNeck to the RoachBody object.

19. When finished, make certain that all the parts of the head (including the DummyNeck) are unfrozen. Then select all the parts of the roach's head. Click on Group in the menu bar, and then click on Group in the pull-down menu. In the Group dialog, type the name **RHead** and then click on OK.

20. Be certain to save your scene file as **rocky01.max** to make sure that you don't lose your work.

FIGURE 3.5

This is view of the DummyNeck object that links the head to the roach's shell and acts as the new pivot point for the head.

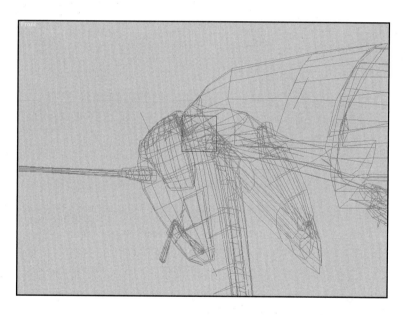

Using Grouped Objects to Create Complex Animations

The technique of animating objects within groups of objects that are themselves part of larger groups of objects is a very powerful technique. It is similar in concept to nesting one software program within another. This is a way to link together many different animated objects in different parts of a scene without actually creating hierarchies. This technique is used in combinations with various animation tools throughout the rest of this chapter. The animated objects within a group can have any number of different modifiers, controllers, and other animations applied to them; the group itself can be treated as a single object and linked to a parent dummy. Then that parent dummy is linked to a larger animated system of grouped objects, to be animated in additional ways.

Here is where the complexity of overlapping objects can move beyond the capability to the mouse to be an effective selection and animation tool. You will switch to using direct data entry through the Transform Type-in to animate many of the more complex portions of this project. The next exercise explains the sequence of steps required to open a group, in this case the cockroach's RHead group, to animate the objects within the group by using the Transform Type-in dialog, and then to close the group.

Using the Transform Type-In

The model is now ready for animation. Figure 3.6 shows the opening shot as described in the script. It is a close-up of the cockroach poised in the correct position to take a bite from the corner of a piece of cheese. Rather than use the mouse to try to select the dummies linked to the feeler and jaws, and then move these small parts with the clumsy mouse, you will use type-in commands. The Select by Name dialog will be used to choose the object to move, and then the Transform Type-in will be used to animate the rotations of the head, feeler, and mouth parts. This method enables you to work on very densely packed models in complex scenes without fear of transforming the wrong object or going too far with your mouse.

As you work in Animation mode, the Transform Type-in dialog stays open as you move the Time Slider along with the mouse. This enables you to type entries into the Absolute and Relative numeric entry fields to set animation keys while you are selecting objects and moving through the animation. In this way, you can create very accurate transform animations without ever using the mouse.

In the next tutorial, you animate the head and antenna moving over the cheese to make it appear that the roach has bitten into the cheese. The action in this part of the animation is subdued, and requires subtle movements, in direct contrast to the frantic motion of the rest of the animation after the rock hits the table. This shot will be called **Scene 1**. The animation has been divided into four scenes that coincide with each major change in camera position.

FIGURE 3.6

Close-up view of the cockroach with all the Dummy objects in place, sitting on the plate just behind the piece of cheese.

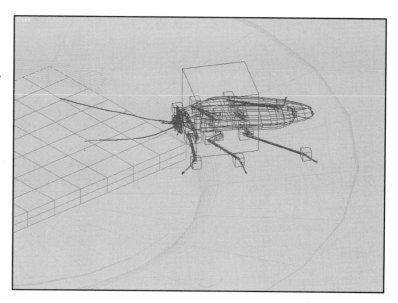

ANIMATE THE HEAD AND ANTENNA OVER THE CHEESE

1. Load croach02.max from the accompanying CD, which includes Camera01 in the correct position. Make certain that the Frame Range is set to 900 frames.

2. Click the Select by Name icon, and in the object list, click on the cockroach's head group, called Rhead, and click Select.

3. To animate the left antenna, you must first open the cockroach's head group. To open the RHead group, click on Group. In the pull-down menu, click on Group, and then click on Open. Now all the objects inside the head group will be accessible, and will be listed in the Select by Name menu.

4. To use Zoom Extents All Selected to bring the cockroach's face into a close-up view, click Select by Name and from the object list click on head. Click select, then click the Zoom Extents All Selected icon.

5. Animate Rocky's left feeler by rotating its parent dummy. Use the Select by Name dialog to select DummyLFeel, and lock the selection.

6. Right-click in the front viewport to activate it, then turn on the Animate button, and move the Time Slider to frame 20.

7. In the Edit menu, click on Transform Type-in.

8. The Rotate Transform Type-In dialog opens. To move the antenna, place the cursor over the Offset Screen Z axis spinner. Drag the spinner up and down to watch the antenna rotate up and down.

9. Rotate the feeler down until it touches the top of the cheese.

10. Use the Select by Name dialog and select DummyRFeel for the right feeler, and then repeat steps 8 and 9.

11. To animate the feelers, click the Animate button and move the Time Slider to frame 40. Using the previous rotation techniques, rotate the feeler dummies so that both feelers move upward to their original frame 0 angles.

12. Click the Time Configuration icon and turn off Real-time playback, then Click on Play to watch the animation of the feelers going down and up.

13. Now animate the head rotating toward the camera. With the Animate button on, move the Time Slider to frame 35. Select DummyNeck in the Select by Name dialog and lock the selection.

14. With the Front viewport active, click on the Offset Screen Y axis spinner in the Rotate Transform Type-in dialog. Drag the spinner up until the head rotates to face the camera at frame 35.

15. Move the Time Slider to frame 50 and rotate the Y spinner in the opposite direction so that the head returns halfway to its original position at frame 50.

16. Turn off Animate, and preview the animation.

Because the head is positioned with its jaws almost in contact with the corner of the cheese, this is all the motion necessary to suggest that Rocky is taking a bite of cheese. You may want to animate the palps wiggling, and the jaws actually taking a bite of the cheese on your own.

17. The first scene ends with a cut. Save your file as **rocky02.max**.

From this point on, you will no longer be given detailed instructions about how to perform any operation that has already been described in previous exercises. An example of this is the use of the Group command. In the rest of this chapter, the instructions will say "group the object" without describing the steps needed to group something. Also Hide and Freeze will no longer be detailed step by step. You should already be very familiar with how to use these commands.

Animating Rocky's Legs for the Run Cycle

In this exercise, you use linked rotation transforms to animate the leg movement for Rocky the Roach's run through the gauntlet of the exterminator's weapons. This will be a simple 30-frame exercise to demonstrate the alternate "reach forward and reach back" insect leg movements necessary to make Rocky run. All of the leg dummies move from the start position at frame 0 to the end position at frame 5. This enables the keys of the animation to "hook up" perfectly for a smooth run cycle using the Out-of-Range Type function curve. Figure 3.7 shows the "starting" position for the legs, and figure 3.8 shows the "ending" position.

When finished, Rocky's short run cycle can be turned into repeat cycles and multiplied in length by applying Out-of-Range Cycle types to each rotation transform track of the leg dummies. Rocky runs continuously.

To move on with the exploration of other methods of advanced transform animation, the Out-of-Range animation technique explanation will not be repeated in this exercise. If you do not recall how to apply it, please return to the first two exercises in this chapter to review.

Only a simple walk or run cycle is needed to get convincing insect run animation for this commercial because much of the viewer's attention is drawn away from Rocky by the rain of weapons attacking him in the final animation.

FIGURE 3.7
The legs of the cockroach are shown rotated into their starting positions at frame 0, the starting frame of the run cycle animation.

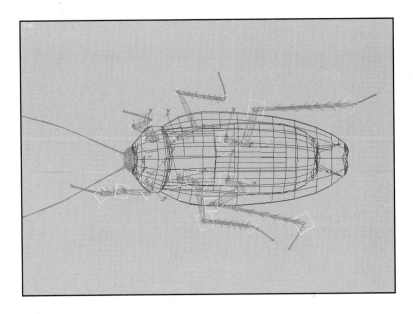

FIGURE 3.8
The opposite or "ending" leg position for the cockroach at frame 5, the opposite of figure 3.7.

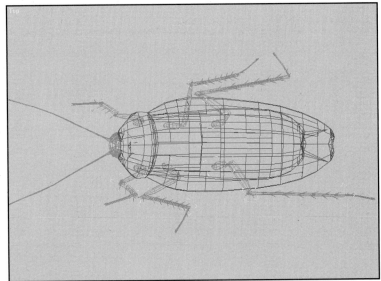

ANIMATING A SIMPLE RUN CYCLE

1. Load croach03.max from the accompanying CD so that you can use the finished cockroach model with linked dummies at each leg joint.

2. In the Top viewport click on Select Object, and then hold down the Ctrl key and select the cockroach's wing, abdomen, and prothorax (front shell).

3. Freeze the objects by clicking on the Display tab and then clicking Freeze Selected.

4. Expand the Top viewport by clicking on the Min/Max Toggle. The legs are at the neutral middle position. To animate the run cycle they need to be rotated into the more extreme starting position as shown in figure 3.7 at frame 0.

5. The leg dummies are easily seen, and can be selected with the mouse in the Top viewport if you are careful. Zoom in on the right front leg. The innermost dummy is named LegRF01, meaning: Leg, Right Front, joint01. Each leg has four Dummies 01 to 04 numbered from the innermost Parent, to the outermost child 04.

6. Click Select and Rotate, restricted to Z. Carefully click one corner of Dummy LefRF01, and drag the mouse downward to rotate the entire leg 15 degrees CCW, or counterclockwise.

7. Go to the next farther out dummy, egRF02. Repeat step 6, except you will rotate this dummy 20 degrees CCW. Continue working, repeating this same procedure until all the legs match the starting position as shown in figure 3.7.

T I P

It is often hard to select a Dummy object overlapped by another object, such as a leg segment. MAX enables you to click once or twice more to shift MAX's Selection tool back along the Z axis to the dummy. You can then lock the selection and rotate it safely.

8. After the legs are at their starting positions at frame 0, move the Time Slider to frame 5.

9. The next operation at frame 5 is almost the exact opposite of what you just did at frame 0, as shown in figure 3.8. Now click on the Animate button to turn on Animation mode.

10. At frame 5 reverse all the leg positions and create the second half of the run cycle.

11. That completes the setup for the run cycle. Now go to the Track View, click the Filter icon and select Animated tracks only. Then apply the Out-of-Range Type curve to each of the leg dummy rotation keys at frame 5. For every key, select Ping-Pong type in the Out-of-Range dialog box.

TIP

I use a Dry Erase Marker pen to trace guide lines over the legs to record their starting angles. I draw these lines right on my computer screen. They rub off easily with a cloth or fingers.

The basic trick I use in creating an insect's walk with transform animation is to think of the legs as two sets of counter-rotating tripods. The insect shifts its weight from one tripod to the other as it walks. Try to keep the legs tucked in close to the sides of the cockroach's body as they move to ensure greater realism.

12. Play the animation in the Top viewport to test the motion. The animation should have no visible jump or hesitation.

13. When you have successfully created the 30-frame run cycle, save the scene file to your MAX directory as **rocky03.max**.

The next step would normally be to apply this animation to the entire project. Because, however, there are areas where you don't want Rocky to run in the final animation, you do not actually animate the run cycle until all the other animation operations are complete. Then you save two copies of the final file— one where Rocky doesn't run and the other where you apply the run cycle animation. By selecting different cameras, you assemble the final animation by rendering cameras 1 and 2 from the non-run cycle file and cameras 3 and 4 from the run cycle file. See the New Riders web site (www.newriders.com) for more detailed instructions on assembling the final animation.

NOTE

It is important to first establish the movement path of Rocky's body through the gauntlet of weapons before applying the run cycle to its legs. For this reason you will see Rocky sliding along without moving his legs during the following exercises.

Use Nested Groups of Objects to Create Complex Animations

The *nested groups* term used here is borrowed from programming language, meaning objects contained within objects. Even though these nested groups are not linked together in a parent/child hierarchy, they do pass on motion from the master group to the sub-group. The transform animation of nested groups require you to open the master group, called FlipObjects, and then apply rotate transform animations to the objects within the group. This can get complicated in big projects, but it is a very powerful and straightforward technique for creating complex motion.

Transforming Groups by Using Offset Dummies

On many occasions, you will want to create animated objects that are part of a larger group of objects. In this animation, you animate an object group that rotates around an offset dummy used as a pivot point. In Scene 2 of the R.E.A. Exterminators commercial, which is called "Flip," the objects on the tabletop stay together as they are flipped into the air.

The script calls for a large rock to drop onto the table from above frame, just after the narrator says the words, "A rock...." The script calls for a cut to a medium camera shot showing the tabletop and some of the space above it. Rather than trying to animate Camera01 to move up to this new location, it is more practical to create a second camera, Camera02, for Scene 2. Figure 3.9 shows the four cameras in place for the four different camera angles. Camera04 is linked to the cockroach and follows it during Scene 4, the big running scene.

FIGURE 3.9

View of four cameras in their starting positions for the four scenes requiring different camera angles.

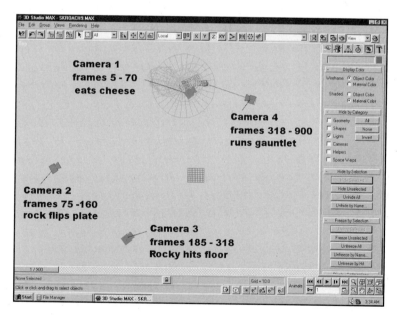

NOTE

To animate this commercial, you will use four cameras in all. You will not completely finish the commercial in this chapter because Video Post procedures will be covered elsewhere. Instead, you will render .AVI movies to see the results of your exercises. If you want to finish the project as it was originally designed, render and output each of the four scenes as individual targa or jpeg frames. Then, in Video Post, create .IFL files for the images, set up the render Queue to assemble them together, and re-render the project as an AVI movie.

In Scene 2, the plate, cheese, and roach should remain visible within the Camera viewport during the arc of their flight. Figure 3.10 is a portion of the storyboard that illustrates the camera angle and the action for the Flip sequence. Figure 3.11 shows the 3DS MAX models built to match the storyboard drawing.

FIGURE 3.10

A storyboard panel showing the main elements of the Flip scene.

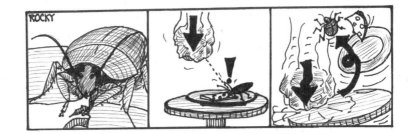

FIGURE 3.11

A view of the 3DS MAX models in a position matching the storyboard drawing.

In the following exercise, a number of dummies have been created to provide different offset rotational pivot points for the grouped objects in the plate Flip scene. Because of the difficulty of explaining in words where each object and dummy should be placed and how their links should be set up, the entire scene has been set up to demonstrate how you could create this scene. This is only one way to accomplish the effect of flipping the plate up into the air. You can easily modify this scene to change the way each object moves.

ANIMATING THE PLATE FLIP

1. Load croach04.max from the accompanying CD, which includes the animated falling rock and Camera02 in the correct position for the Flip scene.

2. Zoom into a close-up of the plate in the top viewport. You will notice a number of dummy objects. The scene is constructed as a combination of groups of objects that are linked to dummies. The cockroach is a group of objects called Roach, linked to its own dummy called RoachRoll.

3. To see how the different dummies are linked, and what they are designed to do, you will select and rotate each one, starting with the RoachRoll dummy located in front of the Roach's head. Use Region Zoom in the top viewport to zoom into a close-up of the cockroach and its associated dummies. Click the Min/Max toggle to enlarge the viewport.

NOTE

You will be testing the way each dummy affects its linked object, but remember to hit the Undo button each time after you move something. All the animation keys are already set, and if you disturb the relationships of the various objects at this point, you may end up seeing the roach pass through the plate during the animation. If you mess up the scene, re-load croach04.max and continue with the exercise.

4. Click on Select by Name and, from the object list, select RoachRoll. Click and drag the selected dummy. Notice that the entire roach moves around the dummy's Z axis in a circle with the dummy as the central pivot point. Be sure to click Undo immediately after rotating the dummy.

5. Try switching the axis from Z to X or Y, then rotate the RochRoll dummy again. Click Undo.

6. To see how the rotation of this dummy was set up for the animation, move the time slider to frame 108 where the movement of the RoachRoll dummy begins. To see what is moving, zoom the viewport out until you can see the entire plate.

7. Click the Next Frame button and step through the animation to frame 113. Notice how in only five frames the plate, the cheese, and the cockroach are all beginning to move in different directions.

8. The RoachRoll dummy has begun to rotate on its X axis to flip the roach upside down.

9. Click the Min/Max Toggle to restore four views. Continue stepping forward until you reach frame 128. The Roach is a child of the RoachRoll dummy which is, in turn, linked to the Plate. That means that the roach will maintain its position relative to the plate's motion no matter where the plates goes, unless you choose to move it.

10. In the front viewport you can see that the rock has already hit the table and that the plate, the roach, and the cheese are now up in the air above the table (see fig. 3.12). This elevation is controlled by the large dummy below the table, DummyFlip.

11. DummyFlip provides the main offset center of rotation that will lift all the grouped objects off the table and send them up into the air and eventually over and down to impact the floor. Click and rotate the DummyFlip dummy in the front viewport to see how it moves the plate, cheese, and roach in a long arc. Click Undo to restore the correct relationships.

12. Try running the animation back and forth and rotating all the different dummies to see how they affect the movement of the objects. They include PlateRoll, and of course, CheeseRoll. Remember to click Undo each time. Also remember that in an animation of this type, the effect is ruined if any of the objects can be seen passing through each other.

13. To experiment with increasing the rate and violence of the movements, you can modify the existing animation keys. Click the Animation button to enter Animation mode, then use the Select by Name dialog to select an object. Try modifying the rotation of the CheeseRoll dummy.

14. Lock the selection. You can use the Key Mode toggle to quickly move between the selected object's keys by clicking the Next Frame and Previous Frame buttons. Use the Select and Rotate tool to change the position and rotation of the dummy at its keyframe. Then turn off the animaton mode and render a preview to see how your changes affect the animation.

15. When you are satisfied, save the file as **rocky04.max**. Activate the Camera02 viewport and Render an AVI movie of the sequence from frame 80 to frame 160, to see your own version of the Flip sequence.

FIGURE 3.12

View of the table, the cockroach, the plate, and the cheese, after the rock has hit the plate and flipped it into the air.

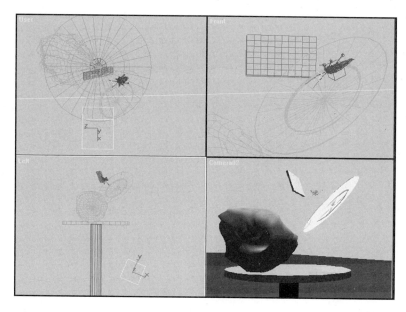

Using XForm and Linked XForm Modifiers

One of the most advanced features of 3D Studio MAX is its capability to animate individual vertices, or sets of vertices, by using the XForm and the Linked XForm modifiers. After the vertices are selected on the sub-object level by an Edit Mesh modifier or a Volume Select modifier, the transform tools can be applied to the vertices. After you have animated the vertices, you can still animate the original object with transform tools. You could rotate a selected set of vertices in an object in one direction, for example, and add a Rotate transform to turn the whole object in another direction. The animated sub-object transform modifies the surface shape in reference to its own axis, ignoring the axis of the object. By experimentation, a number of exotic animated forms can quickly be made from primitive shapes. Doing detailed animated surface modification, however, takes careful planning.

Distorting Objects with XForm

Simulating Squash and Stretch animation can be done by using Volume Select to select the entire object, and then applying XForm. The object's local axis is then scaled by scaling the XForm modifier gizmo in two of the axes.

In the R.E.A. Exterminators animation, the Club object is transformed with an XForm modifier to create a Squash deformation as it hits the floor right behind Rocky the Roach.

In this exercise, you will only apply a Volume Select modifier to the end of the club and then use an XForm modifier to squash only the immediate area of the club that contacts the floor, leaving the rest of the club unchanged (see fig. 3.13).

FIGURE 3.13

The end of the club with a Volume Select gizmo scaled down to select the portion that contacts the floor.

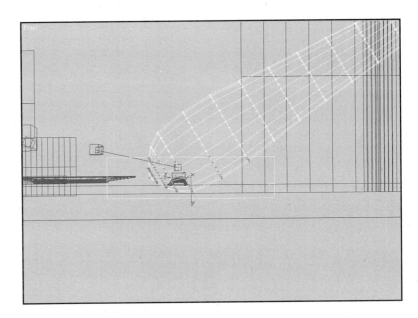

THE "ROCKY ROACH CLUB" INITIATION

1. Load croach06.max from the accompanying CD, select Club in the Select by Name dialog and click on Zoom Extents All Selected. The camera viewport should show the scene through Camera04, which is linked to Rocky and follows right behind him during the rest of the animation.

2. The movement of the club is already animated so that it rotates downward and strikes the floor at frame 334, just after Rocky the Roach runs by. Move the Time Slider to frame 334, where the club hits the floor.

3. Click on Modify/More. From the Additional Modifiers menu, select the Volume Select modifier, and then click on Vertex under Selection Level in the Parameters rollout menu.

4. Click on Sub-object and then scale and rotate the yellow Volume Select gizmo so that it only surrounds the lower half of the tip of the club where it contacts the floor at frame 334. Rotate the gizmo so that it is parallel to the floor as shown in figure 3.13.

5. Next add a XForm modifier to the stack. Click More, and from the Additional Modifiers list, select XForm. An XForm gizmo will replace the Volume Select gizmo. The XForm modifier is animatable.

6. You will now animate the scale of the XForm modifier gizmo. Click Lock Selection. The business end of the Club should expand out horizontally in the X and Z axis just as it hits the floor, giving the appearance that the club is made of semi-hard rubber.

7. Move the Time Slider to frame 325. Turn on Animation mode. You will set a "null" key at this point to prevent the XForm distortion from being passed back to earlier frames. Click and drag upward a small amount on the XForm gizmo at the end of the club. Without releasing the mouse, drag it back downward so that the end of the club looks unchanged. This sets a key that holds the vertices in their original size.

8. Move to frame 331, and repeat the creation of another null key at this point to control the scale of the club. Then move to frame 335 where you will now scale up the end of the club to create a Squash and stretch by scaling up the XForm gizmo. In the left viewport, click on the red selected vertices at the end of the club and drag the mouse upward to scale them up 20 to 30 percent. The selected region of the Club will spread horizontally.

9. Turn off Animation mode. Scroll the time slider to observe the effect of the animaiton. Click the Sub-object button to turn off the XForm modifier, then click the Create icon to close the Modifier panel. This deselects the vertices.

10. Render a preview and save your scene as **rocky06.max**.

In the R.E.A. Exterminators animation, XForm and Linked XForm modifiers are applied to many of the weapons to make them react to the heavy impact as they hit the floor next to the cockroach. The Demon Sphere model uses an XForm modifier to create pseudo-morphing shapes, where selected vertices are animated extruding out of a smooth surface to form threatening points as the roach comes within striking distance.

Use XForm to Animate Portions of Objects

The XForm modifier works in conjunction with other modifiers to animate vertices and modify surfaces. It cannot select vertices by itself, but must inherit the selection set from other modifiers in the stack. It works by generating a gizmo around a selected set of vertices when you open the XForm modifier. In practice, you would select vertices with Edit Mesh, Edit Spline, or Volume Select.

In the next exercise, you animate the shape change of a Demon. It is actually a modified torus that expands and extrudes spiny appendages with two big angry eyes, and then attempts to impale Rocky the Roach by rolling over him. Rocky is barely able to slip by. Figure 3.14 shows the spines created by applying the XForm modifier to the sphere at the vertex level. The eyes are separate objects linked to the sphere and then animated to scale-up by using an animated Uniform Scale transform.

FIGURE 3.14

View of the Demon torus after it has been morphed with the XForm modifier to form the spines.

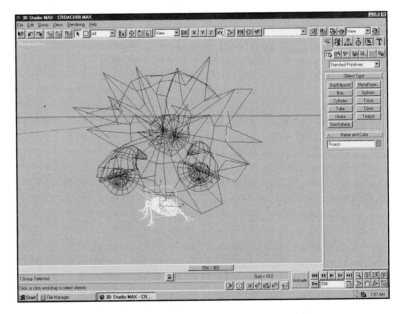

ANIMATING THE SHAPE CHANGE OF A DEMON

1. Load croach07.max and move the Time Slider to frame 600 where Rocky approaches a lumpy ball that will turn into a spiked rolling Demon.

2. Select Demon from the Select by Name object list and click on Zoom Extents All Selected.

3. Click on the Min/Max toggle to expand the Front viewport, and then Click on Modify. From the rollout, select Edit Mesh.

4. Click on Sub-object on the vertex level. You will select small groups of vertices from all over the surface of the Demon torus.

5. Click on Select Object, hold down the Ctrl key, and select every third individual vertex. Spread them out across the underside of the torus. These points will become spines. When you have a number of them, lock the selection.

6. Add XForm to the stack by clicking on the More button in the Modifiers rollout and selecting it from the additional modifiers menu. When it opens, the XForm modifier will create an animatable gizmo around the selected vertices.

7. Make certain that the Sub-object button is yellow. You can now manipulate the gizmo with any of the transform tools.

8. To animate the growth of the selected points into long spines, move the Time Slider back to frame 560. Click the animation button to turn on Animation mode, then click on Select and Uniform Scale. You will set a "null" Scale key, which prevents the vertices from scaling up before frame 560. Click and drag a tiny amount in the Front viewport, then release the mouse—this establishes the null starting key for the scale animation.

9. Move to frame 600 then click and drag upward to scale up the selected points, turning them into long spines. Turn off Animate.

10. Render a preview from frame 560 to 600 in the Camera viewport. You can continue to animate different modifications to the shape of the Demon torus by adding additional XForm modifiers to the stack, which act on different selected vertices.

11. After the Demon grows spines, it should roll forward rapidly, attacking Rocky as he passes. Save your scene as **rock07.max**.

NOTE

The XForm gizmo's center acts as the gizmo's pivot point. When you're manipulating the gizmo, you don't have access to the object's pivot point.

Use Linked XForm to Modify a Lofted Object

When working with a Lofted object, you can animate its shape by inserting a Linked XForm modifier in the stack just above an Edit Mesh or Edit Spline modifier. The Linked XForm enables you to animate the selected vertices to create changes in the shape of the model. This is a very useful technique for bringing organic models to life by making them move and breathe. The Linked XForm controller can effectively animate small or even large parts of a one-piece mesh model, reducing your dependence on plug-in skeletal deformation programs such as Bones Pro or morph targets.

In the following exercise, you animate a change in the shape of the voodoo doll. To animate the doll, you will animate the movement of a Dummy object, which is linked to the vertices of the doll's loft path and which will deform and bend the model forward to lunge downward. The selected and linked vertices of the loft path appear as red crosses (see fig. 3.15).

FIGURE 3.15

This shows the impaled Voodoo Doll Roach with the selected vertices, which are linked to a dummy by the Link XForm modifier, shown here as red tick marks on the loft path.

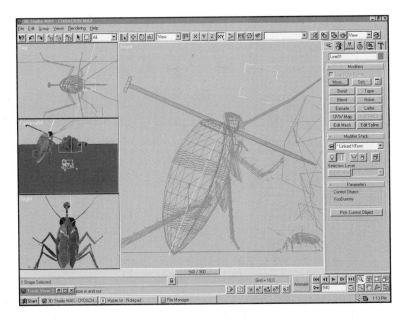

CHANGING THE SHAPE OF THE VOODOO DOLL

1. Load the croach08.max file from the accompanying CD, and then select the Voodoo Doll in the Select by Name dialog.

2. Click on Zoom Extents All Selected, and then move the Time Slider to frame 540, which will place Rocky the Roach near the voodoo doll.

3. Click on Create, Helpers, and then Dummy. Click on the Top viewport to make a dummy a short distance to the right of the Voodoo doll's head. Switch to the Left viewport, zoom out, and move the dummy down to place just above the Doll's head. Rename the dummy **VooDummy**.

4. Select Line01, the doll's loft path spline, from the Select by Name dialog.

5. Click on Modify. The Modifiers rollout will open, showing Edit Spline Modifier in the modifier Stack window.

6. Click on the Sub-object button and then on Select Object, and in the Front viewport, drag a selection box around the top half of the white spline that runs up through the center of the doll's body. The top two vertices will turn red to show they are selected. These are the vertices that you will control with a Linked XForm modifier to distort the doll's body.

7. In the Modifiers rollout, click on the More button. From the Additional Modifiers menu, select Linked XForm.

8. Linked XForm will pick up the selected vertices and open its rollout menu. Click on the Pick Control Object button, then in the Top viewport where it is easy to see, click on VooDummy to link the selected vertices to the VooDummy Helper object. The dummy will now be listed as the control object.

9. You will now be able to use Rotate and Move transform to animate the position of the VooDummy and the spline's vertices. This will now automatically pass its parameter changes back down the stack to the lofter to modify the body mesh.

10. Before you animate the VooDoo doll, you must link the pin, head, and legs of the doll to the VooDummy so they will move as the body mesh deforms. These parts are all grouped in the VooDooPin object. Select the pin through the doll's head, and all the parts will turn white. Click on the Select and Link icon and drag a link from the pin to the VooDummy.

11. To test the dummy to see if it works correctly, click on Select and Move and drag the dummy up and down a short distance. Then click Undo. The Pin and the legs will move with the expanding and contracting body mesh. With the VooDummy still selected, lock the Selection.

12. To animate the VooDoo doll, turn on the Animate button and move the Time Slider to frame 535.

13. Set "null" transform keys at frame 535 by right-clicking on the Time Slider and in the Create Keys dialog, click on OK—this establishes a key to hold the VooDummy where it is.

14. Move the Time Slider to frame 545 and click on Select and Move. Click on VooDummy and move it a short distance forward and down, closer to Rocky the Roach. This causes the doll's head and shoulders to jut forward at an awkward angle. Next, you will rotate the dummy to correct the body angle.

15. Now click Select and Rotate, and drag the mouse downward to rotate the VooDummy object so that the doll's body twists downward, making the pin almost plunge into Rocky's back as he runs by.

16. Render a preview of the animation from frame 525 to 560 to see the action. This section of the animation is all rendered from the Camera04 viewport.

17. Save the scene file as **rocky08.max**.

NOTE

You cannot select and modify vertex and lattice control handles and vertex region curves with an XForm modifier because they are not part of the object's geometry.

Perform Pick Transformations Along Surfaces

This transform animation technique takes advantage of the capability of the Pick Reference coordinate to enable you to transform an object along one axis of another object. Helper objects are especially useful for this purpose because they are easily created and they do not render. Moving objects along a Grid or a helper object that has been aligned to a surface gives you the capability to easily create an effect such as a morphing drop of rain running down an inclined window. The local axis of a tape measure helper object can also be picked as a path of motion for any object.

Using Tape Measure Objects as a Motion Axis

In the R.E.A. Exterminators animation, three Tape Measure objects are used as axes of motion or path for the darts thrown at Rocky the Roach.

In this exercise, you use a Tape Measure helper object as a pick transform Path object to aim and animate the flight of a dart hitting the floor right next to Rocky's legs (see fig. 3.16).

FIGURE 3.16

View of the dart in position aligned to the axis of the tape measure with the Pick command.

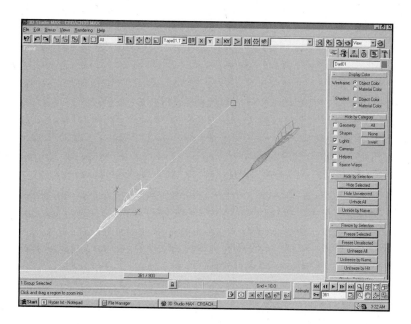

ANIMATING THE DART'S FLIGHT

1. Load the croach09.max scene file and click on Zoom Extents All.

2. Move the Time Slider to frame 380. Click on Select by Name and select the Roach group from the list. Click on Zoom Extents All icon so that you can see where the dart hits the floor next to Rocky as he runs for his life.

3. In the left viewport, zoom out to see the Dart01 object and the yellow tape measure line. You can see that a Tape Measure object is in place and is being used as the axis of travel for the dart.

4. Create two more tape Helper objects for darts 2 and 3. Move the time slider to frame 400. Notice that there is a dummy indicating where the dart will hit the floor as Rocky runs by. You will now make a tape axis to guide Dart02. Zoom out in the Left viewport until you can see both the dummy and Dart02 positioned above it.

5. Click on Create, then on the Helpers icon. From the rollout menu, select Tape. Create a tape by clicking on the tip of the dart and dragging the mouse downward to the dummy beside the cockroach. Lock the selection.

6. Right-click to switch to the Top viewport. Zoom out until you can see the darts, the roach, and the new tape, which is still selected. Click Select by Name and select Tape02 and Tape02target from the list. Select and lock the selection.

7. Click on Select and Move, and drag the tape over until it is directly below Dart02. Switch to the Front viewport and click on Zoom Extents Selected. You will see the tape extending straight down. Zoom out until you can see Dart02 and the dummy beside Rocky the Roach.

8. Click the spacebar to turn off Lock Selection. Click in an empty area of the viewport to deselect the tape and then click and drag the bottom end of Tape02 over to the dummy sitting beside Rocky the Roach. The tape will now be on a 45-degree angle, in alignment with the axis of Dart02.

9. You are now ready to align the dart's local axis with the tape to create a travel path for the dart.

10. Click on Select Object and select Dart02. Open the Reference Coordinate System pull-down menu in the menu bar and click on Pick.

11. Now click on the top end (not the target) of the yellow tape measure to pick it as the local Pick Transform axis for the dart. Tape02 should be displayed in the Reference Coordinate window.

12. The dart can now be animated along the tape by clicking Select and Move, Restrict to Z axis. It will track smoothly along the local axis of the tape measure Helper object.

13. Select Dart02, and lock the Selection. Move the Time Slider to frame 380. The dart should impact the floor at frame 400. Click on the Animate button and drag Dart02 a very short distance down the tape to establish a starting key at 380. Move the time slider to frame 400.

14. Click and drag the dart down along the Z axis until its point is stuck in the floor at the dummy. Rocky should be right next to the dart. The point should just miss Rocky's head. The third dart should hit the floor at frame 420. Animate it on your own.

15. Turn off Animation mode and render a preview. That's it.

16. Save the scene as **rocky09.max**.

Using Grid Objects as Transform Paths

To move an object along a surface (as you may occasionally want to do), the simplest way is to first create a grid helper object. Then you use the Align tool to place the grid object coincident to the surface you want to move along (see fig. 3.17). Select your object. After the grid is in place, you can use the Pick Reference Coordinate command to pick the grid as the surface on which you want your object to move. In practice, you would constrain the axis of movement to the axis on which you want to move.

FIGURE 3.17

View of a polyhedron showing a grid aligned to one face of the polyhedron, and a small sphere set to move along the object's surface.

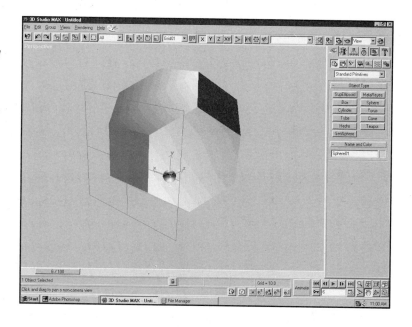

Animating Multiple Object Instances

The Shift key used with any transform will enable you to create multiple instance clones that can be animated with transforms. The convenient feature of this technique is that you only need to animate the first object. All the others will copy the motion exactly. In addition, the instances can be moved, and their keys can be adjusted in the Track View to make them appear to be unique. And if you decide you want one of them to be unique and animatable on its own, you need only click on the Make Unique button in the Track View.

In the R.E.A. Exterminators animation, the second and third darts are instances of this type. Only the first dart is animated. The animation track ranges for the second and third dart have been slid down to create a time lag between the first, second, and third dart.

Instance animation is useful for re-creating natural phenomena such as flocks of birds, schools of fish, and blades of grass. But it can also be used to create a "herd" of cockroaches to simulate an infestation (see fig. 3.18).

FIGURE 3.18

An infestation of instanced cockroaches animated with transform animation.

Transforming Lights

Creating good lighting is a difficult problem for many animators. It is an easy task to use a spot and two omni lights to light a scene, but it is very difficult to equal the real light in a room, a building, or in nature. Many animations contain boring, flat lighting that does not change at all and takes no advantage of MAX's capability to animate lights with transforms. In real life, light changes as you move through an environment. Lights are modified either by being blocked by objects such as walls or trees, or by changing angles of reflection from surfaces of objects that vary as you move past them.

No matter how good an animator you are, your scenes will look lackluster if you do not devote considerable time to lighting. There is no room in this chapter to expand on the definition of what makes good lighting. This topic of lighting is brought up only to remind you to explore some of the special kinds of transformation techniques that can move tiny accent lights along and over surfaces to give them a touch of realism that can never be attained with static key and fill lights. Use your ingenuity and experiment. It is the small details that can turn a good animation into a great one. For more information, read Chapter 15, "Animating Lights and Atmospheres."

Finishing the R.E.A. Exterminators Animation

This chapter does not take you through the entire animation of this project step by step. If you want to continue working on it, however, you can work with croach09.max and try setting up all the different weapon gags. Remember, four cameras are used and the project should be rendered as four separate parts and then assembled. The roach.txt file on the New Riders web site contains instructions for finishing all the weapons animations, the frame number at which the weapon should impact the floor, notes about setting up your camera frame ranges, and the Video Post Queue setup for finishing this animation. Have fun with it!

In Practice: Advanced Transformation Animation

- **Linked transforms.** When you don't want to take the time to set up Inverse Kinematics to create complex motion, linked transforms can do the job simply and quickly.

- **Out-of-Range Type Curves.** Out-of-Range animation will enable you to extend a short animation into a repetitive cycle loop and save having to enter additional keys.

- **Helper objects.** Helper objects are valuable for linking complex objects, for acting as temporary transform movement axes, and for creating offset pivot points.

- **Grouped objects.** Using Nested Grouped objects enables you to treat a group of animated objects as if it were a single part of a larger object, enabling you to create very complex layered animations.

- **XForm and Linked XForm.** Use the power of XForm and Linked XForm modifiers to animate selected portions of your models at the vertex level.

IMAGE CREATED BY DAN O'LEARY

Models courtesy of Viewpoint DataLabs International, Inc.

Chapter 4

by Randy Kreitzman
and Dan O'Leary
with Ted Neuman

ANIMATING WITH CONTROLLERS

3D Studio MAX provides users with an amazing set of tools for animating their scenes. Central to this task are controllers—a group of plug-ins that handle the creation and manipulation of all animation data in 3D Studio MAX.

Controllers handle the user data for any and all animated tracks, storing keyframe information and procedural animation settings. Any time you create a keyframe or adjust a function curve in Track View, data is sent to the animation controller assigned to that track. Controllers also generate all interpolated animation, calculating the value of animated parameters for each frame based on keyframe data.

All animation tracks, including object transformations, creation parameters, and modifier parameters, are assigned a default controller. For most tracks, this assignment is made when the track is first animated. Transform controllers are assigned when the track is first created.

This chapter explores the following topics:

- Path controller

- Euler Rotation controller

- Look-At controller

- List and Noise controller

- Expression controllers

Project: WWII Air Combat

To illustrate the proper use of and applications for animation controllers in 3D Studio MAX, you will use a sample project. Your goal is to animate a WWII air combat scene in which an American B-17 bomber is attacked by a German FW-190 fighter (see fig. 4.1). You will build on this one example throughout the chapter to emphasize the power and flexibility provided by animation controllers. This example will give you a feel for how an animator might approach this kind of assignment.

Before you begin, open bomber.avi on the accompanying CD-ROM to watch the final animation.

Throughout this project, you will be using two 3D models provided by Viewpoint DataLabs. Both the B-17 bomber and FW-190 fighter pictured in figure 4.2 are from their outstanding catalog and are included on the accompanying CD.

FIGURE 4.1
WWII air combat.

FIGURE 4.2
*3D models by
Viewpoint DataLabs
International, Inc.*

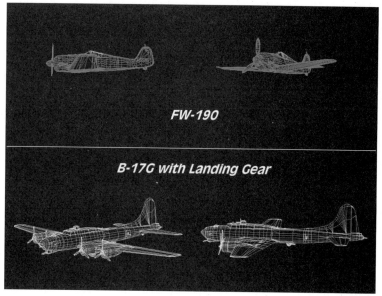

Animating with Path Controllers

The project begins with a static shot of the B-17 with some background clouds. You will keep the camera and bomber stationary, and use other tricks to give the impression of forward motion and relative velocities. This approach helps to keep the action focused on and around the Bomber.

You will make extensive use of Path controllers to animate this scene. The *Path controller* is a compound controller created as an alternative position controller. It receives the output of a subordinate Percent controller that specifies the path position, expressed as a percentage of total path length. This data is combined with the path data itself to determine the X, Y, Z position in time of an object following the specified spline.

First you will make the clouds fly past the bomber by applying a Path controller. Then, you will assign a Path controller to the attacking fighter. Finally, you will add more realism to your animation by adjusting the relative velocity of the plane.

Background Cloud Motion

The clouds in this scene have been created as Combustion objects. Combustion is a MAX atmospheric effect for creating realistic fire, smoke, and explosion effects. Without the animated clouds, this scene would feel extremely static and unconvincing. They create the illusion of forward motion and add a great deal of depth to the scene.

BACKGROUND CLOUD MOTION

1. Load bomber.max from the accompanying CD. Select Combustion01 and open the Motion panel.

2. Under Assign Controller, expand the Transform controller hierarchy and highlight Position.

3. Click on Assign Controller, choose Path, and click on OK.

4. Under Path Parameters, click on Pick Path and select Cloud Path 01 in the viewport.

The Combustion object jumps to the start of the path. If you scroll through the animation, you will see the combustion travel from the beginning to the end of the path.

NOTE

When a Path controller is first assigned, two keys are automatically created at the first and last frame of the active time segment. By default, the value of the first key is 0, the second key has a value of 100.

Now for the second set of clouds, follow these steps.

5. Select Combustion02 and open the Motion panel.

6. Under Assign Controller, expand the Transform controller hierarchy and highlight Position.

7. Click on Assign Controller, choose Path, and click on OK.

8. Under Path Parameters, click on Pick Path and select Cloud Path 02 in the viewport.

Combustion 02 has a slightly longer path and therefore a greater distance to travel in the same amount of time as Combustion 01. The difference in speed between the two cloud objects should give a better sense of depth to the scene. Figure 4.3 illustrates the correct Path controller assignment.

FIGURE 4.3

Animating clouds with the Path controller.

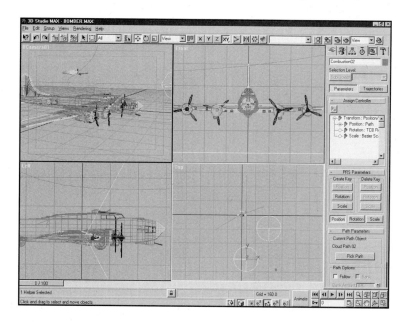

Fighter Attack

Here again, you use the Path controller to animate the attack of the German fighter. The Path controller is truly one of the most useful new controllers included with MAX. Working with keys is often frustrating when it is easy to visualize exactly the path you want an object to follow. In those cases, working directly with the path splines is a very natural way of molding the animation.

FIGHTER ATTACK

In this exercise, you assign a Path controller to the attacking fighter.

1. Open the Select by Name dialog and choose the Fighter Body object. Open the Motion panel.

2. Under Assign Controller, expand the Transform controller hierarchy and highlight Position.

3. Click on Assign Controller, choose Path, and click on OK.

4. Under Path Parameters, click on Pick Path and select Fighter Path in the Top viewport.

5. Switch to the Camera view and slide the playback bar slowly toward frame 100. Compare your results to figure 4.4.

FIGURE 4.4
Creating the fighter flight path.

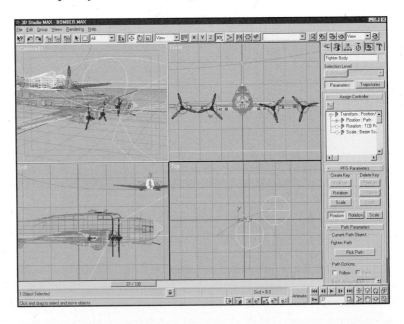

The fighter flies into frame along the path, but something is not quite right. For one thing, the fighter is not banking with the turn and, more importantly, it is flying away from the camera—not a very dramatic effect at all. This is because the Fighter Path spline vertices were mistakenly created in reverse order. You can easily remedy this problem by reversing the key values of the Percent track.

6. Open Track View and expand the Object hierarchy.

7. Select Fighter Body. Right-click and select Expand Tracks from the pop-up list.

8. Find the animated Percent track and right-click on the first key. Change the default value of 0.0 to 100.0.

9. Click on the Next Key button to jump to the key at frame 100. Change the value of this key to 0.0.

TIP

An alternative fix for this problem is to reverse the direction of the spline itself. Apply an Edit Spline modifier to the path, select the last vertex in the spline, and click on Make First. This method does not work for closed spline shapes.

With that minor crisis behind you, look into improving the look and feel of the Fighter's attack run by adding some banking.

10. Select Fighter Body and open the Motion panel.

11. Under Path Parameters, click on Follow and Bank for Path Options.

12. Slide the playback bar slowly from frame 0 to 100.

Now the fighter is moving toward the camera, but it is flying backward! To fix this, you must change its default orientation before adding follow and bank.

13. Uncheck Follow and Bank for the Fighter Body object. Choose the Select and Rotate tool and make the Top viewport active. Verify that the View coordinate system is selected.

14. In the Top viewport, rotate the Fighter Body 180 degrees about the Z axis. It now faces the opposite direction.

15. Again, check the Follow and Bank options for the path controller. The fighter should snap in line with the path, facing the direction of travel as seen in figure 4.5. Verify the results by playing the animation in the Camera viewport.

FIGURE 4.5

Correcting the fighter orientation.

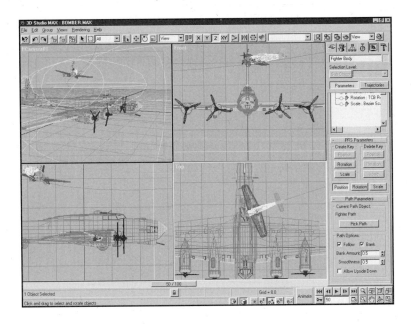

That is better, but the banking of the fighter is very subtle. Go to a good reference frame (about frame 60) and adjust the Bank Amount. A value of 3 gives a very dramatic feel to the attack run. You may want to raise the smoothness to around 1, which will take out some of the jerkiness in the angle correction.

Relative Velocities

Because you are dealing with a locked-down camera and you are simulating objects flying by, you must take into account that the attacking fighter should drift back some during its flight.

Because the path controls the fighter, animating that path sliding backward should do the trick. The fighter will inherit the motion of the path and slide across the screen.

RELATIVE VELOCITIES

1. Switch to your Top view and select the Fighter Path.

2. Go to frame 0 and activate the Animate button.

3. Move the path forward so that it is just in front of the bomber (about −40 units).

4. Go to frame 100 and move the path back until it is at the tail of the Bomber (about 70 units).

5. Turn off the Animate button.

6. Switch to the Camera view and slide the playback bar to view the animation. Compare to figure 4.6.

FIGURE 4.6

Bandits at 8 o'clock!

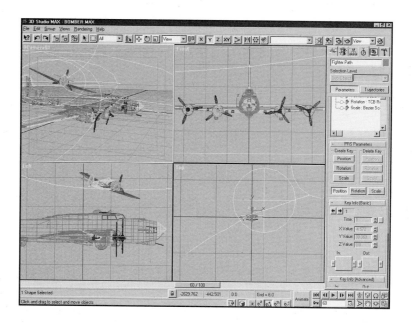

The fighter drifts back as it attacks and scrapes past the camera. Already you have the core of an exciting animation. Next you will add some wobble to the bomber to give it a more realistic feel.

Animating with Euler XYZ Rotation Controllers

There are a couple of ways to rotate the bomber. One of the easiest and most adjustable methods makes use of another powerful 3D Studio MAX animation controller: the Euler XYZ Rotation controller.

The Euler XYZ controller is provided as an alternative to the standard TCB Rotation controller. Anyone familiar with the DOS version of 3D Studio is quite aware of the problems and limitations presented by the TCB controller because it was the only option for controlling rotations in that package. The Euler XYZ controller is superior to the TCB controller in several ways, most notably in that it enables the user to view and adjust rotation values in the Function Curves mode of Track View.

This controller works by decomposing the orientation of an object into discrete X, Y, and Z rotations. A unique track is created subordinate to the Euler XYZ controller for each of these components. This approach provides the user with very precise rotational control, enabling him or her to individually animate the rotation about each of the object's local axes. With a TCB controller, you cannot adjust the interpolation values about one axis without affecting the others.

Unfortunately, the Euler XYZ controller comes with its own set of problems. Key among these is a phenomena known as *gimbal lock*. In any system of Euler angles, orientations exist for which two Euler angles are undefined. When a mechanism is rotated into such a singularity, it locks up—rigid to any rotation about the two undefined axes.

Bomber Wobble

With the Euler XYZ Rotation controller, animating wobble in the bomber is as simple as assigning the controller to the body and creating an appropriate curve for the X rotation.

BOMBER WOBBLE

1. Switch to the Camera view and select the B17 body.

2. Open the Track View.

3. Right-click on the Filters button and select Selected Objects Only and Transforms Only. These filters are very useful in keeping your workspace uncluttered and focused only on what you need.

4. Expand the Transform controller hierarchy for B17 Body and highlight Rotation.

5. Click on Assign Controller from the Track View toolbar, select Euler XYZ, and click on OK.

6. Expand the Rotation controller hierarchy. Beneath the parent Euler XYZ controller are individual X, Y, and Z rotation tracks. Each of these tracks has been assigned a Bézier Float controller as seen in figure 4.7. Highlight the X Rotation.

FIGURE 4.7

Assigning the Euler XYZ Rotation controller.

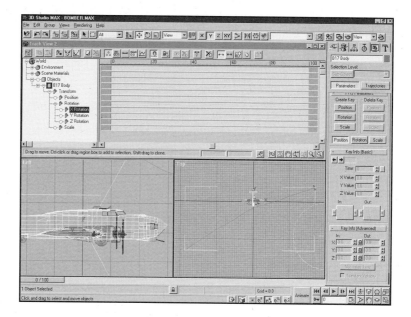

7. Click on Function Curves from the toolbar.

8. Click on Move Keys and select the dotted line that lies at value 0 (right now there are no keyframes laid out).

9. Click on Add Keys and create a keyframe around every 20 frames or so, increasing and decreasing the value and adding a few random keys here and there (see fig. 4.8). Because you want the effect to be subtle, try not to let the values go higher than 0.5 degrees or lower than –0.5.

FIGURE 4.8
Creating the wobble for the bomber.

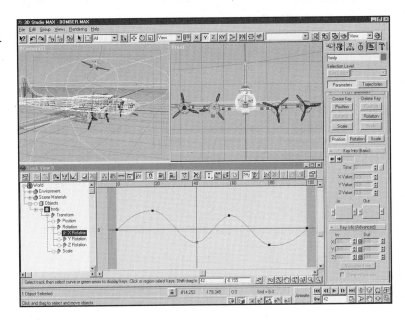

10. Save your scene as **mybomber01.max** and render out a Smooth + Highlights preview of the Camera01 viewport, frames 0–100.

If the motion looks unnatural, try lowering the values of the keyframes or the frequency at which they occur (maybe a key every 30 frames). One advantage of working with Euler controllers is that the function curves enable quick and easy adjustment of your animation. They also provide a better picture of what each key is doing.

NOTE

You may find yourself wondering why you would ever want to use TCB Rotation controllers again. If so, save yourself the trouble of assigning Euler XYZ controllers to every rotation you animate by choosing Make Default in the Replace Controller dialog. This sets Euler XYZ as the default controller for all future rotation parameters.

Another place to try a Euler Rotation controller is the Y Rotation of the Fighter Body. The Banking option for the Path controller takes care of this to an extent, but you may want to try adding some of your own keyframes to spice up the attack a bit. Perhaps a barrel roll in the beginning of the pass or at the end as it flies by the camera? Feel free to experiment before moving on to the next section.

Animating with the Look-At Controller

Another useful controller included with 3DS MAX is the Look At controller. The Look At controller is a compound controller that combines the output of an object's position, roll, and scale controllers. It completely replaces the standard PRS (Position/Rotation/Scale) controller and outputs the transformation matrix of associated objects.

The Look-At controller takes the negative Z axis of an object and points it toward a selected target. The most graphic example is that of a character's head staring at an object, following it automatically as it moves through the scene. Look-At controllers are used by Target Spots and Target Cameras to keep them directed at their point of interest.

Tracking Turrets

In this example, you use a Look-At controller to make the turret on top of the bomber track the fighter as it flies by.

First you link the turret and its guns to a dummy object. You then apply the Look-At controller to the dummy, which in turn affects the turret and guns.

TRACKING TURRETS

1. Before getting started, choose Edit, Hold.

2. In the Top viewport, zoom in on the turret just behind the cockpit of the bomber.

3. Select the Top Turret object and link it to the surrounding Top Turret dummy.

4. Select the Turret Guns and also link them to Top Turret dummy.

5. Select Top Turret dummy, open the Motion panel, and highlight Transform under Assign Controller.

6. Click on Assign Controller, select Look At, and click on OK.

7. In the Motion panel, click on Pick Target and select Fighter Body.

8. Switch to the Camera view and slide the playback bar to view the animation.

So what went wrong? The dummy and turret follow the fighter, but as you can see from figure 4.9, the turret is turned on its side and the guns are pointing straight up. That is because the negative Z axis of the dummy object was pointing in the default world orientation, which is straight down. When the Look-At controller was applied, the dummy rotated itself back (along with the linked turret and guns) so that the negative Z points to the passing fighter. A quick way of fixing this is to adjust the pivot of the dummy so that it and its children face the right direction.

FIGURE 4.9

Creating the turret hierarchy.

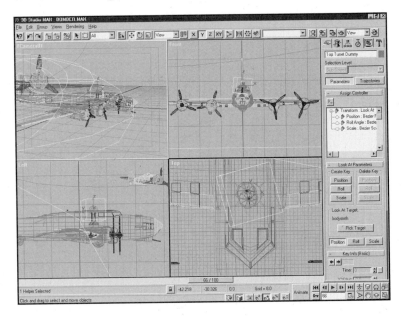

ADJUSTING THE TURRET

1. Select the Top Turret dummy and open up the Hierarchy panel.

2. Click on Pivot and select Affect Pivot Only.

3. With the Local coordinate system active, rotate the pivot –90 degrees along the X axis in the Top viewport.

You won't actually see the pivot rotate, but the turret and guns now face the right way. By scrolling through the animation, however, you might notice a new problem. The rotating turret tilts up and down as it follows the fighter. In reality the turret would only spin and the guns themselves would angle up and down. A little preplanning could have prevented this, but because you performed a hold not too long ago, you can go back and prevent all these problems from occurring.

4. Choose Edit, Fetch and click on Yes.

5. Select Top Turret dummy and open the Hierarchy panel.

6. Click on Pivot and Affect Pivot only.

7. Verify that the View coordinate system is currently selected in the Reference Coordinate System drop-down. Rotate the pivot for Dummy01 90 degrees along the X axis in the Top view as before. The blue Z axis now points toward the rear of the aircraft.

That will save the correction step later. To lock down the turret so that it only inherits Z rotations from its Dummy parent, follow these steps.

8. Select Top Turret and click on Link Info in the Hierarchy panel.

9. Under Inherit, uncheck the X and Y for Rotate.

10. Link the Turret and Turret Guns to the Top Turret dummy.

11. With the Top Turret dummy selected, open the Motion panel and highlight Transform under Assign Controller.

12. Click on Assign Controller, select Look At, and click on OK.

13. In the Motion panel, click on Pick Target and select the Fighter Body.

14. Switch to the Camera view and slide the playback bar to view the animation.

The turret stays level and the guns tilt as they follow the fighter (see fig. 4.10).

FIGURE 4.10

The Look-At controller at work.

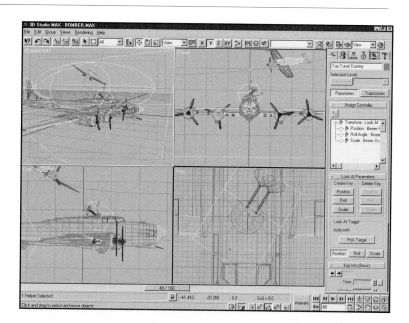

Animating with Noise and List Controllers

The Noise controller is one of two parametric controllers included with 3D Studio MAX. A *parametric controller* is unique in that it automatically creates animation data for an object based on user-specified data values. No keyframes are ever set for a parametric controller, as the user data totally defines the behavior of the animation. Instead, range bars appear in Track View for tracks animated with parametric controllers.

The Noise controller is useful for creating an amazing variety of irregular animated effects. Buzzing wings, rustling leaves, flashing lights, and many, many other effects can be handled quickly and effectively with a Noise controller.

NOTE

The other parametric controller that comes with MAX is the Expression controller. It is significantly different from any other controller and is addressed later in this chapter and more fully in Chapter 5, "Animating with Expressions."

The List controller is a user-defined compound controller used to combine the effects of multiple controllers. It is frequently used to add noise to a predefined motion. The effect can be subtle or drastic, adding natural irregularities to a motion, simulating rough terrain, or similar effects. This combination of parametric and key-based animation is indeed a powerful and efficient technique.

Gunfire Effects

For the gunfire of the bomber turret and fighter plane, you will try a simple but effective approach. You will apply a Noise controller under a List controller for the XYZ scale of the cones, causing them to shrink and expand rapidly during the flyby, giving the illusion of flashing gunfire. A Visibility track can then be used to make the fire sporadic.

CREATING GUNFIRE

1. Zoom in on the Turret object in the Top viewport and select Flash02.

2. Open the Track View. Right-click on the Filters button and select Selected Objects Only and Transforms Only.

3.   Expand the hierarchy until you get to Flash02 and its parameters.

4.   Highlight Scale and click on Assign Controller. Select Scale List and click on OK.

5.   Expand the Scale hierarchy and select Available.

6.   Click on Assign Controller, select Noise Scale, and click on OK (see fig. 4.11).

7.   Click on Properties from the Track View toolbar. Change the X, Y, and Z strengths to 300. Close the Properties dialog and minimize the Track View.

8.   Slide the playback bar to view the animation.

FIGURE 4.11

Creating the List Scale controller hierarchy.

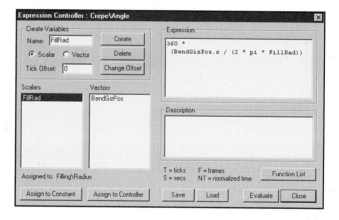

The Flash02 cone scales randomly in all directions. Now copy that same effect to the other gun flashes.

9.   Click on Select By Name and select Flash01, Flash02, Flash03, and Flash04.

10. Maximize your Track View. Highlight Objects at the top of the hierarchy and right-click, selecting Expand All.

11. Select Scale for Flash02 and click on Copy Controller from the toolbar.

12. Select Scale for Flash01 and click on Paste Controller, making certain to select Paste As Instance in the dialog.

13. Repeat step 12 for Flash03 and Flash04, making them instances as well.

14. Minimize your Track View and switch to the Camera viewport. Slide the playback bar to view the animation.

Both the turret on the bomber and the guns on the fighter emit throbbing cones.

15. Select Flash03 and Flash04 of the fighter. Maximize your Track View.

16. Right-click on Filters and select Show All (this is necessary to work with Visibility tracks).

17. Locate and select Flash04.

18. From the toolbar, click on Add Visibility Track. Click on Add Keys and place a key at frame 0.

19. Right-click on keyframe 0, choose Step Tangent for both the In and Out, and close the Properties dialog.

20. Click on Move Keys and Shift-drag a copy of keyframe 0 to frame 1.

21. Right-click on keyframe 1 and change the value to 0. Shift-drag a copy of keyframe 0 to frame 2.

22. Click on the Parameter Curve Out-of-Range Type from the toolbar and select Loop.

23. Open the Function Curve for the Visibility track. Compare your results to figure 4.12.

FIGURE 4.12
Animating the Visibility function curve.

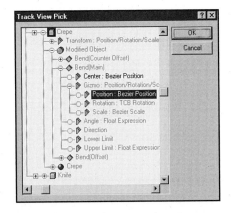

The curve for visibility shifts from 1 to 0 every other frame, causing the gunfire to appear and disappear. Now layer another curve to control when the firing starts and stops.

24. Click on Assign Controller from the Track View toolbar and select Float List.

25. Expand the Visibility hierarchy and select Available. Click on Assign Controller and select Bézier Float.

26. Select Add Key and place a keyframe at frame 0 and frame 60.

27. Click on Move Keys, select frame 0 and 60, and open their Properties dialog.

28. Right-click on keyframe and choose Step Tangent for both the In and Out.

29. Change the value of frame 0 to 0 and frame 60 to −1.

The original Looping Bézier Curve, created in steps 18 through 22, will be unaffected by this second curve from frame 0 to frame 60 (where the value is 0). Beginning at frame 61, the value drops to −1. The gunfire flashes on and off for sixty frames, and then turns off entirely. The combined output of the list controller is best seen by selecting the parent Visibility track in the function curve mode of Track View (see fig. 4.13).

FIGURE 4.13

The combined output of the Visibility List controller.

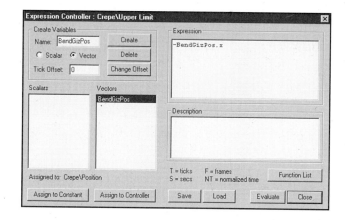

Now to copy this set of curves to the other Flash objects and offset them accordingly, follow these steps:

30. Select Visibility for Flash04 and click on Copy Controller. Find and select Flash03 and add a Visibility track.

TIP

If the Add Visibility Track button is not on the toolbar, remember that you must be in Edit Keys mode to access it.

31. Select Visibility for Flash03 and click on Paste Controller, pasting as an Instance.

Finish up by copying your newly animated Visibility tracks to the guns in the turret of the bomber. Because you want to make a few subtle changes to the firing of those guns, you will paste the controllers as copies.

32. Minimize your Track View and select Flash01 and Flash02.

33. Maximize your Track View and add a Visibility track to both Flash01 and Flash02.

34. Select Visibility for Flash01 and click on Paste Controller, pasting as a Copy, not an Instance this time.

35. Repeat step 34 for Flash02.

36. For both Flash01 and Flash02, move frame 60 of the second Bézier Float to frame 90.

37. Select the first Bézier Float for Flash 01 and offset the three keyframes by one (this alternates the firing of the barrels).

Expression Controllers

The latter half of this chapter introduces Expression controllers as a means to reference and manipulate animation data output by other controllers in the scene. Expression controllers contain a fairly comprehensive set of functions that can be used to create enormously complex equations, if necessary. This advanced level of functionality is discussed in greater detail in Chapter 5.

Project: Making Crepes

The next project uses a few relatively simple expressions to communicate animation data between two separate objects: a crepe and its filling. The goal is to configure the objects to reference specific characteristics of each other so that the crepe can be made to roll up, wrapping the filling as it goes. You will use expressions to affect the following aspects of the scene:

- Controlling the crepe's roll with its Bend(Main) modifier.

- Controlling the crepe's outer radius with the Bend(Offset) and Bend(Counter Offset) modifiers

- Controlling the filling's transforms with the crepe's Bend modifiers

Load the file ch4_1.max from the accompanying CD. Open Track View and expand the objects to display the Crepe and Filling objects' modifiers (see fig. 4.14).

FIGURE 4.14

Track View layout displaying Crepe and Filling objects.

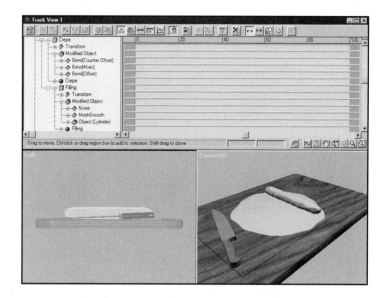

This scene shows four objects: a knife, a conveniently precooked crepe sitting on a cutting board, complete with a filling of your choice. The crepe was once a squashed geosphere with a Noise modifier, but has since been collapsed into an Editable (and edible) Mesh object containing three Bend modifiers. Used in conjunction with one another, the Bend modifiers will precisely control the behavior of the crepe as it is rolled. The filling is a cylinder with MeshSmooth and Noise modifiers. The filling's radius will control how tightly the crepe is wound up. The Bend modifiers will control the filling's position and rotation.

Controlling the Crepe's Roll with the Bend(Main) Modifier

The Bend(Main) modifier will be responsible for the crepe's primary roll component. As the bend's Angle value increases, the crepe winds up tighter onto itself. Moving the modifier's gizmo along its local X-axis causes the wound-up crepe to roll along that axis. Adjusting the Angle value, gizmo position, and Upper Limit simultaneously enables the crepe to start out flat and roll up onto itself. Now take a closer look at these components.

PREPARING THE CREPE

1. Select and hide the Cutting Board, Knife, and Filling objects for the time being while you work with the crepe.

2. Select the Crepe object and go to the Bend(Main) modifier in the Modifier Stack.

3. Use the spinner to adjust the Angle value between 0 and –270.0 degrees.

The bend pivots about the gizmo center positioned at the far-right end of the crepe (see fig. 4.15).

FIGURE 4.15

Adjusting the Crepe object's Bend(Main) Angle value.

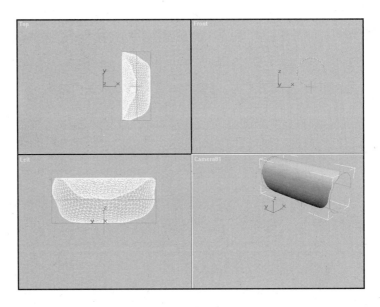

4. Go to the Sub-Object gizmo level. In the camera viewport, select and move the gizmo along the crepe's local X-axis only.

TIP

Turn on the Snap Toggle prior to transforming the gizmo; this will simplify placing it back in its original position when necessary.

The crepe appears to roll through the bend as the Bend(Main) gizmo is moved (see fig. 4.16).

FIGURE 4.16
Moving the Crepe
object's Bend(Main)
gizmo along its local
X-axis.

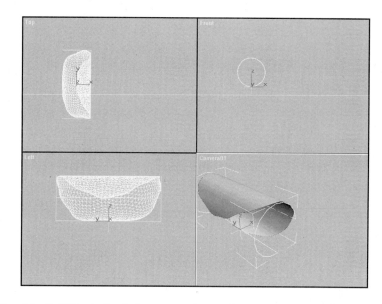

5. Check the Limit Effect check box to activate the modifier's limits.

6. Change the Upper Limit value to 100.0.

7. In the camera viewport, select and move the gizmo along the crepe's local X-axis only.

The crepe appears to curl up and roll over onto itself (see fig. 4.17).

FIGURE 4.17
Moving the Crepe
object's Bend(Main)
gizmo with Limits
enabled.

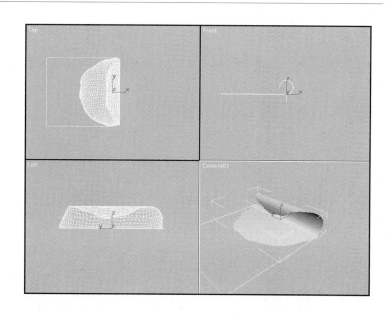

Notice that the roll effect stops working after the right edge of the crepe has passed the Upper Limit value. If you increase the Upper Limit value, you need to also increase the Angle value to maintain a constant radius. For the roll to work properly, the Angle and Upper Limit values must change as the gizmo is moved. You can either manually keyframe these values to keep pace with the gizmo's changing position or you can let expression controllers handle the tasks for you and update the results procedurally.

Using Expressions to Control the Angle and Upper Limit Values

Expression controllers are incredibly powerful, enabling you to represent any parameter with a complex mathematical expression that can include data referenced from other controllers in the scene. Expressions do not have to be complex to take advantage of this capability to relate and interpret values from other controllers. The following exercise uses expressions to update the Bend(Main) modifier's Angle and Upper Limit values, by:

- Converting the gizmo's position into a rotational equivalent

- Moving the Upper Limit value in the opposite direction as the gizmo's position

ASSIGNING EXPRESSION CONTROLLERS TO THE ANGLE AND UPPER LIMIT TRACKS

1. Open Track View and expand the tracks to display the Crepe object's Bend(Main) modifier's tracks (see fig. 4.18).

TIP

Turn on Track View's Controller Types filter when preparing to assign or manipulate controllers (see fig. 4.19).

2. Select the Angle and Upper Limit tracks and click on Assign Controller in the Track View toolbar.

3. Select Float Expression and click on OK (see fig. 4.20).

FIGURE 4.18
Track View layout displaying Crepe object's Bend(Main) modifier's tracks.

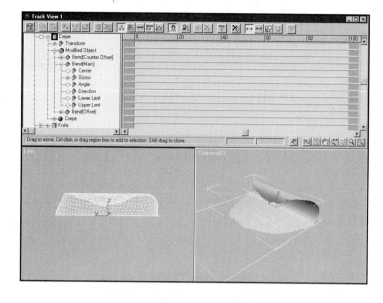

FIGURE 4.19
The Track View's Filters dialog.

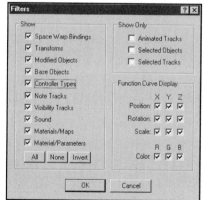

FIGURE 4.20
The Track View's Replace Float Controller dialog.

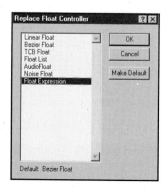

4. Select the Angle track only and click on Properties in the Track View toolbar. The Expression Controller dialog appears (see fig. 4.21).

FIGURE 4.21

Track View's Expression Controller dialog.

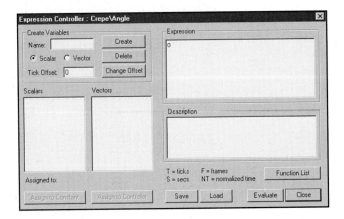

You need two variables to control the angle of the Bend(Main) modifier as its gizmo moves along the local X-axis. One variable will reference the position of the gizmo itself; the other will reference the radius of the Filling object. With this information, the expression can calculate the position and radius of the crepe's curl as it rolls.

5. In the Expression Controller dialog, enter **BendGizPos** in the Name field, select the Vector radio button (if it is not already selected), and click on Create.

Vector variables are used to reference data containing three separate components, such as the gizmo's X, Y, and Z position data.

6. With the newly created BendGizPos variable selected, click on Assign to Controller.

7. In the Track View Pick dialog, expand the tracks to display the Crepe object's Bend(Main) modifier and select the gizmo's Position track (see fig. 4.22). Click on OK.

Expression controller variables can be assigned either to a constant value or to a value output by another controller in the scene. A variable assigned to a controller will update dynamically as that controller changes state.

FIGURE 4.22
Track View Pick dialog with the Bend(Main) gizmo's Position track selected.

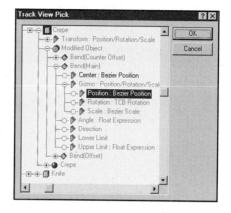

8. In the Expression Controller dialog, enter **FillRad** in the Name field, select the Scalar radio button, and click on Create.

    Scalar variables are used to reference data containing only one component, such as the Filling's radius data.

9. With the FillRad variable selected, click on Assign to Controller.

10. In the Track View Pick dialog, expand the objects and tracks to display the Filling object's Radius track. Select the Radius track (see fig. 4.23). Click on OK.

FIGURE 4.23
The Track View's Pick dialog with the Filling object's Radius track selected.

WARNING

The Expression Controller's "Assigned to" field is designed to display the name of the controller assigned to the selected variable. Although this is usually accurate, it is a good idea always to name your variables so that they remind you which object they are assigned to. Do not rely on the "Assigned to" field.

Now that you have the two variables assigned to their respective controllers, it is time to create the expression. Although expressions can be intimidating, the following simple equation converts the Bend(Main) gizmo's position along its local X-axis into a rotational equivalent with respect to the Filling object's radius.

11. In the Expression field, replace 0 with the expression **360 * (BendGizPos.x / (2 * pi * FillRad))** (see fig. 4.24). Close the Expression Controller dialog.

FIGURE 4.24

The Track View's Expression Controller dialog with new expression.

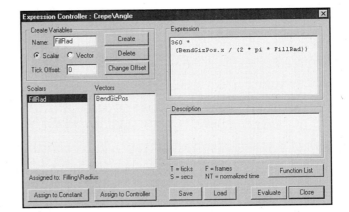

To complete this exercise you now need to configure the Upper Limit's Expression controller. You need only one variable to control the Upper Limit of the Bend(Main) modifier as its Gizmo moves along the local X-axis.

12. Select the Upper Limit track only and click on Properties in the Track View toolbar.

13. In the Expression Controller dialog, enter **BendGizPos** in the Name field, select the Vector radio button, and click on Create.

14. With the BendGizPos variable selected, click on Assign to Controller.

15. In the Track View Pick dialog, expand the tracks to display the Crepe object's Bend(Main) modifier and select the gizmo's Position track (see fig. 4.25). Click on OK.

FIGURE 4.25

The Track View Pick dialog with the Bend(Main) gizmo's Position track selected.

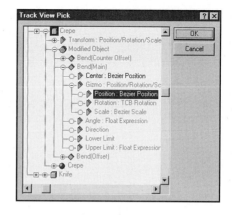

The following expression references the Bend(Main) gizmo's position along the local X-axis and communicates its negative value to the Upper Limit.

16. In the Expression field, replace 0 with the expression **–BendGizPos.x** (see fig. 4.26). Close the Expression Controller dialog.

FIGURE 4.26

The Track View's Expression Controller dialog with new expression.

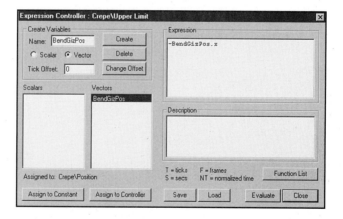

17. In the camera viewport, select and move the Bend(Main) modifier's gizmo along the crepe's local X-axis only. Watch the Angle and Upper Limit values change as the gizmo moves.

The Bend(Main)'s Angle and Upper Limit values now update dynamically as you move the gizmo along its local X-axis. On close examination of the roll, however, you will notice that the crepe's outer radius does not increase as the roll is wound up (see fig. 4.27). To control the outer radius offset, use the crepe's Bend(Offset) and Bend(Counter Offset) modifiers. Because you will be diverting your attention away from the Bend(Main) modifier for a while, first animate its Gizmo's position along the local X-axis to automate its movement.

FIGURE 4.27
Rolled up crepe with constant radius.

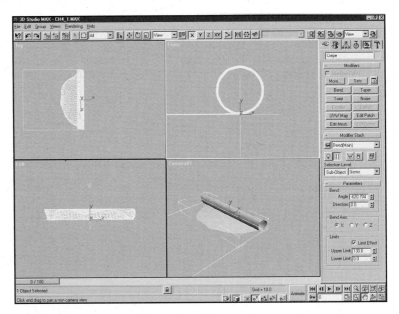

Load ch4_1_1.max from the accompanying CD if you would like to start where the previous exercise left off.

ANIMATING THE GIZMO

1. Select and move the Bend(Main) modifier's gizmo back to its original position so that the crepe lies flat (see fig. 4.28).

2. Go to frame 100. Turn on the Animate button. In the camera viewport, select and move the Bend(Main) modifier's gizmo –200.0 units along its local X-axis (see fig. 4.29).

FIGURE 4.28
Bend(Main) modifier's gizmo returned to its original position.

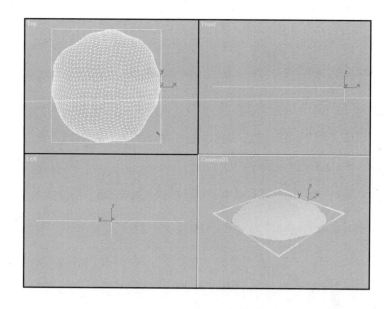

FIGURE 4.29
Bend(Main) modifier's animated gizmo.

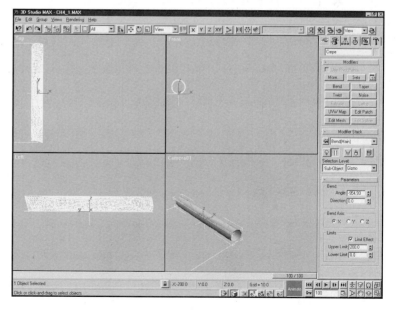

3. Turn off Animate and play back the animation.

Now that you have animated the roll, it is time to take a closer look at the crepe's Bend(Offset) and Bend(Counter Offset) modifiers.

Controlling the Crepe's Outer Radius

To make the crepe look more natural, it needs to grow slightly larger as it rolls up to compensate for its thickness. To achieve this, you will use the crepe's Bend(Offset) and Bend(Counter Offset) modifiers to increase its outside radius by a constant amount. The Bend(Offset) modifier sits below the Bend(Main) modifier in the stack; the Bend(Counter Offset) is above. If the Bend(Offset)'s Angle value is greater than zero, the Bend(Main)'s effect is compounded and the roll radiates outward. The Bend(Counter Offset) modifier is used to correct unwanted sloping that results from the initial offset.

ROLLING UP THE CREPE

Load ch4_1_2.max from the accompanying CD if you would like to start where the previous exercise left off.

1. Go to frame 75 so that the crepe is three-quarters of the way rolled up.

2. Select the Crepe object and go to the Bend(Offset) modifier in the Modifier Stack.

3. Use the spinner to adjust the Angle value between 0 and 15.0 degrees.

The crepe's outer radius increases as the Bend(Offset)'s Angle value moves positively away from zero (see fig. 4.30).

FIGURE 4.30

Bend(Offset) modifier's positive Angle value increases the crepe's outer radius.

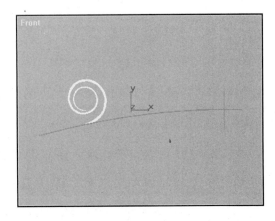

4. Change the Angle value to 8.0 degrees. Play back the animation.

A side effect of the increasing outer radius is that the entire crepe now slopes down by the Bend(Offset)'s angle amount (see fig. 4.31). An examination of the crepe's Bend(Counter Offset) modifier should help you see how to remedy this.

FIGURE 4.31

Side-effect of the increasing outer radius.

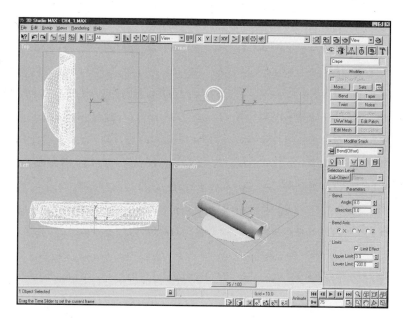

5. Go to the Bend(Counter Offset) modifier in the Modifier Stack.

6. Change the Angle value to 8.0 degrees, matching that of the Bend(Offset) modifier.

7. Play back the animation.

The sloping side-effect has been eliminated (see fig. 4.32). The Bend(Counter Offset) modifier's Direction value is set to 180.0 degrees; this applies the bend effect in the opposite direction to that of the Bend(Offset) modifier. This counters the overall slope, but leaves the crepe's increasing radius intact.

Because the bend offset is only used to compensate for the thickness of the crepe, you can use a much smaller amount.

8. Reduce the Bend(Offset) and Bend(Counter Offset) Angle values to 1.2.

FIGURE 4.32

Rolled-up crepe with increasing outer radius minus sloping side effect.

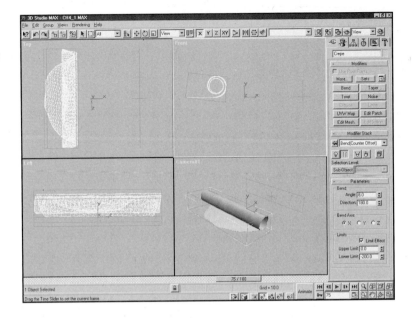

Because the Angle value of both Offset modifiers should always be equal, it makes sense to use two instances of the same animation controller for these parameters. Chapter 24 of *Inside 3D Studio MAX Volume I* discusses copying and pasting of controllers. If you copy either Bézier Float controller to the other Angle track and paste it as an instance, adjusting either the Bend(Offset) or Bend(Counter Offset) Angle parameter will identically affect the other.

Controlling the Filling's Transforms with the Crepe's Bend Modifiers

Your crepe is well on its way to becoming part of a delicious entree (or dessert). Now it is time to reintroduce the Filling object and prepare it for its journey into the culinary arts. Your task is to enable the filling to precisely match the movement and rotation of the crepe as it is rolled up. To control its position, you will use a Position Expression to reference several components of the crepe, including the Bend(Main) gizmo's position, the Bend(Main) and Bend(Offset) Angle values, as well as the filling's own radius. To control its rotation, you use a Euler XYZ compound controller with a Float Expression referencing the crepe's Bend(Main) angle.

PREPARING THE FILLING

Load ch4_1_3.max from the accompanying CD if you would like to start where the previous exercise left off.

1. Unhide the Filling object.

2. Open Track View and expand tracks to display the Filling object's Position track.

3. Select the Position track and click on Assign Controller in the Track View toolbar.

4. Select the Position Expression controller and click on OK (see fig. 4.33).

FIGURE 4.33

Replacing the Filling object's Position Expression controller.

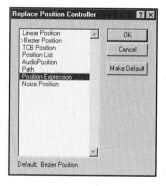

5. With the Position track selected, bring up the Expression Controller dialog by clicking on the Properties button in the Track View toolbar.

For this expression, you will create four variables that will enable the filling to remain centered in the crepe's curl as it is rolled up. The first variable references the Bend(Main) gizmo's position, the second variable references the Bend(Offset)'s Angle value, the third variable references the filling's own height, and the fourth variable references the filling's own radius.

6. In the Expression Controller dialog, enter **BendGizPos** in the Name field, select the Vector radio button, and click on Create.

7. With the newly created BendGizPos variable selected, click on Assign to Controller.

8. In the Track View Pick dialog, expand the tracks to display the Crepe object's Bend(Main) modifier and select the gizmo's Position track (see fig. 4.34). Click on OK.

FIGURE 4.34

The Track View Pick dialog with the Bend(Main) gizmo's Position track selected.

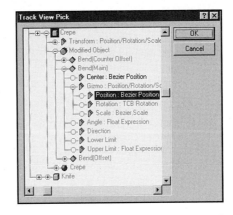

9. In the Expression Controller dialog, enter **BendOffAng** in the Name field, select the Scalar radio button, and click on Create.

10. With the newly created BendOffAng variable selected, click on Assign to Controller.

11. In the Track View Pick dialog, expand the tracks to display the Crepe object's Bend(Offset) modifier and select the Angle track (see fig. 4.35). Click on OK.

FIGURE 4.35

The Track View Pick dialog with the Bend(Offset) Angle track selected.

12. In the Expression Controller dialog, enter **FillHeight** in the Name field, select the Scalar radio button, and click on Create.

13. With the FillHeight variable selected, click on Assign to Controller.

14. In the Track View Pick dialog, expand the objects and tracks to display the Filling object's Height track. Select the Height track (see fig. 4.36). Click on OK.

FIGURE 4.36

The Track View Pick dialog with the Filling object's Height track selected.

15. In the Expression Controller dialog, enter **FillRad** in the Name field, select the Scalar radio button, and click on Create.

16. With the FillRad variable selected, click on Assign to Controller.

17. In the Track View Pick dialog, expand the objects and tracks to display the Filling object's Radius track. Select the Radius track (see fig. 4.37). Click on OK.

FIGURE 4.37

The Track View Pick dialog with the Filling object's Radius track selected.

The Position Expression controller uses a vector expression containing three components to determine the location of an object in space. The following expression (in step 18) uses the four variables to control the precise position of the Filling object as the crepe rolls up.

- The expression's X-axis component references the Bend(Main) Gizmo's position to control the filling's position along the crepe's local X-axis.

- The expression's Y-axis component references the filling's height to keep it centered in the crepe along the crepe's local Y-axis.

- The expression's Z-axis component references the filling's radius along with the crepe's Bend(Offset) Angle value and Bend(Main) Gizmo's position to control the filling's position along the crepe's local Z-axis.

18. In the Expression field, replace the existing values with the expression **[BendGizPos.x + 100, FillHeight / 2, FillRad + tan((BendOffAng/360) * BendGizPos.x) * BendGizPos.x]** (see fig. 4.38). Close the Expression Controller dialog.

FIGURE 4.38

The Track View's Expression Controller dialog with the new expression.

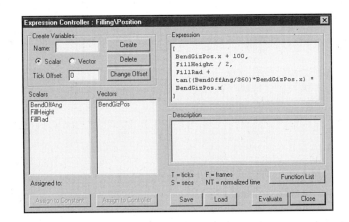

This expression will dynamically compensate for changes to both the filling's shape and the crepe's increasing outer radius. You can test this by altering the filling's radius and height or by changing the crepe's Bend(Offset) Angle.

The last step to controlling the Filling object's motion is to convert the Bend(Main)'s changing Angle into the filling's rotation. You will use a Euler XYZ compound controller in the filling's Rotation track and then assign a simple expression controller referencing the Angle value to its Y-axis component.

NOTE

It would be very convenient to simply copy and paste an instance of the Bend(Main) Angle's Bézier Float controller into the Y-axis component of the Euler XYZ rotation. However, pasting into sub-track controllers (such as Eulers, Lists, Ease, and Multiplier curves) is not supported in MAX 1.x.

ASSIGNING AN EXPRESSION CONTROLLER
(VIA EULER XYZ) TO THE ROTATION TRACK

Load ch4_1_4.max from the accompanying CD if you would like to start where the previous exercise left off.

1. Open Track View and expand tracks to display the Filling object's Rotation track.

2. Select the Rotation track and click on Assign Controller in the Track View toolbar.

3. Select the Euler XYZ controller and click on OK (see fig. 4.39).

FIGURE 4.39

Replacing the Filling object's Rotation controller.

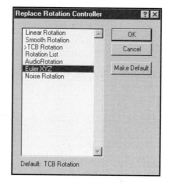

4. Expand the Rotation track to display the Euler's X, Y, and Z components.

5. Select the Y Rotation track and click on Assign Controller in the Track View toolbar.

6. Select the Float Expression controller and click on OK

7. Click on Properties to bring up the Expression Controller dialog. Enter **BendMainAng** in the Name field, select the Scalar radio button, and click on Create.

8. With the BendMainAng variable selected, click on Assign to Controller.

9. In the Track View Pick dialog, expand the objects and tracks to display the Crepe object's Bend(Main) Angle track. Select the Angle track (see fig. 4.40). Click on OK

FIGURE 4.40

The Track View Pick dialog with the Crepe object's Bend(Main) Angle track selected.

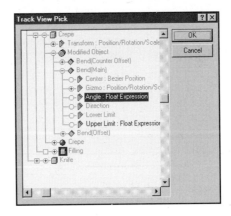

The following expression references the Bend(Main)'s Angle value and converts it from degrees to radians. This conversion is necessary when channeling nonrotation angle values (such as bends or twists) into rotation expressions.

10. In the Expression field, replace the existing value with the expression **degToRad(BendMainAng)** (see fig. 4.41).

FIGURE 4.41

The Track View's Expression Controller dialog with new expression.

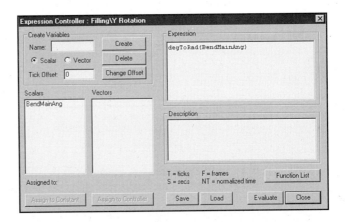

When you play back the animation, you will see that the filling now moves and rotates precisely with the rolling crepe. Load ch4_1.avi or ch4_2.max from the accompanying CD to see the finished scene.

In Practice: Animating with Controllers

- **Controllers.** Understanding how controllers can be made to communicate with each other is an important step toward mastering your animated scenes.

- **Path controllers.** The Path controller is a compound controller created as an alternative position controller. It receives the output of a subordinate Percent controller that specifies the path position, expressed as a percentage of total path length.

- **Euler XYZ Rotation controller.** The Euler XYZ controller is provided as an alternative to the standard TCB Rotation controller. The Euler XYZ controller enables the user to view and adjust rotation values in the Function Curves mode of Track View.

- **Look-At controller.** This controller is a compound controller that combines the output of an object's position, roll, and scale controllers. It completely replaces the standard PRS (Position/Rotation/Scale) controller and outputs the transformation matrix of associated objects.

- **Parametric controller.** A parametric controller is unique in that it automatically creates animation data for an object based on user-specified data values.

- **Noise controller.** One of two parametric controllers, the Noise controller is useful for creating an amazing variety of irregular animated effects, such as buzzing wings, rustling leaves, flashing lights, and other effects.

- **List controller.** The other parametric controller, the List controller is a user-defined compound controller used to combine the effects of multiple controllers.

- **Expression controllers.** Expression controllers contain a fairly comprehensive set of functions that can be used to create enormously complex equations, if necessary. However, they do not have to be complex for you to take advantage of their capability to relate and interpret values from other controllers.

- **Instancing.** Instancing controllers across multiple tracks is a powerful way to simplify complex procedures.

- **Naming Strategy.** Use a sound naming strategy for variables so that you never lose track of your controller assignments.

IMAGE CREATED BY DAN O'LEARY

Chapter 5

by Dan O'Leary

ANIMATING WITH EXPRESSIONS

Expression controllers provide a level of animation control just short of that afforded by scripting plug-ins or the SDK. Without learning a programming language, any MAX user familiar with Expression controllers can mathematically define animations for the transforms and numeric creation, modifier, or material parameters of an object.

Additionally, expressions enable astute users to define relationships between the animation controllers of objects. A wheel's rate of rotation, for example, can be defined as a function of its radius.

This kind of precise control has applications in many animation markets. Forensic animation and scientific visualization are obvious examples because simulation is often the goal. Beyond these niche markets, expressions are a very useful tool for creating behaviors that enhance the primary animation.

This chapter explores the following topics:

- Transform animation with Expression controllers
- Control objects
- Modifier animation

Expression Controllers Overview

Expression controllers are not for everyone. They require the user to take on a different level of understanding than any other tool in the MAX interface. This is largely due to the fact that, by itself, the Expression controller does absolutely nothing. It is a do-it-yourself controller kit that requires the user to do the following:

1. Recognize effects that could be implemented more efficiently or effectively using procedural techniques than by using other key-based controllers.

2. Create an equation or group of equations that produce the required results. Those of you comfortable with math, especially algebra and trigonometry, are at an advantage here.

The time invested in understanding the applications of this unique and powerful tool in your daily work will pay off in increased efficiency and improved effects. The results are limited only by your creativity, ingenuity, and determination.

As powerful as they are, keep in mind that expressions do not work magic. They give users new ways to control the animation of existing parameters only. Anything beyond that requires you to spend some quality time with the MAX SDK or scripting application.

Transform Animation with Expression Controllers

Expression controllers are very useful for creating motion or effects to supplement the primary action in a scene. The work process for most animators begins with a simple representation of the scene to establish the basic motion and timing for the shot. The final animation is arrived at through a series of refinements in which increasing detail is added to the motion. Each iteration improves the look and feel of the animation without making drastic departures from the original timing and composition.

The following series of examples demonstrates the application of Expression controllers to create a complex natural behavior. This discussion approaches this in a way that enables you to layer the effects of each Expression on top of a base animation to create the final effect. In this example, Expression controllers will be used to control the position and rotation transforms of a tornado object.

Tornado Project

This project begins with a tornado animated with a simple Path controller. Some additional keys have been set so that it pauses along the way.

1. Load the file twister.max.

2. Play the animation in the Camera viewport (see fig. 5.1).

FIGURE 5.1
*Tornado motion
animated with a Path
controller.*

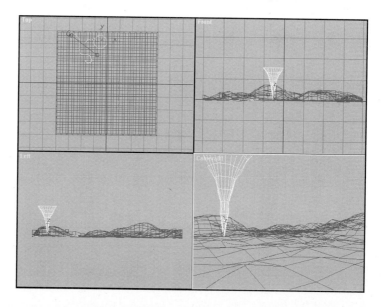

Not terribly exciting stuff, but it is enough to define timing and basic motion for the scene. Open twister.avi on the accompanying CD to see how expressions bring the scene to life.

The goal of this exercise is to create a collection of position and rotation expressions that work together to define a natural tornado behavior. You will use List controllers to add this behavior to the predefined path. Each step along the way refines the original animation, making it more lifelike than before.

Start with the basics. The most obvious problem with twister.max is that the tornado does not spin!

ANIMATING ROTATION

1. Open Track View and expand the Transform tracks for the Twister object.

2. Right-click on the Filters button in the upper-left corner of Track View and select Controller Types on the resulting menu. Verify that the Rotation Transform has been assigned a TCB controller.

To assign an Expression controller to the tornado's Z Rotation, you must first replace this TCB controller with a Euler XYZ controller. If a Euler controller was assigned by default (many users prefer them to the TCB controller), skip the following step.

3. Select the TCB Rotation and click on Assign Controller. Select Euler XYZ in the Replace Controller dialog.

4. Expand the Rotation track to reveal unique Bézier controllers on X, Y, and Z.

5. Select the Z Rotation track and assign a Float Expression controller. A range bar appears in the track to indicate the active controller.

WARNING ———————————————————————————————

Assigning an Expression controller to an animated track overwrites the existing key information. If you wish to use Expressions and keyframe data together, both controllers must be subordinate to a List controller. An example of this is provided in the Position Expressions section later in the chapter.

6. Bring up the Expression Controller Properties dialog by right-clicking on the range bar.

7. Click on Load to import a previously defined expression. Using the resulting file requester, load zrot.xpr.

8. Click on Evaluate to apply the new expression (see fig. 5.2).

9. Without closing the Expression Controller dialog, play the animation in the Camera viewport. The tornado makes one complete rotation as it moves along the path.

FIGURE 5.2

Setting up the Tornado Rotation Expression.

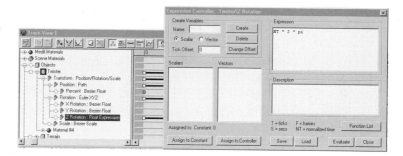

Take a moment to review the mechanics of this simple expression: NT*2*pi.

pi is a static function predefined in MAX. Its value is 3.14159, the number of radians in 180 degrees. 2*pi is the radian equivalent of 360 degrees, a complete circle. When creating expressions that control the rotation of an object, the output must be in radians to match the range of values expected by the parent Transform PRS controller.

NT is a reserved variable for Normalized Time. The value of NT increases linearly from 0.0 to 1.0 as a function of the current frame and active time segment. It is frequently used in expressions to match the timing of an animated effect to the active time segment. In this example, it serves to increase the value of your expression from 0 at the beginning of the animation (when NT=0) to 2*pi at the end (when NT=1). Table 5.1 illustrates how NT and the expression change with time.

TABLE 5.1

Using Normalized Time (NT) to Drive an Animated Expression

Frame	NT	Expression (in radians)	Expression (in degrees)
0	0	0	0
25	0.25	1.5708	90
50	0.50	3.1415	180
100	1.0	6.2832	360

Now that you have the Rotation controller up and running, it is time to make some improvements. After viewing the animation, it seems clear that a single rotation just is not enough. It would be nice to have control over the number of revolutions that the tornado makes during the course of the animation. This can be done simply enough by adding a multiplier to your current expression.

10. In the Name field of the Expression Controller Properties dialog, enter the word **Repeat**.

11. Select the Scalar option and click on Create to create a new scalar variable.

12. Click on Assign to Constant and enter a value of 5.0.

13. Click on the Expression Edit window. Edit the expression to include the Repeat multiplier: Repeat*NT*2*pi.

14. Click on Evaluate to confirm your changes and update the controller. Play the animation in the Camera viewport. The tornado now makes five complete rotations as it moves along the path.

15. Save the new expression as **zrot-r.xpr**.

Expressions were purposely, and with much effort, used in this example as an introduction to their usage—it would have been a trivial matter to keyframe this effect.

Rules of the Road

Next you move on to some more complicated behaviors not so easily animated with traditional methods. But first, take a minute to review some important rules to remember while working with expressions.

- Above all, expressions must be mathematically valid statements. Although this should be obvious, it is often easier said than done. A good way to help make your expressions clean, neat, and error-free is to use "white space." Spaces, tabs, or returns can be used freely when composing your expressions to improve readability. Clean code is bug-free code—or at least easier to make that way.

- Expressions must evaluate to a compatible variable type. Float expressions must output float data; Vector expressions must output vectors.

- Variable names are case sensitive and cannot contain spaces. Variable names may contain numbers, but must begin with a letter.

- Variables are local to the controller—its name and value apply only to the track that it is used in. An Expression controller has no knowledge of variables defined in other tracks.

- Braces and parenthesis must be balanced; open vectors or subexpressions are illegal.

Position Expressions

The Path controller animation for your tornado is too simplistic for the needs of almost any animator. Real tornadoes wander along their way, directed yet chaotic. You want to create an Expression controller that simulates that behavior automatically. Ideally its action would be independent of the path data so that it could be reused—just point the Path controller at a new spline and go!

To pull it off, make use of a List controller and some not-too fancy math.

ANIMATING THE TORNADO'S POSITION

1. Continue from the previous exercise. Close the Z Rotation Expression Properties box and stop the animation playback.

2. In the Track View, select the Path Position controller.

3. Use Assign Controller to replace the Path controller with a Position List controller.

4. Expand the List controller. Note that the old Path controller has been retained as the primary child of the List.

5. Assign a Position Expression controller to the Available slot and open the Properties box (see fig. 5.3).

FIGURE 5.3

Creating the Position List controller hierarchy.

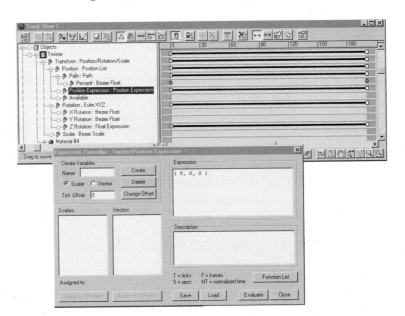

All Position Expression data must be output as vectors. This is indicated by the format of the default [0, 0, 0] expression. With a single controller, you calculate the X, Y, and Z position of the object, output in [X, Y, Z] format. Contrast this with the scalar output of the Rotation controller in the preceding example, where only the Z orientation was output.

The data output by your Position expression is then passed up to the List controller, where it is added as an offset to the output of the Path controller.

6. Load the expression 4leaf.xpr from the accompanying CD.

7. Assign a value of 10.0 to the Radius variable.

8. Assign a value of 2.0 to the Repeat variable.

N O T E

Saved expressions do not include assignments. Any constant or controller assignments must be redefined after loading. It is a good idea to include usage notes and suggested values for user-defined variables in the Description field of saved expressions.

9. Click on Evaluate to update your changes and update the controller.

10. Without closing the Expression Controller dialog, play the animation in the Camera viewport. The tornado now meanders lazily along its path of destruction.

With one expression, you have added significantly to the believability of the animation. You should now examine the components of this motion more carefully.

11. Make certain that the tornado is selected. In the Display panel, check Trajectory under Display Optimizations. The output of the Position List controller and the original spline path are now clearly visible in the Top viewport (see fig. 5.4).

FIGURE 5.4

Comparing the List controller trajectory and spline path.

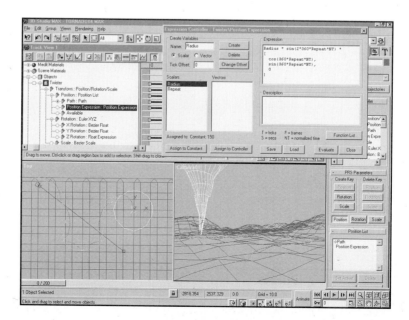

TIP

Trajectories are an excellent visualization tool when working with Position expressions; they provide instant visual feedback to the changes you make.

12. Take a few minutes to experiment with different values for Radius and Repeat, observing the effect of your changes on the trajectory. Remember that you must click on Evaluate after each new assignment to apply your changes.

13. When you are finished experimenting, reset the values of Radius and Repeat to something that creates a natural look.

As the value of Radius increases, the effect of the Position Expression controller becomes much more pronounced, visually overpowering the effects of the Path controller. With very large Radius values, the curves of the expression output are obvious. Large Repeat values tend to make the animation very jittery and knotted.

For the purposes of studying, debugging, and modifying an expression such as this, it would be nice to have a method for isolating its output in the List. Unfortunately, MAX does not provide a mechanism for making the various components of a List controller active or inactive. Here is a quick work-around—not pretty, but perfectly functional.

14. In Track View, find the keyframes for the tornado Path controller. Right-click on the key dot at frame 100 to bring up the keyframe info.

15. Change the value for that key to 0. This simple trick effectively disables the Path controller, enabling you to study the output of the Expression controller in isolation (see fig. 5.5).

FIGURE 5.5

The output of the four-leaved Rose curve Position Expression.

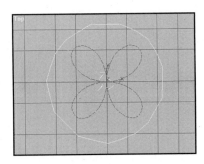

The expression used to create the meandering behavior in this example is a curve known to mathematicians as the Four-leaved Rose curve. In the polar coordinate system (r, theta), it is described by the equation r = a*sin(2*theta). Conversion to the Cartesian coordinate system (x, y, z) is achieved by substituting this for r in the following equations for x and y:

x = r*cos(theta) = a*sin(2*theta)*cos(theta)

y = r*sin(theta) = a*sin(2*theta)*sin(theta)

These equations provide an easy mechanism for determining both x and y position given an angle, theta. Spinning the value of theta from 0 around to 360 traces out the curve in x and y. To vary theta in this manner, borrow from the lessons of the first example, replacing theta with 360*Repeat*NT, to create the following equations:

x = a*sin(2*360*Repeat*NT) *cos(360*Repeat*NT)

y = a*sin(2*360*Repeat*NT)*sin(360*Repeat*NT)

Notice that the first two terms of each expression are the same. Put this into vector format for the Position expression, collecting those shared terms and replacing the variable name *a* with *Radius*, a more fitting description:

Radius*sin(2*360*Repeat*NT)*

[

    cos(360*Repeat*NT),

    sin(360*Repeat*NT),

    0

]

You can pull shared terms outside of the vector without error because of the distributive property of multiplication. In evaluating this expression, MAX multiplies each term of the position vector by the scalar.

As a final experiment, you might want to try replacing the 2 in the first sin() function with other values to vary the number of leaves in the pattern. Any even integer value *n* produces a rose with *2n* leaves. Odd values create roses with *n* leaves. Non-integer values have unpredictable results. Also, try changing that entire sin() function with a cos() to rotate the pattern 45 degrees. See figure 5.6 for an example of an alternate Rose Curve.

FIGURE 5.6

The output of an eight-leaved cosine Rose curve.

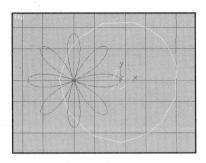

The equation for this and other useful curves can be found in most Analytic Geometry texts and mathematical handbooks.

Adding Wobble

The animation is looking much better now, but it still lacks some character. You need to add some wobbling and teetering action to give it that out-of-control look. This requires a pair of expressions for the X and Y rotation that are similar in nature, yet out of sync enough to complement the crisscrossing pattern of the Position expression.

WOBBLING AND TEETERING

1. If you have not already done so, close the Position Expression Properties dialog and change the Path Position percentage key back to 100 percent.

2. Assign Float Expression controllers to the X and Y Rotation tracks of the tornado model.

3. In the X Rotation Expression Properties dialog, load xrot.xpr from the accompanying CD. Assign a value of 5 to MaxXAngle and a value of 2 to Repeat.

The scalar expression defined by xrot.xpr is similar in some ways to the others used in this example, with a few new twists:

degToRad(sin(Repeat*360*NT)*MaxXAngle)

Again, you are using NT to drive the animation through a repeating sine wave. This time the variable MaxXAngle is your goal and the maximum value for the expression. *degToRad* is a function that MAX supports for converting from degrees to radians as required by the Euler XYZ controller. It is the equivalent of multiplying the value by pi/180.

4. In the Y Rotation Expression Properties dialog, load yrot.xpr from the accompanying CD. Assign a value of 8 to MaxYAngle and a value of 1 to Repeat.

The yrot.xpr expression is the cosine version of xrot.xpr to make its rotation out of sync:

degToRad(cos(Repeat*360*NT)*MaxXAngle)+pi

pi is added to keep the tornado upright.

Before you play the animation, take a minute to view the function curve output of these expressions.

5. Click on the Function Curves icon in the Track View toolbar.

6. Select the X Rotation: Float Expression track label to show its output in the Function Curve display.

7. With the Shift key depressed, select the Y Rotation: Float Expression track label to add its output to the Function Curve display (see fig. 5.7).

FIGURE 5.7

Using Function Curves with Rotation Expressions.

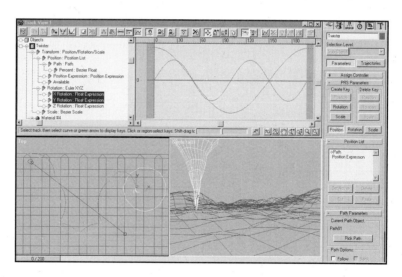

TIP

The Function Curves display is another excellent tool for visualizing your work as you develop, modify, and debug expressions.

The various properties of the X and Y rotation expressions are clearly visible in the Function Curve display, including MaxAngle, Repeat, and the phase difference between sine and cosine functions.

8. Play the animation in the Camera viewport.

You have come a long way from the original scene. With a group of four relatively simple expressions, you created a convincing behavior that can be used with any path- or key-based animation. As a test of that claim, make one last change to this animation.

9. Save the project.

10. Unhide Line02.

11. Select the tornado object and go to the Motion Panel.

12. Click on Pick Path and select Line02.

13. Play the new animation.

FIGURE 5.8

The finished twister.

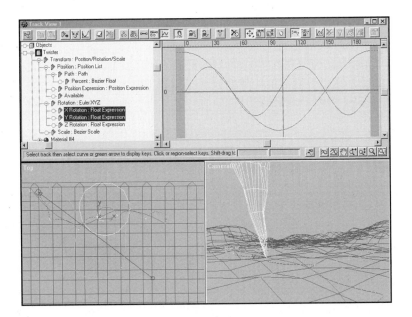

NOTE

Internally, all 3DS MAX Rotation controllers represent the orientation of an object with quaternion math. Developed in the 1840s by Sir William Hamilton, *quaternions* allow for smooth interpolation of rotation values that is impossible with the separate X, Y, and Z rotations required by a matrix solution. Additionally, quaternion interpolation schemes result in more direct, natural, and predictable motions. The output of these controllers consists of four components: a three-component unit vector and a scalar rotation value. Together these describe the orientation of the object in quaternion format for the parent PRS Compound controller.

Remember that expressions recognize (and therefore output) only scalar and vector data types. Because they do not support quaternion data types, you are forced to use Float Expressions in the Rotation tracks of a Euler XYZ controller.

The Euler XYZ controller is a List controller that converts the output of three unique Float controllers into their quaternion equivalent. This approach enables users to work with familiar X, Y, and Z rotations individually without losing the many hidden benefits of quaternion math.

Although it is easy to comprehend the physical significance of the X, Y, and Z float components of a Euler controller, the four-dimensional output of a Quaternion controller is extremely difficult to visualize. Because of this, most of the Rotation controllers that ship with MAX do not support the Function Curves display of Track View. This makes the Euler XYZ controller unique and powerful.

It is not hard to imagine the applications for this kind of flexibility in a production environment. Imagine yourself tasked with animating a tornado in several different shots for a blockbuster feature film with tight deadlines. After making the initial time investment to develop these controllers, a lot of the work is done for you. You finish on time with better effects (because you had more time to focus on them), and you are really looking forward to working on the sequel!

Control Objects and Modifier Animation

In addition to their proven utility in controlling transform animations, expressions are a very powerful tool for animating the parameters of all imaginable modifiers. Imagine creating a simple expression to relate the mix amount of a blush texture map to the bend angle of a smile. How about decreasing the density of a mesh as it moves away from the camera by automatically varying the parameters of an Optimize modifier?

Any effect that can be achieved by animating the parameters of a MAX modifier can be controlled mathematically with an Expression controller. Many secondary motion effects such as bouncing bellies and bending hair can be realistically achieved with a well-placed modifier and a few simple expressions. You can make the belly of a jovial character jiggle by animating the strength of a Displace modifier with an expression tied to Position track of his center of mass.

Another, often overlooked application of expressions is the creation of Controller objects. A *Controller object* is an object created to provide the user a physical input mechanism to an expression or system of expressions. By creating groups of virtual knobs, levers, and sliders and assigning their transformations to expression variables, users can tackle complicated gestures with relative ease.

Imagine creating a virtual lighting panel for controlling complicated systems of animated lights. How about animating the gestures of your next character with a few sliders with labels such as smile and frown? This is the kind of approach that Pixar animators used when creating and controlling AVARS (Animation Variables) for *Toy Story*.

The Whirlygig Project

In the following series of examples, you create a set of expressions controlled by the position of a Control object. By moving that object in the scene, you control the animation of the Fantastic Whirlygig carnival ride.

Start by loading the project and having a look around. Load the file whirl.max and play the animation in the shaded Camera viewport (see fig. 5.9).

FIGURE 5.9

The Fantastic Whirlygig project.

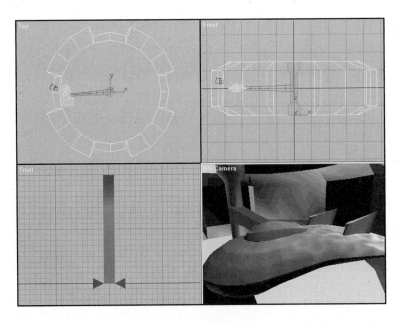

Creating a Control Object

First, you need to create the expression and assignments necessary to control the vehicle's rotation with another object in the scene.

CONTROLING VEHICLE ROTATION

1. With the whirl.max file open, open Track View.

2. Right-click on Objects and select Expand Objects. Right-click again to expand Tracks.

3. Click on Filters in the toolbar and activate Show Only Animated Tracks and Show Controller Types.

TIP

This combination of filters is a quick way to isolate the animation data in complex or unfamiliar scenes.

4. Right-click on the Z Rotation range bar and bring up the Properties dialog for that Float Expression.

As you can see, you are using the standard expression for object rotation, as developed in the previous set of examples. What you need to do is alter it so that Repeat can be driven by the position of another object in the scene. Because variables can only be assigned to controllers of the same data type, you must create a new vector variable.

5. Select Repeat in the list of scalar variables and click on Delete.

6. Type **Repeat** in the Variable Name edit box, choose Vector, and click on Create to define the new, improved vector variable.

7. Assign Repeat to the Position controller of Pointer.

8. Edit the Expression, changing –Repeat to –Repeat.z.

By appending ".z" to the Repeat variable, you specify that only the z component of the vector should be used in the expression. To correspond with the MAX World coordinate system, z was chosen.

9. Click on Evaluate and play the animation in the Camera view.

Nothing happens! This is because the default position of the Controller object is on the Z axis, so –Repeat.z = 0 and the entire rotation expression zeros out.

10. Change the bottom-left viewport to a Front view. Select Pointer and Bar and perform a Zoom Extents Selected.

11. Deselect the bar, and activate Select and Move. With Snap on, move Pointer up in Y by three snaps (30 units). Check your results with figure 5.10.

12. Play the animation in the Camera view.

Even at this low setting, the car is spinning too quickly. You need to find some way to scale the input of the expression.

FIGURE 5.10

Animating the Pointer Control object.

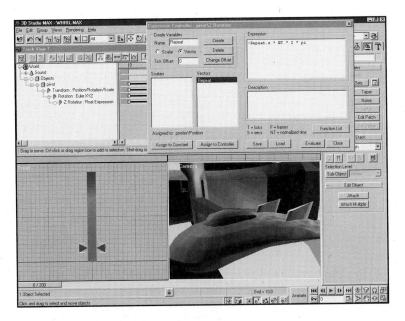

13. Edit the expression to include a scale factor on the Z component of Repeat: –Repeat.z/50*NT*2*pi. Click on Evaluate and play the animation in the Camera viewport. Close the Properties dialog.

Take a moment to think about what is going on here. In this expression, the term –Repeat.z/50 again determines the number of complete rotations or "laps" that your car will make during the course of the animation. At the pointer's current position, Repeat.z has the value of 30—3 snaps on a 10 unit grid. The car will therefore spin 30÷50 or 60 percent of one full lap in the 200 frame animation.

Before adding the scale factor, each click of the pointer increased the vehicle speed by three complete revolutions per second! By dividing –Repeat.z by 50, you desensitized the controls, providing the user much smoother input and cleaner control of the animation.

Animating with Control Objects

Now that you have a means of controlling the rotation of the vehicle, try setting some position keys for the Pointer object to animate the spin-up of the ride.

ANIMATING THE SPIN

1. With the Pointer object at its minimum position on the bar, click on Animate. Go to frame 70 and move the pointer up 3 clicks to 30.

2. Jump to frame 100 and slide the pointer up 3 more clicks to 60.

3. Add another key at frame 130 by sliding the pointer up 6 more clicks to 120.

4. Add one last key at frame 200 with a value of 120. Turn off Animate.

5. Play the animation in the Camera viewport.

The car smoothly accelerates until around frame 160, when it reverses direction for the final second of animation. What is going on here? The keyframes you defined for the animation of the Pointer Control object would not seem to account for any deceleration, let alone backward travel. Take a look at the function curves to get a better idea of what is going on.

6. Bring up Track View and find the pointer position keys you just created. Click on the Function Curves icon and select the pointer Position track to display its profile.

7. Pan up in the Track View list panel to find the arm Z Rotation track. With the Ctrl key depressed, click on the Z Rotation track to add its output to the function curve display.

8. Zoom Horizontal and Value Extents to see the entire animation (see fig. 5.11).

FIGURE 5.11

Troubleshooting with function curves.

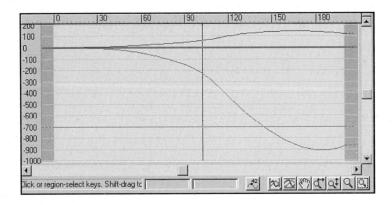

The top blue curve is the position of the Pointer Object, the lower green curve is the rotation of the arm. As you can see, the green rotation curve is decreasing throughout the animation until a point near frame 180, where it clearly reverses direction.

Looking at the blue pointer position curve, you can see the problem. Because of the nature of Bézier controllers, the Pointer Control object does not immediately level off following the key at frame 130. Instead, it overshoots that key and smoothly turns to the final key at frame 200.

Although it may be very comfortable to think of the Pointer object as a gas pedal that directly controls the angular velocity of the arm, it does not actually work that way. Changes in the position of the Pointer object are directly proportional to changes in the position of the arm at any frame.

By animating the position of the pointer upward, you create the impression of acceleration by forcing the arm to catch up with an ever-increasing "total twist" factor.

9. Click on the blue pointer position curve to display its key information dots.

10. Select the key at frame 200 and right-click to display its key information dialog. Change the Z value to 160.

11. Open the In tangent flyout and select the Slow tangent type.

12. Add a key at frame 170 with a Z value of 160. Set the In and Out tangents to Slow. The position curve should now slope smoothly up to this key and flatten out (see fig. 5.12). Play the animation in the Camera viewport.

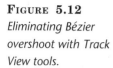

FIGURE 5.12
*Eliminating Bézier
overshoot with Track
View tools.*

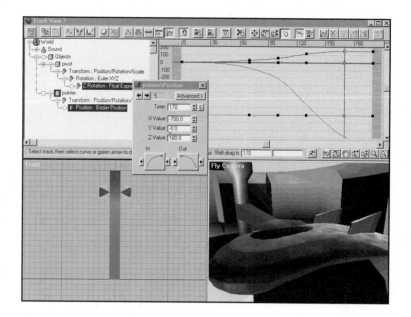

Parametric Modifier Animation

In all the previous examples, you have seen how expressions can be used to create object transform animations. Expressions can also be used to define the numeric creation parameters of an object as well as any modifiers applied to it. This gives users a very unique and powerful tool for animating the geometry in their projects.

In your example, it would be nice to see the support arm bend as the vehicle accelerates. With Expression controllers, it is simple enough to relate that bend angle to the position of the Control object defined in the preceding example.

BENDING THE SUPPORT ARM

1. Select the Arm and Car objects in the Top view. Maximize the Top view and go to frame zero of the animation.

2. Go to the Modify Command panel and apply a Bend modifier to the two selected objects.

3. Activate Sub-Object Selection mode and choose Center to edit the position of the Bend Gizmo Center. Activate the Snap mode.

4. In the Top view, move the Gizmo Center –190 in X to near the World Coordinate Center (0,0,0). This centers the Bend effect at the pivot point of the support arm.

5. Set the Bend Axis to X and the Direction to 270. Spin the Bend Angle up and down to see the effect. The arm bends back and forth about the center of rotation. Unfortunately, the bend is deforming the car as well. Limit the Bend effect to avoid this undesirable effect.

6. Click on Limit Effect at the bottom of the Bend rollup and set the Upper Limit to 268, the length of the arm (see fig. 5.13). Test the Bend effect to see that the car is no longer distorted. Click on Min/Max Toggle to restore the viewports.

FIGURE 5.13
Setting up the bend modifier.

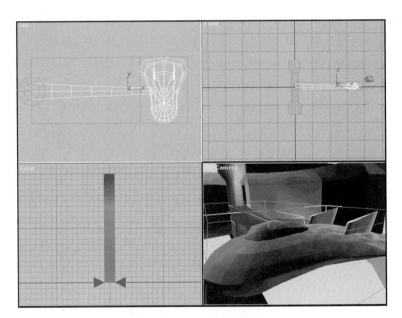

7. Open Track View and expand the arm hierarchy for the Bend modifier. Select the Bend Angle track.

NOTE

The Bend Angle track is one of many that begins life in MAX with no assigned controller. Unlike the Gizmo Position track above it, which has been assigned a standard PRS controller, the Angle track shows no assigned controller type.

To reduce memory usage in MAX, many tracks that can be animated do not have a controller assigned at the time of their creation. This normally has no impact on the animator because an appropriate controller automatically attaches whenever keys for the track are generated.

The main opportunity for this to cause confusion is when assigning Expression controller variables to the output of a track that is not animated. If you wanted to create an expression for the rotation of a wheel based on its radius, for example, you might create a Scalar Variable named Radius and attempt to assign it to the Radius track of the Wheel object. Because the Wheel object radius is unlikely to be animated, that track will be ghosted (grayed out) in the Track View Pick dialog when you try to create the assignment. MAX allows only variables to be tied to tracks that have been assigned controllers. Tracks such as Bend Angle have to be manually assigned a controller in Track View before they can be attached to an expression variable.

8. Assign a Float Expression to the Bend Angle, open the Expression Properties dialog, and create a vector variable named Repeat.

9. Assign Repeat to the Position track of the Control object Pointer.

10. Enter the following equation: **Repeat.z/10**. This causes the arm to bend one degree with each snap (10 units) of the Control object.

11. Find the Car object in Track View. Click on the square plus box to the right of the arm object to show the objects linked to it, including the car.

12. Expand the Car object hierarchy and locate the Angle track of its Bend modifier. As you can see, the Float Expression you just created for the arm Bend Angle track has been assigned here as well. Magic? No. Recall that when you first applied the Bend modifier, both arm and car were selected. Whenever modifiers are applied to multiple selected objects in MAX, the result is instanced for all objects. Any changes that you make to the Bend Float Expression therefore automatically affect both objects!

13. Test the new expression by moving the Pointer Control object up and down in the Front view. If all is well, play the animation in the Camera viewport (see fig. 5.14).

Now add one last expression to keep the camera pointed at the action.

14. Expand the camera hierarchy. Assign a Euler XYZ controller to the camera rotation.

15. Assign a Float Expression controller to the Z Rotation track of the Euler XYZ controller.

FIGURE 5.14

The completed Fantastic Whirlygig.

16. Open the new Expression Controller dialog and create a vector variable named Repeat.

17. Edit the expression to take into account the arm bend: 1.17302 – (Repeat.z/1500).

18. Play the animation in the Camera viewport.

For one last trick, unhide the Counter group in the Whirlygig scene and play the animation in the Front viewport. A pair of expressions has been used to provide a real-time readout of the pointer position.

The Counter group is made up of four objects: one object for each digit and a controller object. A unique Material modifier has been applied to each of the objects, and a Multi/Sub-Object Material called *Digits* has been assigned to the group. The Digits material is comprised of 10 standard materials, one material for each digit bitmap 0–9. By animating the Material ID track of the Material modifier on each Counter object, the digits animate, creating the effect of a numeric counter.

The Material ID track of the Counter Controller object holds the Z component of the pointer position controller. The expression used by each Counter object references that value, which is decomposed with floor and mod functions to provide the appropriate digit. Take some time to study this simple but well-designed set of expressions—it points to yet another powerful area of application for this impressive tool.

In this example you have used Expressions to animate object transforms (rotation in this case), the parameters of an object modifier, and the Material ID assigned to an object. It isn't difficult to appreciate the power of Expressions. With careful planning, they can be used to help you work more efficiently and generate better results.

In Practice: Animating with Expressions

- **Animated Variables.** Before a variable can be assigned to the output of other tracks in a scene, those tracks must have an Animation controller assigned.

- **Rotation Expressions.** Euler XYZ controllers must be used on objects whose rotations will be animated with expressions. A Float Expression controller is then assigned as desired to each of the independent X, Y, and Z tracks.

- **Animated Expressions.** For an expression to produce an animated effect, it must be driven by the output of another animated track or by one of the animated MAX reserved variables (T, S, F, or NT). Additionally, animated expressions can be created using the noise (p,q,r) function.

- **Clean Code.** Use white-space in your expressions to keep things clear and legible. Also, make use of the Description field to keep usage notes and suggested values for user-defined variables in your expressions, because variable assignments are not saved with the expression.

- **Trajectories and Function Curves.** These two visualization tools are invaluable to Expression controller users. Both provide direct and very useful visual feedback of the output of your functions for verification and troubleshooting.

Rendered with *The Incredible Comicshop*™

IMAGE CREATED BY DAN O'LEARY

Chapter 6

by Dan O'Leary

ANIMATING WITH MULTIPLE MODIFIERS

Modifiers in 3D Studio MAX give users the ability to deform and enhance geometry without these alterations being carved in stone. Changes in a model's appearance can be broken up into any number of separate "modifiers" that can be deactivated, deleted, or have their parameters change at any time. These parameters can also be animated. Apply a Taper modifier and animate the object going to a point. Apply on top of that a Bend modifier and animate the object bending as it points. Days could be spent creating abstract animations where every available parameter of an object and its deforms are animated.

Modifiers can be used in this way—where the changes they make to your geometry are the focus of your animation. But more often, they are useful for more subtle effects, enhancing the action taking place rather than directing it. This chapter uses modifiers both as a means to perform broad changes to your geometry as well as a tool for embellishing your scene. This chapter explores the following topics:

- Animating Object modifier parameters
- Using Object modifiers for global animated effects
- Using Object modifiers for subtle animated effects
- Using objects to affect sub-object selections (linked XForm)

Animating Object Modifier Parameters

Modifier animation can start at the most elementary level—the basic parameters that make up an object. A cylinder can have its measurements change over time or have its number of sides and segments increase or decrease as the view gets closer or farther away.

Beyond animation of a primitive object's creation parameters are the Standard modifiers. Bends, Twists, Skews, and so on can have their respective angles, strengths, directions, and so forth, animated, as well as animating the gizmo that controls where and how the modification is made.

To illustrate some examples of using multiple modifiers in animation, you will experiment on a simple character affectionately named Henry. For the purpose of these animations, Henry is basically like a test pilot of old. A model such as Henry should make an interesting and enjoyable subject on which to try out some modifications. Initially, some tortuous ideas came to mind, some of which you'll explore. But also keep in mind the power of using modifiers for less extreme examples.

Air Pump Project

This first scene contains the Henry Editable Mesh, an air hose made up of a Loft object, and a simple pump model (see fig. 6.1). You will start by performing some modifications to the character model.

FIGURE 6.1
Henry hooked up to an air compressor.

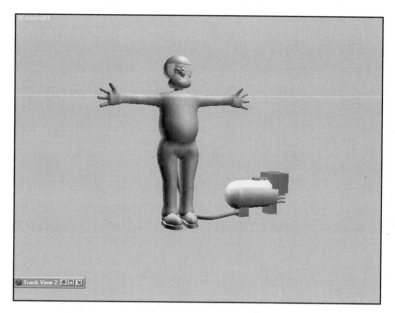

Before you start, open wpumpedcomic.avi from the accompanying CD-ROM to view the final animation to get an idea of what you are going to do.

Pumped Up—Using Displace

Displace, both as a modifier and as a space warp, is commonly used in conjunction with a bitmap, where the luminance values in the image determine the severity of the displacement. In this way, it is an excellent tool for creating effects such as surface detail and terrain. Displace can also be used alone as a force that acts on the geometry. The Displace gizmo can be animated, and so can the settings of Strength and Decay that control it. The effect can be as gentle as a dent or bulge on the surface of an object or as extreme as the inflating of a character with an air compressor.

1. From the accompanying CD-ROM, load wpumped.max.

2. Select Henry Body and open the Modify panel.

3. Add a Displace modifier to the stack. You may have to click on More under modifiers to locate Displace.

4. Open the Edit Stack dialog and click on Displace.

5. In the Name field, add the word **Body** at the end of Displace and click on OK.

6. Change the Mapping parameter from Planar to Spherical.

7. Select the Displace gizmo as your sub-object.

8. Uniform Scale the gizmo 60 percent.

9. Move the gizmo to the center of the torso, just below the chest and above the stomach, making certain to check other views to see whether it is centered (see fig. 6.2).

FIGURE 6.2

Centering the Displace gizmo for the torso-swelling effect.

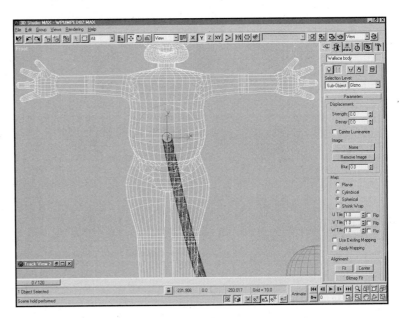

The size of the gizmo ultimately affects the shape to which the stomach will balloon. For the nice round ball effect, it is best to make the gizmo fit just inside the stomach area. A smaller gizmo would result in an oddly elongated displacement; a larger one would carry the displacement too far into the legs and chest. With the gizmo at the proper size, see how things look by performing the following steps:

1. Slide the Strength slider up and down to see the effect, stopping around 5.

The Displace is spreading out too much and scaling the entire body. You want to localize the effect more so that there is less stretching overall.

2. Slide the Decay slider slowly up, stopping around 0.8.

The feet and head stay about where they are; the stomach and chest balloon outward. That's more like it (see fig. 6.3).

FIGURE 6.3

Adjusting the Displace.

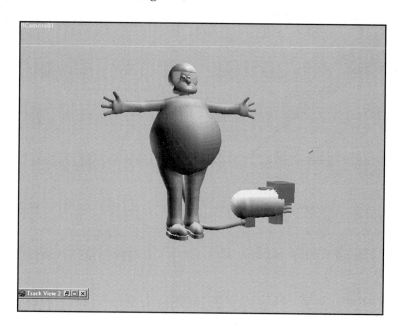

Animating Stomach Pump

Now that you have your first modifier in place, you need to set some keyframes for the inflation. To set the keyframes, perform the following steps:

1. Return the Strength slider to 0, keeping Decay at 0.8.

2. Turn on the Animate button and go to frame 30.

3. Slide the Strength slider to around 8.

4. Go to frame 60.

5. Slide the Strength slider to around 15.

6. Go to frame 90.

7. Slide the Strength slider to around 20. Now you have the beginnings of the pump effect.

8. Save your scene as **mypump01.max** and render out a Smooth + Highlights preview of the Camera01 viewport, frames 0–90.

Not bad, but instead of a steady inflation, make it look more like the pumping is happening in three stages. To do this, set a lag time in between frames, so the effect swells, pauses, swells again, and so on.

9. Open the Track View.

10. Right-click on the Filters button and filter out everything but Animated Tracks, Transforms, Modified Objects, and Base Objects.

TIP

Because these track types are all that you will be animating in this tutorial, you can hide things such as Materials and Maps tracks so that they don't clutter your view. In a scene with as few objects as this, it doesn't matter much, but later on it can make a big difference, and you can save yourself a lot of time scrolling through hierarchies.

Now, add some easing in and out to the pumping keys.

1. Find the Displace Strength controller from the hierarchy list.

2. Select the Strength controller (by clicking on the name in the hierarchy) and open its function curve.

3. Select the spline. The four keys from 0–90 appear at a steady slope.

4. Select Edit Keys from the toolbar to go back to the Range and Animation tracks.

5. Holding the Shift key, select the key at frame 30 and drag a copy to frame 35.

6. Do the same for frames 60 and 90, offsetting a copy of each five frames.

This creates a lag between each phase of pumping. To smooth things out, perform the following steps:

7. Open the function curve for Strength.

The curve now has a slight stair-stepping effect (see fig. 6.4)

8. Open the Properties dialog for keyframe 30 by right-clicking on the key.

9. Select the Custom Tangent type (last one in the pull down) for the In (this automatically changes the Out to a Custom Tangent as well).

10. Repeat steps 8 and 9 for frames 60 and 90.

FIGURE 6.4

The function curve now has extra frames, creating a pause each time the curve levels off.

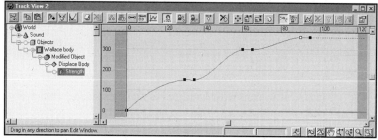

11. Now go back and region-zoom in on frames 30 and 35.

12. Adjust the custom tangent handle, pulling it down to make a shallow dip (see fig. 6.5).

FIGURE 6.5

Easing around the swelling keyframes.

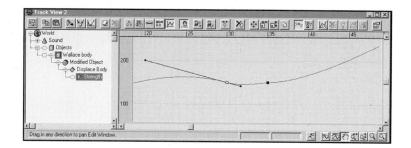

NOTE

If you can't see the tangent handles, make certain that the Show Tangents button on the toolbar is on.

13. Repeat steps 11 and 12 for frames 60 and 90, adjusting the tangent for each so that the In rises gently while the Out slopes down.

14. Minimize the Track View and make another preview of the Camera01 viewport, frames 0–90, saving your scene before you do.

TIP

To avoid having to set the filters every time, try minimizing the Track View rather than closing it completely. Sometimes it is easy to forget that you have a Track View already open (especially when it is tucked away at the bottom of the screen), and you will end up opening a new one even though the other one is still minimized. I like to move the minimized Track View up into the corner of the viewport while animating, so it is less easy to forget about it.

The body swells and pauses as if being inflated by multiple pushes of a bicycle pump. This effect may not be entirely accurate when taking into consideration that the character is being inflated by a mechanical compressor that would supply an even flow. For something this "cartoony" in nature, however, it is sometimes best to illustrate the stereotypical effect rather than the physical reality. Open wpumped.avi from the accompanying CD to see this effect.

Now keeping in the cartoony scheme of things, inflate Henry's head in a similar fashion.

1. Go to frame 0.

2. Select Henry Body and open the Modify panel.

3. Add a second Displace modifier to the stack.

4. This time rename Displace to **Displace Head** in the Edit Stack dialog.

5. Change the Mapping parameter from Planar to Spherical.

6. Select the Displace gizmo as your sub-object.

7. Uniform Scale the gizmo 60 percent.

8. Move the gizmo to the middle of the head (check to make certain that it is centered).

9. Maximize your Track View and select Edit Keys from the toolbar.

To save some steps, copy the Strength keys from Displace Body and paste them onto Displace Head. Then you will adjust the keys so that the majority of the head ballooning happens at the end.

1. Turn off the Animated Objects Only filter so that you can see the tracks for Displace Head (because it currently has no keyframes).

2. Expand your window and scroll down until you can see the tracks for both Displace Body and Displace Head (you may need to expand the Displace Head tracks).

3. Select the Strength controller and click on Copy Controller.

4. Select the Strength controller for Displace Head and click on Paste Controller.

5. Make certain that Paste as Copy is selected rather than Instance (because you will be making changes to the head inflation that you don't want on the body displace).

You now have keys for Henry's head. If you render a preview now, you will see the head inflating to about the same size as the body, giving it a snowman look (see fig. 6.6). A preferred and suggested approach, however, sees the body inflate first, and then, when it almost reaches its capacity, the head swells up. To do this, you need to lower the values of the strength keys for the head.

FIGURE 6.6

The head swells as much as the body and looks a little too extreme.

1. Select the Strength controller for Displace Head in the Track View and look at its function curve. You see the stair-stepping slope from before.

2. Region select frames 30 and 35 and change the value in the Key Value field to 0.5.

3. Region-select frames 60 and 65 and change the value in the Key Value field to 1.5.

4. Region-select frames 90 and 95 and change the value in the Key Value field to 3.

5. Finally, flatten out the custom tangent curves by leveling off the handles for frames 30, 60, and 90 (see fig. 6.7). After all, you don't want as much shrinking and swelling of the head in between pumps.

FIGURE 6.7

Leveling off the ease curves for the Displace Head strength.

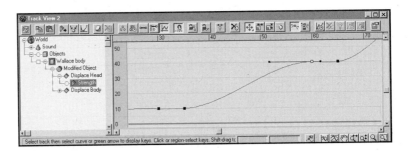

6. Save your scene and render out a Smooth + Highlights preview of the Camera01 viewport, frames 0–90.

Floating Henry—Using Linked XForm

Somewhere during this process, it would be nice to have Henry start to rise off the ground. This can be done simply enough by setting move keys, but Henry has an air hose attached to his back. Realistically this should stretch and follow any vertical movement you give him. This can again be done with modifiers.

The air hose is a Loft object, which means that its basic components (the loft shape and its path) can still be edited and, in this case, animated. For this example, you need the hose to remain connected to his back as he rises off the ground. You do this by selecting the end vertex of the spline that makes up the path for the Loft object and apply a Linked XForm modifier.

Linked XForm allows a sub-object selection (in this case a vertex of a spline) to be linked to another object in this scene. What you do is create a dummy object where the hose meets Henry's back, link the dummy to Henry, and link the end vertex to the dummy. The reason you link the hose to the dummy object and not directly to Henry himself is so that as he swells up, you can move the dummy back so that the hose doesn't pass through him.

1. Create a dummy at the point where the hose meets Henry's back (see fig. 6.8).

FIGURE 6.8

Creating a dummy object to help control the air hose spline.

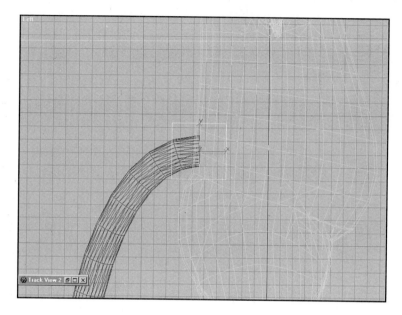

2. Link the dummy to Henry.

TIP

When using the various Select icons (select and move, link, rotate, and scale) it's easy to forget that these remain active until you select another, which is usually harmless. However when you're simply selecting objects to edit their parameters or tracks, having move, link, or rotate selected can cause you to perform an unwanted transform when you simply want to select something. It is a good habit to go back to the basic Select Object icon when you have finished your transforming or linking.

3. Select the Spline object at the center of the air hose loft (Line01).

4. In the Modify panel, apply an Edit Spline modifier to the spline.

5. Activate Sub-Object and select the end vertex where the hose meets the back.

6. Apply a Linked XForm modifier to the vertex sub-object.

7. Click on Pick Control Object and select Dummy01.

All set. Try selecting Henry and moving him around the viewport, undoing any moves you make by right-clicking before letting go of the mouse button or by pressing Undo. You will see the hose stretching to follow him. If you try the same thing from the top view, however, it looks like the hose should move more, especially in the middle where it curves. Because there happens to be a vertex in your path spline there, you can repeat the same Linked XForm technique to give it a little stretch.

1. Select the air hose spline (Line01) again.

2. Add another Edit Spline to the stack.

3. Find and select the middle vertex.

4. Apply a Linked XForm.

5. Create another dummy object centered on the middle vertex (see fig. 6.9).

FIGURE 6.9

Creating a second dummy object to affect the middle of the air hose loft.

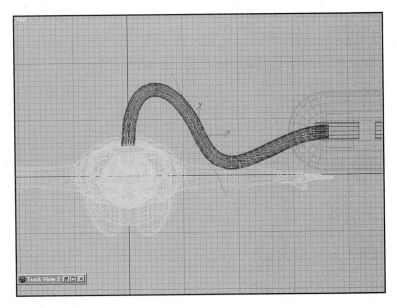

6. Click on Pick Control Object and select Dummy02.

By moving Dummy02 around, the middle of the air hose follows. Now you link Dummy02 to Dummy01.

7. Select Dummy02 and link it to Dummy01.

Moving Henry now moves both parts of the air hose as well, but the middle section doesn't look natural when it rises off the ground with him. You fix this by locking down the inherited links of Dummy02 so that it only slides along the ground.

8. Select Dummy02.

9. Open the Hierarchy panel and click on Link Info.

10. Deselect all the transforms except for Move along the Y axis.

This causes Dummy02 to inherit only translations along the Y axis from its parent, Dummy01. Try moving Henry around and you will see the middle slide along with him. Rotating him (your next step), however, is a different story. Before you do this, you disable the rotational inheritance for Dummy01.

1. Select Dummy01.

2. Open the Hierarchy panel and click on Link Info.

3. Deselect the X, Y, Z options for Rotation.

Now you can move and rotate Henry safely.

4. Go to frame 90 and turn on the Animate button.

5. Move Henry up and to the left about 20 units each.

6. Go to frame 120 and move Henry up and to the right about 15 units each (see fig. 6.10).

FIGURE 6.10
Only the inflated Henry floats upward.

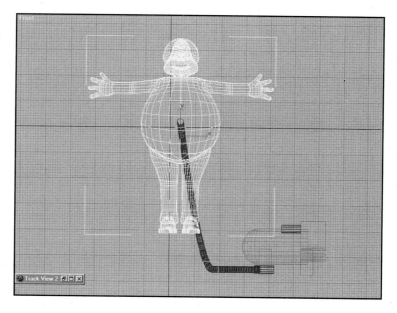

7. Maximize your Track View and find the position keys for Henry.

8. Move the key at frame 0 to frame 40.

9. Repeat step 6 for his X rotation key.

10. Minimize Track View and go to frame 70.

11. Rotate Henry 5 degrees.

12. Go to frame 100 and rotate Henry –20 degrees.

13. Go to frame 120 and rotate Henry –5 degrees.

14. Maximize your Track View and apply Ease Out controller curves to your first position and rotation keyframes and Ease In controller curves to your last.

15. Save your scene and render a Smooth + Highlights preview of the Camera01 viewport, frames 0–90.

That should do it for Henry.

Animating the Hose

You could add another touch to make things a bit more cartoony. How about some bulges pumping through the air hose? You could do this with more Displace modifiers, animating the gizmos along the path of the air hose, but a few steps in between would slow you down. Basically, a secondary object such as a dummy would have to be animated along the path and then that Position track copied to the Displace gizmo in the track view. Because the Displace space warp gives you the same effect and can be assigned a Path controller in one step, you can take the easy way out.

1. Create a Displace space warp from the Create panel about twice the width of the air hose at its base near the pump (see fig. 6.11).

2. Change the Strength to 1.0, the Decay to 0.8, and the Map to Spherical.

3. Bind the air hose to the Displace space warp.

Now to animate the bulge along the path of the hose, follow these steps:

4. Select the Displace space warp and open the Motion panel.

5. Under Parameters, open the Assign Controller rollout and select Position.

FIGURE 6.11

A Displace space warp will be used to ride along the spline of the hose and deform it along the way.

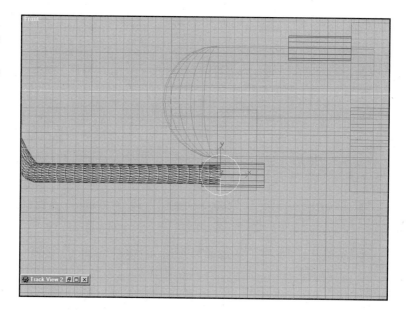

6. Click on the Assign Controller button and select Path. A new rollout entitled Path Parameters appears.

7. Click on Pick Path and choose the spline for the air hose Loft object.

8. Move the Time Slider back and forth to see the bulge's effect.

Now you set up the timing for the bulge. You will also animate the strength so that the effect builds as it comes from the pump and fades as it approaches the character.

9. Maximize your Track View.

10. Move the last Percent keyframe for the Displace space warp from 120 to 45 and click on the Percent heading in the Track Hierarchy.

11. Click on Parameter Curve Out-of-Range Type and select Constant for before the animated range (left arrow) and Loop for after the animated range (right arrow).

12. Minimize your Track View and select the Displace space warp.

13. Turn on the Animate button.

14. At frame 0, set the Displace space warp Strength to 0.

15. At frame 15 and frame 30, set the Strength to about 5.7.

16. Finally at frame 45, set the Strength back to 0.

17. Maximize your Track View.

18. Select Strength from the Displace hierarchy and open the function curve.

19. Apply Ease In and Ease Outs to your four keyframes.

20. Click on Parameter Curve Out-of-Range Type and select Constant for before the animated range (left arrow) and Loop for after the animated range (right arrow).

This creates one looping bulge pumping through the hose. To create a second trailing bulge, copy the first space warp and offset the keys.

1. Minimize your Track View and make a copy of the Displace space warp directly on top of the other.

2. Maximize your Track View and select Edit Keys and Slide Keys from the toolbar.

3. Offset the Percent and Strength keys for Displace02 forward 20 frames (see fig. 6.12).

FIGURE 6.12

Offsetting the timing for the second Displace space warp.

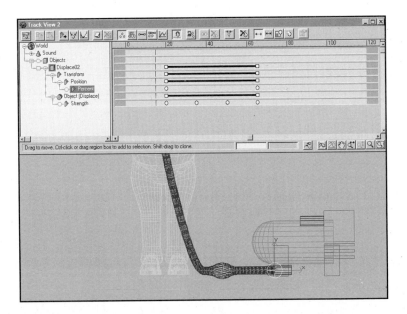

4. Minimize your Track View, save your scene, and render a Smooth + Highlights preview of the Camera01 viewport, frames 0–90.

That's about it. You can add some finishing touches such as moving the hose back as Henry's body swells. For the camera angle you're rendering, however, things work pretty well. A noise controller applied to the position or rotation path of the air pump could add that extra bit of detail. Or if you really want to get carried away, you could try detaching the hose and have Henry wiggle and deflate like a pierced balloon. Perhaps an animated Wave, Ripple, or Noise modifier alone or in conjunction would do the trick?

Magnetic Boots Project

The last test was a bit hard on Henry, so for this next scene you will be little more easy on him. This time he will be trying out a pair of magnetic boots in a wind tunnel experiment.

FIGURE 6.13

Henry ready for the next test.

Open wbootscomic.avi from the accompanying CD and view the final animation.

Starting the Reaction

In the AVI, Henry appears in his latest predicament. A blowing fan blows in his face, his eyes squint, his mouth closes, and his clothes ripple in the wind. Eventually the force becomes too strong, and he bends over backward. To make things somewhat more exaggerated, he begins to stretch off into the distance.

For a final production animation, you would ideally have some arm and head motion added for extra character, but that would involve a skin deformation program, such as Physique, which might not be available to everyone. Instead, everything you see here was done with simple transforms and modifier animation.

First you start with Henry's basic reaction to the fan. The wind is just starting to pick up in the first 30 frames, so start by squinting his eyes. Henry has what might be referred to as "cheap" eyelids. They are basically a pair of squashed torii that have a slightly larger radius than the eye itself. The closing of the lids is performed by changing the Slice From and Slice To values in the basic parameters of the object. These parameters can also be animated.

1. Load wboots.max from the CD-ROM. Switch to the Left viewport and zoom in on Henry's eyes.

2. Select either eyelid object (W Eye L or W Eye R, which are instances of each other and will animate in tandem).

3. Activate the Animate button and go to frame 30.

4. In the Modify Panel, change the Slice From value to 270 degrees and the Slice To value to –90 (see fig. 6.14).

Now that the eyelids are set to close from frame 0 to frame 30, add a quick blink in the beginning for a more natural feel.

1. Select one of the eyelids and open the Track View.

2. Set the filters to Animated Tracks Selected Objects Only.

3. Expand the eyelid tracks and open the Function Curve for Slice To.

4. While holding the shift key, drag a copy of the keyframe at frame 30 to frame 10, making sure the value remains at –90 degrees.

The Slice To and From is touchy because crossing over 360 degrees will cause the object to fold back in on itself and start the slicing from scratch.

5. Select all keys in the Function Curve for Slice To and change the Tangent Type for In and Out to Linear.

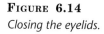

FIGURE 6.14

Closing the eyelids.

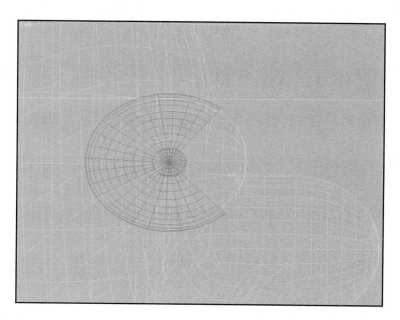

6. Copy the keyframe for frame 0 to frame 8, making certain that the value remains at −37.50.

7. Copy that same key (frame 8) to frame 11, again making certain that the value doesn't change.

8. Switch to the Function Curve for Step From.

9. Copy the keyframe for frame 30 to frame 10, making certain that the value remains at 270.

10. Select all keys in the Function Curve and change the Tangent Type for In and Out to Linear.

11. Copy the keyframe for frame 0 to frame 8, making certain that the value remains at 222.50.

12. Copy that same key (frame 8) to frame 11, again making certain that the value doesn't change.

13. Minimize the Track View and slowly scroll through the first 30 frames.

14. Save your scene as **myboot01.max**.

Simple enough. If you want to add a little flutter to the eyelids as they close, go ahead and copy around the extra keyframes in the function curves. Next you add a Free Form Deformation lattice to the mouth for some extra effect.

Free Form deformations were new to 3D Studio MAX R1.1. They enable you to affect an entire object or a sub-selection of vertices. The deformation is controlled by a set of control points that form a lattice around the object or selection. The selected geometry within the volume of the lattice is influenced by the changing positions of the control points. The effect is similar to that of deforming a spline object. This is great for regular Mesh objects because moving vertices around can often have very jagged and undesirable results. For Henry, you select the vertices of the mouth and apply a Free Form Deformation modifier to this sub-selection.

1. Select Henry Body and zoom in on the mouth in the left window.

2. In the Modify panel, set the selection level to Sub-Object Vertex.

3. Select the vertices of the teeth and the general area surrounding the mouth (see fig. 6.15)

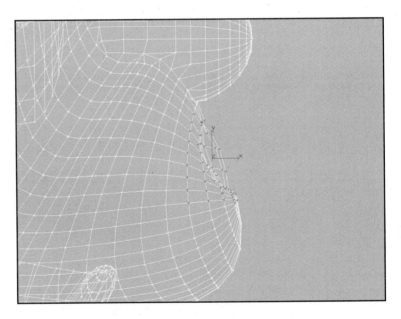

FIGURE 6.15

Selecting the vertices surrounding the mouth.

You don't have to worry about being too exact at this point because you can always change the sub-selection later.

4. Add a 4×4×4 Free Form Deformation modifier.

5. Switch to a Front viewport and zoom in on the mouth.

6. Activate Sub-Object Control Points in the Modify panel and region-select the two inside rows of control points (see fig. 6.16).

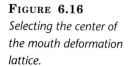

FIGURE 6.16

Selecting the center of the mouth deformation lattice.

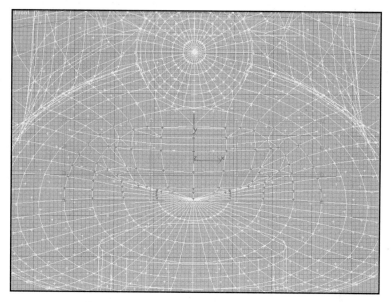

Select Non-uniform Scale and try sizing the center control points up and down, right-clicking at the end to undo the changes. Change your axis to Y and see how the effect is spread throughout the lattice—full intensity in the center and tapering off to the unselected edges. For this exercise, you scale the mouth down to give Henry a bit of a grimace as the wind picks up. True, his teeth are being squashed unnaturally, but the camera is far enough away and, after all, this is a cartoon.

Now set a single keyframe for the mouth at frame 30.

1. Turn on the Animate button and move to frame 30.

2. With the Y axis selected, non-uniform scale the two inside rows of control points about 40 percent. Too little will be unnoticeable and too much will stretch the surroundings too much.

3. Save your scene as myboot01.max and render a Smooth + Highlights preview of the Camera01 viewport, frames 0–30.

Previews are somewhat sketchy, so you might have to render at a higher resolution to make out what's going on. So far you have only animated basic nuances, but don't worry. Things will get a bit more interesting.

Windy City—Using the Noise Modifier

Now that you have Henry's facial reaction set, what about the rest of his body? Ideally his jumpsuit would ripple from the effects of the fan. A simple Noise modifier provides just that sort of chaotic feel.

The Noise modifier is often used to create basic terrain models or enhance existing topography. It is also handy for adding a subtle roughness to surfaces where a bump map just isn't enough. In this case, you apply an animated noise to Henry's suit. It is a more random effect than ripple or wave, which is just what is needed for this example.

1. Switch to the Front viewport and zoom out to view the entire body.

2. Apply an Edit Mesh modifier to the Henry Body object.

3. Select Sub-Object Vertex and region-select all vertices except for the hands, head, and boots (see fig. 6.17).

FIGURE 6.17
Isolating the noise effect.

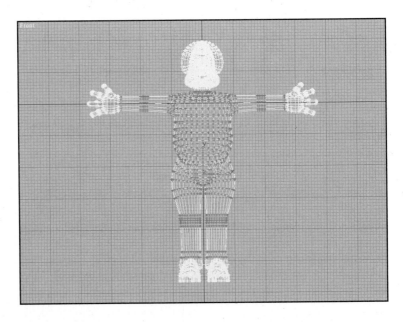

4. Apply a Noise modifier.

5. Set the Scale to 10 and Y Strength to 10.

6. Click on Animated Noise and render a Smooth + Highlights preview of the Camera01 viewport, frames 0–30.

Well, it is doing something. Rather than a wind tunnel, however, it looks as if he's more underwater than anything. This slow crawl of noise results from the low frequency setting.

7. Raise the frequency to 4 and re-render the preview.

That's better. Notice that you did not touch some options, such as the X and Z strengths and fractal noise. Displacing the geometry in Y was sufficient to achieve the desired effect. Adding X and/or Z on top of that would be overdoing things. Also fractal noise (which produces more jagged results) seems inappropriate. Feel free to play with some of these settings before moving on to see whether you agree.

Weak at the Knees—Using Edit Mesh, Bend, and Skew

So far you have been pretty easy on Henry, so it's time to turn things up a notch. What you have so far indicates a windy environment, but you need some additional modifier help to make things more extreme.

1. Save your scene as myboot01.max.

2. Apply an Edit Mesh modifier to the Henry Body object and deselect Sub-Object.

3. Select Henry Body and both eyelid objects.

TIP

At this point, you might want to make a named selection set of Henry and his eyelid objects. Selection sets are a great tool for keeping track of groups of objects. It is easy to forget which objects go together without resorting to groups (which can cause problems later on) or attaching elements (which limits the amount of in-depth animation you can do). Selection sets are a nice alternative to these other, more "permanent" methods.

4. Apply a Bend modifier.

5. Switch to the Left viewport and zoom out to view the entire body.

6. Select Sub-Object Center for the Bend modifier and move the center down in Y to the base of the feet (about 380 units).

7. Change the Direction to 90 and the Bend axis to Z.

8. Slide the Angle spinner up and down to view the effect.

Henry rocks back and forth while his boots stay locked in place. Now it is time to set some keyframes. You will make Henry resist the wind for the first second or so, and then he will bend back uncomfortably and flap in the breeze. You do this by setting a single key that times out when he bends, and then alter the time curve to add a wobbling effect.

1. Go to frame 75 and turn on the Animate button.

2. Drag the Bend Angle spinner down to about –150 degrees (see fig. 6.18).

FIGURE 6.18

Henry bending over backward.

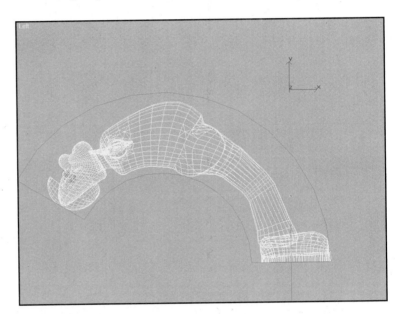

3. Open the Track View and expand the tracks for Henry body.

Notice that there is a ton of tracks for the Free Form deformation 4×4×4 (one for each control point), so you might want to collapse those tracks to avoid cluttering your window.

4. Open the Function Curve for the Bend Angle and select the key at frame 0.

5. Move the keyframe from frame 0 to frame 30, keeping the angle value at 0.

6. Select both keys and change the tangent type to Slow on the In and Out.

Henry will hold steady for the first second, and then ease into his bend. Now you create some wobble frames.

7. Select the key at frame 30 and while holding the Shift button, drag it back to make a copy around frame 25, lowering the angle value to about –15.

8. Repeat this step a few more times, creating a sine wave of sorts that decreases in intensity as it approaches frame 0. Make a key about every three or four frames until you reach 0 (see fig. 6.19).

FIGURE 6.19

Wobbling in the bend.

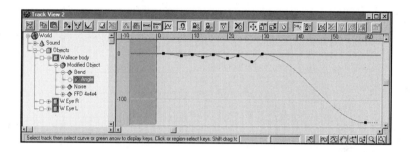

9. Save your scene as myboot01.max and render a Smooth + Highlights preview of the Camera01 viewport, frames 0–75.

The wobble might be a little too extreme. Try softening the effect by zooming in on the Function Curve for the first 30 frames and make the highs of your wave around 0 degrees and the lows starting around –2 degrees and increasing to about –5 before finally bending over all the way (see fig. 6.20).

FIGURE 6.20

Softening the wobble.

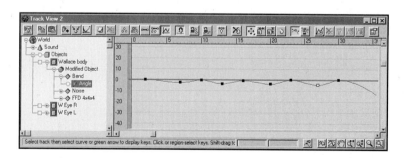

Another problem could be that the final bend seems too smooth in comparison to the wobbly beginning. Try adding a slight stair-step effect to the curve from 30 to 75. Be careful not to level off between keys; this would cause an unwanted delay in the bend (see fig. 6.21).

FIGURE 6.21

Roughening the back bend.

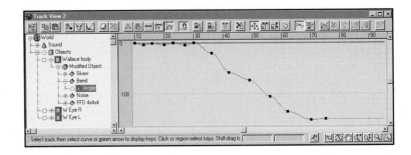

10. Save your scene as myboot01.max and render a Smooth + Highlights preview of the Camera01 viewport, frames 0–75.

Not bad, but is the bend modifier enough, or should another modifier be layered on top? How about a Skew?

Adding a Skew modifier is just like adding a bend. Just change your center and animate the strength. You could also give it the same treatment you gave the bend by wobbling the direction a bit.

1. Minimize any other windows and switch to the Left viewport.

2. Zoom out and select Henry Body and both eyelid objects.

3. Go to frame 0 and apply a Skew modifier.

4. Select Sub-Object Center for the Skew modifier and move the center down in Y to the base of the feet (about 380 units).

5. Change the Skew axis to Z and the Direction to 90.

6. Go to frame 100 and activate the Animate button.

7. While pressing the Ctrl key, drag the Amount spinner up and down to view the effect, stopping around –300.

TIP

The spinner for Skew Amount is slower than most, providing accuracy up to three decimal places. Holding down the Ctrl key increases the rate at which the value changes.

8. Open the Track View and find the keyframes for Skew Amount.

9. Move the key at frame 0 to frame 30.

10. Save your scene as myboot01.max and render a Smooth + Highlights preview of the Camera01 viewport, frames 0–100.

Henry wobbles, bends, and then stretches backward.

1. Go to frame 100 and activate the Animate button.

2. Slide the Skew Direction spinner up and down to view the effect, stopping around 95.

3. In the Track View, open the Function Curve for the Skew Direction and select the key at frame 0.

4. Move the keyframe from frame 0 to frame 60, keeping the angle value at 90 degrees.

5. Select both keys and change the tangent type to Slow on the In and Out.

6. Add a few more frames between frame 60 and 100 by shift-dragging the existing frames to create copies, and make a sine wave similar to the bend wobble. This time, increase the effect by having the strength start off mild and increase in value and frequency as you approach frame 100, dipping to 80 at the valleys and 100 at the peaks (see fig. 6.22).

FIGURE 6.22

Increasing the effect of the back bend.

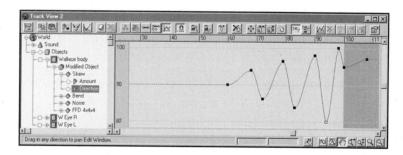

7. Save your scene as myboot01.max and render a Smooth + Highlights preview of the Camera01 viewport, frames 0–100.

One object that has been hidden all this time is the source of Henry's trouble, the fan. Next you add a simple oscillation to the body of the fan for a finishing touch.

1. Unhide the object called Fan Body.

2. Select Fan Body and open the Track View.

3. Expand the tracks for Fan Body and find Radius 1 and Radius 2 under Modified Object/Object.

4. Select Radius 1 and assign a Float List controller.

A List controller enables you to layer multiple controllers that combine their own effects into one. The controllers are calculated in the order you specify in the Properties dialog box.

In this case, you want to oscillate the fan body by changing its radius. A Noise controller would do this, but applied alone would cause the radius to jump from one extreme to the next (try it to see what happens). By applying a Noise float below the existing Linear Float, the Linear takes precedence and the Noise is merely an enhancement.

5. Expand the Float List for Radius 1 and select Available.

6. Click on Assign Control and assign a Noise Float.

7. Click on the Properties button and change the noise frequency to 4 and the strength to 10.

8. Minimize the Track View window and move the Time Slider slowly from frame 0 to frame 100.

The outer radius of the fan body shrinks and expands randomly. Now do the same to Radius 2 by repeating steps 4 through 7. Copying the controller from Radius 1 to Radius 2 is not an option because the initial values for each need to be different (Radius 2 being smaller than Radius 1).

After you have added the Noise Float and adjusted its parameters for Radius 2, unhide the Fan Blade object and render your final preview animation, saving your scene beforehand.

Alright, maybe it is time to leave Henry alone. There *are* other modifiers, not touched on here, that would work well with him. What about a torture rack animation using Stretch and Twist? Maybe combine some of these with the modifying power of Free Form Deformations for some distorting results? Feel free to play around with different combinations and effects, not just on a character model such as Henry, but on any object.

As you work with 3DS MAX, you will discover ways of enhancing your projects by adding an Animated modifier to an element in your scene or setting keyframes for a standard primitive's creation parameters.

One effect I needed to create along the way was an energy sphere encircled by arcs of lightning. I created the sphere itself with an animated material, but I was uncertain as to the approach to take for the lightning effect. Lightning plug-ins were available, but didn't have the look I was after. The solution turned out to be right here in MAX.

Open lsphere.avi from the accompanying CD-ROM and view the final animation.

The arcs that shoot out and surround the sphere are torus primitives with animated Slice values and a Noise modifier on top. Try a quick example.

1. Save any scene you have open and reset MAX.

2. Create a sphere in the center with a radius around 70 units.

3. Create a thin torus encircling the sphere with a radius around 100 (see fig. 6.23).

FIGURE 6.23

Creating a thin torus.

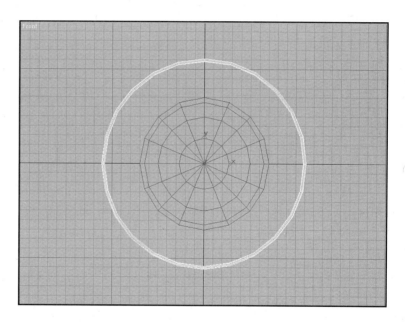

4. Activate the Animate button and move to frame 100.

5. Rotate the torus about 120 degrees in Y and then 120 degrees in X.

6. Slide the playback bar around to get a feel for what you have.

7. Go to frame 0 and click on Slice On under the torus parameters in the Modify panel.

8. At frame 0, set the Slice To value to –0.5.

9. Go to frame 25 and change the Slice To value to –360.

10. Go to frame 50 and change the Slice To value to –600 and the Slice From value to –360.

11. Go to frame 75 and change the Slice To value to –720 and the Slice From value to –600.

12. Finally, go to frame 100 and change the Slice From value to –719.5.

13. Play the animation in wireframe or render a preview.

Now you have a torus chasing its tail around a sphere. Next you apply some noise.

1. Turn off the Animate button and go to around frame 50.

2. Apply a Noise modifier to the torus.

3. Set the Noise Scale to 20, the X, Y, and Z strengths to 20, activate Animate Noise, and change the Frequency to 5.

4. Play the animation in wireframe or render a preview.

That's the basis for the lightning arcs. Try turning off Animated Noise and double the Frequency for a smoother effect. You could also enhance things by adding a Noise Float controller underneath a Linear Float for the Radius 2 of the torus. With a low frequency and strength setting, the torus will randomly change its thickness as it travels around the sphere.

Another quick solution I needed for a project was to animate a cloth banner on a wall being affected by an object flying by.

The banner is a patch grid with an animated Ripple modifier moving through it at the right moment. The extra fold of the corner of the cloth was achieved by applying a Linked Transform to the corner vertex of the patch. A dummy object then takes that vertex and folds over the end. Patch grids are an excellent subject for Linked Transforms because they work with a minimum of control vertices, deforming the object smoothly between them.

In Practice: Modifier Animation

- **Geometry modifiers.** Geometry modifiers are useful tools for broad animation of the dimensions of an object or for subtle changes over time.

- **Linked XForm.** Objects can be controlled on the sub-object level by linking selected pieces to any other object.

- **Function curves.** Adding and adjusting keys directly on the function curve of a controller is a quick and powerful way of animating transforms and parameters.

- **List controllers.** Controller types can be layered much in the same way that modifiers are layered to mix multiple effects.

- **Object parameters.** Keeping a primitive object open to Object Parameter animation (by not collapsing it into a mesh) enables adjustment of the basic parameters of an object and animation later on.

IMAGE CREATED BY PAUL KAKERT

Chapter 7

by Paul Kakert

ANIMATING ACCURACY FOR FORENSICS

The use of multimedia in the courtroom is becoming common-place. So much so that the courtroom of the future will be wired for multimedia. High-tech trials are where the legal industry is heading. Besides the widely recognized vehicular accident recon-struction, animations play a key role in dramatizing crime scenes, personal injury, product liability, fire damage, faulty construc-tion, workers' compensation, and many other situations. Even though admissibility in court should be the basis for all your work, animation also takes part in pretrial settlement discussions. After all, settling out of court is what most attorneys would like to do. Animation can be a "big stick" in negotiations, showing the attorney is prepared to go to great lengths to persuade the jury.

Regardless of the kind of animation you are working on, accuracy is key. MAX aides in your accuracy by offering great support for DXF files, and helpful third-party plug-ins. Because most of the experts working with animators on cases are engineers or reconstructionists with engineering skills, you can often use their DXF files as the basis of your layout. Aside from that, you will discover in this chapter's tutorials that MAX does not do things automatically for you. You will have to figure out speeds of vehicles and pedestrians and keyframe them manually over time. When a car skids to a stop, you must use a third-party program to create the skid marks. If you want to have scratches, gouges, and dents appear on objects throughout the course of the animation, it is easiest to work with yet another plug-in for those effects. These are not downfalls of MAX. They are good points, illustrating the advantage of using a program open for developers to create specialized plug-in tools. This chapter shows how to achieve an accurate level of detail within MAX with the help of some important plug-ins along the way.

This chapter covers the following topics:

- Forensic animation industry overview

- Timing

- Advanced character studio motion

- Details

Forensic Animation Industry Overview

A few key factors affect an animation's admissibility. The following list identifies some of the areas you should be concerned with as you start production:

- **The animation must be based on facts.** A forensic animator takes the role of a visualization expert in a case. The party hiring you, whether an attorney or otherwise, is not like a commercial business client. They cannot direct you to re-create a vehicular accident, for example, in a manner that defies physics or is inaccurate in any way just to suit the needs of their client. To be admitted in court, your animation must be based on facts supplied by experts involved in the case or some other known circumstances, such as eyewitness testimony.

- **The animation must be unbiased.** In criminal trials, for example, the use of low-detail, faceless human figures makes the subjects of your animation unidentifiable. The purpose of the trial is not to prove whether the defendant was or was not the subject portrayed in the animation. The animation should just show the actions of the subject.

- **Only include details relevant to the case.** There is a fine line between making it look realistic and including things just for aesthetic reasons. Bottom line is, if there were not five other cars on the road when it happened, don't put them in.

Regardless of the amount of time you spend working on the details of these admissibility factors, admissibility is out of your control. The judge is the ultimate gatekeeper of the courtroom. If a judge is unfamiliar with what the animator is doing, that may be enough to keep the animation out of the courtroom.

Accuracy—Make It Obvious in Your Animation

Where did you get your information, and how did it become an animation? These key questions come up in almost every trial. A good place to start any animation, therefore, is with diagrams, blueprints, layouts, and photos supplied by experts. Every case you work on will involve an expert in the field of accident reconstruction, engineering, medicine, or some other relevant field. In accident reconstructions, for example, many reconstructionists can supply you with DXF files direct from their reconstruction program, making it easy to establish the accuracy of your work.

It is a good idea to start your animated presentation by setting up a reference to any technical diagrams or material you were supplied. Figure 7.1 shows the diagram of a vehicular accident scene as supplied by the accident reconstructionist in a DXF file. This type of technical drawing provides a great foundation for your work. Transition from this image to the same reference view in your animation. Figure 7.2 shows the first frame in an animation that used the preceding DXF layout. It shows the degree of accuracy in translating data from the expert's reports or diagrams to your animation and the realism of the animation you created.

FIGURE 7.1
*Include a DXF
wireframe reference
viewed from above the
scene and identify it as
a technical drawing
supplied by the expert
reconstructionist.*

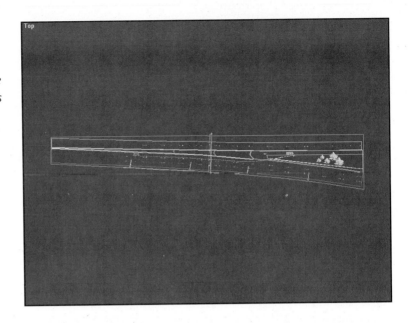

FIGURE 7.2
*Transition between
the DXF wireframe
and a rendered MAX
reference view from the
same vantage point of
the scene.*

If you have the advantage of using an aerial photograph, use it in conjunction with your reference rendering to show how accurately the scene is depicted (see fig. 7.3).

FIGURE 7.3
*An aerial photo
reference view makes
for a great comparison
to the actual layout of
the scene.*

It is a good idea to document the basis for the different aspects in the animation. If one expert gave you the dimensions of a vehicle and another gave you dimensions of pedestrians, make a note of each source. In commercial animation, and even in other technical applications for animation, you are rarely pressed to provide verification of your every keystroke. The courts may not look for a video documentary of how you created the animation, but it is a good idea to document your sources. You will likely be asked where you received the details and how you can prove they are shown accurately in the final product. Overlaying animations over still photographs and wireframe DXF files, as outlined previously, is a great way to show accuracy.

Animation Proves Nothing

Your animation proves nothing more than the fact that you are a competent animator and can accurately portray the facts provided to you. Even high-tech simulations using animation fall into this category. The picture proves nothing; it is always the numbers behind the scenes that are the proof in a case. The pictures just tell the story. Keep this in mind as you accept work from attorneys. Make certain that they are clear on the fact that unless expert findings back up your work, the animation will just be an illustration with no foundation. Attorneys who misunderstand your role may ask you to animate different scenarios of an accident without thinking about involving an expert in crash scene analysis. For an animator to run scenarios after changing starting position of vehicles or pedestrians, for example, would be pure speculation and would not be admissible.

A special case exists when animating eyewitness testimony—which itself, proves nothing. You can validate your work with a reference to the eyewitness testimony. What a witness claims to have seen, however, does not prove or disprove whether it was actually the case or whether it was even possible.

The rest of this chapter focuses on the main differences between a commercial animation and one created for use in the courtroom. The following issues are covered:

- Timing

- Advanced character studio motion

- Details—humans, vehicles, and skid marks

Accurate Timing

Where in MAX do you input that the car was traveling 55 miles per hour or that the pedestrian was walking 3 feet per second? Well, you don't. Not exactly. MAX does have some built-in features, such as constant velocity, that will aide in accurately portraying speeds in your animation. In the following tutorial, you will work with a basic two-car collision scene. You will figure out where to start each vehicle in order to re-create the scene as it happened. You will also create an alternate scenario with the vehicles moving at different speeds.

NOTE

All information in this case was supplied by the accident reconstructionist who worked on the case with the animator.

In this timing tutorial, a passenger vehicle failed to stop at a pedestrian crosswalk due to an obstructed view caused by another vehicle. The speed of the striking vehicle was determined by the reconstructionist. The placement of the obstructing vehicle was determined by eyewitness testimony. The objective in this case was to visualize the obstructed view of the driver and the limited reaction time it created, resulting in the accident.

To create this animation, you need the following details:

- The prebraking speed of the car was 26 mph.

- The car's speed at impact was 24 mph.

- Based on the age of the pedestrian, you will use a walking speed of 3 feet per second (slightly slower than a standard walk of 4 feet per second).

- The position of the view-obstructing vehicle based on witness statements.

- The skid marks for the car start 15 feet north of the crosswalk.

- The point of impact was 3.5 feet south of the north edge of the crosswalk and 17 feet east of the west curb.

NOTE

Walking speed is a variable you will never be able to re-create precisely. The average of 4 feet per second is what is used by civil engineers who design devices such as walk signals at stop lights. The standard has been set by the National Advisory Committee on Uniform Traffic Control Devices and the American Association of State Highway and Transportation Officials (AASHTO). Manuals and books by either group discuss the standards for walking speeds in more detail.

TIMING

1. Load the file fmtiming.max from the accompanying CD-ROM. Save it to your hard drive as **mytiming.max**.

2. Click on Unit Setup from the View menu and set units to Decimal Feet.

3. Maximize the Top viewport to fill the screen and Region Zoom until you see only the crosswalk area. You will do all your measurements with the tape measure from this view.

4. Start with the point of impact and work backward to determine where to set starting points for movement. You know exactly where the car strikes the pedestrian. Select Create-Tape and specify a length of 3.5 feet (see fig. 7.4).

FIGURE 7.4
By using the Tape Measure, you can input your exact measurements.

5. Click on the north edge of the crosswalk and drag the tape south. When you release the mouse, you will have your north-south reference to the point of impact. Name this tape **north-south impact**.

6. Click on the Tape button again and specify a new tape length of 17 feet.

WARNING

Before specifying your second tape length, you must deselect the current tape by either right-clicking or clicking on the Tape button. If you don't, you will be adjusting your current tape rather than creating a new one.

7. Click on the west curb in the middle of the crosswalk and drag toward the east curb. Name this tape **west-east impact**.

8. Before deselecting the west-east tape you just created, select the Move tool, constrain movement to the Y axis, and move the tape until it touches the end of your north-south tape. Figure 7.5 shows the point of impact you just defined.

FIGURE 7.5

The point where the west-east and north-south tape measures meet represents the point of impact.

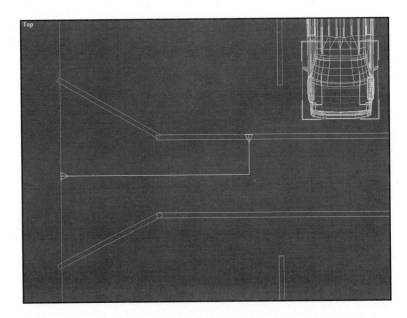

TIP

To select and adjust the position of a tape, make certain that you select both the Tape Measure object (yellow triangle) and its target (blue box). If you select one without the other, you will be adjusting the angle of the tape measure only.

In this case, there is a view-obstructing second vehicle that is stationary and that makes a great reference. It has been placed in the scene for you. There also is an arbitrary starting position for the car. It left the town public square 392 feet north of the north crosswalk line.

9. Click on Create-Tape and specify a length of 392 feet. Click on the center of the north crosswalk line and drag north. Name this tape **392 feet car path**.

10. The car is currently in the wrong position. Click on Named Selection Sets and select Caddy and Dummy.

11. Position the front of the car at the end of the 392 feet car path tape measure in the outside (west) lane, facing the crosswalk.

You need to figure out how long it takes for the car to travel to the point of impact. This will involve two speed translation because the car travels one speed prebraking and another speed after braking is applied. MAX does not support miles per hour (mph), so you must do the translation to feet per second (fps). There are 5,280 feet in one mile. Work with the prebrake speed first, which is 26 mph, and multiply it by 5,280. Divide that number by 60. Take that result and divide it by 60. The resulting number is your fps. The equation looks like this:

26 mph×5,280 = 137,280÷60 = 2288÷60 = 38.13 fps.

Round this to 38 fps. This is the speed of the car from the starting position to the point of braking. You'll have to apply the same equation to the speed after the brakes are applied, which is 24 mph. That result is 35 fps and will be used later.

12. The point of braking (measured from the center of the north crosswalk line to the rear tires) is 15 feet north of the crosswalk.

13. Click on Create-Tape and specify a length of 15 feet. Click on the center of the north crosswalk line and drag north. Name this tape **15 foot skid**. Now you are ready to keyframe the position of your car at the point of braking.

The front of the car is now 392 feet from the center of the north crosswalk line. The brakes are applied 15 feet north from the same reference point. The distance from the front of the car to the rear tires is 14 feet, which means that the front of the car is one foot north of the north crosswalk line when the brakes are applied. Divide the 391 feet the car travels by the prebraking speed of 38 fps, and you get 10.3 seconds. You will use 309 frames (10.3×30 fps).

TIP

The Road Safety and Motor Vehicle Regulation Directorate of Canada has a database of manufacturer's vehicle specs available on disk. The program contains most makes and models. Make requests for copies to

Dr. Alan German
Collision Investigation, Transport Canada
P.O. Box 8880
Ottawa Postal Terminal
Ottawa, Ontario, K1G 3J2
Tel: 613-993-9851
E-Mail: GermanA@tc.gc.ca

14. Click on Zoom Extents to see the entire scene.

15. Click on Select By Name and select dummy caddy front; the dummy aligned with the front of the car. Click on Lock Selection Set.

16. Click on Animate and go to frame 309. Using the Move tool, constrained to the Y axis, drag the dummy toward the crosswalk until the back tires line up with the 15 foot skid tape measure (see fig. 7.6).

The point of impact is now just 4.5 feet away. In that distance, the car slows to 24 mph or 35 fps. That translates to .13 seconds to travel 4.5 feet. That is only 4 frames in this animation.

17. Go to frame 313 and move the front of the car to the impact point. Turn off Animate.

FIGURE 7.6
The car's rear wheels are now aligned with the point where the skid marks started.

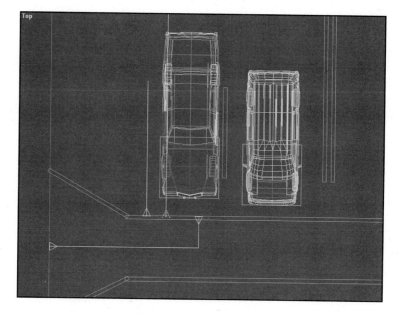

Now you set the starting position of the pedestrian. You want the walking time equal to the car's traveling time, which is 10.4 seconds (313 frames divided by 30 frames per second). At 3 fps, determined by the reconstructionist, the pedestrian will travel 31.2 feet.

18. Unhide the pedestrian. Click on Display-UnhideAll. This unhides Bip01 and all its child objects. Bip01 is a Character Studio Biped already placed 31.2 feet from the point of impact.

19. With the biped selected, click on the Footstep Track in the Motion Control panel.

20. Using the Default Walking Gait, click on the Create Multiple Footsteps button (see fig. 7.7).

21. The only settings you need to adjust are the Stride Length and the Number of Steps. Set the Actual Stride Length to 1.5 feet. This length is an arbitrary setting you can play with to get the effect you want. Leaving the time to the next footstep at 15 frames, the pedestrian will travel 3 feet per second and will take 2 steps per second. This below-average setting is appropriate because the pedestrian is older.

FIGURE 7.7

Character Studio has only one dialog box where you make all of your adjustments for the footsteps of the pedestrian.

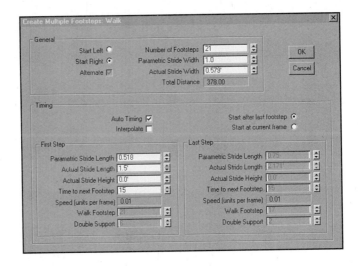

22. Set the Number of Footsteps at 21 (10.4 seconds×2 steps per second).

23. Click on OK. Your footsteps are generated, leading the pedestrian to the point of impact.

24. Click on Create Keys for Inactive Footsteps and preview your pedestrian's motion (see fig. 7.8).

FIGURE 7.8

This represents the point of impact in the final animation, complete with Character Studio footprints.

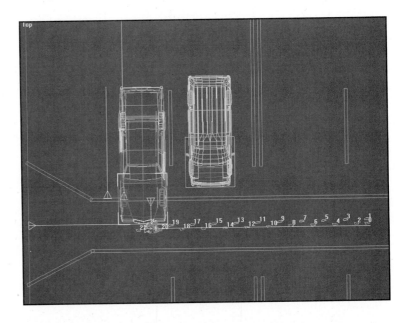

25. Save your file. Load fmtiming.avi from the accompanying CD-ROM to see the final rendered animation. You can load the final animation file in MAX by loading the fmtiming finished.max file from the CD.

Now that you have learned how to set up accurate timing in MAX, the next step is to accurately portray bipedal motion that is suddenly disrupted. One of the most effective and easiest ways to accomplish this is through the Character Studio plug-in.

Advanced Character Studio Motion

The Character Studio plug-in is a great time saver for any animator, not just those interested in forensics. Forensic animations, however, may offer the greatest deviation from normal bipedal motion that you will ever encounter. After all, how many other situations have a walking, running, or jumping person suddenly hit and rolled over by a car? It is a gruesome thought, but animating such incidents is a common necessity in many forensic cases involving personal injury.

Where do you draw the line between using a product such as Bones Pro with inverse kinematics and using Character Studio (CS)? You will have to decide for yourself, but consider this: CS motion is very easy to set up, and it enables quick edits to your motion. One possible drawback is that you cannot place any keys after the last footstep. If you use CS to animate a biped running across the street and being hit by a car, therefore, your last footstep cannot be at the point of impact. If you want the biped to move after impact, you will need additional footsteps. You will also need to utilize free-form editing between footsteps. Free-form editing enables you to turn off the biped's vertical dynamics. In other words, the force of gravity will not affect your biped's motion.

Before looking at how to create unique CS motion, take a quick look at how CS normally constructs a scene's vertical dynamics.

1. Load the file flip.max from the Character Studio folder. This file was installed with Character Studio in the c:\3dsmax\cstudio\scenes folder. Save it to your hard drive as **myflip.max**.

The character in this scene does two backflips. The flip would have to be added by the user, but the height of each jump is determined by CS and is user definable. Play the animation, or drag the Timeline Slider to see the height of each jump and the motion of the character prior to and immediately after each jump. The character crouches and squats for a realistic appearance according to the height of the jump. Both attributes are set by the Gravitational Acceleration spinner in the biped's motion panel (see fig. 7.9).

FIGURE 7.9

Character Studio uses the Gravitational Acceleration setting to automatically determine the height of vertical motion.

2. Maximize the Front viewport. Click on Select By Name and choose the Bip01 object.

3. Enter the Motion panel. In the General section, set the GravAccel spinner to 369.032.

4. Drag the Timeline Slider to see the height of the jump and the pre- and post-landing motion of the character.

5. Adjust the GravAccel spinner to .01.

6. Drag the Timeline Slider again and notice the difference in the vertical motion. Basically, there is no vertical motion. In the real world equivalent of this example, this type of motion would be impossible.

The limitation of the GravAccel setting is that it is a universal setting for the biped for the entire animation and cannot be animated, which is why freeform editing is the best method to change from motion affected primarily by gravity and motion that is unnatural and caused by a force such as an impacting vehicle. Free-form editing enables editing of the vertical dynamics of each airborne interval, independent of the other motion of the character. In simpler terms, it enables you to temporarily turn off the GravAccel setting you adjusted in the preceding tutorial.

You will use the same file as used in the Timing tutorial. In that tutorial, you dealt only with motion up to the point of impact. You will now look at how to keyframe the positions of the pedestrian post-impact. The objective is strictly to work with Character Studio free-form editing.

1. Load the file fmcstudio.max from the accompanying CD and save it to your hard drive as **mycstudio.max**.

2. Start by identifying the ending position for the biped in the animation. The animation already has motion for the vehicle ending at frame 359, so use that frame for your last footstep placement.

3. Go to frame 359 and maximize the Top viewport. Region zoom the area showing the point of impact and the final rest position of the vehicle (see fig. 7.10).

FIGURE 7.10

Use the final rest of the vehicle to set the final footsteps for your biped's final rest position.

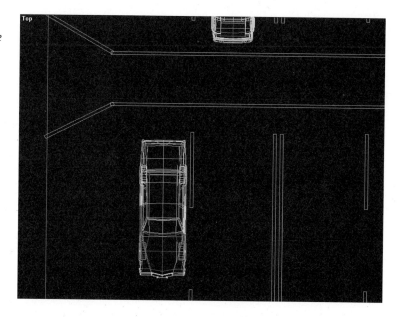

NOTE

From this point forward, you will be adjusting the rotation and position of the biped post-impact. The degrees and amounts of movement are not meant to be precise. You may have to adjust slightly to get the correct positioning in your scene. This tutorial will run through the basics of animating the biped through to its final rest. For a more realistic motion, you could add more upper body rotation, arm movements, and so on.

4. Click on Select By Name and choose the Bip01 object.

5. Click on the Motion panel. Under Track Selection, click on Footstep Track.

6. Because you already have footsteps generated for the biped, add new footsteps starting at the end of the existing ones. Under Footstep Creation, click on the Create Footsteps (append) button (see fig. 7.11).

FIGURE 7.11

Character Studio enables you to append new footsteps to the end of existing ones.

7. This will enable you to manually place alternating left and right footsteps. Notice that your cursor is now an arrow and a footprint. Click on an area in the viewport at a location just to the right of the front tire of the car.

8. Click a second time on an area next to that footstep to generate the second footstep (see fig. 7.12).

FIGURE 7.12

This shows the position of the final rest footsteps of the character.

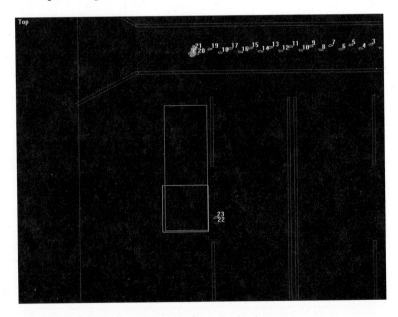

9. In the Footstep Operations section, click on Create Keys for Inactive Footsteps.

10. Drag the Timeline Slider to see the effect on the character's motion. The character takes a huge sideways leap to the final rest footsteps. Not what we need it to look like, but that's the way to get the character to the final rest position.

Now you will do the free-form editing for the airborne period between the impact and final rest to make the character react appropriately. You want to adjust a time period that starts at impact and ends at the final rest. Because the free-form edit is of airborne time only, you have to make certain that the character leaves its feet at impact, around frame 314. You make this adjustment in Track View.

1. Click on the Track View button. Position the Track View window in the lower half of the screen so that you can see the top and front view above it.

2. Click on the Filters button in the Track View menu bar (see fig. 7.13).

FIGURE 7.13

Avoid cluttering your screen by viewing only the animated tracks.

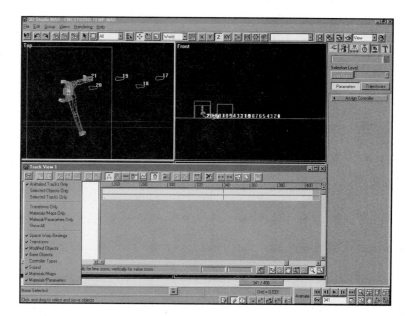

3. Select Animated Tracks Only.

4. Right-click on Objects and click Expand Objects from the pop-up menu. Then click on the plus sign next to Bip01 Footsteps to reveal the footstep tracks (see fig. 7.14).

5. Use the Zoom Region tool within Track View so that you can see footsteps 20 through 23 only. You want to zoom in far enough to see the starting and ending frame for each footstep, especially footstep 21. Depending on the resolution of your monitor, you may at different times throughout this tutorial have to zoom in to see the detail described.

Figure 7.14

These are the biped's footsteps as seen in the Track View.

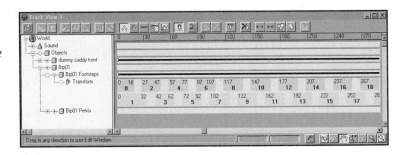

6. Adjust footstep 21 by clicking on the middle of the footstep and dragging it toward footstep 20.

7. Watch the numbers on the left side of the footstep; they indicate the starting frame of that footstep. Stop dragging when it reads 307.

8. Right-click on the footstep to open the Footstep Track window for the biped.

9. Under Footstep Edge Selection, click on the right button. This enables you to scale the footstep.

10. Click and drag the right edge of the footstep until the far right number in the footstep reads 313. Now the last footstep ends at the point of impact (see fig. 7.15).

Figure 7.15

The last pre-impact footstep now aligns with the impact.

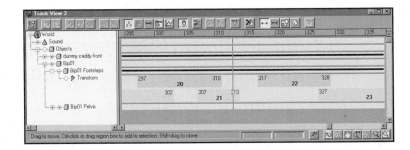

11. Pan to the right until you can see footsteps 22 and 23, the final rest footsteps. You will keep these footsteps together, and want them to occur at the same frame. Click on footstep 22 and drag toward footstep 23. Make certain that each footstep starts on frame 359.

12. Click on the right edge of footstep 22 and drag the duration to be equal to footstep 23 (see fig. 7.16).

13. Zoom out to see footsteps 20 through 23 again.

FIGURE 7.16

By clicking and dragging on the end of the footstep, you make adjustments to the last two footsteps.

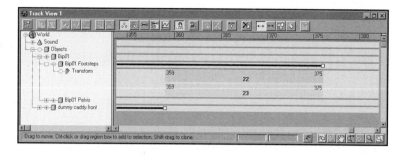

14. The area between footsteps 21 and 22 is the airborne time post-impact. To designate it as a free-form area, right-click on any footstep.

15. In the Footstep Track window that opens, click on Edit Free-form (no physics).

16. The areas between the footsteps are now outlined in yellow. Click on the yellow outlined area between footsteps 21 and 22. The area turns solid yellow, indicating it is a free-form area (see fig. 7.17).

FIGURE 7.17

Free-form editing areas are indicated by the solid yellow boxes.

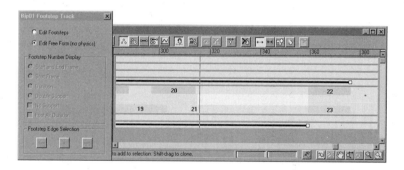

17. Close the Track View window and maximize the Left viewport.

18. Now start adjusting the position of the biped from impact to final rest. Start by going to the final rest position at frame 359.

19. Click on Select By Name and choose Bip01.

20. Adjust the final rest position so that the character is lying flat on its back.

21. Click on the Footstep Track button in the Track Selection section.

22. Because you placed the final two footsteps from the Top viewport, they are not aligned correctly. Click on Select and Rotate and select footsteps 22 and 23.

23. Select the Local Coordinate System and rotate the two footsteps about their Z axis –90 degrees and then rotate the two footsteps about their Y axis –90 degrees. Both feet should be pointing up.

24. Click on Select and Move.

25. Constrain movement to the Z axis and move the footsteps above ground level (see fig. 7.18).

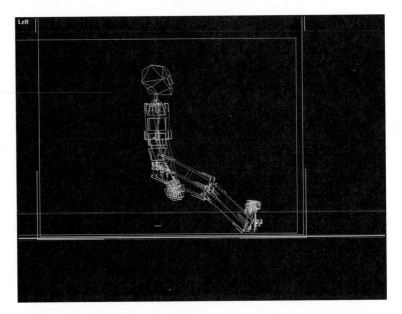

FIGURE 7.18

Place the final footsteps above ground level.

26. Click on Footstep Track in the Track Selection section to leave Footstep mode.

27. With the Bip01 still selected, click on the Select and Rotate tool.

28. Click on Lock Selection set.

29. Constrain movement to the Y axis and rotate –80 degrees.

30. Under Track Operations, click on the Set Key button. This creates a key for the current position.

WARNING

Remember to click on the Set Key button after every move, or your actions will be lost as soon as you move to another frame. This is the same effect as not turning on the Animate button when keyframing motion in MAX.

31. Click on the Select and Move tool.

32. Move down until the biped is on the ground. Click on the Set Key button. This is the final rest position (see fig. 7.19).

FIGURE 7.19
This is the final rest position for the biped character.

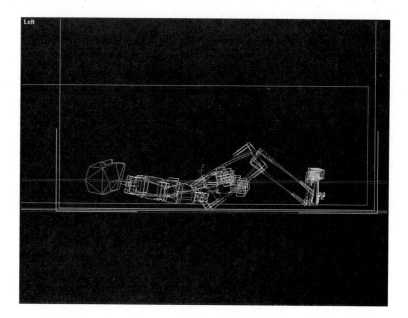

33. Go to frame 316, the frame immediately after impact. With the Bip01 still selected, click on Select and Rotate and constrain movement to the X axis.

34. Rotate –75 degrees and click on Set Key.

35. Click on Select and Move and move the biped up along the Z axis to clear the top of the car. Click on Set Key (see fig. 7.20).

36. Go to frame 340, just about halfway to the final rest.

37. Move the biped up along the Z axis again until it clears the top of the car. Click on Set Key.

38. Rotate about the Y axis –80 degrees and click on Set Key (see fig. 7.21).

39. Go to frame 349 and switch to the Top viewport.

40. Move the biped along its X axis until it clears the car. Click on Set Key (see fig. 7.22).

FIGURE 7.20
Adjustments are made at the point of impact.

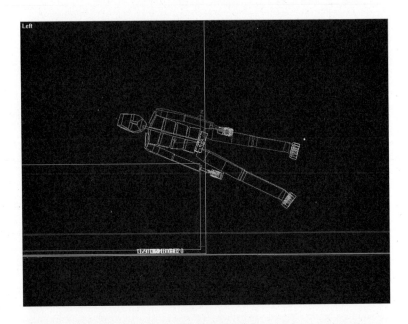

FIGURE 7.21
Rotate the position of the biped along its airborne path as it bounces atop the car hood.

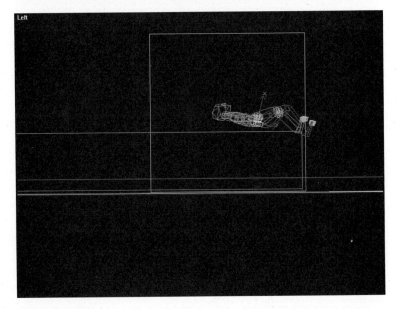

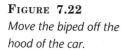

FIGURE 7.22
Move the biped off the hood of the car.

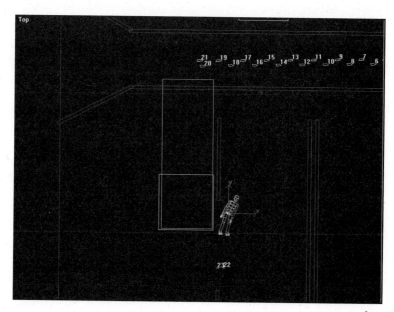

41. Switch back to the Left viewport and rotate the biped along its Y axis −60 degrees, until it is again parallel to the ground. Click on Set Key.

42. Move the biped up along the Z axis to a point about halfway up the car height. Click on Set Key.

43. The biped should now fall into position at frame 359, the end of the animation.

N OTE

Remember that at frame 360, footsteps 22 and 23 begin, ending the free-form editing. Character Studio will again gain control of the vertical dynamics of the character, which is why, in this example, you would end the animation at 359 and only render to that frame.

44. Save your file. Load fmcstudio.avi from the accompanying CD-ROM to see the final rendered animation. You can load the final animation file in MAX by loading the fmcstudio finished.max file from the CD.

The first two tutorials have shown you how to make accurate animations, including speed for objects and movements and interactions between different objects, including people. What's left are the details of those objects that will be accurately moving about in your animation. In forensic animation, the texture maps you use can not only make your animation look more convincing, but they can also play a significant role in the admissibility of your work.

Details

As any attorney will tell you, when they go up against an animation, they look for any inaccuracy to discredit the work of the animator. Ignoring details or including innacurate details opens the door for the "perception" of inaccuracy in the minds of the jury and the judge. When you are making the decision of which details to include, think in terms of relevance to the events that occurred or the subjects involved. Using this as a rule of thumb will enable you to answer questions about why certain things appear in the animation and why others are left out.

Leaving the details off human figures is a good idea. If you make a subject appear as a black person when there is no evidence suggesting this (other than perhaps the accused being a black person), for example, the animation is going to cause trouble. Use a generic mannequin shaded in a neutral tone such as a dull grey color.

It is also best to err on the side of conservatism. Don't speculate or include details based on averages unless expert opinion will be used in testimony to back up the images. In other words, even though the average traffic flow is a certain number of cars every 30 seconds, that average might not be appropriate or relevant to this event; the particular day of the accident might not have been an average day.

You can usually get away with low-resolution models for human subjects and vehicles. The two exceptions to this are when you are working with an injury or surgical animation, or in a vehicular case where some aspect of the vehicle may have contributed to the accident.

In the same way that Character Studio, as a plug-in, gives added abilities to animate bipedal motion in MAX, other plug-ins help you add just the right detail. The following section describes some of the most helpful applications and plug-ins that will save you time and add to your capabilities. The following topics are covered:

- Human Models
- Vehicular Models
- Skid Marks, Tracks, and Trails

Human Models

The ever famous mannequin will do just fine for many reenactments. When you need more detail, however, it becomes a more complex task. Two new programs help produce incredible detail with reduced effort. Poser 2 and Detailer from Fractal Design make a great combination.

Poser 2 enables easy creation of predefined figures. You can adjust the body specifics, such as weight, height, and age. It makes for a great motion and pose study program for your animations. It also directly supports the exporting of 3DS files for use in MAX.

Detailer enables painting directly on your 3D models. The program creates all your texture and bump maps for you as you draw and paint on the mesh. Detailer also directly exports 3DS files for use in MAX. Detailer is great for human figures, especially faces. It also comes in handy when trying to paint gouges and scratches on vehicles and other surfaces.

Detailer works directly on your exported 3DS or DXF files from MAX, but a plug-in called Unwrap is a time-saving tool that literally unwraps the mapping coordinates of your model and saves the flat map as a graphic file. When you open the file in Photoshop, you see the form of the model represented as a flat outline. You can then paint on the map using the lines as a reference for positioning on the mesh in MAX.

NOTE

Each of these programs is highlighted in *Inside 3D Studio MAX Volume II*.

Vehicle Models

A majority of the time, the vehicle does not cause, or even contribute to the cause of, a vehicular accident. Therefore, do not spend a fortune buying highly detailed models, or hours of your time modeling vehicles yourself. Companies such as Viewpoint have growing libraries of vehicles with varying degrees of complexity that will suit most of your needs. If you must have a model custom made, make that decision early. It is not cheap!

The realism of your models will play a large part in how real the scene will appear to the jury. Many programs are now available that enable you to create models based on photographs taken from two different angles. These programs, such as Wireframe Express, create a relatively simple mesh file with the photo serving as a texture map. What you get is a quick rendering, very realistic model. These programs can be great for modeling before and after models of vehicles in collisions where you need to show the details of the damage. The downside is that, as in any modeling task, it takes quite a bit of time. This also is not a good choice if you have to interact with the models. Your car door will look like it is there, for example, but it only exists in the texture map. If you want to open the door, you will need to do some model modification.

Skid Marks, Tracks, and Trails

When did the vehicle start braking? When did it drive off the road? These events are often evident from tire marks, skids, or skuff marks.

One plug-in offers an easy way to create these effects: the MAXTrax plug-in from Sisyphus. It enables you to automate the process of creating procedural tracks and trails. It combines both a geometry-based application and a particle system to create everything from wake patterns in water to trails behind airplanes. The program is a big time saver, especially in forensic work. The key issue in skid marks is the location and duration. Their function is to point out things such as when brakes were applied or when tires left contact with the road as the car skidded across uneven terrain.

TIP

The use of MAXTrax is not limited to skid marks, although that is a common application. It is just as easy to set up the plug-in to create odd markings. Use it to create a gouge or paint mark on the side of a car as two cars bump against each other, or to place a skuff or gouge in the ground as a car tumbles across the side of a road after a collision.

Skid Marks

This first tutorial sets up skid marks from a tire in a simple head-on vehicular collision. This is a basic tutorial on how to apply tire tracks in your scene. You will take it one step further to show areas where the tire loses contact with the ground and the tracks stop and then start again when the tire lands back on the ground. Within the program's parameters, you have control over just about everything except designating multiple starting and stopping points for the same track. An easy workaround enables forensic animators to meet this common need. The following tutorial shows the workaround you will need to use.

1. Load the file trax1.max from the accompanying CD and save it to your hard drive as **mytrax1.max**.

NOTE

The animation in this scene is simple and completed for you. The truck realizes that the car is not going to clear its path and applies its brakes. But it is too late, and the collision takes place. The goal in such a case may be to show one of two things. It may show that the car turned in front of the truck when it should have yielded, or it may show the truck was going too fast to react in time. This tutorial does not deal with these issues.

The basis of MAXTrax is to place an emitter (skidmark or track) between the object leaving the skidmark or track and the object on top of which the skidmark or track should appear—in this case, between the tire and the road. In MAXTrax terminology, the tire is the reference object, and the road is the target object.

2. Maximize the Top viewport and Region Zoom the area that includes the back tires of the truck and the right side of the road (see fig. 7.23).

FIGURE 7.23

Isolate the tires that will produce the tracks, but make certain that you can see a selectable edge of the road.

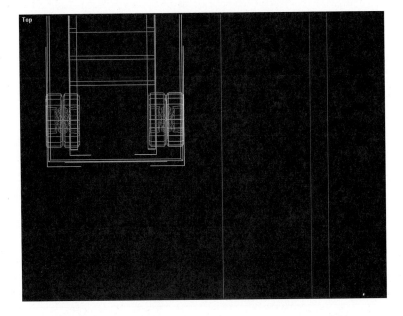

3. Because the roadside is a separate object from the road, it would be easy to select the roadside object when you go to click on your reference object. To avoid this, click on Select By Name and select Shoulder of Road.

4. Click on Display and Freeze By Selection, and Freeze Selected, to make the shoulder of the road unselectable.

5. Click on Create, Geometry, Particle Systems (see fig. 7.24).

FIGURE 7.24

The particle systems selection as it appears in the Create Geometry module in MAX.

6. Click on the MTrack button to enter MAXTrax. Figure 7.25 shows the layout of MAXTrax parameters.

Figure 7.25
The MAXTrax parameters.

7. Enter a start frame of 80 and an end frame of 130 for your first track.

8. Enter the end frame of 157 in the Display Until setting to make certain that the tracks stay visible after they are generated. Accept the rest of the default settings.

9. Click on the PICK button. This process has two steps: clicking on the reference object and then the target object.

10. In the Top viewport, click on the far left tire as the reference object. The emitter, which generates the track, will be made to fit the width of this object.

11. In the Top viewport, click on the edge of the road, making it the target object. The emitter will be aligned by face with your selection. It will be placed just above the road's surface to give the illusion of the tracks being painted on the road itself.

12. If it is not aligned with the tire, select and move the patch in the Top viewport until it is centered on the tire. Make certain that you do not move the patch vertically. Figure 7.26 shows the properly aligned emitter patch.

13. Click on the Select and Link button.

FIGURE 7.26

The emitter, which generates the skidmark or track, is aligned with the tire object.

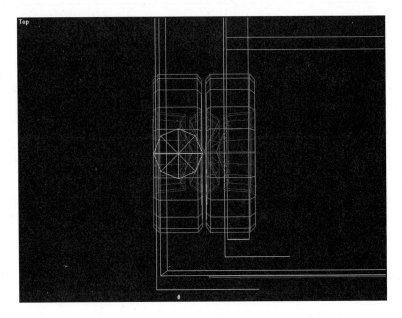

14. Click and hold the mouse button on the emitter and drag the cursor until it is over the tire. When you see the Link Boxes icon, release the mouse. The emitter patch will now follow your tire.

15. Change your viewport to the Shortbird camera and scroll the timeline to see the animation. The track is generated starting at frame 80.

16. With the emitter patch selected, take a few minutes to adjust the settings in the MTrack parameters to see your changes in real time. By adjusting the starting and stopping frame, you can see the track adjusted in the Camera viewport.

17. The only thing missing is the skid mark. Open the Material Editor and start a new material by clicking on the Standard button and choosing a New-Standard material. You will use both a Diffuse and Opacity map to create the tire tracks.

18. Click on Maps and the check boxes next to Diffuse and Opacity.

19. Click on the Map button for the Diffuse map and select Bitmap from the list.

20. Click on the blank button next to Bitmap and select the tireblak.tif file from the accompanying CD.

21. In the Mapping Coordinates section, adjust the UV mapping by setting the tiling factor for U to 24. You must play with this setting for each track you set to get the look you want (see fig. 7.27).

FIGURE 7.27

Adjusting the UV mapping coordinates is critical to get the correct aspect ratio along the length of track.

22. Click on the Map button for the Opacity map and select Bitmap from the list.

23. Click on the blank button next to Bitmap and select the tiretrak.tif file from the accompanying CD.

24. In the Mapping Coordinates section, adjust the UV mapping by setting the tiling factor for U to 24.

TIP

In most cases, unless you want a distorted map for your path, remember to make the exact same settings for mapping coordinates for the diffuse and the opacity maps.

25. Save the material as **tiretrax** and save it to your material library.

26. With the emitter selected, click on Assign Material to Selected and close the Material Editor.

27. Make certain that the shortbird view is displayed and go to frame 130.

28. Render a single frame of the animation, and you will see the tire track left behind the far left wheel.

29. Add a wrinkle to this basic track by making it stop and then start again. The only way to do this is to add a second emitter.

30. Go to frame 0 and Region Zoom to see the far left tire.

31. Click on the Select and Move button and constrain to the X axis.

32. Hold the left Shift key down and click on the emitter object without moving it. When you release the mouse, the Clone Options dialog box appears.

33. Click on OK to make a copy of the emitter.

34. Note that the first emitter is named Mtrack01 and the copy is Mtrack02.

35. Click on Select By Name and select Mtrack01.

36. Adjust the start frame to 30 and the end frame to 60. Leave the other settings the same.

37. Click on Select By Name and select Mtrack02.

38. Adjust the start frame to 90 and the end frame to 130. Leave the other settings the same.

39. Make certain that the shortbird view is displayed and go to frame 130.

40. Render a single frame of the animation. Figure 7.28 shows the broken track effect you just created.

FIGURE 7.28

A broken track effect is achieved by creating two emitters for the same tire.

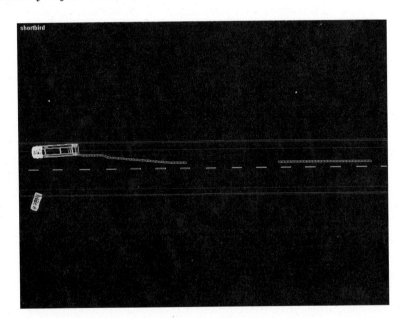

41. Save your file and load trax1.avi from the accompanying CD to see the final rendered animation. You can load the final animation file in MAX by loading the trax1fin.max file from the CD.

TIP

Make certain that you assign the same material to each track. You may have to adjust the UV tiling for each track separately to compensate for any difference in track length.

Footprints

This second tutorial uses MAXTrax to add footprints behind a Character Studio biped. Placement of the footprints is not an exact science in this method, but it will generate a footstep path for your character. The results look great from a distance and good from close up. If your perspective is a tight shot centered on the feet as the character walks, don't use this method because you will see inaccuracies. Similarly, if you are interested in the exact placement of the footprints, this method will not work.

In forensic animation, you quite often need to show footprints because a victim or defendant left some physical evidence showing the path he or she took. Perhaps a pedestrian claims to have been stuck by a car on the side of the road, but she left footprints in the mud or snow that show she was actually in the street when hit. In criminal cases, you may want to show how a burglar entered a building or how a murder suspect stalked a victim. In these situations, you could use footprints solely to identify the path taken. Using footprints enables the jury to see the path as the character walks and to refer back to it even after the walking sequence is complete. When these or similar situations arise, MAXTrax can help.

For short sequences of steps, it is easier to create a ground-level planar object at the point of each footstep and apply an opacity-mapped footprint manually. For longer runs or walks, the MAXTrax solution may be the best option. The main advantage would come if you had to change the path your character takes. If you use MAXTrax to create the footprints, any changes in your character motion would be automatically reflected in the footprints.

TIP

Sisyphus, the creators of MAXTrax, has commented that it would be very difficult to align the footprints with the footsteps precisely. This tutorial comes very close to being accurate by way of some extra steps to create texture maps that closely match the walking distance of each step. You may find that through making modifications to the MAXTrax settings, texture maps, or the walking gait of your character, your animations can be more accurate. If you discover a way to use the program to precisely place the footsteps, call Sisyphus; they would be very interested in hearing your technique.

As you set up your own animations to create footprints behind bipeds, refer to the following list of key areas to make adjustments that affect where the footprints are generated:

- The placement of the emitter patch from MAXTrax
- The size and scale of the emitter patch
- The UV tiling of the footprint texture and opacity maps
- The dimensions of the image files used in the footprint texture and opacity maps
- The footstep pattern of your character

Load the file walktrax.max from the accompanying CD and save it to your hard drive as **mytrax2.max**. The scene contains a hunched over biped character created with CS that takes a basic walk across the screen.

1. Maximize the Top viewport and Region Zoom until the character takes up most of your screen. Make certain that you can see a selectable edge of the floor object. You will need to select it as MAXTrax's target object.

2. Click on Create, Geometry, Particle Systems.

3. Click on the MTrack button to enter MAXTrax.

4. Leave the start frame of 0 and enter a stop frame of 306.

5. Enter the end frame of 306 in the Display Until setting to make certain that the tracks stay visible after they are generated. Accept the rest of the default settings.

6. Click on the PICK button to select the reference and target objects.

WARNING

You must select the reference object first. MAXTrax reminds you of the order in which you are choosing objects; just watch the MAX display bar for the prompts.

7. Click on the character as your reference object.

8. Click on the floor as your target object.

9. Click on My Choice in the Position Relative section of the MAXTrax panel. You should see the emitter patch appear aligned to the Top viewport.

10. Size the emitter patch to match the width of the character's feet by clicking on the Size and Uniform Scale tool and resizing the XY coordinates of the patch. Don't worry about the Z coordinate of the patch; MAXTrax aligned it directly above the floor when you picked the target object.

11. Click on Select and Move and move the patch directly under the character (see fig. 7.29).

FIGURE 7.29

This shows the correct size and location of the emitter patch relative to the character's feet.

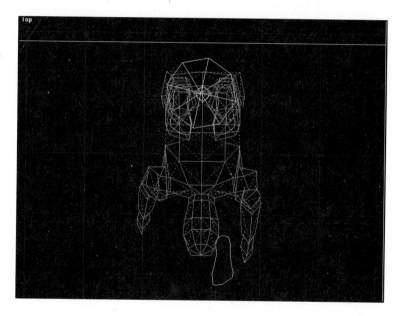

12. Switch views to show the Left viewport and Region Zoom to close in on the character, leaving room to show the first few footsteps.

13. Create a dummy for the character by clicking on Create, Helpers, Dummy. Draw a dummy of any size aligned near the front of the feet of the character. You will link this dummy to the character and the emitter to this dummy (see fig. 7.30).

FIGURE 7.30

It is best to create a dummy object to set the motion in the scene.

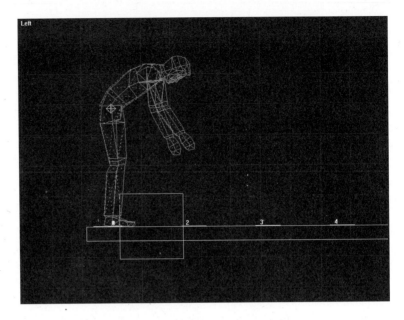

14. Because you need the footprints to stay on the ground, you want the dummy to follow only the horizontal motion of the character. You will do this by limiting the inherited links to only the Y axis by using the World coordinate system. Click on Hierarchy, Link Info, and uncheck everything but the Y check box under Inherit (see fig. 7.31).

FIGURE 7.31

The dummy object needs to inherit only the Y axis data from the character.

15. Click on Select and Link.

16. Select the dummy, drag the cursor over the character, and release the mouse. This links the dummy to the character.

17. Now link the emitter to the dummy. With Select and Link still the active tool, click on Select by Name and select the emitter (Mtrack01).

18. Click on Select by Name again to select the parent object, which is the dummy.

19. Switch views to the top view and drag the timeline to see the dummy and emitter move with the character (see fig. 7.32).

FIGURE 7.32
The emitter and dummy now move with the character. The emitter generates the footprints as it moves.

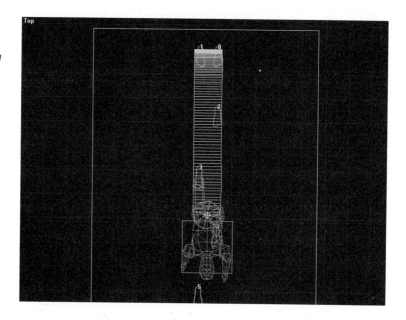

The only thing left to do is to assign the footprint material to the emitter. Use a paint program such as Photoshop to create the maps. To make the best attempt at an accurate map, you will need the following measurements:

■ The distance from heel to heel in the walking pattern

■ The length and width of each foot

■ The distance from the outside edge of the left foot to the outside edge of the right foot

NOTE

These measurements will aid in the creation of the Diffuse and Opacity maps. They will not guarantee easy success in lining up the footsteps with the footprints generated by MAXTrax, but they should reduce the amount of playing around with settings it takes to get the amount of alignment you need.

1. Because you need the measurements in inches, click on Views, Units Setup and make certain that Decimal Inches is selected.

2. Using the Left viewport, drag the timeline to a point where the left and right foot are farthest apart.

3. Click on Create, Helpers, Tape.

4. Click on the viewport at the left heel and drag forward to the right heel. Because you will not use this tape measure again, you don't need to create it. When you reach the right heel, make note of the distance listed in the Parameters section for the length of the tape. In this example, it is roughly 22 inches (see fig. 7.33).

FIGURE 7.33
Gathering measurements from the character will help create an image map more easily aligned with the footsteps.

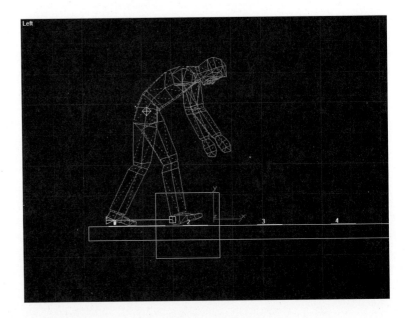

5. Right-click to cancel the creation of the tape measure.

6. Repeat this technique to gather the measurements listed in step 4.

7. With those measurements, create your footprint pattern in Photoshop, consisting of one left and one right footprint. Make the left foot the first print you create, followed by the right (see fig. 7.34).

FIGURE 7.34

This is the image created for the diffuse map of the footprints.

8. After you have created your footprint diffuse map, you will need an opacity map to drop out the surrounding area so that the footprints will appear on top of whatever surface your character is walking on in the animation. In Photoshop, do this by inverting the colors, changing to greyscale, and finally changing to a bitmap using diffusion dithering (see fig. 7.35).

FIGURE 7.35
This is the image created for the opacity map of the footprints.

NOTE

Remember that in the opacity map, everything black will be transparent and will let the underlying elements (in this case, the floor) show through.

9. Back in MAX, open the Material Editor and start a new material by clicking on the Standard button.

10. On the next screen, select Standard and click on OK.

11. Click on Maps and then on the check boxes next to Diffuse and Opacity.

12. Click on the Map button for the Diffuse map and select Bitmap from the list.

13. Click on the blank button next to Bitmap and select the 2steps.jpg file from the accompanying CD.

14. In the Mapping Coordinates section, adjust the UV mapping by setting the tiling factor for U to 1.0 and for V to 6.8. You also have to adjust the angle to get the footprints facing the same direction as the character. You must play with these settings to get the look you want (see fig. 7.36).

TIP

The settings for the UV tiling at 1.0 and 6.8 respectively are not exact. They came from numerous attempts at aligning the footprints. A good place to start is to take the total distance that your character walks and divide it by the distance covered by a left-right footstep sequence (the length of your image map) and to enter that number. If your character travels 21 feet and the length of your map is 3 feet, for example, enter a number of 7.0 for the V tiling and adjust from there.

FIGURE 7.36

To align the footprints, adjust the UV mapping coordinates and the angle of the map.

15. Click on the Map button for the Opacity map and select Bitmap from the list.

16. Click on the blank button next to Bitmap and select the 2stepsop.tif file from the accompanying CD.

17. In the Mapping Coordinates section, adjust the UV mapping and angle setting to the same settings that you used for the diffuse map.

18. Save the material as **walking footsteps** and save it to your material library.

19. With the Mtrack01 emitter selected, click on Assign Material to Selected and close the Material Editor.

20. Click on Display and uncheck Cameras in the Hide by Category section.

21. Click on Select by Name and select both Camera01 and Camera01.target.

22. Click on Select and Link and drag the cursor to the dummy object and release the mouse button. The Camera and its target will now follow the character's dummy so that you can follow the walk and see all the footsteps MAXTrax will generate.

23. Activate the Camera viewport and slide the timeline to various frames along the walking path. Render a single frame at each frame to see how realistic the footprints appear (see fig. 7.37).

FIGURE 7.37
A rendered frame showing the footprints generated by MAXTrax.

24. Save your file and load walktrax.avi from the accompanying CD to see the final rendered animation. You can load the final animation file in MAX by loading the walktrax.max file from the accompanying CD.

3DS MAX is a valuable tool for the forensic animator, and plug-ins are an essential part of the complete toolbox. One of the biggest production advantages you should realize from using Character Studio and MAXTrax is the time they save. The nature of the forensic industry is to create exhibits, such as animation, as a last thought. Attorneys tend to focus on current trial dates, depositions, and similar events. Not a lot of thought is put into exhibits for a trial nine months away. It is not uncommon, therefore, to be producing forensic animations in a very short time. Any tool that speeds up the process is worth its weight in gold. Because of the complexity of scenes and the necessity for accuracy, animators must focus on details, not methods of creation.

There are other means of creating effects such as skid marks and footprints besides the ones mentioned in this chapter. The methods introduced in this chapter were outlined because of their simplicity and automation. New plug-ins are being developed that will aid in the details of real-world physics that may play a large role in further automation of collisions. The main point is that MAX is an intentionally incomplete program. As new plug-ins are announced, the usefulness of MAX will increase, and the animator will benefit even more.

In Practice: Animating Accuracy for Forensics

- Go back to the timing.max file and add a camera in the driver's seat of the car to see what the driver's view would have been in this case. Based on the time the pedestrian is visible from behind the car, an expert could determine whether there was sufficient time to react and apply the brakes.

- To add more realistic movements, use Character Studio's biped in the fmsstudio.max file to adjust the body movements post-impact for the character. Subtle adjustments to the flailing of arms or the abrupt snap of the head at impact can make a more dramatic visual of the force of the impact.

- MAXTrax may be even better suited for group or herd foot- or hoofprints. Try setting up a scene where a large group of people or animals travels across the sand or snow—something that would show tracks. Create your image maps of randomly placed prints at different angles and positions. Make the map a long rectangular shape, filled with the prints, and attach it to a dummy object in the center of the rushing crowd.

- When designing tire tracks in MAXTrax, try making a map that looks more like a skid than a perfect tire track. It will look more realistic because the tires are not turning during the skid. You could do this by creating a distorted image map, or adjusting the UV tiling for the map in the Material Editor.

- There are a number of ways to place distinctive markings in your forensic animations. Scratches in paint where two cars impacted, for example, can be made by painting on the mesh's image maps with a program such as Detailer, or by using Unwrap to make a flat image map with the outline of the mesh visible for painting in Photoshop. For times when there is a dent or gouge (something that penetrates a flat surface), try making a clone of the object to be damaged, linking it to its original/ parent object, and hiding it in the scene until the impact occurs. At impact, unhide the damaged clone, and hide its original.

Part III

CHARACTER ANIMATION

IMAGE CREATED BY GEORGE MAESTRI

Chapter 8

by George Maestri

Setting Up Characters for Animation

Setup is one of the most important tasks a character animator faces. It involves not only building the character so that it looks nice, but also tweaking the models and adding elements such as skeletons and expressions to help the animation process along. If a character is built solidly and is easy to animate, the process goes faster, and the animator's creative flow isn't interrupted by frustrating problems and system delays.

Setup includes deciding how to build your characters and how to manipulate them. Characters can be built in segments so that they are animated at the object level, or they can be built as one solid object and animated at the sub-object level. Characters that are one solid mesh are usually deformed with a skeleton, which also needs to be set up so that it can be manipulated with IK. Characters created out of separate objects also can be manipulated with IK. This chapter covers the following topics:

- Types of characters

- Creating skeletons that deform meshes

- Building a skeleton from scratch

- Skeletons for hands

Types of Characters

3D Studio MAX offers a number of strategies for creating characters. Many of these methods are the same used for creating any object within MAX; the previous volume discussed many of these techniques. How the character is animated depends on how it is built.

Characters can be animated at the object level. Object level animation requires that the character be split up into discrete segments that are linked together in a hierarchy. Object level animation is how most characters in video games are animated.

Characters that need to have a smooth, seamless skin should be animated at the sub-object level, which means that the vertices of the mesh or the patch are affected by using any number of techniques, described in later chapters. These techniques include Physique, Bones Pro, FFDs, and linked Xforms, to name a few.

Object Level Animation—Segmented Characters

The easiest way to animate a character is to separate the body into segments and animate the individual objects. Picture a segmented character as the classic artist's mannequin, constructed of wood and fitted together with pins at the joints. An armored knight or a jointed robot would be other examples of a segmented character (see figs. 8.1 and 8.2).

FIGURE 8.1

A good example of a segmented character.

FIGURE 8.2

This exploded view shows that his body is composed of multiple objects.

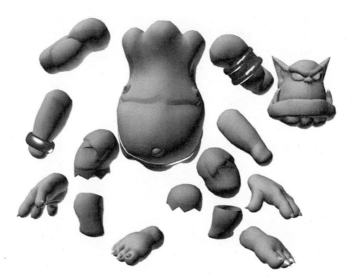

Segmented characters are pretty much required for applications such as video games. Most game machines require that objects be segmented because deforming a mesh requires too much overhead. The same is true for MAX. It animates segments faster because deforming a mesh requires extra calculations.

The many parts of a segmented character are joined together via a hierarchy, which can then be animated using forward kinematics or inverse kinematics (IK).

There are, of course, drawbacks to creating segmented characters. First, the seams always find a way to show themselves—no matter how hard you try to hide them. You can always turn this pitfall to your advantage by purposely designing your character with exposed seams. Pixar's Buzz Lightyear is a good example of such a design.

Solid Mesh Characters

A solid mesh character is built as one solid object and animated at the sub-object level. This character can be built out of any supported MAX geometry, from polygons to patches. Animating such a character requires use of a mesh deformation system (see fig. 8.3). MAX has two such systems, sold as plug-ins: Physique and Bones Pro. Physique is sold as one part of Character Studio by Kinetix, and Bones Pro is a product from Digimation. Operation of these plug-ins is described in Chapters 11 "Mesh Deformation" and 12 "Physique." For now, however, it is important to know that both plug-ins require a skeleton of bones to deform the mesh.

FIGURE 8.03

A solid mesh character can be constructed out of spline patches or polygons, but must be deformed using a mesh deformation plug-in, such as Physique or Bones Pro.

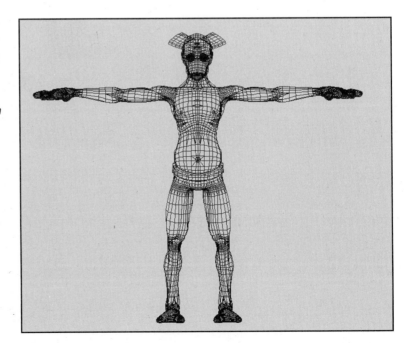

Building Solid Meshes out of Polygons

Historically, polygons have typically been the modeling method of choice for many 3D Studio and MAX animators. One reason to animate with polygonal meshes is because MAX's mesh modeling tools are very robust. This wealth of tools allows for much more control over the modeling process, but the end result of that process is a mesh.

Polygonal meshes definitely have the advantage of a wealth of tools, and this may make them a good choice for characters animated within MAX. The disadvantage of creating polygonal mesh models is that they can be difficult of control when animated at the sub-object level with a mesh deformation tool:

- The first reason is speed. Polygonal meshes require significantly more vertices to create a smooth skin than a patch object does. A larger number of vertices means that the CPU needs to perform more calculations, slowing down the process and hampering interactivity.

- Second, and more importantly, the increased density of a polygonal mesh means that the vertices are closer together, which gives the character a much higher probability of tearing, crimping, or bulging in the wrong places. Deciding which vertex belongs to which skeletal bone can prove to be an exercise in hair splitting.

Still, MAX does have tools such as MeshSmooth, which can allow for a low-polygonal count model to behave in much the same way that a spline model would. This is discussed in detail in Chapter 11.

Building Solid Meshes from Spline Patches

As was mentioned previously, patches are much better for organic characters, particularly in solid mesh characters deformed by a skeleton. The reason for this is that patches cover a much larger area with fewer vertices and remain smooth over a wider range of motion. The fewer things you need to animate, the less you have to worry about. Although MAX's patch modeling tools can be a bit tough to master, models built this way can perform much better at animation time.

The introduction of Digimation's Surface Tools has given animators an easy to use and serious tool for animating patch surfaces. As described earlier in this volume, the plug-in gives animators a much better way of creating a patch surface by defining the outline with simple Bézier curves.

Surface Tools contains a number of modifiers, most important of which are Cross Section and Surface. Cross Section is similar to a skinning tool in that it takes a series of spline outlines and connects them together. Surface completes the process by turning the splines into a flexible patch surface. Bodies can be built using Surface Tools by creating a "cage" out of splines and using the Cross Section tool to stitch them together. The objects created within Surface Tools resolve to patches, which, in turn, resolve to meshes.

Placement of Detail Within a Solid Mesh

Whether you build out of splines or polygons, you should always pay attention to where the detail is in a character. A character needs extra detail at the joints, such as the knees and elbows. This extra detail enables the joints to bend smoothly and realistically. Areas that don't flex, such as the part of the thigh and shin outside the knee, can be spared extra detail. In figure 8.4 the hand is very flexible, so it requires more detail. The forearm is relatively rigid and requires less. More detail is added at the elbow because it also flexes. More vertices in the middle part of the joints only add weight to a character, but doesn't help add detail to the outline of the character.

FIGURE 8.4
This close-up of the alien's arm shows the varying degrees of detail.

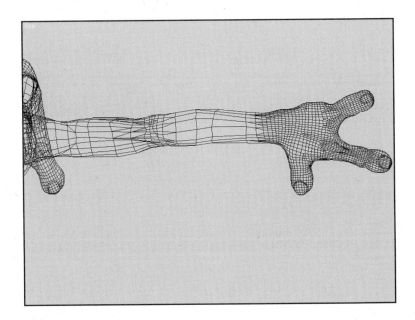

Two other areas that require attention to detail and the placement of it are the groin and shoulder areas. These areas are also flexible, but along a much wider range than the knees or elbows. When constructing the intersection of the legs and the hips at the groin area, try to model extra detail along the "bikini line," roughly a 45-degree line that runs from the inside of the crotch to the top of the hips (see fig. 8.5).

FIGURE 8.5

This close-up of the hip area shows the extra detail along the intersection of the thighs and hips.

The shoulders are probably the most flexible joints in the body and thus need to be modeled properly to allow for proper deformation. Think of the shoulders as a slight funnel shape that leads from the arms to the torso, with extra detail in the upper arm that broadens out into the chest area (see fig. 8.6)

FIGURE 8.6
This close-up of the shoulder area shows how the extra detail is added to the upper arm as it transitions to the chest area.

Metaball Characters

Metaballs can also be used for creating characters. MAX has a number of metaball plug-ins (some of the most innovative on the market). Two of the most notable are Infografica's Meta-Reyes (see fig. 8.7), which can create dynamic muscle-shaped metaballs, and Digimation's Clay Studio, which allows for spherical, ellipsoidal, and rectangular primitives. The simple capability to create non-spherical objects significantly reduces the number of objects needed to construct a character. Animating fewer objects makes for fewer headaches when animation time comes around. MetaReyes is discussed in detail in Chapter 11.

Mapping was a problem with earlier metaball implementations. Both Digimation and Infografica have addressed this with *sticky mapping*, which allows the underlying metaball objects to be animated. The map, however, remains glued to the surface, enabling some very natural and organic animation.

The metaballs created by these programs can be linked among themselves to build a blobby, segmented character without seams. They can also be attached to skeletons, such as those created by Biped. As with a solid mesh character, the skeleton can be animated fairly easily like a segmented character, with the metaballs fusing only at render time.

FIGURE 8.7
This character was created using Infografica's MetaReyes plug-in by Jose Maria de Espona. Notice how the metaball primitives follow the natural lines that muscles normally would.

Hybrid Characters

Because MAX can mix and match geometry types on the fly, there is no reason you cannot mix and match any of the previously discussed methods when building your character. Facial animation, which is covered in Chapter 13, "Facial Animation and Lip Sync," can be accomplished quite effectively with Surface Tools. The entire character can be constructed out of Surface Tools–generated geometry.

Building a hand using Surface Tools, however, might prove to be too much effort, and metaballs can be used to make simple hands quite easily. Metaballs also work well for bodies, but facial animation using metaballs can be difficult to achieve.

Polygons can also be used in any of these situations, from heads to bodies to hands. The choice of tools depends on the individual character and the animation tasks it needs to perform. It might be a good idea to use a Surface Tools–generated head on a polygonal body with metaball-generated hands. Any number of combinations is possible, so it is always a good idea to consider all possibilities and tools at your disposal.

Creating Skeletons that Deform Meshes

If you build a seamless mesh character, you will need to deform that mesh in one way or another. For very simple characters, modifiers such as Bend, Twist, or an FFD might work. Typically, however, this is not enough. In most cases, you must create a skeleton and use a plug-in such as Physique or Bones Pro.

The skeletons required by these plug-ins are very similar to the bones in a human body. Most digital characters built in this way have thigh bones, shin bones, spines, necks, shoulders, and hips (to name a few). Of course, digital skeletons are merely a simplified approximation of the real thing. The human body has dozens of vertebrae in the spine. A digital skeleton may have only three.

Skeletons are put together in much the same way as segmented characters. They are merely objects linked together into a hierarchy. You can build your own skeletons out of MAX's bones or out of simple geometry, such as boxes. If you are building a two-legged creature, you can use the prebuilt skeletons supplied with Biped—the other half of Character Studio (see fig. 8.8).

FIGURE 8.8

Biped provides a good example of a skeleton, though there are many ways of building skeletons in MAX.

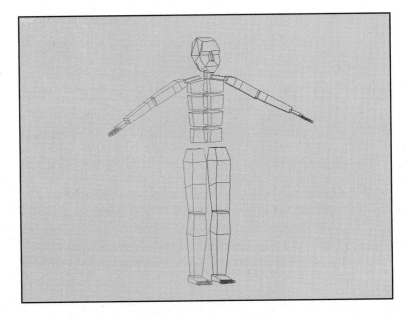

MAX Bones

MAX has the capability to create a system of bones. In the simplest sense, bones are helper objects linked hierarchically. Bones can be found in the Create panel under the systems glyph.

MAX Bones work with jointed characters, but to be used with a solid mesh character, they must be coupled with a mesh deformation plug-in, such as Physique or Bones Pro. Vertex animation can be accomplished through a linked XForm modifier so that the vertices of the mesh are actually controlled and moved by the bones system. All of these methods are discussed in detail in Chapter 10, "Animating with Biped."

The nice thing about bones is that creating them automatically generates a hierarchy. If you look in Track View, you can see that a two-bone chain actually consists of a base object (bone01) plus the two bones.

The bones can be animated and manipulated by clicking on the bones and translating the objects. The bones behave in two ways, depending on whether IK is turned on or off.

- When IK is off, only the end effectors of each bone move, enabling you to reposition and change the length of the bone on the fly (see fig. 8.9).

- When IK is turned on, the bone's length remains fixed. The bone will automatically flex and bend much like the bones in a skeleton. As you will see, the IK rotations of these bones can be constrained in a number of ways (see fig. 8.10).

Bones can also be rotated manually to accomplish forward kinematic-type motions. The trick here is knowing which object to rotate. You must rotate the bone at its base—the joint where the bone begins. The forearm, for example, is rotated at the elbow. This is the same for MAX bones.

When IK is on, the bones are always rigid. This can cause headaches because your skeletons can change shape if you forget to switch on IK. Some animators consider this a detriment; others use this to get stretchy cartoon-like effects because—in both Physique and Bones Pro—stretching the bone stretches the underlying mesh. If you want to move the chain as a whole, you can always select the entire bone structure and move it with IK turned off without affecting the shape.

FIGURE 8.9
Moving a bone with IK off resizes the bone.

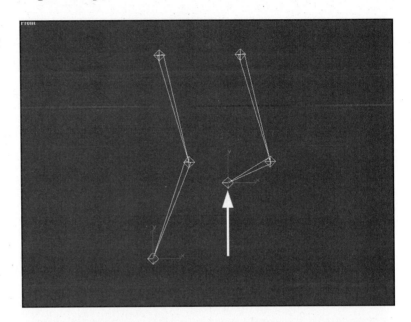

FIGURE 8.10
Moving a bone with IK on, however, keeps the bone rigid and forces the chain to bend.

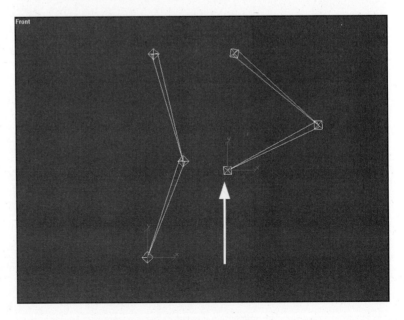

Boxes as Bones

In addition to bones, MAX users are fortunate that both Physique and Bones Pro can use any type of object as a bone. Most animators use simple boxes, though any geometry works. The bones created by Character Studio's Biped module are box-like and are a very good example of how to construct an effective skeleton out of simple objects.

The advantages of using box bones over MAX bones is that the boxes are easier to visualize; you can watch them in Shaded mode and render simple tests. Another advantage is that box bones retain their shape regardless of whether IK is flipped on; their shape must be changed by scaling.

Box bones are a bit harder to model and set up, and the extra geometry adds a bit to the weight of the scene. Boxes must also be hidden before rendering, which adds a step to the rendering process.

Digimation's Skeleton plug-in, provided with Bones Pro, can turn MAX bones into box bones. The plug-in retains the linking from the original bones and enables you to sketch out a skeleton quite easily, changing the bones into boxes after the skeleton is set (see fig. 8.11).

FIGURE 8.11
Two skeletons. The one on the right is made of MAX Bones, and the left is made of box bones.

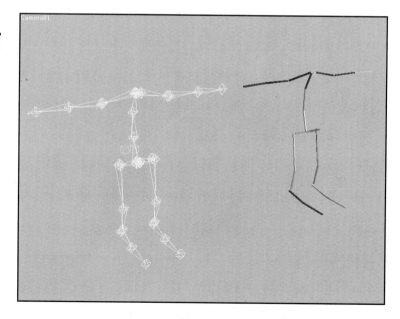

Building a Skeleton from Scratch

If you have Biped, building a skeleton is as easy as clicking and dragging. Still, building your own will give you insight into the entire process of how a skeleton works. Creating a skeleton is similar to creating a segmented character, only the geometry is much simpler. Likewise, setting up IK for a segmented character is the same as for a generic skeleton. This basic skeleton can be used in conjunction with either Physique or Bones Pro.

Creating Bones

Creating a skeleton can be intimidating, but it is simply a matter of creating bones that mimic the bones of your character's body. Your skeleton will have arm bones, leg bones, and a spinal column, to name a few. Typically, it is a good idea to load your target mesh and freeze it, using it as a guide for creating, fitting, and sizing the bones of the skeleton. The following exercise strips away the mesh so that you can see exactly how the bones are built and tied together.

The first step is to build two basic bones: one vertical, one horizontal. Create the vertical bone first.

STRIPPING AWAY THE MESH TO SEE THE STRUCTURE

1. Go to the Creation panel and create a simple box to use as a bone. For demonstration purposes, make a box of 10×10×40 units. (Of course, the size of the box depends a great deal on the size of your mesh object being deformed.)

2. Go to the Hierarchy panel and click on the Pivot button. Under Move/Rotate/Scale, click on Affect Pivot Only. Move the pivot so that it rests neatly along the top of the box and the Z axis of the pivot is aligned with the length of the box. This will be the basic bone.

3. Now create a horizontal box with dimensions of 40×10×10, which will become the basis of your skeleton's hips and shoulders.

4. Again, go to the Hierarchy panel and click on the Pivot button. Under the Move/Rotate/Scale rollout, click Affect Pivot Only. Next, under Alignment, press Center to Object. Check your results against figure 8.12.

FIGURE 8.12

The two basic bones. The horizontal bone has its pivot centered, while the vertical one's pivot is at the base.

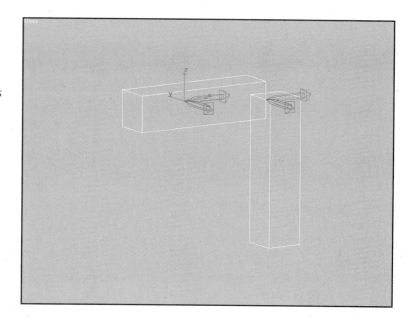

5. If you plan to use IK, it is best to change the default rotation controller to Euler XYZ for both bones. As is explained in *Inside 3D Studio MAX Volume I*, this is the best controller to use with IK. With this default, when you copy the bone, the controller will go with it. You set this controller as the default by clicking on the Make Default button in the Replace Rotation Controller dialog box (see fig. 8.13).

FIGURE 8.13

Select Euler XYZ as the rotation controller for use with IK.

Creating a Skeleton

The next task is to copy and arrange these bones into a skeleton. It may be a skeleton for a human, as is constructed here, or it can vary as widely as your characters.

ARRANGING THE SKELETON

1. Give the first bone a descriptive name. This will be a shin bone in this particular skeleton, so name the bone **R-Shin**.

2. Copy this bone and drag the copy upward so that it rests immediately above the first. Name this bone **R-Thigh**.

3. Copy R-Shin and R-Thigh, and drag these new bones approximately 45 units to the left. Name these **L-Shin** and **L-Thigh**.

4. Copy the horizontal box and place it between the two legs to create the hips. Name this bone **Hips**. Compare what you have to figure 8.14.

FIGURE 8.14

The hips and legs of the skeleton.

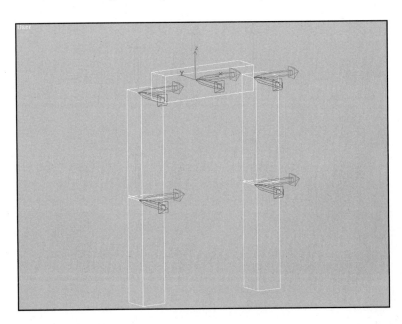

5. Copy one of the leg bones and resize it so that it is 20 units high. This will be the base of the spine.

6. Rotate this bone 180 degrees so that the pivot is located at the bottom of the box. Place this bone directly above the center of the hips. Name the bone **Spine-01**.

7. Copy this bone twice to create the rest of the spinal column. Name these **Spine-02** and **Spine-03**. Typically, three bones are just enough to give the illusion of a full spine, though you can add more if your character needs more flexibility. Check figure 8.15.

FIGURE 8.15

The spine. Notice how the pivots for these bones are located along the lower part of the joint.

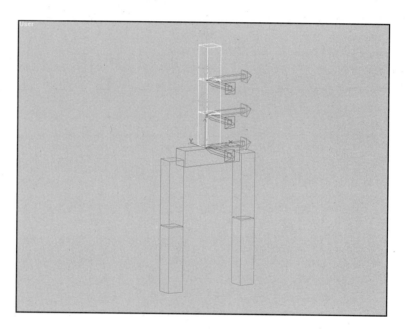

8. Copy the hips and drag the box upward to make the shoulders. Resize this box so that it is 30 units wide. Copy this again and name the two bones **L-Shoulder** and **R-Shoulder**, respectively. Copy it again and make a smaller bone the width of the spine (10 units). Name this bone **Collar**. Reposition the pivots of these bones so that they lie on the end of the spine (see fig. 8.16).

FIGURE 8.16

Positioning of the shoulder and collar bones. The shoulders should pivot along the edge of the bone closest to the collar bone.

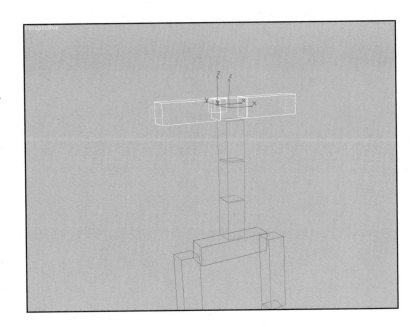

Having two separate bones will help your character shrug its shoulders and such, and will also help you create more natural arm motions. One long shoulder bone can work for simple characters who do not need to perform these types of actions. If all your character does is walk, the extra bone may not be necessary.

9. Copy the leg bones and rotate them 180 degrees to make the right arm. Position these just outside the shoulders. Name these two bones **R-Bicep** and **R-Forearm**. Copy these two to the left side of the body and name those bones **L-Bicep** and **L-Forearm**.

10. You now can link the hand hierarchy to the ends of the arms. If your hands are separate objects, link those in. In this case, use a dummy object as a stand-in for a hand that can be added in later. Name these objects **L-HandDummy** and **R-HandDummy**. Compare your results to figure 8.17.

11. Copy a spine bone and use it to create a neck. Name this bone **Neck**.

12. Many animators like to keep the head as a separate object. If this is the case, just link the head to the neck. In this example, a sphere will stand in for the head. Name this object **Head**.

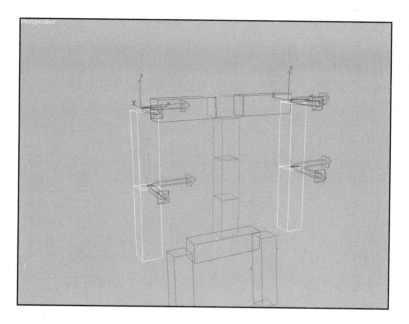

If your body and head are one seamless mesh, the facial animation method must be considered. If you are using bones to animate the face, these bones can be linked into the hierarchy for the rest of the body. If you are using direct manipulation tools such as linked XForms, you will need to link the XForms to the body in some fashion—usually by linking them hierarchically to a dummy, which in turn is linked to the neck.

With some facial animation methods you actually use two heads, one of which is actually attached to the body. The first head contains Bones or linked XForms used to actually animate the shape of the face. The second head is simply a referenced clone of the first and is the one actually attached to the body. Animation performed on the first head is reflected on the second. This allows you to attach a head to the body that is free of helper objects, such as bones, that also need to be attached. The first head can then be placed out of camera range and animated.

13. Finally, create the feet. If your character is barefoot and needs to wiggle its toes, you may need to construct a complete skeleton for the feet, but this hardly ever happens. Most characters wear shoes and toe wiggling is not a common action, so you can simplify the feet with two bones—one for the foot and one for the toes. Name these bones **R-Heel** and **R-Toe**. Copy these two to the left leg and rename the copies **L-Heel** and **L-Toe**. Compare your final result against figure 8.18.

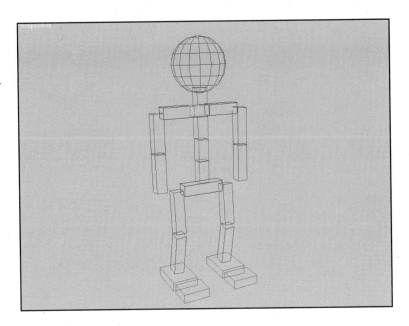

Methods for Linking the Bones Together

After the skeleton is in place, the bones must be linked together into a hierarchy. This speeds animation and enables you to use IK. How the hierarchy is constructed depends on the character and the requirements of the animation.

For a two-legged character, the hierarchy is always centered around the hips in some manner. The hips are the center of the body's weight distribution, and they are where the upper body, supported by the spine, connects to the legs. How the hips are connected to the legs is one of the central questions that you must ask. The hip-centric places the hips at the top of the hierarchy with the legs and spine as children. Other methods break the hierarchy at the hips and keep each of the legs as separate hierarchies.

Hip Centric

By far the most common is a simple hierarchical linkage that uses the hips as the base of the hierarchy.

A hip-centric hierarchy (see fig. 8.19) is the best way to keep the body so that it moves as one. It is also the best method to set up a skeleton for IK.

SETTING UP A HIERARCHY FOR A HIP-CENTRIC HUMAN BODY

1. To link the legs to the hips: On the right side of the body, link the toes to the feet, the feet to the shins, the shins to the thighs, and the thighs to the hips. Repeat for the left side.

2. To link the spinal column together: Link the head to the neck, and the neck to the top of the spine. Link all the spinal joints, top to bottom, and finally the base of the spine to the hips.

3. Link the forearm to the bicep, the bicep to the shoulder, and the shoulder to the top of the spine. Repeat for the left side.

4. Save the model.

FIGURE 8.19
The hip-centric hierarchy has the hips as the parent with the legs and spine as children.

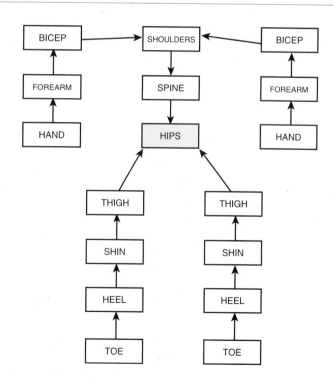

Broken Hierarchies

Using the broken hierarchies method typically turns the hierarchy of the legs upside down, making the toes the parents of the feet, which parent the legs (see fig. 8.20). Because an object can't have two parents, the hierarchy must be broken at the hips. This gives you a total of three chains to work with: one for each leg and one for the upper body, starting with the hips.

FIGURE 8.20

The broken hierarchy has three separate chains, one for the hips and spine, and one each for the legs.

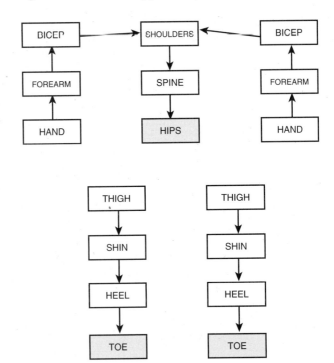

Another thing you need to do when setting up this type of hierarchy is to reverse the pivots of all the leg bones. In a hip-centric hierarchy, the thigh pivots at the hip. In a broken hierarchy, the thigh pivots at the knee, the shin at the ankle, and so on.

The broken hierarchy method is certainly the exception rather than the rule, but it works great if you want to avoid setting up IK for a skeleton. Because the hips are not connected, they must be animated so that they "float" above the legs, which invariably causes some gaps between the joints, and it is best used for skeletons that deform a mesh (because those skeletons are ultimately hidden). It can also be used for characters where the hips are hidden—a character in a dress, for example. Another caveat is that a broken hierarchy may cause problems with single mesh characters and Physique because that plug-in relies on the hierarchy to determine how the mesh is deformed.

TIP

One easy way to get the hips to line up in a broken hierarchy is to create a dummy object linked to the tops of each thigh and add two more to each end of the hips. The dummies on the hips can then be linked to the ones on the thighs by using Bind Position in the IK rollout. This will enable you to move the legs, and the hips will automatically float between them.

Setting Up and Controlling IK

After the hierarchy is in place, you can actually turn on IK and manipulate the skeleton. Doing so, however, invariably makes the skeleton go haywire because, by default, all the joints are completely unconstrained. Without constraints, the IK system comes up with multiple solutions for each joint's position, making the model very hard to control.

To keep the model under control, you first need to limit the actions of the joints so that they rotate naturally and that the solutions generated by the IK system are regular and predictable. The elbow only bends along one axis, for example, so limiting the other two axes so that they don't move will give you a more predictable motion. This is done by setting the rotational limits for each joint.

WARNING

One strong warning needs to be given at this point. MAX's IK does not like any objects created or modified using non-uniform scale at the object level, or mirror, or mirrored clones. Be sure to avoid these religiously when modeling objects intended to be used in IK chains.

TIP

By default all objects are free to rotate in all three axes. If you set an axis constraint for the first bone at the start of the skeleton building process (say x-only) before you start cloning all the bones, IK can be much faster to set up.

Setting Rotational Limits

Rotational limits are found on the IK panel under Rotational Limits. Each axis (X, Y, and Z) has parameters that can be set. Most of these are discussed in *Inside 3D Studio MAX Volume I*. Table 8.1 lists suggested joint parameters for this skeleton. In the table, it is assumed that the Y axis of each joint runs along the length of the bone. Joints with limits of zero can be set inactive.

TABLE **8.1**

Rotational Limits for a Generic Hip-Centric Human Skeleton

Joint	X	Y	Z
Hips	0–0	0–0	0–0
L-Thigh	-90–20	0–30	0–15
L-Shin	0–125	0–0	0–0
L-Heel	-115– -60	0–0	0–0
L-Toe	-40–10	0–0	0–0
R-Thigh	-90–20	0–30	0–15
R-Shin	0–125	0–0	0–0
R-Heel	-115– -60	0–0	0–0
R-Toe	-40–10	0–0	0–0
L-Shoulder	0–0	-6–12	-20–10
L-Bicep	-140–45	0–0	0–180
L-Forearm	-135–0	0–0	0–0
R-Shoulder	0–0	-6–12	-20–10
R-Bicep	-140–45	0–0	0–180
R-Forearm	-135–0	0–0	0–0
Spine-01	-5–10	0–0	0–0
Spine-02	-5–10	0–0	0–0
Spine-03	-5–10	0–0	0–0
Collar	0–0	0–0	0–0

Terminating IK Chains

Rotational limits, however, are only the first step. You also need to terminate some of the chains to further refine the motion. If you pull on the hand, for example, it is usually to position the arm only. The hierarchy of the arm, however, runs through the shoulder to the spine and down to the hips. Without terminating the chain at the shoulder, moving the hand would invoke an IK solution in every joint between the hand and the hips. This would likely cause your skeleton to go haywire again.

The Terminator button can help prevent this from happening. This button enables you to dictate which joints are calculated in an IK chain. The arm, for example, should be terminated at the shoulder to prevent hand motion from affecting the spine (see fig. 8.21). Terminating each chain in the skeleton makes it much easier to control the behavior of the skeleton. The joint that terminates the chain is the one immediately above the chain you want to constrain. The arm is terminated at the shoulder; the legs are terminated at the hips. See figure 8.22.

FIGURE 8.21

Positioning an arm without termination affects the entire upper body.

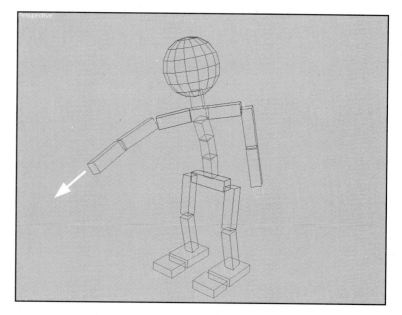

FIGURE 8.22
With the shoulder set as the terminator, only the arm itself is affected, giving you more control over how it is posed.

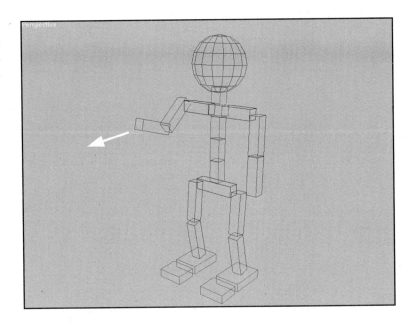

To set termination, simply select the joint you would like to affect, in this case the shoulder; go to the IK panel and toggle the Terminate button on. Once toggled, all IK calculations will stop at the chosen joint. In a hip-centric hierarchy, the spine and legs are naturally terminated at the hips, which, as the top of the hierarchy, are also the end of the chain. This makes the hip bone a natural terminator.

Creating Handles

Handles are an aid to help you simplify the task of animating a skeleton. Typically, they are dummy objects linked into the skeleton at critical points, such as the ends of the toes, fingers, ankles, and so on. The most important place to put these is at the ends of a chain (at the toe, for example). If the toe itself is dragged, IK will not change its angle (to be specific, the toe itself is a handle) (see fig. 8.23). For the toe to be included in the solution, a dummy object must be placed beyond the end of the toe and used as an effector, or, more generically, a handle (see fig. 8.24).

FIGURE 8.23

Pulling the toe flexes the leg, but does not enable the toe itself to flex.

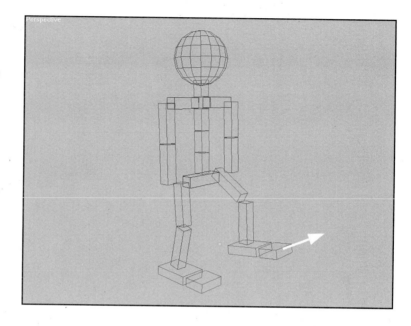

FIGURE 8.24

A dummy object placed at the end of the toe (shown in white) becomes a handle, enabling the toe to flex.

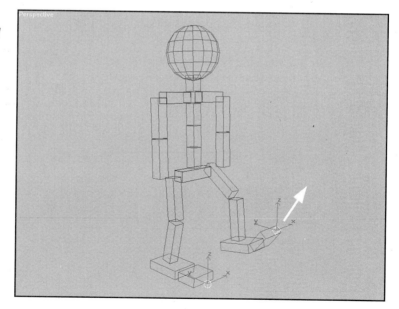

Effectors placed beyond the end of the chain are also very important when using Physique because this plug-in relies on the hierarchy to determine how a mesh is affected. Physique requires that the hierarchy extend one joint beyond the end of the mesh. If the hierarchy stops at the toe, Physique only affects vertices up to, but not including, the toe area.

To further refine the skeleton, you can insert a handle inside the hierarchy to act both as a terminator and as a handle. Again, a good example is the foot. The hips, being the root of the hierarchy, act as a terminator for the leg chain. If a handle at the end of the toe is moved, IK will have to solve for the toe, the heel, the shin, and the thigh. Four joints in the chain increase the possibility of multiple solutions and reduce the amount of control you have over the leg. Using extra dummies in the hierarchy can also allow more complex ranges of motion (the shoulder for example) so that limits can change when certain angles are met.

Introducing a second dummy into the hierarchy between the ankle and the shin (see fig. 8.25) enables it to act as a terminator for the foot. This way, pulling the toe now only affects the toe and the heel. This second dummy can also be used as a handle to manipulate the shin and the thigh. Breaking the leg into discrete IK segments with handles gives you more control. The only objects that need to be animated are the handles, not the actual geometry of the skeleton itself (though this is certainly possible). You can also add such handles at the shoulders and at the spine.

FIGURE 8.25

A handle (shown in white) inserted into the hierarchy between the foot and the leg.

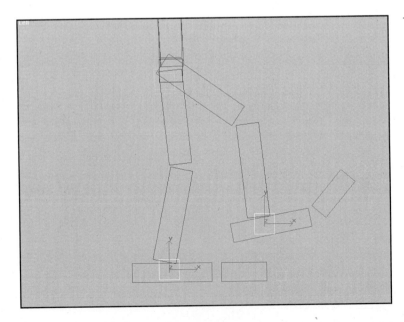

TIP

When placing a handle inside a hierarchy, it is important to set all IK rotation limits to zero (or deactivate them). This way, the dummy will remain fixed in relation to its parent. If it is allowed to rotate, the rotation limits for the lower joint (in this case, the heel) will become skewed.

Testing a Skeleton

The easiest way to test a skeleton is to manipulate it through a wide range of motion. If you have created handles for all the major points of the skeleton, these should be the only objects that need to be animated (see fig. 8.26). To make it easier to select a handle, freeze the bones of the skeleton, leaving only the handles active.

FIGURE 8.26

Typical placement of handles for a human skeleton.

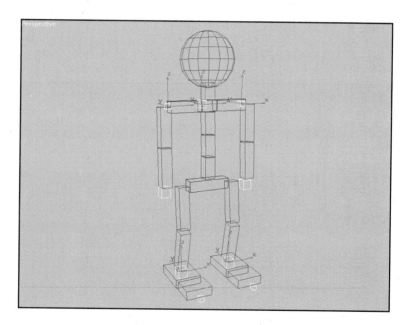

After this is done, manipulating the skeleton is a simple matter of turning on IK, selecting the appropriate handle, and moving it. To fine tune an animation, however, you may need to go back to some joints, such as the hands or feet, and fine tune joint rotations as needed.

The finished skeleton is located in a file named ik-skel.max on the accompanying CD.

Skeletons for Hands

Hands are one of the most complex parts of the human body. A hand has dozens of bones, muscles, and tendons covered with a pliable skin that bends and flexes. Modeling and setting up a skeleton for a hand so that it animates well presents a daunting task.

Construction of the Skeleton

Placement of the bones for the fingers is fairly obvious. Each finger has three joints, and each joint requires a bone. If you want to set up IK for a finger, you need to add a dummy object as the end effector for each finger chain. The upper two joints of the fingers should have their rotations constrained to one axis only. The lowest joint of the finger, however, can also move along a second axis, enabling the fingers to spread.

The palm and the thumb are another matter. The palm of the hand contains many bones, enabling the hand to flex enough so that the thumb can touch the pinky. (If the palm were rigid, this couldn't occur.)

One way to allow for this motion is to model a separate bone through the palm for each finger. If such flexibility is not needed, the palm can be represented by a single bone (perhaps a box).

Another situation involves the knuckle, over which the skin stretches when the fingers curl under the palm. Accurately simulating this stretching motion can be difficult, even with advanced tools such as Physique. Adding knuckle bones to the hand hierarchy can help the situation by giving Physique (and Bones Pro) an extra bone to help define the outline of the hand (see figs. 8.27 and 8.28).

Though only two joints are visible on the thumb, a third joint exists within the body of the palm. This joint enables the thumb to move above and below the plane of the hand, giving humans their opposable thumbs.

FIGURE 8.27

A simple skeleton for the hand uses a box as the basis for the palm.

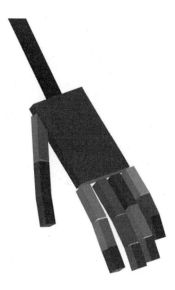

FIGURE 8.28

Adding separate palm bones for each finger gives the hand more flexibility.

Attaching a Hand to the Arm

To attach a hand to the skeleton, the hand hierarchy can be linked to the wrist. One good tactic is to place a dummy inside the hierarchy between the palm and the wrist. This dummy can act as a handle to manipulate the arm and also as a terminator for the hand hierarchy.

Using Reference Objects to Animate a Hand

One problem when manipulating a hand is getting a good view of the hand and its exact pose. Posing a hand can require some very delicate fine tuning, requiring a clear, close-up view of it. Unfortunately, the hand itself can move over a large range if the arms are in motion, which makes it difficult to maintain a clear view of what your character's hands are doing. There are a number of way to keep an eye on the hands, so to speak.

One method is to make a referenced clone of the entire hand, with an instancing of the controller so that both the clone and the original animate in perfect sync (see figs. 8.29 and 8.30). This means that changes to hand #1 are mirrored on the other. The copy can then be placed in front of a camera and posed quite easily. You can find an example of these hands in the file refhand.max on the accompanying CD.

FIGURE 8.29

Make a clone of the hand by setting Object Reference and Controller Instance on.

FIGURE 8.30

When created in this manner, changes to one hand skeleton affect the other.

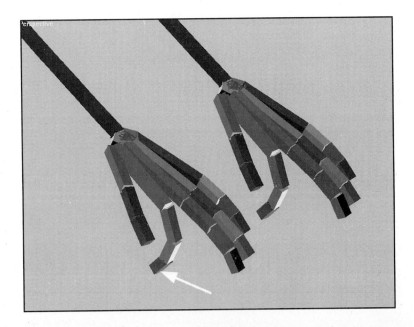

Unfortunately, this form of manipulation does not work on the hands attached to a biped because cloning the hand of the biped clones the entire skeleton. In this case, it is probably best to lock a camera directly on each of the biped's hands.

Create a target camera slightly above the biped's hand, with the target residing on the hand itself. Hierarchically link both the camera and target to the palm (see fig. 8.31). When the hand moves, the camera moves as well, keeping the hand centered in the camera's viewport. Because the camera's target is centered on the palm, the camera can be orbited around the hand at will to get a bird's eye view wherever the hand may be. This method not only works for bipeds, but for any type of character. It works quite well for facial animation, too.

FIGURE 8.31

The camera is locked to the biped's hand by linking it and the target to the biped's palm.

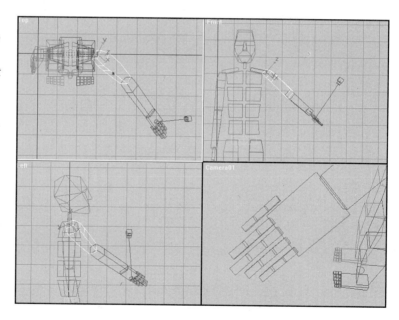

To see a biped with a camera locked to the hand, open camlock.max on the accompanying CD.

In Practice: Setting Up Characters for Animation

- **Building Solid Mesh Characters.** A character needs extra detail at the joints, such as the knees and elbows. This extra detail enables the joints to bend smoothly and realistically. Areas that don't flex, such as the part of the thigh and shin outside the knee, can be spared extra detail.

■ **Using MAX Bones.** Remember to turn on IK when manipulating bones; otherwise, they will change their length. If you want to move the chain as a whole, you can always select the entire bone structure and, with IK off, move it without affecting the shape.

■ **Fitting Skeletons.** When building a skeleton, it is a good idea to load your target mesh and freeze it. This allows you to use it as a guide for creating and fitting the bones of the skeleton so they match up with the mesh.

■ **Limiting Joints.** The key to limiting joints is keeping the chain short enough so that the chain follows a predictable motion. This can be accomplished not only through setting joint limits, but also by using dummy objects as terminators and handles.

IMAGE CREATED BY GEORGE MAESTRI

Chapter 9

by George Maestri

ANIMATING WALKING

A character's walk conveys a great deal about its personality. The next time you are in a crowded place, notice all the different types of walks that people have. Some people waddle, others saunter, and some drag their feet. It is amazing how almost everyone you see has a unique walk. Mae West, Groucho Marx, John Wayne, and Charlie Chaplin were all characters who had very distinctive walks. If you want to know who a character is, figure out how that character walks.

This chapter covers the following topics:

- The mechanics of walking
- Animating a two-legged walk
- Creating a four-legged walk
- Creating a six-legged walk

The Mechanics of Walking

Walking has been described as controlled falling. Every time someone takes a step, he or she actually leans forward and falls slightly, only to be caught by his or her outstretched foot. After a foot touches the ground, the body's weight is transferred to it, and the knee bends to absorb the shock. The leg then lifts the body and propels it forward as the opposite leg swings up to catch the body again, and the cycle repeats.

Walks are very complex. Not only do the feet have to move across the ground, but the hips, spine, arms, shoulders, and head all move in sync to maintain balance in the system. Though complex, if you break down each of these movements joint by joint, the mechanics of walking become clear.

The Feet and Legs

The feet and legs propel the body forward. To keep your character looking natural, you should always keep the joints bent slightly, even at full leg extension. An animated walk usually starts where the feet are fully extended and farthest apart—this is the point where the character's weight shifts to the forward foot (see fig. 9.1).

As the weight of the body is transferred to the forward foot, the knee bends to absorb the shock. This is called the *recoil* position and is the lowest point in the walk (see fig. 9.2)

FIGURE 9.1

The walk usually starts with the feet at the extended position— where the feet are farthest apart.

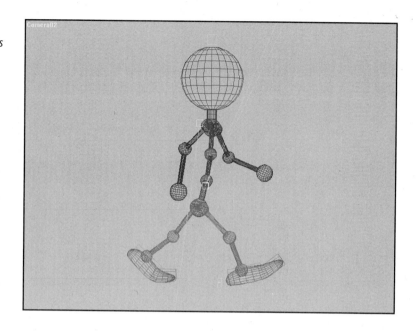

FIGURE 9.2

When the foot plants, the knee bends to absorb the shock.

This is halfway through the first step. As the character moves forward, the knee straightens and lifts the body to its highest point. This is called the *passing* position because this is where the free foot passes the supporting leg (see fig. 9.3).

FIGURE 9.3

As one foot passes the other, the knee straightens to full extension, lifting the body.

As the character moves forward, the weight-bearing foot lifts off the ground at the heel, transmitting the force to the ball of the foot. The body starts to fall forward now. The free foot swings forward like a pendulum to catch the ground (see fig. 9.4).

The free leg makes contact. Half the cycle has been completed (see fig. 9.5). The second half is an exact mirror of the first. If it differs, the character may appear to limp.

The Hips, Spine, and Shoulders

The body's center of gravity is at the hips—all balance starts there, as does the rest of the body's motion. During a walk, it is best to think of the hips' motion as two separate, overlapping rotations. First, the hips rotate along the axis of the spine, forward and back with the legs. If the right leg is forward, the right hip is rotated forward as well. Second, at the passing position, the free leg pulls the hip out of center, forcing the hips to rock from side to side. These two motions are then transmitted through the spine to the shoulders, which mirror the hips to maintain balance.

When the feet are fully extended, the hips must rotate along the axis of the spine. To keep balance, the shoulders swing in the opposite direction. From the front, the spine is relatively straight. From the top, however, you can see how the hips and shoulders twist in opposite directions to maintain balance (see fig. 9.6).

FIGURE 9.6

From the top, the rotation of the hips and shoulders are apparent.

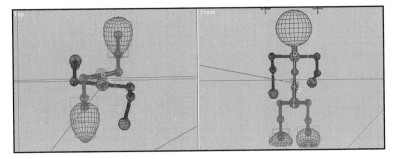

At the passing position, the front view shows the hip being pulled out of center by the weight of the free leg, which causes a counter-rotation in the shoulders. From the top, however, the hips and shoulders are nearly equal angles (see fig. 9.7).

FIGURE 9.7

As one leg passes the other, the hips are even when viewed from above, skewed when viewed from the front.

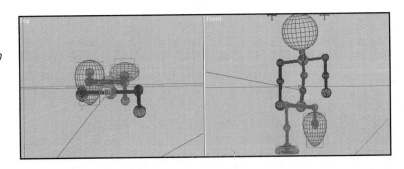

At the extension of the second leg, the hips and shoulders again are flat when viewed from the front. From the top, however, you can see the rotation of the hips and shoulders has completed (see fig. 9.8).

FIGURE 9.8
When the weight shifts from one foot to the other, the hips are again twisted when viewed from above, even when viewed from the front.

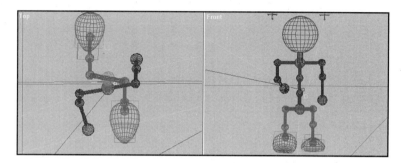

The Arms

Unless the character is using its arms, they generally hang loose at the sides. In this case, they tend to act like pendulums, dragging a few frames behind the hips and shoulders. If the character is running, the arms may pump quite a bit and lead the action by a few frames. Even at full extension, the arms should be slightly bent at the elbows. This keeps them looking natural.

The Head

In a standard walk, the head generally tries to stay level, with the eyes focused on where the character is going. It will then bob around slightly to stay balanced. If a character is excited, this bobbing will be more pronounced. The head may also hang low for a sad character or may look around if the scene requires it.

Body Posture and Emotion

The character's body posture changes, depending on the character's mood. A happy character arches his back and juts out his chest proudly and swings the arms jauntily (see fig. 9.9), whereas a sad character slumps over, barely swings his arms, and hangs his head low (see fig. 9.10). If a character is running scared, he may lean forward quite a bit and push his arms out in front of him, trying to escape the danger (see fig. 9.11). A character who is sneaking around may walk on tiptoe while keeping his hands at the ready (see fig. 9.12). These postures translate beyond walking and should also be used as examples for portraying emotion in non-locomotive scenes.

FIGURE 9.9

A happy character arches his back and sticks out his chest proudly.

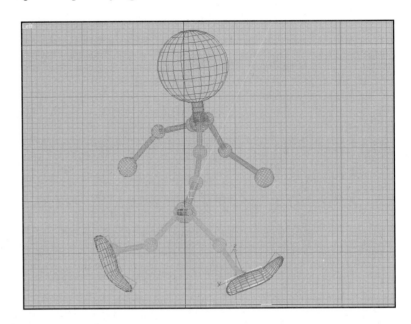

FIGURE 9.10

A sad character hangs his head low and slumps over.

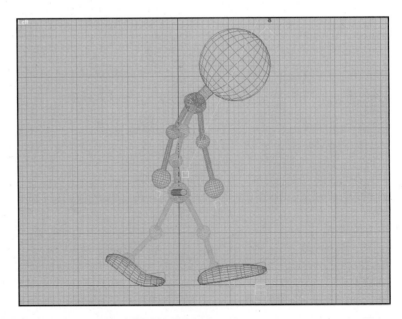

FIGURE 9.11
A character who is running scared leans forward to get away from the danger.

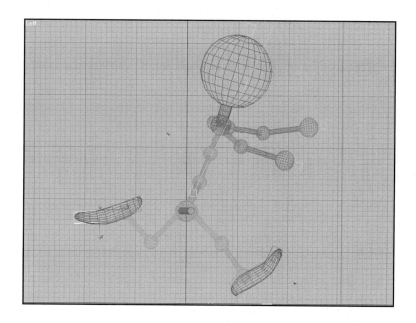

FIGURE 9.12
A sneaky character may walk on tiptoes.

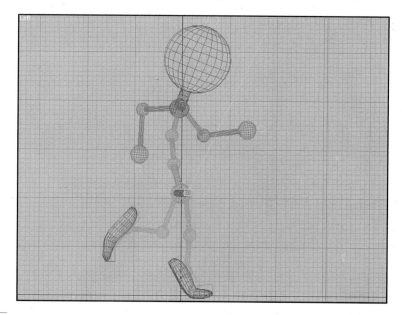

Walk Cycles

Because walking is a cyclical motion, it may behoove the animator to create walking motion as a cycle rather than as straight ahead-animation. If done properly, a cycle can save an inordinate amount of animation time. It can also be applied to a number of different environments, creating a library of motions (perfect for video games).

The use of cycles does, however, have its downside. First, because the cycle is repetitive, it can seem sterile and homogenous, particularly when viewed for an extended period of time. Second, cycles work best on flat terrain. If your character has to walk around a corner or over a hill, the cycle might not match up properly.

Animating a cycle is similar to making your character walk on a treadmill. The body does not move forward—the feet just move beneath it. To maintain the illusion of walking, the entire character must be moved across the ground (or the ground moved past the character) at the exact same rate as the feet are moving. Otherwise, the character's feet will appear to slip. Also, the foot on the ground needs to move the exact same distance on each frame. Not doing this will again cause the feet to slip.

Animating a Walk

With the introduction of Biped, animating a basic walk in 3DS MAX has been reduced to a few simple mouse clicks. Although Biped has become a preferred method for animating walks, it is still entirely possible to animate convincing walks by using basic MAX tools. Also, to truly understand a walk, it is a very good exercise to animate several walks from scratch.

An Animated Walk Cycle

A cycled walk is one of the easier walks to construct. Because walks are repetitive, the first two steps are all that need to be animated; the rest can be duplicated from there. The cycle can also be used as the basis for the cycles and actions used in video game environments. Of course, no two steps are exactly alike, so if possible, make the cycle several steps long and adjust the keys on each step to give the walk a subtle bit of variety, as well as added life.

The following exercise is a good method for producing an animated walk cycle.

CREATING AN ANIMATED WALK CYCLE

1. Load the skeleton you created in Chapter 8. A version of this appears on the accompanying CD-ROM in the file called ik-skel.max in the Chapter 9 folder.

2. This walk cycle is timed at 16 frames per step. At 30 fps, this averages out to approximately one half second per step. Go to the Time Configuration dialog box and set the Animation Length to 32 frames, plus one extra frame for the first frame of the next cycle (see fig. 9.13). This extra frame is not rendered, but helps the cycle repeat smoothly.

FIGURE 9.13

The Time Configuration dialog box.

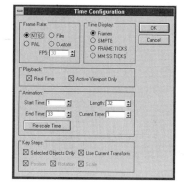

It is best to start such a walk with the hips because all other motions derive from the hips. The hips have two separate, overlapping rotations mirrored by the shoulders. The first rotation is along the vertical axis of the spine and follows the position of the legs and feet.

3. Start the walk with the right foot. This means the right hip must go forward as well. On frame 1, rotate the hips around the axis of the spine so that the right side of the hip bone is forward by 10 degrees. From the top view, rotate the collar bone so the shoulders mirror this rotation in the opposite direction (see fig. 9.14).

FIGURE 9.14

In the Top viewport, you can see the rotation of the hips and shoulders match the back and forth motion of the legs.

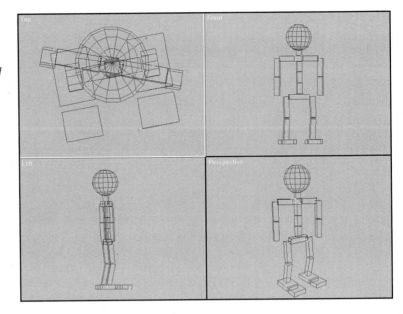

4. Go to the halfway point (frame 17) in the cycle and rotate the hips and collar bones in the opposite direction.

5. Open Track View. Find the rotation keys for the hips and collar. Copy the keys on frame 1 to frame 33 by shift-clicking and dragging. Scrub the animation to make certain that the motions are even.

6. Create the sway of the hips. Go to the frame in the middle of the first step (frame 9). If your rotations are correct, the hips and shoulders should be parallel when viewed from the top. This is the passing position, or the highest leg extension. At this point, the body rests on the right leg, whereas the left pulls the hips out of center. From the Front viewport, rotate the hips 5 degrees around the Z axis so that the right hip is higher (see fig. 9.15). Adjust the spine and shoulders so that you get a smooth line of action and the shoulders mirror the hips.

7. Go to the middle frame of the second step (frame 25) and reverse the rotations. The body rests on the left leg at this point, and the spine curves in the opposite direction.

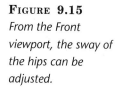

FIGURE 9.15
From the Front viewport, the sway of the hips can be adjusted.

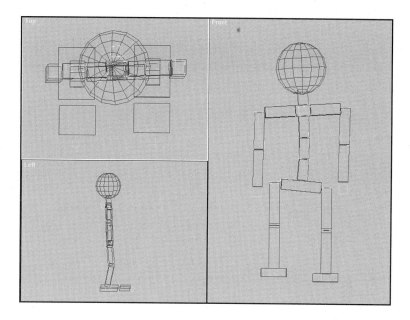

8. At this point, the spinal bones (Spine01–Spine03) will have keys only at frames 9 and 25. Go to frame 1 and, within the Motion tab, create a rotation key for each of the spinal bones. From within Track View, locate these rotation keys located on frame 1 and copy them to frame 33 to complete the cycle. Scrub the animation to check it for smoothness.

9. Go back to each keyframe and add rotation keys to the legs and arms so that they hang vertically and the toes point forward throughout the cycle.

10. The hips also bob up and down during a walk. The lowest point in the walk occurs at the recoil position. In this animation, this is at frame 5. Go to frame 5 and move the hips down slightly (about 4 units in this case). The highest point occurs at the passing position. In this animation, it is at frame 9. Go to that frame and move the hips up (about 6 units above the position at frame 5). Within Track View, copy the keys for frames 1, 5, and 9 to frame 17, 21, and 25, respectively. Copy the key at frame 11 to frame 33 to complete the cycle. Scrub the animation to check it for smoothness.

On the accompanying CD, the file hips-sho.max shows the motion of just the hips and shoulders.

Animating the Legs

How the legs are animated depends to some degree on personal preference. MAX's Inverse Kinematics is one good solution, but Forward Kinematics is often overlooked and is also a valid method. MAX's IK solves the joint motion as rotations and actually places rotation keys into Track View, much like keyframing by hand with Forward Kinematics. This makes it entirely possible to block in the character's broad motions by using IK and then going back over the scene, tweaking the joint rotations with Forward Kinematics.

Using IK to Lock the Ankles to an Elliptical Path

For a cycle, the first method is to lock the ankles to an elliptical path, which enables you to let MAX's IK control the rotation of the legs. The feet, however, remain free and able to rotate.

LOCKING THE ANKLES TO THE ELLIPTICAL PATH

1. First, draw a spline curve similar to that shown in figure 9.16. The curve should start at the front bottom, run back along the ground, and arch over on the return. The section along the ground should be completely flat and the curve needs to have an equal number of segments along the flat part of the path as the curved part. Duplicate this curve. Place one curve over each foot.

2. Create a dummy object. Go to the Motion panel and assign a Path Controller to the dummy. Within the Path Parameters rollout, click on Pick Path. Select the right path. Create another dummy and assign it to the left path in the same way.

3. Select the handle at the skeleton's right ankle. In the IK panel, select Bind Position. Under Bind to Follow Object, press the Bind button. Click on the right ankle's handle and bind the handle to the dummy object. Repeat the procedure for the left side.

4. Select both of the handles at the ankles. In the IK panel, press the Apply IK button. This solves the rotations for the leg joints and places rotation keys within Track View for every frame of the cycle. Go into Track View and observe the tracks for the thighs and shins.

FIGURE 9.16

Create two spline paths, such as this (highlighted in white), and place them over the feet.

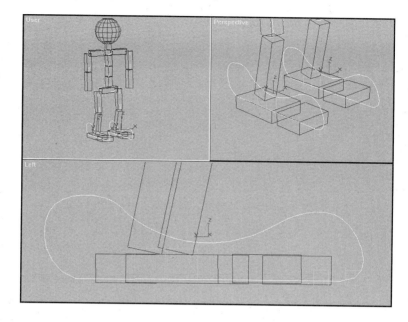

5. Play the animation. The legs will now follow the path. Unfortunately, both legs move in sync, making the skeleton look like it is hopping. This occurs because both paths start at the same point.

6. Select the left path. Under the Modify panel, select the Edit Spline modifier. Under Sub-Object, select Vertex. This shows the vertices that comprise the spline, with the first vertex indicated by a small box. This needs to be offset by exactly 180 degrees. Select the vertex exactly opposite the first vertex and press the Make First button under the Edit Vertex rollout.

7. Select both of the handles at the ankles again and press the Apply IK button. Play the animation. The legs will now appear to walk. If the legs lock or are not quite fully extended, you may use the Edit Spline modifier to adjust the shape or positioning of the paths.

8. Go through the animation and adjust the feet so that they remain flat against the ground while planted and the toes don't scrape the ground while passing.

9. After this is done, the paths are no longer needed. Pressing the Apply IK button in step 7 resolved all the IK tasks to explicit joint rotations. If you so desire, delete the paths and the dummies.

An example of the elliptical path method is found in the file pathwalk.max on the accompanying CD.

Using Guides to Keyframe a Walk Cycle

The path method as previously outlined is a very easy method, but the walk can be keyframed manually by using Inverse Kinematics, Forward Kinematics, or a combination of both. The entire process can be simplified by using a simple box as a guide to help place the feet. In addition to animating a cycle, IK and Forward Kinematics can also be used to keyframe a straight-ahead walk that does not cycle—just move the hips forward at the same constant rate as the feet.

KEYFRAMING A WALK CYCLE

1. First, create the first extreme pose. Turn on IK. Using the Left viewport, go to frame 1 and make the first pose by dragging the handles on the feet into place. You do this by turning on IK and pulling the handle into place, which creates rotation keys for the joints in the chain. If you so desire, you can rotate the joints manually to achieve the same effect, or use a combination of the two methods.

   Regardless of the way in which the pose is achieved, the legs are now at maximum extension (see fig. 9.17). Copy these keys to the end of the cycle (frame 33). Next, go to the middle of the cycle (frame 17) and mirror this pose with the left leg forward.

2. To aid in the animation process, create a guide to help position the feet (see fig. 9.18). To create the guide, model a simple box the length of the stride and place it directly beneath the feet, with the edges of the box at the balls of the toes. This box acts as a guide for the stride length.

FIGURE 9.17
The first frame of the animation has the legs at full extension.

FIGURE 9.18
This guide (highlighted in white) is aligned on its leading edge with the character's forward foot and also indicates the stride length.

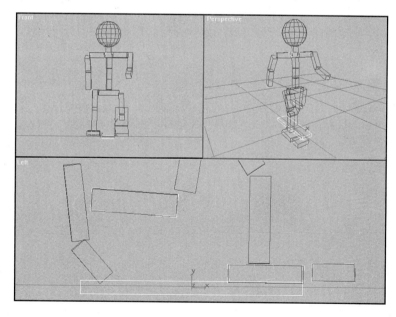

3. Go to the middle of the cycle (frame 17) and position the guide to the exact same place on the toe as in frame 1. Set the guide so that it inbetweens these two positions at a linear rate. This is done within the Key Info rollout within the Motion panel. With a linear inbetween, the guide will now tell you exactly where the toe needs be at any point in the first step.

4. One quarter of the way through the first step on frame 5 is the recoil position—where the leg absorbs the shock and the hips reach their lowest point. Adjust the foot so that it remains even with the guide.

5. Halfway through the first step, at frame 9, the body recoils upward into the passing position. The hips are at the highest point, meaning that the planted foot is fairly well extended. Again, adjust this leg so that the foot rests even with the guide. It is very important to keep the knee bent slightly to make the action look natural.

6. Three quarters of the way through the first step, at frame 13, the weight of the body is on the ball of the foot. The heel lifts off the floor as the body falls forward. The hips are moving down at this point. There can also be problems with the free foot as it swings forward. If the character has extra-big shoes, they will hit the floor unless you bend the toes slightly.

This completes the first step. Create a second guide and repeat these procedures for the left foot on the second half of the cycle. Be careful to make the second half as close to the first as possible. Render a test and go back to tweak any inconsistencies.

Animating the Arms

No matter how the legs were animated, it is still necessary to create the motion of the arms and head. In the simplest case, the arms swing back and forth to maintain balance in opposition to the legs. The arms also drag behind the action a bit, making the arm's extreme poses a few frames behind the legs.

1. Using the same ik-skel.max model, grab the handles on the arms and pull them into the position on frame 1 (see fig. 9.19). Because the right leg is forward on this frame, the right arm will be back, the left arm forward. This is not an extreme pose, but it's close.

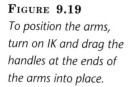

FIGURE 9.19

To position the arms, turn on IK and drag the handles at the ends of the arms into place.

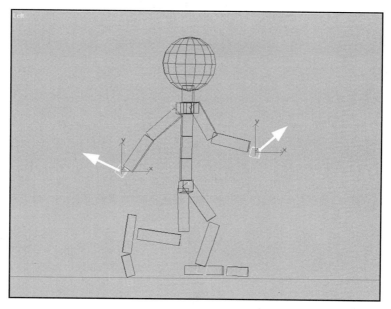

2. Go to frame 5 and set the arm's extreme pose. On the left arm, pull the handle or rotate the forearm back to a nice extension. On the right, pull the forearm up slightly.

3. Go to frame 21 and mirror the extreme from the previous step (on frame 5). Finally, copy the keys on frame 1 to the last frame so the arm will swing through to the end of the cycle. Scrub the cycle and check for smoothness, or render a test.

An example of this walk is on the accompanying CD as walkcycle.max.

Moving the Cycled Character

Now that the cycle is animated convincingly, it is time to get the character off the treadmill and out into the world. This may be as simple as rendering the animation as a sprite for a video game or passing the rotational data to a 3D game engine. You can also move the character by creating an environment within 3DS MAX.

You can move the skeleton through the environment in two ways: by moving the character past the ground, or by moving the ground past the character. Moving the ground is best when you want to use a panning camera locked on the character. Because the character is still, the camera can remain still as well. Moving the character is best in cases when you want the camera stable and the character to walk past.

Calculating the Stride Length

In either example, the character or ground needs to move at a constant rate. This rate can be calculated quite easily. Load the file walkcycle.max and follow along.

walkcycle.max is used as a guide to assist in the animation. Find the absolute position of the guide (Box01) on frame 1, and then again when it stops in the middle of the cycle (frame 16). This is done by opening Track View and looking at the keyframe data for Box01 and doing a little math.

In this case, the guide moves along Y from -10.8 to 82.0 over 16 frames, which works out to 92.8 units for one stride. Dividing by the number of frames gives $92.8 \div 16 = 5.8$ units per frame.

T I P

If an elliptical path is used to drive the legs, the stride length can be calculated by using the Tape object, found under the helper buttons in the Create panel. Set the Time Slider to frame 1 and measure the distance from toe tip to toe tip. Divide this by the number of frames for a stride (16 in this case) to get the same figure.

This number (5.8 units÷frame) is exactly how far the character or the ground needs to move on each frame. If the cycle is replicated four times for a 128 frame animation, this means the character travels 5.8 units÷frame×128 frames = 742.4 units.

Duplicating the Cycle in Track View

To cycle the animation four times, it is just a matter of increasing the length of the animation to 128 frames and copying all the keys for each joint four times. This will create explicit keys for the animation. If you want a strict repeat, with no modification of the keys, you could use the Cycle or Loop function in Out of Range parameters to get a nice repetition. Copying the keys is more flexible because it allows them to be edited individually, should the need arise.

CYCLE DUPLICATION

1. Activate the Time Configuration dialog box and change the length of the animation so that it runs from frame 1 to 129.

2. Activate Track View. Press the Filters button and check Animated Tracks Only. Right-click on the Hips object and select Expand All to bring up all the keys (quite a large number).

3. Select all the keys from frame 1 to 33, which is done by holding down the Ctrl key while clicking and dragging over the keys to select them.

4. After the keys are selected, hold down the Shift key and click on one of the keys. Drag the mouse to the right and the keys will clone themselves. Place the clones from frame 1 at frame 33 and release the mouse. The frames have been copied. Repeat this twice more to create four full cycles.

Play back the animation and watch for any glitches in the transitions between steps.

Moving the Ground to Match

After the cycle has been duplicated, the ground can now be moved to match the footstep rate. To do so, follow these steps:

1. Select the object named Ground, which is a simple patch grid that needs to be moved at a constant rate to match the calculated rate of the character. In the preceding section, this rate was calculated at 5.8 units per frame, or 742.4 units for 128 frames.

2. Set the Time Slider to frame 1. Open the Motion panel and press Create Key/Position. Move to the last frame and press Create Key/Position again.

3. Go back to frame 1. In the Key Info rollout, set the In and Out ramps to linear. In the Y-Value spinner, set the position to –371.2 units. (This number is half of the required distance of 742.4 units.)

4. Go to the last frame and repeat this procedure. Set the In and Out ramps to linear, and in the Y-Value spinner, set the position to 371.2 units. (Along with the 371.2 units in the negative direction, this makes the total distance 742.2 units.)

Play back the animation. The character should now appear to take four steps with the feet locked exactly to the ground. A rendered version of this walk is located on the accompanying CD as walkcycle.avi.

Creating Four-Legged Walks

Four-legged creatures are quite common in animation. Unfortunately, a package such as Biped does not help much with this task. Laying down footsteps for two feet is quite straightforward, but the overlapping footsteps required of a four-legged creature can be difficult for an algorithmic package such as Biped to handle.

A four-legged walk is very similar to the two-legged variety, but multiplied by two. The creature's legs still rock back and forth at the hips, but the upper-body motion happens parallel to the ground rather than perpendicular to it. Whereas human shoulders rock back and forth in the vertical axis, a dog's "shoulders" will rock back and forth horizontal to the ground as the front paws move back and forth.

The center of gravity is also slightly different for a four-legged beast. Instead of being located at the hips, it is further up on the body, roughly centered between the front and back legs. This may cause you to set up the hierarchy of a quadrupedal skeleton slightly differently. Because both the front and back legs move equally, the hierarchy can be set up with the center of the spine as the parent.

The location of the root of the hierarchy is important because it represents the *center of gravity*. If the animal were to leap, for example, the entire body's rotation would center around this point, so it is important to place it properly. The center joint of the spinal column makes a good candidate because many four-legged creatures have a center of gravity that is evenly located between the front and rear legs (see fig. 9.20). If the creature has its center of gravity closer to the chest (a cheetah or a greyhound, perhaps) then the shoulders or the first spinal joint may make a better center of gravity (see fig. 9.21). The head also plays a role in determination of center of gravity. A giraffe's long neck will place it further up the spinal column, near the shoulders.

FIGURE 9.20

The center of gravity of a dog is centered between the front and rear legs.

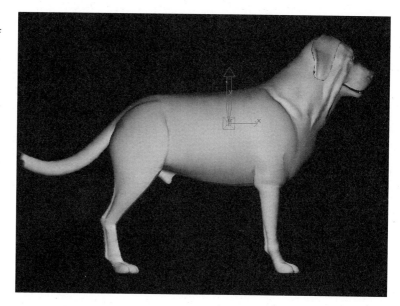

FIGURE 9.21

The center of gravity of a cheetah, however, is closer to the shoulders.

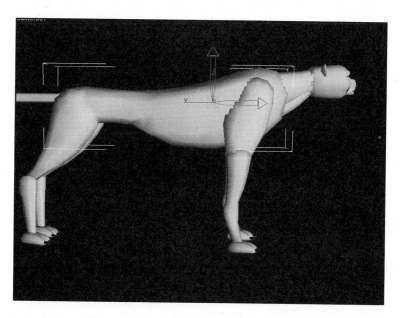

Creating a Quadruped Skeleton

One easy way to set up a skeleton for a four-legged creature is to modify a bipedal skeleton. To do so, follow these steps:

1. Load ik-skel.max from the accompanying CD-ROM. This is the skeleton created in the preceding chapter. If IK is on, turn it off.

2. Select the foot bones and delete them.

3. Select the bone at the base of the spine (Spine01). Using the Unlink Selection button, unlink this bone from the hips.

4. Rotate Spine01 90 degrees so that the spine is now parallel to the ground.

5. While Spine01 is still selected, adjust the bone's pivot so that it is at the top rather than the bottom of the bone. From the Hierarchy panel, press Affect Pivot Only. Move the pivot forward so that it lies even with the top of the bone (see fig. 9.22).

FIGURE 9.22

If the center spine bone is the center of the hierarchy, the pivots of the children should be located next to it.

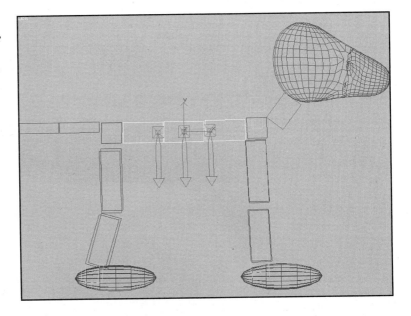

6. Link the skeleton back together. Select Spine02 and press the Unlink Selection. Next, press the Link Selection button and select the hips. Link these to Spine01. Link Spine01 to Spine02, the parent of the hierarchy.

7. Rotate the arms down 90 degrees so that they hang down like legs. If you notice, these new legs bend forward like bird legs, which is exactly how most four-legged creatures' front legs are jointed.

8. Tilt the head up, adjust the lengths of the legs and shoulders as you see fit. A dachshund will have much shorter legs than a greyhound, for example. Also adjust the width of the shoulders so that they match the hips more closely. Finally, add a tail if needed.

Although elementary, this is a basic four-legged skeleton. Building this from a human skeleton shows you just how close our skeletons are to our fellow mammals (see fig. 9.23).

FIGURE 9.23
A bipedal and quadrupedal skeleton are surprisingly similar.

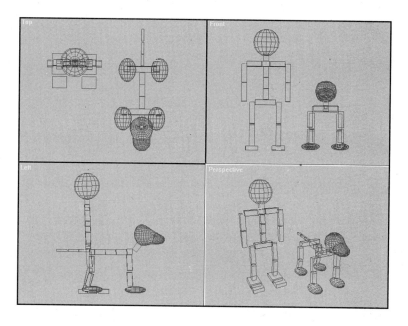

For reference, a version of this skeleton has been placed on the accompanying CD-ROM in the file fourskel.max.

Analysis of a Four-Legged Walk

A four-legged walk is very similar to a two-legged walk in that the hips and shoulders have rotations that mirror each other. When the right hip is forward, the left shoulder is back, and vice versa. This action usually varies a bit in that the front and back legs might be offset by a few frames (see fig. 9.24). Notice how the spine curves much like a human and that the left shoulder and leg are back, mirroring the hip pose. This means that the left front leg, too, is about to plant.

FIGURE 9.24

This step has the right rear leg forward and the foot about to plant.

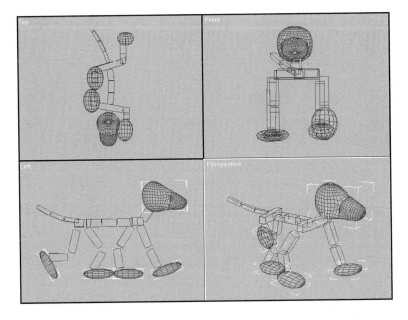

As the legs move forward through the step, the legs that are not currently planted on the ground (the free legs) move forward. The rear legs are fairly similar to a human's, bending at the knee in much the same fashion. The front legs, however, are actually jointed so that they bend forward, much like a bird's (see fig. 9.25). This dictates a slightly different lift motion for the front legs. At this point, the spine is straight when viewed from the top, but it may bow or arch a bit more when viewed from the side. This will be character dependent. A dilapidated horse's back may sag quite a bit.

FIGURE 9.25

Halfway through the step, the free legs are moving forward. Notice how the front leg's joint causes a different bend in the leg.

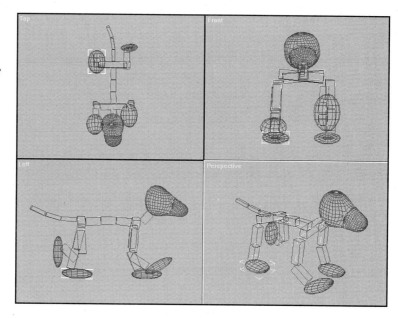

The legs then move through the step and plant the free feet, repeating the first step. In addition to this, a four-legged animal can have several different gaits: the walk, the trot, the canter, and the gallop. The animal will vary the timing and rhythm of its steps as it moves faster and faster. In the walk, the animal's legs behave very much like the arms and legs of a human—if the right rear leg is back, the right front leg is forward, with the opposite happening on the left. This changes as the strides change, however. By the time the creature has reached full gallop, the front legs are in sync—going forward and back nearly in unison, with the back legs operating as a mirror to the front.

Animating a Four-Legged Walk Cycle

This skeleton can be made to walk quite easily. It is a simple matter of getting the back legs to walk much like a two-legged character's and then adding in the front leg motions. A cycle is a good way to create such a walk because keyframing four legs over a large number of frames can be quite tedious.

1. Get the hips and shoulders moving. Like in a two-legged walk, the hips and shoulders mirror each other.

2. Move the feet. This can be done by attaching each ankle to an elliptical path, much like in a two-legged walk. The legs can also be keyframed manually using either forward or inverse kinematics.

TIP

When animating a four-legged walk, it is important that both pairs of legs move the same distance with each step. If the back legs have a larger stride than the front, for example, one set of feet will appear to slip.

3. Make certain that the feet remain planted by rotating them at the ankles.

4. For a cycle, again move the ground in relation to the character, or the character in relation to the ground. Like in the two-legged walk, this rate can be calculated by using a Helper object, such as a tape, to measure out the stride over a series of frames and then dividing this by the number of frames.

You can find on the accompanying CD-ROM an example of a four-legged walk using the supplied skeleton. The file is called fourwalk.max, and it is also rendered to the AVI file fourwalk.avi.

Animating Six-Legged Walks

If four-legged walks seem complex, then six legs might seem intolerably difficult. This, fortunately, is not the case. An insect walk actually follows a definite, repeatable pattern that can be animated on a cycle. A six-legged walk is very similar to the four-legged walk—the front two legs move back and forth, while the second set of legs mirror this motion (see fig. 9.26). The insect's third set of legs simply mirrors the second again, closely matching the motion of the front legs. Generally, insects keep at least three legs on the ground, forming a stable tripod at all times.

FIGURE 9.26

Insect legs and body parts are naturally segmented, making direct animation of the joints possible.

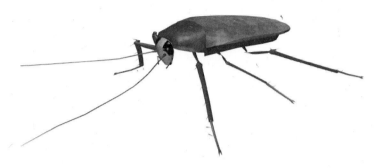

Because insects are the quintessential segmented creatures, their parts can be put together in a simple hierarchy. Shape animation or spinal bones are not needed for such a creature because an insect's exoskeleton does not change shape. The one exception may be antennae on the insect, which can be animated with bones, or more directly, by using a simple bend modifier.

Animating the walk of an insect is simply a matter of getting the front legs to walk, mirroring this motion on the second set of legs, and then mirroring the second set of leg motion on the third. The legs of an insect have three main segments, with the first segment, the one closest to the body, acting like a suspension bridge that holds the body of the bug aloft (see fig. 9.27).

FIGURE 9.27

Insect legs suspend the insect's body like a bridge.

The accompanying CD-ROM contains a file called roach.max, which contains a roach model that has been set up in a hierarchy and is ready to animate. Load this file into MAX and follow along.

Body

Like the body of a two- or four-legged creature, the body of an insect bounces up and down as the creature walks. This rate of bounce is directly proportional to the rate of the walk, which means that the body bounces up and down once per step—the insect bounces twice for a full cycle of right and left leg steps. The bug is highest when the legs are in the middle of the stride.

The rate of an insect walk will depend on the species of bug and its demeanor. Generally, bugs move pretty fast compared to mammals, and a quarter or eighth second per step is not out of the question. When walks get this fast, the frame rate of the animation becomes a limiting factor. At 24 fps, an eighth second stride would only take three frames per step. This is about as fast as a walk could be animated, with one frame each for the forward, middle, and back portions of the step. For this animation, 6 fps gives you a good pace for the insect walk.

1. At frame 0, the insect will be at the bottom of the stride. Move the abdomen object down along Y about 12 units.

2. At frame 6, the insect will be at the top of it's stride. Move the abdomen up 12 units to get it back to center, plus another 12 units to make it the top of his stride, for a total upward movement of 24 units.

3. At frame 12, the cycle repeats. Copy the abdomen position key from frame 0 to this frame.

4. To get enough up and down motion for a full cycle of steps, copy these keys once again to make a second cycle, for a total of 24 frames.

The Legs

The legs are best dealt with a set at a time. The front legs are always a good guide, so these are best animated first. Once the front legs are moving, the rear sets can be keyframed in the same manner (see fig. 9.28).

Front Legs

As mentioned previously, the front legs are a good guide to animating each set of legs. These will be animated in the next exercise.

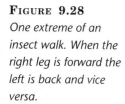

Figure 9.28

One extreme of an insect walk. When the right leg is forward the left is back and vice versa.

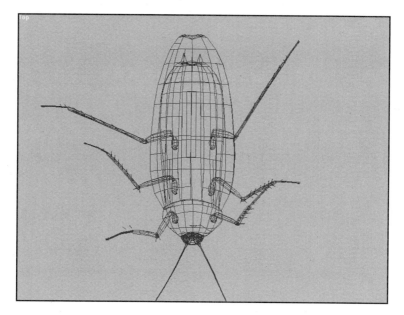

Animating the Front Legs

1. At Frame 0, the right front leg should be rotated forward about 15 degrees, the left front leg rotated back approximately the same amount. Both legs should be touching the ground.

2. At Frame 6, both legs should be roughly centered. The left front leg is moving forward, so it should be raised off the ground. The right front leg is firmly planted. The body at this point is also at its highest point.

3. At Frame 12, the legs switch—the left leg plants and the right leg lifts. The left front leg should be approximately 15 degrees forward, while the right front is 15 degrees back.

4. Repeat the same positions outlined in the previous steps for the opposite legs on frames 12 through 24. The left leg should be planted, while the right leg lifts and moves forward.

5. Scrub the animation and adjust the rotations of the front legs to make sure they remain planted on the ground throughout their respective steps.

Middle and Rear Legs

The middle and rear legs move in an identical manner as the front, but are simply mirrored. This makes creating the animation as simple as repeating the exact same steps for the front legs—creating a key for the beginning, middle, and end of each step, then adjusting the inbetweens as required.

One tactic to take while animating the rear legs would be to copy and paste the controllers from the front legs to the corresponding rear legs. In order for this to work, the pivots of all the joints of the respective legs need to be aligned along the same axis. If they are not, the rotations will not translate properly, and the legs will not mirror exactly the rotations of the front. This is easily done by aligning all of the pivots on the legs to the world before animation begins.

Another problem with copying the controllers may be one of scale. The cockroach, for example, has rear legs that are quite a bit longer than the front legs. Copied rotations from the front leg may not match up exactly. Still, it may prove to be a good starting point, but the effectiveness of this tactic depends on the anatomy of the insect being animated.

Another factor to consider is timing. If all of the legs move at the exact same time, the animation may look unnatural. To compensate for this, it is simply a matter of sliding the keys for each set of legs back a frame or two so that they touch slightly behind the leading legs. This will add an extra touch of realism.

One final thing to consider with insects is their antennae. These act as feelers for the insect, constantly searching out a path for the bug to follow. Antennae can be animated using a number of methods, such as bones with a mesh deformation system, such as Biped or Physique. A simple bend modifier can also be quite effective for this effect, as the angle and direction of the bend can be keyframed to give a nice effect.

To view how a walk cycle such as the one created can be worked into a full animation look at the file roachwalk.max, which is also rendered out to the file roachwalk.avi.

Using Expressions to Automate an Insect Walk

Keyframing six legs can be quite tedious, so the procedure can be sped up quite significantly using MAX's expressions. Expressions enable you to create mathematical relationships between objects. In the case of insect legs, the rotation of one leg can easily control the actions of the other five.

The key to making an expression-driven insect work is that insect legs follow a predictable pattern. As was described previously, the rotations on each row of legs simply mirrors the rotations of the row in front of it. Additionally, the left side of legs mirrors the rotations on the right. These simple rules make it quite easy to set up a series of expressions that can make one leg drive many.

Load the file bugexp01.max. This file contains a simple bug. The body is a simple box, as are the legs. This particular bug only has one leg, which needs to be duplicated to create the other five. Before the leg is duplicated, however, it needs to be properly positioned and aligned to the world.

Position the leg so that it is slightly bent, with the "knee" slightly above the body of the insect. A bent knee gives the insect a more relaxed and realistic pose (see fig. 9.29). In the Hierarchy panel, select Affect Pivot Only and click on Align to World. This simply puts the pivots in world space, which makes each leg movement work along the same axis as the body. Rotations around the leg's local Z axis move the leg forward and back. Rotations along the local Y axis lift the leg off the ground and also plant it. Local X rotations will twist the leg. The two primary rotations used in walking are the Y and Z rotations. The legs must move back and forth along Z to propel the insect forward. Additionally, legs must rotate along Y to lift and plant the feet.

Because Y and Z rotations of the leg need to be isolated to create the expressions, the leg must be assigned the Euler XYZ rotation controller, which is the only controller that separates the X, Y, and Z components of the rotation. To assign this, simply select the object Leg01, the upper part of the first leg, open the assign controller rollout within the motion panel, and assign the Euler XYZ controller to the leg.

FIGURE 9.29

*The proper positioning
of the leg and the
pivots.*

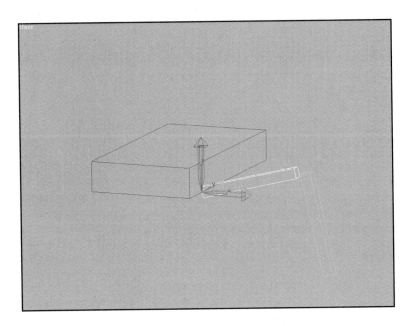

To make the expressions easier to construct, all six of the insect's legs will
need to have their X, Y, and Z axes aligned in the same fashion. The easiest
way to make sure the legs are aligned properly is simply to clone the first leg
to create the others.

ALIGNING THE LEGS

1. From the Top viewport, select both leg joints (Leg01 and Leg02) and
   clone them to create the two other legs on the right side.

2. Now create the left legs from the right. Select all of the legs on the right
   side and click the Mirror Selected Objects button. Select the X axis as the
   mirror axis and create copies of the right legs.

3. Position the left legs along the left side of the insect's body. When they
   are finished, they should look like figure 9.30.

FIGURE 9.30

After all of the legs have been copied and properly placed, their pivots should be aligned.

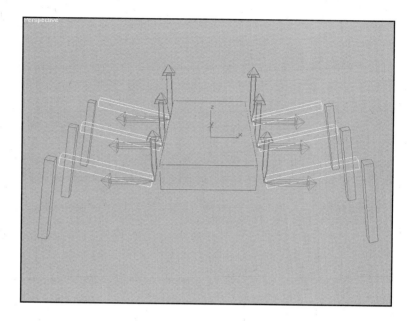

Now that the legs are in position and properly aligned with the Euler XYZ controllers assigned, they can be assigned individual expressions. Select the upper joint of the second right leg. This joint will mirror the rotations of the front right leg. When the front right leg rotates forward along Z, the second right will rotate back. When the front right leg plants itself on the ground, the second right will lift. This is simply accomplished by multiplying the controlling leg's rotation by –1.

4. Open TrackView. Select the track for the second right leg's (Leg04) Z rotation. Change the controller type to Float Expression. Open the properties panel to get the Expression controller dialog.

5. Within the Expression Controller dialog, create a scalar variable named **Leg01Z** and assign this to the Z rotation controller for the front right leg (Leg01).

6. Enter the expression **–Leg01Z**. This will make the second right leg's Z rotation exactly opposite the front right (see fig. 9.31).

FIGURE 9.31

*The Expression
Controller dialog box
with the expression for
the leg rotation
entered.*

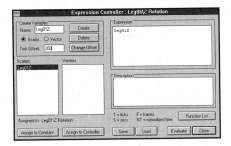

Evaluate the expression and close the dialog.

7. Select the front right leg and rotate it around its local Z axis. The second right leg should mirror it exactly.

Repeat this procedure for the Y rotation of the second right leg. Create a scalar variable named "Leg01Y" and assign this variable to the Z rotation controller for the front right leg (Leg01). Create the expression **–Leg01Z** in the Expression box and evaluate it. The leg's Y rotation will now follow the front right leg.

Work your way around the body, creating expressions for every leg. Each set of legs mirrors the one in front of it, and the left side mirrors the right. Remember that the left legs were created by mirroring the right legs, so their rotations will automatically be mirrored as well, making their expressions the same as their corresponding right leg. The expressions are listed in table 9.1.

TABLE 9.1

Mirrored Leg Expressions

LEG	EXPRESSIONS
Second Right	–Leg01Z ;–Leg01Y
Third Right	Leg01Z ; Leg01Y
Front Left	Leg01Z ; Leg01Y
Second Left	–Leg01Z ; –Leg01Y
Third Left	Leg01Z ; Leg01Y

After all 10 expressions are written, moving the front right leg will move all of the rest in perfect sync. The file bugexp02.max is included on the accompanying CD as a reference. It has all of these expressions in place.

Of course, no living creatures, including insects, are perfect, so this method has its limitations when compared to purely keyframing the animation by hand. The limitations are that the legs may seem too perfect because they move in lockstep. One way to get around this limitation is to add a Tick Offset for each succeeding row of legs to make them move with a slight delay for each step, adding a touch of realism. The Tick Offset is found along with each expression in the Expression controller dialog, accessed by clicking on the Properties panel within Track View. Each variable in the expression created within the dialog can have its own offset.

Recall that each tick is exactly 1/4800 of a second, so a good tick offset would be in the range of 1–3 frames, or approximately 200–600 ticks, depending on the frame rate. Because the tick value is time driven, the effects will only show up when animated. After the expressions have been set up, animating a walk cycle is quite easy. The front leg simply needs to be moved forward and back in a walking motion, as in the previous section, and the other legs will follow.

Another way to create a similar insect walk is to write the expressions so that both front legs are involved. The front left leg would control the second right and the third left, whereas the front right leg would control the second left and the third right. This forces animation to be created for two legs, but the front legs can have slightly varying motions, which can add to the shot's realism. Adding a tick offset to each succeeding row of legs adds even more realism. As can be surmised, using expressions to help drive walks has quite a few other possibilities, so the rest is left up to your imagination.

In Practice: Animating Walking

- **Walking.** The two-legged walk is like a controlled fall, with the legs catching the body on each step. Each step has several major components: the plant, the lift, and the passing position. The spine twists and bends along with the shoulders and hips to maintain balance. Different character attitudes manifest themselves in different body postures.

- **Walk cycles.** Walk cycles are good for environments such as games where cyclical motions are a requirement. An elliptically shaped path can be used quite effectively along with MAX's IK to get the legs moving in a walking motion. After the Apply IK button has been clicked, rotation keys are generated, and the path can be dispensed.

- **Four-legged skeletons.** Four-legged skeletons are very much like the two-legged variety. All of the bones are in similar places, but the spine is parallel to the ground and the size relationships of the bones are different.

- **Four-legged walks.** The key to this is the spine, which moves much like the spine of a two-legged walk, with the shoulders and hips still flexing and bending. Be sure to keep both sets of legs moving at the same rate. If one set of legs is longer than the other, there may be a temptation to move it further, but this causes an apparent slip of the creature's feet.

- **Six-legged walks.** The sheer number of legs makes these a bit vexing, but they follow regular, repetitive motions that makes them easy to set up. This regular motion lends itself to the use of expressions to help animate the many legs.

IMAGE CREATED BY GEORGE MAESTRI

by George Maestri

ANIMATING WITH BIPED

Although creating and animating your own biped skeletons gives you freedom to customize how they are built, these skeletons can typically fall short when it comes to animation. These skeletons typically use inverse kinematics to position the limbs of the skeleton based on the position of their extremities. The position of the arm, therefore, is controlled by the position of the hand. To approach life-like motion of the limbs, the animator must configure the constraints on each skeleton joint to restrict the rotation to the appropriate axis (knees bend but do not twist) and set the appropriate limits for each axis (knees bend backward, but not forward). Even with these constraints properly configured, the resulting motion is still not life-like. The motion of the limbs in-between keyframes uses a spline-based interpolation which, while smooth, does not match the kinematic motion of a biped.

Even more important for bipeds, inverse kinematics knows nothing about the skeleton other than it is a collection of joints. As such, it is easy to have the skeleton in a pose that causes a bipedal animal to fall on its face. An example of this is the forward rotation of the spine. Unless the hips move backward as the spine is rotated, a bipedal animal quickly reaches an unstable position where it would fall forward.

Biped is exactly one half of the Character Studio plug-in. It not only enables automatic construction of "smart" humanoid skeletons with a built-in IK system, it also enables extensive customization of those skeletons' structural details such as the number of fingers and toes, and whether the biped has a tail. Biped is primarily a footstep-driven animation tool, where the position of the biped is controlled by the timing and placement of footsteps. The IK system used in Biped was designed specifically for animating bipeds and takes into account the mechanics and restrictions of how bipedal animals move. Integral to Biped is the handling of gravity and the biped's center-of-mass. This enables Biped to interpolate the position of the biped properly when both feet are off the ground, and to dynamically balance the biped about the center-of-mass to achieve life-like motions.

This chapter covers the following topics:

- Creating a biped

- Manipulating a biped

- Animating a biped with footsteps

- Performing free-form animation of a biped

- Using animatable IK attachments

- Using libraries of biped animation

Creating a Biped

The Biped creation button is located under the Systems button in the Create panel. To create a biped, click on the button and then on a viewport, and drag. A box appears indicating the size of the biped. Releasing the mouse generates the Biped skeleton.

After the mouse is released, the Biped Creation panel appears (see fig. 10.1). From within this panel, you can configure the skeleton exactly to your needs, including details such as how many segments are in the spine and neck, whether the character has a tail, how many links are in that tail, how many fingers and toes, and whether the character has arms. (A bird, for example, has no arms.) Another important parameter to consider is the Leg Links spinner, which determines how the legs are configured. This has two settings: 3 and 4. A human has a setting of 3 (thigh, calf, and foot), and some birds or dinosaurs have a setting of 4 (thigh, calf, shin, and foot).

FIGURE 10.1

From within the Biped Creation panel, you can change the structure of the biped.

Once created, the biped can be controlled through the Motion panel (see fig. 10.2). Select any part of the biped, and all the controls for manipulating and animating the biped appear. Because Biped is essentially a very sophisticated animation controller, its controls appear on the motion panel rather than on the Modify panel.

FIGURE 10.2

*Selecting the Motion
tab brings up the Biped
Control panel.*

Manipulating a Biped

Bipeds have their own built-in IK, completely separate from MAX's native IK. This system has been configured to give smooth, controllable, predictable motion. Biped's IK always works in real time, and there is no need to apply IK as you would within MAX's native IK. The joints of a biped can be manipulated through translation, rotation, and by using footsteps.

With Biped's IK, if you are adjusting a biped's arm by moving the hand, the position of the arm and hand returns to the exact starting position if you return the hand to its original position. This is impossible in MAX's, and most other, IK systems. The typical result with those systems is that, although the hand returns to its original position, the arm's position is different. An additional feature of Biped is the use of IK Blend to blend between forward and inverse kinematics. This feature enables you to link a hand or foot to another object and have that hand or foot follow the object. The amount of IK blending is animatable, so the hand or foot can effectively be attached and detached from the object over time, enabling you to easily animate the biped catching and throwing a ball, dancing with a partner, or performing other actions where the biped interacts with other objects in the scene. The "Attaching the Hands and Feet to MAX Objects" section of this chapter describes IK Blend further.

Translating a biped's joints is straightforward—grab the joint and move it. Unlike MAX's IK, the joints moved need not be constrained with end effectors or terminators for the joint to move properly. All that intelligence is built into the biped. You can just as easily move the biceps as the pinky and still retain a single, predictable solution for the limb, no matter how many joints the move affects.

To move the biped himself, the Center of Mass object needs to be selected and moved (see fig. 10.3). Rather than a hip-centric model, Biped uses the center-of-mass as the top of the hierarchy. As such, the pelvis itself is not translatable. The tetrahedral-shaped object found near the center of the pelvis represents the biped's center-of-mass. Translating this object accomplishes the same effect as moving the pelvis on a hip-centric skeleton.

FIGURE 10.3

To move the biped's body, the Center of Mass object (arrow) must be moved, not the pelvis. The Center of Mass object is represented by a tetrahedron.

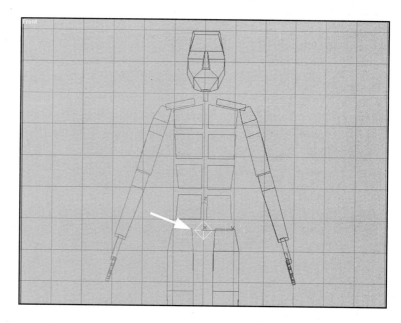

Rotating joints is also possible, giving the animator the flexibility of positioning a skeleton by using any combination of forward or inverse kinematics. Translating joints on the fingers, for example, normally causes a translation of the entire arm. For motions such as hand gestures, rotations are required.

Another thing to be aware of is that not all biped joints can be translated, and not every joint can rotate around every axis. The restrictions on translating joints are that only the Center of Mass object and the leg and arm joints (except for the clavicles) can be translated. The restrictions on rotating joints are more involved. In general, if you cannot rotate a joint in your body about an axis, you cannot rotate the same joint in the biped about that axis. The following are special rotations or restrictions:

- **Elbows and Knees.** The elbow and knee joints can be rotated both on their local Z axis (like a hinge) and along their local X axis (along their length). When rotated along their local X axis, the rotation does not occur at that joint. Instead, the upper and lower leg/arm are rotated together along an axis formed by the hip/shoulder and ankle/wrist.

- **Feet.** If the foot is planted on a footstep, the foot can be rotated on its local Y and Z axes. The foot remains in contact with the footstep, and the leg joints are rotated to maintain the position of the pelvis. A foot cannot be rotated on its local X axis if the foot is planted.

- **Legs.** If a foot is planted and a leg is rotated, the rotation may be limited to ensure that the foot remains in contact with the footstep.

When a joint is selected, the disallowed motions are grayed out on the menu bar, which can prove a bit frustrating for the novice. After the restrictions are understood, however, nearly any pose can be effectively attained.

Other Biped Selection and Manipulation Tools

In addition to the standard MAX translation and rotation tools, the Biped Motion panel contains a number of Biped-specific tools to assist in manipulating your skeletons:

- **Center of Mass.** Found under the Track Selection rollout, it selects the biped's Center of Mass object. Sometimes this object can be hard to locate in a complex scene; this button speeds the process.

- **Symmetrical Tracks.** Found under the Track Selection rollout, clicking on this button mirrors the current selection on the opposite side of the body. If the left leg is selected, pressing Symmetrical Tracks adds the right leg to the selection.

- **Opposite Tracks.** Found under the Track Selection rollout, clicking on this button selects the identical limbs on the opposite side of the body. If the right arm is selected, pressing the Opposite Tracks button selects the left arm and deselects the right.

- **Copy Posture.** Found on the Track Operations rollout, this is a very handy tool that enables you to copy the position of any joint or group of joints.

- **Paste Posture.** Enables you to paste copied postures to another point in the animation or to another biped. Copy and paste posture is also handy for saving the state of a biped if you want to experiment with a pose. If the new pose does not work out, pasting the original pose returns the biped to normal.

- **Paste Posture Opposite.** This is identical to Paste Posture, but this button mirrors the pose to the opposite side of the body, enabling you to take a pose on the right leg, for example, and paste it on the left.

- **Bend Links.** Found on the Track Operations rollout, this tool evenly bends linked joints, such as the spine, tail, or a multi-jointed neck (see fig. 10.4). Activating the Bend Links button causes all joints in the section (the joints in the spine, for example) to be evenly adjusted by adjusting a single joint.

FIGURE 10.4

Bipeds with a single spine joint rotated without and with Bend Links enacted. Bend Links mode makes possible even rotations of the spine.

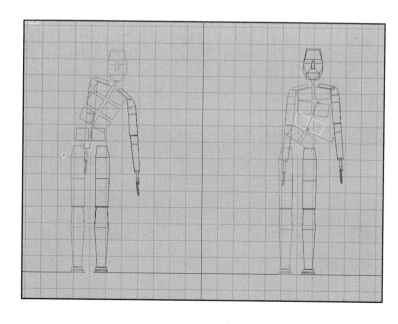

Animating a Biped

There are many ways to animate a biped. Creating and adjusting footsteps are the obvious method. With version 1.1, however, you can also free-form animate bipeds without footsteps. This, however, is a one way street—after keys have been added to a free-form animation, footsteps may not be added to that biped's animation later. If you are in doubt as to whether footsteps will be used in an animation, it is best to assume that they will be and create a free-form area between footsteps. This section takes you through the process of animating with footsteps and free-form animation.

Animating with Footsteps

Footsteps enable you to take advantage of Biped's built-in dynamics to create quasi-realistic motion. The walks, runs, and jumps created by Biped are purposely generic because Biped is a tool that tries not to force a specific style on the animator. The keys automatically generated from footsteps are the minimum required to achieve the motion. This enables the animator to add the desired characteristics without having to delete the many keys that would have to be generated to achieve a realistic default motion. Instead, these keys should be thought of as a motion "sketch" that can be easily modified.

To create footsteps, click on the Footstep Track button within the Track Selection rollout to activate the Footstep Creation rollouts; additionally, Sub-Object Footsteps is enabled for the biped. This means that only footsteps may be selected, created, or manipulated while the Footstep Track button is toggled. After this button has been toggled on, you are free to create footsteps.

Creating Footsteps

There are two methods of creation (footstep creation and adjustment) along with three types of footsteps: walk, run, and jump. The different types of footsteps represent the different timings for the footsteps. Again, you should think of the footstep timing and placement as an easily modified motion "sketch."

- **Walk.** One foot always remains planted, while the other swings forward. At least one foot is always on the ground. There can also be a section in the walk motion—called Double Support—where both feet are on the ground. Both the number of frames that each footstep remains on the ground (Walk Footstep) and the number of frames in a double support period (Double Support) are defined by spinners that activate when the Footstep Track button is toggled on.

- **Run.** One foot is on the ground at a time with no double support. There is also a point in the cycle where both feet are airborne. Both the number of frames that each footstep remains on the ground (Run Footstep) and the number of frames that the biped is airborne (Airborne) are defined by spinners that activate when the Footstep Track button is toggled on.

- **Jump.** Both feet are on the ground equally and are airborne equally. The number of frames that both feet are on the ground (2 Feet Down) and the number of frames that the biped is airborne (Airborne) are defined by spinners that activate when Footstep Track is toggled on.

Biped footsteps can be created singly or in multiples. When creating a set of single footsteps, the footstep can be appended in time to the current footsteps, or created starting at the current frame. Each method has its own button, as follows:

- **Create Footsteps (append).** This button enables you to lay down footsteps by clicking on a viewport—a good method for creating footsteps over tricky terrain or for complex motions such as dance steps. Footsteps are appended to any current footsteps.

- **Create Footsteps (at current frame).** Same as Create Footsteps (append), except that footsteps are added starting at the current frame. If the footstep being added overlaps in time with an existing footstep, an alert appears, and the footstep is not created.

- **Create Multiple Footsteps.** This button creates a user-defined number of footsteps with user-specified spacing and timing. Footsteps created in this manner run along a straight line and are best for walking a character through a scene.

TIP

Using the Interpolate option in the Create Multiple Footsteps dialog, you can change the stride length, stride height, and timing of the footsteps over the footsteps being created.

Activating Footsteps

After a series of footsteps has been laid down, the footsteps need to be activated. To activate footsteps, click on the Create Keys for Inactive Footsteps button in the Footstep Operations rollout. Activation computes dynamics for the biped for any footsteps that have been created, but not yet activated, and creates keys within Track View for the biped. Once activated, you can still modify the walk by manipulating the footsteps or keys. If new footsteps are added after activation, those footsteps must also be activated.

Creating a Simple Walk

You can always get instant gratification from Biped by creating a few footsteps and activating them. The following simple task makes a biped walk and gives you a supply of footsteps with which to work.

CREATING A SIMPLE WALK

1. Load biped01.max from the accompanying CD. This file contains a biped and a ground plane.

2. Select any portion of the biped. Select the Motion tab to bring up the Biped Motion panel.

3. Footsteps are created and modified from within Footstep mode. Click on the Footstep Track button under Track Selection to enter Footstep mode. When this button is toggled on, it enables Sub-Object Footsteps selection on the biped. While in Footstep mode, only footsteps may be selected and modified.

4. There are two ways to create footsteps: single footsteps manually placed with the mouse, or multiple footsteps automatically placed. Footsteps can be one of three types: walk, run, or jump. Click on the Walk button in the Footstep Creation rollout.

5. The fastest way to create footsteps is with the Create Multiple Footsteps button. This creates a number of footsteps with user-specified spacing and timing that can be modified and manipulated later. Press this button to display the Create Multiple Footsteps dialog. Enter **10** for the number of footsteps, make certain that the Start Left option is chosen in the General section, and click on OK.

6. Ten numbered footsteps appear, which need to be activated for the biped to follow them. To do this, press the Create Keys for Inactive Footsteps button in the Footstep Operations rollout (see fig. 10.5).

7. Activate the Left viewport with a right-click and play the animation. The biped now follows these footsteps. Instant gratification!

FIGURE 10.5

Activating the footsteps causes the biped to walk.

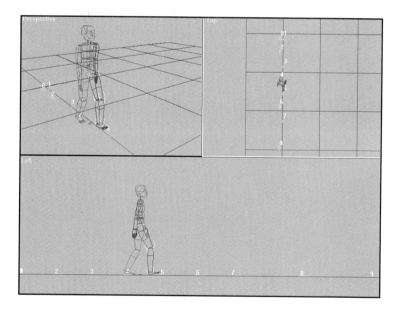

Appending to an Animation

You can append to Biped-created animations quite easily. It is simply a matter of creating additional footsteps and activating them.

APPENDING BIPED ANIMATIONS

1. Click on the Run button and then on the Create Multiple Footsteps button. Type in **4** for the number of footsteps, choose the Start after last footstep option in the Timing section, and click on OK. This appends four footsteps to the end of the animation. Activate the new footsteps.

2. Zoom extents the Left viewport and play back the animation. As you might notice, the biped changes from a walking to a running gait for the new footsteps.

3. Press the Jump button and then the Create Multiple Footsteps button. For the number of footsteps, type in **2**. Activate the footsteps.

4. Zoom extents the Left viewport and play back the animation. The biped now ends the run with a small jump.

An example of this animation is stored on the accompanying CD in the file named biped02.max.

Modifying Footsteps

Once activated, the footsteps can be moved and modified on the fly, with Biped adjusting the biped to match the footsteps automatically.

MODIFYING FOOTSTEPS

1. Using the animation just created, go to the Display panel and click on Unhide All. A small platform with a staircase appears. Play back the animation. The biped should walk right through the stairs because Biped just follows the footsteps, which are laid in a straight line across the ground. Biped does not perform collision detection with other objects in the scene.

2. This obstacle can be overcome quite easily by adjusting the footsteps. Zoom in the platform in the Left viewport. Select any part of the biped and, in Motion panel, toggle the Footstep Track button on. Using the standard MAX selection tools, select footsteps 3 through 15. Move these up so that footstep 3 resides on the first step of the platform. Select footsteps 4 through 15 and move these up so that footstep 4 lies on the second step. Repeat until all the footsteps are properly positioned on the stairs.

3. Play the animation. The biped now walks up the stairs and then runs off the edge of the platform.

4. This can also be adjusted quite easily. Select the biped, go to the Motion panel, and enter Footstep mode. Select footsteps 6 through 8. In the Footstep Operations rollout, adjust the Bend spinner up to 30. The selected footsteps automatically bend. Footsteps prior to footstep 6 are not affected, and footsteps after footstep 8 are rotated to maintain their alignment with footstep 8.

5. Play the animation. Notice how the biped automatically banks as it goes through the turn. A problem still exists, however. The biped still runs off the end of the platform and jumps from and lands in mid-air.

6. In the Front viewport, select footsteps 9 through 13. In the Footstep Operations rollout, uncheck the Width option and adjust the Scale spinner so that footstep 13 resides precisely on the edge of the platform. By unchecking the Width option, the width between footsteps remains the same as the footsteps are scaled downward.

7. Now select footsteps 14 and 15, which are still in mid-air off the edge of the platform. Move these down so that they lie level with the ground plane (see fig. 10.6).

8. Play the animation. The biped now walks up the stairs, rounds a corner, runs, and jumps off the edge. Not bad for a few minutes worth of work.

FIGURE 10.6

Obstacles such as stairs can be overcome quite easily by repositioning the footsteps.

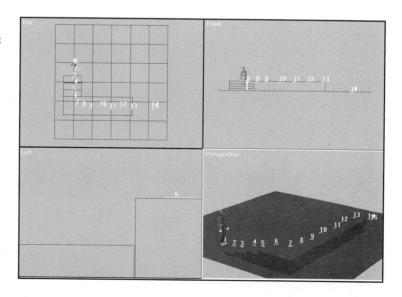

What has this demonstrated? First, by moving the footsteps up the stairs, you saw that footsteps are sub-objects that can be manipulated either individually or in groups. The footsteps can be moved and rotated anywhere in the scene to account for uneven terrain. Also, groups of footsteps can be scaled and bent quite easily by using the Bend and Scale spinners in the Footstep Operations rollout.

The final animation is on the accompanying CD in a file called biped03.max.

Individual footsteps or a selection set of footsteps can also be rotated using Select and Rotate. Rotating the footsteps this way is different than using the Bend spinner in that the unselected footsteps are not moved or rotated. When a selection set of footsteps is rotated in this way, the rotation pivot point is the pivot point of the footstep that the mouse cursor is over when you click and drag. If you change the transform coordinate center from Use Pivot Point Center to Use Selection Center, each footstep is rotated about its local pivot point. Go figure.

Copying and Pasting Footsteps

Biped enables you to select a set of footsteps, copy those footsteps to a buffer, and splice the footsteps into either the middle or end of the footstep sequence. You can even copy and splice a set of footsteps from one biped to another. The section "Saving and Loading Canned Motions" later in this chapter provides an example of this.

In this example, you copy and splice footsteps on a single biped.

COPYING FOOTSTEPS

1. Load cswalk.max from the accompanying CD. This file contains a biped walking forward, turning left, and walking a bit farther. For this exercise, you want the biped to turn left again near the end of the animation.

2. Select any portion of the biped. Select the Motion tab to bring up the Biped Motion panel. Click on the Footstep Track button in the Track Selection rollout.

3. Maximize the Top viewport and select footsteps 4 through 8. To be able to splice a set of footsteps into the middle of a sequence, the first and last footsteps selected need to be for the same leg.

4. Click on the Copy Selected Footsteps button in the Footstep Operations rollout to place the selected footsteps into the Footstep buffer.

5. Click on the Insert Footstep Buffer Onto Footsteps button in the Footstep Operations rollout. A copy of the footsteps in the buffer appears in the viewport.

6. Rotate the footsteps 90° about the Z axis.

7. Using the Move tool, click and drag the footsteps so that the first footstep is over the biped's footstep number 12. This target footstep turns red to signify that a splice is possible (see fig. 10.7). Release the mouse button.

The first buffer footstep replaces the target footstep, and remaining buffer footsteps follow. The original footsteps after the target footstep are automatically copied into the footstep buffer and are now available to paste.

FIGURE 10.7

When you move the first pasted footstep over a valid target footstep, the target footstep turns red.

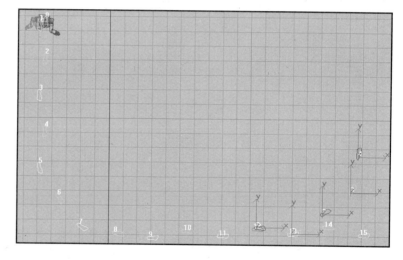

8. Rotate the footsteps 90° about the Z axis.

9. Using the Move tool, click and drag the footsteps so that the first footstep is over the biped's footstep number 16. Release the mouse button. The buffer footsteps are now spliced on to the end of the animation.

10. Minimize the Top viewport. Click on the Perspective viewport to activate it and play back the animation.

After copying the footsteps into the Footstep buffer and before pasting them into the scene, you can edit the footsteps and associated keys that are in the buffer. To do this, click on the Buffer Mode button in the General rollout to toggle on the Buffer mode. The footsteps in the buffer appear in the viewport, applied to the biped. In Track View, the footsteps are shown as the footsteps for the biped, and the associated keys are shown for the biped. These footsteps and keys can be edited just like the normal biped footsteps and keys. To return to the actual footsteps and keys for the biped, toggle off the Buffer Mode button.

Dynamics of Motion

As a biped walks, runs, or jumps, several factors affect the biped's motion: Gravitational Acceleration, Dynamics Blend, Ballistic Tension, and Balance Factor. Each of these factors affects the motion of the biped between keyframes.

N O T E

In the Samples directory of the Character Studio CD-ROM, you can find examples of different settings for the parameters described in this section. You can experiment with the set of AVI and MAX files provided.

A walk cycle is the act of falling forward and then catching yourself. To start walking, you extend one leg forward, which shifts your center of mass forward. As your center of mass moves forward past your planted foot, you start to fall forward. The back of your planted foot lifts off the ground, whereas the ball and toes of the foot remain planted. You continue to fall forward until the heel of the moving foot hits the ground. At this point, the momentum of your body pulls the back leg forward, and as the back foot leaves the ground, it also pushes you forward. This back leg continues forward until it passes the front leg, and you begin to fall forward again. While one of your feet is off the ground, your entire weight is being supported by the other foot. To maintain balance, the body arcs over the moving foot (the hip shifts toward the planted foot). Biped properly animates the hip to provide this motion (see fig. 10.8).

FIGURE 10.8

While only supported on one foot, the hip swings over the planted foot.

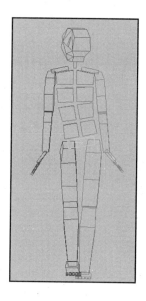

As you walk, the height of your pelvis (and center of mass) from the ground varies. It is at a minimum right after the front foot hits the ground, and at a maximum as the back leg passes the front leg.

A run cycle is similar to a walk cycle, except that instead of falling forward, you throw yourself forward. In a walk cycle, at least one foot is always on the ground. During a run cycle, however, there are split seconds when both feet are off the ground. During these periods, you are either airborne or ballistic. You move forward at a constant velocity during this airborne period, and the vertical height of your center of mass is based on how hard you "push off" and gravity. Leading up to this push off, your legs are typically bent more than during a walk cycle to generate more power with which to push. As the legs are bent, the center of mass also is lowered.

A jump cycle, in turn, is similar to a run cycle. The only difference is that both feet are in the air at the same time, and both hit the ground at the same time. Again, you move forward at a constant velocity during this airborne period, and the vertical height of your center of mass is based on how hard you push off and on gravity.

When you land in a run or jump cycle, your center of mass continues downward and forward due to momentum. Your legs act like springs, absorbing this momentum.

Dynamics Blend

Biped stores both Vertical and Horizontal keys for the biped's Center of Mass object. The Horizontal keys are generated at the middle of each footstep's support period and provide the forward motion of the biped. The Vertical keys are generated at the start, middle, and end of each footstep. The Vertical keys store the extension of the legs and the actual vertical height of the Center of Mass object.

During walking motions, the height is interpolated based on the extension of the legs recorded at each vertical key. This ensures that the supporting leg's knee angle does not change direction between two vertical keys. In effect, when walking, the leg extensions (and rising and falling foot pivots on the ground) control the height of the body in a natural way.

You can defeat this approach (or selectively blend it) with an interpolation of the actual vertical height by setting Dynamics Blend at each vertical key. At a Dynamics Blend setting of zero, Biped performs a spline interpolation of the vertical heights and ignores the leg extension information at each key. At a Dynamics Blend setting of one, Biped interpolates the leg extension distances and ignores the vertical heights at each key. You can change the Dynamics Blend value only while the Center of Mass object is selected, Move is active, and Restrict to Z is active.

During running and jumping motions, or transitions between them, the height is always determined by the vertical heights at each key because running and jumping are governed by the requirements of gravity, the heights of the body at liftoff and touchdown, and the duration of each airborne period. For running and jumping vertical keys, therefore, Dynamics Blend is grayed-out because it is not applicable.

Gravitational Acceleration

While the biped is airborne during a run or jump cycle, the vertical dynamics are controlled by Gravitational Acceleration (GravAccel in the General rollout of the Biped Motion panel) and the length of time between the lift and landing footsteps. If the length of time between these footsteps is shortened, or the Gravitational Acceleration value is decreased, the maximum height during the airborne period is decreased (on the moon, you don't need to jump very high to cover a lot of ground). The Gravitational Acceleration value is not animatable.

Ballistic Tension

The Ballistic Tension value controls how "springy" the legs are before lift-off and after touchdown in run and jump cycles (see fig. 10.9). The higher the value, the stiffer the legs are, resulting in less leg bending. You can change the Ballistic Tension value only while the Center of Mass object is selected, Move is active, and Restrict to Z is active. This value can only be set at the touchdown keyframe, unless three or more Vertical keys are set during the footprint support cycle. In this case, a Ballistic Tension value can also be set at the lift-off keyframe.

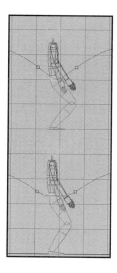

FIGURE 10.9

The follow-through of a landing for bipeds with a low (top biped) and high (bottom biped) Ballistic Tension value.

Balance Factor

The Balance Factor value specifies the biped's weight distribution by positioning the biped weight anywhere along a line extending from the center of mass to the head. A value of 0 places the biped's weight in the feet. A value of 1 places the biped's weight over the center of mass. A value of 2 places the biped's weight in the head. The Balance Factor value has no effect on the walk, run, and jump cycle motions; however, it can be used to your advantage when adjusting the rotation of the spine.

Assume, for example, a biped is sitting on a chair, and you are animating it so that it leans over a table. With the default value for Balance Factor (1.0), as you rotate the spine forward, the pelvis moves backward to maintain a constant position for the Center of Mass object. If you set the Balance Factor to 0, as you rotate the spine forward the pelvis remains at the same location. If you attempt to do this while the biped is standing, however, the biped looks very unnatural—like it should be falling over but isn't (see fig. 10.10). The Balance Factor value is set in the Structure rollout while in Figure mode. The Balance Factor value is not animatable.

FIGURE 10.10
The movement of the pelvis back from the center of mass when the spine is bent forward for bipeds with a normal Balance Factor (left) and a low Balance Factor (right).

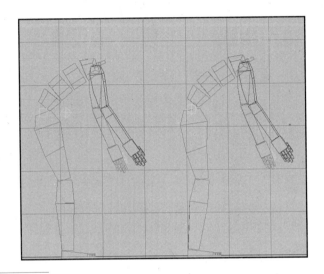

Bipeds in Track View

Although manipulating the footsteps themselves can change the walk quite a bit, the timing of a walk is also very important. A biped's timing can be changed quite radically from within Track View. When viewed as keys within Track View (see figs. 10.10 and 10.11), a Biped animation looks slightly different from ordinary MAX animation. When viewing a Biped animation, notice that the legs, arms, and spine do not have separate keys for each joint—Biped keys span all joints in the limb (arms, legs, spine, tail). A leg does not have separate keys for the thigh and shin, for example; instead, it has only one key that comprises the position of all the limb's joints. This enables Biped to transfer animation between disparate skeletons quite easily.

FIGURE 10.11

Biped tracks in Track View. The footstep keys are represented as blocks rather than dots, and locked Biped keys are highlighted in red.

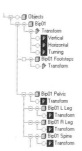
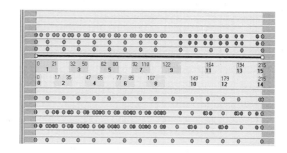

Footstep Tracks

One of the more important tracks is the footsteps track, which has a distinct appearance of alternating green and blue blocks—green are right footsteps, blue are left. The colored blocks indicate exactly when the feet are on the ground. Space between the footsteps for a foot indicates that the foot is airborne. If neither foot has a footstep at a given frame, both feet are airborne, such as in a run or a jump. Walks, by definition, always keep at least one foot on the ground. Places where the blocks overlap means both feet are on the ground. Displaying the footsteps this way enables you to know exactly what the feet are doing.

A footstep key actually spans several frames and has a number of components. By default, each footstep is labeled in its center with the footstep number, and each footstep indicates the start and stop frame in the top corners.

To modify a footstep, click on the center of the footstep near the footstep number and drag. Clicking on the start or stop frame in the corners of the footstep enables you to modify these positions as well, affecting the duration of the footstep. Like with any other key, you can also select, move, and resize groups of keys.

Right-clicking on a footstep key brings up the Footstep Track dialog (see fig. 10.12), which gives you control over how the footsteps are displayed, as well as some additional selection tools. The top portion of this dialog is for turning off vertical dynamics in free-form areas and is discussed in this chapter's "Free-Form Animation" section. The Footstep Number Display section provides options on the frame information shown for each footstep. The

Footstep Edge Selection section enables you to change which portion of previously selected footsteps remain chosen. If you have chosen three footsteps and click on the Left button, for example, only the left edges of these three footsteps remain selected. You can then move these edges to increase or decrease the duration for the footsteps.

NOTE

Release 1.1 of Character Studio enables you to select any combination of left and right edges, and generally improves footstep editing in Track View.

FIGURE 10.12

Right-clicking on the footstep track displays the Footstep Track dialog.

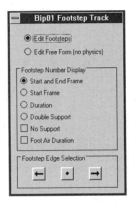

Other Tracks

In addition to the footstep tracks, the Biped also has another class of keys not normally found within MAX. These are keys for skeletal objects, such as the legs, and are calculated by Biped and are shown in red. Called *locked keys*, these are keys that Biped requires for it to perform its calculations. The locked keys cannot be moved or deleted except by changing the footsteps themselves. If you edit a footstep track, the locked keys appear and disappear as the track changes. Finally, Biped also creates normal MAX keys (shown in gray). These are for skeletal elements, such as the arms, spine, and head. These keys can be edited, moved, or deleted, like any other MAX key.

Right-clicking on a Biped track other than the Footstep track displays the Change Multiple Keys dialog (see fig. 10.13). This dialog enables you to select keys based on a number of user-defined filters defined as Tracks and State filters, and to apply the last transform performed on a portion of the biped to a selected set of keys.

FIGURE 10.13

The Change Multiple Keys dialog enables you to quickly select and change the values of multiple keys.

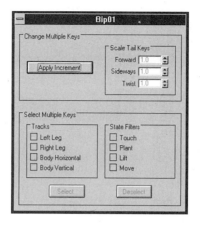

The Tracks section defines which tracks in the animation are marked for selection. These can be the Left Leg, Right Leg, Body Horizontal, and Body Vertical tracks. If you want a character's walking body to bounce up and down more, for example, check the Body Vertical box.

State filters define which portion of the step is selected. Biped defines four states that correlate to the major states of a footstep. These are not to be confused with the major poses of a walk described in the previous chapters—contact, recoil, and passing. States define where the foot contacts and leaves the ground, not the pose of the body.

- **Touch.** The point in the step where the forward foot first touches the ground.

- **Plant.** Any keys where the leg is planted on the ground. This includes the recoil and passing position.

- **Lift.** Where the planted leg lifts off the ground.

- **Move.** Any keys where the leg is off the ground. This includes the recoil and passing position.

By using a combination of Track and State selections, you can select and modify multiple keys. This can change the character of an entire walk quite easily while keeping the walk consistent.

Biped records the last mouse movement and moved body part whenever you do anything with a biped. When you click on Apply Increment, Biped applies that mouse move and updates the key for each selected key in Track View that matches the same moved body part type. If you have keys selected on both arms and legs, and you move or rotate an arm and perform an Apply Increment, only the selected keys on the arms are modified.

If you actually set a key when performing the move that is going to be applied to the entire set, the increment of that key happens twice: once for the Set Key and again for the Apply Increment. In general, you should never be in Animate mode or use Set Key if you are attempting to just modify a selected set of keys in a uniform way. The normal sequence of events is to select a set of keys, perform some interactive transform on the body part in question, and click on Apply Increment. If you do set a key when the interactive move is performed (either via Set Key or if Animate is on), the key should not be selected in Track View when performing the Apply Increment.

The frame number or keyframe for this "last recorded mouse move + body part" makes no difference because Biped is really just recording the "increment," not the actual posture. It is usually convenient, however, to adjust the increment relative to a particular keyframe.

NOTE

A bug is present in release 1.1 of Character Studio where, if you have keys selected for opposing body limbs (for example, both legs), and you perform more than one Apply Increment, the first key on the limb opposing the one transformed is not properly modified. If you perform the transform with Animate on (and deselect in Track View the modified key), Apply Increment properly updates the keys.

You may have noticed in the last example that the biped's feet were passing through the steps as the biped walked up the stairs. In the following exercise, you use the Change Multiple Keys dialog to correct this.

PLANTING THE FOOT ON THE STAIRS

1. Load the file biped03.max, which is the platform animation created previously.

2. Maximize the Left viewport and zoom in to the area of the footsteps 2 through 6. Advance to frame 40.

3. Open Track View and right-click on the Filters button. Choose Animated Tracks Only. Right-click on Objects and choose Expand All. Scroll the Track View windows to display the Footsteps track and the left and right leg transform tracks.

4. Select the right foot. Note that in Track View that a key is already present on the left leg track at this frame. Because the foot is off the ground, this is a Move state key.

5. In Track View, right-click on one of the leg transform tracks to display the Change Multiple Keys dialog. In the Select Multiple Keys section, check Left Leg and Right Leg under Tracks, and Move under State Filters. Click on the Select button. The Move keys on the right and left legs are selected in Track View.

6. The set of keys selected contains more keys than you want to adjust. Deselect the keys at and before frame 40. Deselect the keys after frame 108 (the right edge of footstep 6 is at frame 108). Deselect the last key currently selected on the right leg (see fig. 10.14).

FIGURE 10.14

The keys on the left and right leg selected when performing the first Apply Increment.

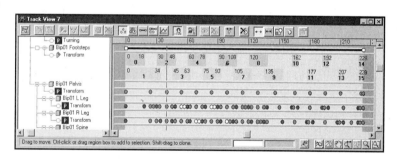

7. Click on the Animate button to turn on Animate mode. Move the right foot up 2 units on the world Z axis.

8. Click on Apply Increment in the Change Multiple Keys dialog.

9. Advance to frame 54 and select the left foot. Move the left foot back 10 units on the world Y axis, and up 1 unit on the world Z axis.

10. In Track View, deselect the second key in each pair of keys currently selected. Deselect the left leg key at frame 54 (see fig. 10.15).

FIGURE 10.15

The keys on the left and right leg selected when performing the second Apply Increment.

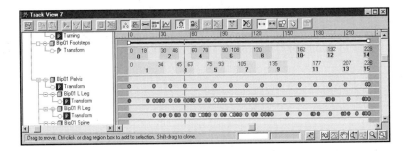

11. Click on Apply Increment in the Change Multiple Keys dialog.

12. Play the animation. As the biped walks up the stairs, his feet no longer pass through the stairs.

The final animation is on the accompanying CD in the file biped04.max.

Manipulating Biped Animation Within Track View

Manipulating a biped within Track View is an easy way to change the character of an animation quite quickly. The timing of the footsteps can be affected just by moving or resizing the footstep blocks.

Walks can also be made into runs or jumps, and vice versa. If the footstep keys are placed so that they overlap, the footsteps are *walk* footsteps (see fig. 10.16). If the footstep keys are moved so that they don't overlap, the double support is eliminated and the walk footstep becomes a *run* footstep (see fig. 10.17). If the run footstep is then moved so that both the left and right foot are airborne at the same time, and both are in contact with the ground at the same time, it becomes a *jump* (see fig. 10.18).

FIGURE 10.16

Footstep 9 is a walk footstep because it overlaps footstep 8 by three frames, giving it double support.

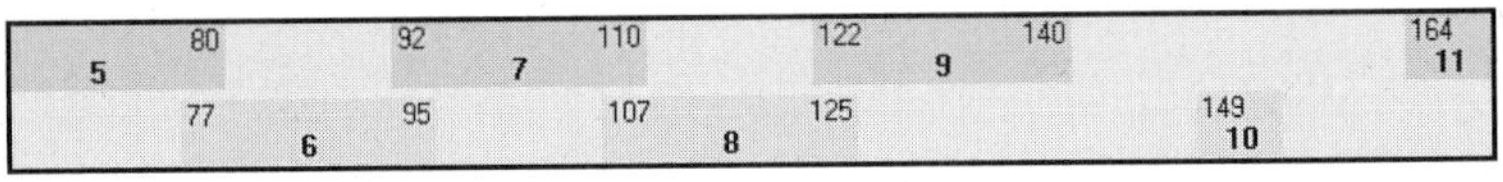

FIGURE 10.17

Moving the edge of footstep 9 so that it doesn't overlap footstep 8 turns the step into a run because double support is eliminated.

FIGURE 10.18

Moving footstep 9 so that it overlaps footstep 10 turns it from a jump into a footstep, because both feet are airborne before the step.

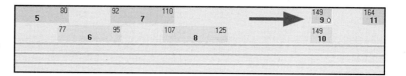

Directly Animating a Biped

Besides animating with footsteps, a biped can also be keyframed directly. The only limits are for a walking biped, because footsteps introduce calculated keys that cannot be deleted or moved outside of changing the footsteps. Outside of this handful of keys, the biped can be keyframed to give a walk more character and life. This animation can be as simple as bobbing the body up and down by animating the center of mass or as involved as introducing complex leg and arm motions—for a dance sequence or gymnastics, perhaps.

Animating a Flip

In this exercise, a gymnastic flip is added to an existing biped animation.

FLIPPING

1. Load the file biped04.max, which is the platform animation created previously. You are going to make the biped do a flip as it jumps off the platform between frames 213 and 233.

2. To make viewing this action easier, maximize the Front viewport and zoom in to the area of the jump.

3. The biped himself can be flipped 360 degrees by rotating his Center of Mass object. Select any portion of the biped and open the Motion panel. To select the Center of Mass object, click on the Center of Mass Object button in the Track Selection rollout.

4. Move the Slider to frame 219. Click on Angle Snap and rotate the Center of Mass object 140 degrees about the Y axis (see fig. 10.19). Press the Set Key button on the Biped panel.

T I P

The Set Key button sets a key for the selected limb(s). If a limb is transformed while the Animate button is toggled on, a key is automatically generated.

FIGURE 10.19

Rotating the body is a simple matter of rotating the Center of Mass object.

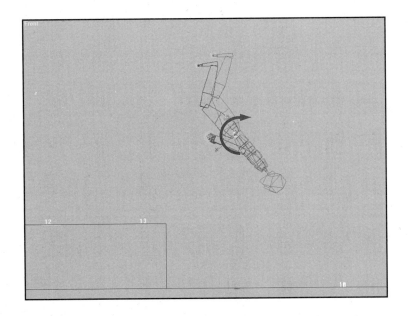

5. Move the Slider to frame 225. As you may notice, the biped tries to reverse his rotation to complete the animation because this is the shortest way to interpolate between the rotation key set at frame 219 and the key at 233. This can be fixed by further rotating the body back in the desired direction and setting another key. With Angle Snap still toggled on, rotate the biped's Center of Mass object an additional 200 degrees. Set a key.

6. Notice how the biped automatically extends his legs because the plug-in automatically computes the dynamics of the biped. As you will see later, dynamics can be turned off. For this animation, it is perfectly acceptable.

7. Play the animation. The biped does the flip. Still, the animation looks rather stiff. This animation can be given a bit more liveliness in many ways. These methods also employ the various Biped tools.

8. The takeoff step (step 13) is 6 frames long. To make the takeoff slightly quicker, this can be shortened to 4 frames. From Track View, locate the footstep block for step 13 and click on its right edge. Drag the edge to shorten the step so that it runs from frame 207 to 211.

9. The biped also seems a little light when it takes off. To give it the illusion of weight, the body needs to move lower before taking off because the legs need to absorb the shock of the body and also anticipate the leap. On frame 207, when the foot makes contact, select the Center of Mass object and move it down approximately 5 units in Z. Set a key.

10. During the flip, the left leg moves forward and kicks backward to make the body flip. Anticipate the kick motion by bringing the left foot forward at frame 207 (see fig. 10.20). Set a key.

FIGURE 10.20

Move the right leg forward by dragging the foot. This helps to anticipate the flip.

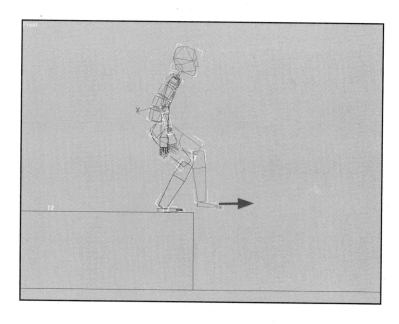

11. Animate the kick of the left foot. Go to frame 200 and drag the left foot back behind the right leg. Set a key.

12. The body should bend forward a bit more before it takes off. This can be done by rotating the spine around the Z axis. The easiest way to do this is by using the Bend Links mode. Toggle the Bend Links button on and then select a spine segment. Go to frame 207 and rotate the segment about 40 degrees around the Z axis. Set a key.

13. Scrub the animation. Notice that the spine motion pops at frame 209. When Biped created the original jump, it placed a key for the spine at frame 209. With the key just set at frame 207, this key is now extraneous. Delete this key either in Track View, or by advancing to frame 209 and clicking on the Delete Key button in the Track Operations rollout with a spine segment selected.

14. Scrub the animation. At the end of the jump, the spine straightens out—which is fine for a standing pose—but the spine straightens out too early. Go to frame 207, where the spine key was set. Select the spinal segments. Click on Copy Posture. Move to frame 223, slightly before the landing, and press Paste Posture. The spine bends. Set a key.

15. To anticipate the jump, the arms swing forward quite a bit. Go to frame 205. Select the right hand and move it forward and up so that it is even with the chest and the arm is slightly bent (see fig. 10.21). Set a key. Do the same with the left arm.

FIGURE 10.21

The arms swing forward before the flip.

16. When the flip begins, the arms pull in toward the body to help give it rotation. On frame 213, move both the right and left hands so that they are roughly even with the hips and the arms are slightly bent. Set keys for both limbs.

17. The head needs to be tucked toward the chest as the body rotates. Go to frame 223 and rotate the head in to the chest. Set a key.

18. Finally, the biped should absorb the impact of the landing a bit more. Go to frame 230 and move the Center of Mass object down about 6 or 7 units (see fig. 10.22). Set a key.

FIGURE 10.22
Upon impact, the body continues moving down to absorb the shock before the character stands.

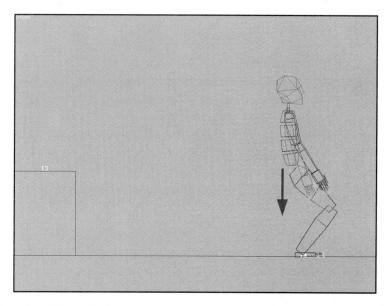

Play the animation. These little tweaks go a long way toward making the flip more realistic and natural. The lesson here is that Biped gives you basic motion only; it is the animator who makes the skeleton come alive. Biped is a very nice tool, but it still needs to be driven by an animator.

This animation can be found on the accompanying CD as biped05.max.

Free-Form Animation

Not every action in every animation requires footsteps. People also stand still, sit, swim, and sometimes fly. As stated previously, with version 1.1, footsteps are no longer a requirement to animate a biped—making the previously mentioned actions easier to animate. If footsteps are in the scene, the free-form animation must be set up in an area between footsteps. Free-form keys cannot be set before the first footstep, nor after the last.

Free-Form Animation Without Footsteps

Free-form animation without footsteps is an all or nothing proposition. After keys have been set, footsteps cannot be added to the shot. If footsteps are required in addition to free-form animation, you can accomplish this by suspending dynamics. This is discussed in the next section.

Animating a biped in free-form mode without footsteps gives you many advantages, most important of which is that the biped's IK remains active, making it very easy to pose the character. Biped keys are still calculated in the same way, with the keys being assigned to limbs rather than individual joints. The only exception is that vertical dynamics is suspended while in free-form mode without footsteps. The vertical and horizontal position of the biped's Center of Mass object between keyframes is based on a spline interpolation of the keyframes. Because there are no footsteps, there will also be no calculated or restricted keys.

Free-Form Animation with Footsteps

Free-form animation with footsteps is very similar to animating a biped without them. The task requires a few extra keystrokes to enable. The free section must be free of any footsteps. Normally, Biped's dynamics want to control the trajectory of the biped, as in a jump. To animate the character completely unencumbered, these dynamics need to be suspended.

FREE-FORM FOOTSTEPS

1. Open Track View and right-click on the Footsteps track to open the Footstep Track dialog.

2. In the Footstep Track dialog, choose the Edit Free Form (no physics) option.

3. The areas between footsteps are highlighted with a yellow box. These are areas where vertical dynamics are being calculated. Clicking on a box turns it solid yellow, causing vertical dynamics to be suspended (see fig. 10.23).

FIGURE 10.23

Free-form areas with vertical dynamics turned off are shown as solid yellow boxes in the Footstep track in Track View.

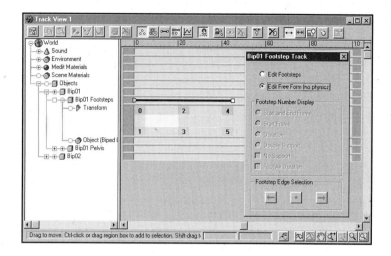

After vertical dynamics is suspended, the biped can be animated in any manner desired—to fly it around the world, for instance, or to mount and ride a bicycle. The only caveat is that the free-form animation must occur between two sets of footsteps, which means that the biped's feet automatically attach themselves to footprints when the free-form section ends.

If the free-form section is at the end of the animation, the end footsteps must be placed a few frames past the end of the animation. The converse goes for free-form animation at the beginning of a scene. In that situation, the footsteps preceding the free-form section are placed before the first rendered frame.

If the character is to resume walking, the free-form animation needs to match up to the footprints at the end of the free-form section, otherwise the biped seems to pop into place.

Standing Still

If your character's feet are firmly planted throughout the animation, you can place only two footsteps in the scene and extend their lengths from within Track View to match the length of the scene. This locks the feet down and gives you the freedom to animate the upper body as desired.

Attaching the Hands and Feet to MAX Objects

Biped has the capability to attach or lock a biped's hands and feet to any object in the scene, which enables Biped skeletons to grip and hold onto things, as well as to keep their feet firmly locked to moving objects (an escalator, perhaps). The object attached to may be a point in the world space or a point relative to another object (the Object Space object).

These attachments can be animated through the use of the IK Blend spinner in the Track Operations rollout (see fig. 10.24). This spinner is the heart of Biped's animatable IK attachments. With it, you can make a biped's hand or foot gradually release his lock. When the IK Blend is set to 1.0, the hand or foot is firmly locked relative to the object space object or at a point in space. If the rest of the biped is moved, the hand or foot remains at the same location. At an IK Blend of 0.0, the motion of the hand or foot is based on the motion of the biped. If the rest of the biped is moved, the hand or foot moves along with it.

Each key for a hand or foot can be set in the Body or Object coordinate space. If two consecutive keys are set in Body space, and the IK Blend value for each is set to 1.0, the location of the hand or foot is interpolated between these keys based on the motion of the object space object. If the object space object is moving, therefore, the hand or foot moves along with that object. To attach a hand or foot to an object or a point in space, use the following steps.

ATTACHING HANDS OR FEET

1. Select the hand or foot.

2. Position the hand or foot in its desired position relative to the object to follow.

3. Click on the Select Object Space Object button.

4. Click on the object to follow. Not selecting an object binds the hand or foot to a fixed position in world space.

5. In the Kinematics section, choose the Object option.

6. Set the IK Blend spinner at 1.0

7. Click on Set Key.

Figure 10.24

The Track Operations rollout with the Kinematics box. All the operations for animating a lock occur here.

To release an object, spin IK Blend to 0.0 and set another key. As the spinner animates to zero, the lock is gradually broken. If you want to keep a hand or foot locked for a period of time and then release the lock, a second IK Blend key of 1.0 is needed to keep it locked for the time up until the release begins. To maintain the position of the hand or foot relative to the object space object, toggle on the appropriate Anchor button in the Track Operations rollout. This action holds the hand or foot in place regardless of the keys set for the hand or foot. Anchors are not permanent, rather they are interactive tools to enable you to set keys with the hand or foot in a fixed position relative to the object space object (or fixed in world space if no object space object has been chosen).

One new feature with version 1.1 is the capability to attach portions of a biped to himself by using the IK Blend function. This enables you to work with closed loops of biped linkages and objects. A sword may be linked to a biped's left hand, for example, and the right hand may be linked via IK Blend to the sword, creating a closed loop of links that can be animated together. As a result, movement of the left hand controls both the sword and the movement of the entire right arm. In addition, you can animate the IK Blend spinner for the right hand to release its grip on the sword during motion.

Using IK Attachments to Dribble a Ball

In this exercise, you experiment with IK attachments, and see how changing the IK attachment parameters affects the biped's motion.

Dribbling a Ball

1. From the accompanying CD, load dribble.max, which contains a biped and a ball. Activate the Left viewport and play the animation.

The left hand has been positioned to be on top of the ball at frame 0. It then moves down to the biped's side at frame 16. The ball moves up, and then down to hit the ground, and bounces back up.

2. Select the biped's left hand and open the Motion panel.

3. Go to frame 0. Click on the Select Object Space Object button and then click on the ball. Object Ball appears as the object space object. Select Object in the Kinematics section of the Track Operations rollout. Set the IK Blend value to 1.0, and click on Set Key.

   Based on the height of the ball, you want the hand to remain locked to the ball until frame 10. If we just advance to frame 10 though, the hand is no longer in its proper position relative to the ball.

4. At frame 0, click on the Anchor Left Hand button to toggle it on. Advance to frame 10, select Object in the Kinematics section of the Track Operations rollout, set the IK Blend value to 1.0, and click on Set Key. Click on the Anchor Left Hand button to toggle it off and play the animation.

   The hand now remains in a fixed position relative to the ball on frames 0 to 10, and then drops away from the ball and moves to the side of the biped. Now you want to catch the ball on its rise.

5. At frame 0, click on the Anchor Left Hand button to toggle it on. Advance to frame 33, select Object in the Kinematics section of the Track Operations rollout, set the IK Blend value to 1.0, and click on Set Key. Click on the Anchor Left Hand button to toggle it off and play the animation. The hand now meets the ball as it is rising.

6. Perform an Edit/Hold to save the file and start playing with the IK attachment parameters, particularly on frames 0 and 10. Note that if Body space is selected or the IK Blend value is 0, the motion of the ball has no affect on the motion of the hand.

The final animation can be found on the accompanying CD as dribble2.max.

Using IK Attachments to Ride a Bicycle

In this exercise, you see how Biped's animatable attachments can help with difficult animation tasks. Locking objects to a bicycle, such as both hands to the handlebars, can easily cause dependency loops in MAX's native IK.

Biped provides a very elegant solution and enables you to lock different parts of the biped's hierarchy to any object or combination of objects.

RIDING A BICYCLE

1. From the accompanying CD, load bipbike.max, which contains a biped and a simple bicycle (see fig. 10.25).

FIGURE 10.25

The biped and his bicycle.

2. Select the biped's Center of Mass object and open the Motion panel. Drag the biped so that his pelvis is over the seat. Go to frame 0 and set a key for both the Vertical and Horizontal tracks. This can be done by selecting the Restrict to X or the Restrict to Y button and clicking on Set Key, and selecting the Restrict to Z button and clicking on Set Key. Alternatively, you can select the Restrict to XZ or Restrict to YZ button and click Set Key. This will create keys on both the Vertical and Horizontal tracks. When you set the first key, a warning stating that you are about to create a Biped animation without footsteps appears. This is fine, so press OK.

3. Link the biped to the bicycle. Press the Select and Link button on the toolbar. Drag a line from the Center of Mass object to the bicycle seat to make the biped a child of the bicycle, enabling him to move wherever the bicycle moves.

4. Bend the biped over a bit so that the arms can reach the handlebars. Select one spine segment and, using Bend Links, rotate the spine approximately 32° about his Z axis so that the chest is over the pedals (see fig. 10.26). Set a key.

FIGURE 10.26

The Biped properly positioned before linking the feet to the pedals. The spine is bent forward.

5. Select the biped's right foot. Drag this up and forward so that it rests directly over the right pedal. Select the left foot and drag it to the left pedal in the same manner (see fig. 10.27).

FIGURE 10.27

The biped with the legs locked to the pedals.

6. Link the right foot to the right pedal. Select the right foot. In the Kinematics section of the Track Operations rollout, choose the option marked Object. Press the Select Object Space Object button. Click on the right pedal to select this as the object space object. Set the IK Blend spinner at 1.0. With the Time Slider on frame 0, set a key for the foot.

7. Repeat this procedure for the left foot and left pedal.

   Both feet are now locked to the pedals. They will move wherever the pedals move. The pedals have already been linked to the crank, so they will rotate at the crank rotates.

8. Scrub the animation. The feet now follow the pedals. Next, you need to attach the hands to the handlebars.

9. Select the hands and position them over the handlebars. To get a more natural pose, you should also rotate the arms so that the elbows are slightly out from the body. At frame 0, set a key for each arm to lock in the angle of the elbows.

10. Using the same procedure in step 6, lock each hand to the Bike-Handle object and set a key for each hand's IK Blend at frame 0.

11. Rotate the handle bars. The hands and arms should follow.

12. Adjust the biped's Center of Mass object so that the pelvis rests firmly on the seat. Set a key at frame 0. Figure 10.28 shows the final position of the biped.

FIGURE 10.28

With the hands and feet locked to bike, the biped's animation is driven by the animation of the bike.

13. Experiment with the animation. Because the links are bound on frame 0, any motion of the bike past that point is reflected in the biped. You can extend the animation by copying the cycle of the pedals, and can make the bicycle move by translating it. Rotations to the handlebars are reflected, and if you want to make the biped stand up on the pedals, translate the Center of Mass object up so that the biped stands.

This final animation is on the accompanying CD in a file called bikefin.max.

Saving and Loading Canned Motions

Biped enables you to save motions from one biped and apply them to another. The motions apply regardless of the differences in size and structure of the two bipeds. This is very powerful in that it enables you to create canned libraries of motions that can be applied anywhere. Biped has two types of motion files: Biped (.BIP) files store the footsteps and associated keyframes of a biped character; and step files (.STP) store just the footsteps.

The STP file format is rarely used because it merely generates the default Biped motions when loaded. This file format was mainly provided for programmers who might wish to write software that parametrically creates STP footstep patterns (crowds of bipeds walking in a building, for example).

A major feature of Biped is its capability to adapt any BIP file to your character without changing its kinematic structure, dimensions, distribution of weight, and so on. Furthermore, any Physique mapping is also completely independent from the motions. You may load any BIP file on to a biped without changing his Physiqued skin, or his pose, kinematic structure, and center-of-gravity in Biped's Figure Mode. The only animation type data not stored in a BIP file are IK attachments to scene-specific objects—because these are, by nature, scene specific. This data is best stored in scenes in the normal MAX file format.

To save a STP or BIP file, select any portion of the biped and, in the Biped Motion panel, click on the Save File button in the General rollout. Select the type of file to save and its path and file name, and click on OK. All footsteps (and keys for BIP files) associated with the biped are saved.

To replace the entire animation currently applied to a biped with that defined in a BIP file, select any portion of the biped and, in the Biped Motion panel, click on the Load File button. Select the BIP file to load and click on OK.

A BIP file can also be read into the Footstep buffer and spliced into the current animation. To do this, you need to be in Buffer mode and then load the BIP file. To enter Buffer mode, however, footsteps need to be present in the Footstep buffer. To do this, you need to go into Footstep Track mode, select one or more footsteps, and click on Copy Selected Footsteps in the Footstep Operations rollout. This action copies the selected footsteps into the Footstep buffer and enables the Buffer Mode button.

Frequently, you will not want to apply the entire animation defined in a BIP file, but only a section of it. Currently, there is no way to do this directly. Although you can load the animation defined by the BIP file into the Footstep buffer and delete the undesired footsteps, this causes the animation keys to be regenerated. This can cause a loss of the very animation data you are trying splice in. The easiest way to get around this is to place another biped in the scene, apply the animation in the BIP to that biped, and copy and paste motions from this biped to the desired biped.

SPLICING MOTIONS

1. Load cswalk.max from the accompanying CD. This file contains a biped walking forward, turning left, and walking a bit farther. You want splice in a motion where the biped walks on tiptoes.

2. Create another biped in the Perspective viewport. This biped will be used as an intermediary, holding the animation imported from the BIP file for application to the original biped.

    Because Biped can properly adjust the animation data while moving between dissimilar bipeds, the details of this biped do not need to match those of the original biped. To prevent the loss of data, however, if the original biped has arms or a tail, this biped also should have arms or a tail. As a practical matter, this biped should be roughly the same height as the original biped.

3. With this new biped selected, in the Biped motion panel click on the Load File button in the General rollout. Load creep.bip from the accompanying CD.

4. Play the animation. As the original biped walks along, the new biped creeps along.

5. With the new biped selected, click on the Footstep Track button. Select footsteps 3 through 5, and click on the Copy Selected Footsteps button in the Footstep Operations rollout. Click on the Footstep Track button to exit Footstep mode.

6. Select any portion of the original biped and click on the Footstep Track button. Click on the Insert Footstep Buffer onto Footsteps button to display the footsteps in the Footstep buffer.

7. Drag the first buffer footstep over the biped's footstep number 10 and release the mouse. The remaining original footsteps are now shown in their saturated colors. Drag these footsteps so that the first one is over the new footstep number 12 and release the mouse.

8. Click on the Footstep Track button to exit Footstep mode, activate the Perspective viewport, and play the animation. At this point, you can delete or hide the biped added to the scene.

When you splice in a set of footsteps, sometimes the leg rotation near the end of the splice is very visibly incorrect—the upper leg is pointing toward the biped's head. A single key has been improperly set in these cases. To correct this, perform the remaining steps:

9. Select the leg with the incorrect rotation.

10. Toggle the Key Mode Toggle button on (the Key Mode Toggle is located at the bottom on the MAX window, with the Time controls).

11. Click on the Select and Move or Select and Rotate button.

12. Click on the Next Frame or Previous Frame button to advance to the keyframe where the leg rotation is incorrect. Note the frame number and the pose of the biped.

13. Click on the Next Frame or Previous Frame button to advance to a keyframe where the biped is in a similar pose.

14. Click on the Copy Posture button to copy the leg's rotation to a buffer.

15. Return to the keyframe where the leg rotation is incorrect. Click on the Paste Posture button to set the leg's rotation from the buffer. Click on Set Key.

By using BIP files, you can set up libraries of motion that can easily be applied to any biped. The capability to share animations between bipeds, regardless of their size or structure, is not found in any other application.

In Practice: Biped

- **Manipulating bipeds.** Using Biped's manipulation tools, such as Select Opposite, can help streamline your work. It is also possible to freeze or hide parts of a biped while working on others.

- **Footstep driven animation.** Although footsteps certainly take a lot of the drudgery out of creating locomotive sequences, they are only the first step. To truly bring your characters to life, you need to go back over the Biped-generated motions and bring them to life by adding animation.

- **Bipeds in hierarchies.** If your biped is a child of another object, the biped and his footsteps move in relation to the parent. This makes scenes that require moving footsteps—such as ice-skating or walking up a moving escalator—possible by parenting the escalator's stairs to the biped.

- **Free-form animation.** Free-form animation between footsteps defaults to having dynamics turned on, which causes the biped to simulate a jump motion. Typically, it is best to turn dynamics off when starting a free-form animation.

- **Animatable locks.** This is a very powerful feature, so be certain to practice its use, and be familiar with the keystrokes. In addition to locking hands and feet to objects or world space, they can be locked in relation to the body itself.

- **Splicing motions.** This is a feature unique to Biped that enables you to apply animation data to bipeds with dissimilar structures. By building and using libraries of canned motions, you can quickly build complex animations for your characters.

IMAGE CREATED BY GEORGE MAESTRI

Chapter 11

by George Maestri

MESH DEFORMATION

In real life, most characters are made out of a single skin. In MAX, this skin can be a single polygonal or patch mesh. This mesh, however, will look like a rigid statue unless you find a way to deform it. In real life, skin is very flexible, and the actions of muscles and bones beneath the skin are all that is needed to bend and flex the skin. In MAX, a number of tools do exactly the same thing. These are known as skeletal deformation tools *because they take a skeleton—a biped or a custom-built skeleton—and use that skeleton to deform a mesh much like it would appear in real life.*

MAX's open architecture allows for any number of methods for deforming meshes, and several plug-ins are on the market. Most popular are Character Studio's Physique and Digimation's Bones Pro. Additionally, several methods for deforming MAX geometry use native MAX tools—most notably the Linked XForm tool.

This chapter covers the following topics:

- Getting meshes to behave
- Basic mesh deformation
- Fitting a skeleton to a mesh
- Bones Pro
- MetaReyes

Getting Meshes to Behave

Although deforming a character with a mesh deformation tool may look easy, getting your mesh to deform smoothly can sometimes be a real problem. No matter which plug-in you decide to use, your joints will find ways to crimp, bulge, tear, or flatten at the wrong places, making your character look worse than when you started. Every animator runs into these problems, but you can use several techniques to help your meshes behave:

- Choose patches over polygons
- Build the mesh with the character's arms outstretched
- Add extra detail at the bends

Patches over Polygons

Spline patches control far more surface area with fewer vertices than a polygonal model does. As such, a patch-based model will be easier to control for two reasons. First, because there are fewer vertices, it will be easier to assign those vertices to the proper bone in the skeleton. Second, and more importantly, patches always keep a smooth surface between the vertices. A polygonal model, on the other hand, has many more vertices, and has flat areas between the vertices. Currently, the best and easiest way to build spline patch-based models is by using Digimation's Surface Tools.

Surface Tools enables the user to generate patch surfaces from interwoven splines. Any segments that form a three- or four-sided closed polygon create a surface that will be patched. Currently, it is one of the best ways to create seamless surfaces within MAX (see fig. 11.1). The surfaces created are also completely compatible with both Character Studio and Bones Pro MAX.

FIGURE 11.1
A cylinder constructed out of a spline patch deforms much more smoothly than the same cylinder constructed out of polygons. The same goes for characters.

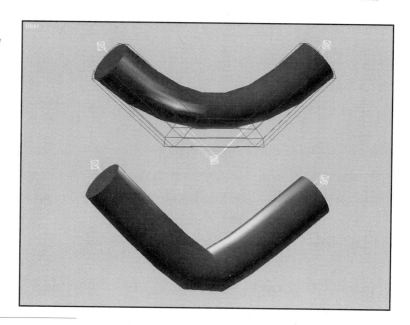

Arms Outstretched

The best argument for building a character this way is that the arms are exactly halfway between the extremes that the arm can take. It is tempting to build a character with its arms at its side. This is one of the more common poses a human takes. Unfortunately, if a character built that way needs to put his arms above his head, the skin around the underarms will have to stretch twice as much as if it were built with the arms outstretched. Centering the arms helps prevent crimping, tearing, and unwanted bulging later on when the character is deformed (see fig. 11.2).

Because the legs don't have nearly the range of motion the arms have, keeping them outstretched is not as critical, particularly for characters that only walk and sit. If the characters are supposed to be performing gymnastics, it might give you a bit more control if the legs were slightly apart when built.

FIGURE 11.2
Building a character
with the arms
outstretched allows for
a much wider range of
motion.

Extra Detail at the Bends

Adding detail only where it is needed will keep your models light and easy to control. Many places on the body don't flex as much as others. The elbow and the skin around it flexes quite a bit, for example, but the forearm itself remains fairly rigid. Therefore, the forearm does not need nearly as much detail to retain its shape as the area around the elbow joint. Extra detail also needs to be placed at the knees, the shoulder, the crotch area, and the areas around the wrists and the many joints of the hand. One good reference is the Viewpoint models supplied with MAX and Character Studio, which are built with detail in the proper places.

Eliminating the detail from rigid areas such as the forearm significantly reduces the number of vertices in the model and also reduces the total weight of the model (see fig. 11.3). A lighter model will animate easier, will deform more quickly, and will render faster.

FIGURE 11.3

Add detail only where it is needed—at the joint areas where the mesh will flex and bend.

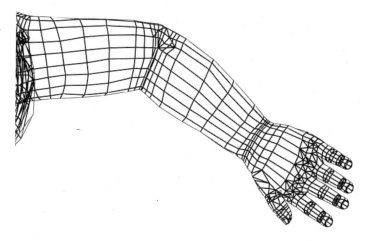

Fitting a Skeleton to a Mesh

After the solid mesh model is built, a skeleton of bones needs to be fit into it for the solid mesh to be deformed. Construction of skeletons was discussed in detail in the previous three chapters. The skeleton can be a biped, a skeleton of MAX bones, or be made from geometry such as boxes. The skeleton is usually tied together in a hierarchy and set up for animation using forward or inverse kinematics.

If you are not using Biped and are building a custom skeleton from scratch, it is best to construct the skeleton with the mesh in mind—even going to the point where you are actually loading the mesh model, freezing it, then building the skeleton within it, and finally linking the skeleton together in a hierarchy and setting up IK last.

However it is done, the key to fitting a skeleton to a mesh is lining up the joints correctly. Typically, the extra detail that was modeled in the joints is the guide to use. Line up the joints of the skeleton so that they match up with the joints of the mesh. The key areas to focus on are

- The elbow and knee
- The hip and pelvis
- The shoulders

The Elbow and Knee Areas

Placement of bones in the elbow and knee areas is fairly straightforward (see fig. 11.4). Center the joint of the bones within the area defined by the joint. If it was modeled properly, the mesh should have a bit of extra detail in this area to help guide the positioning of the bones.

FIGURE 11.4

Placement of bones in an elbow or knee joint.

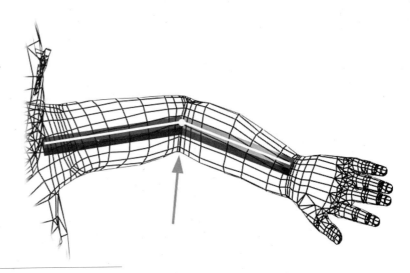

The Hip and Pelvis Area

The hips and pelvis can prove a bit problematic. The hip bone needs to be centered within the hip area, with the leg bones proceeding down through the center of the leg. The detail in the crotch usually flows along an approximately 45-degree angle along the so-called bikini line. Place the joint of the hips and the legs along this line, resizing the hips if necessary (see fig. 11.5).

The Shoulder Areas

The shoulder areas can also be problematic. A flexible shoulder joint aids in placement, particularly if the character is normally sloop shouldered. If this is the case, the shoulder can be rotated downward to match the sloop of the shoulders. The joint between the shoulder and the upper arm should be placed immediately above the armpit (see fig. 11.6).

FIGURE 11.5
The placement of joints in the pelvis area.

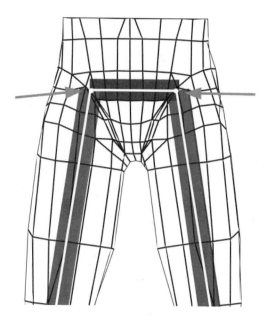

FIGURE 11.6
Placement of joints in the shoulder areas.

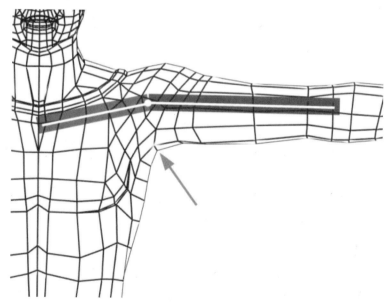

Basic Mesh Deformation

After the model has been built, it will look like a very attractive statue. To animate it so it will spring to life, the model will need to be deformed, much like the bones and muscles deform and shape our skin. Several methods can be employed to accomplish this. The most popular methods are Linked XForms, Bones Pro, and Physique. Each method requires a different procedure. To get a comparative overview, therefore, it is best to show the fundamentals of each procedure on a simple object such as a cylinder, which is very similar to an arm or leg joint.

Deforming a Cylinder with Linked XForms

Using Linked XForms is one method that can be employed without additional plug-ins. The Linked XForm is a very direct manipulation tool that can be used in a variety of situations. It enables you to link a set of vertices to a control object, such as a dummy, a box, or in this case, a MAX bone. This technique leverages on the flexibility of this modifier to attach specific vertices of the model directly to the skeleton.

XFORM DEFORMATION

1. Load the file bone-cyl.max from the accompanying CD. This file contains a simple cylinder with a set of MAX bones inside.

2. Apply an Edit Mesh modifier to the cylinder.

3. From the front or top viewport select the vertices on the right side of the cylinder (see fig. 11.7).

4. Select the Linked XForm modifier.

5. Within the Linked XForm rollout, press the Pick Control Object button.

FIGURE 11.7

Select the vertices on either side of the cylinder and apply a Linked XForm modifier to them.

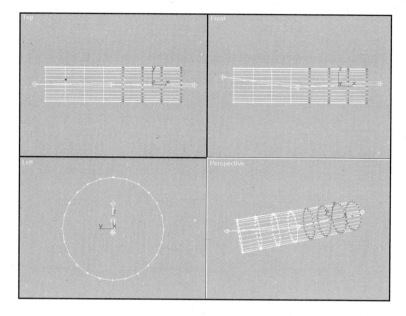

6. Select Bone01 as the Control object. Select by name to avoid mistakes.

7. Select the cylinder once again. Add another Edit Mesh modifier to the stack.

8. Select the vertices on the left side of the cylinder.

9. Select the Linked XForm modifier.

10. Within the Linked XForm rollout, press the Pick Control Object button.

11. Select Bone03 as the Control object.

The mesh of the cylinder will now be deformed by the bones. Turn on IK and translate the end of the bone chain. Because the vertices of the mesh are directly connected to the bones, they move along with them. The one problem with this method is that there is no weighting of vertices, so you can get flat spots in the area between the neighboring Linked XForm modifiers (see fig. 11.8).

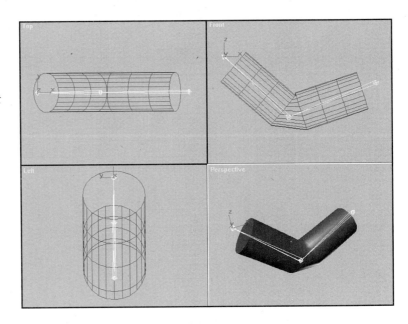

If the cylinder object were created out of spline patches, the flat spots would smooth themselves over automatically. Not all characters are made of splines, however. One way to sneak around this is to introduce a Mesh Smooth modifier in the stack after the Linked XForms. MeshSmooth will actually add vertices and smooth out the flat spots in the mesh.

1. To further smooth the mesh, add an Edit Mesh modifier to the top of the stack.

2. Select those vertices immediately surrounding the joint area.

3. Apply the MeshSmooth modifier.

The file bonexfor.max on the accompanying CD shows an example of this technique.

This procedure adds vertices in the problem area and smooths out the joint (see fig. 11.9). Mesh Smooth could be applied to the entire cylinder, but this is not necessary because it would just add extra vertices where they are not needed. Applying the modifier to only the problem area helps keep the vertex count down and keeps the model as light as possible.

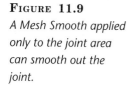

FIGURE 11.9

A Mesh Smooth applied only to the joint area can smooth out the joint.

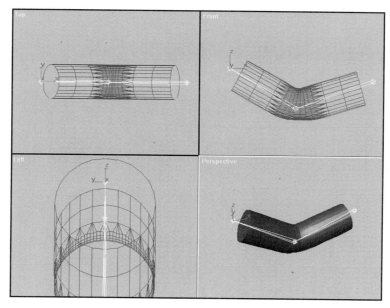

The one problem with the Mesh Smooth modifier is that it adds vertices to the model and can adversely affect topology dependent modifiers, such as texture mapping. All UVW mapping must be placed on the object after the MeshSmooth modifier has been applied.

Deforming a Cylinder with Bones Pro

Bones Pro is a plug-in sold by Digimation. It enables much more discrete control over the mesh than the previous method. As you will see later in this chapter, Bones Pro enables vertex-by-vertex control over the deformation of a mesh, along with weighting of vertices between bones. A demo version of Bones Pro is on the accompanying CD.

BONES PRO DEFORMATION

1. Load bone-cyl.max from the accomanying CD-ROM.

2. The Bones Pro modifier is a space warp. To create a modifier, go to the space warp Creation panel and press Bones Pro.

3. Click in a viewport. A six-sided object appears that resembles a jack. This is the Bones Pro object and will not render.

4. Space warps need to be bound to the object they affect. Press the Bind to Space Warp button on the toolbar. Select the cylinder and drag a line to the Bones Pro object.

5. After the cylinder has been bound, you may select the Bones Pro object and go to the Modify panel. This is where specific bones are applied to the cylinder.

6. Assign some bones. In the box marked Bones, select Assign. A dialog appears with the names of the objects in the scene. Highlight Bone02 and Bone03 and then press Select.

7. Assign the bound node. In the box marked Bound Node, select Assign. A dialog appears with the names of the objects in the scene. Highlight Cylinder01 and then press Select.

8. Bones Pro deforms objects that are animated only and references a "Master" frame (defaulted to frame 0) that indicates the starting position of the deformation (see fig. 11.10). To make the mesh deform, turn Animate on and move the Time Slider a few frames into the scene. Manipulating the bones will cause the mesh to deform.

FIGURE 11.10

The cylinder deformed using Bones Pro.

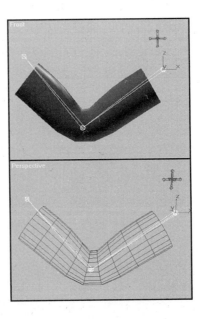

Deforming a Cylinder with Physique

Physique is part of Character Studio. It is a direct modifier and, as you will see in the next chapter, it has a number of features that closely tie it to Biped. The package also supports a number of advanced features, such as the capability to accurately define bulging and crimping of joints.

PHYSIQUE DEFORMATION

1. Load bone-cyl.max.

2. Select the cylinder.

3. From the Modify panel, select the Physique modifier and apply it to the stack.

4. Press Attach to Node. The cursor will change to resemble a stick figure.

5. In the Front viewport, position the cursor over the root node of the bone hierarchy all the way to the right. The cursor turns into a skeleton. This is Bone01. Click on the bone.

The modifier is now attached. Turn on IK and select the end node of the bone chain. Translating the bone will deform the mesh (see fig. 11.11).

FIGURE 11.11

The cylinder deformed using Physique.

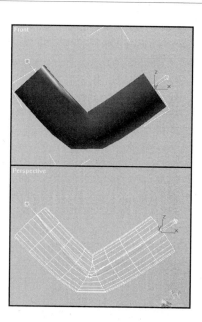

Differences Between Bones Pro and Physique

Although Bones Pro and Physique accomplish the same task, they go about it in two completely different ways. No plug-in is ideal for all tasks, and the plethora of MAX plug-ins gives you more freedom in deciding which plug-in will work for a specific task. Because the mesh deformation plug-ins are so different, it is a good idea to outline these differences.

- Bones Pro is a space warp, Physique is an Object modifier.

- Bones Pro references the pose of the skeleton at a specific frame (usually frame 0). Physique references the pose of the skeleton when the Physique modifier is applied.

- Bones Pro requires that the Animation button be set active and key frames be set to deform the mesh. Once attached to the default pose, Physique always deforms the mesh.

- Physique requires that all bones be connected via a hierarchy. Bones Pro can use any combination of bones, linked or not.

- Bones Pro enables vertex-by-vertex assignment and weighting to any bone in the skeleton. Physique can allocate to a bone only those vertices located within a cylinder defined by the edges that bone.

- Physique enables user-defined bulging and crimping, as well as tendons for maintaining an object's overall shape. To control bulging and crimping in Bones Pro, extra bones may need to be added.

Deformations Using FFD Lattices

Free Form Deformations (FFDs), or lattices, are another way to deform meshes without resorting to third party plug-ins. Lattices are good overall tools for modeling, and their control vertices can be animated, which makes them a good option for performing mesh deformations. The best way to use lattices is for local deformations. Because FFDs cannot be linked together, or the control vertices of the lattice manipulated by Linked XForms, it is not feasible to use lattices as the sole tool used to deform entire bodies. Lattices, however, can help out quite a bit with other tasks, such as creating bulging biceps or making fat bellies jiggle.

To accomplish these sorts of effects, the FFD is best applied as a sub-object modifier, usually in conjunction with edit mesh. The best FFD to use in this context is the 4×4×4 modifier, which enables you to keep one row of vertices stable on each end of the modifier to keep the transition into the lattice deformed area smooth. Once inside, two rows of vertices are available to deform the mesh inside the area.

Creating a Bulging Muscle by Using FFDs

Combined with Linked XForm and MeshSmooth, FFDs can help the plug-in–challenged MAX animator create bulging muscles. For those with Character Studio, the following method can also be used to create deformations that are difficult for Physique to conquer, such as the jiggling of a fat man's belly.

BULGING MUSCLES

Load the file ffdbulge.max, which contains a simple cylinder attached to a set of bones using Linked XForm and MeshSmooth.

1. Scrub the animation to see how the arm bends.

2. Select the cylinder. Apply an edit Mesh modifier to the stack.

3. Select the vertices at the far right side of the Cylinder, from the end of the cylinder to where the Mesh Smooth modifier is applied.

4. Apply the 4×4×4 FFD modifier to these vertices.

5. Enable Animation and scrub the animation to frame 30. At this point, the arm is bent, and the Bicep can bulge. Unfortunately, the lattice remains oriented the wrong way. It will need to be rotated.

6. With the FFD modifier active, select sub-object/lattice. Select the lattice and rotate it so that it is oriented in the same direction as the upper part of the cylinder.

7. Select Sub Object/Control points. Select the points along the top side of the bicep. Move these points upward to create a nice bulge (see fig. 11.12).

Because the animation button was enabled, the bulge should grow as the time slider is scrubbed. This file has been saved as ffdbulg2.max.

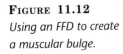

FIGURE 11.12
Using an FFD to create a muscular bulge.

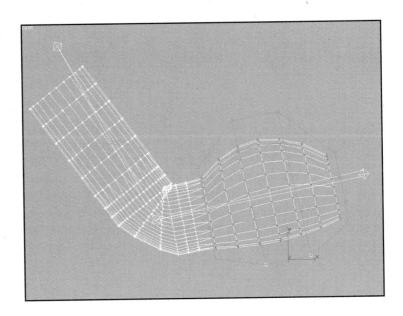

Bones Pro

Digimation's Bones Pro is classified as a space warp. As the previous example illustrated, a space warp needs to be bound to the object it affects. Bones Pro also needs Animation to be active when the body is manipulated for the effect to work.

Bones Pro may use any object as a bone, but it only looks at the bounding boxes of those objects when deciding which vertices to affect. This means that complex geometry used as bones is not necessary. A sphere will still be seen by Bones Pro as a cube because that is the shape of the sphere's bounding box. Because a box's outline is also its bounding box, boxes make for light and easy-to-visualize bones.

Bones Pro Rollout

The Bones Pro rollout is where the bones themselves are selected and assigned to the mesh. You should be aware of certain controls in this rollout (see fig. 11.13):

- Master Frame
- Bones and Bound Node boxes
- Falloff and Strength spinners

FIGURE 11.13

FIGURE 11.13

The Bones Pro rollout.

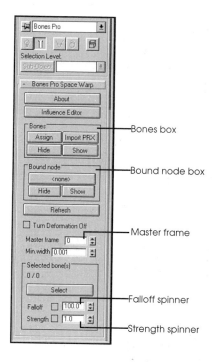

Bones box

Bound node box

Master frame

Falloff spinner

Strength spinner

Master Frame

The Master Frame spinner determines on which frame the vertices are assigned to the mesh. Usually, this is frame zero, but any frame can be selected. What is essential is that the skeleton be fitted properly to the mesh on the selected frame.

The fact that Bones Pro requires a Master Frame may make it a bit tricky to get it working with a biped. Bones Pro does not reference Biped's Figure Mode information, so getting the biped into a stable pose so that it can be fit to the mesh may be a bit tricky. If a biped's animation involves footsteps, the best way to get around this is to create a Freeform section in the animation outside the rendering range, and then pose and fit the biped to the mesh within the freeform section.

Bones and Bound Node Boxes

Within these boxes are buttons for assigning both the bones and the bound node (that is, the mesh) to Bones Pro. Bones and meshes may also be hidden or revealed by using the Hide and Show buttons. This is handy for switching off the mesh while animating. On all but the fastest systems, the calculations required to deform the mesh can slow down the system considerably. Hiding the mesh will prevent these calculations from taking place and speed up real-time playback. Conversely, the skeleton should be hidden before rendering, and the Hide and Show buttons enable this.

Falloff and Strength Spinners

Bones may be selected from the rollout and assigned to Falloff and Strength spinners individually or in groups. The Falloff spinner determines how much of the mesh is affected by the bone. A larger number means that the bone affects a larger area and more vertices. The Strength spinner determines how heavily these vertices are affected. A larger number will pull the affected vertices closer to the bone.

Influence Editor

This is where vertices are assigned to the skeleton. The Influence Editor has a viewport for viewing the skeleton and the mesh, along with a number of tools for selecting, modifying, and visualizing the effects of bones on vertices (see fig. 11.14). Because the Influence Editor has a viewport, there are the standard navigation controls, along with a pull-down menu to select the standard views (Front, Top, Left, and so on).

FIGURE 11.14

The Influence Editor.

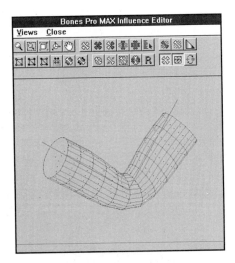

Bone Selection Tools

By default, the Influence Editor is in Bone Selection mode. Clicking on any bone selects and highlights it. Clicking again deselects it. In addition, a number of selection controls are provided to assist in filtering the selection. They enable you to select All, None, or Invert the Current Selection. In addition to this are two buttons named Select Unlinked and Deselect Unlinked. These buttons highlight all bones that are not direct parents or children of the selected bone.

In addition to bone selection controls, tools are provided for assigning falloff and strength values to any bone or group of bones. These replicate the controls found in the space warp Control panel.

Visualization Tools

The Visualize button enables you to see exactly how a selected bone is influencing the mesh. Pressing this button and selecting a single bone will produce a rendered image of the mesh. Highlighted on the mesh will be a gradient that represents the selected bone's strength and falloff. Colors closer to blue are unaffected vertices, and colors closer to red are more strongly affected.

Vertex Selection Tools

Vertex Selection buttons enable you to select groups of vertices so that they can be assigned or excluded from the influence of specific bones. These tools enable you to select or deselect all vertices, select them by region, or select and deselect vertices in the range of a specific bone or groups of bones.

Assigning and Excluding Bones to Vertices

By far the most important group of buttons are the Bone & Vertex Exclusion buttons. These buttons are the heart of the Influence Editor window, because they control the assignation and exclusion of specific vertices to specific bones. This is accomplished by selecting a group of vertices and a group of bones, and then including or excluding the vertices from the bones.

By default, all Bones Pro vertices are influenced by all bones. The Bone & Vertex Exclusion buttons enable you to alter this. One obvious example might be the head. It should not be affected by bones in the hands or feet. If the character were to scratch his head, for instance, the vertices in the head, by default, would tend to be attracted to the bones in the hand. These buttons enable you to exclude the specific vertices in the head from being influenced by the bones in the hand.

One of the more handy buttons is the Exclude Unlinked button. This enables you to quickly exclude bones that should have no direct influence. A good example of where this might be used is the feet and legs. The right leg should be immune from the effects of the left. Exclude Unlinked assigns vertices between bones that neighbor each other in the hierarchical scheme only. This way, the bones in the right shin are affected by the right thigh and the right foot, but not any other bones.

Tip

Assigning vertices with the Select Vertices by Region tool should only be done as a last resort for packets of stray vertices. It is usually better to select vertices by bone influence rather than by regions, because selection by region will invariably produce stray vertices.

Deforming a Body with Bones Pro

One of the more challenging tasks that Bones Pro can be used for is to deform an entire body. This is also a good way to understand the basic tools and procedures contained within the Influence Editor.

DEFORMING THE BODY

1. Load the file bonepro.max.

2. This file has a simple mesh character with a skeleton fitted to it. The skeleton also has a simple animation. This has been added so that it moves the character through a wide range of motions.

3. Create the Bones Pro space warp and bind it to the object named Body.

4. Select the Bones Pro space warp and open the Modify panel. Click on Display Subtree from the selection panel. All of the bones are parented by the hips. Select these objects.

5. From the Bones Pro rollout, open the Influence Editor.

6. Move the Time Slider to frame 30. Notice how the feet are influenced by each other, causing the shoes to distort (see fig. 11.15). Select the bones in the shin, feet, and toes for the right and left side of the body. Press Exclude Unlinked from Selected Bones. The feet should snap into place.

FIGURE 11.15

This situation with the feet can be corrected by selecting the lower leg bones and using the Exclude Unlinked from Selected Bones function from within the Influence Editor.

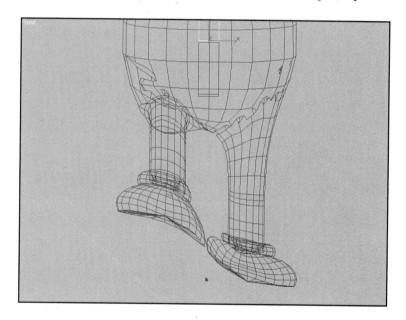

7. Move the Time Slider to frame 10. On this frame, the arms are above the head, and there is a significant bulge underneath the arms (see fig. 11.16). This is a common problem. To visualize this, select one of the upper arm bones and press Visualize Bone's Influence. This will show a bright area around the upper arm and extending down to the rib cage. Selecting the Spine03 bone and performing the same function will show that the spine has little or no influence over this area.

FIGURE 11.16

The Visualize tool
indicates that the
arm's influence over
the rib cage is large,
causing a bulge.

FIGURE 11.16

The Visualize tool
indicates that the
arm's influence over
the rib cage is large,
causing a bulge.

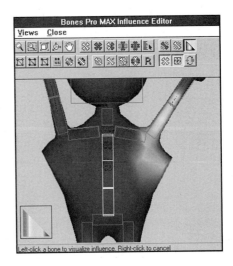

This is because the spinal bones in this particular skeleton are rather small, and their bounding boxes don't extend to the rib cage. Rather than rebuilding the skeleton, you can amplify their influence by increasing the falloff—the volume affected. For the three bones in the spinal column, set falloffs at Spine01 = 150, Spine02 = 200, Spine03 = 250. As these are set, notice how the model begins to snap into place. You can further amplify the effect of these bones by increasing their strength to 2.0. This should pull the model further into place.

8. The arms, however, are still affecting the rib cage area (see fig. 11.17). Because these bones are supposed to affect the area immediately around the arm only, these bones' influences can be reduced. Set the bones in the upper arm to a falloff of 75.

FIGURE 11.17

Adding more strength
and influence to the
spine pulls the bulge
into place.

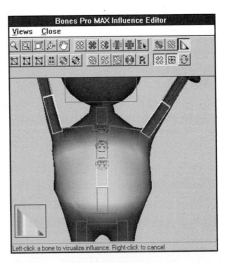

9. Move the Time Slider to frame 30. At this frame, you will see the legs distort the lower belly. To eliminate this, reduce the influence of both thigh bones so that they have a falloff of 60. Increase the strength of the hip bone from 1.0 to 1.5

10. You will see a single vertex being pulled off of the right shoe by the left (see fig. 11.18). From the Front view, zoom into this vertex. Using the Select by Region tool, select this lone vertex.

FIGURE 11.18

This stray vertex can be fixed by selecting it and including it into the proper foot.

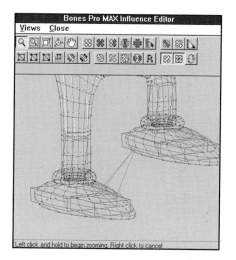

11. Zoom out slightly and use the Bone Selection tools to select both bones in the right foot. Press the Include Selected Vertices into Selected Bones button. The vertex will snap halfway between the two feet. This is because the left foot is still affecting this vertex.

12. Press the Invert Bone Selection button. Now press the Exclude Selected Vertices from Selected Bones button. This frees the stray vertex from any influences, except for those of the right foot. It will snap into place.

The basic setup is now complete. You can continue to work through the model and fine-tune the parameters within the Influence Editor.

Getting the mesh to deform properly over a wide range of motion may give you some headaches. If you are diligent and test every conceivable body position, however, you should have a rock-solid character. Hopefully, you will only have to set up the skeleton one time; after it is set up, you will have a character that you can use again and again. Even if it takes a day or two to set up the skeleton properly, it is worth it. The time you spend tweaking the skeleton pales in comparison to the time you will spend animating your character. Also, having to go back and fix things is never pleasant, so test thoroughly.

MetaReyes

Unlike mesh deformation routines, MetaReyes, and metaball plug-ins in general, work in the opposite way that a mesh deformation plug-in works. There is never a fixed mesh that needs to be deformed. Instead of the mesh being completely fixed and rigid, a metaball-created object generates its own mesh on the fly. This always makes for a smooth surface without any stray vertex-induced crimping and bulging. The one downfall of a metaball-generated character may be that the skin sometimes seems too smooth because it can be difficult to get a good hard crease when you need it.

MetaReyes originated as a plug-in for 3D Studio Release 4. The 3.0 plug-in for 3D Studio MAX takes the metaball modeling process to a new level, allowing for the creation of metamuscles, which operate in much the same way that real muscles do. A metamuscle can be attached to a bone in a skeleton, or a biped, and it will bend and flex the same way that real muscles do. Add to that the smooth surfacing created by metaball style fusion of the metamuscle objects, and you have the basis of a very complete way to create smooth, deformable surfaces. These surfaces can also be textured using dynamic texture mapping, which allows for sticky placement of maps on metaball objects for textures that move with the skin. MetaReyes is covered more thoroughly in Chapter 8, "Character Modeling with Plug-Ins," in *Inside 3D Studio MAX Volume II: Advanced Modeling and Materials*.

Metaball Concepts

The "balls" in metaballs derive their name from simple spheres, which are the building blocks of metaball objects. By assigning each sphere a weight and a sphere of influence, the metaballs modeler fuses many spheres into a single blob. How much the spheres fuse really depends in the weights, influences, and the distances between the spheres. In plug-ins such as MetaReyes, other shapes may also be used in addition to spheres.

Consider two spheres of equal size. The sphere of influence surrounds each of the spheres like a shell. Any other sphere coming within this range will try to fuse with the balls. The weight determines exactly how much fusion actually occurs. In figure 11.19, there are two balls of equal size. They'll fuse together at the intersection of their spheres of influence (see fig. 11.20). The amount that they fuse depends on their weights. As weights and the spheres of influence change, you get different effects. A higher sphere of influence will make an object softer and more willing to fuse with another. On the other hand, if one sphere is given more weight than another, it would appear more stable and solid.

FIGURE 11.19

Each metaball has its own sphere of influence. Where these two spheres of influence cross determines how the two objects fuse.

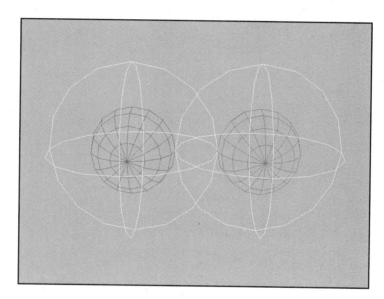

FIGURE 11.20

When they become metaballs, they will blob together.

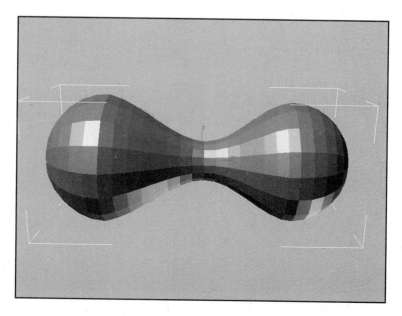

Using MetaReyes

A metamuscle is the standard primitive of MetaReyes. The metamuscle has two main components: control points and radii. *Control points* determine the linear path of the muscle, and the *radii* determine the outline of the muscle at any given point (see fig. 11.21). This metaphor is an outgrowth of the modeling methods used for MetaReyes 2.0 for 3D Studio R4. In that release, metaballs were aligned along a spline path to make complex surfaces in the Keyframer, sometimes making surfaces with dozens of individual balls. This method dispenses with the need for dozens of metaballs, and only requires a radial outline where the surface changes.

FIGURE 11.21

Basic components of a metamuscle are the path and the radii, as seen on the top object. From this the surface is derived.

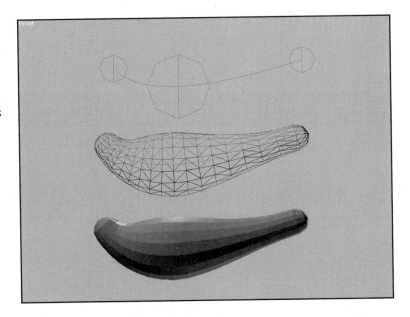

If you still wanted a sphere, you could simply create a surface with only one radius. Two radii would make a pill-shaped surface, while three, four, and more radii can make some very complex primitives (see fig. 11.22). By keeping the primitives simple, manipulation becomes easier as well. Instead of dealing with dozens of primitive spheres, you can work with a handful of spherical primitives and achieve the same results much more quickly.

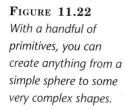

FIGURE 11.22
With a handful of primitives, you can create anything from a simple sphere to some very complex shapes.

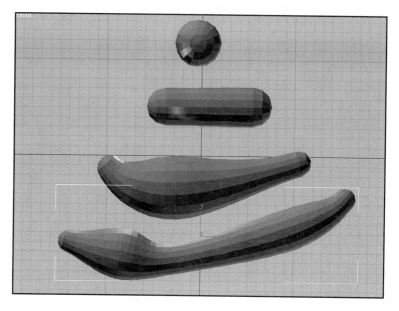

The metamuscles fall into two main categories. *Static muscles* are essentially rigid, but can flex and vibrate dynamically. *Dynamic muscles* can be attached to a skeleton so that they flex and bend much like the biceps and triceps of a human arm.

Static Muscles

Static muscles make excellent modeling tools. They can have any number of radii and can be of any shape. Static muscles can also have a dynamics component, so if a character were to stop or accelerate suddenly, the muscles would flex and vibrate much like real skin.

CREATING A STATIC MUSCLE

1. Click on the Geometry button in the Create menu.

2. Select MetaReyes as the geomtery type.

3. The MetaReyes rollout will appear. In the Muscle Types box, click on the button marked Static.

4. Click in a viewport to start making a metamuscle.

5. The first click determines the first control point of the muscle. After this is set, the radius can be set simply by dragging the mouse. A second left click sets the radius.

6. Clicking again sets another control point and allows another radius to be set. This sequence can be repeated until the muscle is defined. Left-clicking at any point in the procedure terminates the process.

After the muscle is created, you can turn the mesh generated by the muscle on and off by toggling the mesh box in the muscle's modify panel. The resolution of the muscle's mesh can also be adjusted by using the Fast and Seg. Density spinners.

Dynamic Muscles

Dynamic muscles add a new dimension to modeling and animating with metaballs. Dynamic muscles act much like the muscles of the body in that they can vary their thickness dynamically, much like the bulging muscles of a bicep.

Dynamic muscles are structurally more restricted than static muscles. Dynamic muscles can only have four control points, no more, no less. Two of these points are designated as anchors, which affix the muscle to a skeleton much like a biological muscle is connected via tendons at either end. Moving the skeleton stretches and bulges the muscle by moving the end points of the muscle.

CREATING A DYNAMIC MUSCLE

1. Click on the Geometry button in the Create menu.

2. Select MetaReyes as the geomtery type.

3. The MetaReyes rollout will appear. In the Muscle Types box, click on the button marked "Dynamic."

4. Click in a viewport to start making a metamuscle.

5. Like with static muscles, the first click determines the first control point of the muscle. This point should be positioned close to the object that will be used to deform it (a skeletal bone, perhaps). Once this is set, the radius can be set simply by dragging the mouse.

6. The end point of the muscle next needs to be set. Position the mouse near the second anchor point and click. This will make a second radius with the same diameter as the first.

7. A third click sets the default radius for the muscle. This can be adjusted later.

8. After the radius is set, the cursor changes to a question mark. The muscle will now be linked to the skeleton. As the cursor moves over an appropriate object, the cursor changes to read "link 1." The first object to select is where the first anchor point will be affixed.

9. The second anchor point needs to be chosen next. Again, the cursor changes as it passes over an appropriate object. Select the second anchor point.

After the muscles are anchored, moving the control points moves the ends of the muscles. This causes a squash and stretch effect on the metamuscle. The closer the ends are, the more the muscles will bulge, the further apart, the thinner it will get (see fig. 11.23).

FIGURE 11.23

The dynamic muscle follows the joint and stretches as the joint rotates.

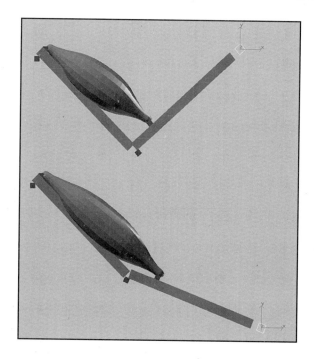

TIP

After the muscle is anchored, you will not be able to move it in relation to the object it is attached to. It is a good idea to attach the muscles to dummy objects, which are, in turn, linked hierarchically to the skeleton or controlling object. This way, the dummies can be repositioned to fine tune the attach points of the muscle.

With a combination of dynamic and static muscles, you can construct a very realistic skeleton. The dynamic muscles should be placed at the places where muscles bulge and flex, where the static muscles are used to fill in the space between the dynamic muscles, and also to even out the profile of the character (see fig. 11.24).

An example of an arm created using metamuscles has been added to the CD as the file muscles.avi.

FIGURE 11.24
Adding a combination of static an dynamic muscles helps even out the profile while keeping the joint flexible.

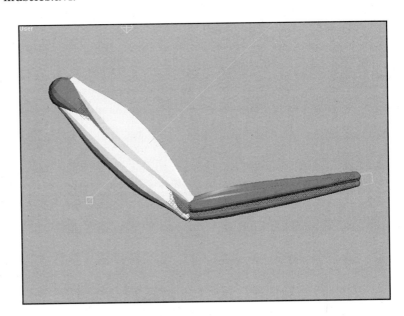

Hierarchies and Linking Metamuscles

In order for metamuscles to fuse, they need to be joined together in a hierarchy. Only muscles that are hierachically linked will fuse. The hierarchy may be one built entirely of metamuscles, or it could contain metamuscles and a combination of other objects.

A good hierarchy to attach a family of metamuscles to is a simple skeleton. This could be a custom-built skeleton made of MAX bones or boxes, or it could be a biped, which takes the muscle analogy to the logical conclusion, as the virtual bones of the skeleton will thus have virtual muscles attached to it.

The *master* object is the metamuscle that contains all of the information about the grouping of the test of the muscles in the tree. This metamuscle is simply the highest one in the hierarchy. If this muscle is deleted, all of the grouping information will be lost.

TIP

If you are connecting the metamuscles to a skeleton, it is a good idea to parent one tiny metamuscle to the skeleton and hide this metamuscle within the body of the character. This muscle will then be easily accessed and be the parent of the entire group. As the parent, the metamuscle will contain all of the grouping information for the entire model.

Fusion

Metamuscle fusion happens very much like the previous version of MetaReyes. Each muscle is assigned a color that indicates how hard or soft the degree of fusion is. Red indicates the softest, and most "blobby" of the fusion settings, whereas blue represents a hard negative value (to subtract matter out of a space). Fusion is applied to each individual muscle either at creation time or through the Modify panel for the individual muscle.

Grouping

After the muscles have been created, assigned fusion values, and linked into a hierarchy, they can be grouped. Grouping simply excludes some muscles from fusing with others. Think of the legs. If they were not excluded from each other, the skin of one leg would tend to fuse with the other every time they got close. By excluding the muscles in one leg from the other, this situation is prevented, preserving the illusion.

Grouping is accomplished through the MetaReyes utility panel, found under Utilities. This panel enables you to select a model (a hierarchically attached organization of metamuscles) and select individual muscles to be added to or deleted from various groups.

Muscles can also be included in more than one group. This is done to preserve the continuity of the skin. The arm muscles would be excluded from the torso muscles, but both would include a shoulder metamuscle, which provides a seamless bridge between them.

The Muscle Edit Modifier

The Muscle Edit modifier is an object modifier that can only be applied to the metamuscle primitives. Muscle Edit enables you to edit the muscles and the components held within. This is accomplished through sub-object editing of the vertices of the control point radii, as well as the capability to add or delete control points. When performing vertex-level editing of dynamic muscles, be sure to avoid the insert and delete buttons because these will convert the dynamic muscle to a static one.

The Muscle Edit modifier also allows for dynamics. This is not to be confused with a dynamic muscle. Dynamics allows both static and dynamic muscles to react to motion and vibrate like rubber as they change speed and direction. This adds considerably to the realism of the muscle. The dynamics has several options:

- **Oscillation Amplitude.** This is the level of amplification. The lower the value, the more rigid the muscle.

- **Contraction Level.** This parameter affects only dynamic metamuscles. Higher numbers increase the thickness of the muscle as it contracts. Lower numbers reduce this effect.

- **Inertia Level.** How the muscle is affected by inertia, or changes in speed. This ranges from VL (very low) to VH (very high).

In Practice: Mesh Deformation

- **Building the Mesh.** Patches work better than polygonal meshes, add extra detail at the joints, and model the character with the arms outstretched.

- **Fitting the Skeleton to the Mesh.** Use the extra detail modeled into the mesh as a guide for placing the bones. If you are creating a custom skeleton, freeze the mesh and use it as a guide.

- **Linked XForms.** These are a handy way to perform skeletal deformations right out of the box. Although they don't give you as much control as more sophisticated plug-ins, Linked XForms can work perfectly well on simple objects needing deformation.

- **Bones Pro.** This program gives you more control over mesh deformation than linked XForms does because it can assign weight vertices to bones in any combination. When animating with Bones Pro, remember to keep the Animate button toggled on at all times, because manipulating a skeleton without this button on will change the Master Frame and affect the way the bones are assigned to the vertices.

IMAGE CREATED BY GEORGE MAESTRI

Chapter 12

by George Maestri

ANIMATING WITH PHYSIQUE

Physique is the second half of Character Studio. It enables some very sophisticated and controllable deformations of MAX objects. Physique gives MAX users the ability to define specific bulging and crimping over a wide range of joint and body types. Combined with Biped, Physique gives MAX users a very robust environment for animating characters. Although Biped is the preferred method for creating skeletons, Physique may be used with any type of MAX skeleton, including custom-built skeletons or, as seen in the previous chapter, simple chains of bones.

This chapter covers the following topics:

- Physique overview
- Using Physique
- Physique and Biped
- Tendons

One of the more vexing problems digital animators face is simulating the realistic flexing and bending of muscles underneath skin. Moving the vertices of an object so that they deform along with the skeletal bones is only the first step. In real life, the bones are actually driven by muscles and tendons under the skin. These muscles relax and contract to pull the bones in the skeleton around. As anyone who has witnessed a Mr. Universe pageant can attest, contracting muscles can change the shape of the skin significantly.

Although not every character animated in MAX needs to be a Mr. Universe contestant, the capability to effectively control and manipulate the shape and appearance of the skin is very important to all characters. Accurate control of the shape of a character enables you to not only bulge muscles, but also to eliminate nasty crimping and tearing of vertices that can be so common in any mesh deformation package.

Physique enables you to store the outlines and bulge angles of any portion of a character's geometry and apply these to the character according to the joint angle. In theory, it works exactly the opposite of nature. In nature, the bulging muscle pulls on the joint and causes it to bend. In Physique, bending the joint causes the muscle to bulge. Although opposite in procedure, visually, the effect is identical.

In addition to bulge angles, Physique's tendons feature gives you the ability to maintain a character's shape over many links, to simulate details such as the small web between the thumb and forefinger, or the stretching of the skin around the shoulders as the arm rotates.

Using Physique

As was demonstrated in the previous chapter, Physique is an object modifier. It is applied like any other object modifier to the object's stack. To be activated, the Attach to Node button must be toggled and the root node of the skeleton must be selected. After this occurs, Physique takes a snapshot of the positions and orientations of all the bones on the skeleton and uses it to assign specific vertices to specific bones.

The Physique modifier has two types of sub-objects: Link and Vertex. Link sub-objects are just the bones themselves; Vertex sub-objects are the vertices of the mesh.

TIP

Physique is an object modifier. As such, it should be placed in the stack above any UVW mapping or sub-object mapping applied to the object because the texture needs to be applied before the mesh is deformed.

Hierarchies and Physique

Physique determines its vertex assignments based on the hierarchy of the skeleton. Bones Pro uses the bounding boxes of the bones themselves to determine vertex assignation, whereas Physique simply looks at the pivot points of the bones and uses that information to create its default vertex assignments.

Physique assigns vertices by placing an imaginary plane at each pivot in the hierarchy and then making a cylindrical projection through the mesh. The imaginary plane is aligned perpendicular to the axis of the joint. Vertices that lie between the two planes are assigned to the joint; vertices residing outside these boundaries are not (see fig. 12.1). The assignment of vertices is strictly controlled by their location in relation to the joints. This makes joint placement of the skeleton of paramount importance.

In the case where these imaginary planes do intersect and overlap, vertices can be assigned to one joint or the other, but not both. A common case would be the vertices surrounding the pelvis area. Because the pelvic bone and the thigh bones are oriented along different axes, significant overlap occurs in the assignment of the vertices. Vertices in these areas typically need to be reassigned during the course of Physique setup. This procedure is discussed in detail in the section "Vertex Control," later in the chapter.

FIGURE 12.1
*Physique assigns
vertices by placing an
imaginary plane at the
end of each joint.*

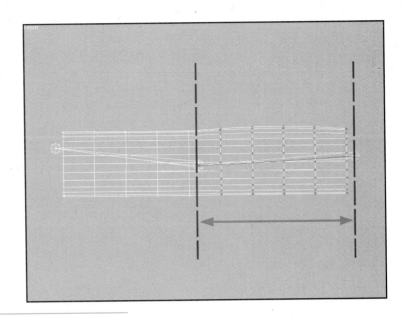

FIGURE 12.1
*Physique assigns
vertices by placing an
imaginary plane at the
end of each joint.*

Creating Realistic Bulges

The easiest way to visualize exactly how Physique creates and manages bulges is to use a simple, predictable object, such as a cylinder. This also introduces a number of fundamental concepts, and by using a regularly shaped cylinder, the effects of Physique are made perfectly clear.

APPLYING PHYSIQUE TO THE CYLINDER

1. Load the file bulge.max from the accompanying CD.

2. Select the Cylinder.

3. From the Modify panel, select the Physique modifier and apply it to the stack.

4. Press Attach to Node. The cursor changes to resemble a stick figure.

5. Position the cursor over the root node of the bone hierarchy. This is Bone01. Click on the bone.

This is the same procedure that was discussed in Chapter 10, "Animating with Biped," but now that the Physique modifier has been added, it can be taken further by adding a realistic bulge to the cylinder. The file contains a short animation where the bone in the forearm flexes 90 degrees and then relaxes. Scrubbing the Time Slider reveals how the cylinder is currently affected—the joint rotates, but the cylinder retains its outline as it deforms with the joints. The joint rotation can be used to create a nice bulge.

The Cross Section Editor

The Cross Section Editor is the heart of many Physique operations, and it is one you will become quite familiar with when using the plug-in. The Cross Section Editor is a floating dialog that enables you to create bulge angles, their cross sections, and, as you will see later, tendons. The Cross Section Editor dialog is shown in figure 12.2. There are two ways to bring up this window, first by clicking on the Cross Section Editor button from within the main Physique rollout, and second, by clicking on a specific joint's rollout when Physique is in joint Sub-object mode.

The Cross Section Editor is modeless, meaning you can use it along with the standard MAX viewports to select and modify parameters on the fly. The window has a toolbar with two windows along the bottom—on the lower left is the cross section view, on the lower right is the link view. In combination, these can be used to create and manage the bulge of the skin around the joint.

FIGURE 12.2
The Cross Section Editor. The circular graph on the left is the outline editor, the one on the right is the link editor.

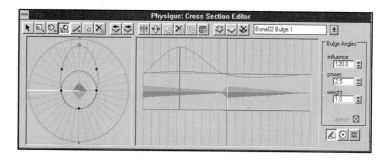

EDITING THE LINK'S CROSS SECTION

To select a specific joint, you need to go into Physique's Sub-object Selection mode.

1. Using the same cylinder as before, press the Sub-Object button and select the sub-object type as Link.

2. From within the MAX viewport, select Bone02. The bone's link parameters appear.

3. To enable the Cross Section Editor, click on the Cross Section Editor button in the Physique Link Parameters rollout.

4. To create a bulge, you first need to tell Physique at what angle the bulge will be defined. The default angle is the angle at which the bone was positioned when Physique was applied. The second angle should be where the joint is rotated the most. In this animation, the maximum rotation is at frame 30. Move the Time Slider to frame 30.

5. To add a bulge, press the Insert Bulge Angle button. A new bulge angle is created and automatically named Bulge 1.

6. Next, you need to tell Physique exactly where the bulge occurs. This is known as a cross section. Press the Insert CS Slice button. The cursor changes. Click on the Link view portion of the Cross Section Editor dialog near the center of the leftmost link. A red line appears, indicating the cross section has been added.

7. You can now use the Cross Section Editor to resize the bulge at that angle. Press Select and Scale Ctl Points and, within the Cross Section View, click on the topmost control point and drag it upward. This movement is reflected in both the Link view and also within the normal MAX viewports.

8. Scrub the Time Slider. The muscle now bulges, as shown in figure 12.3. When the joint is flat, there is no bulge, when the joint is flexed, the bulge appears.

FIGURE 12.3

A cylinder bulges according to the angle of the joint.

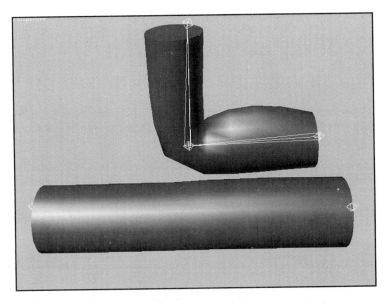

9. You can further modify the shape of the bulge by adding more cross sections or by adding more control points.

Physique Link Parameters

The bulge can be even further modified by using the Physique Link Parameters in the Link Sub-Object panel. These parameters give you additional control over how the skin stretches and compresses as the joint bends, twists, and scales.

Bend

Bend parameters control the flow of skin over a bending joint, such as a knee or elbow. They apply to hinge-like movement perpendicular to the axis of the bend.

Tension determines the tightness of the crimp at the bend. A higher number produces a more arc-shaped bend, and a lower number causes the joint to crimp more.

Bias determines the angle of the crimp. At 0.5 it is evenly centered between the joints. When it moves higher, the crimp is angled toward the link's child; when it is lower, it is angled toward the link (see figs. 12.4 and 12.5).

FIGURE 12.4
Cylinder bent with different Bias settings.

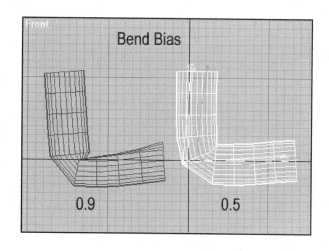

FIGURE 12.5
*The figure on the
bottom has a high
bend tension, the one
on the top has a low
bend tension.*

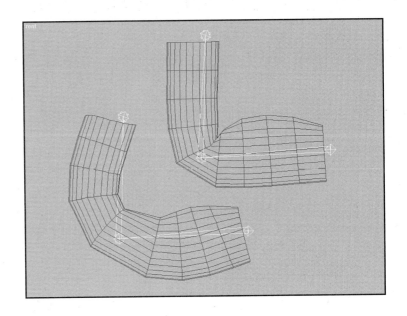

Twist

Twist parameters determine how the mesh is affected when the joint is twisted along its length, such as when a hand turns a screwdriver.

Tension determines how much the skin rotates around the length of the joint. A value of 1.0 causes all skin along the length of the joint to rotate evenly. Lower values emphasize the twist closer to the rotating link, and higher values add extra twisting to the skin farther away from the point of rotation. The effects of Twist are shown in figure 12.6.

Bias shifts the twist effect toward or away from the link. A value lower than 0.5 puts more of the twist on the skin covering the child link, and a higher value puts more of the twist on the selected link.

Scale

The scale parameters affect how the skin and any underlying cross sections are affected by the scaling of the links. Because Physique looks at the hierarchy, not the physical bones themselves, the links can be scaled by turning off IK and translating the bones to increase or decrease the distance between the links.

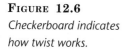

FIGURE 12.6
*Checkerboard indicates
how twist works.*

Activating the Stretch and Breathe buttons is one easy way to get squash
and stretch effects when using Physique. Stretch and Breathe enable you to
create this effect automatically by moving or scaling the bone. Stretch pulls
out the mesh along the length of the link, whereas Breathe expands the mesh
radially (see fig. 12.7). You cannot use this technique with Biped bones,
however, because they cannot scale over time.

FIGURE 12.7
*Bone scaled with and
without Breathe option.*

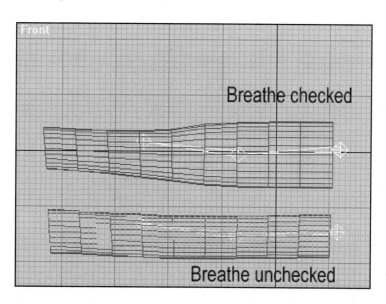

Physique Joint Intersections

Joint intersections determine how and where the joint creases. Physique tries very hard not to have skin vertices cross over each other because this would cause one part of the skin to penetrate another—not something that would happen in real life.

To prevent this, Physique places an imaginary plane between the joints and restricts vertices on either side from crossing over. This keeps the skin seamless and can cause a natural crease. A good example is the skin around the fingers. It tends to crease along a nice, flat plane. Sometimes, however, you may want the joint intersections to be less planar, to create a dimple, perhaps.

Typically, the default planar joint intersections are fine, but they can sometimes "go flat" before the skin actually touches, particularly when the skin bulges dramatically. This can be tweaked using the Joint Intersections dialog. This determines how the plane affects the crease. A bias value of 1.0 means that the plane is fully active, causing a planar crease; a lower value reduces the planarity of the effect. The From and To spinners determine how much of the skin around the joint is affected by the plane.

Physique and Biped

Although Physique can be used with MAX's native bones or any hierarchy of objects, marrying the two halves of Character Studio enables Physique to be affected by a Biped skeleton. This gives you a very good solution for creating a lifelike character.

Any class of geometry works with Physique, but it is much easier to deform a spline-based surface because this kind of mesh has fewer vertices. Digimation's Surface Tools provides a very good solution because you can animate just the spline cage while turning off the surface, making manipulation much faster.

TIP

If you are using prebuilt polygonal models, you can use optimize modifiers to reduce the face count and help improve manipulation performance. When you are ready to render the model, delete the Optimize modifiers from the stack.

Fitting a Biped to a Mesh

For Physique to work correctly, the Biped must be properly fitted to the mesh. The joints of the Biped must line up with the joints of the mesh. The most critical area is the area where one joint intersects the other. Because Physique uses the intersection of the joints to define vertex assignment, a misplacement can cause vertices to go astray.

Figure Mode

To facilitate the fitting of a Biped to a mesh, you need to place the Biped in Figure mode, which is a special pose that Biped remembers and can always be returned to at the press of a button. Figure mode also allows for resizing and positioning a Biped freely.

NOTE

You must have an authorized copy of Character Studio installed on your computer to do the exercises in this chapter.

FITTING A BIPED TO A MESH

1. Load your character's mesh file, which is a file on the accompanying CD entitled meshman.max that can be used for practice.

2. Create a Biped roughly the same height as the mesh. In the Biped's Structure rollout, set the number of fingers and toes to match the character. If your character is wearing shoes, one toe will suffice.

3. Select the mesh. Go to the Display panel and press Freeze Selected. This way, the mesh will not accidentally get selected while the Biped is being manipulated.

4. Select the Biped. Go to the Motion panel and place the Biped in Figure mode. In Figure mode, you are free to rotate and scale every joint of the Biped.

5. Select the Center of Mass object, and position the Biped over the body so the hips rest inside the Pelvis area. One thing to remember is that manipulating a Biped in Figure mode puts the navigation tools in world space. This means that, from the front, the Biped moves along the XZ axis (see fig. 12.8).

FIGURE 12.8

Proper placement of biped inside mesh (note that ZX is the front plane).

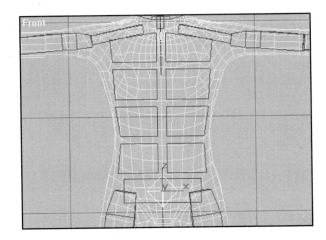

6. Non-uniform scale the PELVIS in Z so that the joint between the hips and thighs rests along the V-shaped area that defines the crease between the tops of the thighs and the crotch (refer to fig. 12.8).

7. Scale the spinal segments so that the shoulders are slightly beneath the shoulders of the mesh, and so the joint between the shoulder and the upper arm resides above the mesh's armpit.

8. Scale the legs in X so that the biped's knees are properly aligned within the joint area of the mesh. Rotate the legs to align them with the mesh. The Symmetrical tracks button can be used to easily select both legs for manipulation. Do the same for the arms and scale them so the elbows of the Biped line up with the elbow area of the mesh. Rotate the arms to fit into the mesh (use the Top viewport to do this).

9. If your character has fingers that move, adjust the bones in the hand to match the fingers. The Biped's fingers can not only be resized and rotated, but they can also be moved along the edge of the palm bone to get an exact fit.

10. When positioning joints at the end of a chain, such as the head or toes, be certain to place the ends of the bones slightly beyond the edge of the mesh. Because Physique uses the bounding planes of the joints to determine vertex assignment, any vertices not included within these planes will be left behind (see fig. 12.9). In this example figure, the head is too small, so when it tilts forward, the top of the skull remains stationary.

FIGURE 12.9

If the vertices of the mesh do not lie inside the bounding planes of the joints, the vertices will get left behind.

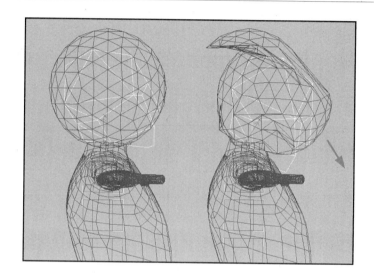

Applying Physique to a Biped

After the mesh has been fitted, you can link the skin to the Biped. The important thing to remember is that the Physique modifier needs to be attached to the pelvis of the Biped, not the Center of Mass object. The Center of Mass object moves on every frame to reflect the changing mass distribution of the Biped. This means that the joint between the center of mass and the rest of the Biped will stretch and change shape, causing all sorts of problems.

If parts of the body or clothing are modeled as separate objects, such as a head or a hat, select all the objects and apply a single Physique modifier to them all. Later, you'll need to make some of the vertices rigid so that they do not deform (see the next section for a description of how to do this).

Refining How Physique Affects the Mesh

If the character is being used for a wide variety of shots, the model needs to be tested over a wide range of motion to ensure that the skin behaves the way that it should. To test this, it is a good idea to have a test animation that puts the character through its paces. This animation should have the character move its arms and legs through the extremes of motion.

The file phystest.max on the accompanying CD is a good example of a test animation to put a Biped and its attached mesh through a wide range of motion. The animation is also saved as a biped file (phystest.bip) so that you can easily apply it to other models.

Conversely, if the character is only being used for a very specific set of actions, those actions are the only ones that need to be tested. In this case, it might be faster to animate a rough version of the action and then correct any deficiencies in the vertex assignment for those actions only.

Regardless of how you test the motion, if the joint placement of the Biped is correct, most of the vertices in the mesh will follow along with the Biped's joints. Unfortunately, nothing is perfect, and there will almost always be stray vertices that cause unwanted bulges.

Vertex Control

If a joint affects an unwanted area of the mesh, the vertices in those areas may need to be reassigned to another joint. To do this, select the Vertex Sub-Object rollout from the Physique panel and reassign the vertices or change their behavior. In Physique, vertices are assigned colors, either red, green, or blue. The specific color of the vertex defines the way the individual vertex behaves. The Vertex Sub-Object rollout is shown in figure 12.10.

The following list describes the three different types of vertex assignments.

- **Red Vertices.** These vertices are deformable. They flex, bend, and move with the joint to which they have been assigned.

- **Green Vertices.** These vertices are rigid. They move along with the joint, but they do not flex or change shape. This is good for areas such as the head and skull, which remain relatively rigid.

- **Blue Vertices.** These vertices are not assigned to any specific joint and are known as root vertices. They will not move with the skeleton.

Figure 12.10

The Vertex Sub-Object rollout.

By default, each vertex is assigned as deformable, so every vertex in the body should be red. If a vertex is defaulted as root (blue), it means that the vertex did not lie within the bounding planes of any joint within the skeleton and could not be assigned. This is often caused by joints at the end of the chain, such as the top of the head or the ends of the fingers, which did not protrude through the ends of the mesh when Physique was applied. In this case, the Biped needs to be refitted and the Physique modifier reapplied.

One of the most common situations encountered is when the joints in the upper arm affect the area under the arm along the side of the rib cage, causing the skin to bulge as the arm lifts above the head. This happens because the vertically oriented bounding planes of the upper arm intersect the horizontally oriented bounding planes of the spinal bones. In cases when a vertex can be assigned to more than one joint, Physique assigns the vertex to the closest joint. Unfortunately, the closest joint is not always the correct joint. One common situation is bulging along the ribcage (shown by the arrows in figure 12.11), which happens because the vertically oriented bounding planes of the upper arm intersect the horizontally oriented bounding planes of the spinal column.

The Physique Vertex Assignment rollout contains the tools for selecting and assigning (or reassigning) vertices to the correct links.

- **Vertex Type.** This set of three buttons gives you control of which vertices are selected and assigned. These buttons affect the selection set that you create with the Select, Select by Link, and Assign to Link buttons (described on the following page). For example, if the red button is depressed, only deformable (red) vertices will be selected or assigned.

- **Select.** This button enables you to use the standard MAX selection tools, such as the box or fence, to select groups of vertices.

- **Select by Link.** This button enables you to select all the vertices currently assigned to a single joint. The type of vertices selected depends on the settings of the Vertex Type buttons.

- **Assign to Link.** This button assigns the currently selected vertices to the selected link. The setting of the Vertex Type button determines how these are assigned. If the button is red, the vertices are assigned as deformable, green assigns them as rigid, and blue as root.

FIGURE 12.11
Incorrect vertex assignment causes the mesh to deform incorrectly around the chest.

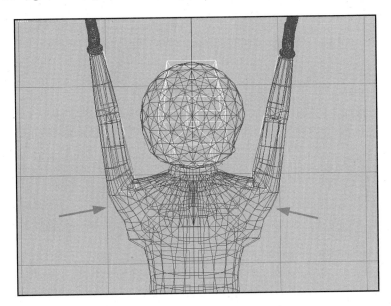

TIP

In Character Studio Release 1.1, there is a new checkbox labeled Initial Skeletal Pose in the Vertex Assignment rollout. This checkbox enables you to toggle between the initial pose (typically with arms outstretched) and whatever pose the figure happens to be in when you enter Physique Vertex Sub-Object level.

MODIFYING THE VERTICES

1. Load the file meshbipd.max from the accompanying CD. This file contains the same character contained in meshman.max, but with a Biped fitted to it. The Biped also has a short animation to help test the mesh attachment.

2. Select the Biped. From the Motion panel, place the biped in Figure mode.

3. Select the object MeshMan. From the Modify panel, add the Physique modifier to the stack.

4. From the Physique panel, press Attach to Node. Select the pelvis of the Biped as the root node. Be sure not to select the Center of Mass object. Zoom in so you are sure to hit the right object. By default, the Pelvis object is a yellow-colored rectangular box.

5. Reselect the Biped. Go to the Modify panel and turn off Figure mode.

6. Move the Time Slider to frame 10. This is where the Biped moves its arms above its head. Notice the bulge under the arm. This must be fixed by reassigning the vertices within Physique's Vertex Sub-Object mode.

7. Select the mesh. In the Modifier Panel, with the mesh selected under Sub-Object Vertex, press Select by Link and select the shoulder link. This action highlights all the vertices affected by the shoulder. Notice how the vertices extend down to the underarm area and up into the head.

8. Click on the Select button and, while holding down the Alt key and using the Fence Selection tool, deselect the vertices along the upper half of the shoulder, leaving only those along the underarm highlighted (see fig. 12.12).

FIGURE 12.12
The vertices in the bulge are best assigned to the spinal column.

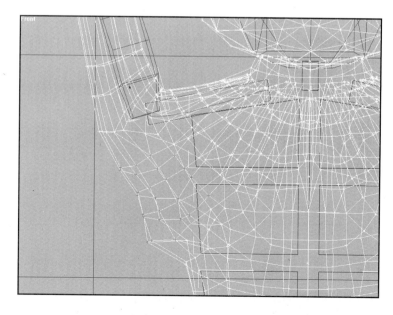

9. Click on Assign to Link, select the joint Bip01_Spine3. Most of the vertices pop into place and remain red. A few turn blue, meaning these are out of the bounding plane of the selected joint.

10. To select only the blue vertices, click on Select by Link. Within the Vertex Type box, turn off the Red and Green vertex type buttons, leaving only the Blue button depressed. Select the joint Bip01_Spine3. Only the blue vertices are selected.

11. Assign these vertices to the spine link immediately below the clavicles. The vertices change color to red.

TIP

Steps 10 and 11 show the "long way" to get the results. In step 10, you can simply Ctrl+click on the desired link to assign the root vertices to that link.

The head is another area affected by the shoulders. On this character, the head should be rigid. To accomplish this, make the vertices comprising the head green, or rigid.

12. Set Vertex type to all three (red, green, and blue). Click on the Select button and, using the Box Selection tool, select the vertices in the head.

13. Set the vertex type to rigid (green) and click on the Assign to Link button. Select the head joint. The vertices turn green.

14. Continue through the rest of the body, modifying and reassigning vertices as needed.

15. Save the file as meshphys.max (note that this file is also provided on the CD-ROM).

TIP

If it is difficult to get vertex assignments exactly right in critical areas such as the pelvis, linking a dummy object to the offending joint can give you an extra joint to assist in assigning vertices. If this is done, the Physique modifier's default pose must be reapplied.

TIP

In Character Studio Release 1.1, you can save the vertex assignments that you've made to one figure and then apply them to another figure, using a new file format called .VPH. This can be a great time-saver, assuming that the two models are very similar and start from more or less the same pose. You can use this feature, for example, to replace a low-resolution model with a high-resolution version of the same model.

You can use the Cross Section Editor not only for creating bulging muscles, but also to fix problem areas of the mesh, such as bulges or creases. This is not an obvious use of the Cross Section Editor, and it is not described in the Character Studio manual. However, it is such a useful technique that an exercise is included to show you how to do it.

As previously described, a particularly common problem occurs when the arms raise above the head and the underside of the arm bulges out, and the vertices under the arm tear or cause creases in the body. The Cross Section Editor can be used to further refine the behavior of these joints.

USING THE CROSS SECTION EDITOR TO FIX PROBLEM SPOTS

1. Open the file meshbip2.max (this file already has the Physique modifier applied to the mesh). Within the Physique panel, go to Link Sub-Object mode.

2. Select the shoulder joint and open the Cross Section Editor from the Physique Link Parameters rollout.

3. Move the Time Slider to frame 10 and insert a new bulge angle from within the Cross Section Editor. Name this bulge **Frame 10 Bulge** by using the text box at the top right. Move the slider to frame 20 and insert a second bulge angle. Name this bulge **Frame 20 Bulge**.

4. Move the Time Slider back to frame 10 and select the appropriate bulge angle (Frame 10 Bulge). Select default CS slice on the joint between the shoulder and the upper arm. Within the Section view, scale down the part of the outline representing the underside of the arm to reduce the size of the bulge (see fig. 12.13).

FIGURE 12.13

Adjusting the bulge angle by scaling the cross section.

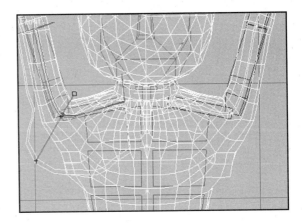

5. Move the Time Slider to frame 20 and select the second bulge angle created (Frame 20 Bulge). Select default CS slice on the joint between the shoulder and the upper arm. Within the Section view, scale the part of the outline representing the underside of the arm. This also reduces the size of the crease. Adjusting this bulge angle also reduces the bulge at frame 10.

6. If you need more control, you may add a second CS slice on each arm and scale those appropriately as well.

Figure 12.14 shows the meshman model after modification. Even though the vertices have been reassigned, when the arm is raised above the head, a slight bulge still exists. This is fixed by adding a cross section to the Bulge angle on the joint between the shoulder and arm. A second bulge angle on the same joint can also help prevent crimping when the arm is at its side (see fig. 12.15).

Tendons

Tendons are used to further refine the way the character's skin behaves across many joints when cross sections and bulge angles aren't enough. They enable you to make one joint affect the outline of another joint's vertices over many links. They can be best used in areas such as the shoulder and pelvic areas, where T-shaped branching exists. They can also be used in skinning hands, particularly the fleshy webbing between the thumb and forefinger. A tendon has three main components:

- **Base.** The base is where one or more tendon cross sections originate. A base may be applied to any link in the skeleton. Usually the base resides in the torso.

FIGURE 12.14

The bulge under the arm is reduced after using the Cross Section Editor.

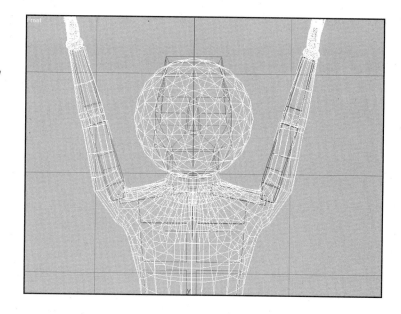

FIGURE 12.15

The second bulge angle is added to the shoulder joint.

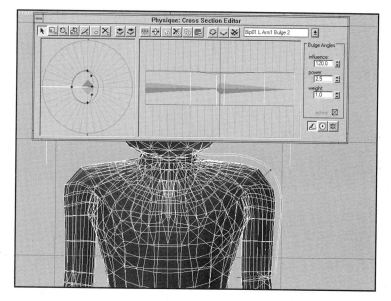

- **Cross sections.** These are much like the cross sections used to create bulges; attach points are located at radial subdivisions of the outline of the cross section.

- **Attach points.** These are the points on the cross sections that can be tied to another link. The attached link is usually a shoulder or pelvic bone. Each attach point may be tied to a different link.

How Tendons Work

For a good example of how tendons affect the skin across multiple joints, use a simple T-shaped mesh and attach a few tendons between the joints as it flexes.

HOW TENDONS WORK

1. Load the file tbone.max. This file contains a T-shaped mesh and a set of tendons attached to it. The tendons run from the middle joint of the vertical branch to the middle joint of the right horizontal branch (see fig. 12.16).

FIGURE 12.16
This T-shaped object can be used to demonstrate how tendons affect the skin across multiple joints.

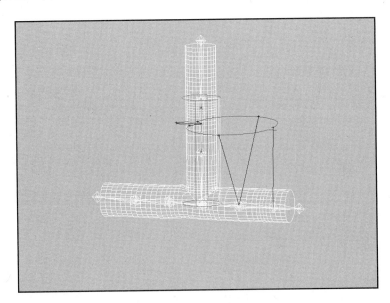

2. Move the Time Slider to frame 25. Notice how the middle joint on the right limb affects the vertical joint. This is due to the action of a tendon (see fig. 12.17).

3. Move the Time Slider to frame 50. As the middle-right joint flexes down, it affects the skin on the vertical joint.

FIGURE 12.17

As the far joints rotate, the skin on the vertical shaft is affected, even though the two joints are not adjacent.

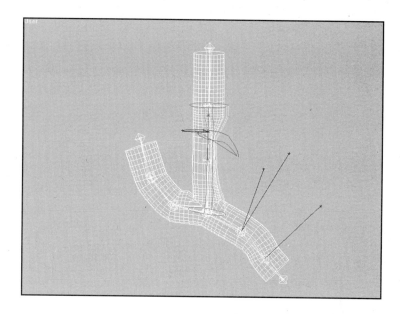

4. Move the Time Slider to frame 75. Again, the skin on the middle joint bulges, even though many other joints are active.

This shows that tendons can give a more globalized effect than just bulge angles, enabling skin to flow across many joints. The T-shaped branch is very similar to the branches that occur in the human body—between the spine, shoulders, and arms; between the spine, pelvis, and legs; and even between the thumb and forefinger. Tendons can be used to the same effect with a biped or with other types of skeletons, such as 3DS MAX bones.

Creating Tendons

Tendons are created in the Link Sub-Object mode from the Physique panel. You just need to select the link that will become the base and press the Create button on the Physique Tendons rollout. This panel has a number of parameters.

- **Sections.** This is the number of cross section bases created for the link.

- **Attach Points.** This is the number of radial attach points around each of the cross sections.

- **Resolution.** The radial resolution of the cross sections.

A pair of tendons can be used to help maintain the outline of the belly where it meets the pelvic area. Many times creasing occurs in this area. Tendons can help maintain the shape of the character.

ATTACHING TENDONS

1. Open the file meshphys.max. This file has an animation to test the flexibility of the character. Move the Time Slider to frame 50.

2. Select the mesh and go to the Physique Modifier panel. Select Link Sub-Object mode.

3. Select the central spinal joint (Bip01 Spine 2), scroll down to the Physique Tendons rollout, and set the default sections parameter to 1. These must be set before the tendon's base is created.

4. Click on the Create button. This action creates a base for tendons originating from this joint.

5. Open the Cross Section Editor by clicking on Cross Section Editor. Activate the Tendon panel within the Cross Section Editor. Select the attach point along the front right of the torso, as shown in figure 12.18.

6. Attach this point to the right clavicle joint. To do this, click on the Attach button within the Tendon panel of the Cross Section Editor, and then click on the right clavicle joint from within the Front viewport.

7. Repeat the same procedure for the front-left attach point and the left clavicle joint. The tendons are now attached. The tendon, however, does not yet pull the mesh correctly (see fig. 12.19).

8. Save the file. You will modify the tendons in the last exercise.

Modifying Tendons

After being attached, the tendons may need to be modified so that they affect the way the skin behaves across the joints. A number of parameters within the tendon panel of the Cross Section Editor enable you to modify the tendons as needed. These parameters are described in the following list.

FIGURE 12.18

The tendon is in place on the spine link and is ready for attachment.

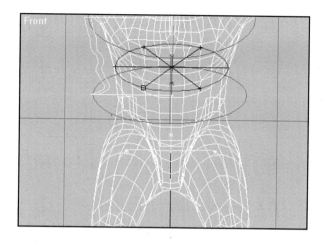

FIGURE 12.19

After the tendons are properly attached, they look like this.

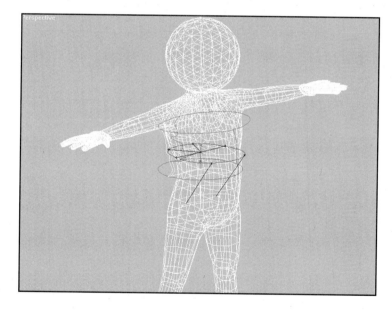

- **Radial Distance.** This is how far out the attach points lie from the body. If you look at the tendons from within a MAX viewport, you see a purple outline that roughly matches that of the character's skin. Increasing or decreasing this amount affects the size of the outline.

- **Pull.** This determines how much the skin is pulled by the attached joint. A good example is the chest and shoulder area. As the arms move outward, the skin of the chest is pulled outward along the surface of the skin as well.

- **Pinch.** This determines how much the skin are pushed inward by the action of the tendon attached joint. A good example is the crease that forms in the web of the hand as the thumb moves next to the forefinger.

- **Stretch.** This determines how much the skin is stretched by the tendon attached joint. This gives the skin more or less pliability.

Normally, the values for all these joints are set at 1.0 to give a good skin behavior when the tendons are attached to a nearby link. If the tendons span multiple links, these numbers should probably be reduced somewhat because the effect of a change on a link normally decreases the further away from the link you are. For example, the clavicle should have more of an effect on the upper spine than on the lower spine.

Tendon Boundary conditions are also important for tendons that span multiple links. These determine exactly how far the skin is affected. If these are off, only the joint with the tendon is affected. When the upper bound value is high, the skin on the spanned joints is also affected by the tendon. This is very important for getting a smooth behavior across the skin.

If you enable boundary conditions, it is a good idea to turn off the joint intersection parameters for each of the spanned joints. This action prevents the two features from trying to create different outlines at the joint intersections, and causing unpredictable results.

MODIFYING TENDONS

1. Continue with meshphys.max.

2. In the Cross Section Editor, select the two front attach points. Change Radial Distance to 16, Pull to –0.25, and Pinch to 0.0.

3. In the Tendons rollout, change upper bound to 2.0 and pull bias to 0.0, and then change the lower bound to –1.

4. Unhide the biped skeleton turn on Animate, and, at frame 10, rotate the clavicles up 30 degrees in the Y axis.

These modifications have the effect of lifting the skin evenly over the front of the chest as the clavicles raise. The file meshtend.max on the accompanying CD contains the completed tendons. The figure has a texture map applied so that the effect of the tendons is more visible.

5. Make a preview of frames 0–20 to see the effect.

In Practice: Physique

- **Bulge Angles.** Bulges can be used not only to create bulging muscles, but also to help prevent unwanted effects such as crimping and tearing of the skin.

- **Vertex Reassignment.** Vertices can only be assigned to one joint, and thus must be reassigned to the proper joint from time to time.

- **Using Biped.** Always assign the Physique modifier to the pelvis, not the Center of Mass object. If you need additional control, you may link dummy objects to the Biped skeleton to get additional joints to help control the skin.

- **Tendons.** Tendons affect the skin across multiple joints and are very helpful in branching areas of the body, such as the shoulder and pelvis areas.

IMAGE CREATED BY GEORGE MAESTRI

Chapter 13

by George Maestri

FACIAL ANIMATION AND LIP SYNC

Animating the face is one of the most challenging and rewarding tasks that animators encounter. People are all experts in the subtleties of expression and emotion. A bad actor elicits instinctively negative reactions, typically because his emotions seem forced rather than genuine. The same goes for animation—great facial animation looks seamless and does not draw attention to itself. Bad animation seems curiously off for some unknown reason.

Within MAX, there are many ways to accomplish the shape deformations necessary to animate the face, each method approaching the problem from a slightly different angle. The vertices of the face can be directly manipulated, either by attaching them to a control object via a Linked XForm, or through morphing to one or many targets. Bones can also be used for facial animation, and the mesh of the face deformed by using either Physique or Bones Pro.

Anatomy of the Face

Animating the face requires a good eye and a strong knowledge of acting and emotion. You also need to understand the underlying anatomy of the human head and face to understand exactly how it moves. The face is by far the most important part of the equation because this is where emotion is shown. The face is the most flexible area of the head. It is driven by approximately a dozen muscles that connect the skin to the skull. As with muscles in the body, these muscles affect the shape of the skin by bulging, stretching, and pulling it.

The trick is to understand how these muscles pull and shape the face to create expressions. The groups of muscles fall into two categories: lower face muscles, which control the mouth and jaw (see fig. 13.1); and upper face muscles, which control the eyes and brows (see fig. 13.2).

FIGURE 13.1

The muscles surrounding the mouth pull the lips outward radially. Another set of muscles compress and purse the lips.

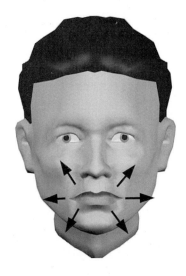

FIGURE 13.2

In addition to opening and closing the eyelids, muscles on the upper half of the face raise, lower, and furrow the brow.

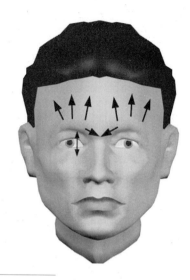

How Muscles Move the Face

At the mouth, the muscles make the following three major types of movements:

- The muscles that lie across the cheeks and jaw pull the lips outward radially from eight major anchor points.

- The muscles surrounding the lips contract to purse the lips, forcing them together and forward.

- The jaw can drop.

At the eyes, the muscles make the following three major movements:

- They open and close the eyelids.

- The Frontalis muscles on the brow raise and lower the eyebrows.

- The Currogator pulls the eyebrows in toward the bridge of the nose, furrowing the brow.

Human anatomy, especially an understanding of muscle action and reaction, provides an exceptionally useful model when you are constructing a face. Human anatomy can also be used as a model for the construction of the face. If the face you create within MAX moves easily along the same lines that these muscles are pulling, you have a much better chance at animating the face.

Modeling and Setting Up Faces for Animation

Before the face is animated, however, it must be modeled and set up for proper animation. How a face is modeled relates intimately to the way that it is animated. A face made from Surface Tools has very few vertices controlling a large surface. It may be animated quite easily using Linked XForms. This method is not useful on denser polygonal models, however, which may be more effectively animated by using a single or multiple target morphing package.

As with bodies and their associated skeletons, faces need to be set up properly and tested over a wide range of motions. Thorough testing prevents difficult problems that can interrupt the creative flow when animating.

Surface Tools

Digimation's Surface Tools has quickly become one of the preferred methods for performing facial animation within MAX. This suite of tools enables you to create very flexible and easy to manipulate mouths and faces. Anyone attempting facial animation should consider Surface Tools to be a standard plug-in. It should be in every MAX animator's toolkit.

Surface Tools contains a number of modifiers, most important of which are Cross Section and Surface. Cross Section is similar to a skinning tool in that it takes a series of spline outlines and connects them together. Surface completes the process by turning the splines into a flexible patch surface.

Modeling a Simple Face with Surface Tools

When building a facial model, a simple and effective way is to build the mouth by using a radial topology—the splines created for the face are oriented so that they stretch out from the mouth radially, in much the same way that the muscles of the face affect the underlying skin. A radial face can also be modeled purely from quadratic patches, so you can avoid tangency problems that crop up when triangular patches are added to the mix.

To picture such a face, think of a cylinder with one end folded inside itself. A face like this can be easily constructed by taking a number of circular splines as outlines, attaching them together, and using the Cross-Section modifier to create a cage of splines that can be surfaced.

CREATING A RADIAL FACE

1. From the Create/Shapes panel, select Line.

2. Draw an egg-shaped outline with eight vertices (for a complex face, more detail may be required).

3. Copy this simple outline three or four times (see fig. 13.3). Using the Edit Spline tool, reshape these outlines so that they taper toward the mouth.

FIGURE 13.3

A simple outline copied four times to create the front part of the face.

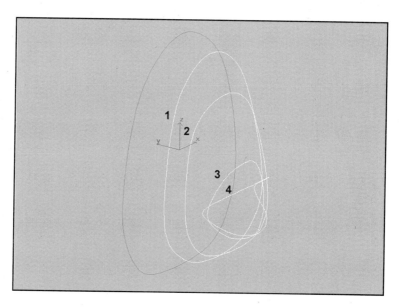

4. Copy the original outline three or four more times. Use these outlines to shape the back portion of the head. The last outline needs to be scaled to zero because it will be the back of the head. If you want, the outlines can also be rotated and tapered so that they become the neck of the character (see fig. 13.4).

FIGURE 13.4
Copying the original outline to create the back of the head.

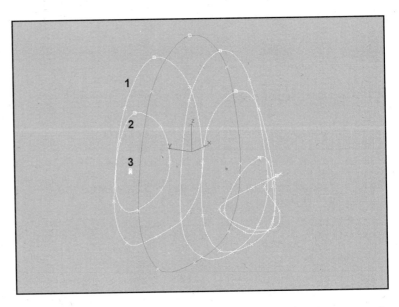

5. Select the outlines near the mouth. Copy these three more times and reshape them to make the throat. Rotate the last outline so that it angles the throat downward into a trachea-like tube (see fig. 13.5).

FIGURE 13.5
The trachea is also created from the same outline.

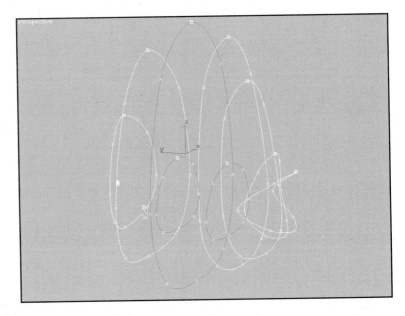

6. Select this spline. Using the Attach tool on the Edit Spline modifier, attach the other splines in order, up the throat, across the face, to the back of the head.

7. Apply the Cross Section Modifier to this spline (see fig. 13.6).

8. Apply the Surface modifier to the stack.

FIGURE 13.6

The original splines, the splines with Cross Section applied, and the final Surface.

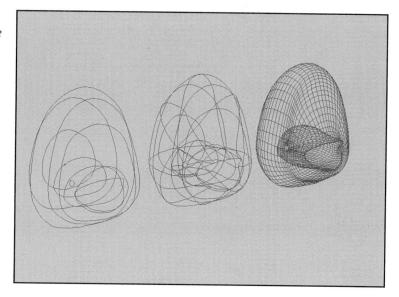

9. Reshape the splines as necessary to create the proper shape. For additional reference, it is a good idea to create a referenced clone of the surfaced face. This can then be used as a live reference of the face while the original splines are being modified.

You can view a simple head created by using Surface Tools. Take a look at the file named splinehd.max on the accompanying CD. A more complex head using the same topology is also on the CD, and is in a file named splineh2.max.

Another important thing to remember is that too much detail in the splines themselves is self-defeating when it comes time to animate. Creating an easily animatable face is an exercise in minimalism. The goal is to get the most detail out of the fewest number of vertices. Typically, 8 or 12 radial subdivisions should be enough to create a usable face.

Because Surface Tools supports triangular patches, it is also possible to use these to help add detail only in those areas that need them, such as around the nose and eyes (see fig. 13.7).

FIGURE 13.7

This face is more realistic and was created using the same basic topology, but with slightly more detail to help define the nose.

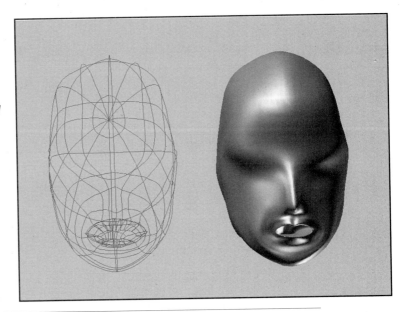

Setting Up a Surface Tools Face for Animation

One very direct method of animating a Surface Tools created face is to use MAX's Linked XForm modifier to attach parts of the spline cage to objects that become handles for the vertices held within. The handle objects, typically dummy objects, can be freely manipulated and keyframed to give the face a wide range of motion.

The face can then be surfaced and textured, while the Linked XForm attached handles give the animator control over the underlying structure. It also enables you to manipulate the underlying vertices while the face is surfaced, giving you a visual cue as to how the skin is behaving. In a typical radial face, eight handles for the mouth and one for the jaw are all that are needed to create convincing mouth animation.

The procedure for creating the handles is very straightforward. The Linked XForms need to be applied to the vertices of the splines used to create the face. On the accompanying CD is a simple, but effective head. It is in the file named xformhd.max. Load this file and follow these steps:

CREATING THE HANDLES

1. Create eight small objects to be used as handles. Any geometry may be used, but dummy objects work best because they don't render. Place

these handles near the vertices of the face you wish to control. In the example head, there will be a total of eight objects arrayed radially around the mouth, each distanced approximately 45 degrees apart.

TIP

Some people use text objects for facial animation because they do not render handles (see fig. 13.8). The text itself serves as a label for the associated handle.

FIGURE 13.8
Arrangement of the handles around the mouth. The white cubes are the handles.

2. Select the spline that represents the head and apply an Edit Spline modifier to it.

3. Activate Sub-Object/Vertex, and select the vertices that comprise the top center of the lip.

4. With Vertex Sub-Object mode still active, add a Linked XForm modifier to the stack. Because this was applied while Sub-Object mode was active, it only affects the selected vertices.

5. Within the Linked XForm rollout, click on Pick Control Object and select the handle object nearest the top center of the lip. The handle now controls these vertices.

6. Add another Edit Spline to the stack, and select the next set of vertices—those on the top left of the lip. Add a Linked XForm modifier to this and attach it to the handle.

7. Repeat this procedure for the remaining handles.

8. Now use a dummy object or a simple piece of geometry to create a handle for the jaw. Place this handle underneath the chin.

9. After all the XForms are in place, apply the Surface modifier. This action creates the skin as the last step in the procedure. Because the Surface modifier is computationally intensive, it slows down manipulation times considerably. It is very easy to switch this modifier off to get additional speed while animating.

The one catch with this method is that the handles themselves are not attached to the head. This means that when the surface of the head is moved, the handles do not follow along. The handles also cannot be bound to the head in a hierarchy because a dependency loop will result.

The easiest way around this problem is to make a referenced clone of the head (see fig. 13.9). The clone can then be attached to the body quite easily, and the original tucked safely away in a separate viewport, so the face can be viewed directly as it is manipulated.

FIGURE 13.9

Creating a referenced clone of the original head.

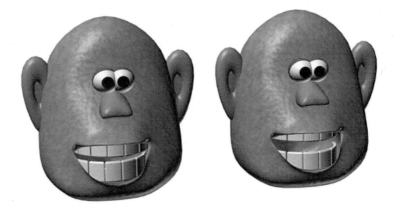

An additional problem concerns the bottom teeth. Because the bottom teeth are attached to the jaw bone, they need to move along with the skin of the jaw—controlled by the jaw handle. On the master model, this can be accomplished by binding the lower teeth to the jaw handle.

The clone, however, has no handles with which to attach the teeth, forcing other solutions to be considered. One way is to use Digimation's Object Glider space warp, which will constrain any object to a surface. This can be used to attach a dummy to the bottom of the chin, which can then be used to parent the lower teeth, forcing them to move along with the skin.

Another sly way to do this without using a third-party plug-in is to apply an Edit Mesh modifier to the objects representing the lower teeth. Select all the vertices in the object and add a Linked XForm modifier to the selection, linking these vertices to the Jaw handle. Because all the vertices are being affected by the Linked XForm, the teeth appear to move as if linked. Technically, however, the teeth are changing shape relative to their pivot. They can be cloned and placed inside the cloned head. They will appear to move just like in the master.

To attach the cloned head to the body, just create a dummy to parent all the objects in the head—the skin of the head, the teeth, tongue, eyes, and so on.

This dummy can then be attached as a child to the body and used to rotate and manipulate the position of the head. If you are using a biped for the body's skeleton, the skull of the biped could be used in place of the dummy object.

You can view the final version of this head by loading the file named xformhdf.max from the accompanying CD.

Morphing

One way to animate faces is with shape animation, also known as morphing. In its simplest sense, morphing just changes the shape of one object into another. MAX has a number of methods for morphing objects, including third-party plug-ins such as MorphMagic, which is discussed later. Included in the base package is a single target morphing function, which is implemented as an animation controller.

Single Target Morphing

Single target morphing changes the shape of one object into another over time. The controller in MAX is of the TCB variety, which gives adequate control over how the morph takes place.

Modeling Morph Targets

To set up your model for animation, you just have to model a library of the appropriate poses. This method works for both spline and polygonal models. MAX requires that the models being morphed have the same number of vertices in the exact same order. This is easily accomplished by modeling a single stock, expressionless face, copying it, and reworking the one face into the many expressions and facial poses required.

Morphs can be created under the Compound Objects Creation panel. The morphs are selected and added to a scrolling list of objects. The trick here is to keep the Instance button toggled as the morph targets are selected, thereby keeping the overhead of the shot lower. After the targets have been selected and the animation has been authored, the geometry for the morph targets are no longer needed, and can be safely deleted from the shot. This deletion keeps geometry counts lower when rendering.

FIGURE 12.10

The Compound Objects Creation panel.

One downfall of this method (and any single target method, for that matter) is that it seems as though you never have enough poses (see fig. 13.11). The number of expressions a human face can make is essentially infinite, so you need to pick your battles and model the broad expressions needed most. Many of the delicate subtleties can get lost when using such stock poses. Strictly morphing between poses can also look mechanical. Having a few different versions of the same pose, therefore, can be one way to avoid this problem. This, of course, adds more geometry to the scene.

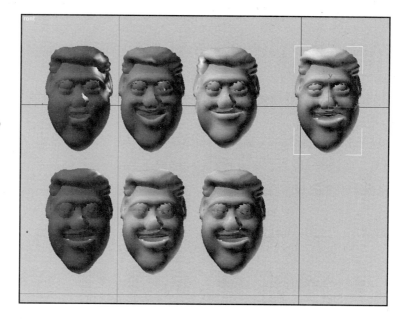

FIGURE 13.11

For MAX's morph manager and for MorphMagic, the models need to be constructed from a master, neutral face so that the vertex counts and vertex order is identical.

Multiple Target Morphing

MorphMagic, a plug-in available through Platinum Pictures, gives MAX the capability to accomplish morphing with multiple targets, along with a number of other features. MorphMagic operates as an object modifier in the standard 3D Studio MAX interface. Because MorphMagic allows for multiple targets, the targets will be much more specific than those used for MAX's single target controller. You may model a single target for a left eye blink and another for a right eye blink, for example, as well as individual extremes for the right and left sides of the face.

MorphMagic enables you to load up to 100 different shapes into a Channel Control menu, and then morph between any number of those shapes at any ratio, or "weight." You can overshoot by using negative values or values greater than 100 percent to amplify the distortion of your objects. You can also limit the effects of the morph to certain areas of your individual objects by first making a selection of vertices in individual targets by using the Edit Mesh modifier.

Morph Magic Interface

The interface is centered around the concept of channels. A *channel* contains a shape, which can be an individual model, a combination of models, or selected vertices within a model. For best use, the MorphMagic modifier should be applied to a neutral, relaxed face, with the extremes applied to the channels. MorphMagic has 10 pages of 10 channels each, for a total of 100 channels (see fig. 13.12). Each channel may be labeled, and each may contain any one of the following three types of targets:

- **Morph Target.** This enables you to select an entire object as a channel.

- **Compound Target.** Compound Target enables you to take a snapshot of any shape you have created by combining channels and inserting them into another channel as a new morph target without remodeling. Then you can just drag one slider to make the "compound" facial expression, rather than remixing the original channels.

- **Selected Vertices.** Using selected vertices enables you to save modeling time and memory by isolating parts of a model as channels. A good example is blinks. Rather than creating two separate models with the right and left eyes closed, you can create a single model with both eyes closed and select the vertices representing the right and left eyes.

FIGURE 13.12

The Morph Magic interface.

Weighted Channel Morphing

After the targets have been selected, you must animate the spinners that represent the individual channels. By combining and mixing multiple channels, you can get any number of combinations. You could model individual shapes for expressions such as anger, fear, joy, surprise, disgust, and so forth, and then combine them so that a pose is 30 percent surprise and 70 percent joy, for example. If you want to transition that to 100 percent joy, animate the surprise channel down to zero, while moving joy up to 100 percent. You can combine two, three, four, or as many channels as you want; all you really need to animate is the relative weights. This makes it much easier to create the exact right pose for the given moment, and also requires that fewer poses be modeled.

The accompanying CD contains a demo version of the MorphMagic plug-in. This demo can be used only with the supplied file mmdemo.max. It gives you a good overview of how this plug-in can be used.

Setting Up a Face with Bones

Using bones to animate the face is another method that can be employed. This method is similar to using the Linked XForm method that can be used with Surface Tools. The similarities lie in the placement of the bones.

Digimation's Bones Pro is a good tool to use for the mesh deformation portion of the process, because this plug-in allows for overlapping influences of bones and allows multiple bones to affect a single vertex. The deformations created with Bones Pro work well on a face.

Bones can also work on a Surface Tools generated face. In this case, however, Physique is the preferred mesh deformation tool to use. One problem with using Bones Pro with a Surface Tools face is that the modifier always floats to the top of the stack, disallowing bones to directly manipulate the underlying splines themselves.

Boning a face is very similar to creating the Linked XForm handles described previously with Surface Tools. The placement of the bones follows the same radial pattern with eight or more bones arrayed approximately 45 degrees apart around the mouth.

If you use bones to animate a face, proper placement of those bones is essential. This face is made out of polygons, but the principles apply equally as well to a patch face. For this exercise, Bones Pro is used. Bones Pro uses the bounding boxes of the bones for initial vertex assignment, so the bones should roughly match the volume of the area of the head they are affecting.

BONING A FACE FOR ANIMATION

1. Load the file head.max. Place a large bone in the center of the head to define the skull.

2. Add a jaw bone. This is a simple box that fills the volume from slightly in front of the ear to the tip of the chin.

3. The jaw bone needs to be pivoted somewhere near the bottom front corner of the ear. Link this bone to the skull bone.

4. Like with the Surface Tools face, create a radial array of eight bones around the mouth.

5. Link the bones along the upper part of the lip to the skull.

6. The bones in the lower part of the face move with the jaw bone. Link or constrain these bones to the jaw bone so that when the jaw pivots down, the bones and the vertices they affect move with it.

7. Placement of the bones around the eyes is very similar to the mouth, but one or two bones per lid is sufficient. Be certain to pivot the bones along the center of the eyeball, so the lid moves along its surface. Link these bones to the skull bone.

8. Add a bone for the nose to help keep it rigid, and add bones for the eyebrows, and maybe even a bone or two to help puff out the cheeks during a smile. See figure 13.13 for a rendering of a basic face.

After the bones are in place, you can continue the exercise and create a Bones Pro space warp to apply to the head. From within the Bones Pro rollout, assign the bones that were just created and the head as the bound node.

Turn on the Animation button and create a simple test animation for the face. Rotate the jaw to open the mouth, move the lip bones to test the range of motion of the mouth, and blink the eyes. Do not worry too much about stray vertices; this animation helps to find them. After this is done, enter the Influence Editor.

FIGURE 13.13

The arrangement of bones for a simple face.

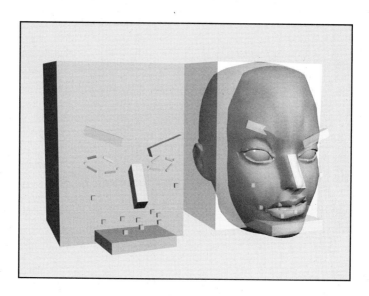

1. Assign the vertices representing the solid portions of the head to the skull bone. These vertices remain rigid, so exclude them from other bones.

2. Assign the vertices of the chin and lower face to the jaw bone (see fig. 13.14).

FIGURE 13.14

The vertices in the lower face need to be assigned to the jaw.

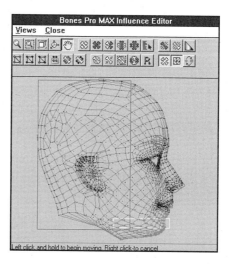

3. You will probably notice some tearing in the lips, where stray vertices from the top lip are influenced by the bottom and vice versa. Go to the mouth and select the vertices representing the upper lip and exclude them from the lower lip bones.

4. Do the same for the lower lip vertices (see fig. 13.15). Exclude them from the upper lip bones.

FIGURE 13.15

*The vertices in the top
lip need to be excluded
from the bones in the
bottom lip.*

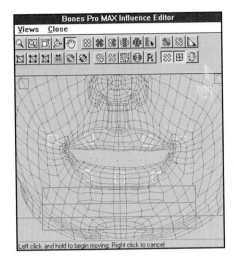

5. To get a smoother transition of vertices, it is a good idea to increase the influences of the bones surrounding the mouth so that they overlap significantly with their neighbors.

6. Locate and reassign any stray vertices in the eye area. The eyes are very similar to the lips in that the upper lid vertices need to be excluded from the lower lid bones and vice versa.

Continue to test and reassign stray vertices as required. A version of this file is located on the accompanying CD as bonehead.max.

Setting Up Eyes and Other Facial Features

Setting up the skin of the face so that it deforms properly is only half the process. Other components of the face need to be set up for animation, such as the eyes, eyebrows, teeth, and tongue, which is heavily involved in speech and lip-sync.

The eyes are by far the most important of these components. Eyes not only need to blink but also need to express emotion. Many emotions and moods are expressed through subtle changes in the eyes, and stiff, unnatural eyes make your character look like a doll rather than a living creature. Eye motions as simple as a blink can add a tremendous amount of life to a character, and more subtle changes in eye shape can add significantly more dimension to the character. On a broad scale, a shifty character may squint his eyes, a surprised character would open his eyes wide, and sad character would furrow his brow. With this in mind, it is essential to have eyes that are controllable in every respect. The lids of the eyes need to follow the surface of the eyeball, and eyebrows need to be able to lift and furrow themselves.

Internal Eyes

Internal eyes are akin to realistic eyes. The eyelids are part of the facial surface with the eyeball inside the skull. If your character design dictates internal eyes, you need to plan for this by modeling eye sockets when constructing the head. This can add a lot of detail, however, particularly when using Surface Tools.

The eyeball itself can be either a sphere or a hemisphere because only the front part of the eye ever shows through the skin (see fig. 13.16). The pupil can be made with a simple texture map, or second hemisphere sitting on the first.

FIGURE 13.16

Eyes inside the head can be constructed out of simple spheres or hemispheres.

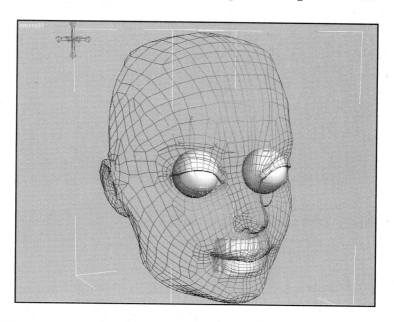

The big problem with internal eyes is that you need to keep the eyeballs locked in the socket while the head moves. This is usually accomplished with a hierarchy—the head being the parent of the eyes. Another issue is the movement of the eyelids. They must move along an arc that is the same radius as the eye.

One way to do this is to place a bone or Linked XForm on the eyelid to close it. To make certain that the skin of the lid follows the arc of the eyeball, place the pivot point of the bone at the center of the eyeball. That way, rotating the bone automatically makes it track the surface of the eye. In this case, a tool-like MorphMagic becomes very useful because the eyelids can be selected out as groups of vertices and morphed into a blink.

Another way to go about this is to create a second lid that animates and remains hidden until the eyes close. For fast eye closures, such as blinks, this can be fine. If the lid is closed too long, however, the audience may pick up the seam where the second lid pokes through the skin.

External Eyes

External eyes have a more cartoon-like appearance, and are easier to control than internal eyes. These eyes are separate objects made from spheres or cylinders that sit on the surface of the face. Because they do not have to line up exactly with the eye sockets on the face, you have much greater control over how they are placed. They are great for Tex-Avery style eye popping, and afford the animator a variety of stylistic choices.

The following are very simply constructed eyes that can be used in many situations. The lids of these eyes are not directly attached to the surface of the face, but rather are separate objects linked to the eyeball itself. This allows for simple construction and gives the lids the capability to change shape along with the eyes, the lids following the surface exactly, even when the eyes are scaled to an oblong shape.

MODELING EXTERNAL EYES

1. From the Geometry Creation panel, create a standard sphere that is 30 units in diameter and has 32 radial subdivisions. Name this sphere **R-Eye**.

2. Select the sphere and then Shift-click on the sphere to clone it as a copy. Name this object **R-Eyelid**.

3. Select the copy, being careful not to move it. (If you accidentally jog it, you might want to use grid snap to align the two pivots exactly.) Within the Modify panel, increase the diameter to 31 units.

4. Remaining in the Modify panel, set the hemisphere spinner to 0.5. This makes the eyelid half a sphere.

5. Clone the object R-Eye again to make the pupil. Name this object **R-EyePupil**.

6. Set the diameter of this object to 30.5 units, and the hemisphere to 0.9.

7. Select R-Eyelid and R-EyePupil and link them to R-Eye.

8. Duplicate these three objects to make the left eye.

Because the objects all rotate around the same center, eye rotation is as simple as rotating the pupil, and blinking is as simple as rotating the lid.

Cartoon Eyes

The method just described produces spherical eyeballs. Not all characters, however, have perfectly round eyes. Sometimes, it is nice to place oblong or asymmetrical eyes on a character to get a cartoony effect.

This can be accomplished quite handily by making certain the Inherit Scale boxes under the Hierarchy/Link Info panel are checked. Because the eyelid and the pupil are children of the eye, the eye's scaling information is inherited. This enables you to scale the eyes in any manner possible, including non-proportional scale to make the eyes oblong (see fig. 13.17).

FIGURE 13.17

A non-proportional scale stretches the eye, and yet still allows the lid to follow its surface.

Furthermore, the scaling can be animated to give the eyes a very flexible squash and stretch effect. This enables you to use the eyes far more expressively on the character. Some examples of this expressive behavior might include the following situations:

- During a blink, the eyes can be scaled along the horizontal axis for two or three frames to help give the blink itself more snap.

- When a character is surprised, his eyebrows raise up. Scaling the eyes along the vertical axis accentuates this even further.

- If a character is loopy or has been knocked senseless, the eyes can be scaled along different axes to give a crazy or mixed-up look.

- Shifty-eyed characters would have their eyes elongated along a horizontal axis.

Blinks happen all the time, and they are a very useful tool for the animator. Blinks can be used to help shift the direction of the eyes or to convey emotion. They also help keep your characters alive—blinking the eyes every few seconds gives your characters believability. In a squash and stretch cartoon environment, animators emphasize motions, such as blinks, by animating the shape of the objects as they move in order to help exaggerate the differences and to help add contrast to the animation.

ANIMATING A CARTOON BLINK

1. Using the eyes just created, turn on the animation button and use the Non-Proportional Scale tool to make the eyes slightly elongated along the vertical axis.

2. Move the Time Slider to frame 6. This is the start of the blink. Within the Motion panel, set keyframes for the scale of the eyes and rotation of the eyelids.

3. Move the Time Slider to frame 9. This is the middle of the blink. Rotate the eyelids 90 degrees so that they cover the eyes. Notice that, even though the eyes are scaled, the lids still follow the surface of the eyes.

4. Select the Squash Scaling tool and squash the eyes down so that they are elongated along the horizontal axis (see fig. 13.18).

FIGURE 13.18
To get a more "cartoony" effect, squash the eyes as they blink.

5. Move the Time Slider to frame 12. Rotate the lids open and use the Squash Scaling tool to put the scaling of the eyes back to normal (for complete accuracy, the keys on frame 6 can also be copied to frame 12 from within Track View).

TIP

Eyes never blink at exactly the same time. Offsetting the blink of one eye by a single frame can add more life to your shot.

Run the animation. Notice how the extra squash added to the blink helps make it look more cartoony. Also notice how the lids stay along the surface of the eye no matter what the shape. For reference, a file is located on the accompanying CD—eyes.avi.

Eyebrows

Depending on the design of your face, the eyebrows can be on the surface of the face or separate. Eyebrows go a long way toward indicating emotion, so be certain to plan for them when designing your characters. If the eyebrows are on the surface of the face, they can be painted on as a texture. For a more complex effect, you can use a displacement or bump map to further define the illusion of hair. Moving these eyebrows requires moving and animating the surface of the face.

MorphMagic makes a good tool for creating surfaced eyebrow motion. Because bitmap textures and displacement maps can be morphed from within the plug-in, the eyebrows can be created as a bump or displacement map that morphs from within MorphMagic.

Eyebrows separate from the face are less realistic, but can take a wider variety of shapes and positions. These can be constructed from a variety of shapes and can float free or ride along the surface of the forehead. Bones Pro or Physique can be used to change the shape of the eyebrow and also help keep it attached to the surface of the face.

Tongues

The tongue is particularly important when animating speech. The tongue is a very flexible object and needs to be animated with bones or some form of shape animation. The tongue is invariably a separate object that just floats in the mouth cavity. The back of the tongue is rarely seen. Directors, after all, rarely fly digital cameras down characters' throats.

The easiest way to build a tongue is by squashing a sphere and putting a dent down its length. Texture and bump maps can also be used to make a more detailed surface. It is a good idea to fade this texture to black at the back of the tongue so that the back of the tongue remains hidden.

The tongue is easily animated using either morphing or a chain of bones and a package such as Physique or Bones Pro. Using MAX's bones with IK turned off makes a particularly good tongue controller, because the mesh stretches along with the bones as they themselves stretch.

Animation and Lip Sync

After the face is properly set up for animation, the actual process of animation becomes easier. Faces set up well can be controlled easily and new expressions can be created on the fly. This can be done by manipulating the bones or Linked XForms, or manipulating and reshaping the morph targets.

Creating a Library of Poses

No matter which animation method you choose, it is a good idea to build up a stock library of expressions that you can draw from when creating your animation. If you use Linked XForms, bones, or single target morphs, the library will actually be keyframes sitting within Track View.

If you animate a Surface Tools face, for example, the positions of the handles at each keyframe determine the individual expression. By copying these keys to other parts of the timeline, you can make animation easy. You can separate the components of each expression and copy them where needed. The keyframes of the handles that control the eyes, for example, can be manipulated and copied separately from those controlling the mouth.

One easy way to create a library is to create keyframes or groups of keyframes on the timeline that can be copied (see fig. 13.19). The negative frame numbers before frame zero serve as one convenient place to store these keys. That way, you do not have to worry about offsetting your animation.

FIGURE 13.19

Store groups of keyframes in the timeline before frame 0 (grayed) to create a library of stock poses.

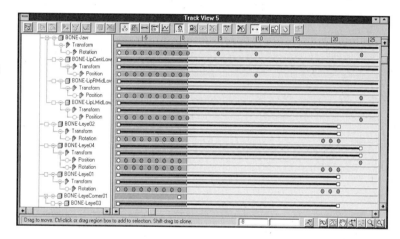

When creating a library, which sort of expressions do you want to model? For a plug-in such as MorphMagic, these are not keyframes, but most likely are the extremes of each of the major muscles of the face. This way, you can have a slider for each extreme, theoretically being able to create all expressions from a handful of sliders. Added to this could be mouths used for lip sync and a number of stock expressions.

The muscle-based method also translates to keyframe-based methods, such as Bones and Linked XForms. These methods, however, lend themselves to groups of keys to create stock or novel poses that your character's face may make. These could be as simple as the mouths used to animate dialogue. Also, as you animate a character, you may create new expressions that strike you as ones that you may need to use again.

The Eight Basic Mouth Positions

The mouths used to create lip sync are a good start to creating a library of poses. Because many characters that do facial animation also perform lip-sync, these poses always come in handy.

Position 1 is the closed mouth, used for consonants made by the lips, specifically, the *M*, *B*, and *P* sounds (see fig. 13.20). In this position, the lips may usually be the normal width. For added realism, you can add an additional position with the lips slightly pursed, for sounds following an "ooo" sound, such as in the word "room."

Position 2 has the mouth open with the teeth closed (see fig. 13.21). It is a very common shape and is used for consonants made within the mouth, specifically those made by *C*, *D*, *G*, *K*, *N*, *R*, *S*, *TH*, *Y*, and *Z*. All these sounds can also be made with the teeth slightly open, particularly in fast speech.

FIGURE 13.20
Position 1 is the closed mouth.

FIGURE 13.21
Position 2 has the mouth open with the teeth closed.

Position 3 is used for the wide open vowels such as *A* and *I* (see fig. 13.22). The tongue should be visible at the bottom of the mouth, and the jaw relatively slack.

Position 4 is used primarily for the vowel *E* (see fig. 13.23). It can also be used on occasion for *C*, *K*, or *N* during fast speech.

FIGURE 13.22

Position 3 is used for the wide open vowels such as A and I.

FIGURE 13.23

Position 4 is used primarily for the vowel E.

Position 5 has the mouth wide open in an elliptical shape (see fig. 13.24). It is used for the vowel *O*, as in the word "flow." Sometimes, particularly when the sound is at the end of a word, you can follow this shape with the one in position 6 to close down the mouth.

Position 6 has the mouth smaller, but more pursed (see fig. 13.25). It is used for the "oooo" sound, as in "food." This can also be used for the vowel *U*.

Position 7 has the mouth wide open with the tongue against the teeth (see fig. 13.26). This is reserved for the letter L. It can also sometimes be used for *D* or *TH* sounds, particularly when preceded by *A* or *I*. If the speech is particularly rapid, this shape may not be necessary, and position 2 might be substituted.

Position 8 has the bottom lip tucked under the teeth to make the sound of the letters *F* or *V* (see fig. 13.27). In highly pronounced speech, this shape is necessary, but the shape can also be replaced with position 2 for more casual or rapid speech.

FIGURE 13.26
Position 7 has the mouth wide open with the tongue against the teeth.

FIGURE 13.27
Position 8 has the bottom lip tucked under the teeth to make the sound of the letters F or V.

Loading Sound into MAX

MAX has the capability to load sound directly into Track View, which makes it excellent for lip sync applications. Sound is loaded by right-clicking on the Sound Track object and selecting Properties from the pull-down menu that appears.

MAX then displays the audio waveform from within Track View, giving you the ability to read the track directly in MAX. Simply sliding the time slider audibly scrubs the audio, allowing you to read the phonemes of the dialog frame by frame. This is best done before animation begins because a properly read track serves as a good roadmap when animating.

Also, reading the track after animation has been added to the shot may prove troublesome due to machine speed and animation complexity issues. If shape animation is being used, the calculations required to perform this can tax even the most powerful systems, so real time playback may not be possible.

Using an Audio Controller for Automatic Lip Sync

One of the easier ways to do lip sync is to use MAX's audio controllers. These controllers enable you to translate, rotate, and scale objects based on the volume of a standard Windows .WAV file. The lip sync produced by this method is not exceptionally accurate; it produces a simple lip flapping effect, which is not particularly convincing. Still, for stylized characters, the method may prove more than adequate.

The Rotation controller is the one chosen most often because it can be used to rotate and flap the lower jaw (though the Translate and Scale controllers can also be put to similar use). These controllers can be applied from within Track View or within the Motion panel.

Once applied, the Rotation controller is accessed from within Track View. The controller's dialog has a number of parameters (see fig. 13.28). First is the name of the sound file to be loaded. It must be noted that the sound file does not have to match the sound file used for Audio sync. This allows for multiple sound files to be used as controllers—perhaps to flap the lips of a dozen people in a crowded room.

FIGURE 13.28

The Audio Controller Rotation controller dialog.

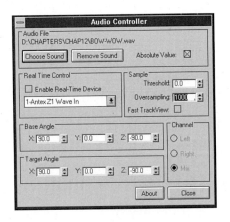

A sound file does not even have to be used because the controller has a check box to enable a live audio source to be used as the controller. This can be useful for real-time or performance-animation applications.

The oversampling spinner is the most critical for smooth operation. A CD-Quality audio waveform changes 44,100 times per second, rising and falling constantly. The audio controller takes the value of the waveform on the given frame and uses that number to calculate the rotation. This can cause jittery behavior because the waveform could coincidentally be at zero, maximum, or somewhere in between when it is sampled.

Oversampling prevents this jittering movement, by smoothing out the waveform seen by MAX. The procedure averages the waveform over a large number of samples (maximum 1,000), giving the effect of a much smoother motion (see fig. 13.29).

FIGURE 13.29

The Waveform display within MAX. The top waveform is the audio itself, and the bottom two are controllers.

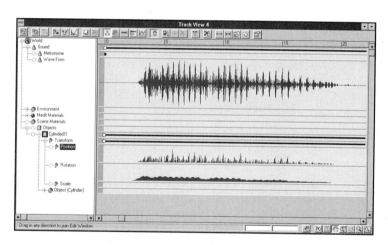

TIP

Sometimes if your audio sample rate is high (44,100 kHz), you may still see some unwanted jitter, even though oversampling spinner is cranked to 1,000. To eliminate this, load the audio file into a sound editing program and convert it to a lower sample rate (11,025 kHz, for example). Fewer samples force the controller to oversample over a wider range of time, effectively doubling or quadrupling the oversample effect.

Along the bottom of the dialog are the limits for the rotation controller. This enables you to set a Base angle, which is the position when the sound is silent, and a Target angle, which is the position when the waveform is at 100 percent.

The following exercise demonstrates the oversampling principle using a barking dog.

MAKING THE DOG BARK

1. Load the file toondog.max. It has a simple cartoon dog with a very simple skeleton inside. The skeleton is configured for use with Bones Pro, although Physique works just as well. The skeleton is set up so that the lips flap when the bones in the mouth and nose rotate around their Y-axis.

2. Select the bone named BONE-Mouth. From within Track View, apply the Audio Rotation controller. Open the controller's dialog.

3. Select the sound. On the accompanying CD is an audio file named bow-wow.wav.

4. Set the Oversampling spinner to a high number between 250 and 1,000. Notice how the waveform shown in Track View smooths out as this number increases.

5. The bone is set to rotate along its local Y-axis. Set the Target angle to 30.0 degrees.

6. Repeat the preceding procedure for the bone named BINE-Nose. Set its Target angle to –70.0 degrees.

Scrub the Time Slider. The skeleton moves and the lips flap along with the sound. On most systems, it may be necessary to render a test to see the effect in real time.

Using a Third-Party Sound Editor

Third-party sound editors can provide more flexibility when reading a track. Some packages enable you to scrub the audio quite accurately in real time, and also to label the tracks as they are read for further reference.

Several third-party lip-sync applications also run under Windows. One popular application is Magpie, distributed over the World Wide Web at http://www.cinenet.net/users/rickmay/CGCHAR/magpie.htm.

Magpie enables you to load a series of bitmap files that represent the key mouth poses as found in your library of poses. These bitmaps can then be timed to the track on a frame-by-frame basis; the final result output is a text file that looks very much like an animator's dope sheet.

Reading the Track

Now that you understand the basic mouth positions, it is time to break down the track. If you have animator's exposure sheet paper, use it. Otherwise, get a pad of lined paper to read your track on, using one line per frame. If you want, you can also create a spreadsheet for this purpose and do it all digitally. There is an example Excel spreadsheet on the CD entitled xsheet.xls. You may use this or print it if you so desire. Load the dialog in a sound editing program.

The first thing you should do is match your sound editing program's timebase to the timebase you are animating—30, 25, or 24 frames per second, for example. After your timebase is set, selecting out a snippet of dialogue should enable you to listen to the snippet and read its exact length on the editor's data window. The visual readout of the dialogue gives you clues as to where the words start and stop. Work your way through the track, and write down each sound as it occurs on your exposure sheet, frame by frame. It is a tedious, but necessary chore.

3DS MAX enables you to play back audio in sync with the animation. This is particularly helpful because you might be able to skip the step of reading the track and instead just eyeball the sync. Still, it is always a good idea to have read the track methodically before animating so that you know exactly where all the sounds occur.

TIP

In MAX, Realtime Play Back must be checked in the Time Configuration dialog for sound to play back.

When reading the track, be certain to represent the sounds accurately. In human speech, most consonants are short, and usually won't take up more than one or two frames. Vowels, however, can be of any length. If a person is shouting, for instance, you may have vowels that top 30 frames in length.

In these cases, it is important that you don't just hold the mouth in the exact same position for over a second; it would look unnatural. Instead, create two slightly different mouth positions and keep the mouth moving between them so that the character looks alive.

READING A TRACK

1. On the accompanying CD, there is an audio file called dial.wav. Load this into your favorite sound editing program. The dialogue says, "Hello, how are you?" At 30 fps, the dialogue measures 46 frames.

2. Highlight the first 14 frames of the sound file. This is the word "Hello." Play this section back. Highlighting smaller sections to get the individual phonemes HE - L - OOO. Notice how vowels are usually taller and louder than the consonants.

3. Work through the entire track, writing down the positions of each phoneme. Here is a graphic representation of where the phonemes fall.

4. On paper, you should have something similar to table 13.1.

TABLE 13.1

Corresponding Frame, Phoneme, and Mouth Positions for this Exercise

Frame	Phoneme	Mouth Position
1	H	4
2	E	
3	L	7
4	L	
5	OH	5
6	OH	
7	OH	
8	OH	
9	OH	
10	OH	
11	OH	

Frame	Phoneme	Mouth Position
12	OH	6
13	OH	
14	OH	
15	OH	
16	OH	
17	OH	
18		
19		
20		
21		
22		
23		
24		
25		
26	H	4
27	H	
28	OW	5
29	OW	6
30	OW	
31	AH	3
32	AH	
33	AH	
34	Y	6
35	OO	
36	OO	
37	OO	
38	OO	
39	OO	

After the track is read, it is just a matter of copying the appropriate keys to the appropriate places in the timeline.

1. The *H* and the *E* sounds are really one vocalization. This can be best represented by mouth position D.

2. Next, you have the *L* sound at frame 3. Again, copy the appropriate keys for position 7 to frame 3.

3. Finally, the *OH* sound. Because this sound is fairly long, it is probably best to close down the mouth from position 5 to position 6 over the course of the sound.

As you can see, it is really just a matter of placing the keyframes at the right position on the timeline. Go through the rest of the dialogue and finish animating the mouth positions.

In Practice: Facial Animation and Lip Sync

- **Surface tools/Linked XForms.** Surface tools enables you to construct a simple surface with a few vertices, controlled by Linked XForms. This method produces a huge stack, however, which can become memory intensive. Keeping the geometry as light and as efficient as possible prevents the memory hit from becoming too large.

- **Morphing.** The facial poses required for a good morph need to be modeled from the same basic head so that vertex order is maintained. One way of manipulating the morph targets is by using bones, Linked XForms, or any of the other methods as modeling tools. The models created can then be reworked with additional tools to get a perfectly smooth surface.

- **Eyes.** It cannot be stressed enough how important the eyes are to facial expression. This is one of the major spots where animation can fall flat. Characters should blink every few seconds, and the position of the lids, and brows should change as the mood changes.

- **Creating a library of poses.** Track View does not have any way of identifying which frame number of the library contains which facial animation pose. To help keep track of the poses in your library, it might be a good idea to render out the frames containing the library to a small AVI file and insert the frame numbers. That way, you can scrub through the AVI from within MAX and find the pose you want, simply by indexing the frame number.

Part IV

ANIMATING THE ENVIRONMENT

IMAGE CREATED BY ERIC GREENLIEF

Chapter 14

by Eric Greenlief

ANIMATING CAMERAS

In today's world, people are used to seeing through the eye of a camera. Television, movie theaters, and VCRs have become everyday elements of peoples' lives. Because of this, people are very aware of how their "electronic eye on the world" should behave. The capability to animate cameras in 3D Studio MAX enables production of animations having the look and feel audiences expect.

As an animator, you have the ability to involve the audience through camera motion. Viewers want to feel as though they are participating. How do you accomplish this? You must uphold the suspension of disbelief. That is, do not allow the audience to realize they are watching still images moving by at 30 frames per second on a flat screen. Create your animation so that they believe they are looking at this other world directly.

One element of 3DS MAX that gives you the capability to suspend disbelief is camera animation. It gives you capabilities that can make a director of photography or a cinematographer of any major movie jealous. These tools enable you to increase the professionalism of your animations enormously. This chapter covers how to achieve success in camera animation, including examples and details on the following topics:

- Traditional film camera techniques and history
- Creating an architectural walkthrough
- Camera work for a moving character
- Special camera motion styles
- Creating camera special effects

Traditional Film Cameras

Virtually any film or television show you have seen has been produced by a professional, experienced staff. One of the primary and integral people involved in the production of films is the cinematographer. The cinematographer is responsible for setting the camera shot and deciding what movement is necessary to tell the story. Cinematographers have typically been trained in film school, studied camera motion, and worked around film for many years before being given the responsibility of capturing the film sequences that you take for granted.

As a CG animator operating a "virtual camera," you have probably not been trained in film school, studied camera motion, or even been on the set of a film in production. But you are suddenly given the same responsibility as the cinematographer—to involve the audience in the scene through the use of a camera. Camera placement and movement is an art that is not easily mastered and should be studied and practiced. All the methods of cinematography that are taught in film school are also valid in CG animation. If possible, take some classes in filmmaking and study the ways of the master cinematographers and directors.

Computer animation often suffers from the intrusiveness of the camera. This can happen when the freedom of using a virtual camera in a virtual world tempts the animator to get away from the constraints a real-world camera operator faces. When you push the envelope of what is expected, whether it is by moving through a scene at supernatural speed or by being able to fly above, below, and through anything, the audience is more likely to notice the camera work rather than the message of the work itself.

You can avoid the obtrusive camera by using it in ways that people understand. Nearly everyone in today's world has viewed thousands of hours of moving pictures on television and in theaters. Mimicking real-world camera techniques in computer animation gives viewers visual cues they already understand.

One characteristic of computer generated animation, for example, is the machine-driven precision of the virtual camera. This precision can make the presence of the camera obvious. Computer-animated camera moves often tend to be very uniform in pacing and direction. Working to simulate a human camera operator adds a quality to the animation that brings it closer to the type of camera work people are used to seeing.

A good way to learn about refined camera work is to step back and take an objective look at motion picture and television footage. Ignore the content and focus on what the camera actually is doing. Try turning down the sound while watching TV and analyzing what you see. You are likely to be surprised by the complexity.

The following elements are what cinematographers must consider when recording moving images:

- Field of view
- Transitions
- Camera angle
- Camera moves
- Panning
- Dolly shot
- Crane shot
- Lenses

Field of View

Field of view is the angle described by an imaginary cone, the vertex of which is at the camera's location. This angle is determined by the focal length of the lens being used.

Short focal length lenses (28mm or 35mm on a 35mm SLR) give a very wide angle of view. Objects in the scene tend to appear far apart from one another. Something appearing on the horizon is nearly invisible, although an object near the camera looks huge. If you take a close-up portrait of someone with a wide angle lens, he or she will appear to have a huge nose and tiny ears. See figure 14.1 for an example of different lens sizes.

FIGURE 14.1
The same scene shot with 20, 50, and 200mm lenses.

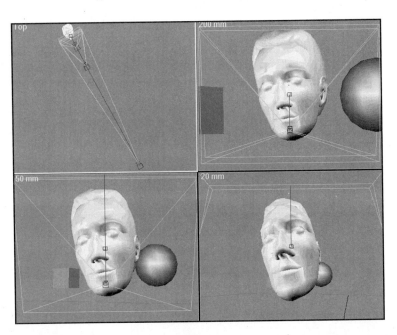

Wide angles of view are useful for showing many objects in a scene simultaneously, for establishing shots of buildings and other large subjects, for building interiors, and to show emphasis by exaggerating perspective.

Medium focal length lenses ("normal" or 50mm on a 35mm SLR) cover a moderate angle of view. The perspective in the resulting display seems to be about what people "normally" perceive with their own vision. The spatial relationships of objects in the scene look normal.

Long focal length, or telephoto, lenses (135mm to 500mm on a 35mm SLR) cover narrow angles of view. Because only objects at the very center of a scene fill the frame, those objects appear to be very close to the camera. Spacing of objects in the scene appear to be compressed.

Narrow angles of view are useful when you want to show objects both near to and far from the camera in the same shot, or when you just cannot get close enough to the object to view it with a normal or wide-angle lens.

Because the computer camera can go anywhere and do anything, you won't need a long focal length to get near something, but because people are used to seeing shots using long lenses, you may want to use them anyway. Refer to table 14.1 for standard lens lengths.

Table 14.1
Standard Lens Lengths, FOV, and Names

Lens	Field of View	Type of Lens
15mm	115.0°	Extreme wide-angle
20mm	94.29°	Very wide-angle
28mm	76.36°	Wide-angle
35mm	63.0°	Moderate wide-angle
50mm	46.0°	Normal
85mm	28.0°	Moderate long/portrait
135mm	18.0°	Long
200mm	12.0°	Very long

Note

In 3DS MAX R1.0, as well as 3DS DOS, the method used to calculate FOV is different from real world lenses. In these programs, the FOV is measured along the *width* of the frame. If you are using these programs and attempting to match the angle of view between your computer-generated images and live-action scenes, it is always best to refer to the focal length of the lens instead of the FOV.

In 3DS MAX R1.1 and later, as well as real world lenses, the FOV is measured *diagonally* across the frame. This eliminates the discepancy between the CG lenses and real world lenses concerning FOV.

When you observe a scene on film or television, you will notice that it consists of a series of shots, each made from a different perspective, joined together. Even though the shots are distinct and separate, the way they are joined makes each sequence appear seamless. This joining of the individual scenes is accomplished through a technique known as *transitions*.

Table 14.2 shows the basic types of shots and their uses.

TABLE 14.2

Standard Camera Shots and Their Traditional Uses

Shot Name	Visual Composition	Use
Extreme Long Shot	Characters small in frame, all or major part of buildings appear.	Establishing physical context of action. Show landscape, architectural exteriors.
Long Shot	All or nearly all of a standing person shows. Large parts, but not all, of a building show.	Show large scale action (athletics, and so on). Show whole groups of people. Display large architectural details.
Medium Shot	Character shown from waist up. Medium size architectural details show.	Face plays important role. Two or three people shown in conversation. Moderate sized architectural detail.
Close-up	Head and neck of character shown. Small architectural details. Objects about the size of a desktop computer fill the frame.	Focus on one character. Facial expression very important. Small architectural details.
Extreme Close-up	Frame filled with just part of a character's face. Very small objects fill the frame.	Show small objects entirely. Very small architectural details. Emphasize facial features in character.

Transitions

Effective transitions are an art form and some gesture to that fact should be made. In a cross-fade, for example, the editor often tries to align the compositions in such a way that the fade is not overly abrupt (looking for a strong vertical contrast, and so on).

The transition from one camera to another determines the overall effect of an edited sequence. Again, as a CG animator, you are taking the place of someone on a professional film crew. This time it is the editor. And again, film editors have typically been through film school to study the art of filmmaking. One of the techniques editors learn is to focus on a specific element that is consistent between the two shots. This element is often a physical object in the scene, such as a door. Imagine approaching the outside of a door, then seeing the inside of the door in the next shot.

The focus element, however, does not have to be an object. It can just as effectively be a compositional element, such as a specific motion, color, direction (such as looking down a long row of starkly vertical telephone poles, then transitioning to a low shot in a cornfield looking down a row of tall corn stalks), and even contrast or balance. Remember, filmmaking is an art, and the artistic relationship between shots must be taken into consideration to achieve an effective transition.

The easiest transition in traditional filmmaking, as well as computer animation, is a straight cut. A straight cut is an abrupt transition between shots. It is the most common edit and, depending on the nature of the adjacent shots, can either be nearly unnoticeable or very obvious.

Another family of transitions depends on an effect called *fade*, in which the overall value of the scene increases or decreases until the entire frame is just one color. When one scene fades out as another fades in, the result is a *dissolve*.

Generally, fades from or to a black frame indicate the beginning or end of a sequence. It is appropriate to fade out and then fade in again when two sequences are different in location or time. Fades in animated sequences fill much the same purpose as chapter divisions in writing. A fade is accomplished in 3DS MAX with a fade image filter event in Video Post.

Dissolves, in which one scene fades out while the next fades in so that the images overlap, most often indicate passage of time. In an animated walkthrough of a building, for example, you may choose to compress part of the journey by dissolving from a shot at the base of a long staircase to a shot of the room at the top of the stairs. The dissolve can be accomplished in 3DS MAX through Video Post using a cross fade transition image filter event.

There are other transitions in which a scene *wipes* across the frame, displacing the previous scene. These wipes can move in any direction or start in the center or edges of a frame and move out or in. Wipes call attention to themselves and are best used conservatively when necessary for the telling of your story. An example of a wipe would be to show the passage of time. Imagine the exterior of a country barn during the day. A wipe begins at the right side of the screen to reveal the same shot, but this view is at night. Wipes are accomplished in Video Post using a simple wipe image filter event. To achieve more complex wipes you can use image alpha or pseudo alpha filter event, and animate a bitmap in whatever wipe you want.

Another transition effect is the *swish pan*, in which the camera suddenly pans (rotates horizontally on its axis) so fast that the image becomes a blur. This is cut into another swish pan at the beginning of the next shot. The effect is of the camera jumping a great distance instantaneously, as if to say, "Meanwhile, back at the ranch...." A swish pan can be accomplished with the combination of scene motion blur and video post.

Camera Angle

Determining the point of view of the camera is very important in setting up scenes in an animation. Years of exposure to film and television have conditioned viewers to interpret the camera's "eye level" as conveying meaning.

Generally, viewers expect the camera to show a level horizon. If the camera is rolled sideways from the horizontal, thus tilting the horizon—as was often done in the 1960s TV series *Batman*—viewers expect something sinister to happen.

In terms of the camera's height above ground level and its angle in relation to the ground, expectations reflect real life. A "bird's eye" or "worm's eye" view is not part of a viewer's natural experience, and so draws attention to itself. These "unnatural" views are appropriate if the effect matches the message. When the camera is outside the normal range of experience, however, it may detract from the content of the animation. The ease of placing a virtual camera anywhere often leads to excessive use of inappropriate camera angles in computer animations.

It is good practice to observe existing footage and try to determine how far above ground level the camera is, and then use that information when placing cameras for animated scenes. When surveying a scene in a wide-angle shot, the camera's lens is usually where your eyes would be if you were sitting in a comfortable lawn chair. In close-ups of characters, males are usually shown from just below eye level, females from just above.

NOTE

Placing a camera at eye level of a standing person actually looks too high under most circumstances. You should determine whether placing your camera above or below the subject is appropriate in each situation.

Camera Moves

Not long after the invention of motion picture cameras, several basic moves evolved, forming the backbone of camera movement technique today. The same techniques apply to the use of virtual cameras in computer animation. You are by no means restricted to these basic moves because cameras are not constrained by time and space. Knowing "real world" camera techniques, however, is essential because audiences have learned to read moving images through these basic moves.

The fundamental moves are as follows:

- Pan
- Tilt
- Dolly
- Track
- Crane

All these moves create motion by moving the camera itself. Pan and tilt are rotations around the camera's axis. The others are translations of the camera's location in space. Another category of moves involves changing the focal length of the camera lens during a shoot. It is not really a move, however, in that the camera remains stationary. A move is simulated because the changing angle of view makes objects appear to move closer to or farther away from the screen.

Panning and Tilting

Panning is used to follow a moving object or character, to show more than can fit into the frame at one time (such as when panning across a landscape), and as a transition between one camera position and another.

Inexperienced camera operators often make the mistake of panning too fast. You have probably seen home videos that cause motion sickness. When looking from one thing to another, you are panning with your eyes. Panning a camera as fast as you move your eyes just does not work.

Video is played at 30 frames per second. Computer animation is often played back at slower speeds, such as 15 or even 8 frames per second. Panning too quickly causes the difference between one frame and the next to be so great that the illusion of motion is broken. In cinematography, that effect is called *strobing*. In computer animation, it can also be referred to as *tearing*.

There are two ways of dealing with strobing in computer animation. One is to make certain that pans are not too fast. The following table gives some safe pan speeds for various conditions. Again, observe film and television footage to see just how slow most pan moves are. Refer to table 14.3 for recommended pan speeds.

TABLE 14.3

Number of Frames Needed for a 45° Pan

Type	15 fps	24 fps	30 fps
Quick turn	11	18	22
Comfortable turn	15	24	30
Casual turn	33	54	66

Another way of correcting strobing is to use motion blur when rendering. Two kinds of motion blur are available in 3DS MAX: scene and object. *Scene* motion blur shares information between frames. Most of the information comes from the current frame, but some is from the previous and following frames. The effect is to have less difference between frames, expanding the acceptable limits of camera motion. *Object* motion blur produces motion blur for individual objects in a scene, not the entire scene itself like scene motion blur. For this reason it is not used to prevent strobing.

In addition to preventing strobing, motion blur allows the computer animator to simulate the effects of real world cameras. In the real world, the shutter of the camera is open for a specific amount of time. If, during the time the shutter is open, the camera moves quickly, the scene moves a significant distance in relation to the camera, and appears to blur, or streak. Because virtual cameras do not have a shutter to open and close, this streaking or blurring does not occur automatically. Instead, you must explicitly tell the camera to add motion blur. In 3DS MAX, scene motion blur is done in Video Post. This small extra step can be invaluable in simulating the realism of real world cameras.

To see the unrealistic effects of not having motion blur, animate the rotation of a propeller on an airplane or the rotor of a helicopter at a very high speed. When you play the animation back, the propeller or rotor appears to jump around, but does not look like it is rotating. Apply object motion blur to the propeller or rotor and re-render. With motion blur, you get a much more realistic motion that simulates the mechanics of a real camera. Although this example uses object motion blur, the concept is exactly the same for scene motion blur.

NOTE

One of the other ways to simulate real world optics in a computer-generated scene is with depth of field. Depth of field is covered later in this chapter.

Tilting is functionally similar to panning, except that the camera rotates vertically. The same precautions should be followed when tilting as when panning.

Dolly and Tracking Shots

A *dolly* is a small wheeled vehicle used to move a motion picture camera and its operators about in a scene. It is piloted by a *dolly grip* whose job is to smoothly start and stop the dolly and synchronize its motion with the pans and tilts of the camera operator. When you design camera paths, you take on the role of dolly grip. The most challenging part of the job is achieving smooth, subtle starts and stops. As a virtual dolly grip, you need to re-create the human touch in your camera paths.

When the camera moves in and out of a scene (generally on the same axis as the lens), it is referred to as a *dolly move*. When the move is perpendicular to the lens axis, it is called a *tracking shot*. The same precautions must be observed when tracking as when panning. Because you do not have the ability to get inside your virtual scene, you do not have a very good frame of reference to judge the speed at which you should dolly your camera. The speed of dolly and tracking moves are usually based upon how fast a person moves. Refer to tables 14.4 and 14.5 for recommended speed tables.

TABLE **14.4**

Pedestrian Gaits

Type	Miles per Hour	Feet per Second	Inches per Second
Casual stroll	1.5–2.0	2.2–3.0	26–36
Average walk	2.5–3.5	3.6–5.0	43–60
Brisk walk	4–5	6–8	72–96
Average jog	6–8	9–12	108–144
Average run	8–10	12–15	144–180
All out sprint	12–16	18–24	216–288

TABLE **14.5**

Number of Frames Needed to Move 10 Feet

Type	15 fps	24 fps	30 fps
Casual stroll	50–68	80–109	100–136
Average walk	30–42	48–67	60–83
Brisk walk	19–25	30–40	38–50
Average jog	12–17	20–27	25–33
Average run	10–12	16–20	20–25
All out sprint	6–8	10–13	13–17

Crane Shot

When the camera moves up or down, the shot is traditionally called a *crane shot*. It may also be referred to as a *boom shot*. Observe the same timing and rendering practices with a crane shot as you would with a tilt.

Zoom Lenses

The invention of zoom (variable focal length) lenses made it possible for camera "moves" to be made without actually moving the camera. Orthodox cinematographers use the zoom lens only to change the angle of view between shots and prefer to move the camera itself when a move is called for. (Home videographers love to zoom in and out while making fast pans and tilts to enhance the nauseating effect.)

It is as easy (or easier) to move the camera itself rather than to zoom when creating a computer animation. The zoom, however, can be a very effective tool. Because people are accustomed to seeing zoom effects in films and on television, you can use it to accomplish the same effects in computer space. On the surface, zooming appears to move the camera closer to or farther from objects in the scene. In reality, the angle of view is changing, so perceived spatial relationships also change.

The "Vertigo" Effect

Vertigo is a technique made famous in the Alfred Hitchcock film of the same name. It takes advantage of the zoom lens's capability to change the angle of view dynamically during a shot.

In this effect, the subject moves toward or away from the camera (or the camera moves and the subject is stationary). As the distance between the two changes, the zoom lens' focal length is changed to keep the size of the subject constant in relation to the frame. The effect is that the background appears to "zoom" in or out while the subject stays the same size.

Achieving vertigo in 3DS MAX has been a very tricky proposition. With the release of 3D Studio MAX 1.2, however, the process became much simpler. The 1.2 upgrade contains two MAX sample files that demonstrate how to achieve vertigo. For you to be able to complete the next exercise, you must have at least version 1.2 installed. This upgrade can be found on the Kinetix web site at www.ktx.com. If you need to install the upgrade, be certain to read the readme file that comes with it.

VERTIGO

1. Open the vertigo.max file installed by the 1.2 upgrade (you can find it on the accompanying CD-ROM).

2. Select camera01 and open Assign Controller in the Motion Control panel.

3. Right-click on the Position Expression Controller and select Properties. This expression controller contains the formula for creating the vertigo effect. Save this expression as **Vertigo.XPR**.

TIP

Choose Summary Info from the File menu to read more information about this sample file.

4. Load vertigo2.max from the accompanying CD.

5. Create a target camera as shown in figure 14.2. Change the camera lens to 85mm.

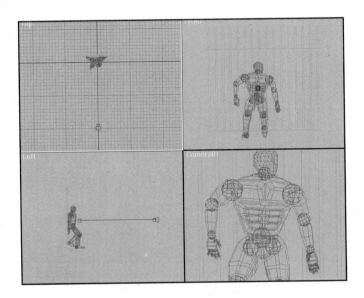

FIGURE 14.2
The position of camera for the vertigo effect.

6. Link the camera to its target.

7. Turn on the Animate button and move to frame 150. Change the lens length to 24mm. Turn off the Animate button.

8. Open Track View, copy the FOV key at frame 0 to frame 30, and change the Bézier tangent to slow in and slow out for each of the three keys.

9. Assign a Position Expression Controller to the camera. Select and right-click on the controller and choose Properties. Load the vertigo.xpr created in step 3.

10. Select W in the Scalars box and assign it a constant of 200.

11. Select FOV in the Scalars box, click on Assign to Controller. Expand the tracks if necessary and select the FOV: Bézier Float under Camera01. Close the Expression Controller box.

12. Unlink the camera from its target. Move to frame 150. With the Animate button off, move the target directly upward until you can see the top of the fence in the Camera viewport.

NOTE

The Expression Controller evaluated the position of the camera while it was linked to the target. During this evaluation, the motion of the camera was set. After the motion of the camera is set, you can unlink the camera and move the target to a position where the vertigo is enhanced by the viewer seeing the top of the fence come into view. This approach enables you to have the camera move in a horizontal line, while not moving directly toward the target.

13. Play the animation in the Camera viewport and render the animation to a flic or AVI.

The vertigo.avi included on the accompanying CD shows the completed animation for this exercise.

Architectural Walkthrough

Architectural walkthroughs have been a major selling point for computer animation from the beginning. Imagine the possibility of being able to walk through your dream home before it has been built. Imagine choosing the color of the carpet, walls, all the furniture, and experiencing them in your home before the plans are even finalized. Unfortunately, this has hardly become the norm for building a new home, or even for expensive commercial buildings. As an animator, you know all the time and effort that goes into creating an architectural animation on the computer. You also know how much more time and effort goes into creating an environment that enables the audience to believe that what they are seeing is real.

After the architectural model has been built, materials applied, and lighting created, your next job is to put the audience into the scene. The camera enables the audience to believe they are moving through the building. They are an observer taking part in the animation.

All too often, camera motion in walkthroughs has the objective of showing off everything that the animator has built in one lengthy shot. The animator chooses specific points of interest in the building, chooses a point outside the building to enter from, and then proceeds to draw a spline path that connects all these points. The results are similar to what early movie makers attempted before the subtleties of editing were discovered. A brilliant 3D model that may have taken weeks or months of work is cheapened by unrefined camera work.

A good example of consistently bad camera moves is in the show *Cops*. Each time the camera is inside the car and the police are chasing a vehicle, the camera typically points directly out of the front of the car. How many times is the suspect's car lost from the frame, and you are disoriented because you can't see the car? Unfortunately, this is the exact same motion that occurs when the camera and target are put on the same path throughout the building with no concern for the composition of the scene.

As you work through the next exercises, and as you are composing your architectural animations, keep the following points in mind:

- Analyze sequences created by professional cinematographers for ideas on timing, composition, camera motion, and transitions.

- Don't waste time getting from one point of interest to another. Use transitions to eliminate boring or insignificant material.

- Avoid moves that draw attention to the camera at the expense of the subject.

- Compose and evaluate your camera moves by using the camera viewport as a viewfinder, not by looking at the top view of the floor plan.

- Avoid camera moves that would not be possible with traditional cameras. Don't do the "death dive" over a railing just to get to the next floor.

- Give the audience time to observe significant objects and points of interest, then move on.

- Do not move the camera too quickly just because you want to save time rendering or animating. Move at a comfortable pace.

TIP

Use a stopwatch to time yourself walking through a building or other interesting space to give yourself a feeling for how long it should take for certain sequences in a walkthrough. A stopwatch is also useful when examining live-action film sequences and transitions.

NOTE

When you visit a space, you remember the important features of that space. You don't waste memory on the uninteresting walks down the hall or across the parking lot. As an animator, you are responsible for the same selective memory when creating a walkthrough.

Creating the Establishing Shot

The first step in many film sequences is to create an establishing shot. The *establishing shot* shows the exterior of a building or area in which the action will be taking place. The establishing shot serves many purposes, including the following:

- It associates the building with the environment.

- It enables the viewer to identify with the character of the building. Architects strive to achieve harmony between the interior and exterior of a building. This harmony is essential to the building's character. The establishing shot serves as the audience's introduction to the building.

- It gives the audience a frame of reference to begin their journey. After experiencing the introduction, they feel more comfortable in exploring the interior of the building. The audience understands where their journey will be taking place.

THE ESTABLISHING AND OPENING SHOTS

1. Load church-e.max from the accompanying CD. The scene consists of the exterior of a church in a simulated environment.

2. Choose Configure Paths from the File menu. Click on the Bitmaps tab and add the path to the CD Maps directory. You may optionally copy the necessary map files to your local hard drive.

3. Create a target camera at the position and angle shown in figure 14.3. Name the camera **es-cam1**. While still in the Create panel, change the lens length to 24mm.

FIGURE 14.3

The placement of camera es-cam1.

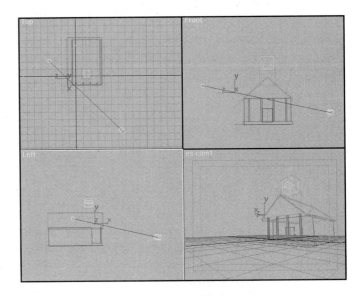

TIP

In a walkthrough, you generally want to create a camera that sees more than the standard 48° seen by the human eye. This can help simulate peripheral vision, and also enable the audience to feel more involved in the animation.

4. Activate the Perspective viewport and press C to change the view to the current Camera view.

NOTE

It is important to adjust the camera position and rotation while observing the Camera viewport. This is the "viewfinder" that enables you to see what the camera sees. Do not simply place the camera in the Top viewport and aim it at something you want to show. Throughout this chapter, pay particular attention to what is shown in the Camera viewport, and try to match the composition shown in the figures.

5. Move to frame 90. Use the Motion Control panel to create a position key for the camera and target. Change the Bézier tangents to slow in and slow out for the target and camera. This setting enables the camera to be motionless for the first 90 frames, enabling the audience to become stable and comfortable in the shot before moving.

6. Turn on the Animate button, and change to frame 360. Move the camera and target to match figure 14.4. After you have established the camera, turn off the Animate button.

FIGURE 14.4

Position of es-cam1 at frame 360.

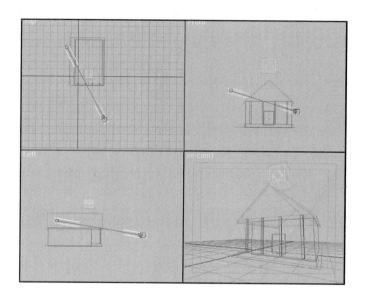

NOTE

It is important to keep the audience moving slowly throughout the animation, avoiding any sudden movements that might detract from the suspension of disbelief. Keep in mind that you are taking the audience on a pleasant trip, not a roller coaster ride.

You do not need to show the entire building at this point. The motion in the camera is needed only to enhance the three-dimensionality of the scene and make it come alive to the audience.

TIP

If you need to show the entire exterior, create a second animation that follows the walkthrough. A good technique is to introduce facts about the building in this second animation. Facts could include square feet, number of rooms, interior and exterior finishes, and so on. It will also enable you to create a more technically oriented animation using simpler geometry that can release you from the necessity of creating a fully realistic 360° environment.

Exterior Detail Shot

The next shot enables you to transition from the initial exterior establishing shot to the inside of the building. You should not just appear inside the building. Each camera shot you create must be a logical progression from the previous one. This progression is called a *transition*. Often, a director focuses on a particular object at the end of a camera shot. This object is then seen at the beginning of the next camera shot, but from a different perspective, enabling the audience to remain oriented throughout the sequence.

For the transition to the interior of a building, it is common to use the main entrance as the transition focus area. Again, you want to add motion to the scene as you did with the last camera. The motion in this case should progress toward the entrance to communicate the feeling of entering the building. After this, the audience knows the next logical place to be is inside.

THE EXTERIOR DETAIL SHOT

1. Continue from the previous exercise. Create a free camera at the position and angle shown in figure 14.5. Name the camera **es-cam2**. While still in the Create panel, change the lens length to 24mm and change the Camera viewport to this camera.

2. Move to frame 315 and create a position and rotation key.

TIP

When using multiple cameras in a scene, animate them at the same time coordinates at which they will be presented in the final animation. Resist the temptation to create all the camera motions at the beginning of the scene. This enables you to compose the timing of your scene more logically, without having to remember exactly how many frames and in what order each camera is to be shown. This also keeps the frame numbers correct when rendering to individual files in the final rendering. Create a Note track in the Track Editor for each camera that shows exactly in which frames this camera will be rendered. Place the note key at the first frame in which the camera will be rendered.

FIGURE 14.5

The position of camera es-cam2.

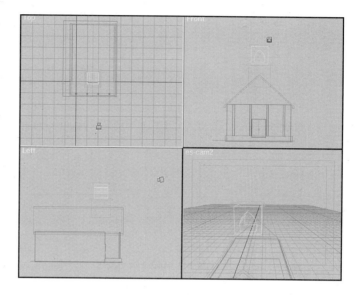

3. Turn on the Animate button and change to frame 530. Move and rotate the camera to match figure 14.6. After you have established the camera, turn off the Animate button.

FIGURE 14.6

The position of escam2 at frame 530.

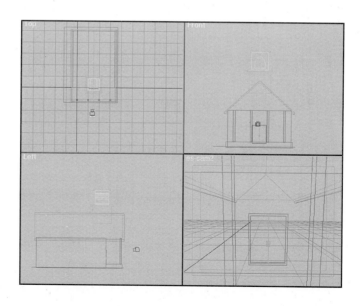

It is important to determine at this point what kind of Video Post transition will be made between cameras. Will it be a fade to/fade from black, or a dissolve from one camera to another? The length of the transition needs to be incorporated into the beginning and ending of each camera move so that the motion does not stop.

For the transition between es-cam1 and es-cam2, you have a 1.5 second (45 frame) dissolve from one camera to the other. In other types of animation, this transition time might be too long, but in the case of an architectural walkthrough, you want to ease the audience from one camera to the other and keep them moving comfortably.

For the transition between es-cam2 and the first interior camera, have the audience pause at the entrance, fade to black, and then fade from black to a motionless camera. This transition helps the audience relate more easily to the change from interior to exterior.

4. Change the in position tangent for the camera to slow in at frame 530.

5. Save your MAX file.

Creating the Interior Shot

Before you begin creating cameras for the interior shots, take a few moments to preview the cameras you have animated and save them as flic files. Keep these files so that they can be examined later as well.

The interior of the chapel is created by using a separate MAX file. Using separate files can help you in the following ways:

- Lowers polygon count for rendering because you do not have exterior geometry for interior shots, and interior geometry for exterior shots.

- There are fewer objects to sort through in object lists.

- The file size is smaller and more manageable.

WARNING

If changes are made to one file that will affect the other, you must be certain to change both files simultaneously. This can be done easily by making the changes in one file, temporarily merging it into the other, making changes, and then deleting the objects from the merged file.

THE INTERIOR SHOT

1. Load the file church-i.max from the CD. This scene consists of the interior of the church.

2. Create a free camera at the position and angle shown in figure 14.7. Name the camera **int-cam01**. While still in the Create panel, change the lens length to 24mm and change the Camera viewport to this camera.

FIGURE 14.7

The position of camera int-cam01.

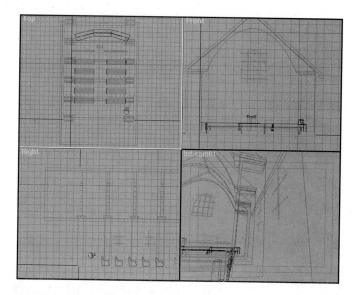

3. Turn on the Animate button, and change to frame 305. Move and rotate the camera to match figure 14.8.

The transition between the three interior cameras uses a 1.5 second (45 frame) moving dissolve. This overlap needs to be incorporated into the timing of the cameras as it did in the establishing shots. Also keep in mind that during the dissolve, neither of the camera views will be clearly visible.

Because the composition of each camera shot is critical to the success of the animation, be certain to compose the beginning and ending shots through the Camera viewport, and then adjust the path between them.

4. Select the camera and click on the Trajectories button in the Motion Control panel. At this point you can see the path your camera will take.

5. Change the end time to 305 in the Spline Conversion section, and the samples to 2. Press the Convert To button.

FIGURE 14.8

*Position of camera int-
cam1 at frame 305.*

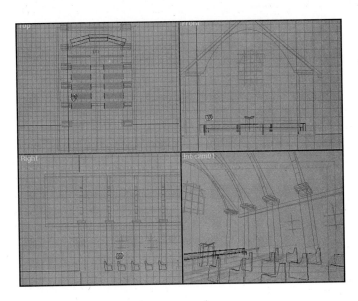

6. Access the Modify panel and select the spline just created. Change the name to **spline int-cam01** and add an Edit Spline modifier. Change the endpoints of the spline to Bézier and modify the spline to approximate the one shown in figure 14.9.

FIGURE 14.9

*Shape of path spline for
int-cam01 after
modification.*

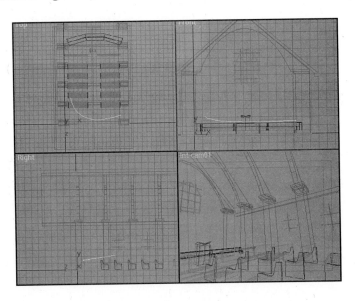

7. Select the camera and access the Motion Control panel.

8. Change the samples to 10 in the Spline Conversion section. Press Convert From and select spline int-cam01.

9. Play the animation in the Camera view.

By using this technique, you can maneuver the camera path around walls, furniture, and other objects while still maintaining the beginning and ending frame composition. If necessary, add a few vertices to the spline. You may also adjust the timing of the camera by adjusting the start and end times in the Spline Conversion section of the Motion Control panel.

If you add vertices, keep in mind that the more vertices in the spline used for a path, the more radical the camera movement will tend to be. It will also become increasingly difficult to edit the spline and keep it smooth. Keep the fewest possible number of vertices in the spline to ensure smooth motion.

TIP

If you need to edit the path more, do not convert the camera path to the spline again. Simply edit the existing spline and then convert the camera trajectory from that spline.

Because camera timing is critical, try to view the animation in as close to real time as possible with a minimum of strobing. To aid in this, keep the camera view set to wireframe. If needed, you can also hide unnecessary objects and change the viewport to Box mode. You may also want to pause at this point and create a preview animation. To keep the animation close to real time, keep the resolution low. You are only evaluating camera motion, which can usually still be distinguished sufficiently at low resolution.

10. Create a free camera as shown in figure 14.10. Name the camera **int-cam02** and change the lens length as before. Change the camera view to this camera.

NOTE

If one camera is selected from multiple cameras in the scene, and you change a viewport to a Camera view using the C shortcut, the view automatically changes to the currently selected camera. If you want to select a different camera, either deselect the camera and press C again, or select the desired camera by right-clicking on the viewport title.

FIGURE 14.10
The position of int-cam02.

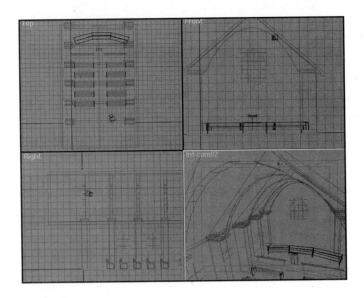

FIGURE 14.10
The position of int-cam02.

11. Move to frame 261 and create a position and rotation key for the camera. Activate the Animate button, move to frame 670, and modify the camera and camera path by using the technique shown earlier (see fig. 14.11).

FIGURE 14.11
The position of int-cam02 at frame 670 and its spline path.

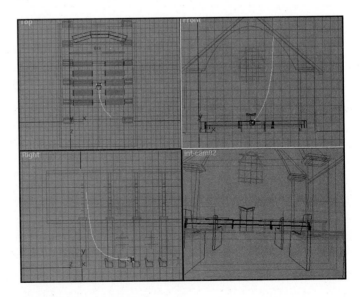

12. Create a preview for the camera.

Closing Shot

The closing camera shot can be the most important one. It is the last picture of the interior of the building that the audience will see. To aid in determining the final shot, think of the impression with which you want to leave the audience. You may choose to show a wide view of the lobby of the building, or the view of a beautiful sunset from the penthouse. Whatever you choose, be certain that you compose the last frame carefully. Use your knowledge of color, composition, balance, and so forth to help you.

After you have determined the last frame of the closing shot, use the animation of the camera to lead up to it. Swing the camera around the room to enable the audience to discover other interesting details. As they are focusing on the smaller details, they will soon discover the sunset out the window, and realize they have come to the end of their journey. As the camera comes to the end of its move, be certain to allow the audience to settle into their last glimpse by using a slow in on the last key, and then pause. After the audience has had a chance to enjoy the last frame, use a slow (45–60 frame) fade to black.

THE CLOSING SHOT

1. Create a free camera as shown in figure 14.12. Name the camera **int-cam03** and change the lens length as before. Change the Camera view to this camera.

FIGURE 14.12

Position of int-cam03.

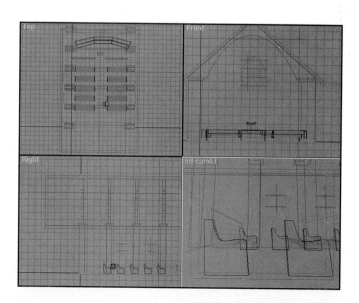

2. Create a rotation and position key on frame 626.

3. Move to frame 945, activate the Animate button, and modify the camera as shown in figure 14.13. Change the position Bézier tangent to slow in, the rotation TCB continuity to 0, and ease in to 25.

FIGURE 14.13

Position of int-cam03 at frame 945.

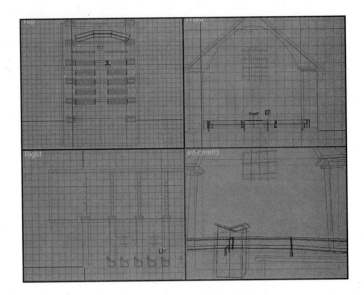

4. Preview the last camera for motion.

Previews

As you completed animating your cameras, you created a preview for each one. These previews can help you determine proper timing for your animation. They also enable you to determine whether the length of the entire animation is correct. To view your preview animations in sequence, it is best to use a viewer outside of 3D Studio MAX. This enables you to script your animations together and view them sequentially. One of the standard viewers, AAPlay for Windows, is available at the Kinetix web site (www.ktx.com).

Unfortunately these previews do not enable you to examine the fades and dissolves that are important to the animation just completed. To accomplish this, use Video Post. When creating these files, keep the resolution as small as needed to keep the animation playing near real time. If you are using two separate MAX files for your animation, and the transition between them is a fade to/from black, just script them together in your animation player. If the transition is a cross fade (dissolve), render the first MAX file out to individual files rather than a flic, and then add them as an Image Input event in the second file's Video Post.

TIP

Using separate image files rather than flics for the individual camera shots makes the creation of the final rendering run more quickly because Video Post must examine each preceding frame to obtain all the color information for a frame in the middle of a flic. This is not necessary when individual image files are used.

A copy of the Video Post VPX file is included on the CD for your reference. You may load this file while in Video Post to render your preview animation.

NOTE

AVIs could also be used for your preview. AVIs tend to have a larger number of colors, many different possible codecs, and drop frames to keep the animation playing at the desired speed. They also tend to be more portable to other systems because they are more popular at this time.

Flics are limited to 256 colors and are compressed with a delta compression scheme. They play back every frame and, if necessary, slow the frame rate of the animation to accomplish this. Although there are fewer colors when using a flic, as long as the resolution is kept low, flic playback is generally superior to AVI playback.

Camera Animation for Characters

Study almost any movie or television sequence showing people and you will see the basic camera techniques involved for animating characters. Most sequences can be built from basic shots: long, medium, and close-up.

The "long" or full shot, shows all or most of the character's body. This is used to show the context in which the character appears, or to show large body actions such as running or tumbling. In a full shot, the body is the most important visual element of the character (see fig. 14.14).

Figure 14.14
A figure in a long camera shot.

When framing a character in full shot, try to avoid centering in the frame. Use the "rule of thirds" to place the character on one of the two axes that divide the frame in thirds. When tracking or panning with a character in full shot, make certain that there is plenty of "nose room" between the character and the edge of the frame he is facing.

A "medium" shot generally shows a character from the waist up. It shows more facial expression. Most conversations in which both speakers appear together in one frame are shot in medium format. The same rules apply regarding "nose room." If a character in a medium shot is facing the side of the frame, allow more space on that side of the frame (see fig. 14.15).

A "close-up" focuses on the character's face. A medium close-up shows the head and neck, where an extreme close-up closes in on the face itself and lets hair and so on go out of frame. It is especially important in close-ups to make certain that the framing is comfortable. Keep an eye on that nose room (see fig. 14.16).

FIGURE 14.15

A figure in a medium camera shot.

FIGURE 14.16

A close-up shot.

Real people have a very difficult time sitting or standing still—only television news anchors have mastered the technique. Most people also move hands and body a great deal to add meaning to verbal communication. One of the challenges a real-world camera operator faces is maintaining a pleasing composition in a frame in which the subject is constantly moving. A skillful operator "floats" with the person, always maintaining appropriate visual relationships in the frame. When studying live action footage, notice that the camera is very seldom locked down when a person appears in the frame. There are constant subtle moves. For computer animation to simulate real life effectively, the same techniques should be adopted. As a character moves from left to right, or turns and faces a different direction in the frame, adjust the framing to compensate.

Use the established live action camera techniques when animating characters, and thereby move your animation into the realm of "film grammar" your audience understands.

The following exercise shows you successful camera placement and animation for a moving character.

CAMERA PLACEMENT FOR A MOVING CHARACTER

1. Load robot.max from the CD.

Similar to the establishing shot of the walkthrough, you will have an establishing shot of your character. In this case, however, the character suddenly enters from above. You want to establish the audience's attention on the scene before the character enters.

2. Move to frame 50 and create a free camera as shown in figure 14.17. Change the lens length to 35mm.

The ominous shot is often used in establishing a character's attitude. See whether you recognize this shot from virtually any action movie you have seen. When you see this shot, you know something exciting is going to happen.

3. Create a dummy object and center it on the character's head using the Align button on the main toolbar. Name the dummy object **camera02**.

4. Move to frame 150 and create a target camera as shown in figure 14.18. Align the camera's target to the center of the dummy object. Use this camera for the active Camera view. Link the camera to the dummy object.

FIGURE 14.17

Position of camera01 using frame 50 as a reference frame.

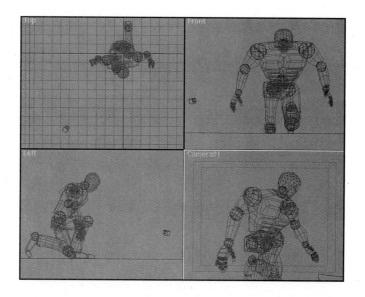

FIGURE 14.18

The dummy object and camera02 at frame 150.

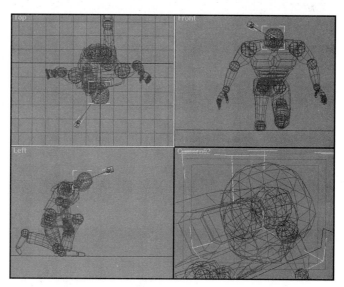

5. Select the dummy object and create a rotation key at frame 150. Move to frame 310, turn on the Animate button, and then rotate the dummy 67 degrees on its local Z axis. Change the continuity to 0 for both frames.

6. While still on frame 310, move the camera approximately 28 units straight down (see fig. 14.19). Turn the Animate button off.

FIGURE 14.19
Camera02 at frame 310 after dummy rotation and camera movement.

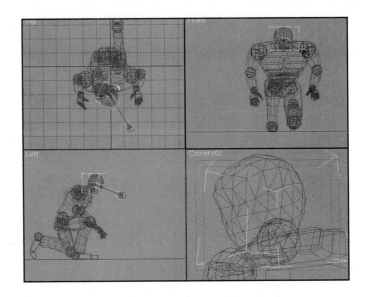

7. Change the camera's position controller to linear position.

8. Change to frame 505 and create a target camera as shown in figure 14.20. This is camera03.

FIGURE 14.20
Camera03 at frame 505.

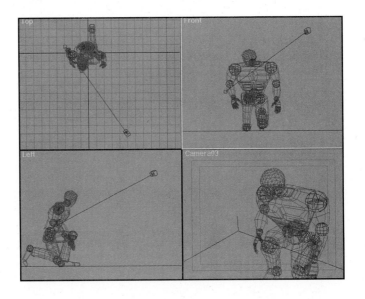

9. Change to frame 570 and create camera04, a target camera (see fig. 14.21). Create a position key at this frame for the target of camera04.

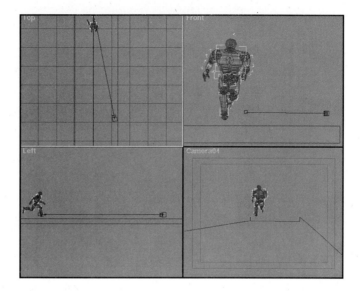

10. Turn on the Animate button and move to frame 600. Move camera04's target straight along the path of the robot so that the robot is approximately centered in the view. You will be modifying this key, so its exact location is not important now.

11. Change to frame 650 and move the camera's target to put the robot right of center in the view.

12. Turn off the Animate button and play the Camera viewport from frame 570 until the end. Determine whether the camera movement as the robot goes by will keep the robot sufficiently in the frame. The entire figure will not be in the frame, you are just looking at the timing of the movement. Do not allow the robot to move completely out of the frame at either side during the move. Also keep in mind the "nose room" principle mentioned earlier (see fig. 14.22).

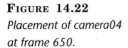

FIGURE 14.22

Placement of camera04 at frame 650.

Preview and Video Post

As with the last exercise, many cameras are being used, and they must be composited in Video Post. Unlike the walkthrough, however, this exercise is used to show action. Straight cuts from one camera to another on the same subject tend to raise the audience's excitement level, so you will not use any dissolves or fades except at the end.

Preview each camera for the frames shown in table 14.6. As before, save the individual files out and script them together to get an idea of the timing of the final rendered animation. After you have verified the timing and made any corrections, render to a FLIC or AVI.

TABLE 14.6

Video Post Setup for Robot

Camera	Beginning Frame	Ending Frame
camera01	0	120
camera02	121	505
camera03	506	560
camera04	561	690
camera04 fade out	660	690

"MTV" Camera Style

In computer animation work, you will likely be asked to generate material for use in what might be described as "MTV-style" footage. Music videos have developed a visual style related to their musical content and youth culture audience. This style has been around long enough that it has spread well beyond just music videos.

The music video style is characterized by camera and editing techniques often just outside the boundaries of the normal and expected. Thus you find unusual camera angles, extreme field of view, unorthodox camera motion, and fast, sometimes jarring, cutting from one scene to another. This style has become a staple in television commercials and other non-music areas (for an excellent example, watch *Bill Nye the Science Guy* on your local Public Broadcasting Station).

The best way to adopt the music video style in your animations is to objectively observe the type of footage you are trying to emulate. Visualize how the camera was used, in terms of lens focal length, placement, motion, and so on, and decide what must be done in 3DS MAX to duplicate the effect. Most of the techniques needed can be derived from information and examples given in this chapter.

Shaky Cam

For many years, cinematographers have faced the challenge of keeping the camera steady while moving it through rough terrain. At first, this problem was overcome by building tracks, using cranes and cherry pickers, and using other engineered solutions that generally cost a great deal and chewed up a lot of time.

Of course, a camera operator could just grab the camera and run overland with it on her shoulder. The resulting images would have an unsteady, jerky action that we have come to associate with documentary and television news footage. The implication to the viewer when they see shaky camera images is that the footage is immediate, spontaneous, and somehow more "real" than carefully locked-down and smooth studio shots.

Even though a device was invented several years ago (the Steadicam) that can eliminate undesirable motion in hand-held shots, many contemporary directors and cinematographers deliberately hand-hold the camera to imply spontaneity. You see this most often in television commercials and music videos.

In the real world, achieving a steady image is not easy. In the computer realm, however, perfect steadiness is the default. You may want to use random camera motion to add a "documentary" effect to an animation, in which case you will need to corrupt that perfection with a virtual "shaky-cam."

The concept behind creating a shaky cam in 3DS MAX is fairly simple. You will assign a noise controller to the position controller of the camera (see "Earthquake!" later in the chapter).

One of the challenges is creating a shaky cam combined with live action footage. Luckily, this can also be solved easily in 3DS MAX. Film your live-action with a stationary camera. In your MAX scene, create a flat plane object or box in the backround of the scene. Create a material for this object that includes the live-action footage as a diffuse map and adjust the mapping so it appears as a "movie screen" to project the live footage onto.

NOTE

The mapping can be accomplished best through a camera mapping plug-in. One is available on the Kinetix web site in the Yost Group "Fun Stuff" plug-ins.

This setup enables you to have the live footage appear as a backround, similar to what you would accomplish in Video Post, but the camera movement is independent of the backround. If you shake your computer camera in the scene, the "movie screen" is stationary and achieves the proper illusion. Another valuable benefit of this setup is that it allows scene motion blur to be applied to the virtual movie screen, and you can add motion blur to your live footage *after* it has been filmed!

Earthquake Cam

Another effect seen in film and TV is the "earthquake cam." This is where the camera shakes to simulate ground motion. This effect can be easily dupli-cated in 3DS MAX.

EARTHQUAKE!

1. Load earthqua.max from the CD.

2. Select camera01 and open the Motion Control panel. Apply a Position List Controller to camera01. A List Controller enables you to use multiple controllers on an object at the same time.

3. Apply a Noise Position Controller to the available controller slot in the Motion Control panel. The Noise Position Controller gives the camera a random position simulating the earth shaking.

4. Open Track View and expand the camera01 tracks. Select Noise position, right-click, and select Properties. This action opens the Noise Controller settings. Here you can control specifics about the randomness of the position.

5. In this camera effect, you want to have the camera move suddenly at the beginning. This is shown on the characteristic graph as a spike at the left side. You may scan through the seed possibilities to find a suitable graph. This exercise will be using seed 1.

6. Change the X, Y, and Z strength values to 20, and ramp out to 90. The ramp makes the camera motion settle down as time passes. Close the Noise Controller box.

7. Drag the Noise Position range bar to begin at 96 and end at 150. Minimize Track View.

TIP

Because there is no way to type in frame numbers to set the range for this kind of controller, it can be helpful to set the current frame to where you want the beginning or ending of the range. The current frame is represented by a thin vertical line in Track View and can help in the alignment of ranges.

Play the animation in the Camera viewport to see the effect. Play the animation in the Right viewport as well. Notice that the camera position in the Right viewport changes as the animation cycles to the beginning. Generally, you will want specific, predictable control of the camera position before and after the shaking. As you can see, the randomness of the Noise Controller placed the camera at a different position at the end of the shaking than at the beginning. The Position List Controller assigned earlier will enable you to compensate for this difference in position.

8. In the Motion Control Panel, change the Bézier Position Controller to Linear Position Controller.

9. Move to frame 96 and create a position key.

The dummy object around the camera has been aligned with the pivot point of the camera at its original position. This positioning enables you to realign the pivot point of the camera to the center of the dummy after the Noise Controller has placed it out of position.

10. Be certain that the camera is still selected, move to frame 150, and turn on the Animate button. Align the X, Y, and Z coordinates of the camera pivot point to the center of the dummy object by using the Align button on the main toolbar. Turn off the Animate button.

11. Hold your MAX file. You will be coming back to this point.

To make the effect a little more realistic, you will also want to add a little random rotation to the camera.

12. Open the Motion Control Panel, and assign a Rotation Noise Controller to the camera.

Notice that the camera has oriented its Local coordinate system to the World coordinate system and the camera is pointing at the ground. To avoid this, assign the Noise Rotation Controller to the dummy object, and then link the camera to the dummy.

13. Undo the Noise Rotation Controller or perform a fetch. Assign a Noise Rotation Controller to the dummy.

14. Open Track View, select the Noise Rotation, right-click, and select Properties. Set the seed to 22, the X, Y, and Z strength to 5.0, and ramp out to 40. Close the Noise Controller box.

15. Drag the range bar to begin at 96 and end at 150.

16. Link the camera to the dummy object and play the animation.

17. To add a little more to the effect, animate the camera to move and rotate as the ground ripple hits.

18. Render to a FLIC or AVI.

NOTE ——————————————————————————————————————

You can also render the scene in Video Post and turn on Scene Motion Blur to increase the realism in the camera motion.

To view a version of the final animation with the final camera motion, play quake.avi from the CD.

Depth of Field

One of the problems faced by users of real-life camera optics is that depth of field is limited. When an object in the foreground of a shot is in focus, the background is out of focus. This characteristic is a problem in some circumstances, but it can also be very useful when trying to emphasize an element of the visual composition. Virtual cameras have unlimited depth of field. This leads to computer-generated images that are sharply focused from foreground to background.

You may want to introduce limited depth of field to re-create the "realism" people are used to seeing in film and television. Shallow depth of field enables you to isolate specific objects in a scene. You can also shift the plane of focus during a shot to move emphasis from one object to another. That effect was used to great advantage in *Jurassic Park* when the game warden is surprised by a velociraptor emerging from the undergrowth.

Included on the accompanying CD is a shareware version of a depth of field plug-in. Other excellent depth of field plug-ins are available on the market today. The two popular ones are Cebas' Real Lens Flare and Digimation's LenzFX MAX (not yet released at this writing). Each of them has specific advantages and features. The one included on the accompanying CD has the advantage of low price, while still creating a very realistic effect. At the time of this writing, however, it does not have the capability to animate the focus plane independently of geometry in the scene. The next exercise is designed to simulate this effect with the included plug-in.

TIP

Although this exercise is designed for a plug-in without an object-independent, animatable plane of focus, the same technique can be used to save large amounts of rendering time on plug-ins that do have this feature as well.

ANIMATING DEPTH OF FIELD

1. Install the plug-in and read the accompanying documentation.

2. Load the demoscen2.max from the plug-in installation.

3. Select geosphere06, right-click, and select Properties. Change the G-buffer object channel to 1. Follow the same procedure to assign geosphere02 to object channel 2, and geosphere05 to object channel 3.

Because the plug-in is a Video Post filter, all the rendering is done in Video Post. In this animation, you create three separate images, each focusing on a different sphere. You then composite the three images to simulate the animated focus plane.

4. Open Video Post and clear the entries by selecting New.

5. Add a Scene event of camera01 with a range from 0 to 0.

6. Highlight the Scene event and add an Image Filter event. Select the Fields of Depth filter plug-in. Select Setup, set the Object Focus object ID to 1, and set aperture size to 14.

7. Add two more Scene and Image Filter events as previously described. One with a range of 1 to 1 and an object ID of 2, and the other with a range of 2 to 2 and an object ID of 3 (see fig. 14.23).

FIGURE 14.23

Use Video Post to create the three images to be composited.

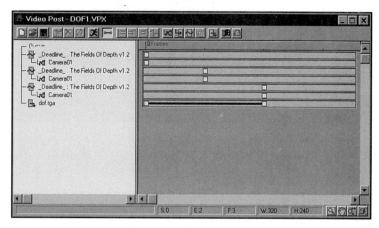

8. Add an Image Output event from frame 0 to 2. Type **dof.tga** for the output file name.

TIP

It is always a good idea to save the Video Post VPX files as you complete them. Save this file to DOFI.VPX.

9. Execute the sequence to render the 3 TGA images and clear Video Post again. It is not necessary to include the alpha channel for this exercise; 24 bit is sufficient.

10. Add an Image Input event from frame 0 to 30 with the file DOF000.TGA.

11. Add an Image Input event from 31 to 45 with DOF000.TGA and another with DOF001.TGA for the same frames. Select these two entries and add a cross fade transition between them.

12. Use the same cross fade technique for frames 46 to 60 using DOF001.TGA and DOF002.TGA.

13. Add an Image Input event for frames 61 to 90 with DOF002.TGA.

14. Add an Image Output event from frame 0 to 90 to a FLIC or AVI (see fig. 14.24).

FIGURE 14.24

Use Video Post to composit the three images into an animation.

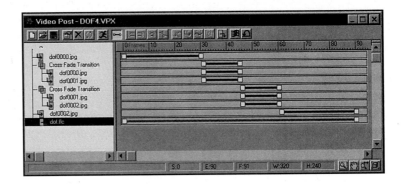

15. Save the VPX file and execute the sequence.

NOTE

For most applications, only two different focus planes are needed, not three as were used in this exercise.

As you can see, just doing a cross fade transition between different image files achieves a fairly realistic effect and suits most circumstances. If examined closely, however, the technique is apparent.

If the animated focus plane needs to happen while the camera is moving, you must render out the entire camera move to sequential images for each different focus plane. This takes considerably longer because the computer not only calculates the entire range of frames for depth of field, but also must calculate it again for the second focus plane.

A workaround for this can be achieved with the included plug-in with the use of an object that has a completely invisible material applied to it. Use the object focus option, set the object ID for the invisible object, and then animate the position of the invisible object. The focus plane then follows the object as it moves. To achieve the desired effect, you will probably need to experiment with the shape and size of the object as well as use a lower aperture setting.

Another less automatic workaround is to use the manual focus option and change the distance one frame at a time.

In Practice: Animating Cameras

- **Study established camera technique.** Viewers understand an established camera "grammar" derived from years of watching television and film. Using the same techniques in computer animation helps the artist communicate effectively.

- **Architectural walkthroughs.** Effective walkthroughs depend on using multiple cameras and creative transitions between shots. Make the camera's presence as unobtrusive as possible so that the viewer can be drawn into the scene. Use motion blur where appropriate and pace camera moves, such as pans and tilts, to avoid strobing.

- **Character animation.** "Float" the frame so that there is always a comfortable composition as characters move. Use multiple shots in a scene. Observing existing live footage will help you learn effective camera technique.

- **"Shaky cam" and "earthquake cam."** Adding random motion to the camera path can duplicate the kind of motion that disturbs cameras in real life. The effect can be used to dramatically emphasize the force and impact, or to simulate a hand-held camera for a documentary effect.

- **Vertigo.** Dynamically altering angle of view during a shot creates a captivating effect. Use it to dramatize the relationship of a character or object to its background.

- **Depth of field.** Simulating real-world optics is possible by using a depth of field plug-in. Controlling depth of field enables selective emphasis on different objects in the field of view.

"Sunnyvale Open House" by Steve Burke

Chapter 15

by Steve Burke

ANIMATING LIGHTS AND ATMOSPHERES

Animated lights and atmospheres can add texture and character to a scene. With these tools, you can add drama to an otherwise simple animation. They also help to establish mood, because most animated light and environment effects evoke some type of emotion. The tranquillity of a candlelit room is one example. Compare this to the tension and foreboding created by a powerful lightning storm. A good way to use these tools is to suggest an effect—to provide strong visual clues and invite the viewer to imagine what he or she cannot see. This chapter uses animated lights and environments to create a range of rich lighting and atmospheric effects. The focus—always—is on achieving an aesthetic result as efficiently as possible, using all the tools 3D Studio MAX has to offer.

The tutorials in this chapter cover animated light effects and touch on animated environmental effects. Further, the tutorials describe modeling, material, and other considerations necessary to create these effects. When describing the techniques in this chapter, the most pertinent steps are presented first, followed by additional steps that complete or refine the techniques. Often, this type of comprehensive approach is necessary for an effect to look convincing.

The following tutorials all use a variation of the same basic scene file, a cozy living room. By varying the lighting and animation, a number of effects and moods can be obtained.

This chapter covers the following general topics:

- Candlelight

- Moonlight

- Lightning storm

- Volumetric light

To get the most out of this chapter, follow the tutorials in order because each tutorial builds on the previous one. The end results of these tutorials comprise some very intricate effects.

The first scene presented is a candlelit room. Aside from the flame effect, candlelight presents another lighting problem you will encounter in many situations—too little light. Nighttime, cave, and underwater scenes fall into this category. The techniques discussed are as applicable to these situations as they are to candlelight.

As a course of habit, a scene should be built, texture-mapped, and lit before beginning any animation. First establishing the scene in this way provides a solid foundation for animating lights and environments. You will examine the next scene and complete it before beginning to animate.

Using Candlelight to Create Ambience

The concepts and techniques presented in this section of the chapter are quite extensive, covering every element of lighting a candlelit room. This includes special materials, creating and animating lights, some aspects of Video Post, and much emphasis on aesthetic concerns. Later in the chapter, you build on these techniques to create some great variations on the simple candlelight theme.

Candlelight produces a warm, low-intensity, flickering light. 3DS MAX makes creating this effect simple. Low-light scenes, however, can be difficult for the viewer to read. These scenes must have enough illumination to make the composition clear without being over-bright. Too much light spoils the candlelight effect, too little light produces a dim incomprehensible image.

Examining the Lighting

Load candle.max from the Chapter 15 directory of the accompanying CD. This file contains a pleasant living room scene illuminated with several low-intensity lights (see fig. 15.1). In the foreground of the scene is a TV tray and candle. At present, only the background of the scene is lit. Later, you will create the candle flame effect, and create the illumination from the candle. First, take a moment to examine how the scene is lit.

FIGURE 15.1

The candle.max scene as seen from the Camera viewport.

The scene contains several spotlights and one omni light. Each affects a different part of the scene. It may seem unnecessary to have so many lights for such a dimly lit room, but actually the opposite is true. Because the scene is very low-key, every bit of light is important and needs to be exactingly directed. One or two lights could not adequately do this.

Some lights affect several objects, but most are focused on a specific object or an edge or corner of an object. Combined, the lights hit every part of the scene. Using several lights in this way enables you to brighten or darken any area by changing the multiplier of one or more lights. Using lights in this way enables you to fine-tune a scene with relative ease.

NOTE

If you are getting missing bitmap file errors when rendering, copy the bitmaps from the Chapter 15 Maps directory on the accompanying CD to the 3DSMAX maps directory on your hard drive.

Render the scene from the Camera viewport. Although it is dimly lit, notice that the background of the scene is clearly visible and that the foreground is very dark (see fig. 15.2). If too much background light hits the foreground objects, the foreground objects appear washed-out when more lights are added to the scene. Remember, the foreground lighting still needs to be created and the darker the foreground objects are now, the deeper their shadows will be after these additional lights are added.

By adding a relatively strong light source to the foreground and retaining the deep shadow color already present, the foreground will have strong contrast. This contrast helps to separate the foreground items from the background. When working with a dimly lit scene, proper contrast can make the difference between a clean, readable image or a murky, indecipherable one.

Select some of the lights in the scene and examine their parameters. Notice that all the lights are gray or blue and have very low multiplier settings (see fig. 15.3). This setup helps create the illusion of diffused and reflected nighttime light. Further, these lights are kept minimal so that they will not overpower the candlelight in the foreground. The candle flame is the focal point of the scene, and the background should be lit only enough to make the background visible; it needs to be much less intense than the candlelight.

Now that you are familiar with the background lighting, it is time to add some foreground light to the scene. The foreground light in this scene is emanating from a single source, the candle flame. You will, however, need to add more than one light to the scene to create the foreground lighting. This is a common practice in computer graphics where lights don't behave quite as they would in real life.

FIGURE 15.2
*The candle.max scene
as seen from the
Camera viewport.*

FIGURE 15.3
*To create a subdued
light effect, each of the
many lights has a very
low multiplier setting.*

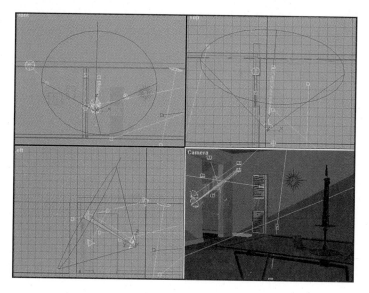

CREATING THE PRIMARY FOREGROUND LIGHT

The first light you add to this scene simulates the light of the candle flame
shining down on the foreground objects. To create this effect, place a
spotlight above the candle aimed downward toward the floor.

1. If it is not already loaded, load candle.max from the accompanying CD. All of the bitmaps for this file are located in the Chapter 15 Maps directory on the CD; you may want to copy them to your 3DSMAX maps directory.

2. From the Viewport Controls section of the interface, Click on the Min/Max Toggle button. This action minimizes the Camera viewport and makes the three orthogonal views visible.

3. Create a new Target Spotlight in the Front viewport. Name this light **Spot_Candlelight**. It does not matter where you place it, you will type in the exact coordinates next.

4. With the light selected, choose Transform Type-In from the Edit menu. This dialog can be used to enter exact coordinates for any object (see fig. 15.4). You use it to precisely place each new light.

FIGURE 15.4

A new spotlight is added to the scene and precisely placed with the Move Transform Type-In dialog.

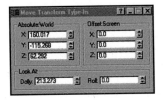

5. Make certain that the Select and Move tool is active. Place the light up and to the right of the wall (at about X: 180, Y: –50, Z: 75).

6. Select the target of the new spotlight. Set the Absolute:World coordinates as follows: X: 159.992, Y: –115.266, Z: –13.727.

NOTE

The Transform Type-In dialog affects objects based on the currently active transform tool; Move, Rotate, or Scale. If you type coordinates into the dialog and nothing happens, check to make certain that one of these tools is active. When the Select tool is active, the Transform Type-In dialog has no effect on these parameters.

Entering the previously designated coordinates places the new spotlight directly over the candle. The next step is to enter the spotlights parameters.

7. Select Spot_Candlelight and open the Modify panel. Set General
   Parameters as follows:
   Set Color to RGB 216, 194, 126.
   Set Multiplier to 0.65.
   Under Attenuation, check Use.
   Set Attenuation Start Range to 97.
   Set End Range to 187.

   Set Spotlight Parameters as follows:
   Set Hotspot to 98.
   Set Falloff to 147.2.

   Set Shadow Parameters as follows:
   Check Cast Shadows.
   Set Map Bias to 2.5.
   Set Size to 320.

The preceding settings create a soft, yellow-orange light that casts shadows
and fades over distance (see fig. 15.5).

FIGURE 15.5

The Modify panel for
Spot_Candlelight.

8. Render the scene to see how this single light has changed the scene (see
   fig. 15.6).

FIGURE 15.6

The foreground cleanly separates from the background with the addition of a well-placed spotlight.

The foreground, except for the candle and flame, is now well-lit and separates nicely from the background. You still need to add candlelight shining on the walls. Later you will create special materials for the candlestick and flame and then animate the scene.

The illumination from a candle flame can be simulated with a single omni light or a single spotlight with overshoot enabled. This method, however, is not as flexible as using several lights. When using multiple lights, each light can have a different multiplier, shadow setting, attenuation, and so on.

You have already built the first spotlight for the candle illumination, next you continue with the scene, adding two more lights to enhance the candlelight effect. You will merge these lights into the scene.

ADDING SECOND AND THIRD FOREGROUND LIGHT

1. Select Merge from the File menu. Choose the file candle_2.max from the accompanying CD and click on OK. From the Merge dialog, scroll to the bottom of the list and select the last two items: Spot_Candle-Sidewall and Spot Candle-Wall. Click on OK.

2. Click on Select by Name in the menu bar. Click on None to deselect any objects. Now select Spot_Candle-Sidewall and click on OK. With the first light selected, you can examine its parameters in the Modify command panel.

    This light has a very low multiplier and is aimed at the wall toward the left of the image. It provides a very subtle effect. Note that the light itself is not positioned anywhere near the actual candle flame. The light could have been positioned near the flame and angled to hit the wall in the same place. Lights that are nearly perpendicular to the surfaces they are illuminating, however, are easier to control.

3. Click on the Exclude button in the Modify panel to see which items have been excluded from the light's illumination. The Exclude/Include dialog should look like that shown in figure 15.7. Including only the aforementioned objects minimizes the effect the light has on the room, ensuring that this additional light does not destroy the lighting already created for the background.

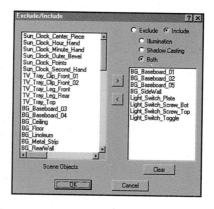

FIGURE 15.7

The Exclude/Include dialog is used to limit the effect of the spotlight Spot_Candle_Wall.

4. Examine the second new spotlight Spot_Candle_Wall. This is the light aimed from the candle toward the rear of the room (see fig. 15.8). It creates a nice yellow glow on the back wall.

FIGURE 15.8

Only the new spotlights you added to this scene are visible; the other lights have been hidden to reduce clutter. Spot_Candle_Wall is selected.

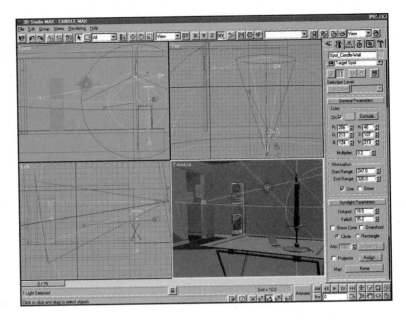

5. Render the scene to see the combined effect of the new spotlights (see fig. 15.9).

FIGURE 15.9

The candlelight scene as rendered, with final lighting arrangement. The candle and flame still require special materials.

The rendered scene now looks complete except for the candle and flame, which at present, look quite dreadful. You will create the flame material first.

Creating the Flame Material

You can use various means to create fire and flame effects; particles, combustion, compositing, and so forth. They all have their strengths. Often you will find the simplest solution is also the most effective. The flame effect described in this tutorial is a combination of modified geometry, materials, and a Video Post Glow filter.

The flame itself is a sphere that has been elongated and tapered with an FFD 3×3×3 (Free Form Deformation) modifier. It was then given a Cylindrical UVW Mapping modifier and a Material modifier. Last, it was assigned a Multi/Sub-Object candle material (see fig. 15.10). Next, you create the material for this object.

FIGURE 15.10

The flame object is a sphere, tapered and elongated with an FFD 3×3×3 modifier. It has been given a Cylindrical UVW Mapping modifier.

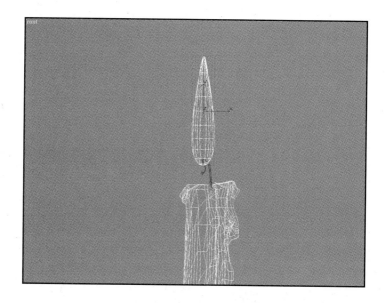

NOTE

The FFD modifier plug-in is an indispensable modeling and animation tool. You can download it free from the Kinetix web site. This modifier enables you to manipulate object surfaces by manipulating a lattice object.

CREATING A CANDLE FLAME MATERIAL

1. Load candle_2.max from the accompanying CD. This file contains the candle scene with the final lighting setup in place. If you have been following along during the last few tutorials, you do not need to load this file.

2. From the Display Command panel, choose Hide by Category Lights to make the screen less cluttered (see fig. 15.11).

FIGURE 15.11

The candle_2.max scene file. Lights are hidden to reduce screen clutter.

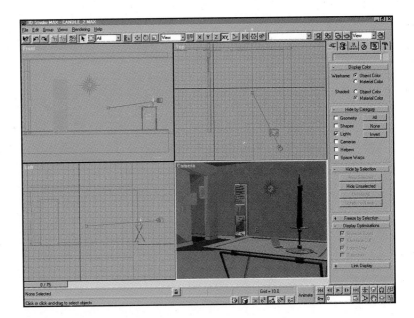

With the lighting in place, it is time to create special materials for the candlestick and flame. Because these objects exhibit some self-illumination, they cannot be lit with lights alone. The material for the flame needs to be created first. The brightness of the flame defines how bright the candlestick needs to be. There is already a Multi/Sub-Object material applied to the flame and candle, but it needs to be adjusted.

3. In the Material Editor, select the Multi/Sub-Object material in Slot #1.

4. Click on the Material 2 button to edit the flame material.

5. From Basic Parameters, Set Shininess and Shin. Strength to 0. Set Self-Illumination to 100.

6. From Extended Parameters, set Opacity Amt to 10. Leave Opacity Falloff at In. Set Type to Additive. These settings make the flame material slightly transparent and behave more like a natural light source. Next you add a diffuse map.

7. From the Maps rollout, click on the Diffuse Map button. From the Material/Map Browser, select Browse From New, select material type Gradient, and click on OK. Set the Gradient settings as follows (see fig. 15.12):
Set Color #1 to RGB 255, 205, 77.
Set Color #2 to RGB 62, 20, 0.
Set Color #3 to RGB 14, 32, 69.
Set Color 2 Position to 0.16.

FIGURE 15.12

Defining a gradient diffuse map for the candle flame material. The colors are kept dark because they will brighten considerably when applied to the scene and a glow effect is added.

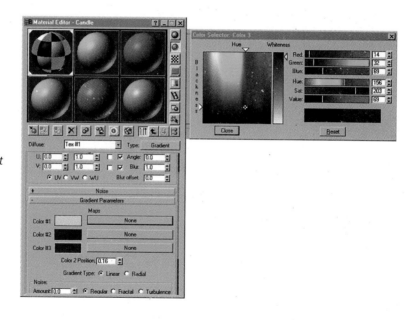

TIP

When defining more than one color, it is helpful to keep the Color Selector dialog open until all colors have been defined. After defining the first color, click on the next color swatch you want to edit. There is no need to close and reopen the dialog each time.

These flames' color settings are subjective and have been tailored to fit this particular scene; they will not fit every situation. The colors previously specified have been kept very dark because they will not be used directly.

Rather, because Transparency Type is set to Additive, the flame colors will be added to the colors behind them, making them appear much brighter in the scene. In addition, you will add a glow to the flame through Video Post. This step also brightens the flame color. If you start with too bright a flame color, the flame turns white. If the settings are kept low, the flame retains some of its color.

The next step is to add an opacity map to the Flame material. The purpose of the opacity map is to fade the flame toward its bottom, much like a real flame.

8. Click on Go to Parent and return to the Maps rollout. Drag a copy of the diffuse map to the Opacity Map slot. Select Copy from the Copy Map dialog and click on OK.

9. Click on the new opacity map to edit it. Set the Gradient settings as follows:
    Set Color #1 to RGB 255, 255, 255.
    Set Color #2 to RGB 131, 131, 131.
    Set Color #3 to RGB 128, 128, 128.
    Set Color 2 Position to 0.02.

You are almost finished. In the last few steps, you set the material effects channel for the material and set up Video Post for rendering. Setting the material effects channel is necessary when using some filters, such as glow, in Video Post.

10. Click on Go to Parent to return to the top level of the Flame material. Click on the Material Effects Channel pop-up, located just above the material name, and select channel 1.

11. Choose Video Post from the Rendering menu. To use the Glow filter in 3DS MAX, it is necessary to render from Video Post. It makes rendering slightly more tedious, but is definitely worth the added effect.

12. From Video Post, click on the Add Scene Event button, choose View Camera, and click on OK.

WARNING

For tutorials in this chapter, it is important not to add new events with any item in the queue selected. Doing so affects the way events are handled and prevents you from getting proper results.

13. Click on the Add Image Filter Event button, choose Filter Plug-in, Glow (frame only). Click on the Setup button. Set the Size to 7. Leave the other settings intact. By default, this filter affects all materials assigned material ID 1. Double-click on OK to return to Video Post.

NOTE

Glow (frame only) has a rather odd name. "Frame only" signifies that the filter can only render full-frames and does not support field rendering.

Your Video Post queue should like that shown in figure 15.13. Note that the queue is organized into a hierarchy and that both the Camera and Glow events are indented by the same amount.

FIGURE 15.13
The Video Post queue includes a Glow filter for the candle flame effect.

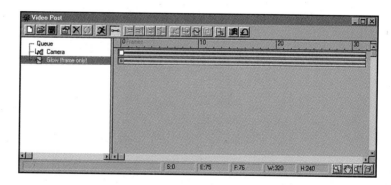

14. Click on the Execute Sequence button, Set Time Output to Single, Output Size to 640×480, and click on the Render button.

You now have a decent candle flame material (see fig. 15.14). You will next create the candlestick material by using the same scene file.

FIGURE 15.14
*The flame material
with a Glow filter
applied.*

FIGURE 15.14
*The flame material
with a Glow filter
applied.*

CREATING A CANDLESTICK MATERIAL

1. In the Material Editor, select the Multi/Sub-Object material in Slot #1. Navigate to the top of the material hierarchy.

2. Click on the Material 1 button to edit the Candle material.

3. From Basic Parameters, set Shininess to 55 and Shin. Strength to 52. Check Soften to enable.

4. From the Maps rollout, click on the Diffuse Map button. From the Material/Map Browser, select Browse From New, select material type Gradient, and click on OK. Set the Gradient settings as follows:
   Set Color #1 to RGB 255, 220, 136.
   Set Color #2 to RGB 255, 255, 234.
   Set Color #3 to RGB 255, 255, 255.
   Set Color 2 Position to 0.65.

5. Click on Go to Parent and return to the Maps rollout. Drag a copy of the diffuse map to the Self-Illumination slot. Select Copy from the Copy Map dialog, and click on OK.

6. Click on the new Self-Illumination Map to edit it. Set the Gradient settings as follows:
   Set Color #1 to RGB 200, 200, 200.
   Set Color #2 to RGB 99, 99, 99.

Set Color #3 to RGB 55, 55, 55.
Set Color 2 Position to 0.52.

7. Render the scene from Video Post (see fig. 15.15). The still image is complete. The gradient maps applied to the candle produce a realistic light effect. You can load the final scene file, candle_4.max, from the accompanying CD. The next step is to animate the scene.

FIGURE 15.15

The scene with final lighting and materials. The next step is to animate the flame effect.

Animating the Scene

Animating the scene brings the illusion to life. In the next tutorials, you create a five-second, looping animation. The flame effect will be animated in three different ways:

- The flame itself will gently sway with unseen air currents.

- The shadow-casting spotlight centered above the candle will move with in time with the flame.

- All three spotlights that comprise the candle's illumination will flicker slightly.

The flame object will be animated with two Bend modifiers. The first animates the flame very quickly back and forth over a very small distance, creating a jittery motion. The second Bend modifier animates more slowly and gracefully. The combined effect of both types of movement creates a realistic flame.

NOTE

Before you begin animating any scene, you should consider carefully the requirements of the animation. For this chapter, each animation is five seconds in length, at 15 fps, for a total of 75 frames. Each is rendered as an AVI file at 320×200 pixels and each is be scored afterward. Establishing the parameters up front can prevent rework and obviate confusion.

For this chapter, knowing the exact frame count is critical to making the first and last frames of the animation synchronize properly. For smooth looping, each animated parameter needs to have the same value at frame 0 as on frame 75. To meet this requirement, all animation cycles need to multiply evenly into 75. Animation cycles of 5, 15, 25, and 75 frames, for example, would all loop properly.

ANIMATING THE CANDLE FLAME

1. Load candle_3.max from the accompanying CD (see fig. 15.16). If you have been following along during the last several tutorials, you do not need to load this file.

2. From the Front viewport, select the Flame object and open the Modify panel.

3. Add a Bend modifier to the Flame object. Click Selection Level Sub-Object and choose Center from the drop-down list.

4. From the Front viewport, move the center of the Bend modifier downward so that it aligns to the top of the candle wick (see fig. 15.17). Turn off Sub-Object mode.

5. Turn on Animate and set keyframes for the Bend modifier as follows:
    Frame 0: Set Bend Angle to 8.
    Set Bend Direction to 0.
    Frame 6: Set Bend Angle to 0.
    Frame 10: Set Bend Angle to 9.5.
    Set Bend Direction to 237.5.

FIGURE 15.16
The Flame object is ready for animating.

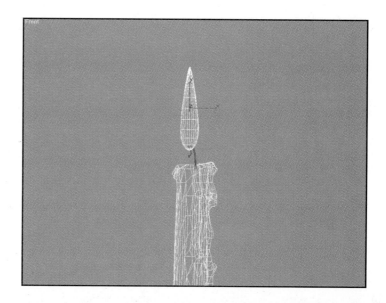

FIGURE 15.17
The center of the Bend modifier is aligned vertically to meet the candle wick.

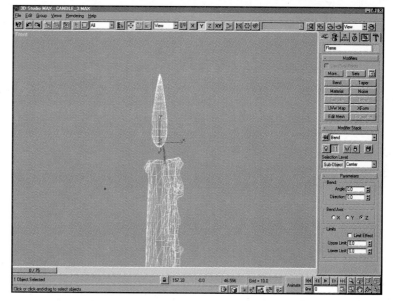

6. Turn off Animate. You will Ping-Pong this animation in Track View.

7. Open Track View. Right-click on the Filters button, and choose Selected Objects Only. Navigate down the Objects hierarchy to the Bend modifier. Select both Angle and Direction in the hierarchy window, and then click on the Parameter Curve Out-of-Range button. Set the Out Type to Ping Pong (see fig. 15.18).

FIGURE 15.18

*The Track View and
Parameter Curve Out-
of-Range windows for
the first Bend modifier.*

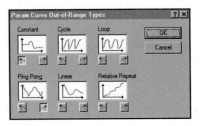

Preview the animation in the Front viewport. The flame now has a jittery movement. Next you add a gently swaying movement.

8. With the flame still selected, add a second Bend modifier. As with the first Bend modifier, align the Bend Center with the top of the wick. Set Bend Direction to 90.

9. Turn on Animate and set keyframes for the Bend modifier as follows:
   Frame 20: Set Bend Angle to 31.
   Frame 40: Set Bend Angle to –49.5.
   Frame 60: Set Bend Angle to 26.

   Turn off Animate. The animation needs to be completed in Track View.

10. From Track View, navigate to the Angle parameters of the new Bend modifier. Click and drag to select all the keys for Angle. Without deselecting anything, right-click on one of the Angle keys. Set the tangency In and Out types to Linear (see fig. 15.19).

FIGURE 15.19

*The tangency In and
Out types for the
second Bend modifier
are set to Linear.*

11. Select the Angle key at frame 0. Shift-click and drag to copy this key to frames 30, 50, and 70.

12. The flame animation is now complete. Make a preview of the animation from the Camera viewport to see the result.

The flame animation has been kept simple and understated and the animation is well-suited to most purposes. The next step is to animate the lights in the scene.

TIP

Keep movements subtle and flowing when making a looping animation. Because the motion will be viewed many times in sequence, any harsh or drastic movement will become obvious and the looping more noticeable.

ANIMATING A SHADOW-CASTING SPOTLIGHT

1. Create a dummy object in the Front viewport. Name it **Dummy_Candlelight**. Use the Align tool to center it to the Flame object. Move the dummy upward so that it lies above the flame (see fig. 15.20).

NOTE

Often, the best way to animate the movement of lights is to link them to one or more dummy objects. The primary advantage is that any number of objects can share the same animation—a spotlight and target can both be animated simultaneously, for example, by linking each to the same dummy. In addition, any animation can be removed just by unlinking the object in question.

FIGURE 15.20
A dummy object is created and positioned over the flame.

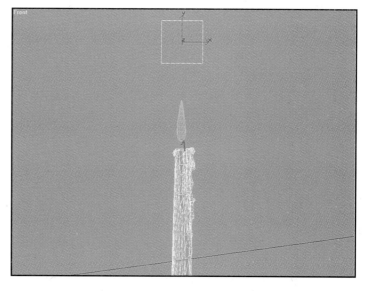

2. From the Display panel, uncheck Hide by Category Lights, making the lights visible again.

3. Link Spot_Candlelight and Spot_Candlelight.Target to the dummy object. The dummy will be used to control the movement of both the light and target objects.

4. Select the dummy object and open Track View. Right-click on the Filters button, and choose Selected Objects Only. Navigate down the Objects hierarchy to the Dummy_Candlelight Position track. Click on the Add Keys button and add a new keyframe at frame 0.

5. Right-click on the new position key at frame 0. Set tangency In and Out to Linear. Enter a new X Value of 160.02. This moves the dummy to the right slightly.

6. Ensure that the Move Keys tool is active. Copy the key at frame 0 to the following frames, adjusting each key's X Value as listed:
   Frame 20: Set X Value to 160.21.
   Frame 28: Set X Value to 159.99.
   Frame 37: Set X Value to 159.75.
   Frame 42: Set X Value to 159.84.
   Frame 62: Set X Value to 160.08.
   Frame 71: Set X Value to 159.95.
   Frame 75: Set X Value to 160.02.

After entering the preceding values, the Dummy_Candlelight object, and the attached spotlight and target, move left and right in-time with the flame movement. The synchronization of this movement is purposefully imprecise so that the effect is not too rigid. Before you render the scene, complete the animation by adding some variation to the strength of the lights.

ANIMATING THE INTENSITY OF CANDLE ILLUMINATION

1. Select Spot_Candlelight from the scene. Open Track View. Right-click on the Filters button, and choose Selected Objects Only. Navigate down the Objects hierarchy to the Multiplier track for Spot_Candlelight. Click on the Add Keys button and add a new keyframe at frame 0.

2. Right-click on the new key at frame 0. Set tangency In and Out to Linear.

Note that the multiplier is currently set to 0.65. You will animate the multiplier to create a flickering effect. Keep in mind, however, that the flicker needs to be very subtle and that the variation in the multiplier will be minimal.

3. Ensure that the Move Keys tool is active. Copy the key at frame 0 to the following frames, adjusting the multiplier value as specified:
   Frame 0: Set Value to 0.65.
   Frame 6: Set Value to 0.69, Tangency to Fast In, Fast Out.
   Frame 12: Set Value to 0.65.
   Frame 16: Set Value to 0.66.
   Frame 21: Set Value to 0.63.
   Frame 25: Set Value to 0.65.

N OTE

Bézier tangent types are described in Volume II of the *3D Studio Max User Guide* on page 32-13. Familiarity with the different tangent types is critical to creating good animation.

4. Select Multiplier in the hierarchy window, and then click on the Parameter Curve Out-of-Range button. Set the Out Type to Loop. The animation will loop every 25 frames.

5. With Multiplier still selected, click on the Copy Controller button. You will paste the multiplier settings into two other lights.

6. Select Spot_Candle-Wall from the scene. Look at the Modify panel and make a note of the current multiplier setting for this light. It should read 0.2.

7. In Track View, navigate down the Objects hierarchy and select the Multiplier track for Spot_Candle-Wall. Click on the Paste button, select Copy, and then click on OK (see fig. 15.21).

FIGURE 15.21

The animation from one light is copied to another.

Copying the multiplier animation from one light to another is a useful shortcut. There is a downside to this method, however. By pasting one light's multiplier into another, the second light is sometimes adversely affected. In this case, your second light is now much too bright. As you noted, the second light's original multiplier was 0.2. By pasting a new multiplier track into the light it has become over three times brighter. The solution is to use a Multiplier Curve to restore the brightness level of the second light while retaining the pasted multiplier animation.

TIP

Copying animated multiplier tracks from one light to another often causes an unwanted change in the recipient light's intensity. This can be corrected with a Multiplier Curve. The setting for the Multiplier Curve can be calculated by dividing the Multiplier setting of the recipient light at frame 0 by the Multiplier setting of the copied light at frame 0.

If you copy an animated multiplier track with a value of 0.65 at frame 0, into a light with a multiplier of 0.2 at frame 0, the correct Multiplier Curve setting will be 0.2 divided by 0.65 or 0.31.

8. With Multiplier still selected, click on the Function Curves button and then click on the Apply Multiplier Curve button. Return to Edit Keys mode.

The Multiplier Curve is placed beneath the Multiplier track in the Track hierarchy and will contain a key at frame 0 and frame 75 (see fig. 15.22).

TIP

If you can't find the multiplier curve, it's a flyoff from the ease curve.

9. In the Multiplier Curve track, delete the key at frame 75. Right-click on the key at frame 0 and set the Value to .31. This action restores the light to its original intensity. Only one more light to go.

10. Select Spot_Candle-Sidewall from the scene. Look at the Modify panel and make a note of the current Multiplier setting for this light. It should read .07.

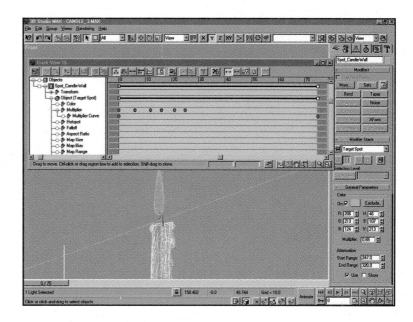

FIGURE 15.22

A Multiplier Curve is used to decrease the value of a multiplier track without compromising the animation keyframes.

11. In Track View, navigate down the Objects hierarchy and select the Multiplier track for Spot_Candle-Sidewall. Click on the Paste button, select Copy, and then click on OK.

12. With Multiplier still selected, click on the Function Curves button and then click on the Apply Multiplier Curve button. Return to Edit Keys mode.

13. In the Multiplier Curve track, delete the key at frame 75. Right-click on the key at frame 0 and set the Value to 0.1077. The scene is complete.

14. Render frames 1 to 75 from Video Post to see the final result. Make certain to add an Output Event first or your file will not be saved. You can also view the file candle.avi from the ch15_avi directory of the accompanying CD.

The finished candle animation is very subtle but makes good use of several animation and lighting techniques. Next you add moonlight streaming into the scene from a pair of off-camera windows.

Using Moonlight for Effect

Like candlelight, moonlight produces a low-intensity, diffuse light. Unlike the warm yellow-orange hue of candle light, moonlight illuminates with a cool, bluish color. Because orange and blue are complementary, placing the candle in front of the moonlit wall makes both their colors appear brighter and more vibrant. In addition, this makes the scene more legible by clearly separating the foreground, lit with candlelight, from the background, bathed in moonlight. Using color theory is especially helpful in this scene because both candlelight and moonlight are low-intensity and therefore do not allow for a great deal of contrast.

TIP

When defining colored lights, such as blue lights to simulate moonlight, keep the light color as close to white as possible. Reduce the necessary RGB components only enough to arrive at the correct hue.

White light, or any shade of gray light, is very predictable; it lights all colors evenly. Saturated light, such as a deep blue, has a strong impact on like-colored objects (blue objects in this example) and little impact on anything else. The end result of over-saturated lights can be strange—uneven lighting and objects that appear to glow.

Realistic Moonlight

You will create a realistic moonlight effect by using almost the exact same setup as the previous file. To give the impression of light beaming in from unseen windows, two additional spotlights will be added to the scene, each projecting a bitmap of a paned-window on to the far wall. You complete the effect by adding a swaying tree in front of the two windows. The tree is not visible in the animation. The shadow from the tree, however, falls on to the far wall, framed by the two windows.

CREATING A MOONLIT WINDOW EFFECT

1. Load moonlit.max from the accompanying CD. This file contains the familiar candle scene (see fig. 15.23).

2. Create a new Target Spotlight in the Front viewport. Name this light **Spot_Window_Right**. The exact placement of the light is not important.

FIGURE 15.23

The file moonlit.max needs some lighting effects.

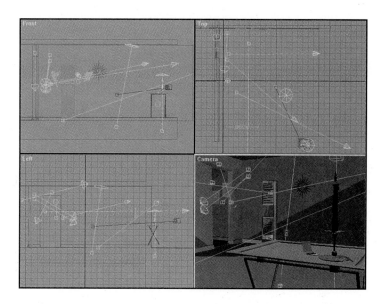

3. With the light selected, choose Transform Type-In from the Edit menu. Make certain that the Select and Move tool is active.

4. Set the Absolute:World coordinates for the light as follows: X: 53.397, Y: –130.203, Z: 57.12.

5. Select the target of the new spotlight. Set the Absolute:World coordinates as follows: X: 106.955, Y: 79.517, Z: 52.512.

6. Select Spot_Window_Right and open the Modify panel.

   Set General Parameters as follows:
   Set Color to RGB 51, 121, 226.
   Set Multiplier to 0.9.
   Set Attenuation Start Range to 191.
   Set Attenuation End Range to 251.
   Check Use to enable attenuation.

   Set Spotlight Parameters as follows:
   Set Hotspot to 11.3.
   Set Falloff to 13.7.
   Enable Rectangle and set Asp:(Aspect Ratio) to 0.57.

   Set Shadow Parameters as follows:
   Check Cast Shadows.
   Set Size to 110.

These settings create blue rectangular light that casts blurry shadows. The blurry shadows help make the tree effect, delineated in the next tutorial, more believable.

The next step is to add the pane effect for the windows. To accomplish this, turn on the projection option for this light and assign a black and white bitmap of window panes.

7. Check the Projector option and click on the Assign button to bring up the Material/Map Browser. Choose Browse From New, select material type Bitmap, and click on OK. The light now has a bitmap assigned but you still need to tell MAX which bitmap to use.

8. Click on the Map button and put the bitmap to slot #2 of the Material Editor. Click on OK.

9. Open the Material Editor and select the new Bitmap in Slot #2. Load window_m.tga from the CD. Leave the other settings intact.

The spotlight is finished. You will make a clone of it to create the second window.

10. From the Top viewport, select Spot_Window_Right and its target object.

11. Press the Shift key and drag a clone of the spotlight 53 units to the left. From the Clone/Copy dialog select Instance and click on OK.

12. Your scene should like figure that shown in 15.24. If it doesn't, load moonlit2.max from the accompanying CD.

13. Render the scene from Video Post to see the result of adding the new spotlights. The window effect adds a nice touch of color to the scene (see fig. 15.25).

FIGURE 15.24
The two projection spotlights will create a convincing moonlight effect.

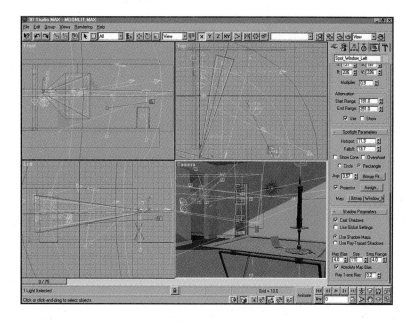

FIGURE 15.25
The rendered scene shows the effect of the two additional spotlights.

Casting the Tree Shadow

Looking at the rendered image, you may be wondering where the tree came from. The tree is a collection of flat, leaf-like geometry sitting in front of the two new spotlights. The shapes that comprise the tree are very low detail. This is one reason why you lowered the Size parameter of the spotlight shadows. The second advantage to a blurry shadow is that it lightens the shadows and helps distinguish the tree from the window panes.

The next step is to animate the tree leaves using dummy objects and Bend modifiers.

ANIMATING THE TREE GOBO

1. Maximize the Front viewport. Select Tree_Gobo from the Named Selection Sets pull-down. This action selects the tree objects. Click on Zoom Extents to select it, giving you a better view of the Gobo objects (see fig. 15.26).

FIGURE 15.26

The tree gobo is comprised of several small leaf objects. These will be animated with dummy objects and Bend modifiers.

Note

A *gobo* is a cutout used to reduce light. In this case, the gobo is shaped like a tree and is comprised of flat geometry.

The tree gobo objects are split into two groups, one for the left window and one for the right. This split is necessary because your window effect is created with two separate lights that do not overlap or touch. The windows would have to be touching or overlapping for them to hit a single group of objects.

Between the two groups of gobo objects are four dummy objects. These have already been assigned a wavelike motion. Preview the animation in the Front viewport. The motion of the dummy objects increases in magnitude with the dummy object on the left being the most dramatic; the dummy on the right is the least dramatic. The dummy on the left is most appropriately assigned to the leaves most distant from the trunk and vice-versa.

By assigning groups of leaves to the dummy objects in this way, the tree leaves can be animated with relative ease. Note also that the leaves overlap other leaves and create subtle new shapes with every frame.

2. Select Gobo_1_Leaves from the Named Selection Sets pull-down list. Click on the Select and Link button and link the leaves to the rightmost dummy object. When linking the leaves to the dummy, it may help to lock the selection with the toolbar and to limit the Selection Filter to Helpers to avoid linking the objects to the background objects.

3. Select Gobo_2_Leaves from the Named Selection Sets pull-down. Link these leaves to Dum_Gobo_02, the dummy second from the right.

4. Select Gobo_3_Leaves from the Named Selection Sets pull-down. Link these leaves to Dum_Gobo_03, the dummy second from the left.

5. Select Gobo_4_Leaves from the Named Selection Sets pull-down. Link these leaves to Dum_Gobo_04, the dummy second on the left.

Preview the animation. The leaves should be moving up and down with a certain rhythm. Now add the Bend modifiers to complete the illusion.

6. Select Gobo_Trunk_Left from the Named Selection Sets pull-down. Apply a Bend modifier to this object. Set Bend Axis to Y. Choose Selection Level Sub-Object and select Center. Move the center to the right 3 units and down 13 units (see fig. 15.27). Exit Sub-Object mode.

FIGURE 15.27

A Bend modifier is applied to the first tree trunk gobo object and the center is moved to the bottom right of the object.

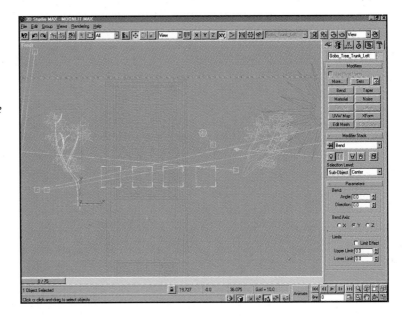

7. Turn on Animate. Set Angle to 1.33 at frame 52. Set Angle to 0 at frame 75. Turn off Animate.

8. Select Gobo_Trunk_Right from the Named Selection Sets pull-down. Apply a Bend modifier to this object. Set Bend Axis to Y. Choose Selection Level Sub-Object and select Center. Move the center to the left 7 units and down 12 units (see fig. 15.28). Exit Sub-Object mode.

9. Turn on Animate. Set Angle to 1.33 at frame 52. Set Angle to 0 at frame 75. Turn off Animate.

The purpose of the Bend modifiers in this example is just to add a little motion to the tree trunks. Next you apply a second bend to each group of gobo objects to enhance the movement.

10. Select Tree_on_Left from the Named Selection Sets pull-down. Apply a Bend modifier to this object. Set Bend Axis to Z. Choose Selection Level Sub-Object and select Center. Move the center to the right 3 units and down 10 units. Exit Sub-Object mode.

FIGURE 15.28

*A Bend modifier is
applied to the second
tree trunk gobo object
and the center is
moved to the left and
below the object.*

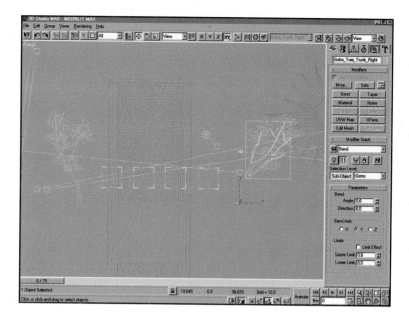

11. Turn on Animate. Set Angle to –3 at frame 38. Set Angle to 0 at frame 75. Turn off Animate.

12. Select Tree_on_Right from the Named Selection Sets pull-down. Apply a Bend modifier to this object. Set Bend Axis to Z. Choose Selection Level Sub-Object and select Center. Move the center to the left 8 units and down 12 units. Exit Sub-Object mode.

13. Turn on Animate. Set Angle to –3 at frame 38. Set Angle to 0 at frame 75. Turn off Animate.

The trees are now animated and you can preview the animation in the front window before doing a final rendering.

14. Render frames 1 to 75 from Video Post to see the final result. You can also view the file moonlit.avi from the CD. You can load the final scene file, moonlit3.max, from the accompanying CD.

The scene is starting to come to life. How about adding some rain and lightning?

Creating a Lightning Storm Effect

Animated lights can be used to create some great lightning storm effects. Following is a discussion of how to create a realistic lightning and storm effect. Lightning requires animating a scene's lights between two states: with lightning and without. These lighting techniques can also be applied to other situations, such as explosions, X-rays, bug-zappers, or any lighting situation that requires two distinct states. You will be navigating through a finished scene file to learn how this effect was created. You can view the animation by loading storm.avi from the CD.

NOTE ────────────────────────────────

Sound is very important in animation. Neglecting this element can rob your work of much of its potential. The soundtracks for the animations in this chapter were scored by Maurice Jackson, of Strategic Simulations, Inc.

The animation is an extension of the last scene. It portrays the same burning candle in a moonlit room but with the addition of rain streaking down the windows and flashes of lightning illuminating the scene. You will add some new spotlights and materials to the scene, and examine how the effect was created from start to finish.

Load storm.max from of the CD. You use this file for the rest of this tutorial.

Examining the Basic Lightning Effect

A basic lightning effect is created by establishing two different lighting conditions. The first lighting condition is the scene in normal light. In this case, normal light is warm candlelight in the foreground and cool bluish moonlight filling the background. The second lighting condition is the scene illuminated by lightning. Compare the two lighting conditions (see fig. 15.29). At this point, the lightning effect is almost full-force.

Creating the second lighting condition was troublesome because it essentially required relighting the scene. To do this, several existing lights had to be animated and new lights were added to the scene.

FIGURE 15.29
The image on the left
shows the scene at
frame 1 under normal
lighting conditions; the
right shows the
animation at frame 38.

To facilitate the light animation, the timing of the lightning was established first. You can more clearly see the pattern of the lighting by viewing the Multiplier Curve of a typical light in the scene.

1. Select Spot_Window_Left and open a Track View window. Right-click on the Filters button and choose Selected Objects Only. Navigate to Spot_Window_Left and select Multiplier. Click on Function Curves.

A very large spike appears, followed quickly by a very small one (see fig. 15.30). This light was used as the basis for animating the other lights in the scene. The multiplier track for this light was copied and pasted into the existing scene lights that needed to animate with the lightning. Using the techniques described earlier in the chapter, a Multiplier Curve was then added to most of the lights to scale down the strength of the light.

FIGURE 15.30
The Multiplier for a
typical light in the
scene shows the
rhythm of the lightning
flashes.

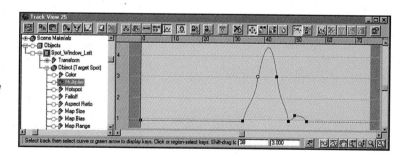

Other elements needed to be adjusted for the lightning effect to work. The color of the windows shining on the wall, for example, needed to be more white. The animation keys for this were created in the Track Editor and matched to the animation of the Multiplier.

2. Select Edit Keys in the Track window and examine the keys for both Color and Multiplier. Notice that the color of the light is animated in time with the Multiplier (see fig. 15.31).

FIGURE 15.31

*The Color and
Multiplier settings for
this light are animating
in the same manner.*

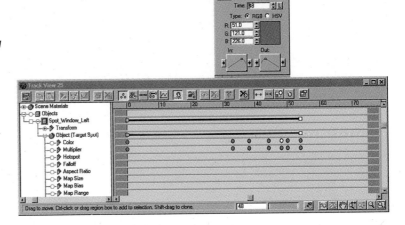

Additionally, the material created for the candlestick also needed to be animated. The candlestick was mapped with a self-illuminated material. The material was well-suited to the normal lighting conditions of a dark room, but did not look good when illuminated by the lightning. The self-illumination of the material overpowered the lightning. Animation keys were added to eliminate the self-illumination during lightning flashes.

The last effect to be added to the scene was the illusion of water running down the window panes. This effect was accomplished by modifying the bitmap the projector spotlights use.

3. Open the Material Editor and examine the Window_&_Rain material in Slot #2. This bitmap contains a noise map and a bitmap of window panes used as a mask.

4. Click on the Map button to view the Slow_Rain map. This map is a standard noise map. The Y offset has been animated to give the map movement.

The animation was looped by animating the Y offset from 0 to 20 over the first 38 frames and animating the Y value from –20 to 0 over the remaining frames. This created an abrupt break in the animation at frame 39, but the lightning hides the switch.

That covers the basics of creating a lightning effect. You may want to examine this file further on your own to learn more about the effect.

Animating Volumetric Light

Volumetric light is a combination of a light and an atmospheric effect. For this tutorial, you create a small living room illuminated by a television set. The TV screen is not visible in the animation because the set faces away from the camera. The light from the television will be provided by a volumetric spotlight.

The volume light for this tutorial appears as one light, but is actually a combination of three different lights. The first is the actual volumetric light. This is the foggy cone of light visible in the scene. You place the second light in a similar fashion to the volumetric light and provide the illumination for the light. To achieve the right effect, it is often necessary to give a volumetric light a high multiplier or a short falloff region. Both of these make illuminating surfaces with volumetric lights difficult. The best solution is to create two separate lights: one for the volume effect and one to simulate the lighting effect. In this way, the volume light can be fine-tuned for appearance without consideration for how it actually disperses light.

The third light simulates light reflecting from the volumetric light back toward the light source. Together, the three lights create a very nice effect.

TIP

When creating artificial light sources, give each light character by assigning a unique color, intensity, or animation. Doing this adds believability to your scene and comes at almost no cost to rendering times or file size.

CREATING A VOLUMETRIC LIGHT

1. Load tv.max from the accompanying CD (see fig. 15.32).

This file contains some new objects and similar lighting to the previous tutorials. Render the Camera viewport to see how the new scene looks rendered (see fig. 15.33).

2. Create a new Target Spotlight in the Top viewport. Name this light **Volume_Light_TV**. The exact placement of the light is not important.

FIGURE 15.32
The tv.max file demonstrates volumetric lighting.

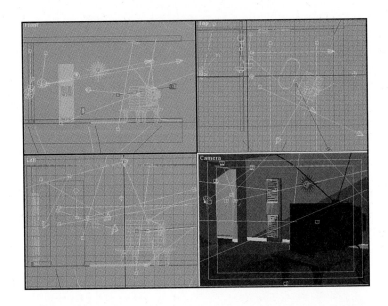

FIGURE 15.33
A rendering of the tv.max file prior to adding the volume light effect.

3. With the light selected, choose Transform Type-In from the Edit menu. Make certain that the Select and Move tool is active.

4. Set the Absolute:World coordinates for the light as follows: X: 148.465, Y: –32.274, Z: 32.582.

5. Select the target of the new spotlight. Set the Absolute:World coordinates as follows: X: 58.258, Y: 12.126, Z: 33.4.

6. Select Volume_Light_TV and open the Modify panel.
   Set General Parameters as follows:
   Set Color to RGB 210, 211, 208.
   Set Multiplier to 2.
   Set Attenuation Start Range to 68.
   Set Attenuation End Range to 105.
   Check Use to enable attenuation.

   Set Spotlight Parameters as follows:
   Set Hotspot to 57.
   Set Falloff to 59.6.
   Enable Rectangle and set Asp:(Aspect Ratio) to 1.38.

   Set Shadow Parameters as follows:
   Check Cast Shadows.
   Leave Size to 256.

These settings create the foundation for the light. A bitmap assigned to the light as a Projector image enhances the final look of the light.

7. Check the Projector option and click on the Assign button to bring up the Material/Map Browser. Choose Browse From Material Editor, select the bitmap TV_Projection and click on OK.

   Assigning this bitmap to the volume light rounds the edges of the volume light cone, removing the sharp, unrealistic edges created by using a rectangular shaped light.

The basic spotlight is finished. You still need to create a new volume light, however, in the Environment dialog and assign the Volume_Light_TV.

8. Choose Environment from the Rendering menu. Under Atmosphere, click on the Add button and choose Volume Light, and then click on OK.

9. Click on the Pick Lights button and select the spotlight Volume_Light_TV.

10. Edit the parameters of the volume light as follows:
    Set Fog Color to RGB 225, 232, 255.
    Set Density to 2.5.
    Check Noise to enable it.
    Set Noise Amount to 0.14.
    Set Noise Uniformity to 0.06.
    Set Noise Size to 0.9.

Next you add a spotlight to provide the illumination for the volume light.

CREATING A SECOND SPOTLIGHT FOR ILLUMINATION

1. Create a new Target Spotlight anywhere in the Top viewport. Name this light **TV_Illumination**.

2. With the light selected, choose Transform Type-In from the Edit menu. Make certain that the Select and Move tool is active.

3. Set the Absolute:World coordinates for the light as follows: X: 132.369, Y: −20.612, Z: 33.645.

4. Select the target of the new spotlight. Set the Absolute:World coordinates as follows: X: 17.072, Y: 34.202, Z: 33.645.

5. Select TV_Illumination and open the Modify panel. Set General Parameters as follows:
   Set Color to RGB 172, 203, 210.
   Set Multiplier to 0 (you animate this later).
   Set Attenuation Start Range to 107.
   Set Attenuation End Range to 180.
   Check Use to enable attenuation.

   Set Spotlight Parameters as follows:
   Set Hotspot to 38.8.
   Set Falloff to 77.2.

These settings create a bluish light aimed in the same direction as the volume light.

CREATING A THIRD SPOTLIGHT FOR REFLECTED LIGHT

1. Create a new Target Spotlight anywhere in the Top viewport. Name this light **VL_Reflected_Light**.

2. With the light selected, choose Transform Type-In from the Edit menu. Make certain that the Select and Move tool is active.

3. Set the Absolute:World coordinates for the light as follows: X: 29.579, Y: 36.67, Z: 89.046.

4. Select the target of the new spotlight. Set the Absolute:World coordinates as follows: X: 117.039, Y: −7.609, Z: −12.988.

5. Select VL_Reflected_Light and open the Modify panel.
Set General Parameters as follows:
Set Color to RGB 156, 190, 216.
Set Multiplier to 1.
Set Attenuation Start Range to 109.
Set Attenuation End Range to 146.
Check Use to enable attenuation.

Set Spotlight Parameters as follows:
Set Hotspot to 37.9.
Set Falloff to 73.5.

Set Shadow Parameters as follows:
Check Cast Shadows.
Set Map Bias to 1.

After adding this last light, your scene should look like that shown in figure 15.34. If your scene doesn't match the one shown, you can load tv2.max from the accompanying CD.

The last step is to animate each of the lights. You animate the Multiplier to create a flickering pulsing television effect.

FIGURE 15.34
The tv.max file with the three new spotlights added. The other scene lights have been hidden.

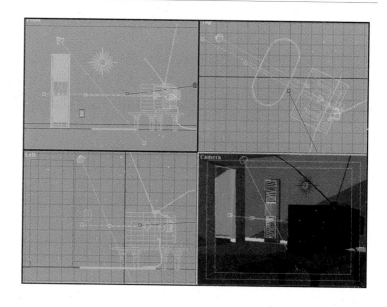

ANIMATING THE VOLUME LIGHT EFFECT

1. With the VL_Reflected_Light spotlight still selected, open Track View. Right-click on the Filter button and choose Selected Objects Only. Navigate to the light's Multiplier track and add keyframes as specified below:
Frame 0: Set Multiplier to .2 Linear In, Out.
Frame 10: Set Multiplier to .22 Linear In, Out.
Frame 16: Set Multiplier to .2 Linear In, Out.
Frame 33: Set Multiplier to .24 Slow In, Smooth Out.
Frame 39: Set Multiplier to .2 Smooth In, Smooth Out.
Frame 44: Set Multiplier to .21 Smooth In, Smooth Out.
Frame 58: Set Multiplier to .18 Smooth In, Smooth Out.
Frame 75: Set Multiplier to .2 Linear In, Out.

2. Select the TV_Illumination spotlight and navigate to the light's Multiplier track. Add keyframes as specified below:
Frame 0: Set Multiplier to 0 Linear In, Out.
Frame 10: Set Multiplier to .22 Linear In, Out.
Frame 16: Set Multiplier to 0 Linear In, Out.
Frame 33: Set Multiplier to .24 Slow In, Smooth Out.
Frame 39: Set Multiplier to 0 Smooth In, Smooth Out.
Frame 44: Set Multiplier to .21 Smooth In, Smooth Out.
Frame 58: Set Multiplier to .18 Smooth In, Smooth Out.
Frame 75: Set Multiplier to 0 Linear In, Out.

3. Select the Volume_Light_TV spotlight and navigate to the light's Multiplier track. Add keyframes as specified below:
Frame 0: Set Multiplier to 2 Linear In, Out.
Frame 10: Set Multiplier to 2.4 Linear In, Out.
Frame 16: Set Multiplier to 2 Linear In, Out.
Frame 33: Set Multiplier to 2.8 Slow In, Smooth Out.
Frame 39: Set Multiplier to 2 Smooth In, Smooth Out.
Frame 44: Set Multiplier to 2.2 Smooth In, Smooth Out.
Frame 58: Set Multiplier to 1.6 Smooth In, Smooth Out.
Frame 75: Set Multiplier to 2 Linear In, Out.

4. You are finished. Render the animation to see the results of all your hard work (see fig. 15.35). You can also view the animation by loading tv.avi from the accompanying CD. You can load the completed scene file, tv3.max, from the CD.

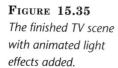

FIGURE 15.35
The finished TV scene with animated light effects added.

In Practice: Animating Lights and Atmospheres

- **Animation Requirements.** Establish the requirements of your animation in advance. How long is your animation going to be? How many frames per second? And so on.... Ask yourself these questions before beginning a project.

- **Value and Contrast.** Proper value and contrast are necessary for foreground objects to separate from background objects. Good lighting can mean the difference between a great-looking animation and something quite atrocious. Color theory should also be used to enhance your imagery.

- **Lighting Control.** Using many low-intensity lights can provide great control over a scene's lighting because each light can be minutely adjusted to get subtle effects.

- **Simple Effects.** Simple geometry placed in front of lights can produce very nice effects. The swaying tree in this chapter was comprised of flat, low-polygon objects.

- **Simple Approach.** The simplest approach to a problem is often the best. Creating a candle flame from a modified sphere is an example of a practical technique.

- **Dummy objects.** Dummy objects are great for animating lights. They enable you to create complex animation effects that would be difficult to do any other way.

- **A quality soundtrack.** A quality soundtrack can greatly improve the appeal of an animation.

- **Volume lights.** Volume lights work best when combined with other lights. In this chapter, two additional spotlights were used to create the illumination from the volume light.

IMAGE CREATED BY RALPH FRANTZ

Chapter 16

by Ralph Frantz

PARTICLES, SPACE WARPS, AND PHYSICS

This chapter attempts to help you get a firm grasp on the wonderful world of 3D Studio MAX particles and space warps. Particles are a great way to simulate a myriad of objects, such as rain, snow, bubbles, or blowing dust. They simulate real-world effects that just can't be represented efficiently by modeling in MAX. As you go about everyday life, you will soon recognize many objects in nature (or even imaginary objects) that can be represented this way. A single particle system can represent hundreds or even thousands of tiny objects that all act similarly but are still slightly different from one another.

Space warps are a great way to affect and deform your MAX objects and particles in world space. This should not be confused with modifiers that affect objects in Object Space.

- **World Space.** The universal coordinate system used by MAX to keep track of objects in the scene. Represented by the Home Grid.

- **Object Space.** The coordinate system used by MAX to keep track of everything that is applied to an object.

Space warps automatically alter objects after they are set up and bound to the object. In this chapter, you use particle systems and space warps together to create several different natural and man-made effects. The following topics are covered:

- Snow particle system

- All Purpose Particles plug-in by Sisyphus Software

- Sand Blaster Particle plug-in by Digimation

- Spray particle system

- Deflector space warp

- Path Deform space warp

- Bomb space warp

Particles and Their Space Warps

The first three exercises in this section have been set up to further teach you about using particle systems and their associated space warps. In these exercises, you use the following systems and space warps:

- **Particles.** You use particles to simulate confetti falling from the sky. Snow particle systems are used because of their natural tumbling capability.

- **The All Purpose Emitter from Sisyphus.** You use the All Purpose Emitter (APE) to create smoke coming from a train. APE particles react very well to the train's starting and stopping motions on the tracks.

- **Sand Blaster by Digimation.** You use Sand Blaster for a unique number countdown. It has a wonderful feature called target simulation that enables you to dissemble objects particle by particle and then reassemble them into a new object.

The next two exercises, as described in the following list, explore the Spray particle system with different space warps. A particle system has yet to be developed that allows particles to follow a path after being emitted, so a series of wind space warps is used to coax them along. Note that Digimation's Sand Blaster comes close to achieving this through its use of multiple targets.

- The first exercise uses spray and a series of Wind space warps to cause the particles to flow aerodynamically over a sports car, as if in a wind tunnel.

- The final Spray exercise utilizes a Gravity space warp and a couple of Deflectors to simulate the sparks emitted from a welding head. Spray is pretty versatile in this respect, and along with the judicious use of space warps, can be made to simulate all kinds of natural phenomena.

The Snow Particle System with Deflector Space Warp

In the following exercise, you create a ticker-tape parade down a New York City street. To simulate thousands of small colorful pieces of confetti falling from the buildings, you use the second MAX core particle system, Snow. Consistent with its name, Snow produces 2D flakes that can spiral and tumble as they fall. Think creatively: This particle system has many uses other than simple snow. The falling confetti created in this exercise is but one example.

TIP

Snow is created as a coplanar set of faces. A snow "flake" thus has only one orientation and can only be seen in one direction. If you want to see both sides of the flake as it tumbles, use a 2-Sided material.

TICKER-TAPE PARADE

Go ahead and load imx16f.max from the accompanying CD and check out the scene. The scene represents a typical New York City street and is just the type on which you would expect to see a ticker-tape parade.

1. In the Particle Systems drop-down list of the Create panel, click on Snow.

2. In the top viewport, click and drag to create an emitter just longer than the street and the length of the five city blocks. A width of about 50,000 and a length of about 3,000 should do. Name it **Snow_OH**.

3. Center the emitter down the middle of the street and move it above the street surface about 7,000 units (see fig. 16.1). With the front viewport active, you can right-click on the Move icon and type **7000** in the Type in Transforms Offset: screen Y field.

FIGURE 16.1

Place the snow emitter down the center of the street and off the ground about 7,000 units.

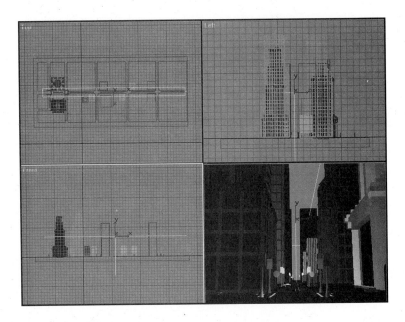

Notice that the emitter's direction vector is pointing away from you in the orthographic viewport. Notice also that because the scene is in such a large scale, most of the Snow parameters need to be adjusted.

4. With the emitter active, go to the Modifier panel and set the Viewport Count at 500 and the Render Count at 10,000. Raise the Flake Size to 40 and the Speed to 20. Also, choose to Render Triangle Faces.

Play the scene. Even with these parameters raised, the lazy way snow particles fall keeps them too close to the emitter before they die. It takes a major adjustment in the timing section to get them to reach the ground.

5. Set the Start Frame to −1000 and the Life to 900.

6. In the Named Selection Set drop-down list, choose NYC Street to select all the geometry in the scene except the snow particles. Click on the Display tab, and under Hide by Selection, choose Hide Selected. Then play the scene.

TIP

It is a good idea to create selection sets for the sole purpose of the hiding and unhiding of geometry to speed up your work. This is especially true when working with thousands of particles. It takes only two steps to select all geometry and to use your hot key to hide selected geometry. When you want to unhide the geometry, select it from the Named Selection set and answer yes to the alert dialog that asks whether you want the objects unhidden.

Naturally, pieces of paper tumble as they fall, and the MAX Snow particle system gives you two parameters to get just the tumble you need. *Tumble* is the amount of random rotation; *tumble rate* is the speed of rotation. MAX provides built-in rotation chaos by randomly generating a different axis of rotation for each particle.

7. Set Tumble to .5 and Tumble Rate to .5. This setting gives you medium tumble at a slow speed. Set Variation to 3, which will vary the initial speed and direction of the particles.

8. Open the Material Editor and assign the multi-sub-object material from slot 5 Red/Wht/Blue Multi to the snow particles.

When multi-sub-object materials are assigned to particle systems such as Snow, each particle receives a different material ID number according to the number of material IDs in the multi-sub-object material assigned to it. Thus each particle as it is emitted gets a different material and will cycle through these different materials in a continuous loop.

NOTE

There is currently an anomaly in using two-sided multi-sub-object materials on snow particles. Using a standard material maps one side only, clicking on 2-Sided maps both sides. It seems that using multi-sub-object materials, whether two-sided or not, does not map both sides of the flakes. The same thing applies to a double-sided material type.

Use the "Force 2-Sided" option in the Render dialog if you really must have both sides of the particle rendered and want to use a multi-sub-object or blend material.

9. Render a frame to the Video Frame Buffer. Then assign the double-sided material Red/Blue Double from slot 6 in the Material Editor and render last.

Notice that the scene appears to have twice as many particles because both the facing and back sides of each particle are now mapped—one side red, the other blue.

Because you should always think about efficiency, use the double-sided material—you get two for one: Each flake does not disappear as it turns its normal away from the camera. This also gives you the opportunity to use more and varied particles. As the flakes rotate to show the color on the other side, the particle confetti seems to sparkle in the sunlight.

10. Set the Render Count down to 5000. In the toolbar, select Edit, Clone, and make a copy with the name **Snow_OH2**. Because Snow has no "seed" parameter, you should set the Variation parameter to 4 so that each particle of the copy is not in the exact same position as the original particles.

11. In the Material Editor, assign the double-sided material in slot 3 Wht/Yelo Double to the copy.

TIP

If you're not planning to animate the camera down the street, you could create your emitter smaller and farther from the camera, enabling the use of fewer particles. Then by borrowing a gag from the movie industry, you could place a small snow emitter close to the camera to give added depth.

12. In the Create panel, click on the Space Warp icon and pick Deflector. Drag in the top viewport to define the Space Warp about twice as wide as the particle emitter (see fig. 16.2).

13. Select both Snow systems, click on the Select and Bind icon, and drag from the Snow systems to the Deflector space warp.

NOTE

You can bind any number of particle systems to a space warp simultaneously by selecting them all and dragging to the space warp.

FIGURE 16.2

Create the deflector big enough to catch all the particles as they hit the ground.

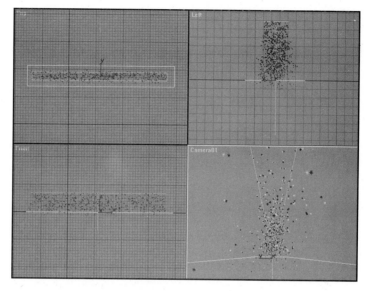

14. Select the Deflector. In the Modifier panel, set the deflector's Bounce parameter to 0.1. This setting provides a collision as the confetti reaches the ground and gives it just a slight movement as it hits.

15. In the toolbar's Named Selection Sets drop-down list, choose NYC Street. This usually would just select the geometry, but because it is hidden, answer yes at the alert to unhide.

To give the scene added depth, you want to add a few small individual snow particle systems emanating from the individual buildings. These individual systems represent people throwing the confetti into the street from a balcony or window. Because you should have a good understanding of snow by now, you can either experiment with this yourself or go ahead and merge the file "more confetti" from the accompanying CD.

This merged file contains four smaller snow emitters streaming confetti from the closest buildings.

16. Choose File Merge from the top menu and pick moreconf.max from the accompanying CD. Select all but the camera from the Merge dialog and click on OK.

17. Hold down the Ctrl key and click on the Gravity space warp to de-select it, leaving the merged Snow systems selected (snow sml1 through snow sml4). Now bind them to the Deflector space warp.

The particles are not affected correctly because they seem to move too far away from the deflector. The particles should not react this way, but it seems to be a viewport refresh thing as witnessed by the following step.

18. Press the Next Frame button and then the Previous Frame button. Then the binding to the deflector will be as you expect (see fig. 16.3).

FIGURE 16.3

The finished scene showing the addition of individual confetti throwers.

Notice that these snow particles are assigned a multi-sub-object material with 64 sub-object materials. This shows that a maximum of 64 different sub-object materials can be assigned to a particle system, and that the particles cycle through these 64 materials.

Feel free to experiment with this file by changing the materials or animating the camera down the street. It would be really interesting if you animated the camera and placed a windshield up front (as if you were in a car, for example). By using your knowledge of the Wind space warps that you will gain later in this chapter, you could simulate the effect of wind turbulence. A Wind space warp used with a bit of Decay would push the confetti out of the way of the windshield as the confetti came into close proximity of the windshield.

19. Save your scene. Take a look at the rendered file nycparade.avi on the accompanying CD.

All Purpose Particles Plug-In

You will use the following exercise to create smoke pouring from the smoke-stack of a train. Creating smoke or vapor can add realism to a scene. In this exercise, you will use the third-party particle system All Purpose Particles from Sisyphus Software.

NOTE

This is the only particle system that provides sub-frame launching of particles. These routines from Sisyphus are very inexpensive. In my opinion, everyone in the MAX community should encourage and support companies that provide quality affordable plug-ins.

All Purpose Particles includes the following particle systems and space warps:

- **The All Purpose Emitter.** A general particle system with many options and built-in presets.

- **Halo.** A particle system with generalized circular motion about an axis.

- **Phasor.** A particle system that creates and animates particles along the long dimension of a box emitter object.

- **Molasses.** A space warp that provides the viscous damping of particles.

- **Vortex.** A space warp that binds particles into a vortex-like swirling mass.

SMOKIN'

Start by loading the file 16himx.max from the accompanying CD. This is a simple scene of a train building up steam and then traveling down the tracks. Put the viewport in Wireframe and play.

Make things easier for the next few steps by clearing the scene of all but the train by hiding the tracks and ground plane, changing to four viewports, and then performing a Zoom Extents All.

1. Hide the tracks and ground and perform a Zoom Extents All. In the Create panel, choose Particles from the drop-down list and pick APE (All Purpose Emitter). In the top viewport, click and drag to create an emitter with a width of 20, a length of 20, and a depth of 35. (Check size in the Display roll-up.)

2. Move the emitter to position it directly over the train's smokestack with barely less than half of the emitter overlapping the stack (see fig. 16.4), and then link it to the Train Dummy object.

FIGURE 16.4

Place the All Purpose Emitter just above the smokestack as the particles emit from the center.

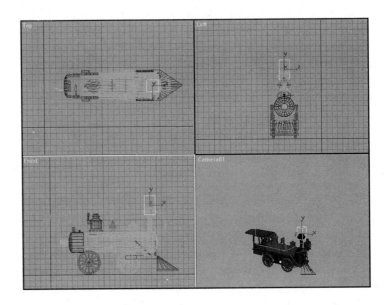

APE has six discrete roll-ups, each pertaining to a different set of particle parameters. It may seem a bit daunting at first, but the roll-ups are organized logically. To make life a little easier, they have included the following six presets and a return to default to get you started:

- Bubbles
- Fireworks
- Hose
- Shockwave
- Trail
- Weldsparks
- Default

APE presets can be used as is, or they can be used as the basis for your own custom particle effects.

3. Choose the Hose preset and move the Frame Slider to see that you are emitting particles that are somewhat close to the effect you are trying to achieve.

The first roll-up section enables you to set up Particle Count, Size, Life, and Timing.

4. Open the Particle Generation roll-up. Increase the Viewport Count to 500, change the Size to 14, and raise the Variation parameter to vary the particle size by 80 percent.

5. Change the End Frame to 400 to match the length of the scene. Also change the Life to 45 and add a variation of 50 percent. Close the roll-up.

Next is the Velocity Settings roll-up, which is an important part of this routine because it sets up the speed and direction of the particles.

6. Go to frame 50 and open the Velocity Settings roll-up. Set both Vertical Velocity Angle and Horizontal Velocity Angle to 0—straight up. To spread the particles out a bit from straight up, set the Vertical Variation to 25 and the Horizontal Variation to 45.

7. To speed up the particles coming up from the emitter, set Vertical Speed to 2.8 and its variation to 50 percent.

The emitter velocity section of this roll-up controls the particles' secondary motion data, which controls the amount of influence the emitter's speed has in relation to the particles' own velocity. As you can see, the Hose preset has set up 100 percent influence because the water leaving a hose takes on quite a bit of secondary influence as the hose is whipped around. You can experiment with this later. For now, however, turn this off because you do not want the particles flung forward as the train stops.

8. Set Emitter Velocity Influence to 0 percent. This effectively turns off secondary motion data and renders null the Multiplier and Variation parameters. Close the Velocity Settings roll-up.

The following roll-up, Gravity/Bounce, carries over the parameters from their original IPAS routine. Because you have better control and flexibility by using built-in gravity and deflector, you can turn these off.

9. Open the Gravity/Bounce roll-up and turn off Gravity's Z influence. Bounce is off, so go ahead and close this roll-up.

Skip down to the last roll-up, which contains the Display settings. Here you set the Viewport Display of dots or ticks, ticks being preferred. Display also contains the Emitter Size parameters and the option to hide the emitter box.

NOTE

Changing the emitter size has no bearing on any parameter and will not affect the appearance at all. All APE parameters are based on the emitter's local coordinate system.

The last part to set up is particle Type/Mapping. This, along with the material assigned in the editor, is what controls the final appearance of the rendered particles. This control is important when trying to create a smoke effect.

In terms of particle type, you will see the familiar types of Triangle and Facing. A few new types are presented:

■ Cube renders cube-shape particles.

■ Special is the old Yost group IPAS type, which renders particles as three intersecting square planes.

■ Pixel renders rangeless anti-aliased pixels.

Cube, Facing, and Special have been specifically set up to accept face-mapped materials. Face mapping enables you to use a graduated radial opacity map to hide the geometric shape of the particles that would ruin a smoke effect. Smoke is, of course, a series of soft-edged, semitransparent, somewhat rounded shapes.

10. Open the particle Type/Mapping roll-up and choose Facing as the particle type. Because you are using a face-mapped material, the Mapping section becomes moot.

NOTE

It seems that the Cube particle type—used with a larger particle size (about 40) and a two-sided material—also shows promise as smoke.

11. Open the Material Editor and assign the material Smoke from slot number 1. Examine this closely; it is key to the smoke's appearance. The following text provides an explanation.

TIP

The use of a face-mapped radial gradient or radial gradient bitmap with Facing type particles effectively smooths out and hides the abrupt edges of the Quad Face particles. This also works well with Cube and Special type particles.

Because it is so important to this exercise, some time must be taken here to explain this Smoke material.

Notice that the Smoke material is a face map. This enables the mapping of the material to individual particles. In the map section, a graduated radial dot bitmap—white inside, black outside—is used in both the diffuse and opacity slots (see fig. 16.5). The use in the opacity slot effectively hides the edges of the Quad Facing particles. Notice that the opacity channel has been cranked way down to 6 to provide semitransparency throughout the particle, even in the whitest (most opaque) part of the bitmap. The dot bitmap in the diffuse slot tints the edges of the visible texture gray. Note that the tiling has been adjusted to give just the right amount of edge opacity and grayness. Noise has also been added to give more randomness to the smoke puffs. This could even be animated.

FIGURE 16.5
This soft white dot bitmap used as an opacity map provides great transparency falloff to the Quad Facing particles.

12. Lastly, right-click to get at the particle properties and turn off Cast and Receive Shadows. You can also turn on Motion Blur.

13. Unhide the tracks and ground objects.

WARNING

Motion Blurred particles can sometimes add quite a bit to the final effect, but can be very costly in terms of processor time as the particle count goes up. Be certain to do a few test renders to ensure that motion blurring is not only necessary, but also worth the extra CPU cycles.

Save your scene and take a look at the final rendered file smokin.avi on the accompanying CD.

Sand Blaster Particle Plug-In

In the following exercise, you will work with the third-party particle plug-in Sand Blaster from Digimation. Sand Blaster is quite a particle package that does much more than just simple particle emitting, although it can be used that way. Sand Blaster's strengths include its capability to use an arbitrary object as an emitter and its ingenious way of using a series of target objects to guide the particles. Don't worry if you do not own Sand Blaster; a demo of the plug-in has been supplied on the accompanying CD. This demo enables you to follow through this exercise, but it does not enable you to render, which is okay because you are also supplied with the rendered animation.

COUNTDOWN

In this exercise, you will create an animation suitable for the intro of a demo tape. You will create a five-second countdown by using a series of numbers that blow apart into particles that rebuild themselves into the next number exactly one second (30 frames) later.

Load 16iimx.max from the accompanying CD and take a look at the scene. It is composed of the numbers 1 through 5 and a sphere. The sphere will be your emitter and the numbers will be the targets.

1. In the Create panel, Particle System drop-down, click on Sand Blaster. In the top viewport, click and drag to create a Sand Blaster icon about 12 units in size.

2. Go to the Modifier panel, in the Sand Blaster Setup section, and click on Set Emitter. Then use Select By Name to pick the hidden Sphere01 object.

3. Click on the check box to turn on particle activation.

Notice that the Sphere01 name is placed as the emitter in the roll-up and also that a new roll-out panel has been created called Emitter: Sphere01. Particle ticks are seen covering the sphere ready to go. If you make the front viewport active and maximized, you can scrub the frame bar to see that the particles are drawn off the sphere in the direction of the Sand Blaster icon arrow, which was created pointing down in the top viewport.

4. Open the Particle Parameters section, raise the Particle Render Count to 1000 and leave the default particle, Pyramid, chosen.

5. All the way at the very bottom, open the Emitter: Sphere01 section. The only change you will make here is under the Speed and Direction section, where you will choose From Icon Out. Notice that the Sand Blaster icon changes to point in all six directions. It does so because you have instructed the particles to move away from the icon in all directions. Go ahead and use the Align tool in the toolbar to center the icon to the numbers.

You are not adjusting the emitter parameters much because you are only using this emitter to get set up for the numbers. It is easier to get the movement of the particles to behave consistently between numbers, as is needed here, by adjusting them all as targets.

6. Close the Emitter roll-up and scroll back up to the Setup section and click on Set Target. Use the H key select-by-name shortcut to choose the object 5 Text.

Notice how its name is placed as the target and that a new roll-up has been created called Target: 5 Text—just as the emitter name was placed and a roll-up created for the emitter earlier.

7. Scroll down to the bottom and open the roll-out Target: 5 Text. In the Timing section, set the Begin Assembly to 30 and the End Assembly to 40. Set Chaos to 10 and Influence Time to 15. Because you want the particle simulation to hold for a bit at the numbers instead of just using them as a path, check the Transition Delay box and set Delay to 10 frames.

8. In the Assembly Direction section, check Center. In the Speed After Transition Delay section, set Speed to 5. Also click on From Icon Out.

9. In the Particle Location section, click on Target Simulation to present a great feature: As the particles leave the target, they appear to disassemble the object face by face.

The number objects have all been given a different-colored metal material. This enables you to change colors as you build the new numbers. Sand Blaster enables you a wide range of options over how to use materials and how change will be timed.

Sand Blaster uses a master/slave method for changing materials, whereby the resultant particle material and mapping can be inherited by the master object. You can elect to use the emitter's or particle's own material instead. In this exercise, you change the particle's color at each number by using the Master option from the targets.

10. In the Material and Mapping section, click to assign this target as a Master and then check Use Target Material. Set Stable Before and Stable After to 5. Set Transform Time to 20. Select and hide all objects except the Sand Blaster itself (Sphere01, 5 Text, 4 Text, 3 Text, 2 Text, and 1 Text).

TIP

In this author's opinion, the following functions are worthy of F key shortcuts.

F2   Unhide by name

F3   Hide unselected

F4   Hide selected

These have become second nature to me and are used often during production. In step 10 of this exercise, it would be more efficient to select the Sand Blaster icon and hit F3 to hide everything unselected.

11. Because you are going to start the countdown animation from here, go into the Time Configuration dialog by clicking on the Time Configuration button and set Start Time to 40.

This finishes the set up of the number 5 object as the first target. Notice that the 5 Text object's outline shows up telling you that the particles are assembled into this configuration at this frame as part of the target simulation.

From here on out, it is just a matter of calculating the begin and end assembly times for the remaining targets and setting the other parameters identical to the first target. First, get all your targets assigned, remembering that this is a seconds countdown that is played at 30 fps.

12. In the Setup section, just above the Set Target button, click on the up spinner next to the target # field to set it to 2. Then click on the Set Target button and press the Select by Name button (or H key) and select object 4 Text as target 2. Notice that hidden objects appear in the Pick Object dialog.

13. Repeat this for target #3 as 3 Text, target #4 for 2 Text, target #5 for 1 Text, and finally set target #6 as Inside 3D Text.

NOTE

During the preceding steps, you had Particle Activation on to see the effect along the way. You get a much quicker response in production, however, if you turn Particle Activation off. This proves especially effective when you want to set a series of Sand Blaster parameters quickly.

14. Turn off Particle Activation in the Setup section.

15. Expand the target: 4 Text roll-out section and set Begin Assembly to 60 and End Assembly to 70.

16. Expand the target: 3 Text roll-out section and set Begin Assembly to 90 and End Assembly to 100.

17. Expand the target: 2 Text roll-out section and set Begin Assembly to 120 and End Assembly to 130.

18. Expand the target: 1 Text roll-out section and set Begin Assembly to 150 and End Assembly to 160.

19. Expand the target: Inside 3D Text roll-out section and set Begin Assembly to 180 and End Assembly to 190.

20. Then in each of these roll-ups, set the following parameters to match that of the first target, object 5 Text:

    Chaos—10
    Influence Time—15
    Check Transition and Set Delay—10
    Set Assembly Direction to Center
    Start Speed 5, Variation 2
    Check From Icon Out
    Check Target Simulation
    Check Master and Use Target material
    Set Stable Before and After to 5 and set Transition Time to 20

21. Close all the roll-outs. In the Setup section, turn on Particle Activation and Render Activation. Make a preview of the scene to test the movement of this particle simulation.

22. Turn on the Sand Blaster particle's Motion Blur property and save your scene.

Render the scene if you like or load the rendered file countdwn.avi from the accompanying CD.

Spray Particle System with Wind Space Warps

In this section, you explore the use of the Spray particle system in combination with the Wind space warp. You use Spray to act as the visible air flow to check the aerodynamics of a sports car in a wind tunnel. You use numerous Wind space warps to make the particles conform to the aerodynamics of the sports car. Because a particle system has yet to be created to implicitly cause particles to follow a path, you use a series of four Wind space warps to persuade them to follow the path over the sports car's contour. The Wind space warp, as well as most of the other particle space warps, have a feature called Decay, which allows the use of a series of space warps to modify the path of particles by setting them up with a fall-off to the space warp effect. Thus, each Wind space warp only affects a specific portion of the particles.

WIND TUNNEL AERODYNAMICS

Before you start, load 16aimx.max from the accompanying CD. This is the sports car model from the World Creating Toolkit.

1. From the Create panel, choose Particle Systems from the drop-down list. Then choose Spray from the list.

2. In the front viewport, click directly in front of the sports car.

3. Drag the mouse and click to create an emitter with a width and length of about 5 (see fig. 16.6).

Notice that the emitter is placed on the home grid with its vector pointing away from you. This is typical of creating particle systems in an orthographic viewport.

Note also that no particles are showing yet because the default timing starts the generation of particles at frame 1. If you move the Frame Slider, they are generated at the default sustainable rate of 3.3 particles per frame.

4. Now, you are going to increase the number of particles. With the Spray Emitter selected, go to the Modifier panel.

5. Increase the Viewport Count to 200 and the Render Count to 1000.

6. Open the Material Editor and apply the White Self Illuminated material from material slot 1 to better see the rendered particles.

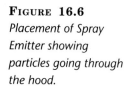

FIGURE 16.6

Placement of Spray Emitter showing particles going through the hood.

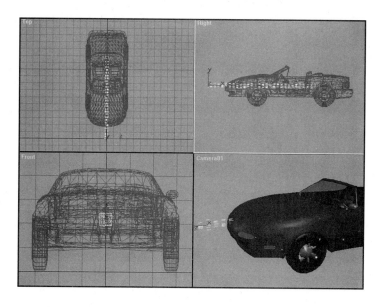

Now you have your first Spray particles. Obviously, however, it does not look right—the flow of particles goes through the roadster (see fig. 16.6). This is where Wind space warps come in.

7. From the Create panel, select the Space Warps icon, and then choose Wind from the list of space warps.

8. In the front viewport, click on an area just under the body of the sports car and drag to an icon size of about 10, and center it in front of the sports car.

Notice that the default Wind is planar (you will get into spherical in a moment), and the Wind space warp is created with its vector pointing toward you in orthographic viewports.

9. Rotate the Wind in the right viewport –135 degrees around the Z axis (pointing upward and toward the back of the sports car).

10. Click on Bind to Space Warp in the toolbar.

11. Select the Spray emitter (notice the cursor changes to the bind cursor) and drag to the Wind and release.

The cursor changes to the green ready bind cursor when over an appropriate space warp. You can use the hit key (Select By Name) and select the space warp from there. MAX conveniently filters the list to show only space warps.

Now you see the effects of the Wind space warp on the flow of particles.

WARNING

It is possible to Bind in reverse by selecting the space warp and binding to the particle system. This is easy to do because you usually bind directly after creating the space warp. Be careful though: In this way, the bind cursor changes to enable you to bind a space warp to geometric objects, even though a space warp can only affect particles.

12. Pick Select and Move from the toolbar.

13. Select the Wind and move it. Notice that no matter where you move the Wind, the particle effect is unchanged.

Remember that space warps influence world space. It is the vector coming off the space warp that tells the particles which direction to turn toward. Without a Decay setting (or effect from another space warp), moving this wind has no affect in the scene.

Seeing the effect the wind space warp has had in figure 16.7, you realize the particles are being coerced in the correct direction but they are not exactly right yet. The particles need to be sent over the hood by this wind. What you need is a stronger wind effect and a way to cause a fall off of the effect. You will use the Decay setting to give a fall off to the wind space warp effect.

FIGURE 16.7

Placement of the first wind space warp gets the particles moving in the correct direction, but not over the hood yet.

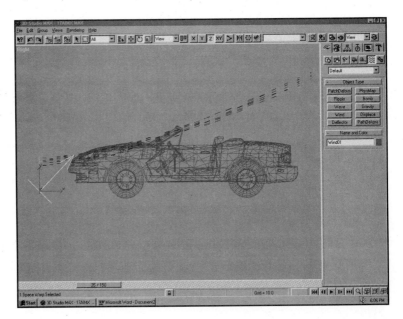

14. Go to the Modifier panel. With the Wind selected, set the Strength to 2.1 and Decay to 0.04.

Now adjust the Spray.

15. Select the Spray object.

16. Click on the drop-down list in the Modifier stack and select Spray.

17. Adjust the Speed to 6.5 (which also shortens their travel) and raise the Life to 40 to compensate for the shortening of distance that the particles will travel with this reduced speed.

Now you have coerced the particles over the hood as seen in figure 16.8.

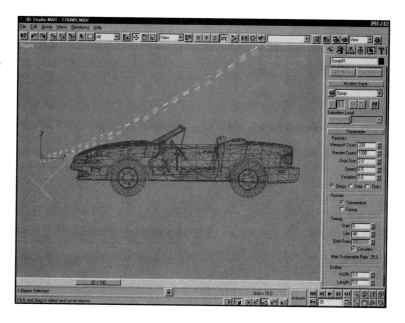

FIGURE 16.8

By raising the wind strength, adding decay, and slowing the speed of the particles, they now go over the hood.

Notice that if you move the Wind space warp now, it makes a difference in the effect because of the fall-off effect of the Decay setting.

Now that the particles are starting to push over the hood, it is time to create another Wind space warp to keep the particles hugging the hood.

18. From the Create panel, choose Wind again.

19. Under the Force section, click on spherical and create a Spherical Wind space warp with an icon size of about 10.

20. Place the new Wind space warp about a third of the way up the hood, just above it (see fig. 16.9).

21. Select and Bind the Spray to this space warp.

FIGURE 16.9

Positioning Spray and the two Wind space warps.

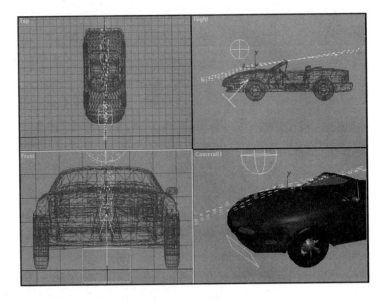

Because a spherical Wind space warp has a vector pointing directly out from the center in all directions, it needs at least some Decay to create the effect you need.

22. Change from Select & Bind to the Select icon, then select the spherical Wind object that MAX has named Wind02 by default.

23. In the Modifier panel, set the Decay at 0.055 and set the Strength at 3.1.

Now you need to do some position adjusting to get the particles to follow the contours of the sports car.

24. Drag the Frame Slider to frame 80 or so and position the two warps so that the particles appear to be flowing over the hood.

25. Move the planar space warp horizontally until it is directly under the spherical Wind space warp.

26. You might have to move the Spray emitter up or back a bit to prevent the particles from going into the hood (refer to figure 16.9).

Now you can make a third Wind space warp that will be used to push the particles up and over the windshield.

27. Shift+Clone (copy) the spherical Wind02 space warp to just below the intersection of the hood and windshield.

28. Set its Strength to 1.9 and its Decay to 0.045

29. Bind to space warp as before.

30. Position this warp to get the particles to flow over the top of the windshield (see fig. 16.10).

FIGURE 16.10

Positioning third Wind space warp to coax particles to flow over windshield

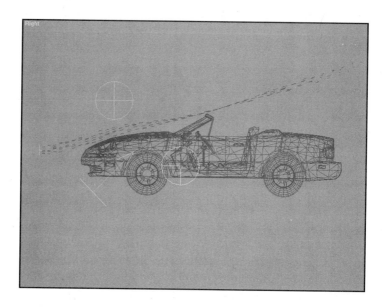

Now you just need one more Wind space warp to push the particles back horizontal after they flow over the windshield.

31. Shift+Clone (copy) Wind03 and place it just past the windshield.

NOTE

All the existing files have a net render directory default in Save File/Render. Change to your local drive before rendering.

32. Set its Strength to 18 and its Decay to 0.09.

33. Bind to space warp as before.

34. Position the Wind04 to push the particles back into a horizontal direction after passing over the windshield (see fig. 16.11).

35. Save your scene. (You may have to adjust these space warps a bit differently than outlined here, depending on exactly where they were placed.)

FIGURE 16.11

Positioning the fourth Wind space warp to coax the particles horizontally.

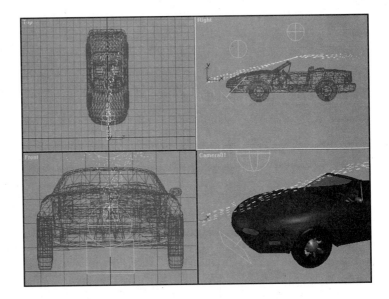

Load wtunnel.max from the accompanying CD to see the final version of the scene. Make a preview of the Camera View. Notice how the particles flow nicely over the roadster.

Notice that all the Spray particles seem to be aligned as they leave the emitter. This is one of the biggest caveats of using Spray. The problem is that the Spray particles are generated from the emitter on a per-frame basis. You would much prefer sub-frame generation of particles. When particles are generated per frame, a particle ends up being in the same position as the last particle in the next frame, which is very apparent as they leave the emitter, but is somewhat hidden as they are affected by the space warps. The best way to lessen this problem is to assign Motion Blur to the Spray particle system.

You can take a look at the renderings with and without Motion Blur by loading and viewing wtunnel.avi (without Motion Blur) and wtunnelm.avi (with Motion Blur).

Spray with Deflector and Gravity Space Warps

In the last exercise, you saw how you could affect Spray particles through the use of multiple Wind space warps. In the next exercise, you use the Spray particle system again, but this time you affect them by using the Gravity space warp and multiple Deflector space warps. Gravity, just as it sounds, adds a gravitational pull to the particles and a Deflector in a 2D plane that acts as collision detection.

In this exercise, you add Spray particles to a robotic welder to simulate the welding arc and flying sparks. You then explore the Deflector space warp that is used to bounce the sparks off the sled as it's welding. A second Deflector is used to bounce some of the sparks along the conveyer table. A Gravity space warp is used to add gravitational force to bring the particles back down to Earth.

ROBOTIC WELDER

Get started by loading 16bimx.max from the accompanying CD. This file consists of a robotic welding arm and a conveyor table with metal rails of a sled waiting to be welded together.

Slide the Frame Slider, and you see that the robotic arm has already been hierarchically linked, and interactive IK was used to place the welding head at a few weld spots. Go ahead and put the first weld together.

1. From the Create panel, choose Particle Systems from the drop-down list, then choose Spray.

2. In the top viewport, create a Spray Emitter at the tip of the weld head with an icon size of 4.

Notice that the emitter is created with its vector pointing down, away from you in the view. In the Front viewport, place the emitter at the end of the weld head and link it to the weld head.

3. Move and rotate the emitter as necessary to place it at the tip of the weld head with the vector pointing out from it (see fig. 16.12).

4. When it is in position, link the emitter to the weld head.

FIGURE 16.12

Position the Spray emitter at the tip of the welding head.

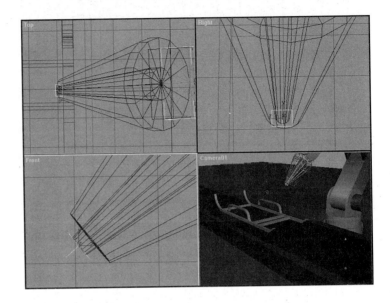

Scrub the Frame Slider and notice how the particles behave now that the emitter is animated. The particles seem to have a secondary motion to them because after a particle is emitted, it travels in that direction until acted on by another force. This happens as subsequent particles are emitted in a new direction, which gives you a nice "water out the end of a moving hose" effect. File that thought away for future use.

In the preceding exercise, you let the particles be emitted in a continuous stream starting at frame 0. Here, this will not work. You need to start emitting the particles when the weld head comes to a stop.

5. Move to frame 25 when the weld head is in position.

6. Be certain that the Spray emitter is selected and go the Modifier panel and set Viewport Count at 200 and Render Count at 1000.

7. In the Timing section, set the Start to 23, a couple frames before the weld head stops.

You'll see the particles on the frame after this start frame. You'll leave the start frame here to get a jump on the particle creation just before the weld head stops.

Now as you scrub the Frame Slider, the particles appear to be emitted as the head comes to position. You need to stop the particles as the weld head lifts up. A bit of calculation is called for here.

The weld head begins to lift off the mark at frame 40. You could probably stand to overshoot this a bit. Assume, for example, that you want to spray for 20 frames, from frame 23 to frame 43. If you want to exhaust all 1,000 particles over 20 frames, you need to birth the particles at 50 particles per frame because 1,000 particles/20 frames = 50 particles per frame.

8. Turn off the Constant button and set the Birth Rate at 50.

NOTE

You don't have to do the calculation here. You can do it interactively.

9. Set the Birth Rate back to about 15.

10. Go to frame 43, the frame at which you want to stop emitting particles.

11. Click on and drag the Birth Rate slider and drag to increase its value.

While you are raising this value, watch the emitter, and you will see the particles slowly stop being emitted. This should be around frame 50.

You will want the particles to last longer than 30 frames.

12. Make certain that the Birth Rate is set to 50.

13. Set the Life to 50.

Scrub the Frame Slider and see that the particles do indeed appear to start as the Spray head comes to rest, and end as the Spray head moves again.

The problem now is that Spray particles, once destroyed, are always regenerated again. This regeneration would be okay if the next stop of the weld head were to pause to coincide with the next release of particles, but this is unlikely—although it almost happens here.

To stop particles from being emitted altogether, you'll have to animate its Birth Rate to 0.

You can do this at any frame after frame 44 (when they stop being emitted) and before frame 74 (when they start after being reborn).

14. Go to frame 60.

15. Turn on the Animate button.

16. Set Birth Rate to 0.

17. Turn off the Animate button.

Doing this, you know that a Bézier float key is created at frame 60. You also know that another key is created automatically at frame 0, resulting in the particle birth rate animating from 50 at frame 0 to 0 at frame 60. Nice effect if you want a tapering off of the effect, but it is not what you want here. As good animators though, you should file this information away for another time.

Now, drop the Birth Rate from 50 to 0 over just 1 frame.

18. Go into Track View, scroll down to Spray01, and get to the Birth Rate track. Right-click on the first key and change the Out Tangent to Steps. This automatically changes the next keys in Tangent to Step. (As an alternative, you could just move the key at frame 0 to frame 59.)

During welding, the sparks usually bounce around a bit—so use your Deflector space warp to create this effect. Remember, a Deflector is a 2D plane that causes particles that come in contact with the deflector plane to bounce off of it. A Deflector provides collision detection for particles.

19. In the Create panel, click on the Space Warp icon.

20. Click on Deflector and, in the Top View, drag to create a Deflector with a width and height of 20.

21. Move the Deflector to the height of the top of the cross bar to be welded, centered on the weld head (see fig. 16.13).

22. Select the Spray object and bind it to the Deflector space warp.

FIGURE 16.13
Position the Deflector directly under weld head, just above the cross bar.

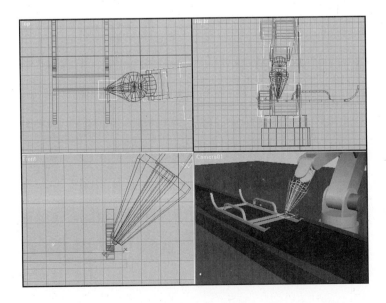

As you scrub the Frame Bar, you see the particles bounce off the Deflector.

Because you left the default Bounce parameter at 1, the particles bounce off the Deflector at the same speed that they collide with it.

NOTE

It does not matter which way the Deflector is facing. Particles bounce off either side of a Deflector. You can witness this by rotating the Deflector 180 degrees.

The effect does not look quite right because the particles bounce off at a predictable angle. Add some randomness to help the effect.

23. Select the Deflector and open Track View.

24. Select the Transform Rotation Track and click on Assign Controller.

25. Assign the Noise Rotation Controller and open its Properties.

26. Because there is no need to rotate on that axis, drop the Z Strength to 0.

27. Set Frequency to 0.35.

28. Set Fractal Noise Roughness to 0.4.

Go back to the Spray to give the particles a longer drop size. You should also add a bit of variation for even more randomness. Variation varies the speed and direction of particles, spreading them out. You should also slow the speed.

29. Select the Spray, go to the Modifier panel, Modifier Stack, and select Spray from the drop-down list.

30. Set Drop Size to 4 and Variation to 1.

31. Set Speed at 7.

Scrub the Frame Slider. You are starting to get the effect that you want now. Notice the randomness of the sparks as they hit the sled's frame and bounce about.

WARNING

Notice as you scrub the Frame Slider that it is possible to upset the Spray to Deflector collision detection when animating the Deflector in certain situations. A few of the particles can get by the Deflector (see fig. 16.14).

FIGURE 16.14
Some particles may go through a Deflector when the Deflector is animated.

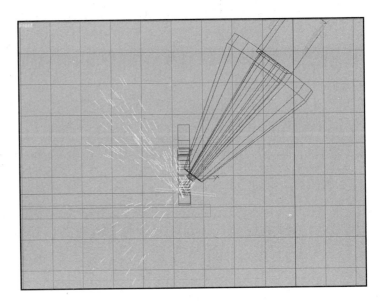

Don't think of the particles going through this deflector as a problem. Think of it as a feature. Do what any good animator would do: Use it to your advantage! These non-deflected particles give you a great opportunity to place a second Deflector at the table height to bounce the missed particles across the table. Besides, in real life, not all the welding sparks would bounce away anyway; some would hit the table.

32. Create a Deflector with the same width (114) as the table and a length of about 120.

33. Set Bounce to .5.

34. Move the Deflector to the top of the table (see fig. 16.15).

35. Bind the Spray to this Deflector.

For realism, you can add one more thing. Make the particles fall under gravity. To do so, use a Gravity space warp.

36. Go to Create panel, choose the Space Warp icon, then pick Gravity.

37. Click on an area in the top viewport and drag to create a Gravity space warp with an icon size of about 50.

Notice that the default Gravity space warp is planar and that it is created with its vector pointing away from you in an orthographic viewport. The force of gravity is in the direction of the vector.

38. Bind the Spray to this Gravity space warp.

FIGURE 16.15

Placing a second Deflector to bounce some particles across the table.

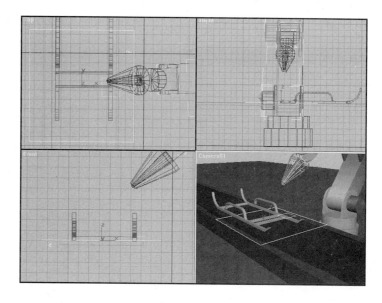

Instantly, the particles are affected by gravity. Note that it does not yet matter where the icon is placed in the scene. Gravity is simply a force in the scene in the direction of the vector. Because Decay controls the falloff of the effect from the icon, it matters where the icon is placed when used with Decay.

39. Move the icon above the scene until its vector arrow touches the table as seen in figure 16.16.

FIGURE 16.16

Place the Gravity space warp here so the vector arrow just touches the table.

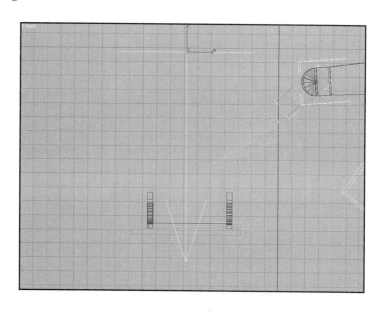

40. Set the Decay to 0.01

Now assign a better material to get the particles to stand out better.

41. Select the Spray emitter, open the Material Editor and assign the Red Hot Particle material from slot number 5 to the emitter.

You now have some nice spark action going on. You may want to play with a few of these settings to get an effect you like. You might want to have the particles last longer. To make them last longer, raise the life of the Spray to 75. You might want to see the particles dance a bit more as they scoot across the table. In that case, increase the Deflector Bounce parameter to 0.8.

42. Save your file.

Load up welder.max from the accompanying CD. Take at look at the rendered version welder.avi.

Object Space Warps

The next two exercises deal with object space warps. As the name implies, these are space warps that are meant to be used to deform objects (as opposed to particles). Note that the Displace space warp is a universal space warp in that it can be used to deform particles as well as to deform objects.

- **Displace Space Warp.** This is a two-part exercise that delves into the use of Displace to deform a tire on a surface. The first part causes the tire to deform on a flat road; the second has the tire deform on a bumpy road. The bumpy road exercise uses the bitmap mapping option that is available for the Displace.

- **Path Deform Space Warp.** This is a new space warp that the Yost Group included with the MAX 1.1 upgrade CD. The Path Deform has many uses, such as flying text along a path, deforming to the path as it goes. In this exercise you use Path Deform in two ways. One way is to use it strictly for modeling as you will do to create piping; the other is to use the same Path Deform as an animation path for objects to travel inside of the pipe.

- **Bomb Space Warp.** Here you blow up the sun for a bit of Big-Bang fun. The Bomb space warp is used to explode an object into its individual faces. The importance in this exercise is to minimize the effect of seeing the individual faces as they blow apart.

The Displace Space Warp

The following exercise presents you with the task of creating the illusion of a car tire as it rolls down the road. How about creating a car tire that doesn't just rotate, but also bounces a bit? That would be great, but what would you do to solve the tire contact with the road? In real life, the air-filled rubber tire deforms a bit against the road as it rolls along.

This is a great job for a MAX space warp. In particular, look at Displace—the only MAX space warp that works with both particles and geometry.

ROUGH ROAD AHEAD (PART 1)

Before you begin, load 16cimx-1.max from the accompanying CD. This file consists of a tire rotating down the road with a bit of bounce happening. The camera is linked in such a way as to keep the tire in view and not bounce with the tire. Unfortunately, as the tire goes down the road, it goes right through the road. The following steps take care of that.

1. In the Create panel, choose the Space Warp icon and pick Displace.

2. Create a Displace space warp in the top viewport about the same size as the ground surface (see fig. 16.17).

3. Select the tire. Using the Bind to Space Warp icon, bind it to the Displace space warp. Make certain that you bind the Geometric object to the space warp. This way the bind cursor only allows binding to space warps.

FIGURE 16.17
The Displace space warp in relation to the ground plane.

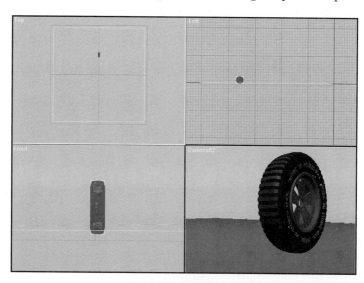

T I P

Use the H key to assign the Bind object.

There currently seems to be an anomaly in the Tire object that flips the normals of the tire after it is bound to the Displace space warp. The problem can be traced back to a mirrored spline before the tire was lathed, which can mess with the object's data flow. The cause of this is reviewed a bit later in the second part of this Rough Road Ahead exercise. For now, it is easy enough to fix.

4. Go to the Modifier panel and, with the tire selected, apply a Normal modifier and check Flip to reverse the normals.

5. Nothing is deforming yet because the Displace space warp has no strength. Therefore, select the Displace space warp, go to the Modifier panel, and set Strength at 2.

Notice that the whole tire object, which is the parent of the rim, moves away from the rim object. Because they are separate objects, albeit linked objects, the tire is affected by the space warp but the rim is not. This is not yet the effect we are looking for anyway because a space warp is applied in world space and goes on forever, which has moved the entire tire off of the rim. The Decay setting, which acts as a falloff for the effect, takes care of this by deforming only a small portion of the tire at a point where the tire meets the road surface. This will leave the parts of the tire surrounding the rim unaffected, and the effect will look correct.

6. Still in the Modifier panel, grab the Decay Spinner. While holding Ctrl for acceleration, drag the spinner up.

You see the effect interactively begin to fall off. The tire returns to the rim and the effect is concentrated at the bottom.

7. Set Decay to 100.

Take a look at figures 16.18 and 16.19 to see the difference between No Decay and Decay at 100.

You must do some tweaking to get the tire to meet the road surface. As it is now, the tire's deformation happens, but not exactly at the road surface. Also, as the tire bounces along, it goes above the road surface at certain

FIGURE 16.18
Displace with No Decay causes the whole tire to move off the rim.

FIGURE 16.19
Displace with Decay of 100 concentrates the space warp at the bottom of the tire.

frames. The following steps correct this.

8. In the Front View, zoom in to the bottom of the tire.

9. Drag the Time Slider to frame 3, where the tire is at a low position.

10. Select the Displace space warp and move it along the Y axis until the tire meets the surface (see fig. 16.20).

11. Move to frame 12, where the tire is a bit in the air.

FIGURE 16.20
*Move the space warp
down until the tire
meets the surface.*

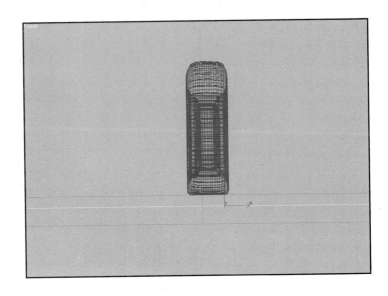

FIGURE 16.21
*Move the tire down to
meet the surface.*

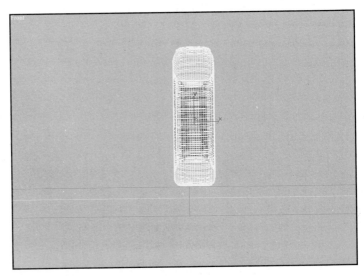

12. Select and move the tire to meet the surface (see fig. 16.21).

Play the animation in the front viewport or play the bounce.avi file from the accompanying CD. Notice how nicely the rubber meets the road as it bounces along.

Save your scene and load bounce.max. Take a look at the rendered file bounce.avi on the accompanying CD.

ROUGH ROAD AHEAD (PART 2)

Now, take this exercise a bit further. What if the road surface you're traveling is not flat? How could you solve the illusion of the tire riding on a bumpy surface?

You know there are different types of Mapping parameters: Planer, Cylindrical, Spherical, and Shrink Wrap. If you had a rock in the road, you could use Spherical mapping to deform the tire going over the rock. If you had an obstacle such as a pipe, you may be able to use Cylindrical mapping. But a bumpy surface does not lend itself to these types of mappings. In such cases, use a bitmap to adjust the strength of your planar mapping.

Take a look at the next scene.

Load 16cimx-2.max from the accompanying CD. This file shows the tire riding over a bumpy surface. Animation keys cause the tire to go up and down according to the bumps.

You could tweak the keys to cause the tire to ride perfectly over the bumps, but that would be very tedious—especially if the surface you're traveling over is randomly bumpy. The bumps here are somewhat repeatable to help you see the effect you will try to create. The tire was also purposely animated not to go completely over the bumps, but goes through the top of them.

The MAX Displace space warp helps you correct the tire's ride over the bumps. In particular, you can use the Luminance Value of a bitmap to influence the amount of displacement.

Now is the time to create a Displace space warp.

1. In the Create panel, choose the Space Warp icon and pick Displace.

2. Maximize the top viewport. In that view, click and drag, starting in the center of the ground surface. Try to make this the same size as the ground surface

Because of how the ground surface was created, it is important for this exercise that the Displace space warp be the same size and in the same position as the ground surface. It is pertinent to this exercise to know how it was done, but you will not go through the steps.

The ground surface started out as a 500-by-500-by-5 box. Because a Displace modifier was to be used to shape the surface, it was given 100 segments in the X and Y. An Edit Mesh modifier was then applied. Next, all the faces not on the top plane were selected and deleted. Note that there is now a parametric object plug-in called Grid, created by Peter Watje, that was uploaded to the CompuServe Kinetix forum libraries that will create a 2D planar grid object. Had this been available earlier, it would have greatly reduced the amount of steps and time needed to create this preceding ground surface. The remaining faces were then tessellated. Next, the Displace modifier was applied using a bitmap (2bump.tga) to deform the surface of the box, which transformed it into the bumpy ground surface you see.

Lastly, an Optimize modifier was applied to lower the number of faces. The stack was then collapsed to an editable mesh for memory and viewport speed reasons.

Remember that the Displace modifier is like the Displace space warp. Modifiers, however, work in Object Space; space warps work in world space.

TIP

Always save a copy of an object before collapsing the stack. You may have to come back and adjust the object later. In which case, you will be glad you saved it.

3. With the space warp still selected, click on the Align icon.

4. Click on the ground surface and then Align in the X and Y axes.

There are no Width and Length parameters, so you must scale the Displace space warp by using the Select and Scale icon in the toolbar. If you had a Width and Height parameters, you could just set them to the same measurements as the ground surface.

5. Select Scale from the toolbar.

6. Scale the space warp to a size very close to the size of the ground surface (see fig. 16.22).

Back to your scene, bind the tire to the displace space warp.

7. Select the tire.

8. Bind it to the space warp.

FIGURE 16.22

The space warp must be the same size as the ground surface.

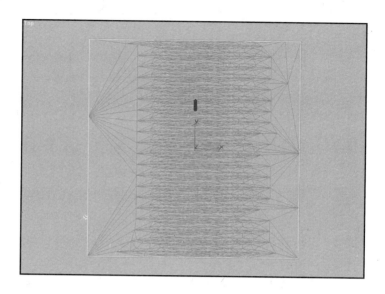

WARNING

Strange things seem to happen to an object when, during its creation, Transform Scale or Mirroring (Negative Scale) has been used. The tire was created from a line that was mirrored to make both sides symmetrical before lathing. This is a result of Object Data Flow; because MAX transforms are evaluated at the end of the stack and modifiers are evaluated earlier, there is no "mirror" occuring for the modifier stack to affect. The result here is that the face normals get flipped. Basically, mirror and non-uniform scale should only be performed in conjunction with the Xform modifier. It is easily enough fixed with a Normal modifier though.

9. Go back to the four viewports, apply a Normal modifier to the tire, and flip the normals.

Notice that when you apply a modifier to the stack after you have applied a space warp, the modifier is placed *before* the space warp. It is very important for MAX users to understand this. 3DS MAX has a very specific order in which it calculates object data. The following a list shows the order in which objects are evaluated.

■ Master object (creation parameters)

■ Object modifiers (Bend, Normal, Lathe, and so on)

■ Transforms (Position, Rotate, and Scale changes)

■ Space Warps

■ Object properties (Name, Material, and so on)

This is not the place to get heavily into this. You must, however, understand object data flow to understand why the normal modifier was placed where it was in the stack and why space warps are always evaluated after transforms. For more information about Object dataflow, refer to *Inside 3D Studio Volume I* (pages 20–26) and the *MAX User Guide* (pages 1–14 through 1–17).

Now, to get back to setting up your Displace space warp. The trick is to set up and vary the strength of the Planar space warp by using the Luminance Value of a bitmap image. You use the same image in your Displace space warp as was used in the ground surface Displace modifier.

10. Select the Displace space warp and go to the Modifier panel.

11. In the Image section, click on None and select 2bump.tga from the accompanying CD.

12. Before clicking on OK, click on View to take a look at the image.

The image is but a single white radial gradient dot on a middle gray background (refer to figure 16.5).

13. Click on OK to select this bitmap.

14. Set Strength to 4 and Decay to 100. Set Blur to 2.

The ground surface modifier was tiled in the V direction to create long bumps. Your Displace space warp must also be tiled.

15. Set the Map V Tile Setting to 20.

16. Maximize the left viewport and play the scene.

Notice how the tire now deforms according to the Luminance Value of the bitmap. The same bitmap was used to deform the ground surface and influence the strength of the Displace space warp (both were lined up and the same size). The result is that the tire appears to deform as a result of the bumps of the surface.

The illusion is completed by making a few adjustments to the tire and space warp to bring the tire into better contact with this surface.

17. As necessary, move the Displace space warp down to effect a better contact between the tire and ground surface (see fig. 16.23).

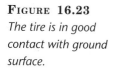

FIGURE 16.23

The tire is in good contact with ground surface.

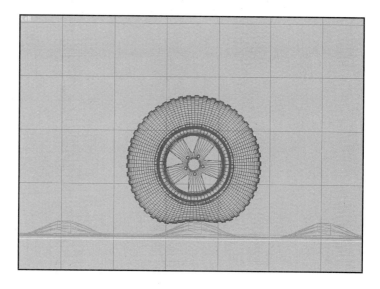

18. Save your scene.

Load bumps.max and see how the illusion has been completed. View the rendered animation bumps.avi on the accompanying CD.

Path Deform Space Warp

In the following exercise, you use the Path Deform space warp, which was not included in the original shipping of MAX 1.0, but was one of the new features added with the 1.1 update. This space warp enables you to deform an object along a spline path. You use that capability in this project of the new and improved Flexible Head Roto-Rooter. This space warp is quite unique compared to the other space warps. For one thing, it deforms in Object Space rather than World Space.

THE ROTO-ROOTER

1. Load imx16e.max from the accompanying CD. This file consists of a Tube object, a Roto-Head, and a spline. This spline serves as the basis for both your modeling and animation.

2. In the Create panel, choose the Space Warp icon, then pick Path Deform.

The only parameter is a Pick Path button. All object deformation is controlled through the Binding parameters in the Modifier Stack—another difference from the other space warps.

3. Click on the Pick Path Button.

4. Click on the spline.

The name of the referenced spline is placed above the Pick Path button and a space warp gizmo is shown in the viewport. Notice that the splines first vertex is used as a start for the gizmo.

NOTE

The spline's Step settings have no effect on the space warp. You can crank the line steps down to 0 and, although the line will be linear from vertex to vertex, the Path Deform gizmo is not affected. It uses true spline interpolation. If you go to the Edit Spline level of the modified line and move the vertices, however, the gizmo conforms.

5. Select the Tube Pipe object and Bind it to the Path Deform space warp

6. Go to the Modifier panel and click on Move Object to Path.

Notice that the length of the tube is shorter than the path. This was done purposely to show that the object is deformed along the path and not modified to fit the path. No problem though, just adjust the height of the tube.

7. Go to the Tubes Creation parameters and increase its height interactively until it matches the length of the path (or type **475**).

The process of binding to the space warp effectively deforms the tube to the gizmo, and the Move to Path places the object directly on the path. Your Tube Pipe should resemble that shown in figure 16.24.

Note that it is important to have a sufficient number of segments to get a good deform around the bends.

TIP

The Path Deform space warp is not just an animation tool; it is also a great modeling tool. Used in place of lofts in some instances, it takes care of the problem of a shape being scaled non-uniformly as it gets lofted around bends.

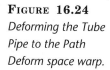

FIGURE 16.24

Deforming the Tube Pipe to the Path Deform space warp.

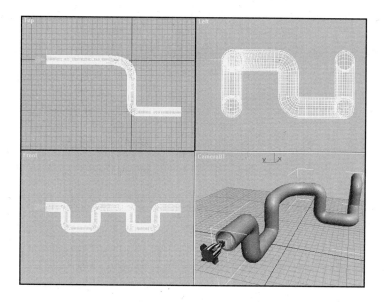

8. Select the Roto-Head object and Bind it to the Path Deform space warp.

9. Click on Move Object to Path.

Now, explore the animation capabilities of the Deform space warp.

10. Go to frame 200 and turn on the Animate button.

11. Set the Percent parameter to 100.

12. Turn off the Animate button.

13. Select the Tube, and open the Material Editor and apply the Glass Piping material.

Play the scene and notice how animating the Path Deforms percent value animated the Roto-Head object from the path start (0 percent) at frame 1 to the path end (100 percent) at frame 200.

NOTE

See how the object deforms according to the gizmo as it goes around the bends. Notice that as the Roto-Head rounds the bends, certain parts deform more smoothly than others. When the Roto-Head was created, it was created to have enough faces where the object was to bend freely. Other parts were kept face simple to simulate the semi-rigid scraping extrusions. There will always be some deformation though, especially closest to and opposite of the apex of the bends. Figure 16.25 shows a close-up view of the Roto-Head object.

FIGURE 16.25

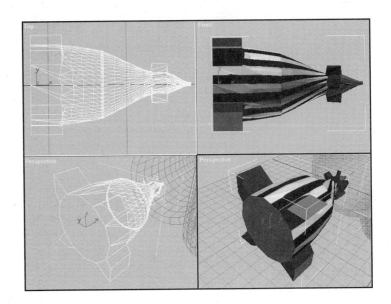

Controlling the Deform by using various face densities.

The Roto-Head must now rotate because it's scraping the pipe.

14. Click on Rotate and try to rotate the Roto-Head.

Another difference from other space warps is that animation of an object bound to a Path Deform space warp is fully controlled by that space warp's parameters. The bound object does not respond to Transform Move, Rotate, or Scale. To rotate the head, you must use the space warp's parameters.

15. Go to frame 200 and turn on the Animate button.

16. Set the Rotation parameter to 2000.

17. Turn off the Animate button.

Play the scene. Now you have a rotating Roto-Head. Now, have a cable follow the Roto-Head.

18. Unhide the Cylinder Cable.

19. Select and Bind it to the space warp.

20. Click on Move object to path.

The cable has a Striped material running down its length. Use your Path Deform parameters to simulate the twist of the cable.

Remember the Twist parameter twists the end of the object while the start of the object is held still. This parameter is also animatable, but is not animated here.

21. Set the Twist parameter to 20,000.

As the Roto-Head travels along the path, you need to have the cable appear along the path, with these steps.

22. Turn on the Animate button.

23. Set Stretch to 0.

24. Go to frame 200.

25. Set the Stretch parameter to 1.

And then you need to rotate to match the Roto-Head animated rotation by using the following steps.

26. Set the Rotate parameter to 2000.

27. Turn off the Animate button.

WARNING

Track View displays some Path Deform space warp parameters at 1/100th of their actual parameters, including the Stretch and Twist parameters. So be careful when doing work in Track View with Path Deform. If you open Track View and look at the key info for stretch at frame 200, you see it displayed at a value of 100, and yet the display shows 1.0.

28. Unhide the Tube Dirt object.

29. Select and Bind it to the Path Deform space warp.

30. Click on Move object to path.

Now animate to simulate the dirt being scraped away, a reverse of the cable animation.

31. Go to frame 200 and turn on the Animate button.

32. Set the Stretch parameter to 0.

33. Set the Percent parameter to 100.

34. Turn off the Animate button.

Play the scene. The Tube Dirt object seems to be scraped away by the Roto-Head. Animating the Stretch parameter from 1 to 0 shrinks the Tube Dirt to 0 height, and animating the Percent from 0 to 100 makes the shrinking begin from the opposite end.

35. Save your scene.

Load rooter.max. Take a look at the rendered animation file rooter.avi on the accompanying CD-ROM.

The Bomb Space Warp

In the following exercise, you work with the Bomb space warp. The Bomb space warp explodes objects into their individual faces. You use it in this exercise to create a sun exploding for a big-bang explosion effect.

THE BIG BANG THEORY

To begin, load 16gimx.max.

1. In the Create panel, pick GeoSphere, click in the Camera View, and drag to create a geosphere in the center of the home grid with a radius of 12. Leave it at the default isoca type and raise the segments to 5. Turn on Generate Mapping coordinates.

2. Open the Material Editor and assign the material Sun from slot 1.

Notice that the Sun material is composed of an orange and red noise map for the diffuse map channel, and that UVW is checked so that it maps to object coordinates rather than world coordinates. Modified versions of this noise map are also used for the self illumination and bump map slots. Render to see the effect.

3. In the Create panel, Space Warps icon, pick Bomb. Click in the Camera View to place it inside the geosphere.

Because the Bomb effect originates from the position of the Bomb object, go ahead and align it to the geosphere.

4. Pick Align from the top menu and click on the geosphere. Then click on the X, Y, and Z position.

5. Select the geosphere, pick Select and Bind from the toolbar, and bind the geosphere to the bomb.

6. Select the Bomb space warp, go to the Modifier panel, and set Detonation to 25. This is the frame at which the bomb begins to explode the sun.

Scrub the frame slider past frame 25 a couple times to see the effect. Notice how symmetrical the explosion looks—not very realistic (see fig. 16.26). Go to frame 27 so that you can see the effect of changing the following parameters.

7. Set the Strength at .4 to slow the exploding faces, and set Gravity at 0—after all, there would be no gravity in space to pull the pieces downward.

8. Turn on the Animate button, go to frame 100, and set Chaos to 2.5. Turn off the Animate button.

9. Open Track View and filter down to selected objects only. Expand Bomb01 and Object (bomb) to get to the Chaos track. Select the key at frame 0 and slide it to frame 25. Minimize Track View. Notice the difference in the apparent randomness (see fig. 16.27).

FIGURE 16.26
Default bomb parameters showing a very symmetrical explosion.

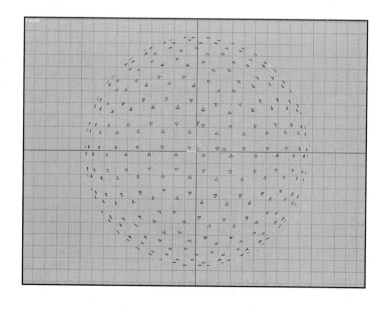

FIGURE 16.27

Adding chaos to the Bomb space warp can add a bit of randomness.

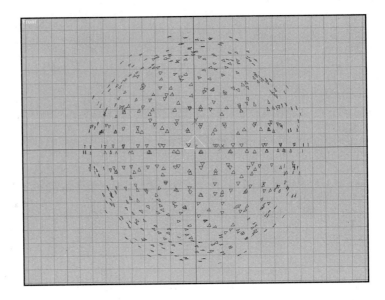

WARNING

The Bomb Detonation parameter does not update in the viewport if it has been animated. It shows the setting of the current frame at the time that the panel is opened. Always check in the Track View, Track Info dialog for the true setting.

The following two parameters were included in the original Yost Group explode IPAS for 3DS DOS and are sorely missing in this space warp.

- More control over the fragmenting of faces. It would be nice to be able to set a min/max fragmentation range instead of exploding every face.

- Capability to assign a rotation or tumbling amount to the exploding faces.

TIP

The following shows workarounds for the missing parameters.

You can animate an increase in the number of faces (segments) as the explosion happens to simulate larger pieces of the object being broken up into smaller pieces. Motion Blur also helps, if appropriate.

You can fake the tumbling of faces by animating the Chaos parameter.

10. Select the geosphere and open the Modifier Stack to get to the geosphere Creation parameters. Go to frame 35, turn on the Animate button, and set Segments to 14. Turn off the Animate button.

11. Restore Track View that is still filtered to selected objects only. Expand the GeoSphere01, Object (GeoSphere) track to get to the Segments track. Select and move the key at frame 0 to frame 26. Minimize Track View.

Scrub the frame bar to see the effect. Between frames 27 and 35, the number of segments is increased by one per frame until frame 35. Also, the animated chaos from step 8 creates a nice scattering of these faces. Notice the difference in the number and size of faces (see fig. 16.28).

FIGURE 16.28
The sun after animating its segments to increase their number and make them smaller.

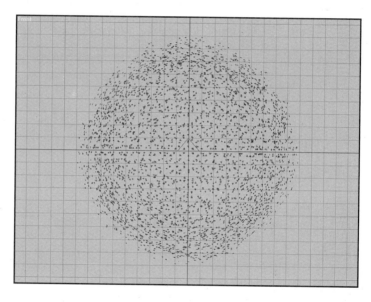

The explosion is so sudden that it seems to need some anticipatory characteristics before the actual big bang—the sun should shudder a bit before blowing apart.

12. Restore Track View, get to the geosphere Position track. Highlight position, click on the Assign Controller button, and pick Position List. Expand the tracks to get to the "available" track. Click on the Assign Controller button again and pick Noise Position.

13. Open the Noise Controller properties, set Seed to 13 and set X, Y, and Z Strength to 2. Raise ramp-in to 25 and Fractal Roughness to .5. Drag the right end of the range bar to coincide with the start of the explosion at frame 26.

Scrub the frame slider to see that the sun now starts to shudder in anticipation of the big bang.

14. Unhide the combustion apparatus that is already set up. Select and link it to the sun.

The big bang is just about ready to render, but to help make it as realistic as possible, you should lessen the look of the triangular faces during the explosion. These can ruin this effect.

15. Right-click on the Sun and turn on its Motion Blur parameter in the Properties dialog. Also set the G-buffer channel to 1. The Render dialog's Motion Blur parameter has already been set.

16. Open the Video Post dialog and notice that Glow has been added to the sun pieces after the explosion. This has the dual purpose of adding a nice glow to the exploding faces and helps blur the triangle face edges.

Notice also that Tom Hudson's starfield generator has been added to the queue. This freeware plug-in has been provided on the accompanying CD-ROM for your convenience.

17. Minimize Track View and change the Camera View to the *Cam-shake* Camera View. This camera is animated to add to the realism of being affected by the shockwave of the explosion. This camera dollies out to show more of the explosion and has a noise controller added at the time of the explosion to simulate the impact of the shockwave.

18. Save your scene.

View the rendered file bigbang.avi on the accompanying CD-ROM.

NOTE

After this chapter was written, a new freeware plug-in called Bomb2 was released to the CompuServe forum by Johnny Ow. This plug-in can be installed in your 3DS MAX plug-in directory and will appear under the Space Warps icon in a new listing in the drop-down list called Johnny Ow. Bomb2 adds the Fragmentation Min/Max parameters (for chunks) and Spin parameters mentioned in the preceding exercise, as needed by an Explosion space warp. It also adds a Scale parameter for scaling the chunks over time. Bomb2 is included on the accompanying CD, please send a note thanking Johnny Ow (Johnny@ywd.com) for this fine contribution to your MAX toolbox and for his support of the MAX community at large.

Feel free to repeat this exercise, using his Bomb2 space warp to create chunks of the sun exploding, rather than just faces.

In Practice: Particles, Space Warps, and Physics

- **Particle systems can simulate many objects.** As these exercises show, particle systems are very versatile and can be used to create the illusion of all sorts of natural and unnatural phenomena. Smoke, dust, jet exhaust, rain, laser blasts, and welding sparks are all possible with particles. As you explore them further, you will find many more uses. How about a little dust kicked up by the tire as it rolls down the street? How about a ring of space dust particles as the sun explodes?

- **Each of the particle systems has similarities, but each also carries its own particular strengths for a given effect.** Each particle system has some similar parameters, but it is the differences between them that make them versatile. Use each particle's differences to your advantage.

- **Particle systems can be used alone, but are often used in combination with Particle space warps.** Depending on what is called for in the shot, a space warp can usually be added to change their original path or to give the particles a more professional look. Particles that behave more believably result in a better-looking scene. The welding sparks bouncing along the table top is a good example of this.

- **Space warps are a great way to coax particles to move according to your plans.** The speed and direction particles take is solely dependent on the particle parameters and emitter orientation at the time of birth for that frame in time. The only way to change that is for the particles to be affected by a space warp. A little bit of Gravity or a Deflector plane can go a long way.

- **All space warps influence world space.** Whether you are using an Object space warp or a Particle space warp, remember that they affect the scene in world space.

- **Space warps are always evaluated last in the stack.** MAX uses a predefined data flow to evaluate objects in your scene. Space warps are at the end, after Object modifiers and transforms.

IMAGE CREATED BY RALPH FRANTZ

Chapter 17

by Ralph Frantz

HYPERMATTER

HyperMatter is a physically based animation system being developed by Second Nature Industries as a plug-in for 3D Studio MAX. It should be shipping by the time this book is published. HyperMatter enables you to apply real-world material properties, according to physical and dynamic laws, to MAX objects. These properties include elasticity, dampening, incompressibility, friction, and gravity. Objects can stretch and wobble according to the values you give these parameters. HyperMatter objects are capable of collision detection with infinite plane walls and with each other.

Because HyperMatter is a soft body system, objects can also be bounced around and off each other with full deformational collision detection.

Although HyperMatter excels at representing highly deformable, soft-bodied objects and it is in this manner that the majority of work will be done, it can also be made to represent rigid objects. One of the exercises in this book, which deals with tossing dice, covers rigid HyperMatter objects.

- Doing its own thing

- Rigid objects, dynamics, and one-way collisions

- Fully deformable collision detection between two objects

- Inheriting the keyframed momentum

- Sub-object solidification of a HyperMatter control object

- Animating substance parameters and the follow constraint

Doing Its Own Thing

After an object is turned into a HyperMatter Control object, the whole object or only parts of the object may be acted upon by HyperMatter. The object, or part thereof, is then said to be *solidified*—or *cladded*, if you will— in a cubic volume element. This cubic volume element is what the HyperMatter effect is applied to. This cladding, in turn, then influences the underlying geometry and is referred to as a HyperMatter *solid*. Each whole object or sub-object solid is then able to be controlled to behave like a real object according to the laws of physics and dynamics. HyperMatter is controlling the object according to these laws, and, as such, the HyperMatter Solid reacts as any real object would. The HyperMatter Solid falls and accelerates according to gravity, and squashes, wobbles, and spins when involved in a collision. The HyperMatter Solids are allowed to "do their own thing" according to these physical and dynamic laws.

Because HyperMatter objects do their own thing, constraints can be set up to act upon the HyperMatter cladding, to constrain selected points (the corner of each cube in the cubic volume element) to a place in the scene where you need them to be and when in time you need them to be. The rest of the cladding will react accordingly. The points can be positioned anywhere in the scene through the use of numerous constraints, such as Fix and Follow. (See figure 17.1 for a view of different types of the Constraints rollout.) These point constraints can be given a lifespan, and their parameter values can also be animated. There is also a Forces panel for adjusting gravity (-Z force) or adjusting the force in the X or Y.

FIGURE 17.1

The Constraints rollout.

HyperMatter may at first seem to be a complicated plug-in, and there is no argument that it can do some incredible things. Some of the cause and effect deformation can truly amaze. You will soon learn that HyperMatter Solid deformations can be easily and quickly achieved. This chapter will help you achieve them and further your understanding at the same time.

NOTE

This author has had some of the most enjoyable times "playing" with the dynamics and physics of HyperMatter. It has been truly enjoyable to participate (in a small way) with the developers on this plug-in. Hopefully, you will receive the same enjoyment I did as you begin learning what HyperMatter can do for you and your scenes.

In this chapter, you will witness a MAX object turned into a deformable object, receiving a sudden impact and observing the rest of the object react. This physical process adds greatly to the realism of motion in your scenes. The illusion of real-world properties and cause and effect are what HyperMatter is all about.

Keep the following rules in mind while going through this chapter:

- When working with HyperMatter, you should try to avoid jumping around between frames as much as possible because of the time-stepping concern discussed previously. It is important, therefore, to turn off Real Time in the Time Configuration dialog box during these exercises. This is very important when you are asked to play the scene.

- It is okay to experiment with the stated parameters, but please return to the stated parameters before proceeding.

- All steps that do not explicitly call for you to be at a specific step should *always* be performed at frame 0. This is important with HyperMatter because it will set certain parameters automatically for you depending on the current frame—most importantly, when applying constraints.

Processing and Time Stepping

You may notice at times in the following exercises that MAX has to wait while a *HyperMatter Processing* progress bar comes up. Attempts have been made to minimize this wait time in the exercises, but maybe an explanation is in order.

MAX can procedurally calculate objects at any time. Given a certain frame number, all objects can calculate their shape and position/orientation at any other random frame number. HyperMatter objects cannot. To calculate a HyperMatter object at a certain frame, it has to time step sequentially through each frame, one by one, to arrive at its new shape and position/orientation. In fact, this is done on a much finer scale than frames, as HyperMatter time steps according to a "sampling rate" or sub-frame calculation. *Sampling rate* refers to the number of internal calculations performed per MAX frame. This is the reason the progress bar comes up. HyperMatter is stepping sequentially through the frames. Generally speaking, you should get to a particular frame by typing in the frame number rather than scrubbing the frame bar.

Substances

The way a HyperMatter Solid reacts and is made to simulate many different real world materials is by means of the Substance Editor rollout. In this rollout you will find the different properties that define how rubbery or soft an object is. The properties you adjust here not only dictate the softness or hardness of the HyperMatter Solid, but also set its friction attributes and mass. The following explains each of these substance parameters.

The following are the substance properties associated with HyperMatter:

- **Elasticity.** The capability of an object once deformed, to try to return to its natural state. An elastic object maintains internal forces that try to make the object return to its natural shape. The higher the elasticity (more rigid), the harder and more bouncy the object is. The lower the elasticity (less rigid), the softer and more stretchy the object is.

- **Damping.** The force within a deformable object that tries to prevent its changing shape. Damping reduces the elastic wobble of an object and fights its momentum.

- **Incompressibility.** A HyperMatter object's attempt at maintaining volume throughout a deformation.

- **Friction.** The degree of slipping when objects collide with each other or when objects slide along the ground or bounce off walls. With less friction, objects slide more freely. With more friction, no relative motion occurs between colliding surfaces.

- **Density.** The mass per unit volume. Remember from your physics lessons that force equals mass times acceleration. The heavier (more dense) an object is, the less inclined it is to react to an implied force. Heavy objects will dominate lighter objects in collisions and move more lethargically. The lighter (less dense) an object is, the faster an object will respond and the higher it will bounce.

Rigid Objects, Dynamics, and One-Way Collisions

In the following exercise, you solve the task of animating a dice roll. This is extremely difficult to animate by traditional keyframing methods, but by using HyperMatter's built-in dynamics, it becomes an easily attainable prospect and can look very natural, as well as more dynamically accurate. Just how would you keyframe the intricate movements of a dice toss?

You will be rolling the dice across a craps table with multiple collision detection against the table surface and sides. Because the title of this exercise is "Snake Eyes," you will have to ensure that both dice end up rolling a number 1. Note that a demo version of HyperMatter was not available at the time of this printing

NOTE

The following exercise assumes that you have a copy of HyperMatter installed on your system. If you do not, install the demo version included for your convenience on the accompanying CD. This demo version enables you to go through the steps, but does not enable you to render the deformed HyperMatter objects.

SNAKE EYES

Load 17aimx.max from the accompanying CD-ROM and examine the scene. It is a simple craps table and a pair of dice. The camera has been animated to enable you to see a large part of the table for the initial toss, but animates a zoom-in that enables you to see the intricate collision with the sides of the table. This also facilitates the close-up view as HyperMatter does the subtle movements of the dice coming to rest.

1. Select Dice #1. In the Create panel, select Second Nature from the drop-down list. Then click on HyperMatter to make Dice #1 a HyperMatter Control object named **H_Dice#1**.

NOTE

When you create a HyperMatter Control object, HyperMatter automatically hides the original object and builds a new copy of the geometry as it is at that frame with all the modifiers collapsed. This is an important feature because it always enables you to go back to this original object if you need to. Do an Unhide by Name to see that the original Dice #1 is there.

2. In the HyperMatter rollout, click on Solidify Object to make all of the dice a HyperMatter Solid object. You can leave the default resolution of the HyperMatter Solid at 2.

What you have now is a copy of Dice #1, solidified in a cubic volume element. Default substance properties, Elasticity of 1 and Damping of 1, have been applied to this H_Dice #1. Knowing that a HyperMatter object "does its own thing" by acting according to physical laws, you will see that playing the scene from the Left viewport shows the object falling pursuant to gravity's effect.

The first thing you will want to do is set up one-way collision detection—one-way because HyperMatter has two ways to do collisions.

- **HyperMatter Walls.** One-way collision detection can be set up with HyperMatter Walls, which are represented like a Box object in the scene. A HyperMatter Solid, once set up, senses a HyperMatter Wall for collision detection and animates/deforms accordingly. This is very CPU-efficient.

- **Collide Constraint.** Full deformational collision detection between two HyperMatter objects can be set up. Each object senses collisions between each other by sensing when the selected solid cladding points surrounding the object collide and thus animates/deforms accordingly. This is much more CPU-intensive.

You should use HyperMatter Walls in this case because you need the dice to sense the tabletop and sides only, but don't need or want the tabletop to deform.

3. In the Create panel, while still under the Second Nature drop-down, click on Walls. In the Top viewport, drag to define the walls to the same size as the inside of the craps table (see fig. 17.2). The following values should define the length, width, and height of the walls to fit the inside of the table.

   Length = 590
   Width = 1480
   Height = 500

4. In the viewports, move the Wall object to coincide with the surface of the table, as well as with the inner sides. Play close attention to the table surface and upper-right corner of the table because this is where you will be throwing the dice and doing the collisions (again, see fig. 17.2).

If you play the scene in the Left viewport, you will see that the dice still drops according to gravity and does not collide with the walls yet. To have the walls be "seen" by H_Dice #1, you must set up a constraint (in this case, a Walls constraint). Because HyperMatter Solids "do their own thing," you need and will use constraints to get them to behave according to your script in the scene.

FIGURE 17.2

Create and position the HyperMatter Walls object to fit the inside of the craps table.

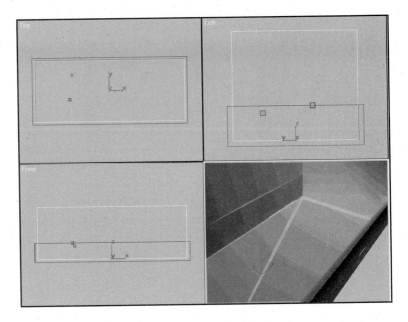

5. Select H_Dice #1 and go to the Modify panel. This is where most of your tweaking will be done to a HyperMatter Solid. Click on Sub-Object and select HyperMatter from the drop-down list. This will enable the Substance, Constraints, and Forces icons. Click on the Constraints icon (see fig. 17.3).

FIGURE 17.3

A shot of the HyperMatter Control panels, showing the Substance, Constraints, and Forces icons with the Constraints icon selected.

Notice that the various constraints are greyed out and are not ready to be used because all constraints need to be set up to affect a certain set of points in the cubic volume element. Constraints can then be set up to act on the whole object or only a sub-object selection. These *named selection sets* (of points) are created and can be selected from the top toolbar. When a HyperMatter Control object is solidified, three named selection sets of points are automatically created and named for you. These auto assigned points are the Exterior points, Interior points, and All points. Remember, the constraints act on the cladding points, and the deformation of the cladding points causes a deformation of the underlying geometry.

6. Choose the Exterior set of points from the Named Selection Set drop-down list. The exterior points in the clad will turn red, which immediately enables the various constraints. You are now able to constrain these selected points.

7. Click on the Walls constraint and click in the viewport on the H_Wall01 object you created in step 3. The Constraints drop-down list will note "WAL [Exterior]->H_Wall01," showing you that all was done correctly.

8. Get out of Sub-Object mode, and select and hide the H_Walls01 object. It is no longer necessary to see it in the scene because you will not need to see the walls for the collision to happen.

Play the scene in the Left or Front viewport and observe the collision. You have now successfully set up collision detection between the H_Dice #1 HyperMatter Solid and the HyperMatter Walls, which will appear to look like collision detection against the tabletop. Also notice how fast the display playback is; one-way collision detection is very CPU-efficient.

TIP

HyperMatter works on the basis of *time stepping*. In other words, HyperMatter Solids are calculated a frame at a time starting from the first frame and every frame sequentially thereafter. You should get in the habit of moving through frames by playing the scene or typing the frame number. Scrubbing the frame bar may cause unnecessary processing and cause your display to wait. This is evident by a *HyperMatter: Processing* progress bar while it is calculating, frame by frame, the HyperMatter effect. This will be more apparent as your scene gets more complicated.

As you may have noticed during playback, the die is kind of soft and squishy—because the default substance property given to all HyperMatter objects is soft and squishy. HyperMatter is by definition a soft-body dynamics system. It is capable of representing rigid objects as well, and this is the purpose of the Substance parameter rollout. Go ahead and make the die a bit harder.

9. Select H_Dice#1, go to the Modify panel, select Sub-Object HyperMatter, and click on the Substance Editor icon. Set Elasticity to 10, Damping to 30, Incompressibility (Incompress.) to 0, Friction to 0.75, and Density to 2.

Now play the scene in the Left viewport and notice how rigid the die appears. The lists provided in the "Throwing the Dice" exercise give a quick reference of Substance parameters.

See the HyperMatter manual for more information about substance properties. Now is a good time to hold your scene.

Using the HyperMatter Velocity Constraint

Now that you have been successful in creating a rigid die and causing it to collide with the table, examine the ways that you can toss the die down the table. As is true for most operations in MAX, you can accomplish this task in many different ways, including the following:

- Keyframe the die to move down the table and have HyperMatter take over the velocity at the first key.

- Apply HyperMatter forces to push the die down the table. You are already using default forces in the negative Z (–100) for gravity.

- Use the HyperMatter Velocity constraint.

All of these are viable choices, but you will use the last option in the following steps. You may want to experiment on your own with the other two later. You will also be working with HyperMatter's capability to inherit an object's momentum in an exercise later in this chapter.

THROWING THE DICE

1. While still in the Modify panel, select All points from the Named Selection Set drop-down list. Choose the Constraints icon, and then click on the Velocity constraint. VEL[All] appears in the Constraints list.

2. Click on VEL[All] from the constraints list (below the various constraints buttons) to highlight it and bring up the Velocity panel controls. Click on the Enable check box to the right of X in the Velocity rollout and type **250**.

Most constraints are animatable, and they all have a lifespan during which the constraints are enabled. Lifespans can be set separately for each constraint. What you have to do here is give the die some initial velocity to get it moving and then turn off the velocity at a latter frame. If you were to keep the velocity constraint active throughout the entire animation, the die would try to push through the Walls object collision and strange behavior might occur.

WARNING

As was mentioned at the beginning of this chapter, it is important always to be at frame 0 when applying constraints. If you are at a frame other than frame 0, say frame 50 when you apply a constraint, HyperMatter will automatically set its lifespan to start at the current frame, frame 50 in this case.

3. Just above the Velocity rollout is the Start and End Lifespan for this Velocity constraint. Leave the Start at 0 and set the End of its lifespan to frame 60. This should give the die enough momentum to create the toss.

4. Click on the Refresh button in the HyperMatter Control section of the rollout.

You have done quite a bit of tweaking to the Substance and Constraints of this die, so it is advisable to manually refresh the dynamics of the scene now and then when dynamics are as important as they are here. HyperMatter automatically refreshes itself under most conditions.

Play the scene from the Camera view and notice how the velocity of the die rolls it down the craps table. Look at how nicely the collision is with the surface and how the die tumbles as it collides. Notice the collision at the end of the table and the subtlety as the die comes to rest. Smile because you appreciate how difficult this would have been to keyframe so naturally.

Velocity in the X is okay, but a bit of Y velocity is in order to make the action of the die and its collisions more interesting.

5. While still in the Modify panel, Velocity rollout, and VEL[All] still highlighted, click on the Y Enable check box and set this to 30.

Play the scene again from the Camera viewport. Notice that the animation has changed, providing better action with the die as it also is striking the other side wall of the table.

How about rolling snake eyes? How do you roll the die to end up with a 1 rather than a 6 (as it does now)?

You'd hate to retweak the animation and dynamics to try to find a toss that ended up rolling a 1. The numbers on the sides of the dice are maps in a Multi-Sub-Object material. The best way to accomplish this is just to swap the maps between the 1 map and the 6 map. If your die rolls a 1 skip step 6.

6. Open the Material Editor. Select the Dice #1 Multi-Sub-Object material from slot 1 and click on the Material 1 Dice 6 material. Change the Diffuse texture map Dice 6.tga to the Dice 1.tga bitmap. This replaces the 6 on the die at rest with 1. You must also replace the Dice 1.tga bitmap for Sub-object material 6 Dice 1 to Dice 6.tga, so as not to be cheating with non-standard dice.

Play the scene and notice that H_Dice#1 now rolls a 1.

When satisfied with your HyperMatter dynamics setup—and especially if you are about to go further with the scene by adding more HyperMatter objects—it is advisable and highly recommended to lock in the dynamics by making the object a Record object.

A Record object is basically that: a recorder. A HyperMatter object turned into a Record object behaves the same way as the original HyperMatter object did, but is no longer a HyperMatter Solid as its actions become set. It does not change when influenced by other HyperMatter objects, constraints, or walls, and you will not be able to change any of its HyperMatter attributes. Think of a Record object as a sort of Morph object set up to behave like the original object did at the time it was made a Record object.

Basically, Record makes a new copy of the HyperMatter Control object (with an R_ prefix) and uses a special HyperMatter Record Controller with associated keyframes to match the original position and rotation and deformation.

7. Select the HyperMatter H_Dice #1 object, go to the Create panel, Second Nature drop-down, and choose Record. In the HyperMatter Record rollout, choose Auto Create Keys. HyperMatter will take a minute to calculate the Record Object. In the Create Record Keys dialog box, change the Key Creation Timing to every 2 frames and then click on OK. Select and hide H_Dice #1.

Now that you are somewhat familiar with the setup of the first die, go ahead and experiment with the second die or use the following settings to set Dice #2. Don't be afraid to change any of these settings. Observe the difference in action after each change.

8. For Dice #2, make it a HyperMatter object, and Solidify Object.

9. In the Modify panel, Substances Editor set:
   Elasticity 10
   Damping 30
   Incompress 0
   Friction .75
   Density 2

10. In the Constraints rollout set a Velocity constraint to All constraint points:
    VEL [All]
    Lifespan: Start 20
    Lifespan: End 100
    X: 220
    Y: 60

11. In the Constraints rollout, set up a Walls constraint using Exterior as the selected set of points. Then pick the H_Walls01 object by using Select By Name. Using the Pick Object dialog box enables you to select the Walls object without first unhiding it.

    WAL[Exterior]->H_Wall01 appears in the drop-down list.

12. If you used these settings and all went well, this die should roll a 1. If your die rolls anything besides a 1, assign the Dice #2 material from the Material Editor and swap bitmaps for the actual number rolled with the Material 6 Dice 1 bitmap DICE1.tga (see fig. 17.4).

FIGURE 17.4

This is the Camera view of the dice after they have come to rest with a roll of snake eyes.

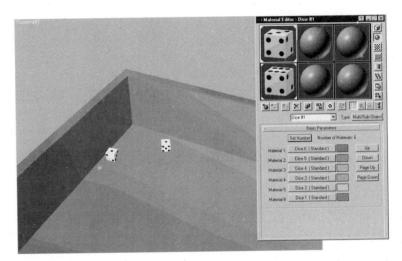

13. Make this H_Dice #2 HyperMatter Solid into a Record object as you did in step 7 for H_Dice #1.

Play the scene and notice how well HyperMatter has dynamically rolled the dice. Also note how well the subtleties of the dice, as they come to rest, have been represented.

View the rendered animation snakeyes.avi from the accompanying CD.

Fully Deformable Collision Detection Between Two Objects

In the following exercise, you use HyperMatter to create a silly carnival duck shoot animation. Silly because it will not be a plain old wooden duck that just falls down when hit. Not that HyperMatter would have a problem with this, but it would be more interesting if the duck were not so rigid. What would be the reaction if a ball hit a rubber duck?

In the last exercise, you did simple one-way collision detection with HyperMatter Walls. In this exercise, you will use the Collide constraint to do fully deformational collision detection between two MAX objects. You will also explore the Fix constraint and see how HyperMatter deals with the velocity of a keyframed ball.

DUCK SHOOT

Go ahead and load 18bimx.max. The scene consists of a dual duck target set up on a shaft. You will be tossing a ball at the upper duck to win the prize. Set that up now.

1. In the Create panel, select Second Nature from the drop-down list. Select the duck. Then turn it into a HyperMatter Control object by clicking on HyperMatter, and then solidify it by clicking on the Solidify Object button.

TIP

Keep the solidify resolution down to the lowest setting you can use and still be able to get the job done. This saves CPU cycles and speeds up the interaction of your scene.

Notice that the default resolution setup for the duck is 2. You have the ability to change this default by clicking on the Options button at the bottom of this rollout. Remember, it is the clad surface itself that will do the checking for collisions, so you should examine the fit direction. Because you will be tossing the ball at the duck from the front, you should make a change from the default fit in the X direction.

2. Go to the Modify panel and try cladding in the different fit directions X, Y, and Z (see fig. 17.5).

FIGURE 17.5

The result of "fitting" the solid cladding in the different X, Y, and Z directions.

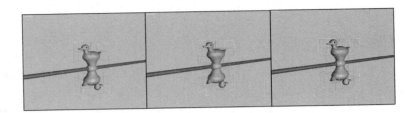

The difference in the fit directions may seem subtle at first and they are in fact very similar. The important point here is that the duck is being set up to swing around the pole when hit, so you will need to hold in place a row of points in the very center (of the duck and the pole) for the duck to swing around, which will have a result of looking like the duck is indeed held to the pole. Not choosing the correct fit direction in this step is important enough to make the difference between whether the gag will work or not.

Although the Fit Y direction seems to give the best fit for a collision from the front, a compromise will have to be made to make the duck swing around the pole. Therefore, you will need a set of clad points in the very center for the constraint and a Fit Z seems to be best.

3. Because the Fit Y has no point in the center, the next best fit would be in the Z direction. Choose Fit Z. Note that this may seem to go against the intended use of fit direction, but it should not impact your collision accuracy enough to be a problem.

Next you need to set up a couple of constraints. Remember that HyperMatter objects "do their own thing" according to physical and dynamic laws. You use constraints to place any point in the solidify clad anywhere in the scene you want it, at any time you want it. The order in which you set up constraints will have no bearing on the outcome, but you will set up the collision constraint first.

4. Go to the Modify Panel. Select Sub-Object HyperMatter mode. From the Named Selection Sets drop-down list, select the auto assigned Exterior points.

Notice how many points will be collision tested. You can minimize this by using the MAX selection tools.

5. Click in a viewport to unselect the Exterior points. Then from the Left viewport, select just the top front points of the duck cladding (see fig. 17.6). Name this selection **Duck front** in the Named Selection Set drop-down list.

TIP

Doing collisions between two HyperMatter objects can get very CPU-intensive so you should always be thinking of ways to minimize the number of points being examined for collision.

6. Click on the Constraints icon and click on Collide. COL[Duck front] appears in the *constraints* list.

FIGURE 17.6

Select the top front set of points on the Duck clad for use with the Collide constraint and name them Duck front.

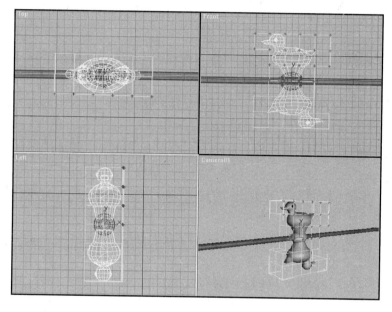

Besides the use of Exterior, Interior, and All Named Selection Sets that are automatically assigned, you are free to select your own as you have just seen. You can save and constrain any number of Named Selection Sets. Because the action required here is to have the duck spin around the pole after the ball hits it, you will need a way to hold the duck to that pole.

Examine the Fix Constraint

A "fixed" point may not move in the scene, but it can rotate around itself. The fixed point can rotate in place, but it is not allowed to rotate around any selection center because this would "move" the point in the scene. This was the reason you selected the Fit Z in step 3 to get the row of points in the center of the duck.

1. In the Left viewport, select just the row of points in the center of the duck (see fig. 17.7). Call this Named Selection Set **Center** and click on Enter to enable the Constraints buttons. Click on the Fix constraint. FIX[Center] appears in the constraints list.

FIGURE 17.7

Select the center row of points for the Fix constraint and name the selection set Center.

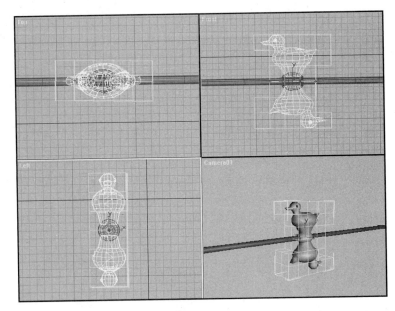

Play the scene from the Camera view and notice that even with the default gravity, the center points stay fixed in space. The rest of the duck can wobble about slightly, all within the constraint of the fixed points and the default substance properties.

The duck is a bit too wobbly, so you should tighten it up a bit.

2. Still in the Modify panel, click on the Substance icon. Open the Library roll-up, click on Use Library and pick Vibrate from the drop-down Library list of pre-assigned substances.

This is a great HyperMatter feature. It enables you to quickly set up a substance in terms that you can quickly grasp and identify with. It is often advantageous to use a Library material to get close to the substance you want. From there you can easily tweak it to fit your needs by means of the Copy Library Substance to Local icon. This enables the adjustment of Elasticity, Damping, and the rest of the Substance properties as usual starting from the settings of the Library Substance.

Now that the Duck is set up, go ahead and throw the ball at it.

3. Play the scene and notice that it is already keyframed to be thrown at the duck through frame 40.

4. Make certain that you are at frame 0. Go to the Create panel and make the sphere a HyperMatter Control object and Solidify object.

Play the scene and notice that the object keeps the keyframed info and HyperMatter makes it fall under its own gravity. More important is the fact that HyperMatter calculated the speed of the sphere from frame 0 and maintained that velocity from there. HyperMatter then ignores the keyframed stop at frame 40, because this keyframe was only used to set up the velocity for HyperMatter to assume.

NOTE

HyperMatter is capable of precisely interpreting the keyframed velocity of an object. This provides a transparent transition from keyframed animation to real-world physics.

It seems the ball's gravity may be a bit much for your scene; your ball is moving in slow-motion. HyperMatter even enables you to play with the effects of gravity. Actually, you can set forces in any direction. You could even use a force of Y to throw the ball, although it would accelerate much differently than it does now.

5. In the Modify panel, Sub-Object HyperMatter, select the Forces icon. Set the Z force to –50.

6. Click on the Constraints icon, select the Exterior set of points from the Named Selection Set drop-down in the toolbar, and click on Collide.

7. Click on the Substances icon and open the Library rollout. Select the library substance Power Ball from the drop-down.

Play the scene and notice that the ball just doesn't have enough *oomph* to knock over the duck. Going back to your memory of physics, you remember that force equals mass times acceleration. Therefore, heavy objects will dominate lighter objects in collisions. The duck has a density (mass) of 1 and the sphere also has a density of 1. You should increase the density of the sphere so that it will dominate in the resultant collision.

8. While still in the Modify panel, H_Sphere01 selected, and in Sub-Object HyperMatter mode, select the Substance icon. Under the Library Substance rollout, click on the Copy Library Substance to Local icon. Then under the Properties rollout, Attributes section, raise the Density to 4.

Play the scene in the Camera viewport now and notice the difference. The heavier, or denser, ball knocks the duck pretty good. In fact it hits it hard enough to spin the duck completely around the pole.

View the rendered animation duck_col.avi from the accompanying CD.

This is a very interesting file to experiment with, especially the Density settings of both the duck and ball. Also notice the effect different substance settings such as Elasticity and Damping have when applied to the duck. You can get some wild effects from a little experimentation here. You may even be able to get a double collision as the ball stops its forward momentum just enough to bring it into contact with the duck a second time. Note here that you would have to redo the Collide constraint to use the Exterior set of points, not just the Duck Front selection set that was originally set up for efficiency's sake.

There are a couple of extra rendered versions on the accompanying CD, created during experimentation for this exercise. Feel free to view them, and maybe come up with a few cool duck shot animations of your own.

Inheriting the Keyframed Momentum

In the following exercise, you work with HyperMatter to help with animating the game of curling. If you are not familiar with the sport of curling, it has to do with bowling a "stone" with a handle toward a target laid out on ice. It is kind of like shuffleboard. Perhaps you remember the Beatles in the movie *Help* playing a game of curling? (Although you would think that Ringo would surely have noticed that one of the stones was actually a bomb.)

HyperMatter will help you in the exercise because you will be using HyperMatter's Friction parameter to take care of the deceleration of the stones as they come to rest on the ice. You will also set up one of the stones to knock another out of the target, which HyperMatter's Collide constraint will solve for you. You will use another constraint not previously covered in these exercises called Fix Orientation. The Fix Orientation constraint prevents a HyperMatter from tumbling or rotating. This file also shows how wonderfully easy it is to have HyperMatter inherit the momentum from traditional keyframed objects.

CURLING

Begin by loading 17cimx.max from the accompanying CD. Examine the scene to see that the rink and targets have been set up, and that a single stone has been placed at one end. Notice that there are also three dummy objects and that these dummies have already been keyframed.

1. Select the object STONE rubber. In the Create panel, choose Second Nature from the drop-down list and click on HyperMatter to turn it into a HyperMatter Control object. Then solidify it by picking Solidify Object.

To keep the object from falling and to give it a surface to travel across and sense friction from, you will create a HyperMatter Wall object.

2. In the Create panel, Second Nature drop-down, click on Walls. Drag in the Top Viewport to create a Walls object totally surrounding the curling target layout (see fig. 17.8).

FIGURE 17.8
Create the Walls object to totally surround the curling target layout.

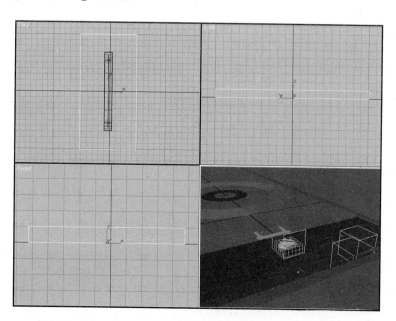

3. Unhide the ICE Plane object. Zoom in enough to the stone, in the Front or Left Viewports, to enable you to see that the Walls object is a bit above the ICE plane. Move the Walls so that they are level with the ICE plane and be certain that the stone is sitting on the ICE plane and Walls object (see fig. 17.9.).

4. Hide the Walls object.

FIGURE 17.9

Be certain to move the HyperMatter Walls object so that it is on the same Z plane as the second ICE plane object.

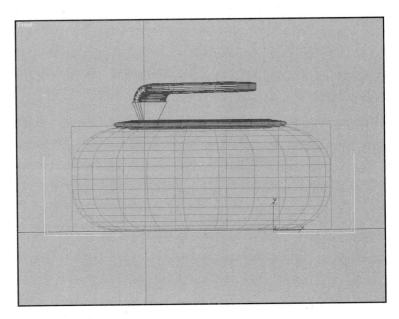

5. Select the Stone and go to the Modify panel. Go into Sub-Object HyperMatter mode and click on the Constraints icon. In the Named Selection Set drop-down, choose All the HyperMatter points and then choose the Walls constraint. Choose Select by Name from the toolbar or press the H key, and then pick the H_Wall01 object. The constraint list should read Wal[All]->H_Wall01.

Play the scene. The stone now rests on the ice but is a bit more rubbery than needed.

6. While still in the Modify panel, Sub-Object HyperMatter mode, click on the Substance Editor icon. In the Attributes section, click on the Elasticity/Damping lock and set the Elasticity to 4 (which also sets Damping to 4).

Playing the scene shows that the stone is a harder rubber and about right for the scene's needs. This would be a good time to Hold your scene.

Now for the task of throwing the stone toward the target. As mentioned previously, there are numerous ways to accomplish this task. In this instance, dummy objects have already been created for the initial throw of the stone, and thus the movement will be nicely created with HyperMatter inheriting that momentum.

7. Release Sub-Object mode. Link H_STONE rubber to the dummy surrounding it. Link the Stone Handle to the H_STONE rubber. In the Dispay panel, turn off Hide by Category, Cameras. Select the Camera (linked) and the Camera (linked) Target and link them to the stone.

8. Maximize the Camera (linked) view and play the scene.

NOTE

HyperMatter is quite heavy in terms of a plug-in. It may even be stretching the limits of the MAX 1.x SDK (Software Developers Kit). It may be necessary and advisable at times to click on the Refresh button located in the HyperMatter rollout of the Modify panel. If your scene is not responding to the link in step 7, this may be one of those Refresh times.

At this point, you should take notice of the following:

- Notice how well the stone has inherited the motion from the keyframed dummy object.

- Notice that although the dummy object has a keyframe at frame 59 to stop, a HyperMatter object ignores this. Only the initial velocity at the time of HyperMatter initialization is assumed by the HM object.

- Notice that the default friction creates such a drag on the stone that the stone actually flips and tumbles after a few frames.

9. In the Modify panel, Sub-Object HyperMatter mode, Substances icon, set Friction to 0.45.

Play the scene. Now the motion is starting to look good. Congratulations, you have thrown the stone inside the red outer circle.

Perhaps you could calm down the slow wobble of the stone as it glides. The substances seem fine for this stone rubber, so you will go elsewhere to solve this tweak.

10. Still in Sub-Object HyperMatter mode, select the Constraints icon. Select All set of points from the Named Selection Sets drop-down list. Select the Fix Orientation button. Notice ORI[All] appears in the Constraints list indicating that the HyperMatter object is not allowed to spin. ORI = Fix Orientation (No spin)

Play the scene. The stone no longer spins or wobbles but still maintains its substance characteristics. It may not be apparent while playing the scene, but if you create a preview (or view 17c-pre.avi from the accompanying CD), you will see the wonderfully subtle secondary motion as the stone comes to rest. The camera link enables you to *feel* this effect. This overshadows the dynamically correct deceleration caused by friction that was automatically computed by HyperMatter.

11. Select the H_STONE rubber and STONE Handle objects. Hold down the Shift key and, from the Top viewport, drag (copy) them into the lowest dummy object, Dummy02. While they are still selected, click on the Unlink icon on the toolbar to release their link from the first dummy.

12. Link H_STONE rubber01 to Dummy02, and then link STONE handle01 to the H_STONE rubber01.

Play the scene from the Top viewport. Notice that the link is apparently not working; this stone does not move with the dummy to which it is linked when you play the scene. If you select and move the dummy, however, you will see that the link is working. Why isn't the HyperMatter object moving with the animated dummy?

NOTE

If you remember, it was explained earlier in this exercise that "only the initial velocity at the time of HyperMatter initialization is assumed by the HyperMatter object." HyperMatter initialization starts at frame 0 by default and this dummy object starts moving at frame 50. Therefore HyperMatter does not see the velocity at frame 50. It has inherited the dummy's velocity at frame 0, which is, of course, a velocity of zero.

13. With Dummy02 and H_STONE rubber01 selected, go into Track View and filter for selected objects only. Expand the H_STONE rubber01 track, and the Object (HyperMatter Control) track to get to the Lifespan track. Grab the left end of the range bar and drag that end to line up with frame 50. This will correspond with the dummy's first key, and thus HyperMatter will initialize at frame 50 to "see" the momentum of the dummy to which it is linked.

Play the scene and see that the HyperMatter initialization has correctly linked the stone to the dummy. Press the Refresh button if necessary.

14. Change the Camera (linked) view to the Camera02 view. Play the scene now to see that the stone decelerates and ends up in the inner blue target.

Now throw one more stone.

15. In the Top viewport, select the second stone and handle and shift copy them into the third dummy. With the two objects still selected, unlink these objects. As before, link the H_STONE rubber02 to the dummy and the STONE handle02 to the H_STONE rubber02.

16. Go into Track View and move the start of the Range bar for the Lifespan of H_STONE rubber02 to frame 100 (as you did before). This now matches the start keyframe for the dummy to which it is linked.

Play the scene and see that you have thrown this stone through the last stone throw. Click on the Refresh button if necessary. This path is lain on purpose because you can now set up a collision to push the second stone out of the way.

17. Go to frame 275, which is just before the two stones collide. Zoom in to these stones in the Top viewport and Maximize the view.

18. Select H_STONE rubber01 and go into the Modify panel, Sub-Object HyperMatter mode. Click on the Constraint icon. Select the front row of points and call this Named Selection Set **Front** in the Named Selection Sets drop-down list, and then press Enter (see fig. 17.10).

FIGURE 17.10

Select these points in the clad, call the selection set Front, and set up a Collide constraint to start at frame 275 for the second stone.

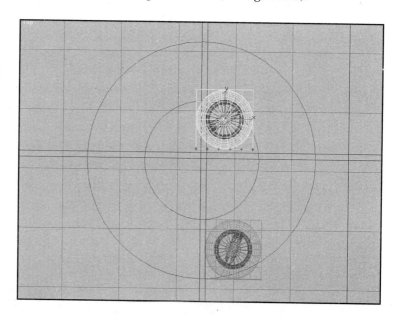

19. Click on the Collide constraint. COL [Front] appears in the Constraint drop-down list. Highlight this COL [Front] and notice that HyperMatter has automatically set up the Lifespan for the Collide constraint to start at frame 275, the current frame.

20. Click on the Select Next HyperMatter Object button to quickly change to the third stone. Select the back row of points, call this Named Selection Set **Back**, and then press Enter (see fig. 17.11). Click on the Collide constraint.

FIGURE 17.11

Select these points, call the selection set Back, and set up a Collide constraint to start at frame 275 for the third stone.

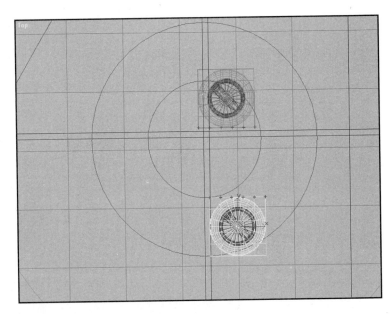

Play the scene from this top view. Remember that you may have to click on the Refresh button. A great collision has been created, and you have been successful in knocking the second stone out of the target and replacing it with this last stone throw.

View the rendered animation included on the accompanying CD as Curling.avi.

Sub-Object Solidification of a HyperMatter Control Object

You should now be familiar with most of HyperMatter's command panels and parameters. You have touched on most of them in the last few exercises and should be somewhat comfortable moving around in them. The one thing common to the previous exercises is that all the HyperMatter Control objects were solidified using the whole object. This may be acceptable in quite a few instances, but sooner or later you will want to have HyperMatter influence only a portion of an object, or influence different portions of an object in different ways. For this reason, you are given the separate Sub-Object mode of Geometry.

In this exercise, you add a bit of motion to a running mouse. Perhaps you remember watching the Olympics and observing how radically the faces of the sprinting runners were affected by the motion of the run itself. You will try to duplicate some of that here. Specifically, you will be using HyperMatter to sub-object solidify portions of the head of a running mouse, using the motion of the mouse head to affect the different parts of the head geometry with different substance attributes.

RUNNING MOUSE

Load 17dimx.max from the accompanying CD and meet Mortimer Mouse courtesy of Viewpoint Datalabs. Play the scene and observe that Mortimer has already been keyframed with a basic running motion, and that his head has a good movement from which HyperMatter can work.

1. From the Create panel, choose Second Nature from the drop-down list. Select Mortimer's head and click on HyperMatter. Do not click on Solidify Object. (Sub-object solidify is done in the modify panel.)

2. Go to the Modify panel and click on Sub-Object to get into Sub-Object Geometry mode. Change the viewport to the Front view. In the top toolbar, change the Rectangular Selection Region icon to Fence Selection Region. Zoom in so the head fills the viewport.

Now you are ready to select the faces from the mouse head from which you will sub-object solidify. You will be creating a few separate selections including the ears, snoot, nose, and eyebrows.

3. Drag a fence selection in the Front viewport to select just the ear on your left (Mortimer's right ear) (see fig. 17.12). Make certain that you select all the ear. Perform an Arc Rotate Selected and spin the viewport around to make certain. Name this selection set **Ear Right** in the Named Selection Sets drop-down list.

FIGURE 17.12

Select all the faces of Mortimer's right ear for the first sub-object solidification. (3D models by Viewpoint Datalabs International, Inc.)

4. Scroll the HyperMatter Control panel down to get to the Automatic Solids rollout. Notice that in this mode of sub-object geometry, the Solidify button reads Solidify Sub-Object. Click on this Solidify Sub-Object button. Rename the Sub-Object HyperMatter Solid from SO_face_1 to **SO_Ear Right**.

You have now made a HyperMatter sub-object solid out of Mortimer's right ear. Notice that the cladding at sub-object level has a default resolution of 6 as opposed to the default for object level solidify of 2. Generally speaking, a higher resolution is needed for sub-objects.

NOTE

The default resolution for both solidify whole and solidify sub-object is an option you can set. If you take a look at the bottom of this Automatic Solids rollout, you will see an Options button. Click on this button to set the default resolutions. Of note here is that these settings (and other HyperMatter preferences set elsewhere) are saved in the Windows Registry, making them configurable per user. Therefore, if another user were to log on after you and change your preferences, he would still be working with the default preferences.

Note the following two differences when working with sub-object solids:

■ There is a separate default resolution set up for whole object solidify and sub-object solidify when performing an automatic solidification.

■ HyperMatter automatically creates a Named Selection Set of points called Join. Furthermore, a Fix constraint is automatically set up to use these points to hold it to the HyperMatter Control.

Play the scene to see how the sub-object solidified ear reacts to Mortimer's head movements. Notice that it is a bit too soft.

5. Go into Sub-Object HyperMatter mode, click on the Substance Editor icon to get to the Substance panel, and set Elasticity to 2.5 and Damping to 2.0.

Go ahead and sub-object solidify Mortimer's left ear.

6. Change to the Front viewport, go into Sub-Object Geometry mode and select the faces of Mortimer's left ear (see fig. 17.13). Name this selection set **Ear Left**. Click on the Automatic Solidify icon and then click on the Solidify Sub-Object button. Rename this sub-object HyperMatter Solid to **SO_Ear Left**.

FIGURE 17.13
Select the faces of Mortimer's left ear for the second sub-object solid. (3D models by Viewpoint Datalabs International, Inc.)

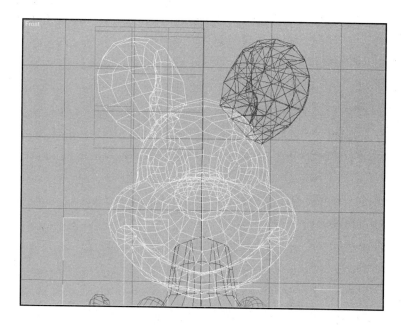

7. Go into Sub-Object HyperMatter mode, click on the Substance Editor icon to get to the Substance panel, and change Elasticity to 2.5 and Damping to 2.0.

Now go ahead and create a HyperMatter sub-object solid out of Mortimer's snout. This is a good time to Hold your scene.

8. Change the viewport to the Left view and zoom in close to the snout. Go into Sub-Object Geometry mode, and with Fence Selection mode still active, select the faces making up the snout (see fig. 17.14). Name this selection set **Snout** in the Named Selection Set drop-down.

FIGURE 17.14

Select these faces of the snout in preparation of sub-object solidification. (3D models by Viewpoint Datalabs International, Inc.)

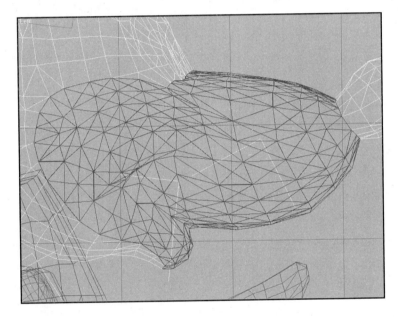

9. Select the Automatic Solidify icon and choose Solidify Sub-Object. Rename the Sub-Object solid to **SO_snout**.

10. Go into Sub-Object HyperMatter mode and click on the Substance Editor icon, set Elasticity to 5 and Damping to 4. Change the viewport to Camera view and play the scene.

Notice that with these substance settings, the snout appears to react well to the running motion and jiggles as if the face were actually reacting to the force of the footsteps. Now go ahead and create a HyperMatter sub-object solid out of Mortimer's nose.

11. Change the viewport to the Left view. Go into Sub-Object Geometry mode and use the Fence Selection tool to select just the faces of the nose (see fig. 17.15). Name this selection set **Nose**.

FIGURE 17.15

Select these faces of the nose for sub-object solidification. (3D models by Viewpoint Datalabs International, Inc.)

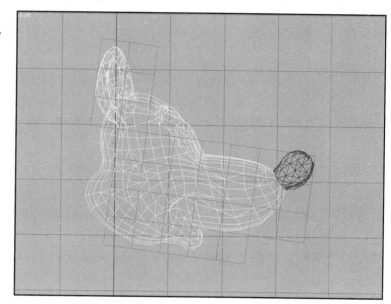

12. Select the Automatic Solidify icon and choose Solidify Sub-Object to rubberize his nose. Rename this sub-object **SO_Nose**. Change the viewport to the Camera view. Get into Sub-Object HyperMatter mode, Substance panel, and change the Damping to 4.

Play the scene and notice how Mortimer's nose is now reacting to the movement of the head and also to the HyperMatter deformation of the snout. Mortimer Mouse is getting very cartoon-like.

NOTE

Feel free to experiment with these substance parameters. These exercises, after all, were created so that you could gain insight into HyperMatter's parameters. And like any other project, experimentation can lead to wonderful new insight.

Just be certain to return to the parameters mentioned here before going on with the exercise; otherwise unexpected behavior may result and cause confusion in later steps.

The great thing about sub-object solidifying a HyperMatter Control object such as this is that you can continue to the sub-object solidify portions until the object has just the dynamic motion you like. Remember how different parts of the Olympic runners' faces were affected by the force and power of the sprint? Mortimer's eyebrows seem to be crying out for a bit of this reaction, don't you think?

The faces of the eyebrows are going to be a bit trickier to select. It would be advantageous to simplify the scene as much as possible before proceeding.

13. With Mortimer's head selected, go into the Display panel and Hide Unselected (or use your keyboard shortcut). Back in the Modify panel, go into Sub-Object HyperMatter mode and click on the Display Preferences icon.

In this rollout, you can turn on or off much of HyperMatter's display attributes. Not only can you show or hide the solidify cladding, you can also adjust how you would like it displayed. The default is to show all faces of the clad, but you also have the choice of showing just the edges or points.

You also have the choice of showing just the solidify cladding and hiding the geometry. Taking that a step further, you can also highlight the geometry of the selected sub-object solidify.

One more button at the bottom of this panel enables you to set the options for the color used to display Solids, Sub-Object selections, and so forth. Remember that these are saved in the Windows Registry, and thus are configurable by each user.

14. In the Display Preferences rollout, click on Hide All to hide all of the sub-object solidify claddings. Change the viewport to the Front view, then perform an Arc Rotate Selected and spin the view so that Mortimer's right eyebrow is isolated with no other geometry behind it. Make certain that you are in Sub-Object Geometry mode and Fence select the eyebrow faces (see fig. 17.16).

15. Arc Rotate again to get a straight-on view of the selected eyebrow, and while holding down the Ctrl key, add to the existing selection set by selecting the faces immediately adjacent to the eyebrow faces. Name this selection set **Eyebrow Right** (see fig. 17.17).

FIGURE 17.16

Arc Rotate the view to select these faces of the eyebrow. (3D models by Viewpoint Datalabs International, Inc.)

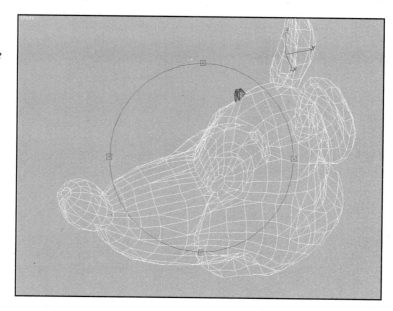

FIGURE 17.17

Arc Rotate again to select these faces surrounding the eyebrow, adding the faces to the last selection. (3D models by Viewpoint Datalabs International, Inc.)

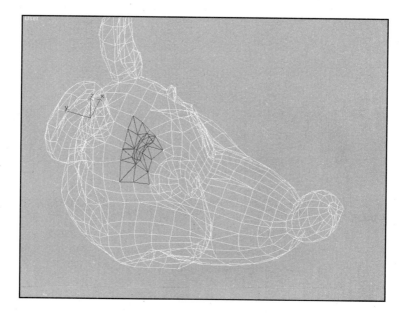

16. Select the Automatic Solidify icon and Solidify Sub-Object. Rename this sub-object selection **SO_Eyebrow Right**. Get into Sub-Object HyperMatter mode, Substance panel, and change Elasticity and Damping to .7. Change the viewport to the Camera view.

Play the scene. This character is starting to get some real personality. You can finish by doing a HyperMatter sub-object solidify to the other eyebrow.

17. Repeat steps 14, 15, and 16 for Mortimer's left eyebrow. Select the same area of faces around this eyebrow (see fig. 17.18). Use the same substance values and substitute the name **Eyebrow Left** in both the Named Selection Set drop down and the sub-object solidify solid name.

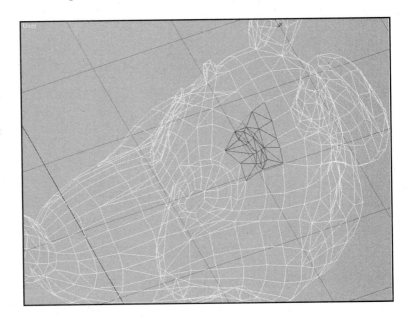

FIGURE 17.18

Select these faces for Sub-Object Solidification of Mortimer's left eyebrow. (3D models by Viewpoint Datalabs International, Inc.)

18. Change to the Camera view. Unhide all the objects except for the original Face object that was copied by HyperMatter and then hidden.

Play the scene. Notice the sub-object solids reacting, all in their own substance ways, to the keyframed motion of Mortimer Mouse running.

View the rendered scene. It is included on the accompanying CD as mouserun.avi. The same file rendered without HyperMatter is included for comparison as nohm.avi.

Animating Substance Parameters and the Follow Constraint

In this exercise, you will work again with Mortimer Mouse. You will actually be working with a manufacturing line of rubber mice on a conveyor. This part of the manufacturing line is testing the mice for the consistency of the rubber material. As the conveyor starts and stops, any inconsistency in the rubber material is detected. When an overly soft mouse is found, it is taken (or rather thrown) off the line.

In the following exercise, you are introduced to a new HyperMatter parameter, Follow. The Follow constraint is a very useful constraint, one that enables you to have any point in the HyperMatter Solid follow any other object in the scene. This constraint, like the other constraints, has an adjustable lifespan, which enables you to follow the particular object during the frames you deem necessary only.

NOTE

The Follow constraint, in certain regards, can be thought of as a specialized type of link. This link would have two big differences from what you normally think of as a Hierarchy link. One is that the link can be used with the whole HyperMatter Solid or with any sub-object portion of the HyperMatter Solid using point selection sets. The other difference is that you can set up as many Follow constraints as needed, making it possible to give each Follow a different lifespan—thus having multiple links to different objects within the same animation.

You will set up multiple follow constraints in this exercise and will even go so far as to overlap the lifetime of the Follow constraints for an interesting stretching effect.

Although you have been told that HyperMatter substances can be animated, you have not animated any Substance parameters in the exercises yet. You will animate both the Elasticity and Damping parameters in this exercise, causing a very nice tightening of the substance over time, which can be useful if you want a very elastic object, and yet want to control how long it continues to wobble.

This exercise is quite involved, so it has been broken up into two parts. In the first part, you set up the mice as HyperMatter Solids and move them on the conveyor. The second part includes a mechanism that picks up the mouse and throws it off the conveyor.

MOUSE REJECT, PART 1

Load 17eimx.max from the accompanying CD and check out the scene. Notice that three mice are on the conveyor and that a dummy object is animated below. This dummy will be the impetus that moves the mice down the line.

1. Select the first mouse named Mouse 1. In the Create panel, choose Second Nature from the drop-down list and click on HyperMatter to turn the first mouse into a HyperMatter Control object. Click on Solidify Object. Make Z the Fit Direction so that the solid cladding is tight against the feet.

2. In the Modify panel, go into Sub-Object HyperMatter mode and select the Substance Editor icon. Set Elasticity to 18 and Damping to 15. This will be the normal mouse substance property.

3. Go back to the Create panel, select the third mouse, named Mouse 3. Choose Second Nature from the drop-down list and click on HyperMatter. Click on Solidify Object. Set Fit Direction in the Z direction if necessary, although the Fit Direction choice should be sticky within the MAX session.

4. Go to the Modify panel, Sub-Object HyperMatter mode, and select the Substance Editor icon. Set Elasticity to 18 and Damping to 15 (just as you did for Mouse 1).

5. Go to the Create panel, select the mouse named Mouse 2, Choose Second Nature from the drop-down list, and click on HyperMatter. Click on Solidify Object and raise the Resolution to 3. Be certain that Fit Z is active.

You have raised the resolution of the solid clad on Mouse 2 because this mouse will be defective and as such will be acting differently than the others. You will be having some real fun with this mouse, so more detail will give you better action. By the way, this creates the perfect solid cladding resolution for the tail. With a resolution of 2, the solid cladding holds the tip of the tail rather rigidly to the body as witnessed by the continuous cladding across the bottom, from front to tail tip. With a resolution of 3, the tail is separated from the body much better.

6. In the Modify panel, with H_Mouse 2 still selected, get into Sub-Object HyperMatter mode, and choose the Substance Editor icon. Set Elasticity to 5 and Damping to 2.

If you play the scene, you will notice the typical HyperMatter Gravity affecting the mice and making them fall.

(Be certain that Real Time is off in the Time configuration dialog box.) You have used HyperMatter Walls before to keep this from happening, but walls and their associated collision and friction is not what is needed here. You need to keep the mice from falling and move them effortlessly forward. This is where the Follow constraint comes in.

7. Select the first HyperMatter mouse H_Mouse 1 (use the Select Next HyperMatter Object button). Click on the Constraints icon. Change the view to the maximized Left viewport and zoom in closer to the first mouse.

TIP

Use the Select Next HyperMatter Object and Select Previous HyperMatter Object icons if you need to go from working on one HyperMatter object to the next. This saves a few steps because you will not have to get out of Sub-Object mode, select the next HyperMatter object, and get back into Sub-Object HyperMatter mode.

8. Select the bottom front four points of the solid clad (see fig. 17.19). Name this point selection set **Bottom4**.

FIGURE 17.19
Select these points for use with the Follow constraint. (3D models by Viewpoint Datalabs International, Inc.)

9. Zoom out a bit so that the dummy is partly in the viewport. Click on the Constraints icon. Click on the Follow button; it presses in and turns green while putting you into an Object Pick mode. Place the arrow cursor over the viewport to see the pick cursor as it passes over objects. Pick the Dummy object. Change to the Camera view.

FOL[Bottom4]->Dummy01 appears in the Constraint list. Play the scene and notice that this first mouse no longer falls from gravity because the Bottom4 points will not allow it; they can only follow the dummy. Notice that the rest of the mouse is still affected by gravity though, and that the mouse moves forward, dragged by his feet.

The Bottom4 points, moved by the Follow constraint, have created in the rest of the mouse what HyperMatter is best at—Cause and Effect motion according to soft body dynamics. This is the kind of motion you would not want to keyframe/morph, and now you don't have to.

10. Go to frame 0. Repeat steps 7, 8, and 9 on the third mouse. Use the same selection set name **Bottom4** and pick the same Dummy01 as the follow object. Change to the Camera view.

Now that these two mice have been set up, you can concentrate on the rubbery reject H_Mouse 2. First you can get these two mice out of the way and clear up the scene a bit to speed up your interaction with the scene and to speed up playback.

11. Get out of Sub-Object mode. Select the first and third mouse in preparation of hiding them. From the Display panel, click on the Hide Selected button (or use your keyboard shortcut). Also select and hide the Floor, Conveyor, and Conveyor Belt objects.

12. Maximize the Left viewport and do a zoom extents.

13. Select the mouse (H_Mouse 2) and go to the Modify panel. Go into Sub-Object HyperMatter mode and select the bottom three points directly below the feet (see fig. 17.20). Name this point selection **Bottom3**.

14. Click on the Follow constraint and then pick the dummy. Change this viewport to Camera.

FIGURE 17.20

Select these points for use with the Follow constraint. (3D models by Viewpoint Datalabs International, Inc.)

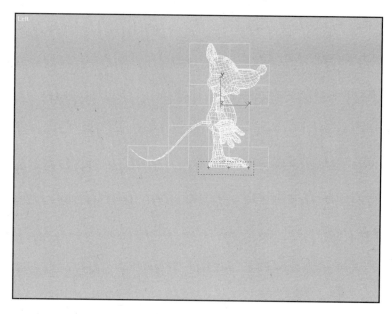

Play the scene. You should see some great cause and effect motion to this rubbery mouse. Notice the tail and how well it reacts. Okay, the tail goes below the conveyor, so you should take care of this now.

15. Go to frame 0 and put the viewport into 4 View mode. Go to the Create panel and choose Second Nature from the drop-down list. Click on Walls. In the Top viewport, drag to create HyperMatter Walls surrounding the mouse and its travels. Make the wall 600 in Length, 150 in Width, and 150 in Height. Position the wall bottom halfway between the dummy and the bottom of the mouse feet. This will position it just below the conveyor (see fig. 17.21).

You are moving the Wall object down below the top of the conveyor for an important reason. A collision occurs between the wall and the solid cladding, not the actual geometry. Because the illusion you need is that of the tail colliding with the conveyor, and the tail's solid cladding is a bit away from the actual tail, you can compensate for this by moving the wall below the conveyor top—about the same distance below the conveyor as the solid cladding is from the bottom of the tail (see fig. 17.22).

FIGURE 17.21

Position the Wall object surrounding the entire path of the mouse with the bottom halfway between the dummy and mouse feet. (3D models by Viewpoint Datalabs International, Inc.)

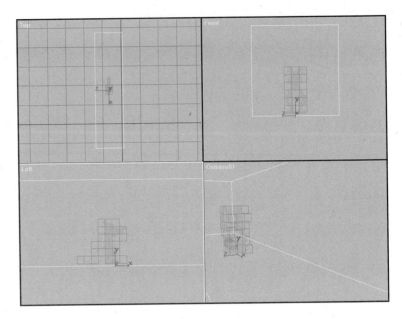

FIGURE 17.22

Position the Wall object below the conveyor belt top to compensate for the difference between the tail geometry and the solid cladding surrounding the tail. (3D models by Viewpoint Datalabs International, Inc.)

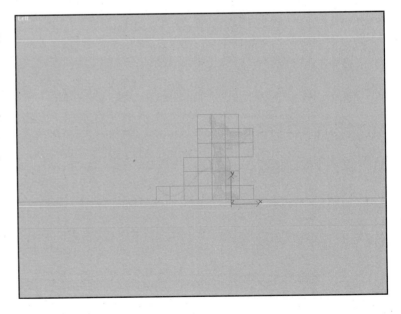

16. Select the mouse, go to the Modify panel, and get into Sub-Object HyperMatter mode. Maximize the Left viewport and select the two points directly under the tail, but do not include the tip of the tail (see fig. 17.23). Name this point selection **Tail**. Click on the Walls constraint and click on the H_Wall01 object. Hide the Wall object. Unhide the conveyor and conveyor belt.

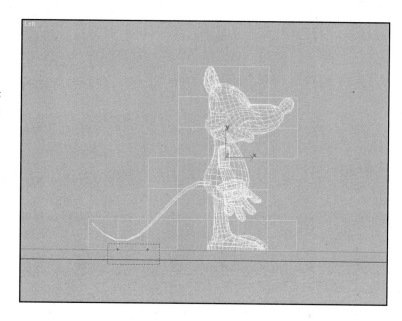

FIGURE 17.23

Select these points under the tail for use with the Walls constraint. (3D models by Viewpoint Datalabs International, Inc.)

Play the scene and observe that the tail no longer goes through the conveyor but bounces nicely against it. Notice also that the tip of the tail actually unwinds as it slaps against the conveyor in a few spots. See the file 18e-pre.avi on the accompanying CD for a preview of the Left viewport. Adjust the wall in your scene if necessary.

A new camera was set up and linked to the mouse just for rendering. Check out the rendered file Ch17e-1.avi. You may notice a minor irregularity in the tail. It seems that on certain frames the tail appears to stick to the conveyor. This seems to be caused by the friction of the tail selection set points as they collide with the wall.

17. Select the mouse, go to the Modify panel, Sub-Object HyperMatter, and choose the Substance Editor icon. Set Friction to 0 to eliminate any friction of the solid clad points as the tail whips across the HyperMatter Walls (conveyor).

Check out ch17e-2.avi from the accompanying CD and compare the new tail action—a minor change, but a big improvement. No other points in the solid cladding will be affected by changing the friction parameter.

This exercise is getting a bit long, and because there is a lot more to be done to this mouse, now would be a good time to save your work and take a break. When you come back, you will finish up the scene as well as throw the mouse off the conveyor belt.

MOUSE REJECT, PART 2

Load your saved scene from part 1 of the preceding exercise or load 17e-hold.max from the accompanying CD. The mice are all set up and the first and third mice are still hidden. The conveyor and floor are also hidden. Now it is time to remove this defective mouse from the conveyor line.

1. Unhide the Clamp assembly and Clamp 1 through 4. Do a Zoom Extents All. This is the mechanism that will take care of the defective mouse. Also unhide Strap 2a and Strap 2b. These keep the mouse in place as it travels along the conveyor. Select these straps and link them both to the dummy. Return to the Select icon from the toolbar.

Play the scene from a maximized Left viewport. You will notice that this Clamp assembly starts moving toward the mouse at frame 175. The individual clamps tighten up and the mechanism stops at frame 200. Only problem is that the mouse is so rubbery that it has not stopped wobbling enough to be picked up yet. Sure, you could change the substance properties of the mouse, but what if you really like these parameters and want to keep them?

You can have the best of both worlds with HyperMatter because all the substance parameters are animatable. What is called for here, therefore, is an animated tightening of the Elasticity and Damping parameters.

2. Select the mouse. Open Track View and filter for selected objects only. Expand the H_Mouse 2 track, Object track, SO_Mouse 2_1 track, and finally the Substance track.

3. Click on the Add Keys icon and add 3 keys for both the Elasticity and Damping tracks somewhere between frames 100 and 200.

4. Right-click on the keys to use the Key Info dialog.
   Set Elasticity keys:
   Time 100 Value 5 Slow-Out Tangent
   Time 175 Value 35 Fast-In / Step-Out Tangent
   Time 200 Value 8 Step-In Tangent
   Set Damping keys:
   Time 100 Value 2 Slow-Out Tangent
   Time 175 Value 35 Fast-in / Step-Out Tangent
   Time 200 Value 4 Step-In Tangent

What you have done is animate the Elasticity and Damping parameters to become more rigid from frames 100 through 175. Then at frame 200, coinciding with the grasping of the Clamp Assembly, the mouse will instantly soften back up. You could just as well have turned on the animate button and adjusted these values in the user interface. It is better and faster (in this author's opinion) to use Track View because you don't need to have HyperMatter process frames as you set up the keyframes.

Play the scene again in the Left viewport to see the mouse turn more rigid between frame 100 and 200. In fact, if you have the Substance Properties rollup visible, you will see the values animate.

5. Go to frame 200 by typing it in the Current Frame Number field and pressing Enter. With the mouse still selected and being in Sub-Object HyperMatter mode, choose the Constraints icon. Select the two rows of points in the solid cladding directly through the ear (see fig. 17.24). Name this selection set **Ears**.

6. Click on the Follow constraint and then pick the Clamp assembly from the scene.

FOL[Ears]->Clamp assembly is added to the constraints list. Highlight this entry and notice that HyperMatter has automatically set the start frame (lifespan) to coincide with the current frame, frame 200.

Play the scene in the Camera view until the clamp assembly stops. Notice that the Clamp is further animated to rise up, resulting in a stretching of the mouse. The mouse is still stuck to the conveyor because of the Follow constraint to the dummy.

Notice also that because the Clamp assembly is still at frame 200, the Follow points will also be still. This results in quick stopping of ear motion and a resultant shudder of motion through the rest of the mouse: Cause and Effect at its finest! Remember that Elasticity and Damping has been animated with a step tangent to be more rubbery at precisely this frame to emphasize this shudder.

FIGURE 17.24

Select these points by the Ear for the Follow constraint. (3D models by Viewpoint Datalabs International, Inc.)

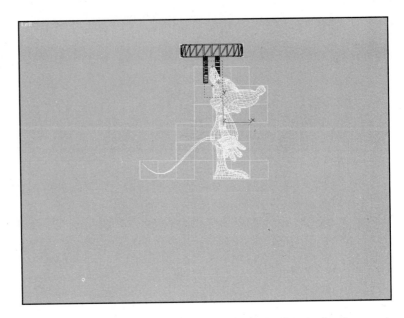

7. Go to frame 260 by typing the Current Frame field. This is the frame at which the Cable assembly reaches the top of its travel and the frame at which you should release the feet.

8. With the mouse selected and still in Sub-Object HyperMatter mode, click on the Constraint icon. Highlight the first Follow constraint from the Constraint list FOL[Bottom3]->Dummy01 and make the current frame the end frame by clicking on the Set End To Current Frame icon next to the End Frame parameter. It will change to 260.

9. Get out of Sub-Object mode and unhide space warps Bomb01 and Bomb02. Bind Strap 2a to Bomb02 and Bind Strap 2b to Bomb01. Hide the Bomb space warps. They have already been set up to detonate at frame 260, completing the release of the mouse feet.

Play the scene for a few frames and stop. Notice that at frame 260, when the Follow constraint to the dummy is released, the stretched mouse springs about as it tries to get back to its original shape.

If you continue playing the scene, you will see the Clamp assembly rotate back and forth, during which time the clamps open up to release the mouse. That is fine except that the mouse does not release. The Follow constraint to the Clamp is not letting the mouse be released from the Clamp assembly for the throw.

10. Go to frame 395, the frame at which the Clamp assembly reaches the end of its travel. Select the mouse, go to the Modify panel, Sub-Object HyperMatter, and choose the Constraints icon. Choose the Ears Follow constraint, FOL[Ears] -> Clamp assembly, from the Constraint list and change the end frame to 392. This is 3 frames before the current frame.

Play the scene starting from frame 0 and check your work. Although it may be fun to see the mouse bounce off the wall object at the end, there is no object there and it doesn't make any sense.

11. While still in the Constraints drop-down list, select the Walls constraint WAL[Tail] ->H_Walls01. Change the end frame to 275 as the walls are no longer needed after the mouse is lifted off the conveyor.

12. Unhide objects Conveyor, Conveyor Belt, H_Mouse 1, H_Mouse 2, Strap 1a, Strap 1b, Strap 3a, and Strap 3b.

Play the scene again in its entirety and admire your handiwork. This has been a lengthy exercise, and you have made it through. Save your scene and make a preview if you would like. Load Mreject.avi from the accompanying CD to see the final rendered animation.

In Practice: HyperMatter

- **HyperMatter Solids react according to the laws of physics and dynamics.** Use HyperMatter whenever you need a MAX object to act as if it were a real-world object. Whether you need a realistic bounce or a deformable collision, HyperMatter is there to help you get it right.

- **When you need to take control of a HyperMatter Solid "doing its own thing," use the available constraints.** You have full control over your HyperMatter Solid through the use of the various constraints. Whether you need to have HyperMatter Solids follow another object, collide with another object, or you just want to prevent it from spinning/tumbling, the HyperMatter's Constraints panel is available.

- **HyperMatter gives you complete control over your objects substance attributes.** HyperMatter's Substance panel gives you full control over your objects' elasticity requirements. HyperMatter objects can represent a highly elastic rubbery substance that deforms easily or a rigid object, such a pair of dice.

- **HyperMatter can be used on the whole object or selected parts of the object.** The versatility of using HyperMatter on the geometry as a whole or on a sub-object selection level gives you much freedom. Use HyperMatter dynamics to influence just one part of your object or many parts of the same object with varied substance attributes.

- **Have fun.** HyperMatter can be a blast and turn a complicated keyframing task into a smooth and realistic joy to behold.

Part V

Video Post

IMAGE CREATED BY ANDREW CROSS

18

by Adam Silverthorne

COMPOSITING AND EDITING

This chapter familiarizes you with some of the powerful and exciting elements of 3D Studio MAX's Video Post module. For many, the words "exciting" and "powerful" don't come to mind when they think of Video Post. Instead, when people think Video Post, they conjure up negative connotations of confusing icons and range bars. Others think of Video Post as just a utility used to splice animations together. Many animators even work productively without ever touching Video Post.

This chapter shows you, however, that Video Post is indeed a very powerful and exciting aspect of 3D Studio MAX. Video Post enables you to composite and edit your animations, which ushers in a whole new world of 3D possibilities. After you realize what MAX Video Post can do for you, you may entirely change the way you animate in MAX.

This chapter covers the following topics:

- Compositing basics
- Using the Alpha Compositor
- Understanding shadows and compositing
- Screen mapping and compositing
- Camera mapping and compositing
- Shadow/Matte and Matte/Shadow
- Masking
- Bluescreening
- Other methods of compositing
- Editing your animations

Compositing Basics

Compositing refers to the act of combining two or more images together to make one image. Video Post enables you to perform this action and also to extend it by performing a composite of two images a multitude of times. Because an animation is just a string of images, Video Post enables you to composite animations. Video Post also enables you to composite a single image with an animation.

System Performance

One of the strongest arguments for compositing is system performance. You might find that when you animate a small scene, it is nice to have all your objects in the scene simultaneously. This way you can animate them and see them in relation to one another. As your scenes become larger and you begin to tax your system resources, however, you might find yourself yearning for a faster machine (or taking a lot of coffee breaks). Even if you have the fastest machine money can buy, a serious face count coupled with some special effects can make it extremely painful to animate with everything in the same scene. The more complex your scene, the slower MAX responds to your commands. Even fast 3D acceleration hardware does little to help out when you have extremely complex scenes. If you use motion blur, volumetric lighting, or render at a high resolution, you also gobble up a lot of RAM. If you use up all your RAM, your computer is forced to use Virtual Memory, which is not good. Compositing enables you to break up your animation into pieces. Because each piece is a fraction of the total face count, the computer handles the file much more efficiently. You might find that an animation you create through compositing might otherwise be impossible.

NOTE

Virtual Memory is memory allocated on your hard drive to store information that your computer cannot fit into its RAM. Because hard disk drives access data much more slowly than RAM does, using virtual memory in a scene can dramatically slow down render times. In many cases, buying more RAM can be a more effective upgrade than a faster processor for 3D work.

Modular Design Approach

Splitting up your animation also facilitates a modular design approach. Working with the pieces frees you to concentrate on individual areas. If you are working on character animation and have an elaborate 3D background, compositing enables you to concentrate on your character animation exclusively. You can get the motion you want for your characters, and then composite on top of a background prepared separately. This approach also enables you to use that same background for any other animation while simultaneously freeing you from the headache of merging the MAX files together and re-rendering. Furthermore, many animators find that approaching animation from a modular point of view works well because it enables them to focus on one element of the animation without getting confused or distracted by other elements. Compositing also enables multiple animators to tackle the same scene without stumbling over one another. After you get used to compositing, you might find yourself using it even when memory and hardware constraints are not an issue. Despite these benefits, compositing does have a few pitfalls. If objects are not rendered together, they are not picked up in reflections or shadow casting. Ways to get around the shadow problem exist, however, and are discussed later in this chapter.

This modularity also forces the animator to be a little bit more organized. It is important to create subdirectories for your file renders, for example, to avoid cluttering up one directory with long lists of sequential files.

Using the Alpha Compositor

Because of the tools MAX provides, the Alpha Compositor is arguably the best way to composite your animations. The *Alpha Compositor* is an Image Layer event that composites two images based on an image alpha channel. The images are combined based on the alpha data present in the second image. This means that to see the top child, the bottom child of a layer event must contain alpha data (see fig. 18.1). Layer events are like plates that cover one another. The alpha data provides a method for seeing through one plate and on to another. If the bottom child of your Layer event is a Scene event, MAX renders that image and automatically provides transparency data wherever nothing obstructs the background in your scene. If the last layer in the Video Post queue is a Scene event such as a Camera viewport, for example, that viewport is rendered as if it had an alpha channel, and the blank areas become transparent automatically.

FIGURE 18.1

The bottom child covers the event above it.

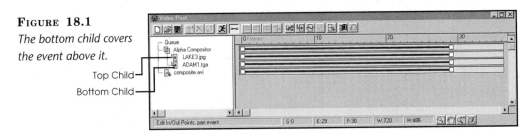

NOTE

You should be aware that transparency data adds an extra 8 bits of information to an image. Consequently, when you need transparency data in an image, the file needs to be 32 bit instead of the default 24 bit. When you composite, you might need this transparency data to see through one layer and on to another. You need to be aware of when you need which type of file, however, so that you don't needlessly waste disk space on 32-bit files if you only need 24-bit files.

For this chapter, you need to understand certain aspects of MAX directly related to compositing, but not necessarily part of the Video Post module. Therefore image setup parameters, the virtual frame buffer window, the graphics buffer (G-Buffer), and the Image File List (IFL) are explained prior to diving into some compositing examples. If you already know some of these concepts, you may want to skim the familiar parts.

Image Setup Parameters

When you have your scene ready to render, and you specify a file in the Render Scene dialog, you are given options specific to a particular file type. If you render a JPG file, for example, you can specify the level of compression versus the quality of the image. With TGA files, you can specify whether you want the rendered file to have an alpha channel. You do this by setting the Bits-Per-Pixel to 32 in the Image Setup dialog (see fig. 18.2). The parameters that you set for an image file type stay that way until you change them again. If you set the Bits-Per-Pixel for TGA images to 32, for example, all TGA images you render from now on are automatically saved with alpha data even if you close and reopen MAX. With this in mind, be certain to check the Image Setup dialog to make certain that you set up the image properly. This dialog also gives you an option called Alpha Split. An *Alpha Split* creates a separate 8-bit image, in addition to the 24-bit rendering. This 8-bit separate image contains the alpha data only. Alpha Split is useful because you could then use this 8-bit Alpha Split image or image sequence in masking operations (see the section on masking later in this chapter).

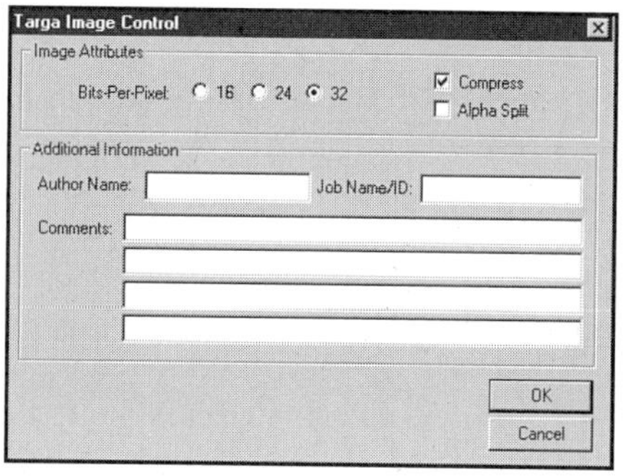

FIGURE 18.2

By setting the Bits-Per-Pixel to 32, you tell MAX that you want to include an alpha channel in the rendered image.

The Virtual Frame Buffer Window

Figure 18.3 shows an image of the Virtual Frame Buffer window. Notice the buttons at the top of the window. On the left, buttons labeled with red, green, and blue circles are followed by a button with a half black, half white circle. Each button represents one of the four channels in an RGBA image. RGBA stands for red, green, blue, and alpha—the four standard channels in a 32-bit image.

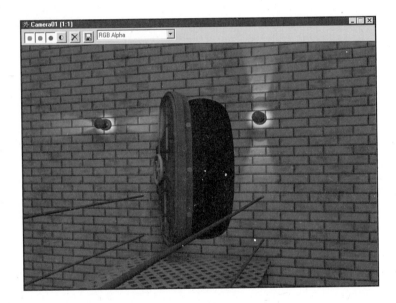

The half black, half white button is the Display Alpha Channel button. If you press this button, the image in the window changes and reveals the alpha channel (see fig. 18.4). The white areas represent opaque sections of the image, and the black areas are transparent. Notice that the alpha channel for this image provides an area of transparency where no geometry is present. In this image, the transparent area is present in the area revealed by the opening door. The space beyond the door can be a background that you composite in later. The Display Alpha Channel button proves particularly useful when doing compositing because it enables you to visualize your areas of transparency. The buttons with the red, green, and blue circles toggle the corresponding channel in the image. If you press the Red button, for example, the red channel of the image no longer displays in the Virtual Frame Buffer window. By clicking on the various buttons, you can toggle the corresponding channel on and off. Visualizing the individual channels that use these buttons is useful when you want to perform masking operations (see the section on masking later in this chapter). Notice the two other buttons next to the RGBA channel buttons. The button labeled with an X clears the current frame buffer. The button with the disk icon enables you to save the image to a file—useful when you do test renders and don't necessarily want to specify an output file in the Render Scene dialog. The pull-down menu shows what G-Buffer information is available in that particular file.

FIGURE 18.4

The Display Alpha Channel button enables you to visualize your areas of transparency.

The G-Buffer

The term *G-Buffer* (graphics buffer) refers to a method of storing geometric information about objects in 3D images. The geometric information is stored so that it may later be calculated and used by image processing programs. The information is stored in various channels similar to the way an alpha channel is stored. Within a G-Buffered image, for example, there might be data that describes how far a pixel is from the camera. This information can then be used to calculate fog or distance blur effects. 3D Studio MAX implements G-Buffer technology. If you specify a material effects channel or an object channel, for example, you set data within the G-Buffer. The Virtual Frame Buffer window enables you to view this data by selecting the appropriate channel from the pull-down list. If no G-Buffer data is available, no channels are listed in the pull-down menu. MAX supports 10 total possible channels, but not all are added automatically. Not all image types support G-Buffer information. The G-Buffer information recorded by MAX is in a format unique to MAX's renderer. This format is public, but it is not extensible. For this reason, MAX uses Silicon Graphics' popular RLA image format for saving images with G-Buffer information.

The Image File List

IFL stands for Image File List. An *IFL file* is a standard text-only file that contains a list of images. Each image in the list corresponds to a 3D Studio MAX frame. MAX reads the file line by line and loads each listed file for a particular frame of animation. Creating IFL files is easy. You must first have a sequence of images. If you rendered an animation to sequential TGA files and called the output file Homey.tga, for example, the sequence of files would look like the following:

Homey0001.tga

Homey0002.tga

Homey0003.tga

And so on...

To create this particular IFL, in the File Selection dialog, navigate to the directory that contains the sequential images and type **Homey*.tga** as the input file. The list continues until it reaches the number of rendered frames. MAX automatically creates a file with an IFL extension. The file contains the list of sequential files that matches the Homey*.tga wild card.

MAX creates the IFL file in the directory that contains the list of images. You cannot, therefore, create an IFL file if the images you intend to use are on CD-ROM. Because CD-ROM is read-only media, MAX cannot create the IFL file because MAX will try to write the file to the CD-ROM.

WARNING

If you are on a network or if you plan to network render, IFL files can slow down your renders significantly. This slowdown occurs because the network needs to send each file specified in the IFL over the network for every frame being processed by Manager. 100BaseT networks seem to handle this increased traffic without too much difficulty. 10BaseT or coaxial networks bottle neck, however, if they must send large TGA files around on very limited bandwidth.

Now that you are familiar with some of the core concepts important to compositing, you should discover the power of Video Post's Alpha Compositor. The following exercise illustrates how to perform a composite by using the Alpha Compositor. In this example, a door swings open and reveals an image that you composite behind it. The door is one layer of your composite, and the background revealed as the door swings open is the other layer.

USING THE ALPHA COMPOSITOR

1. From the accompanying CD, load ch18ex1.max.

2. Activate the Camera viewport and scroll the Time Slider.

Notice the animation of the door opening. This scene presents a good scenario for compositing. The file does not contain complex geometry, but remember that when you have an animation that can be broken up into elementary pieces, that animation makes a good candidate for a composite. If you want, you can now render this animation as a set of sequential images. The images are included on the accompanying CD, however, so this is not a necessary step. With the rendered images ready and waiting, you have what you need to perform a composite.

3. From the Rendering pull-down list on the MAX main screen, select Video Post.

Notice the buttons along the top of the window. Some of the buttons are grayed out, meaning they are inaccessible. Certain buttons are only accessible when events upon which they can perform an action are within the Video Post queue.

4. Click on the Add Image Input Event button.

The Add Image Input Event dialog appears (see fig. 18.5). This dialog enables you to specify a file, a sequence of files, or a device. An example of a device you might use is the Accom WSD Digital Recorder. For this exercise, it is assumed that you are using standard images.

FIGURE 18.5

The Add Image Input Event dialog.

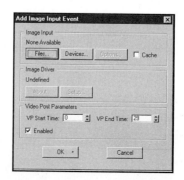

5. In the Image Input section of the dialog, click on the Files button.

6. Navigate to the CD-ROM and highlight back1.tga.

7. Click on the View button.

The View button is a useful button included in the MAX File Selection dialog. The same dialog appears whenever you are called upon to choose an image file regardless of whether you are in Video Post, the Material Editor, or any other section of MAX. While viewing the image, notice that the buttons available to you while viewing rendered images in the virtual frame buffer are available to you now.

8. Click on the Show/Hide Alpha button.

Notice that this file has no alpha channel. Because you use this file as your background, it is essentially the ultimate layer of your composite. It is not necessary to see past it because it is the last one. Remember that you only need alpha data if you need transparency. Because there is no need to see through the background, no alpha channel is necessary in the image.

9. Close the Image Display window.

10. Click on the Cache check box to enable the cache.

11. Click on OK to accept the file and return to the Video Post window.

TIP

The Cache check box instructs Video Post to load the image into RAM and then to use that same information throughout the sequence. This should always be checked if you are using a single image in an Image Input event. By loading the image information into RAM, MAX does not reload or scale the image for every frame. Reloading and scaling takes time and that makes the render take longer. If you are using a single image, checking the Cache check box saves a lot of time. Do not use this option if you are using a sequence of images. It is necessary to load each image for each frame if you want your background animation to correspond with your foreground animation.

You now have the background ready and waiting in the Video Post Event queue. Because compositing requires two images, you need to add another Image Input event.

1. Deselect the current event in the Video Post queue by clicking on a blank area in the Video Post window.

2. Click on the Image Input button to select another Image Input event.

3. Navigate to the CD-ROM and select dooro.ifl in the Dooropen folder.

4. Click on OK to accept the image and return to the Video Post window.

You should now have two Image Input events listed in the Video Post queue. One event is a single image and another event is a list of images. Make certain that the range bars for the two events both span 60 frames. By stretching the range bar for the background image over 60 frames, you are instructing Video Post to use the same image for all 60 frames of your animation.

5. Click on the back1.tga event to highlight it.

6. Hold down the Ctrl key while simultaneously clicking on the dooro.ifl event.

Both events should now be highlighted. Notice that when both events became highlighted, some of the buttons in the Video Post window became active. Notice also that the range bars turned red when events are selected, indicating that the event is active. When both events become active, the Add Image Layer Event button becomes available.

7. Click on the Add Image Layer Event button.

8. Select Alpha Compositor from the pull-down menu and accept it as the Image Layer event.

After creating an Image Layer event, both of your Image Input events lined themselves up below the Alpha Compositor Layer event. This arrangement graphically illustrates that the Input events are now children of the Layer event. The Alpha Compositor is ready to combine these two images.

Warning

Make sure that the background image is listed above the animation sequence in the Alpha Compositor hierarchy (see fig. 18.6). If it is not, the opaque background will be rendered on top of the animation sequence. The result will be an animation of the background only. Thus, the order of children is very important. If you need to switch the order, you can highlight both children and click on the Swap Events button.

FIGURE 18.6

Notice the background event is listed on top of the animation event in the hierarchy.

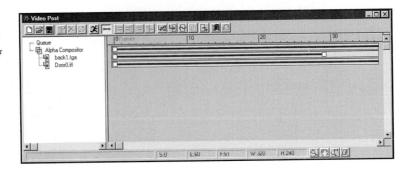

9. Deselect any events in the Video Post queue by clicking on empty space within the Video Post window.

10. Click on the Add Image Output Event button.

11. Navigate to the \3dsmax\images directory on the accompanying CD, specify ch18ex1.avi as an output file, and then click on OK.

12. If you want, you can specify parameters for the AVI file by clicking on the Setup button for the Image Output event, and then click on OK to return to the Video Post window.

13. Click on the Execute Sequence button (the running man) and render frames 0–60 at any resolution you want. If you prefer not to render the animation, you can skip this step.

14. From the 3D Studio MAX file pull-down menu, select View File, navigate to the \3dsmax\images directory and double-click on ch18ex1.avi to view the composited animation. If you chose not to render the animation, you can view it from the accompanying CD.

Congratulations, you just performed a composite entirely within 3D Studio MAX. Using the Alpha Compositor will prove to be a valuable tool to add to your 3D Studio MAX arsenal. In the previous example, you composited a single image with an animation. You could also have specified an animation as the background Scene event. You could use an AVI file, for example, or you could create an IFL from sequential images to use as the background. You should now be beginning to realize the power of the Alpha Compositor.

Multi-Layer Compositing

One great thing about Layer events is that they can be children of other Layer events. Earlier you learned that the Alpha Compositor must have two scene events to perform a composite. This is true only at the bottom of each branch in the hierarchy. The term *branch* refers to a subset of the hierarchical list of parents and children. You could have an Alpha Compositor event with two more Alpha Compositor events as each of its children, for example. The children of the children could be Scene events, or they could be other Alpha Compositor events (see fig. 18.7). This kind of setup is referred to as a *multi-layer composite*. Consider the previous example of the door swinging open. Suppose that you want the door to begin its motion in the open position and then swing closed, blocking out the background temporarily. Suppose further that when it swings back into position, it reveals a different background. This kind of scenario is made possible with a multi-layer composite.

FIGURE 18.7

The children of an Alpha Compositor Layer event can be Alpha Compositor Layer events themselves.

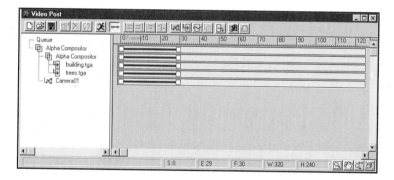

1. From the CD, load ch18ex2.max.

2. Drag the Frame Slider and notice the animation of the door closing over frames 0–60 and then swinging back open over frames 60–120 (see fig. 18.8).

3. Select Rendering from the MAX pull-down menu and choose Video Post.

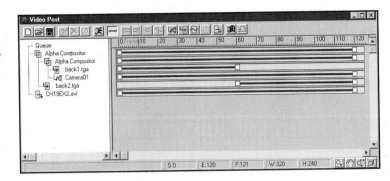

Here you have a Video Post layout that contains multiple Alpha Compositor Layer events. One child of the root of the hierarchy is an Alpha Compositor event. The root of the hierarchy itself is also an Alpha Compositor event. The child Alpha Compositor Event has an Image Input event and a Camera Scene event as its own children. Notice that the range bars in the Video Post window for each event correspond to the frames that you want the image to be viewed in the scene. Because you want back1.tga to be present over frames 0–60, the range bar for that event covers frames 0–60. The back2.tga event picks up where the back1.tga event ends, and covers frames 60–120. The Output event range bar spans the total animation of 120 frames. You can execute this sequence and render the files, or you can view the pre-rendered ch18ex2.avi file from the accompanying CD.

In this instance, a multi-layer composite was used because you wanted to change a background image during an animation. The range bars do the work here. At a specified time, one Image Layer event ends and another event picks up where the first event left off. You might also want to perform a multi-layer composite during one specific time frame. You might need to do this if you want to separate a complex background into various different layers. You can have, for example, some buildings on a bottom layer, some trees on a middle layer, and a character on a foreground layer. To accomplish this task, you might set up the Video Post queue like that shown in figure 18.7.

Notice the first child of the main Alpha Compositor event is another Alpha Compositor event with two Image Input events as children. The building.tga image on top is the background layer. If you think of the events like plates that cover one another, you can see that this Image Input event will be covered up by the trees.tga Image Input event. It is necessary, therefore, that the trees.tga Input event be an event that contains a 32-bit image or images.

If this event did not contain 32-bit files with alpha data, the image would have no transparency and consequently it would completely cover the buildings. The second child of the main Alpha Compositor event is a Camera Scene event. In this instance, the camera would be pointed at a character in the scene. Remember that Scene events in the Video Post queue are rendered as if they had alpha data automatically. The result of this Video Post sequence would be the trees and buildings composited together, and then the character in the scene composited on top of the buildings and trees.

Understanding Shadows and Compositing

Sometimes an animation requires certain elements that make compositing a little more difficult than just laying images on top of one another. If you use the Alpha Compositor to composite a character on a background, for example, it might look like the character is floating in space while the background is pinned up behind her. In other words, it might look like a composite. A good composite should not give away the fact that it is composited. To avoid this dilemma, you need to "ground" your composited objects in their backgrounds. You need to make an object feel like it is a part of its environment, and that it could interact with the background if it wanted to. To make an object feel like it is part of the scene, the object should cast a shadow. Shadows give the illusion that an object is present in its environment. For a long time, a strong argument against compositing in many animation studios was the fact that it has been difficult (if not impossible) to achieve realistic shadows in a composite. While compositing in MAX, however, techniques enable you to achieve realistic shadows. These techniques are outlined here. Furthermore, lights that might be present in your foreground should affect the background and vice versa, and there is a method for achieving this effect as well.

Screen Mapping and Compositing

Using screen mapping to achieve realistic shadow effects in a composite is considered by many to be a "hack" or a workaround. It is only useful in certain situations. It is worth discussing and understanding because it does work for particular situations, and it can work in conjunction with other compositing methods. The main limitation of the screen mapping method is that the camera in the scene must be static. The general term *screen mapping* might sound familiar if you have ever used a background image for an environment map. Essentially, a screen-mapped background remains in a direct facing orientation to the camera and fills the screen. If you are using a background and you use screen mapping, you would not want to animate camera movement because the background would move exactly with the camera. If you moved the camera 45 degrees, for example, it would still be looking at the same exact background scene. The result would be a foreground that moved against an unchanging background. This is a quite unrealistic and unwanted effect. For this reason, if you use an environment map and you have camera movement, you want to use one of the other mapping types such as spherical. If you use the screen mapping method to perform a composite, you encounter the same problem with camera movement. If you have a stationary camera, however, screen mapping can be used to fake shadow and light effects.

The screen mapping method entails setting up a background image in your Camera viewport. You then create geometry and move it so that it matches the perspective of the part of the background image on which you want to cast a shadow. By applying a material that contains the same image as the background in the diffuse channel and specifying screen mapping as the mapping type, the object is mapped with the background image. Because the mapping type is screen, the object has only a section of the map visible. The section of the map visible on the object is exactly the part that the object obstructs from the background. The effect is that the geometry disappears into the background. The geometry, however, is still present and can receive shadows and lighting. Confused? The following example illustrates exactly how this works.

1. From the CD, load ch18ex3.max.

2. Make certain that the Camera viewport is active, select Views from the MAX pull-down menu, and then select Background Image.

The background image feature can be useful for referencing what is happening in a composite. A shaded viewport with a background image displayed can give you a good idea of what to expect from your final render. The background image can be a single image or an animation. You can specify an IFL file (discussed previously in this chapter), or you can specify an AVI file. When using screen mapping for compositing, it is important to display the background image or animation because you need to match the image's perspective with geometry you create in the viewport.

3. Click on the Files button and select back3.jpg from the accompanying CD.

4. Under Aspect Ratio in the lower-left corner, check the box titled Match Rendering Output.

5. Click on the Display Background button in the lower-right corner to enable it, and click on OK to dismiss the dialog (see fig. 18.9).

FIGURE 18.9

The Viewport Background dialog enables you to display a background in the viewport.

You should also turn off the viewport grid by right-clicking on the viewport label and selecting Show Grid to toggle it off. The grid can obstruct your view of the background image and consequently make perspective matching more difficult. Notice the object in the scene named Ground. This geometry is a simple box that has been aligned to match up with the ground plane in the image. By applying a material with screen mapping, you can make the object seem to disappear into the background image.

6. Open the Material Editor, select a material slot and name it Screen Map 1.

7. Set Shininess and Shininess Strength to 0.

8. Click on the gray button next to the Diffuse color selector. From the ensuing dialog, double-click on Bitmap.

9. Under Bitmap Parameters, click on the long gray box next to the Bitmap label and select the same file that you selected for your background image, back3.jpg from the accompanying CD.

10. Under the Coordinates rollout, change Texture to Environ, and then from the list box, change Mapping to Screen.

11. Make the object named Ground in the scene the currently selected object, and then click on the Assign Material to Selection button from the Material Editor toolbar.

12. Render the scene to the Virtual Frame Buffer window (see fig. 18.10).

FIGURE 18.10

By using Screen Mapping in the Material Editor, you can make the object seemingly disappear into the background.

You should now see an object in the scene with a material applied that matches the background image. Notice, however, that the background image didn't show up. Setting the background image in the viewport is not the same as setting a background image for rendering. To set up the background image for rendering, follow this procedure:

1. From MAX's Rendering pull-down menu, choose Environment. Click on the Assign button and change the Browse From section of the Material/Map browser to Scene.

2. Find back3.jpg in the list and double-click on it. Make certain that the Use Map check box is checked and click on the X in the upper-right corner to dismiss the Environment window.

Now when you render the scene, you should see the background image and the CG telephone pole. The Ground Plane object has almost disappeared into the background image. One problem you might notice is that the ground plane is not lit correctly to match the lighting in the background image.

1. Select the Spot01 spotlight that is above the telephone pole, open the Modify panel and adjust the multiplier to approximately 1.5 to correctly match the lighting.

2. Check the Cast Shadows check box in the Shadow Parameters section.

3. Make certain that the Camera viewport is active and re-render the scene.

You should now see that the telephone pole is seemingly casting a shadow on the background image. The shadow makes the object feel as if it is present in the scene. You can also use this method for lighting effects.

4. Select the Spot02 spotlight, open the Modify panel, and check the On check box that is next to the color selector. You might also adjust the color of the spotlight to match the color of your typical pale yellow street light.

5. Render the scene.

Notice that the light appears to affect the ground in the background image as well. To add to the realism of the scene, you might create some telephone wires connecting the CG telephone pole with the real one in the image. Using screen mapping in this manner can be quite useful for creating shadow and light effects over real images or CG backgrounds. This effect is not limited to ground planes. You can cast shadows over buildings or other objects by making simple boxes and perspective matching them to the objects. The backgrounds that you use can be animated, but remember that screen mapping is not the way to go if there is camera movement. If there is camera movement and you need shadow effects, you should use the Shadow/Matte material (discussed in the Shadow Matte/Matte Shadow section later in this chapter). The Display Background feature proves very useful for all types of compositing because it gives you an idea of what to expect from the background and enables you to place foreground objects in relation to the background.

Camera Mapping

The Camera Mapping plug-in works similarly to the way the screen mapping method does. Camera mapping maps the background image on to an object by using a modified planar projection from the camera's point of view. The result is that the object with camera mapping applied disappears into the background image the same way that it did with screen mapping. You could use camera mapping to achieve shadows in a composite. The plug-in contains two parts: a modifier and a space warp.

The *modifier* sets the objects mapping to the background image for a specified frame. The modifier doesn't work properly if there is camera movement for the same reason that screen mapping doesn't. If you use the modifier, the background image is mapped properly only for the current frame you are on when you choose a camera to use for the mapping. If the camera moves, the other frames disorient the mapping from the background.

Essentially, the Camera Mapping modifier is another way to do screen mapping. Screen mapping has some advantages because camera mapping relates to the tessellation of the geometry. For the mapping to be accurate, the object needs to have a high number of faces. Screen mapping works with the minimum number of faces. The second part of the plug-in, the space warp, recalculates the mapping for every frame of animation. The result is that the object is mapped with the correct background perspective for each frame, enabling you to move the camera. You could use this to composite an animation that has a moving camera with a static or moving background. It can be difficult, however, to match the background camera movement with the foreground camera movement. Typically, you must merge the same camera you use in the background MAX file into the foreground MAX file. Furthermore, using this method to match the lighting in a file that has camera movement can be tough. If you want to composite an animation that has a moving camera with shadows, it is easier to use the Shadow/Matte Material described in the next section. This plug-in is quite useful, however, if you are doing special effects. You can blend an object into the background with the space warp, for example. You can then animate the self illumination of the material, or do a morph material and make the object "cloak" in and out of the background. The Camera Mapping plug-in is included on the accompanying CD.

Shadow/Matte and Matte/Shadow

There are ways to composite with shadows that get around the static camera problem that limits Screen Mapping and the Camera Map modifier's functionality. Shadow Matting is one such method. Shadow Matte is a plug-in for 3D Studio MAX written by an invaluable member of the MAX development community, Peter Watje. The Shadow/Matte plug-in is a material that doesn't visually render, but instead functions by receiving shadows. The received shadow is stored in the alpha channel of the rendered image. Then, when you use the Alpha Compositor, the alpha channel darkens the area that the shadow occupies.

Shadow/Matte is essentially an extension of the built-in Matte/Shadow. Matte/Shadow is a material that doesn't render either, but it does not store the shadow in the alpha channel. Matte/Shadow, in essence, functions by poking a hole in your rendering wherever the material is present in the scene. This hole lets the background image through. The object to which Matte/

Shadow is applied can receive shadows. By allowing the background image through, it can give the illusion that something in the background image is casting the shadow. Although Matte/Shadow works, using Shadow/Matte and saving the shadow in the alpha channel is generally the superior method because it is easier and more accurate. For a more complete description of Matte/Shadow, refer to *Inside 3D Studio MAX, Volume I*, pg. 821.

The following example illustrates how to use Shadow/Matte in conjunction with the Alpha Compositor to create realistic shadows within a composite. Before doing this example, you need to copy the smatte.dlt file from the accompanying CD into your \3DSMAX\PLUGINS directory and reload MAX.

1. Open the ch18ex4.max file from the accompanying CD and activate the Camera viewport.

2. Render a single frame to the virtual frame buffer.

3. You should see an image of the IK walking man on a ground plane. Click on the Show Alpha button to display the alpha channel. Notice that the opaque areas of the alpha channel completely cover the ground plane and the character.

4. Close the Virtual Frame Buffer window, right-click on the label for the Camera viewport, and click on Show Background. If you composited this file over the background, the ground plane covers the ground plane in the image.

5. Open the Material Editor. Activate a material slot and click on the gray button labeled Standard, which defines the material type. Make certain that New is selected in the Browse From section and double-click on Shadow Matte to change the material type. Notice that the material preview in the material slot disappeared. This indicates that the material will not render visually.

6. Under Shadow Matte parameters, there are a few options (see fig. 18.11). Beneath Matte, a check box called Don't Effect Alpha toggles whether the material will save the shadow in the alpha channel. This option is what Peter Watje added to the Matte/Shadow material. If you disable this feature by clicking on this check box, the material functions exactly like Matte/Shadow. Leave this button unchecked. You can also make atmospheric effects such as fog affect the Matte object by checking the Apply Atmosphere button.

FIGURE 18.11

The Shadow Matte material options.

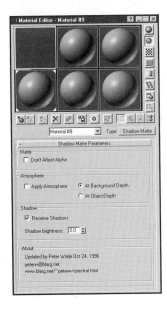

7. Under Shadow is an option called Receive Shadows. Make certain that this box is checked. The Shadow Brightness spin box enables you to adjust the brightness of the shadow. Because the background image is dark, set the shadow brightness to 0.

8. Make certain that the ground plane is selected, and then apply the Shadow Matte material to the selection.

9. Render the scene to the Virtual Frame Buffer window. Notice that the ground plane has disappeared from the rendering. Click on the Show Alpha button to view the new alpha channel. The Shadow Matte material has created an accurate representation of the shadow within the alpha channel.

10. Open Video Post. The Video Post window is set up for a simple composite using the Alpha Compositor. You can execute the sequence and render it on your hard disk, or you can view the ch18ex4a.avi from the accompanying CD. Notice that the shadow is accurately represented and appears to fall on the image in the background.

Using Shadow Matte for shadow effects is usually the best way to go. If you are compositing because of rendering time considerations, you can create a "dummy" scene composed of simple primitives that represent your complicated background. Suppose, for example, you have a scene that calls for characters to chase each other through the aisles of an intricate junkyard. Stacking up bunches of junked up car meshes, barrels, and other miscellaneous objects could create an incredibly complex scene quickly. Trying to concentrate on character animation within this scene would be futile. You should therefore create the complex background and render it on its own. Then you can animate your characters and use simple geometry to stand in for the complex background. Apply the Shadow Matte material to these simple primitives, render, and then composite your character animation over the complex background that you rendered previously. Shadow Matte offers the best choice here because you would likely have lots of camera movement in a chase scene. As long as the dummy background and the real background are laid out in same manner, the shadow effects should be accurate enough to fool the eye.

You can also combine the different methods outlined so far. Although Shadow Matte enables you to move the camera, you cannot use it to receive lighting. Therefore, certain scenes might call for a combination of Screen Mapping and Shadow Matte. ch18ex4b.avi on the accompanying CD shows a combination of Screen Mapping and Shadow Matte.

Masking

Sometimes the images you need to composite are 24 bit and have no alpha channel. If you hope to composite such images, you need some way of creating areas of transparency. You can use a program such as Adobe Photoshop to create an alpha channel in your source images. This can be difficult, however, if the colors in the image are not distinctive. In certain situations, you may need to use a mask to obtain good results in a composite. A mask enables you to use a separate file to get your transparency data and create your areas of transparency. You can use a separate file's alpha channel for your transparency data, for example. Commonly, the alpha channel is used to create the mask. MAX, however, enables you to use any of the image channels, as well as G-Buffer information to create a mask. You can use G-Buffer channels such as Material Effects or Object channels to mask out certain objects. If you intend to use G-Buffer information for masking, be certain to use the RLA image format to save your files (see previous section in this chapter on G-Buffer). If you had one object in an animation that you wanted to mask out, for example, you can set the object to have an object channel and then render out to RLA. You can then specify object as the mask type and wherever that object is present in the scene shows up transparent or opaque. It would be opaque by default and transparent if you checked the Inverted button next to the mask type.

Using the Red, Green, or Blue channel to create a mask is often useful and functions similarly to the way an opacity map works. When you use these color channels to create your mask, the intensity of each pixel (0–255) controls the level of transparency. Because different channels have different intensities in different images, you can pick and choose which color channel you want to use for your particular needs. The following example illustrates how you might use one of the color channels to composite flames over an animation. The flames used come from the Pyromania CD-ROM available from Trinity Enterprises (`http:\\www.trinity3d.com`). These flames make a good illustration for masking because they ship without an alpha channel. Furthermore, you can experiment with which channel to use to get varying levels of transparency.

1. Open MAX or save and reset. Open Video Post.

2. Add back1.tga from the accompanying CD as an Image Input event. Be certain to check the Cache check box so that MAX doesn't load and rescale the same file for every frame of animation. This is going to be the background that you will be compositing flames over.

3. Add another Image Input event and navigate to flames.tga from the accompanying CD. With the image highlighted in the directory list, click on View to view the image. Click on the Display Alpha button and notice that the file has no alpha channel. Click on the Red, Green, and Blue buttons in turn to see the different channels of the image. Accept the image and return to the Video Post window.

4. Select both Image Input events by holding down Ctrl and clicking on both events. Add the Alpha Compositor Layer event. The Flames event should be listed below the Engine Room event in the hierarchy. Because flames.tga does not have an alpha channel, a straight alpha composite will not work. If you render this sequence, only the flames appear because they have no transparency information yet.

5. Double-click on the Alpha Compositor event to bring up the Layer Event window (see fig. 18.12). Under the section labeled Masking, click on the Files button, navigate to the CD, and select flames.tga. Notice that the Enabled check box became checked automatically. Check the Inverted check box to invert the mask.

FIGURE 18.12

The mask feature enables you to use the different channels in an image to create custom areas of transparency.

FIGURE 18.12

The mask feature enables you to use the different channels in an image to create custom areas of transparency.

6. In the pull-down list box, select Blue Channel from the list. You use the blue channel of the flames.tga image as a mask for your composite. Areas containing information other than black in the blue channel represent varying levels of opacity.

7. Render a single image to the Virtual Frame Buffer window.

You should see the flames over the image of the engine room. You can view the rendered sequence, ch18ex5.avi with animated flames, from the accompanying CD. You might experiment with using different channels in the image for the mask. You can render the image by using the red channel instead of the blue, for example. Fire makes for a particularly tricky composite because the flames need to be semi-transparent themselves. For this example, the blue channel seems to work best, but you should experiment depending on each particular project. Masking is a powerful way to composite animations because it enables greater flexibility than the standard alpha channel.

Bluescreening

Bluescreening is a widely used method for compositing. Bluescreening is a chromakey technique. *Chromakeying* is a process whereby a foreground image is shot against a monocolored screen. The monocolored screen represents a background that can be replaced by film, video, or computer graphics. Chromakey techniques such as bluescreening are commonly used in film and television to composite different layers of action together. An actor filmed against a bluescreen in a small studio, for example, could seemingly be placed anywhere on earth or beyond. The method involves shrouding the background in a particular color, commonly blue or green, and then keying the area filled with that color in the image to be the transparent area. To successfully bluescreen, you need to use a material with a little or no shininess or luster. Special blue or green screen material is available from certain mail-order outlets and specialty stores, but you can also use standard color board available at any art store if you are careful with how you set up and light it. The background must be solid and consistently lit for the computer to successfully find every instance of the color. Inconsistencies such as shadows or crumples can cause the computer to miscalculate the areas you intend to be transparent.

Probably the most difficult part of setting up a successful bluescreen is lighting. You need to place high-powered lights behind your subject and point them at the bluescreen material. You should be careful not to create a hotspot on one part of the bluescreen material. The light you use to illuminate your subject cannot be brighter than the lights used to illuminate the bluescreen material, or you will create a shadow. The color you choose for the bluescreen material should also be a color that doesn't conflict with what you intend to be the foreground. You do not want to key a color close to the color of skin, for example, if you want to have an actor in your foreground. This is why a bright solid blue color is normally used. You can, however, theoretically use whatever color you desire.

3D Studio MAX itself does not provide tools necessary to perform chromakey operations. A company called Photron (`http:\\www.photron.com`), however, makes a plug-in for MAX called Primatte, which performs this function. A demo version of Primatte is on the CD. The following example illustrates how you might use Primatte to perform a simple chromakey composite of a person shot against a bluescreen background over a background that comes with MAX. Before doing this example, you need to install the demo version of Primatte into MAX. Copy the primatte.flt file from the accompanying CD to your \3dsmax\plugins directory and then restart MAX.

1. Reset or load MAX. Open Video Post.

2. Add lake3.jpg from your \3dsmax\maps directory as an Image Input event in the Video Post queue.

3. Add adam1.tga from the accompanying CD as an Image Input event. This image was shot with a Kodak DC40 digital camera against a bluescreen background using Savage Widetone bluescreen material from the Savage Universe Corporation.

4. Highlight both Image Input events and add the Primatte Chromakey Compositor as an Image Layer event. Click on OK to return to the Video Post window. You must have the Layer event set in Video Post before you can change the setup for the filter.

5. Double-click on the Primatte Chromakey Compositor Layer event, and then click on Setup. In a few moments, the Primatte plug-in window appears.

6. Click-drag the mouse cursor from the left side of the background area to the right side without dragging over the person. This function tells Primatte what area you intend to be transparent. Notice that part of the person has also become transparent. You need to give Primatte some more information.

7. Click on the button labeled FG (Select Foreground Pixels) on the button bar and click-drag around the torso of the person. You may also need to click-drag around the head area or any area that you see is transparent that shouldn't be.

8. Click on the button labeled with the black/white man (View Matte) to see the matte. You can now activate the FG and BG buttons, and then click-drag within the matte display to modify your chromakey settings with this view active. This view can help you visualize what your final Matte object will look like (see fig. 18.13).

FIGURE 18.13
Primatte shows the Matte object only.

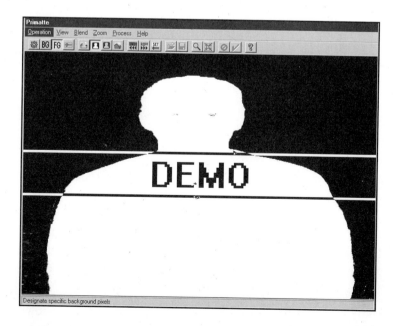

9. Click on the View Composite button to return to the Composite Preview window. You have now set up Primatte to chromakey accurately. The result of this composite is Adam standing in front of a beautiful lake rather than in front of a bluescreen (see fig. 18.14). By choosing OK from the Operation menu, you can accept this composite and render. The demo version, however, is functionally crippled, so select cancel. Feel free to play with the various settings within the Primatte plug-in.

FIGURE 18.14

The final chromakeyed image.

Other Methods of Compositing

So far in this chapter, you have used the Alpha Compositor exclusively when using the tools MAX provides to perform compositing. The reason for this is a simple one. The Alpha Compositor is the best tool that MAX provides for compositing purposes. You should be aware, however, that the following compositing functions are available in MAX, as well:

- Pseudo Alpha
- Simple Additive Composite

Pseudo Alpha

Pseudo Alpha is a method of compositing that obtains the color value of the first pixel of the image and uses it to make all other pixels with the same value in the image transparent. The first pixel in the image is the pixel in the upper-left corner. This method has limited functionality. You might use it if you want to use a particular image for transparency, but the image has no alpha channel. In practice, however, you can only use images that you render with MAX or some other computer program. The reason for this is that the exact value of the first pixel is used to locate all other transparent pixels throughout the image. If you tried to use Pseudo Alpha to do chromokeying, for example, all the blue would not have the exact same value (even with great bluescreen material). The tiny variations in the color that occur as a result of film or video transfer and compression render Pseudo Alpha useless. You end up with many random holes where the values happen to have exactly the same value as the first pixel. If you use computer-generated images, however, this is not as much of a problem because you can set the background color to be exactly one solid color, and one consistent HSV value. You can use Pseudo Alpha as either a Layer event or a Filter event, and it performs the same function in either instance. A useful plug-in would be to rewrite Pseudo Alpha so that you could pick the color you want and then set a threshold to determine the tolerance of the HSV value.

Simple Additive Composite

The *Simple Additive Compositor* composites the two images by using the second image's intensity or HSV value to determine transparency. Areas of full intensity 255 are opaque, areas of 0 intensity are transparent, and areas of intermediate transparency are translucent. This method also has limited functionality. In practice, the only time you would want to use it is if you want to do a funky blend of two images.

Editing Your Animations

You have now seen how you can composite different images and animations within Video Post. You have your composited animations rendered, and they are ready to impress your clients and friends. You might find that you could really knock the socks off some people, however, if you could add some nice transitions and turn all your individual animations into one cohesive unit. You just took out a second mortgage to buy that nifty new dual Pentium Pro, and there's not much left in the coffers for video editing software. What do you do?

Fortunately, Video Post enables you to edit your animations as well as composite them. MAX ships with a few filters that enable you to do fades and wipes, and third-party plug-ins are certain to follow, enabling you to extend MAX's functionality as an editing system. In addition to using the Filter events that ship with MAX, you can use the Alpha Compositor with animated masks to create great transitions. The following examples show how you can use Filter and Layer events as well as masks to edit your animations and create transitions.

Video Post Event Transitions

This example illustrates how you might arrange a Video Post queue by using layers, filters, and range bars to string together some of the animations used in previous examples in this chapter and do transitions between them.

1. Load MAX or save and reset.

2. Add ch18ex2.avi, ch18ex4b.avi, and ch18ex5.avi as Image Input events in the Video Post queue.

3. Select ch18ex2.avi to highlight it and then click on the Add Filter Event button. Select Fade from the list of filters, click on the Setup button, and make certain that In is currently checked active.

4. Select ch18ex2.avi to highlight it, hold down the Ctrl key and click on ch18ex4b.avi, highlighting both events. Align the animations from the end of one to the beginning of the other by clicking on the Abut button on the toolbar. The ch18ex4b.avi event's range bar should now begin where the ch18ex2.avi event's range bar ends, which is at frame 120.

5. With both events still highlighted, click on the Add Image Layer Event button and select Simple Wipe from the pull-down list box. Click on the Setup button to bring up the Setup dialog for Simple Wipe (see fig. 18.15). Set the direction and mode to whatever you wish. When you have a setup you like, click on OK and specify frames 110–120 in the VP Post parameters as a start and end time for the event. Click on OK to return to the Video Post window.

FIGURE 18.15

Simple Wipe enables you to create wipe transitions between animations.

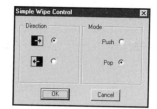

6. Use the Ctrl key to highlight both the ch18ex4b.avi event and then the Wipe event. It is important that you highlight the ch18ex4b.avi event first so that Video Post knows that you want to align the AVI file to the beginning of the Wipe and not align the Wipe to the beginning of the AVI. Click on the Align Selected Left button to align the beginning of ch18ex4b.avi to the beginning of the wipe. You just set up a simple wipe between ch18ex2.avi and ch18ex4b.avi.

7. Now highlight ch18ex5.avi and Abut, align it to ch18ex4b.avi to align the two animations back to front.

8. Click on the Zoom Extents button in the lower-right corner to make the range bars fit within the Video Post window.

9. Use the Ctrl key to highlight ch18ex5.avi and the Simple Wipe. Add a Cross Fade Transition Image Layer event. In the Video Post parameters, set the VP start time to 200 and the end time to 210.

10. Control highlight ch18ex5.avi and the Cross Fade Transition event, and then click on the Align left button to align them properly.

11. Highlight ch18ex5.avi and add a Fade Filter event (see fig. 18.16). Set the VP start time to 279 and the end time to 289. Click on Setup and make certain that Out is specified. Click on OK to accept this event.

12. Click on blank space within the Video Post window to deselect everything. Add an Image Output event and specify the range from 0–289.

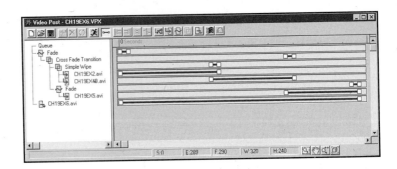

You can render this sequence to your hard disk or view the final rendered ch18ex6.avi from the accompanying CD. If you're uncertain whether you set up the Video Post queue correctly, you can load the ch18ex6.vpx into Video Post from the accompanying CD.

Video Post Masking Transitions

You can use masks (see section on masking in this chapter) within the Alpha Compositor to do transition effects as well. The accompanying CD comes with many useful images and texture maps. The following example illustrates how you might set this up.

1. Load or reset MAX and open Video Post. Load the ch18ex7.vpx Video Post file.

2. Double-click on the Alpha Compositor Layer event. In the Masking section, click on the Files button to bring up the file selector. Navigate to the accompanying CD, highlight TIDE.FLC, and click on the View button to view the animated mask.

3. The TIDE.FLC file is on the accompanying CD. Because this file is made up of either absolute black (0) or white (255), you can use the luminance of the image for the mask. Luminance indicates that a value of 0 is transparent, 255 is opaque, and intermediary values are translucent. Because the FLC is only solid black or white, it works well for transitions. In the list box for the mask, select Luminance.

4. Add an Image Output event and render the sequence, or view the rendered, ch18ex7.avi file from the accompanying CD.

In Practice: Compositing and Editing

- **Alpha Compositor.** You can use MAX's Alpha Compositor to combine images or animation. The ordering of Image Input events is important because it relates to which files need to contain alpha channels. Alpha channels provide a way to create areas of transparency, which are necessary for seeing through one layer event and on to another. Multi-layer compositing enables you to combine as many layers of background and foreground images as you want.

- **Shadow and Light.** You can composite and retain shadow and light effects by using the screen mapping method, the Camera Map plug-in, and Peter Watje's Shadow/Matte material.

- **Masking.** You can achieve complex compositing effects by using MAX's powerful masking feature. With masking, you can use any channel in the image to create a custom area of transparency. This includes using alpha data or even using any of the channels specific to 3D (G-Buffer).

- **Chromakey.** You can use chromakey techniques to composite live action with CG. The Primatte plug-in provides a method of doing chromakeying within MAX.

- **Other Methods.** MAX provides methods other than the Alpha Compositor for doing compositing. Pseudo Alpha and Simple Additive Composite are both limited in their functionality. They do, however, provide an opportunity for a creative programmer to expand and improve upon them. Thanks to MAX's open architecture, this is a likely possibility.

- **Editing.** You can edit your animations in Video Post by using the range bars and Filter and Layer events. You can also use masking to create transitions and achieve new effects that add impact to your animations.

IMAGE CREATED BY ADAM SILVERTHORNE

Chapter 19

by Adam Silverthorne

VIDEO POST EFFECTS

This chapter introduces you to producing specialized effects with MAX's Video Post module. Video Post enables you to produce some amazing effects within your animations. Most effects are used as standard Video Post filters that you add to the Video Post queue. MAX ships with only a few Video Post effects as part of the standard package. Despite the lack of included special effect-oriented Video Post filters, plug-in developers are producing some fantastic software geared toward special effects. For this reason, the bulk of this chapter focuses on plug-ins. Some of the plug-ins discussed are freeware, and the fully working versions are included on the accompanying CD-ROM. Other plug-ins are commercially available from their respective vendors for various prices.

The sheer number of plug-ins available today is phenomenal, especially considering the relatively short time that MAX has been out. Furthermore, new plug-ins are becoming available on a daily basis. Consequently, many more effect-oriented plug-ins are likely to be available by the time this book goes to print. The best way to keep track of the new plug-ins is to regularly check the Kinetix forum on CompuServe and the Kinetix web page (www.ktx.com). You may also find many other MAX-oriented web pages while browsing the web.

Even though many more effects plug-ins are on the horizon, what is available now is enough to make some eyes bulge. Therefore, the overall goal of this chapter is to get you excited about MAX's special effects capabilities. Hopefully, this chapter's examples will inspire you to integrate some of these Video Post effects into your own animations.

This chapter covers the following topics:

- Glows

- Lens flares

- RealLensFlare

- LenzFX MAX

- Blurs

- Adobe Photoshop plug-in filters

- Fractal flow

- Miscellaneous Video Post effects

Glows

Glows are achieved with MAX's Video Post filter events. Glows are useful for heat effects, such as glowing coals or exhaust, surrounding lights in a soft halo, planetary space scenes, lasers, and just about anything else you can think of. MAX ships with a Glow filter that adds glowing luminosity to objects in your scene. The effect is that the objects in your scene that are intended to appear like they give off light will glow near the source as they would in reality. The glow effect is based on G-Buffer information (see Chapter 18, "Compositing and Editing"). The effect is applied to either a Material ID channel or an object channel. Some Glow filter plug-ins enable you to choose either Material ID or Object channel, and some enable use of one or the other without giving you a choice.

You have a few different options when choosing a Glow filter. The standard Glow filter that comes with MAX is simple, but is very useful; in many situations, it is all you will need. A freeware plug-in that is an extension of the standard Glow is available. This plug-in is called Animated Glow, and it enables you to cycle the glow to produce interesting animated effects. Another freeware plug-in, called Super Glow, adds some different features and is designed to function with the freeware lightning plug-in. Arguably the most powerful and flexible glow utilities are available in the commercial packages: RealLensFlare and LensFX MAX. The following sections outline and use the various Glow filters to illustrate how they are similar and how they differ. The last section outlines some glow tips to help you achieve more realistic glow effects.

Glow (Frame Only)

The Glow (frame only) filter is the one that ships with the MAX standard package. This glow affects only the current frame, and therefore cannot be animated. Hereafter in this chapter, Glow (frame only) is referred to as standard glow.

Standard glow functions similarly to the other Glow filters. You can affect objects in your scene in two ways. You can choose the material you want to affect by setting the Material Effects channel to a particular value, or you can specify Object channel in the Video Post filter setup.

The Material Effects channel value is adjusted in the Material Editor, and you must adjust it for the materials you want to be affected by glow (see fig. 19.1). The Video Post filter then finds instances of that Material Effects channel in your scene and glows the corresponding material, or sub-material (in a multi-material).

FIGURE 19.1

The Glow (frame only)
dialog.

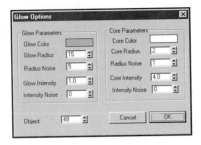

If you choose to apply the glow based on the Object channel, the glow effect will be associated with a particular object or set of objects. You set the ID value for the Object channel in the Properties dialog for the corresponding object. (The properties dialog is accessed by right-clicking on an object and choosing Properties from the list of options.)

In the Properties dialog, the G-Buffer section enables you to set the Object channel to any positive value. The Video Post filter finds instances of corresponding Object channels in your scene and glows the matching object. The color section determines the color of the glow. You can make the glow color the same as your material by selecting the Material radio button, or you can choose the color of the glow by selecting User and choosing a color from the color picker. The size spinner determines how much glow to apply. The higher the value, the more intense the glow is inside the object.

Tip

You should be careful not to set this number too high. Otherwise, the intensity inside the object will wash out the material, and all you will see in your render will be a washed-out blob. Generally, the closer the glowed object is to the camera, the lower the glow size should be and vice versa.

The following example provides a scene containing a construction area stand. These objects usually have a flashing warning light attached to them. In the following example, you use the Glow Video Post filter to re-create how, in reality, the flashing object would glow when lit.

Re-creating Flashing Object Glow

1. Load or Reset MAX and open the ch19ex1.max file from the accompanying CD.

2. Open the Material Editor. The first material slot in the Material Editor contains the material for the warning light's bulb. Change the Material Effect ID from 0 to 1 (see fig. 19.2). This material is already applied to the Light object, so you do not need to apply it.

Figure 19.2

You set the Material Effect ID on materials you want Glow to affect.

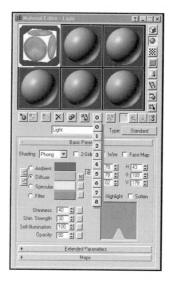

3. Open Video Post. Add a Camera01 scene event. Highlight the Camera01 scene event and add the Glow (frame only) filter.

4. Click on the Setup button to set the Glow parameters. Notice that the default source value is a Material Effects channel value of 1. You can set this to any positive integer. In the Material Editor, you leave this value at 1. Because the Glow filter is set at 1 also, the filter will glow the corresponding material.

5. Set the Glow size to 6. Accept the Glow Control values and return to the Video Post window. Execute the sequence to render a single frame to the Virtual Frame Buffer window.

6. With the Virtual Frame Buffer window displayed, click on the G-Buffer pull-down and change the value from RGB Alpha to Material Effects. The Virtual Frame Buffer window displays a representation of the Material Effects channel that you activated in your scene. This representation displays the area on which the Glow acted. Figure 19.3 shows the final scene.

FIGURE 19.3

The construction area stand with glow applied to the light.

The image looks realistic. The standard glow filter, however, works on every frame the same way. Consequently, you cannot animate the blinking of the light. The Animated Glow plug-in described next enables you to realistically create the flashing light.

Animated Glow

Animated Glow is an extension of the standard glow (see fig. 19.4 and refer to fig. 19.2). Animated Glow functions by cycling the glow effect based on a mathematical equation. You can choose to have the glow cycle based on a Sine wave, a Square wave, an Exponential wave, or a Sine(x)/x wave. With the standard Glow filter, you set a single size parameter. With the Animated Glow plug-in, you must set two size parameters, which determine the maximum and minimum values that the equation will use to determine its cycle. If you are using a Sine wave, for example, the maximum and minimum values determine the crest and the trough of the wave.

FIGURE 19.4

Animated Glow enables you to cycle the glow effect over time.

In the previous example, the glow effect that you applied to the construction area stand worked only for a still frame. With Animated Glow, you can cycle the glow of the light to achieve a realistic flashing effect. The procedure is essentially the same as that of the standard glow, except you must set the additional options that Animated Glow provides. The files ch19agl1.avi, ch19agl2.avi, ch19agl3.avi, and ch19agl4.avi show the geometry from the standard Glow exercise rendered with Animated Glow using each of its four equation options. View each file with the graph of the mathematical equations in mind. The maximum and minimum size values for these examples were left at the default values, but it is possible to change these values to achieve more or less intense flashes.

Did you notice the flaw in the four Animated Glow renderings? If the bulb were flashing the way it does in the renderings, the light emanating from the bulb would illuminate the stand in sync with the flashing of the bulb. It is possible to achieve this effect with the Animated Glow filter by animating the multiplier with Track View to match the Animated Glow cycle. This can be difficult to do manually, however, because you cannot directly visualize where the glow cycle will be at a particular frame aside from doing test renders. You could get around this problem by using the Waveform Controller plug-in.

Waveform Controller

The Waveform Controller is a plug-in animation controller that sets animation values based on a mathematical waveform. You can use the Waveform Controller on the multiplier track of an omni light, and it will sync with the

Animated Glow filter parameters. The following example shows this. Before you can do this example, you need to copy the wavectrl.dlc file from the accompanying CD to your \3DSMAX\PLUG-INS directory.

1. Open or Reset MAX. Load the ch19ex2.max file from the accompanying CD.

2. Open Video Post. Double-click on the Animated Glow filter event. Click on Setup. Notice that the equation is set to Sine and the cycle is set to 20 frames. Accept the settings and close the Video Post window.

3. Open Track View. Expand the omni light named Omni Hazard. Expand the Object parameters. Highlight multiplier by clicking on the text.

4. Click on the Assign Controller button on the Track View toolbar. Select Waveform Float from the list and click on OK.

5. With Multiplier still highlighted, right-click and select Properties from the list to bring up the Waveform Controller dialog (see fig. 19.5).

FIGURE 19.5

The Waveform Controller enables you to control parameters based upon a mathematical waveform.

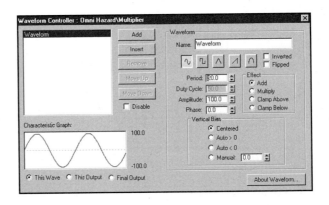

6. Notice that the first button in the row of equation options is the Sine wave. Keep this option selected because it corresponds with the equation set in Video Post for the animated glow filter. Because the period was set to 20 for the Animated Glow filter, you also need to set the period to 20. Increase the period spinner until it reads 20.

7. Close the Waveform Controller dialog and close Track View. You can now open Video Post and render a sequence, or you can view the rendered result in the file ch19ex2.avi from the CD.

You can use the other equations as well. Note that the two plug-ins name the functions differently. Animated Glow's Exponential equation corresponds with Wave Controller's sawtooth. Animated Glow's Sine (x)/x corresponds with Wave Controller's triangle. Make certain that the periods coincide, and you can sync secondary lighting to glow with this combination of plug-ins.

Super Glow

Super Glow is a little different from standard glow or Animated Glow. The advantage that Super Glow has over the standard Glow is that you can specify two different settings for the glow. One setting affects the inside portions of the glow, or the *core*. The other setting affects the falloff of the glow. The core is very close to the object being glowed, and the *falloff* is the rest of the glow. This effect is useful if you need to have two different colors for your glow.

Super Glow works on an Object channel. Both the glow and the core have the same options. The color determines the tint of the glow and partially affects the intensity. Brighter colors result in a brighter glow. The Radius parameter measures a distance in pixels from the edge of the object toward the center. The distance determined by the radius parameter affects the intensity of the glow. The Radius Noise parameter creates variations in the size of the radius. The Intensity determines how much glow will be applied. The Intensity Noise parameter creates variations in the intensity of the glow.

TIP

Super Glow works well with another plug-in, Lightning, which generates a randomly jagged mesh in the shape of a lightning bolt. By applying Super Glow with an intense core and a slightly less intense falloff, you can get something that looks like a lightning bolt (see fig. 19.6). Lightning is available for free download from 3D Café (http://www.3dcafe.com).

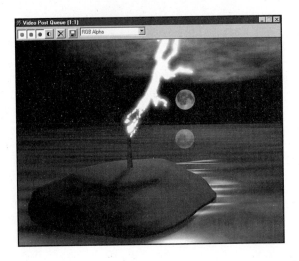

Real Lens Glow

The RealLensFlare plug-in (see the "Lens Flares" section in this chapter) contains its own glow module. Real Lens Glow is a highly optimized glow procedure that processes extremely quickly. Real Lens' glow procedure is roughly three times faster than the standard glow procedure. Real Lens Glow adds flexibility as well. In addition to being able to control the size of the glow and animate it, you can also adjust the density and luminance and animate those aspects of the glow. You can choose to glow the edges if you want. These additional options give you finer control than the other glow plug-ins. You might, for example, want a really subtle glow around an object. With standard Glow, you might find that a size setting of 6 is too little, and a setting of 7 is too high. The additional controls that Real Lens Glow provides enable you to make subtle changes to different aspects of your glow.

Real Lens Glow works as a Helper object, which is another advantage. Because the glow effect is a Helper object, the parameters you set for the glow are fully animatable. Furthermore, you have access to the parameters in Track View. In the sample AVI files you viewed in the "Animated Glow" section, you saw that the glowing bulb did not illuminate the stand. Because Animated Glow cycles its glow effect based on an equation, it is difficult to sync the light with the glow. With Real Lens, however, you can animate the values in Track View and make them correspond with the multiplier of an omni light in the scene. The ch19rlg1.avi file on the accompanying CD shows the construction stand and light glowed by using Real Lens Glow synced with the animated multiplier of the omni light.

LensFX Glow

Glow packages typically enable you to choose a user-defined color, or they automatically base the glow color on the material assigned to the specified object. Although LensFX Glow is still in beta, early indications are that the LensFX Glow module of LensFX MAX will add significant flexibility and power to MAX glow effects. Perhaps its strongest attribute is the implementation of gradients for all aspects of glow color. With LensFX Glow, you can choose a single color or a rainbow of colors to use for both the radial and circular glow colors.

Additionally, with LensFX Glow you can use greyscale gradients to determine different amounts of transparency for various portions of the glow. You can also load and save gradients you or others create. A large preview window enables you to preview your glow settings interactively. You can adjust the position and the color of gradients over time to create animated glow effects. A special scroll bar in the Preview window enables you to preview what the final animation will look like. Almost all the glow parameters are available for editing in Track View. An Inferno tab enables you to use a fractal noise procedure (Fractal Noise is discussed in the section on lens flares later in this chapter) to distort various regions of the glow effect.

Glow Tips

Many animators live for subtlety. Some have found that glow effects go a long way toward improving the visual impact of images and animation. This is especially true when glows are coupled with good lighting. Consequently, you may spend many hours tweaking with glow settings and trying different methods to achieve specific glow effects. Consider the following tips when you use glow in a scene.

Glowing Behind Objects

In certain instances, you may want the glow effect to come from behind your object. One way to achieve this effect is to render the scene with glow applied to the whole object, saving the file or files to disk. Then render the same scene with no glow applied, saving the file or files with Alpha data. You can then composite (see Chapter 18) the no-glow rendering over the glow rendering. This results in a glow behind object effect. The glowcomp.tga file on the accompanying CD is an image rendered using this technique.

Using Glow with Animated Parameters

You can achieve certain animated effects by using any of the glow procedures outlined in this section (including standard Glow) by applying the glow to a material that has animated parameters. If a material uses an animated map or procedural texture such as noise, for example, the glow effect will change based on the state of the material. You can also animate a material's self illumination, and the glow effect will change based on the self illumination value. This technique works well for flashing lights or objects. The technique is also useful for creating effects such as the back of an engine on a spacecraft. The NOISEGLW.AVI file on the accompanying CD is an example of what you might get by using standard Glow on a material that has animated noise in the Diffuse channel.

Glowing Text

Sometimes it is better not to glow an entire object. If you want to create a glowing logo and you apply the glow to the entire object, for example, you might find that the glow appears to slightly shroud and fade out your text. This happens because the glow is being applied to every surface in the text. The surfaces on the inside of the text are glowing inward, slightly obstructing the geometry. In this case, it is usually best to apply the glow only to the faces normal to the camera. This way only the surfaces facing the camera are glowed. The following exercise illustrates this:

1. Load the ch19ex3.max file from the accompanying CD.

2. Select the Extruded Text object and apply an Edit Mesh.

3. In the Sub-Object list box, change Vertex to Face, click on the Window Selection button at the bottom of the screen under the Time Slider, and select only the faces facing toward the camera. This is easily done from the Left or Top viewports.

4. With the faces selected, go to the Edit Surface section of the Edit Mesh modifier rollout and change the Material ID spinner to 2.

5. Open the Material Editor. The first slot in the Material Editor contains a Multi/Sub-Object material. Because you just activated Material ID 2 for the front faces, material number 2 will be assigned to those faces. Therefore, material number 2 is the one you want to glow. Notice that material 2 is a slightly different color than material 1. Another advantage to glowing only certain faces in an object is that you can change the color or texture of those faces to obtain different glow results. Set Material 2 to Effects channel 1 to enable Glow to act on it. Assign this material to the selected text.

6. Open Video Post. The glow size is currently set at 11, but you can adjust this value if you wish. Execute the sequence and render a frame to the Virtual Frame Buffer window. The text appears to glow like neon (see fig. 19.7).

FIGURE 19.7
Using the Glow filter adds realism to a neon sign.

Animating Glow Location

You can also animate the location of the glow on an object to achieve interesting special effects. You can have a ring of glow travel down the arm of a magician character, for example. To achieve this effect, you use the Volume Select modifier. The Volume Select modifier selects a volume of vertices or faces without using the Edit Mesh modifier. The key aspect of Volume Select is that it enables you to animate the movement of the gizmo. You can, therefore, animate a selection volume moving around an object. After you apply the Volume Select modifier, you apply a Material modifier and set the Material ID value to 2. This results in an animated selection volume that changes the Material ID value of the faces it selects while moving around on an object. If you then assign a multi-material that has glow turned on for Material ID 2, that which the selection volume is currently selecting will glow. The following example illustrates this procedure:

1. Reset or load MAX.

2. Create a cylinder of Radius 10 and Height 60. Change the Height Segments value to 50.

3. Apply a Volume Select modifier.

4. Under Stack Selection level, click on the radio button labeled Faces. Activate sub-object selection by clicking on the Sub-Object button. From the Front viewport, non-uniform scale the gizmo down to 10 percent along the Y axis.

5. Move the gizmo so that it is just above the cylinder. Click on the Animate button to activate it. Move the Time Slider to frame 100. Move the gizmo so that it is just below the cylinder. Click on the Animate button to deactivate it.

6. The gizmo should now be animated moving down the faces of the cylinder and selecting the faces that fall within its volume. Add a Material modifier. Change the Value Next to the Material ID spinner to 2.

7. Open the Material Editor. Create a Multi/Sub Object material. Set the number of sub-materials to 2. Click on the color selector for material number 1 and set the color value to Red: 12, Green: 0, Blue: 255. Accept the settings and click and drag the color swatch from material 1 to material 2 to copy the color values. Click on the button for material 2 and change the material's Material Effects channel from 0 to 1.

8. Open Video Post. Add a Perspective or Camera Scene event, highlight it and add a Glow Filter event. Set the value for the Glow to 12. Add an Image Output event and render an AVI to see the results. You can also view the pre-rendered ch19volg.avi file from the accompanying CD.

Lens Flares

Lens flares are optical effects that occur in the lenses of real cameras, but not in MAX's virtual cameras. The effect occurs when light bounces around inside the glass material of a camera's lens. The image is captured while the light beams are in this state of flux, resulting in a photograph containing a bright star-like flare. The term *lens flare* is often used when referring to blemished photographs taken with low-quality camera lenses. If you see a light source through glass in daily life, or if you squint at a bright light source, you should also see a lens flare. If you look at oncoming traffic through the windshield of your car at night, for example, you will see a lens flare.

In 3D animation, lens flares are often used to create added realism in a scene. Furthermore, if you are creative with how you use a lens flare, you can use it to simulate many other interesting special effects. You can use a lens flare to simulate the bursting of a bright star in the galaxy, for example. You can also use it to create more realism for car headlights or streetlights. If you have an object in your scene that gives off light, adding a slight lens flare to it can go a long way toward adding visual impact and realism. Essentially, any time the effect you desire is to make the viewers of an animation know that a specific light is particularly bright, you should consider using a lens flare.

The only Lens Flare package currently available for 3D Studio MAX is a commercial product called RealLensFlare from Cebas software. Another commercial product, LenzFX MAX from Digimation, is in the works. This product is currently in beta and may be available by the time this book is in print. Both plug-ins extend the notion of the lens flare significantly. They enable you to create many special effects beyond the bright star flare traditionally associated with lens flares. You might use RealLensFlare (RLF) to create the sparks of a welders torch, for example. You could also use it to create an animated space nebula or an electrical explosion (see fig. 19.8).

FIGURE 19.8
RealLensFlare 1.5
Fractal Fury.

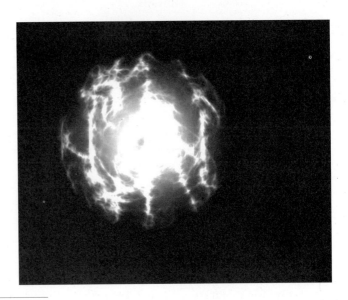

RealLensFlare (RLF)

Release 1.0 of RLF has brought fast and accurate optical effects based on the physics of real-world glass lenses to 3D Studio MAX. Nearly every aspect of RLF is animatable and expression-controllable. In the lenses of real cameras, four types of optical effects occur: lens flares, glows, highlights, and focal blur. RFL uses four distinct modules to re-create these effects as accurately as possible. RFL's corresponding modules are called Flare, Glow, Starfilter, and Depth of Field.

- **Flare.** This module re-creates about every possible optical lens flare that could be brought about by shining different light sources directly into the glass lens of a real camera.

- **Glow.** This module adds powerful and fast glow effects to your MAX renderings.

- **Starfilter.** This module re-creates the star-shaped sparkle that might appear close to extremely shiny materials such as chrome. You can also add twinkling highlights to objects or particle systems to create sparkly fireworks and other special effects.

- **Depth of Field.** This module enables MAX's virtual camera to blur objects that are a specified distance from the location of the camera. This effect can give your animations the cinematic realism of a real camera by focusing the viewer's attention on the foreground action. The module is optimized to handle the borderline between foreground and background objects seamlessly and without jagged lines.

RLFs as Helper Objects

RealLensFlares are added to your scene as Helper objects. You access RLF settings in two places. You can open the Modify panel and access all of RLF's parameters from the standard MAX rollouts. With the Modify panel open, you can also right-click on the Helper object and select Properties. This action brings up the RLF graphical user interface. This GUI is where RealLensFlare's biggest strength lies. The interface is intuitive and fun to use. It provides a preview window where you can see a fully rendered image of the lens flare (see fig. 19.9). When you change the settings in RLF, the preview window updates to show the result of the change. The update rendering is extremely fast.

FIGURE 19.9
RealLensFlare has a fast lens flare preview window.

When you work with lens flares, it is often useful to attach, or *bind*, the lens flare to an object or a light. If you have a light with a lens flare in your scene and you want to animate it, for example, you need the lens flare to move with the light. One of RLF's coolest features does this. This feature is called the Automatic Analytical Binding System (AABS). Despite its complicated name, AABS is extremely simple to use and is extremely powerful. AABS is seamless and invisible to the user. To activate AABS, you need only create the lens flare helper on the object, light, or particle system you want to bind it to. The RLF helper detects and attaches itself automatically.

Binding RLFs to Particle Systems

Binding lens flares to particle systems is great for creating all kinds of special effects. You can bind an RLF Helper object to MAX's standard Spray and Snow particle modules. RLF also binds to Sisyphus's All Purpose Particles and Digimation's SandBlaster particle system. When you bind a lens flare helper to a particle system, each particle becomes an individual lens flare (see fig. 19.10). If you are interested in doing special effects, this feature should cause your imagination to run wild. Sparks from a welder's torch or pulses from a laser rifle are just the beginning. Release 1.5 will extend the power of AABS and particle systems with an added system called Particle Magic. This system will enable you to generate variation on each particle. The result is a particle system that generates different looking light particles. Particle Magic is also capable of analyzing the rotational position of each particle in 3D space, enabling you to make your highlights rotate with the spin of the particle.

FIGURE 19.10
RealLensFlare enables you to make each particle of a particle system a lens flare.

RLF 1.5

At the time of this writing, version 1.5 of RLF is still in beta. It should be publicly available by the time this book is in print. Release 1.5 is a free upgrade to registered owners of 1.0. Version 1.5 greatly extends the functionality of RLF, as the following list illustrates:

- **RLF Files.** A drawback of release 1.0 was that you could not save lens flare settings, which meant that if you had a lens flare looking just the way you wanted, and you wanted to use the same flare in another scene, you would need to write down all of your settings. Now you can save an RLF file and load the settings into your new scene. You can also build a library of effects, download other settings, or share settings with coworkers.

- **Gradients.** RLF 1.5 enables you to adjust the lens flare effect by using gradients. You create a gradient that determines the transparency of the lens flare area, which is useful if you want to soften or feather the lens flare in your scene. Another new feature is the added support of motion blur. You can use motion blur to simulate realistic special effects. One way to create interesting smoke is to apply motion blur to a particle system made up of lens flares. This might sound scary if you have used motion blur in the past. RLF, however, handles motion blur very quickly. Adding motion blur to lens flares with RLF only adds approximately 30 percent to your render time. Motion blur with lens flares is also useful for doing trailers. You can give your 3D animation the *Akira* look, for example, by trailing fast moving objects with motion blurred lens flares.

- **Fog.** RLF is now fog aware. As you move the lens flare into the fog, the lens flare fades and eventually dies out. This proves useful for underwater scenes where an object, such as a submarine, slowly disappears into murky water. The lens flare also inherits the color set for your fog.

- **Alpha channel blur.** RLF 1.5 adds the capability to blur the alpha channel. This is useful for compositing glowing or focal blurred objects.

- **Glow Edges.** The Glow Edges function gives you greater control over where the glow appears on an object. This is particularly useful for glowing text and logos because it saves you from needing to set the glow for certain faces only.

Fractal Fury

One very cool addition to RLF is a module called Fractal Fury. Fractal Fury is a procedure that distorts the lens flare and the glow halo that RLF generates. The procedure uses fractal noise, which is a mathematical procedure that produces random perturbations based on fractal mathematics. The distortion results in gaseous clouds of intense color and variety, wispy electrical arcs, and fire tendrils. Fractal Fury can generate realistic looking space nebula, science-fiction–type explosions, and other special effects.

Like the other modules in RLF, Fractal Fury renders very quickly and its parameters are fully animatable. Because Fractal Fury is a distortion, the setup of your original flare affects your result. You can, therefore, get a different Fractal Fury result by adjusting the basic lens flare parameters. The Fractal Fury module contains three basic types of effects: electrical, glowing clouds, and burning flames. Electrical randomly generates thin electrical arcs. The glowing clouds effect creates globular and swirling gaseous systems. The burning flames effect creates twirling, threadlike flames. Figure 19.11 illustrates some of the effects you can generate with Fractal Fury.

FIGURE 19.11
Some of the possibilities you might achieve with Fractal Fury.

LensFX MAX

LensFX was the best selling special effects package ever for 3D Studio DOS (for good reason). It enabled 3D Studio animators to add beautiful special effects to their animations while providing great flexibility. The LensFX legacy has migrated out of the DOS world and into the world of 3D Studio MAX with a new lens flare package called LensFX MAX. At the time of this writing, LensFX MAX is undergoing beta testing and is not currently publicly available. By the time this book is in print, however, it will likely be shipping. Although LensFX MAX inherits most of the features of its DOS predecessor, it is not simply a direct port of the DOS software. LensFX MAX is completely redesigned to follow 3D Studio MAX's 32-bit object-oriented architecture.

The new interface contains four distinct modules: Lens Flare, Glow, Hilight, and Depth of Field.

- **Lens Flare.** This module re-creates optical lens flares brought about by shining different light sources into the glass lens of a real camera.

- **Glow.** This module adds glow effects to your MAX renderings.

- **Hilight.** This module adds brilliant, photorealistic effects to shiny metals and glass. Hilight simulates a photographic cross star effect and comes with dozens of user-definable settings.

- **Depth of Field.** This module blurs objects based on their distance to the camera. LensFX MAX module enables you to easily create rack focus effects to add an extra touch of realism to your work.

The lens flare module enables you to select from pre-built flare effects, load and save .LZF LensFX MAX lens flare settings, or set your own settings manually. You can create your flares by combining any combination of glows, rays, rings, and secondary reflections. Figure 19.12 diagrams these various lens flare parts.

FIGURE 19.12

The parts of the LensFX lens flare.

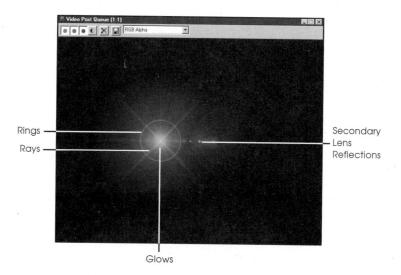

LensFX MAX enables the user to control the color, transparency, intensity, shape, and size of the lens flare effect. Custom animation parameters allow effects to be animated as well. LensFX MAX is accessed as a Filter event in the Video Post queue. Lens flares are created by choosing a source object in the Filter Setup dialog. Anything selectable from within 3D Studio MAX is a valid source object. A large preview window enables you to preview your lens flare, and a special Time Slider enables you to cycle the preview window to see how your parameters affect your lens flare over time.

Another new feature is called Auto Secondaries, which automatically creates any number of secondary lens reflections. For specialized flash effects, LensFX MAX provides a feature that enables the user to control the amount that the flare will brighten the entire scene. This feature proves useful when creating explosions and other effects that require a bright burst of light. LensFX MAX also has special commands that enable you to control the positioning of secondary flares in your scene, enabling you to have secondary lens reflections that follow different paths and change size based on the camera's field of view. LensFX MAX also has a channel soften feature that enables you to blur your scene based on G-Buffer channel information.

One of the neatest features of LensFX MAX is its extensive use of gradients. Every section within the flare module has at least one color selector for the corresponding part of the lens flare. Each color selector can be set to a solid color or a gradient range of colors. The range for the gradient can contain an unlimited number of flags. The flags set the color for the gradient at the location of the flag (see fig. 19.13). The result of these gradient selectors is unparalleled control when choosing a color combination for your lens flare. You can have, for example, a gradient that cycles from blue to red to green for the glow radial color of the lens flare. LensFX MAX also has a special new feature called Inferno, which is a fractal noise procedure similar to RealLensFlare's Fractal Fury module. Inferno adds realistic fire and smoke effects to LensFX MAX. Although LensFX MAX is still currently in beta, the indications are that it will be a solid lens flare package when it ships.

FIGURE 19.13
LensFX MAX makes extensive use of gradients.

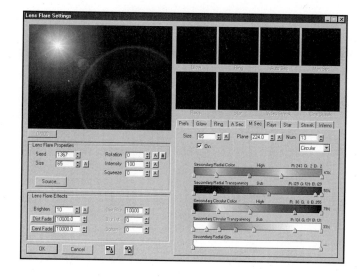

Blurs

Blur effects are useful in a number of situations. Blur effects are commonly used to create a depth of field. When your eyes focus on an object, that object comes into focus and objects on the periphery of your field of vision become slightly blurred. The effect occurs in real cameras and is often exaggerated in motion pictures. When viewing a scene, the effect serves to focus the viewer's attention on a particular spot. By using fields of depth in your MAX scenes, you can force your viewers to focus their attention on the action. This technique can also save modeling time. Because certain areas of your scene are blurred, you don't need to spend a lot of time detailing those areas. The effect can give your animations the cinematic realism of a real camera. Blurs are also used for special effects, such as the atmospheric distortion created by heat. By using blurs, for example, you can re-create a jet engine's exhaust system and be faithful to reality. This section outlines four methods you might choose for depth of field or other blur effects.

Blur (Frame Only)

The Blur (frame only) plug-in is a freeware plug-in written by Johnny Ow. The plug-in blurs the scene based on a Material ID channel or an Object channel. Because the plug-in blurs the scene based on G-Buffer information and not on computational physics, it is better suited for special effects than it is for depth of field. The Blur plug-in is accessed as a Video Post filter event. Figure 19.14 shows the Filter Setup dialog.

FIGURE 19.14

You can blur a scene based on the Material ID or Object channel.

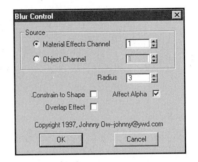

The Source section enables you to specify the particular Material Effects or Object channel you want to use. The Radius parameter controls the level of the blur. A higher radius results in a blurrier area. The Radius parameter also controls the size of the soft edge that surrounds the blurred portions of the image. The Constrain to Shape check box instructs the blur to limit its effect to the exact pixels occupied by the specified Material Effects or Object channel. If Constrain to Shape is checked, the Radius parameter no longer controls the size of the soft edge because the soft edge is eliminated. The Affect Alpha check box instructs the blur filter to blur the alpha channel, which allows for seamless compositing of blurred images. The Overlap Effect check box instructs the blur filter to computationally overlap the pixel sections that it blurs. The effect is usually an increased blurriness, but it also tends to distort and smear the affected regions. The following example illustrates how you might use the blur plug-in to create heat distortion effects. Before you do this example, you need to copy the Blur.flt file from the accompanying CD to your \3dsmax\plug-ins directory.

1. Reset or load 3DS MAX and load ch19ex4.max from the accompanying CD.

2. Select the Exhaust01 object, right-click on it, and choose Properties. Set the Object channel to 1. The Exhaust01 geometry already has a material applied that has Opacity, Shininess, and Shininess Strength all set to 0.

3. Create a Ripple space warp with amplitude 1 set to 5.0, amplitude 2 set to 6.0, and wave length set to 50. Bind the Exhaust01 object to the space warp. For the heat effect to appear realistic, you need it to animate. Because the Blur filter works on each frame the same way, you need to change the form of your Exhaust object to get the effect you want.

4. Click on the Animate button, go to frame 100, and set the phase for the Ripple space warp to 15.

5. Open Video Post. Double-click on the Blur filter to edit the Filter event, and click on Setup to bring up the Blur Setup dialog. Activate the Object radio button and be certain that the value is set to 1. Set the Radius to 4 and leave everything else unchecked. Click on OK to exit the Blur dialog and click on OK again to return to the Video Post window.

6. Execute the sequence and render a single frame to the Virtual Frame Buffer window. You can add an Image Output event to the Video Post queue and render an animation, or you can view the pre-rendered ch19ex4.avi file from the accompanying CD.

TIP

You can also use the Blur filter to create a faux depth of field effect. Essentially, you leave your foreground object focused and blur your background. By setting the object channel to 0 in the Filter Setup dialog, everything in your scene will blur unless you change the default value on your objects to a number other than 0. You can blur everything except specific objects, or you can blur everything and then composite a focused foreground.

Fields Of Depth

The Fields Of Depth plug-in is an inexpensive utility written by Andrew Cross. A demo version is provided on the accompanying CD—if you send the author $15, he will e-mail (or snail mail) you a fully registered version. The shareware registration form is in the fodreg.txt file on the CD. Fields Of Depth is a Video Post filter. The plug-in uses computational physics to simulate a real camera lens, and thus enables you to simulate camera focus (see fig. 19.15). The Fields Of Depth plug-in provides broadcast-quality depth blur in an easy and understandable interface. The plug-in renders relatively quickly and supports alpha channel processing for seamless compositing. The Fields Of Depth plug-in has an elegant interface with understandable icons that illustrate the various options available (see fig. 19.16).

FIGURE 19.15
These images illustrate the focal blur effect.

FIGURE 19.16
The Fields Of Depth plug-in enables you to blur areas of your image based on real camera lens physics.

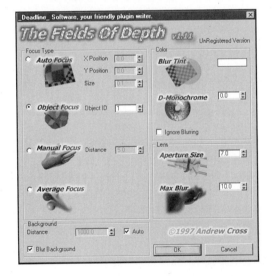

The various options of Fields Of Depth that follow enable you to specify and adjust the focus region:

■ **Auto Focus.** This optional mode enables you to position an area of focus in your scene. The X and Y values correspond to the horizontal and vertical positioning of the focus area. The values for these settings range from −1 to 1, with 0 being the center of the screen and −1 and 1 being the antipodes. The size parameter determines the size of the focus area. The value ranges from 0 to 1, and the value determines the size relative to the size of the screen to keep in focus. A value of .1, for example, means that the focus area will occupy a circle 1/10 the size of the screen.

■ **Object Focus.** This option enables you to specify an Object channel. Objects with the corresponding value set for their property direct the camera's area of focus. This is different than the Blur (frame only) method because it is based on the camera, and consequently the focused area extends beyond the proximity of the object. Object Focus is the easiest and most useful of the focus types that Fields Of Depth offers and is probably the method you should use in most situations. The area of focus follows the object specified if it is animated. The ch19ex6.avi file on the accompanying CD shows an example of Object Focus in action.

■ **Manual Focus.** This option works somewhat like a standard camera's manual focus feature. You specify the distance from the camera, and Fields Of Depth adjusts its area of focus on the specified distance.

■ **Average Focus.** Average focus calculates the average of all distances in the scene and creates its area of focus at the average point. This is useful if you want the area of focus to be in the center of your scene. Average focus requires no user-definable parameters.

The color section of the Fields Of Depth plug-in enables you to tint the out-of-focus objects. The D-Monochrome parameter works in conjunction with the Blur Tint Color picker. If you adjust the D-Monochrome value without choosing a blur tint color, the most blurred objects become monochrome. You must set a value in D-Monochrome if you want the Blur Tint Color picker to function. The value ranges from 0.0 to 1.0. A 1.0 value fully tints the most out-of-focus areas to the specified color. If no color is specified, the most out-of-focus areas are turned completely monochrome. If you check the Ignore Blurring check box, the color section affects the image but no blurring occurs.

The Aperture Size setting determines the size of the area to be blurred. A higher number results in a smaller blur area and vice versa. The MAX Blur spinner adjusts the maximum amount of blur. The higher the number, the more the blur, and the longer it will take to render.

The Background section enables you to adjust how Fields Of Depth will blur the background image if there is one. Auto Blur, however, works fine for most purposes. If you uncheck Auto, you can specify a distance to the background. The further the distance, the blurrier the background image will be. You may want to uncheck the Blur Background check box if the image you are using for your background is already blurred.

RealLensFlare: Distance Blur

One of RealLensFlare's modules is a depth of field plug-in. Like the other modules of RealLensFlare, Distance Blur is created as a Helper object. You place Distance Blur helpers in your scene, which allows for easy placement of focus points. Distance Blur can blur the background, adjust focal depths, and has an auto focus feature for quick and easy blur effects. You can access the Blur parameters in Track View, and you can animate the position of the Helper object. This is useful for creating rack focus effects, where blurred objects in the background suddenly come into focus and vice versa. In version 1.5 of RLF, the Distance Blur module has been enhanced. It now supports alpha channel processing so that you can composite focal blurred images seamlessly. Another added feature, 3D Space Blur Radius, enables you to set near and far ranges for the Distance Blur helper. You can then animate the helper moving smoothly through your scene to create realistic fly through and other effects. A Fancy Blur option enables you to blur specified objects only, based on their distance from the camera. This feature enables you to create object-based distance blurs.

LensFX Focus

The LensFX Focus module of LensFX MAX enables you to do depth of field effects as well. Like the other modules in LensFX MAX, LensFX Focus is a modeless window. This means that with the LensFX Focus module open, you can still access other parts of MAX. When you bring up the Setup dialog for LensFX Focus, a phantom Control object is automatically created. You can set or edit the parameters of the Control object in Track View. LensFX Focus enables you to set values for horizontal and vertical focal loss, which adjusts the overall level of the blurriness. You can lock these values so that they adjust symmetrically, or you can create streaking blurriness and other effects by making the horizontal and vertical blurriness values different.

- A *Scene Blur* option blurs the entire scene based on the values set for horizontal and vertical focal loss.

- A *Radial Blur* option creates a circular target area that remains in focus. You change the focal area with focal range and focal limit spinners. The focal range sets the distance for the cameras focus, and the focal limit sets the distance at which the scene will become completely out of focus.

- A *Focal Object* option enables you to use a selectable item in your scene to create your focus area.

Alpha channel support is available for seamless compositing of focal blurred scenes and a Preview button enables you to generate a preview of how your settings will affect the Video Post queue.

Adobe Photoshop Plug-In Filters

Release 1.1 and later of 3D Studio MAX includes a Video Post filter that enables you to run Adobe Photoshop-compatible filters on images and renderings from within Video Post. Hundred of filters are currently available for Photoshop and other image processing, editing, and enhancement programs. You can create all kinds of interesting effects by using Photoshop-compatible filters with your MAX renderings. Most any image processing effect you can think of probably has a corresponding Photoshop-compatible filter. You can use Photoshop-compatible filters, for example, to make your rendering look like a painted fresco, to add a film grain look, or to tweak out the colors in creative ways.

The MAX Photoshop Plug-in Filter event will work only with 32-bit Photoshop-compatible filters. Consequently, not all the available Photoshop filters will work with MAX. Older 16-bit filters will not be recognized. Furthermore, some of the plug-ins that ship with Adobe Photoshop are programmed to work only with Photoshop. Figuring out which ones will work and which won't is a matter of trial and error. If you attempt to use a Photoshop filter designed to work only with Photoshop, MAX will crash. You should save or hold your file, therefore, if you intend to experiment in this manner. Photoshop-compatible filters have an .8BF file name extension. You can find many 32-bit Photoshop-compatible filters available for free download on the web.

T I P

The following is a list of fun and useful filters you might try applying to some of your animations. You are likely get some extremely psychedelic results. All of the filters in this list are included with Adobe Photoshop 4.0 and have tested well with the Adobe Photoshop MAX plug-in.

- Diffuse Glow
- Glass
- Ocean Ripple
- Film Grain
- Smudge Stick
- Watercolor
- Plastic Wrap
- Rough Pastels
- Paint Daubs
- Sponge

The MAX plug-in uses the native interface of the Photoshop filter to give you an interactive preview of the effect. In most cases, the parameters you set for the filter are saved with the .MAX file and the Video Post .VPX file. This feature enables you to return to the filter to make modifications of the parameters. Some plug-in filters do not allow MAX to access the settings, and therefore MAX cannot save them. The Kai's Power Tools third-party Photoshop plug-in utility pack does not allow MAX to save settings. If you intend to use filters from this product, you should make certain that they are set correctly before exiting the setup, or you should write down the settings for use in future sessions. The Adobe Photoshop Plug-in Filter event can be nested, enabling you to use multiple filters on one image or rendering. You cannot animate the effect, however. If you apply the filter to animation, for example, the filter is applied with the same settings to every frame. When the Filter event is applied to an Image or Scene event, the Image or Scene event appears as the child of the Filter event in the queue. The Filter event then applies to the Image event that is a Child event of it.

Figure 19.17 shows the Photoshop Plug-In Setup dialog. You must first add the filter to the Video Post queue. You can then double-click on the event to bring up the Edit Filter Event dialog and then click on Setup to bring up the Setup dialog for the filter.

FIGURE 19.17

The Photoshop Plug-In Setup dialog.

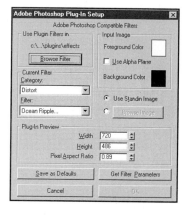

The Use Plugin Filters in section is where you specify the directory where the Photoshop-compatible plug-in filters reside on your hard disk. Click on the Browse Filter button and navigate to the directory to select it. After a directory containing filters is specified, select the category you want from the Category list box in the Current Filter section. The category is encoded in the plug-in file and typically is the name of the developer or the name of the filter package.

Beneath the Category list box is the Filter list box, where you specify the filter you want to use. The Input Image section enables you to specify a foreground and background color, which is needed for some Photoshop filters to function correctly. The KPT Page Curl filter, for example, curls the corner of the image like a turning page. To work properly, this filter needs to know the background color because it places the background color into the area revealed by the upturned page.

The Use Alpha Plane check box determines how the filter handles the alpha channel in an image. Typically, if an alpha channel is available, the Photoshop filter affects only the opaque areas of the image. If the Use Alpha Plane check box is unchecked, the alpha channel information is discarded and the filter affects the entire image. If you are using a mask for the filter (see the section on masking in Chapter 18), for example, the mask is still used and serves to replace the alpha channel. If the Use Alpha Plane check box is checked, only pixels designated as opaque in the alpha channel and pixels that are not masked are affected by the filter.

The Use Standin Image radio button sets the background for the preview window to a standard checker pattern. You can specify an image to use instead by activating the Browse Image radio button and clicking on the Browse Image button to select an image.

The Plug-In Preview section sets the size of the image that you want to use in the preview window. These settings determine how faithfully the preview window will represent what you will see in your final rendering. You should set these parameters to correspond with the image you are using for the preview. Clicking on the Get Filter Parameters button brings up the Interactive Preview window and enables you to adjust the settings to use for the selected Photoshop-compatible filter. Figure 19.18 illustrates an example of the Ocean Ripple Distortion Photoshop-compatible filter applied to the Tutvally.tga file that ships with MAX.

FIGURE 19.18

The Adobe Photoshop Plug-in Filter enables you to use Photoshop-compatible plug-in filters from within Video Post.

Fractal Flow MAX

Fractal Flow, the popular 3D Studio DOS image processing IPAS routine, is currently making its way into the world of 3D Studio MAX. Currently, Fractal Flow MAX is in beta, but it should be available by the time this book is in print. Fractal Flow uses fractal mathematics to distort an image or specific parts of an image in various ways. Fractal Flow is useful for simulating cloaking spaceships, creating heat distortion, or creating realistic fire, smoke, clouds, water, and other special effects.

Although Fractal Flow is a Video Post filter, the Setup dialog is modeless. Modeless dialogs enable you to access other parts of the program while they are open. Because it is modeless, when you bring up the Setup dialog for Fractal Flow, the Video Post window vanishes. You can minimize or move the Fractal Flow Setup dialog and continue to work in MAX. When you hit the Setup button for the first time, Fractal Flow places a phantom Control object in your scene. The Control object enables you to edit and modify the animatable parameters within Track View. The Setup dialog also has its own Time Slider and preview window, which is linked to the MAX Time Slider. By pressing the Time Slider's play button, you can view your Fractal Flow effect in the preview window interactively. Fractal Flow is divided into four main panels: Control, Fractal Distortions, Waves, and Ripples.

Within the Control tab, the *Settings* section enables you to load and save your Fractal Flow settings (see fig. 19.19). One of the most powerful aspects of Fractal Flow is that it contains the capability to use the saved Fractal Flow setting as a standard bitmap. This means that you can use your Fractal Flow settings as bitmaps in the Material Editor.

- **Preview Size.** Enables you to set the image size that Fractal Flow will use for its preview window.

- **Render Preview.** Determines how much of the Video Post queue will be used for the preview.

- **Up To Filter Only.** Creates a preview image containing the Video Post image as it appears in the queue up to the point of the Fractal Flow filter.

- **Whole Queue.** Makes the preview contain the image as it would appear if the entire queue is processed.

- **Bitmap Background.** Enables you to use a background image for the preview.

FIGURE 19.19

*The Fractal Flow
Control tab.*

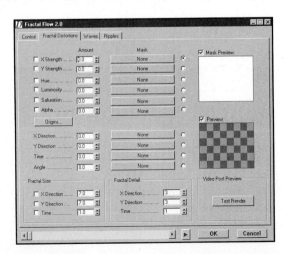

TIP

If you intend to save your Fractal Flow settings and use the corresponding .FLO file in the Material Editor, you need to specify a background image. Using the background image is necessary for Fractal Flow to export the settings correctly for use as a material.

The Fractal Distortion tab is where you set the general Fractal Noise parameters that distort your images (see fig. 19.20). The check boxes on the left activate the corresponding parameter. After you activate a parameter, you can adjust the value and view the results in the preview window. You can also animate the parameters by moving the Time Slider at the bottom of the dialog and set checked parameters to different values at different frames. MAX's Animate button does not need to be activated to set keyframes.

FIGURE 19.20

*The Fractal Distortion
tab is where you set
your general Fractal
Noise parameters.*

WARNING

Because you can set frames without the Animate button being active, you may end up setting keyframes inadvertently. If your results seem erroneous, you should open Track View and make certain that you have not accidentally set extra keyframes.

The preview window at the bottom right corner gives you a preview of the effect against a checkered background. If you click on the Test Render button, Fractal Flow renders the Video Post queue and shows you a rendered preview of your settings. The mask buttons next to the various animatable parameters enable you to create a mask for the effect. Clicking on the radio button next to the mask buttons activate the corresponding mask. After you select a mask, the Mask Preview window updates to show what your mask looks like. Fractal Flow has very powerful masking features. You can mask using linear or radial gradients. You can create a mask by using bitmaps as well. Seven buttons enable you to specify the alpha channel, the RGB color channels, the M channel (Maximum luminance) or the Y channel (Chrominance value) to use as your mask. You can also specify a specific Material ID or Object channel, and you can limit the mask to a depth range or face normals. A Blur parameter softens the edges of your mask.

The Waves tab enables you to create a wave distortion across an image. You can set the number of waves, the height of the wave, the angle at which the waves cross the image, and the speed at which they move across the image (see fig. 19.21). You can animate and mask these parameters in the same manner as those in the Fractal Distortions tab. The Waves tab also enables you to specify the highlight and shadow color and the direction and intensity of the light that will accentuate the waves.

FIGURE 19.21

The Waves tab enables you to create a wave distortion on your images.

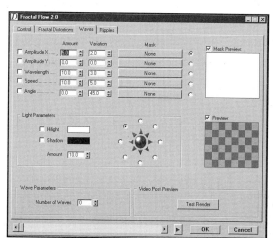

The Ripples tab enables you to create circular ripples across an image. The options for ripples are similar to those of Waves (see fig. 19.22). You can, however, also control how the ripples will decay as they move away from their origin. You can set the origin of the ripples and use a mask for the origin.

FIGURE 19.22

The Ripples tab enables you to create a ripple effect on your images.

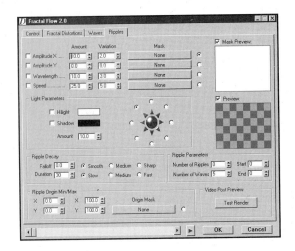

Miscellaneous Effect Plug-Ins

Many miscellaneous plug-ins are available in addition to the ones discussed so far. Some are quite useful, and because of MAX's open architecture, many more are sure to follow. This section outlines a few miscellaneous plug-ins that have proven most useful.

Negative

The Negative filter ships with MAX. This filter inverts the colors of an image. The result looks like the negative of a color photograph. You might use this filter if you need to model a film reel. You can render a frame through the Negative filter and use that image as a tiled map on some celluloid film geometry. You might also use this filter in an abstract or psychedelic animation. Negative requires no setup parameters.

Outline

The Outline plug-in is a Video Post filter written by Harry Denholm. This plug-in creates an outline around specified objects or materials. The outline can be a user-definable color. This plug-in is particularly useful for creating reference frames and examining motion. By surrounding specific objects with an outline, it is easier to dissect subtle animated movement. It is also useful for *rotoscoping*, the process of compositing computer graphics over live action. In certain situations, the computer graphics match the background closely, and it is useful to have a mechanism whereby you can easily discern the CG and the live action as separate elements. By outlining certain objects, you can achieve this goal. The plug-in works on a Material ID or an Object channel.

Stamper

Stamper is a nifty Video Post filter written by Andrey Zmievski. It takes an embossed image and stamps it into a background image. Stamper is a charityware plug-in, meaning if you find it useful, the author asks that you make an appropriate contribution to your favorite charity. The stamp looks like an inverse imprint (see fig. 19.23). This utility is useful for placing logos and copyright information on images and animations. Stamper also supports .IFL files to use as the input image, so you can animate the movement of a stamped image around the screen. This effect is similar to the identification tag that T.V. stations sometimes place over their shows. If you use Adobe Photoshop, you just take your logo, make it black and white if it is not already, and then run the Stylize/Emboss filter on it. After you have an embossed image, you are ready to stamp it. The Stamper interface has a few options. Browse to select the embossed image you want to stamp. After you have an image selected, the four buttons in the Location section determine where the embossed image will appear in the final image. After you choose a location, you can offset the stamp from that location by adjusting the X and Y value spinners. The Stamper plug-in (stamper.flt) is included on the accompanying CD.

FIGURE 19.23
The Stamper plug-in enables you to stamp an embossed image on to your MAX renderings.

Starfield Generator

Starfield Generator is a Video Post filter written by Tom Hudson. It is useful for creating realistic space scene backgrounds. The plug-in is included on the accompanying CD. There are many ways to create star fields in MAX. You can create them with environment maps by using bitmaps or procedurals such as noise. Starfield Generator's advantage over other methods, however, is motion blur. If your scene requires camera movement, the Star Field generator enables you to control the amount that the stars will blur in relation to the movement of the camera. Motion blur is great for creating added impact in space scenes. Motion blur can also be useful for creating special effects such as warp speed star streaks and other effects. Starfield Generator works off of a camera in your scene. You should apply the filter to a Camera Scene event. Access the Setup parameters by clicking on the Setup button in the Edit Filter Event dialog (see fig. 19.24).

FIGURE 19.24

Starfield Generator Setup parameters.

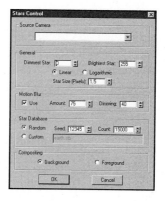

The Source Camera section enables you to select a camera for Starfield Generator on which to base its calculations. If you have multiple cameras in your scene, you should specify the same camera that you add to the Video Post queue. If you specify another camera, the stars will not match the motion of the camera that you render.

The General section enables you to specify the general parameters that determine how your starfield will look. The Dimmest Star and Brightest Star spinners range from 0–255, with 0 being completely black and 255 being solid white. If you want your starfield to be composed completely of dim stars, for example, you can lower the value of the Brightest Star spinner.

The Linear and Logarithmic radio buttons mathematically determine how the brightness changes from dim to bright. The Star Size spinner determines the size of the star dots in pixels.

The Motion Blur parameters determine how the streaking effect occurs when the camera moves. The Use check box turns Motion Blur for the stars on or off. The Amount spinner determines how much motion blur to use and ranges from 0–100. The Dimming spinner sets the amount that the motion streaks will dim as their trails get longer. This value also ranges from 0–100. The default values for Amount and Dimming work fine in most cases.

The Star Database section determines how many stars appear and where they are generated. The Random button uses the number in the Seed spinner to generate a random number of stars and to place them. The Custom radio button enables you to read in a star layout from a specified file. There is currently no way to save your own star layouts.

Finally, the Compositing section determines whether the stars are placed behind your rendering or in front of it.

In Practice: Video Post Effects

- **Special effects.** Special effects go a long way toward adding visual impact to a scene. By using Video Post filters, you can include a variety of effects in your images and animations. Most of the special-effects–oriented filters available today are plug-ins. Keeping track of all the new plug-ins can be both a daunting and exciting task. The Internet and CompuServe are both great resources for obtaining new MAX plug-ins.

- **Glow.** Glow effects are useful in many situations. Currently, a number of glow plug-ins are available. You should experiment with the various free plug-ins to determine whether they will suit your needs. If not, the commercial plug-ins RealLensFlare and LensFX MAX contain more powerful and flexible Glow modules.

- **Lens flares.** Lens flares can be a striking addition to any scene. The most common criticism of lens flares has been their gratuitous overuse. You should make certain that your scene warrants using a lens flare before you start tossing them into scenes. Subtle use of lens flares will take your images further. Slight or barely noticeable flares around light sources give extra realism to your scenes. Remember that lens flares can also be used for special light effects. The Fractal Fury module of RealLensFlare 1.5 and the Inferno module of LensFX MAX both add the capability to create realistic special effect phenomenon.

- **Blur.** Blur effects are useful for creating special effects and reproducing camera focal blur. You can use blur effects to reproduce atmospheric heat distortion, for example. You can use depth of field blur to more faithfully reproduce the look of a real camera.

- **Adobe Photoshop Plug-in filters.** These filters enable you to modify your images and animation in a great variety of ways. The Internet is a great resource for obtaining Adobe Photoshop compatible 32-bit filters, and a variety of third-party commercial collections are available.

- **Fractal Flow MAX.** This makes special image processing effects possible from within Video Post. You can create general fractal distortions, waves, and ripples within your images and animations.

IMAGE CREATED BY JEREMY HUBBELL

Chapter 20

by Jeremy Hubbell

SOUND IN MAX

Over the past few years, multimedia has become an explosion of sight and sound. Sound has always been a part of computers, but really nothing more than blips and bleeps from a four-inch speaker. Today, sound in computers has changed the way we communicate, the way we are entertained, and the way we are informed.

This chapter introduces you to what sound is all about as it relates to your PC and 3DS MAX. The following topics are among those covered in this chapter:

- The basics of sound
- Sound technologies
- Sound hardware
- Sound mixer controls for NT
- Using sound in MAX
- The Audio Controller plug-in

The Basics

Sound on a PC comes in various *flavors,* which means that there are varying levels of quality and file size to suit your needs. A review of the basic concepts of digital sound is a good place to start this discussion.

Digitizing

When your computer records sound, it takes electrical signals from an analog source, such as recording from a microphone, and turns them into digital information—essentially ones and zeros. The computer interprets the digital information and displays it to you as a two-dimensional representation—a waveform.

The waveform displays a great deal of information, such as the given amplitude and the length of the sound. It does not display, however, the third dimension—the medium in which the sound travels. This medium is normally air, but it could be water or even rock.

If you look closely at the waveform, you will see where it derives its name. The waveform is really a graph of peaks and troughs. The distance from the peak to the trough is known as *amplitude,* and the lateral distance from one peak to the next is a *cycle.*

FIGURE 20.1
A display of a waveform.

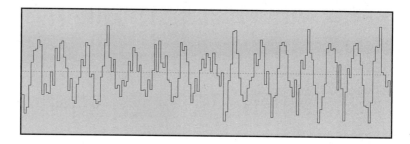

The best way to think of how cycles and amplitude relate to what you hear is that amplitude is usually associated with how loud a sound is, and cycles are governed by the pitch (how high or low).

NOTE

A WAV file in Windows contains all cycle and pitch information of a digital sound.

Sampling Rates

When the computer records a sound, it must do so by taking several samples of that sound and piecing them together to represent that sound digitally. This technique, known as sampling, can greatly affect sound quality and file size. Recording at a sampling rate of 44,100 Hz, for instance, is comparable to CD quality; half that is more akin to "radio" quality.

Waveforms of identical sounds recorded at different sampling rates differ noticeably in appearance. Notice that the steps are very visible on the 8,000 Hz example. The 44,100 Hz sample, on the other hand, is much more smooth. You are essentially just looking at the resolution of the waveform. Much like an image, the more "chunky" it appears, the more information has been lost from the original.

FIGURE 20.1
The same sound file at 8 kHz, 22 kHz, and 44.1 kHz. Notice the amount of "stair-stepping" in the 8 kHz sample.

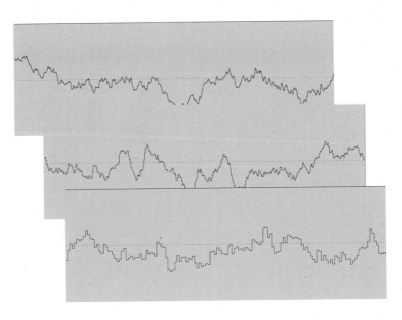

Bit Depth

Much like your display has different bit depths for the number of colors you can have in an image, sound on your PC possesses the same quality. Most sounds have one of two bit depths, 8 or 16.

As with sampling rates, as bit depth increases, so does sound quality. The bit depth setting is controlling the number of levels of amplitude per sample you can have for a digital sound. A wider amplitude range reproduces better high frequencies such as a cymbal and much deeper low frequencies such as rumblings from a kettle drum in the same sample.

An 8-bit sample can have a maximum of 256 levels of amplitude. A 16-bit sample can go as high as 65,536 levels of amplitude. The differing end results are quite dramatic both in sound quality and file size. You can expect a doubling in file size by choosing a 16-bit sample over an 8-bit sample. If sound quality is important, however, then you will need to work with 16-bit samples.

NOTE

A 16-bit sound recorded at 44,100 Hz (CD-quality) is a standard referred to as *Redbook Audio.*

3D Studio MAX is designed to use any size or type of waveform that your PC supports. Before you start animating your WAV recordings of your favorite CDs, make certain that you take the following into account.

Higher sampling rates produce higher quality recordings but can take up enormous amounts of storage space. This is especially true of lengthy recordings. You must weigh what is critical when using sound in MAX.

It is often better to work with sound in a lower quality form. There is really no need to load a 60 MB WAV file into MAX and sacrifice interactivity when you can use a scaled down version in sampling rate and bit depth that maybe only uses 10 percent of that. Programs such as SoundLab, part of Autodesk Animator Studio, have this type of conversion functionality. Save the high-quality sound for final output.

PC Sound Technologies

The important thing to remember is that 3D Studio MAX only reads WAV files, by default. Therefore, if you only plan to synchronize your animation to an already existing sound, all you need to have is a sound card capable of digital audio playback. Basically, any standard sound card you buy these days will have digital audio playback and recording capabilities. The following are the "must haves" for sound cards in MAX:

- 16-bit digital audio playback

- Stereo sound

With MAX's release 1.2, you can now use WAV files to control an object's animation. This new feature is called the Animation Controller. The audio controller animates objects based on the amplitude of a WAV file. For that to be possible, the sound card must have some kind of input. This could be a Line-In, Mic-In, or CD-In, or all three. The following sections describe some of the other technologies that you may want in a sound card.

MIDI

A set of instructions called MIDI is the key to the computer talking to the sound card. MIDI stands for Musical Instrument Digital Interface, a standard that has been around for many years in the music industry. A MIDI signal contains all the necessary information to play a sound for a specific length of time at a certain pitch. Because the file contains only instructions and not the actual digital sound, MIDI files (.MID) are much smaller in size than their WAV counterparts. With a plug-in, MAX could, easily animate objects based on MIDI instructions. Both FM and Wavetable technologies, discussed in the next few sections, use MIDI for playback and recording.

FM Sound Chips

The FM (frequency modulation) sound chip has been around since PC sound cards were first produced. FM chips work off the principle that they can create duplications of real sounds by using the chip's circuitry. The result is that sounds from a drum to an environmental sound such as wind can be re-created by the FM chip.

The main downside of the FM chip is that the re-created sounds don't often sound like the real life counterpart, resulting in very computer-generated sounding music.

Wavetable Synthesis

FM chips still have their uses but are being quickly replaced by a newer technology called Wavetable synthesis. Wavetable synthesis on a PC is equivalent to what transistors were for the computer. Instead of having a computer play wimpy, tinny sounds out of your speaker system, you can now have an orchestra!

Here's how it works. Wavetable technology incorporates a lookup table of digital samples of real instruments or real sounds. An entire table is referred to as a *bank*. A bank of sounds can be various samples of different instruments or sounds, or it can be one specific type of sound. When the computer requests to play a sound, the Wavetable chip determines which type of sound needs to be played, the length of playback, and the pitch. It then makes the necessary modifications to the digital sample stored in the table and plays the modified sample through your sound card—all in about a millisecond. This technology will make your projects, presentations, games, and anything that uses music seem more real.

Wavetable synthesis uses compact MIDI information to play back real sounds that would normally be too large if used in a file. In the past, MIDI information only sounded good when played back on a PC if you had expensive hardware. Today more and more sound card manufacturers are using Wavetable synthesis combined with 16-bit digital audio to provide consumers with the complete sound experience.

Digital Signal Processing (DSP) and 3D Sound

Digital signal processing is a technology that allows a sound being created or played back by the sound card to be modified to change the way the sound is heard. The most common forms of DSP are changing the acoustical properties of a sound, making you feel like you are sitting in a different space. A sound that was recorded in a studio, for instance, sounds like it was recorded in a studio when played back. A DSP chip could add the effect of reverberation (basically an echo), however, to make it sound like you are sitting in a concert hall.

DSP is at the heart of 3D sound, the latest technology to hit the PC airwaves. With 3D sound, not only can you get an effect of being somewhere else, but you can also hear sound coming from different locations other than your speakers! The amazing thing about 3D sound is that you really don't need extra hardware. You can use your existing sound card with your speaker system and still get many of the benefits.

More and more sound cards are implementing DSP. Both DSP and 3D sound play perfectly into the MAX production environment because that environment is simulating a different 3D space. That 3D space could be the one you are designing in the viewports! Best of all, DSP works with both MIDI and digital sound playback.

Speakers

Speakers are the remaining link in your PC sound system and are probably the most critical. Consider that you could have bought a $500 sound card only to realize its capabilties on a pair of $30 speakers. You have come this far, now is not the time to skimp.

When considering what type of speakers you might like, ask yourself the following questions:

- What will be the primary use?

- Where will I be listening?

- How much space do I have for speakers?

- Will the speakers need to be portable?

These are probably not the only questions you could ask yourself, but you should at least consider them before making a speaker purchase.

You have many brands and types of manufacturers to choose from when buying speakers. Obviously, the best test of all is to listen for yourself. Don't buy speakers before you have listened to them. When shopping around, you should follow a few guidelines:

- Make certain that the speakers are magnetically shielded.

- Make certain that the speakers contain the necessary cabling to hook up to your sound card.

- If the speakers are not right, can you return them?

If you are serious about speakers, plan to spend some time shopping. Sometimes your best selection and deal might be where you least expect it. You might be wondering how much speakers will cost you. On average, a good set of speakers sells for about $100. The price ranges from $20 to $700, however, depending on the setup.

The next few sections review what is available in speaker technology and attempt to demystify how speakers work.

Traditional Desktop Speakers

Almost every computer store you go to now has some form of "multimedia" speakers that you can add on to your PC or purchase with an "upgrade kit." Unfortunately, most of these stand-alone speaker types are of poor quality and deliver relatively little in terms of sound.

The Ranks of the Non-Amplified

Perhaps at the bottom of the speaker food chain, besides your internal PC speaker, is the un-amplified (passive) four-inch multimedia speaker set. These speakers sell for usually less than $20 and don't do much except produce small sound amplified only by the two watts coming from your sound card.

Although small, non-amplified speakers normally are not used for production, they do have some good uses—especially when portability is an issue. For a small presentation that needs to be portable, these speakers are a great solution. They are light because there are no batteries or power transformers to lug along, and they can be placed anywhere around the computer. You do not, after all, usually need a massive speaker system when giving a presentation in a small boardroom.

Getting Powered

The next level up in the traditional system is a powered (active) speaker—powered in the sense that it can amplify the signal coming from the sound card. Even the slightest bit of power amplification in your speakers can make them sound much bigger than they really are. You can pick up some powered speakers for only a little more than the non-powered. You will be glad you did. Even if portability is an issue, you might be able to get some speakers that require small batteries and don't necessarily need to be hooked up to a power socket.

Amplified speakers tend to have a few more features than non-amplified ones. If you are trying to get the best bang for the buck, make certain that the speakers have at least the following:

- Bass control

- Treble control

- Balance

- Separate A/C or battery power options

You could substitute tone control for a separate bass/treble control, but this limits you. A tone control acts as sort of a fulcrum. When tone is balanced, there is an even ratio of bass to treble. If the tone leans toward bass, however, bass increases while treble decreases. The result is a heavy bass, but it sounds rather muffled because the treble is gone. The reverse happens if tone is altered in the opposite direction.

Having separate bass and treble control gives you the flexibility to boost both levels or raise one while the other remains normal. It is to your advantage to spend a little extra to get this functionality.

The Satellite/Subwoofer Combination

Perhaps the most popular speaker combination in the marketplace, the satellite and subwoofer combination, can produce an enormous amount of high-quality sound.

The combination works very well in small- to medium-sized spaces. The addition of the subwoofer breathes a whole new life into your computer's sound system. You can now experience the low to lower mid range frequencies most traditional speakers can't reproduce.

The satellite speakers—smaller speakers that handle mid- to high-range frequencies—can be purchased separately, but you will usually find that most are sold in conjunction with the subwoofer. The satellite speaker's placement is fairly crucial. You may not want the speakers to be sitting immediately to the left and right of your monitor, but you certainly don't want them sitting three or four feet from either side. Left and right speakers in a computer system handle 90 percent of the sounds that come from your sound card. They should be placed in such a way that a monaural sound appears to be coming directly from the center of your screen.

The subwoofer is the next step in this combination. The subwoofer can really go anywhere in a room, but is best placed near the computer in a corner somewhere. Corners provide some of the best bass response but can also produce what are known as standing waves—bass that hangs around longer than it should. If you find that occurring, just move the subwoofer farther away from the walls. Your hearing cannot really perceive where a low frequency (such as a rumble) is emanating from, so placement is not as critical. Subwoofers are also usually monaural. They will combine left and right low frequencies and produce one sound. Again, this is okay because you really can't hear the difference at such a low frequency.

This combination of satellite speakers with a subwoofer is what most people will get because they produce great sound at an affordable cost.

Other Speaker Types

There are other speaker combinations for you to choose from besides the standard computer speakers. As a matter of fact, you might find that an alternate solution is better for your needs.

Three-Dimensional Sound Speakers

Three-dimensional sound speakers rely on licensed 3D sound technology to modify the sound coming from your sound card and to add 3D spatialization effects. Usually these speakers are designed to work with any sound coming from your computer, and make it sound as if it is all around you—making your speakers seem as if they are everywhere.

When used in conjunction with software, 3D sound speakers can place sounds in certain locations. A good example of this is a jet flying straight at you and passing overhead. Normal speakers would just treat this as a sound starting softer and then getting louder as the jet passes. 3D speakers would actually make adjustments in the acoustics of the sound so that your ears perceive something to be flying overhead and behind you.

3D sound speaker systems usually look just like a satellite/subwoofer combination, but they have special circuitry to handle the 3D effects.

Proper placement of 3D speakers is as crucial, if not more so, as a traditional speaker setup. Usually, you want the speakers to be immediately to the left and right of your monitor. The manufacturer will usually provide you with the optimum placement settings.

Surround Sound Speakers

Surround Sound (Dolby Pro-Logic) speakers might sound like a frivolity at this point. After all, when would you have a usage for surround sound from your computer? If you are involved in any production work designed for broadcast, you know why. Surround sound is used by hundreds of television stations and every network utilizes it somehow. Almost every household that has purchased a home-entertainment system in the past five years has some type of surround sound unit. Only recently, however, has the PC industry adopted surround sound.

Dolby Pro-Logic uses what is known as *matrix* technology to encode all four channels of sound into just two (left and right). This makes WAV files a perfect technology for playing back surround sound on your computer, because they only incorporate left and right channels.

The technology incorporates a six-speaker system, three front speakers, two surrounds, and usually one subwoofer. Here is how the decoding process works:

- Left and right audio is fed from your VCR, LaserDisc player, or computer to your Dolby Pro-Logic receiver/decoder.

- The Dolby Surround matrix is decoded by the Pro-Logic circuitry. The two channels are broken into four.

- The four channels (Left, Center, Right, and Surround) are then sent to the appropriate speakers. The subwoofer usually just takes the front channel information and uses an electronic crossover to cut out all the high frequencies.

Although you don't have the ability to directly access these individual channels by default in MAX, you can play a WAV file recorded in surround sound. You can then edit your animation not only based on the sound heard, but also the sound's location in 3D space!

There are several ways to get this technology for your PC. Manufacturers produce multimedia speakers with the Pro-Logic circuitry built in. This is a compact solution that gives you great results, especially when you are strapped for desktop space. If you have a little more room, you can purchase a "traditional" home system and just hook it up directly to the PC. Magnetic shielding for the speakers is the only important thing here, because the magnets in your speakers can produce some rather colorful patterns on your monitor if they get too close.

After sorting out your hardware, it is time to get your computer talking to it. Software configurations vary from computer to computer. Make certain that you follow the manufacturer's installation instructions for both hardware and any drivers that need to be set up.

Windows NT and Sound

Windows NT 4 brings a level of sound functionality in high-end PC operating systems not previously found before. In a nutshell, Microsoft has now provided many of the sound board mixing and configuration controls previously only available on actual physical sounds mixing consoles.

Volume Control

When your sound card is installed and configured properly, a little picture of a speaker appears on the taskbar. Click on it to adjust the main volume of the sound card with the Volume Control slider that appears (see fig. 20.3). There is also an option to mute. This controls the overall volume of all inputs of your sound card. If you want to control those outputs individually, double-click on the speaker icon to bring up the Mixer.

FIGURE 20.3

The Windows Volume Control slider. Single click the speaker on the Taskbar to get this dialog.

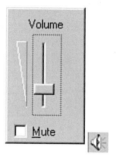

The Windows NT Mixer

After double-clicking on the speaker icon, you will be presented with the main Volume Control panel, which is very similar to many mixer utilities that come with most sound cards (see fig. 20.4).

FIGURE 20.4

The Volume Control panel is used to mix the sound as you might with an "analog" soundboard.

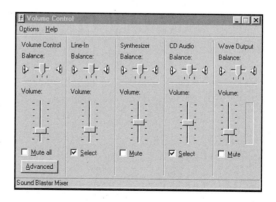

This panel is comprised of the following components:

- **Main Volume Control.** This is a duplicate of the volume control available by single-clicking on the speaker icon. The main difference is the balance control available for all outputs.

- **Line-In.** This volume control enables you to specify the volume output of whatever source is plugged in to your line-in input of the sound card. This is the volume control you use if you have an external CD-ROM drive.

- **Synthesizer.** Next to that is the Synthesizer output control, which controls the MIDI output volume from either your sound card's MIDI device (OPL chip or Wavetable synthesis) or a dedicated MIDI interface connected to an external MIDI instrument.

- **CD Audio.** The CD volume control sets the input level of the digital audio tracks coming from your CD player. Note that it does not control the volume of a program running from a CD. In that case, you would use the Wave Output control. The CD volume control is only useful if you have your internal CD playing through your sound card. Most sound cards have internal hookups to connect the audio-out of the CD so that you can use this feature. You can also use the line-out of your external CD player to connect to the line-in on your sound card.

- **Wave Output.** Next to that is the Wave volume control. This enables you to adjust digital audio volume control. Notice also that it has an empty box next to it; that is the output level meter—a critical component when making recordings because it can tell you whether your settings are too high and might result in distortion. The level meter will come on when you are playing back WAV files in Windows.

- **Advanced.** If you select Advanced Controls from the Options pull-down menu, an Advanced button appears underneath the main Volume control. Clicking on this button brings up a panel to control the Bass and Treble settings during playback (see fig. 20.5). Adjust these as necessary to produce the best sounding playback possible.

FIGURE 20.5

The Windows Advanced Controls dialog. You can control bass and treble amounts for your sound card here.

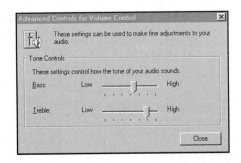

■ **Recording.** If you click on the Options pull-down menu and choose Properties, you are presented with a dialog to choose a Mixer panel for various controls, one of which is Recording. Click on Recording and then on OK. A new panel that has many of the same controls as the playback Volume Control panel appears. These settings enable you to adjust how sounds are recorded.

Animating to Recorded Sounds

One of the best parts of animating in 3DS MAX is using its sound features. Out of the box, MAX can play back WAV files through a sound card as well as a metronome played through your PC internal speaker. This is useful when you are animating objects based on pre-recorded sounds. You can load up any length WAV file and position it in Track View. Figure 20.6 shows a WAV file loaded into the Sound Track of Track View.

FIGURE 20.6

The Track View with a WAV file assigned.

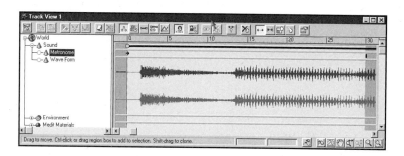

WARNING

Large WAV files consume precious amounts of RAM and may lead to hard disk paging. Use caution when working with long or high-resolution WAV files. Chop up your sound into smaller pieces so MAX can eat it.

Using WAV Files in Track View

To add WAV files in Track View, first click on the Track View icon in the MAX toolbar or choose Track View from the Edit pull-down menu. Click on the Sound entry in the Track hierarchy list, and then either click on the Properties button in the Track View toolbar or right-click and choose properties (see fig. 20.7).

FIGURE 20.7

*Track View with the
properties dialog for
sound track.*

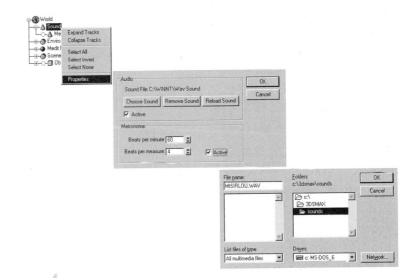

To add a sound, click on the Choose Sound button. By default, MAX looks in
its Sounds directory or whichever directory is chosen for sound in the
Preferences section. You can choose any file that has an audio stream
attached to it. This is typically an AVI file or a WAV file. Click on OK to add
your sound.

Once loaded, the sound's waveform appears in the Track View track display.
By default, the beginning of the sound is aligned with frame 0 of your
animation. You can use the Range Bar to position the sound anywhere in
time. If the sound is shorter than the length of your animation, it is repeated
as many times as necessary to reach the end. Otherwise, the sound is
terminated at the end of your animation. MAX does not enable you to modify
the sound in any way except altering its starting position in your scene.

To hear your sound, just click on the Play button in the MAX interface. You
can also scrub the sound—that is, play it from the Frame Slider by dragging
the slider back and forth along the Timeline. Sound can be scrubbed forward,
but not backward.

NOTE

To hear sound during playback or scrubbing, the Real Time box must be checked in the Time
Configuration Panel. Access this with a right click on the Time Icon in the lower-right corner.

Sounds loaded in Track View can be attached to an *.avi* rendering. By default, when you have a sound active in Track View, it will automatically be attached to *.avi* output. This includes previews and full renderings. If you want to use the sound merely as a guide and not to be included with the final output, you must uncheck the Active option beneath the file assignment buttons within Track View.

If you are editing the sound file in a sound editing package, you can use the Reload Sound button to load the newly saved version. That way, you can just Alt+Tab between MAX and your sound editing tool. To remove a sound, click on the Remove Sound button.

Using the Metronome

The metronome is designed to provide a rhythmic, repeating beat with which to synchronize your animation. It consists of two parameters and an Active check box.

The Beats per minute value specifies how many beats the metronome will play every minute of animation. The default, 60, means that your PC speaker will beep every second with a "low" tone. The minimum is one beat per minute.

The Beats per measure value specifies which beat of the Beats per measure value is played in a high tone. This places emphasis on that beat. The default is four, and the minimum is two. With a value of two, every other beat is emphasized.

Both values are dynamically displayed in Track View's Track display. As you adjust the Beats per minute variable, small vertical lines appear to move farther apart or closer together depending on the values you are selecting. Beats per measure are displayed graphically by black dots in the Metronome track.

NOTE

You cannot scrub the Metronome track. It can only be heard when using MAX's Playback button with the Real Time option checked on.

FIGURE 20.8
The Metronome with different settings.

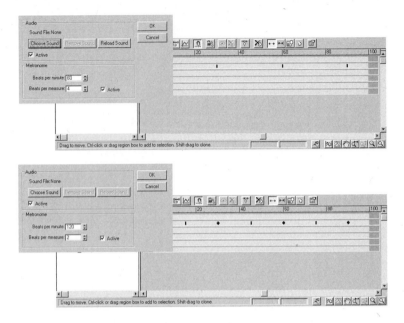

The Audio Controller Plug-In

Developers have taken it upon themselves to take advantage of the extensibility of MAX and add new sound capabilities. One of these is the Audio Controller from Kinetix. Like any other animation controller in MAX, it is used to control the behavior of an animatable property over time. In this case, instead of using math functions like the other controllers, Audio Controller uses sound. The sound can be a WAV file or recorded in real time from a microphone or CD source.

Setting Up the Audio Controller

First, make certain that the file auctl.dlc is in your Plug-ins directory or in a directory where MAX knows to find them. After that's done, all access to the Audio Controller's parameters will be in Track View. Apply the controller as you would any other controller from within Track View. After you have applied it, you can access its properties by selecting the Track name from the hierarchy display and then clicking on the Properties button.

NOTE

You cannot control the plug-in from within the Motion panel. You can, however, apply it to any of the Transform tracks there.

FIGURE 20.9

Assigning the Audio Controller to the Rotation track.

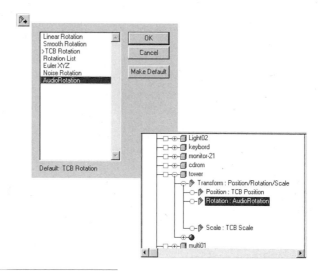

Audio Controller Parameters

The Audio Controller has several functions that you can edit. This section presents what those parameters are and how they can affect your overall animation. The following tutorial shows how to apply the controller and use its functions.

Choosing and removing sounds works just like assigning a sound to the sound track. The Absolute function, however, is new. Use the Absolute option when you want a sound to utilize all 256 possible levels of amplitude when working with the audio controller—even if it does not use it. This function works best when you have a recorded sound of something quiet. Because the Audio Controller works from amplitude, the resulting animation would be minor. Using the Absolute option causes the sound to be stretched out across the entire possible amplitude range, however, sending more dramatic changes in amplitude to the controller and therefore resulting in better animation.

The real-time control enables you to use an input device hooked up to your sound card to animate your objects. The devices displayed in the drop-down list are what NT knows are valid recording sources. This is typically a function of the sound card and its drivers.

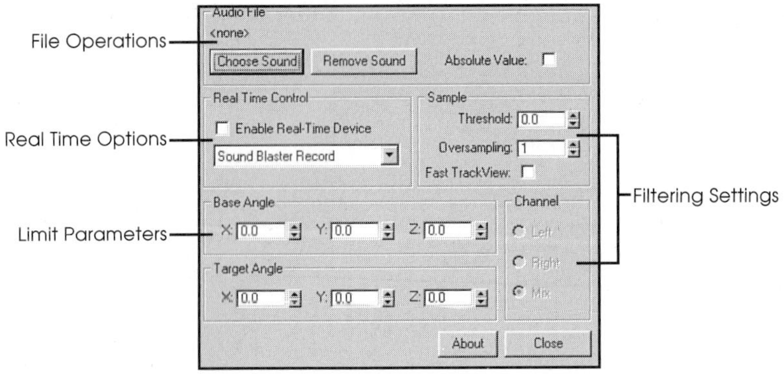

FIGURE 20.10

The Components of the Audio Controller window.

File Operations

Real Time Options

Limit Parameters

Filtering Settings

To use the Real Time option, just choose the input device from the pop-down list and then check Enabled. Animating with the Real Time option can be one of the easiest ways to do lip-sync animation. All you have to do is talk into a microphone, and you can make a character's mouth jaw flap. Mouth morph targets or animating bones or other control devices will give a more professional lip-sync, but this method is perfectly acceptable in more limited animation productions. The following paragraphs describe how to control the various animation parameters for an object.

The Sample section is for fine-tuning the values sent by the controller to the track you have assigned it. This works for both sound files as well as real-time recording. The best way to think of the Sample parameters is as a filter from the sound to the values input to the track itself. When you look at a WAV file, for example, you can usually see sharp peaks and troughs. This can cause the audio controller to send rather sharp values and result in "jumpy" animation. The Oversample value enables you to smooth out those peaks and troughs. The higher the Oversample value, the smoother the waveform becomes. The other value, Threshold, acts like a faucet. Based on values between 0 and 1, you specify what the cutoff point is for a sound. The higher the number, the less of a sound that actually comes through. You would use this value only if you have serious amounts of noise in the sound.

NOTE

A value of 1 for Threshold will effectively cancel out the sound's effect on that track because it filters out everything.

Another Filtering option is which channel of the sound to use: left, right, or both. If you are using a monaural WAV file or a microphone input, these options are greyed out because both channels are equal. With stereo sounds, however, you can isolate the left or right channels to suit your needs. Normally, you will leave this set to both, but sometimes one channel is louder than the other or has more distortion. In that case, choose the channel that animates your objects best.

Beyond the Filtering parameters and channel selection, you also have the ability to specify what range of movement, rotation, scaling, or values will pass from the sound to the track itself. The Audio Controller actually exists in five forms. As a result, the animating parameters or limits differ based on which type of track you have assigned them to. The five types of Audio Controllers are:

- Audio Position

- Audio Rotation

- Audio Scale

- Audio Float

- Audio Point

The three audio transforms obviously map to the respective Transform track. The Float version works with other types of animatable parameter that wouldn't use audio for position, rotation, or scaling. The Point version works with tracks where multiple limits are used (the RGB values for a diffuse color on a material, for example). Figure 20.11 shows the versions of the limits section for each type of controller.

If you are interested in seeing what the Audio Controller is capable of, the next exercise explores the application of the controller to bells of an alarm clock to cause them to vibrate wildly to an alarm clock sound.

FIGURE 20.11

The limit values for each of the different types of audio controllers. Note that depending on which controller you use, you may have several values to work with.

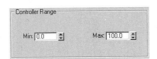

Making an Alarm Clock Ring with Audio Controller

In this exercise, you will take a look at how to use the Audio Controller to animate alarm bells on a clock character by using a WAV file. First start by opening the file of the model.

TIME TO WAKE UP

1. Select File, Open. Choose clock.max and click on OK.

The next step is to bring up Track View and expand out the display so that you can see the left Bell object's Rotation tracks.

2. Click on the Track View button in the toolbar and expand the hierarchy to Clock/Left Bell/Transform/Rotation. This displays the Clock object's hierarchical structure.

The Audio Controller is assignable to any type of track. In this case, apply it to the Rotation track.

3. Click on the Rotation label to highlight it.

4. Click on the Assign to Controller button (see fig. 20.12). This brings up the Controller Assignment dialog.

FIGURE 20.12

Click on this button to assign the Audio Controller to the rotation track.

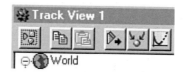

5. Choose Audio Rotation and click on OK. This exits the dialog and assigns the new controller to the Rotation track (see fig. 20.13).

FIGURE 20.13

The Audio controller is now assigned to the rotation track. Note that a blank area now exists in the main track display.

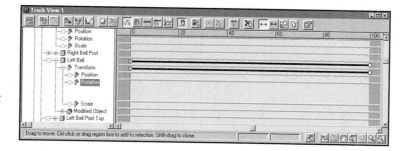

After you have applied the controller, the Rotation track's display changes a bit to make room for the WAV file you will use. As it stands right now, there are no parameters for the controller, so there is no animation. You will assign the sound file of an alarm clock's alarm going off in the Audio Controller's Control panel.

6. Right-click on the Rotation label and choose Properties.

7. Click on the Choose Sound button.

8. Select alarm.wav and click on OK. This loads the alarm clock sound and displays it in the Track display.

As soon as you assign the sound, its waveform display appears in the Rotation track. Right now, it is a bit small. You will change that through various settings in the Control panel. The first thing is to turn on the Absolute parameter.

9. Check on Absolute Value (see fig. 20.14). The displayed peaks of the alarm waveform are increased.

FIGURE 20.14

*The Audio Controller
configuration
parameters for the
rotation track.*

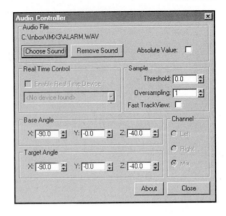

The next step is to use the Oversampling feature. With it, you can smooth out a waveform—they are generally rough. Rough sounds can make an object animate rather strangely, so it is best to use this feature most of the time.

10. Set 10 for Oversampling to smooth out the waveform.

The next set of parameters to define are the Start and End ranges for an object's animation when it uses the sound. The Base value represents an object's rotation state when the sound is at an amplitude of 0. The target value is the maximum rotation an object will have at an amplitude of 255.

11. Set the Base angle value for Y to 60.

12. Set the Target angle value for Y to 20. This changes the target angle for when the WAV file is at maximum amplitude.

13. Click on the Close button of the Audio Controller's Control panel to exit.

NOTE

Currently, there can only be one Audio Controller per scene. You can have multiple *instances* of the controller in the scene, however, to control various parameters for the object.

14. Expand the hierarchy to Clock/Right Bell/Transform/Rotation.

15. Click on the Assign to Controller button. This brings up the Replace Controller button.

16. Choose Audio Rotation and click on OK. This exits the dialog and assigns the new controller to the Rotation track.

17. Right-click and hold on the Rotation label and choose Properties to bring up the Audio Controller's Control panel.

18. Click on the Choose Sound button to bring up the Select File dialog.

19. Click on OK to load alarm.wav and display it in the Track display.

TIP

Because the Audio Controller can only work with one sound at a time, the last sound loaded is stored in any Audio Controller you apply. All you have to do is click on OK after you have clicked on Choose Sound.

20. Turn on Absolute and set Oversampling to 10 to assign the same parameters to the new controller.

21. Set the Base angle value for Y to –60. This changes the base angle so that there is no sound from the WAV file.

22. Set the Target angle value for Y to –20. This changes the target angle for when the WAV file is at maximum amplitude.

23. Click on the Close button of the Audio Controller's Control panel to exit the Control panel.

NOTE

The reason why you didn't instance the Audio Controller from the left bell to the right was that all values, including base and target angles, would be instanced. Because the bells are rotated at different angles, instancing would have produced the wrong result.

You are done! All that's left is to make a preview. If you like the preview, you can do a complete rendering afterward.

24. Make certain that the Perspective view is active and choose Rendering/ Make Preview. This brings up the Make Preview dialog.

25. Click on Create to create the preview.

NOTE

The Audio Controller does not play back the audio in MAX. If you want to create a preview with the sound attached, assign the alarm.wav file to the Sound track in Track View.

Remember, the Audio Controller is assignable to any track. The main difference to you is what you see in the dialog. Applying the Audio Controller to the Rotation track, for instance, uses the Audio Rotation controller. That controller has parameters specific to rotation when using sound. On the other hand, applying it to the Angle track of a Bend modifier will use the Audio Float controller, which has slightly different settings.

The Absolute parameter makes the sound file use a complete range of 256 levels of amplitude, even if it doesn't have it originally. This parameter helps when you have a relatively minor sound by making the highest amplitude be a value of 255 and the lowest 0. Think of it as scaling the sound file's amplitude to fit the entire range possible for digital sound.

By changing the Oversampling, you can see a visible difference in the waveform display. If the object's animation is too smooth or "watered" down, set the value lower. If it is still too "jumpy" or rough, increase the value. Displaying a large oversampled sound file can tax the Track View display and cause slow redraws. If this is happening to you, check on the Fast Track View parameter. This returns the display to the original waveform, but still uses the oversampled sound file for animation purposes.

If you want to enhance the animation a bit, you can assign the Noise modifier to the clock's body for both scale and position. That way, when the bells go off, the clock's whole body shakes. See the file clockcmp.max on the accompanying CD to get a better idea of how to set this up.

In Practice: Sound

- **Sound in the 3D world:** Traditionally, audio has never been part of the world of 3D modeling and animation packages. Today, with sight and sound merging more and more through multimedia, companies such as Kinetix and the Yost Group realize the need to implement sound into a visual software package. In the future, you will see even better integration. MAX's sound features are a testament to that fact.

- **Out-of-box capabilities:** Audio capabilities in MAX are quite extensive out of the box. You can completely animate a scene based on a WAV file or to a metronome.

- **Sound plug-ins:** With the extensibility of MAX, it is now possible to add in your own types of sound features through plug-ins such as the Audio Controller. Expect to see more of this in the future.

Index

Symbols

2D compositing, organizing, 46-49
3D animation
  G-Buffer information, 671-672
  lens flares, creating, 713
  motion picture development, 10-12
  organizing, 46-49
  SoftImage versus 3D Studio MAX, 28-33
  software
    Alias/Wavefront, 11-12
    Prisms, 11-12
    Renderman, 11-12
    SoftImage, 11-12
3D artists
  career ruts, 52
  career specialization, 52-53
  work environment, effects of deadlines, 57
3D Café web site, 707
3D Max Spray and Snow module, 715-716

3D sound
  DSP (Digital Signal Processing) format, 747
  speakers
    circuitry, 751
    importance of placement, 751
3D Studio MAX
  Adobe Photoshop filters, 727-730
  application development by Sony Pictures Imageworks, 20-23
  Bones Pro plug-in, solid mesh characters, 256-259
  Combustion objects, background cloud motion, 110-111
  compositing tools
    Alpha Compositor, 668-679
    Pseudo Alpha, 693
    Simple Additive Compositor, 693
  computer games development
    DreamWorks Interactive, 24-27
    Westwood Studios, 27

development
    ISDN modems, 16-17
    market release, 17-19
    team members, 13-19
    The Yost Group, 13-19
  earthquake cam effect, creating, 510-513
  file formats
    RLA, 51-52
    Targa, 51-52
    TIFF, 51-52
  file output, 50-52
  file translation programs, 62-63
  Fractal Flow
    purpose, 731-734
    settings, 731-734
  future goals
    low cost versions, 19
    plug-ins, 19
    Yost Group (The), 19
  G-Buffer technology, 671-672
  growth, 42
  importing
    Detailer creations, 231
    Poser 2 creations, 231
  Kodak Cineon digital image format, 62

lack of compatibility with
Unix-based software,
50-52
limited to IBM platforms,
50-52
loading sound, 463-464
low to medium budget
effects, 52
market share, 42
MorphMagic, 445-447
motion picture develop-
ment, 10-12
motion picture effects
Blur Studio, 33-36
Digital Phenomena,
36-38
Pyros Pictures, 39-41
visual effects, 33-38
multiple platforms, KA
Share software package,
61-62
Negative plug-in, 734
Outline plug-in, 735
particle systems
All Purpose Emitters
(APE), 573-578
Deflector, 589-596
Sand Blaster, 578-581
smoke, 573-578
snow, 567-572
Spray, 582-588
Wind space warp,
582-588
Physique
overview, 407-408
plug-in, solid mesh
characters, 256-259
plug-ins, HyperMatter,
617-618
production organization,
division of labor, 49-52
"shaky-cam" technique,
creating, 510
sound card require-
ments, 745
Stamper plug-in, 735
Starfield Generator plug-
in, 736-738
tools, RealLensFlare
(RLF), 714-715

using with
Alias software, 63
Flame software, 62
Matador software, 62
SoftImage software, 63
Wavefront software, 63
versus
Renderman Pro, 50-52
SoftImage, 28-33
"Vertigo" effect, upgrade,
485-487
Windows NT platform, 12
16-bit linear colorspace,
21-23
35 mm Anamorphic Wide
Screen Format, 59-60

A

AAPlay for Windows,
animation previews,
500-501
activating
Automatic Analytical
Binding System
(AABS), 715
Cross Section Editor
(Physique), 411-413
footsteps, 338
Add Image Input Event
dialog, 673
adding
Air Pump project,
pumping keys, 180-181
Magnetic Boots project
Noise modifier,
196-197
Skew modifier,
200-204
secondary foreground
light to candlelight,
526-529
tertiary foreground light
to candlelight, 526-529
tick offsets for mirrored
expressions, 324-325
WAV files (Track View),
755-757

Adobe Photoshop filters
alpha channels,
728-730
background images,
728-730
Diffuse Glow, 728-730
directory location,
728-730
Film Grain, 728-730
Glass, 728-730
Ocean Ripple, 728-730
Paint Daubs, 728-730
Plastic Wrap, 728-730
Rough Pastels, 728-730
saving settings,
728-730
Smudge Stick, 728-730
Sponge, 728-730
Watercolor, 728-730
Air Pump project
bulges in hose, 188-191
Displace modifier,
animating, 177-179
dummy object, rotating,
187-188
Edit Spline modifier, 185
head
inflating, 182-184
strength keys, 183-184
hose
animating, 188-191
attaching, 184-188
pumping keys, adding,
180-181
stomach pump, animat-
ing, 179-184
wpumped.avi animation,
182-183
alarm clock animation
(Audio Controller)
creating, 762-766
Noise modifier, 766
oversampling feature,
764-766
Alias
.DXF files, 63
.OBJ files, 63
features, 63
polygonal modeling, 63
spline-based modeling, 63

All Purpose Emitter (APE)
creating smoke effects, 573-578
Halo space warp, 573-578
Molasses space warp, 573-578
Phasor space warp, 573-578
smoke effects, 566-567
bubbles, 574-578
emitter velocity, 575-578
fireworks, 574-578
hose, 574-578
opacity channels, 577-578
shapes, 576-578
shockwave, 574-578
trail, 574-578
weldsparks, 574-578
Vortex space warp, 573-578

Alpha Compositor
animations, compositing, 668-669
composited images, viewing, 676-679
image setup parameters, 669
images, compositing, 673-676
layer events, 668-669
multilayer compositing, 677-679
transparency data, 668-669

American Association of State Highway & Transportation Officials (AASHTO), 213

amplified PC speakers, components, 749-750

Animated Glow, glow effects
based on mathematical waves, 704-705
CD-ROM contents, 705
cycling, 704-705

animated walk cycles
animating, 298-301
hips-sho.max animation, 301

animating
Air Pump project
Displace modifier, 177-179
hose, 188-191
stomach pump, 179-184
animated walk cycle, 298-301
architectural walkthroughs, 487-489
arms, 306-307
bipeds, 336-370
directly, 355-359
Track View, 348-354
bomber wobble (WWII Air Combat animation), 116-118
bones, inverse kinematics, 263-264
box bones, 265
candlelight, 535-544
illumination intensity, 540-543
shadow-casting spotlight, 539-540
cartoon eyes, 455-457
blinks, 456-457
curling games (HyperMatter), 636-642
depth of field, 514-516
designing glow effects, 710
dice
face total, 628-630
HyperMatter, 621-626
Euler XYZ Rotation controllers (WWII Air Combat animation), 115-118
Expression controller (WWII Air Combat animation), 126-146
expression controllers, parametric modifiers, 169-173

faces
bones, 450-452
eyebrows, 457-458
fighter attack (WWII Air Combat animation), 112-114
flames for candlelight, 536-539
footsteps in bipeds, 336
gunfire effects (WWII Air Combat animation), 122-126
gymnastic flips for bipeds, 355-359
hands, 284-285
legs, 302-306
List controller (WWII Air Combat animation), 122-126
Look-At controller (WWII Air Combat animation), 119-121
Magnetic Boots project
eyelid reaction, 191-195
wobbling effects, 198-204
mouth positions, 460-462
Noise controller (WWII Air Combat animation), 122-126
object modifiers, 176
organic models, Linked XForm modifiers, 96-98
Path controller (WWII Air Combat animation), 110-115
running mouse, head movement, 643-650
segmented characters
forward kinematics, 254-256
inverse kinematics, 254-256
six-legged creatures
front legs, 318-319
rear legs, 320
speech, tongues, 458

twister.max animation
  position, 156-160
  rotation, 152-154
  teetering effect,
    160-163
  wobble, 160-163
vertices, XForm modifers,
  94-95
volumetric light,
  candlelight flickers, 560
walk cycles, four-legged
  creatures, 315-316
walking in six-legged
  creatures, 316-317
whirl.max animation,
  spins, 167-168
animation
  AAPlay for Windows,
    previewing, 500-501
  automatic lip synching,
    frame lengths, 467-470
  AVIs versus Flic files, 501
  bipeds, appending,
    339-340
  calculating values (Wave-
    form Controller),
    705-707
  camera movement, speed
    warning, 490-492
  characters, camera
    placement, 504-507
  compositing
    Alpha Compositor,
      668-669
    masking process,
      687-689
  earthquake cam effect,
    510-513
  editing, 694-697
  expression controller
    overview, 150
  facial tools, Surface
    Tools, 438
  forensics
    accuracy in courtroom,
      209-211
    admissibility in court,
      208-209
    car-pedestrian accident
      scenario, 212-219

  eyewitness testimony,
    211-231
  importance of details,
    230-231
  overview, 207-208
  timing, 212-219
  walking speeds,
    213-214
  free-form, 359-361
  looping, out of range type
    curves, 70
  modular design approach,
    667-668
  multilayer compositing,
    677-679
  multiple object instances,
    102-103
  normalized time (NT),
    153-154
  object level, segmented
    characters, 254-256
  transformation types,
    68-70
    grouped objects, 79-86
    helper objects, 74-79
    Linked XForm
      modifiers, 91-98
    nested objects, 86-90
    out-of-range curve
      types, 70-74
    Pick Reference
      coordinate, 98-101
    XForm modifiers,
      91-98
  transition effects, 694
    arranging, 694-696
    masks, 696-697
animation controllers
  Euler XYZ Rotation,
    115-118
  Expression, 126-146
  List, 122-126
  Look-At, 119-121
  Noise, 122-126
  Path, 110-115
applying
  Displace Space warp to
    tires, 597-605
  glow filters, 701-704

  Gravity space warp, weld
    effects, 594-596
  Physique to bipeds, 419
  screen mapping, 680-683
  space warp effect in wind
    tunnel aerodynamics,
    584-588
**architectural walk-
  throughs**
  animating, 487-489
  camera eye, peripheral
    vision, 490
  camera movement,
    488-489
  closing shot, creating,
    499-500
  design guidelines,
    487-489
  establishing shot,
    creating, 489-492
  exterior detail shot,
    creating, 492-494
  interior shot, creating,
    494-498
arms
  animating, 306-307
  attaching hands, 283
  walking mechanics, 295
arranging
  animations, transition
    effects, 694-696
  bones in skeletons,
    268-272
**ascending stairs in
  bipeds, 352-354**
assigning
  expression controller
    angle tracks, 130-137
    upper limit tracks,
      130-137
  vertices
    bones, 391-392
    Physique, 409
**attach points in tendons,
  426-427**
attaching
  Air Pump project, hose,
    184-188
  feet (Biped Utility),
    362-363

hands
arms, 283
Biped Utility, 362-363
tendons (Physique), 430
Audio Controller
Absolute option, 759-761
alarm clock animation
creating, 762-766
oversampling feature, 764-766
automatic lip synching, 464-466
configuring, 758-759
filtering option, 761
float option, 761
oversampling spinner, 464-466
point option, 761
position option, 761
real time option, 759-761
rotation option, 761
sampling section, 759-761
scaling option, 761
Automatic Analytical Binding System (AABS), 715
automatic lip synching
consonants, 467-470
frame lengths, 467-470
Magpie Sound Editor, 466-467
oversampling spinner, 464-466
vowels, 467-470
AVIs (Video for Windows) versus Flic files, 501
axes, transforming (Pick Reference coordinate), 98-101

B

background
clouds, creating (WWII Air Combat project), 110-111
lighting in candlelight, 522-523
balance factor in bipeds, 347-348

ball
dribble2.max animation, 364
dribbling, 363-364
ballistic tension, setting in bipeds, 347
Bend (Counter Offset) modifier, Crepe project, outer radius, 138-140
Bend (Main) modifier, Crepe project, 127-130
Bend (Offset) modifier, Crepe project, outer radius, 138-140
Bend Links tool (Biped Utility), 335
Bend modifiers for candlelight, 535-544
bending
knees (Magnetic Boots project), 197-204
skin (Physique), 413
bicycle
bikefin.max animation, 368
riding, 364-368
Big Bang Theory
creating Bomb space warp, 610-614
detonation parameters, setting, 612-614
bikefin.max animation, 368
binding
RealLensFlares (RLFs), particle systems, 715-716
space warps, particle systems, 570-572
Biped Utility
biped files (.BPD), 368-369
creating bipeds, 330-331
feet, attaching, 362-363
footstep states
lift, 351-354
move, 351-354
plant, 351-354
touch, 351-354

hands, attaching, 362-363
inverse kinematics, 332-334
launching, 330-331
manipulating bipeds, 332-334
simple walks, creating, 338-339
step files (.STP), 368-369
tools
Bend Links, 335
Center of Mass, 334-335
Copy Posture, 335
Opposite Tricks, 335
Paste Posture, 335
Paste Posture Opposite, 335
Symmetrical Tricks, 334-335
versus Physique, 407-408
biped03.max animation, 342
biped04.max animation, 354
biped05.max animation, 359
bipeds
activating footsteps, 338
animating, 336-370
directly, 355-359
footsteps, 336
gymnastic flips, 355-359
appending animations, 339-340
applying (Physique), 419
Biped Utility
creating, 330-331
manipulating, 332-334
biped03.max animation, 342
biped04.max animation, 354
copying footsteps, 342-344
creating
footsteps, 336-338
simple walk, 338-339
dribbling ball, 363-364

files (Biped Utility),
368-369
fmcstudio.avi anima-
tion, 229
footsteps
jump option, 336-338
run option, 336-338
stair ascent, 352-354
free-form animation
with footsteps, 360-361
without footsteps, 360
joint restrictions
elbows, 334
feet, 334
knees, 334
legs, 334
loading motions, 368-370
meshes, fitting, 417-419
modifying footsteps,
340-342
motion dynamics
airborne pedestrian,
220-230
attributes (Character
Studio), 219-230
balance factor, 347-348
ballistic tension, 347
dynamics blend, 346
footprints, creating,
239-249
GravAccel spinner
(Character Stu-
dio), 219-230
gravitational accelera-
tion, 346
jump cycle, 344-345
overview, 344-345
post-impact, 220-230
run cycle, 344-345
walk cycle, 344-345
pasting footsteps, 342-344
riding bicycle, 364-368
rotating joints, 333-334
saving motions, 368-370
Track View, animating,
348-354
translating joints,
333-334
walktrax.avi anima-
tion, 248

bit depths
amplitude level, 744-745
quality selection, 744-745
sound, 744-745
blinks, animating cartoon
eyes, 456-457
blue vertices, vertex
assignments, 420
bluescreen spill, 58-60
bluescreening
chromakey process,
689-692
defined, 689-692
images, compositing,
689-692
materials, 689-692
television/film applica-
tions, 689-692
Blur Studio
creating blurs, 722-723
launching, 722-723
motion picture effects,
33-36
visual effects, 33-36
blurs
creating, 722-727
defined, 721
LensFX MAX Focus
module, 727
RealLensFlare, Distance
Blur, 726
bodies
configuring dice, 625-626
deforming (Bones Pro),
392-396
six-legged creatures, walk
cycles, 317-318
walking mechanics,
295-296
Bomb space warp, 596
Big Bang Theory
creating, 610-614
detonation parameters,
613-614
objects, exploding,
610-614
bomber.avi anima-
tion, 108

bone-cyl.max anima-
tion, 383
bonehead.max anima-
tion, 452
bonepro.max anima-
tion, 392
bones
animating
faces, 450-452
inverse kinematics,
263-264
box versus MAX, 265
configuring faces, 449-452
hands, creating, 282
horizontal, 266-267
link methods
broken hierarchy,
274-275
hip-centric hierarchy,
272-273
naming, 268-272
placement in skeletons
elbows, 378
hips, 378
knees, 378
shoulders, 378
Replace Rotation Control-
ler dialog, 267
rotational limits, setting,
276-277
selecting (Influence
Editor), 391
skeletons
arranging, 268-272
creating, 263-267
vertical, 266-267
vertices
assigning, 391-392
excluding, 391-392
selecting, 391-392
Bones Pro
bodies, deforming,
392-396
bone & vertex exclusion
button, 391-392
controls
bones nodes boxes, 389
bound nodes boxes, 389
Falloff spinners, 390

Master Frame
  spinner, 389
  Strength spinners, 390
creating bones, 263-264
cylinders, deforming,
  383-384
faces, bone configura-
  tions, 449-452
Influence Editor features,
  390-392
meshes, deformation
  tools, 383-384
overview, 388
solid mesh characters,
  256-259
versus Physique, mesh
  deformation tools, 386
**bouncing particles in
  weld effects, 593-596**
box bones
  animating, 265
  converting, 265
**bubbles, smoke effects,
  574-578**
building
  meshes, outstretched
    arms, 375
  solid mesh characters
    polygon meshes, 257
    spline patches, 257-258
bulges
  creating, 410-413
  hose (Air Pump project),
    188-191
  muscles, free form
    deformations
    (FFDs), 387

C

calculating
  field of view, 477-478
  objects (HyperMatter),
    620-621
  walking stride length, 308
  Waveform Controller,
    animation values,
    705-707

camera mapping
  creating shadows,
    683-684
  defined, 683-684
cameras
  angles
    "bird's-eye view",
      480-481
    horizon tilting,
      480-481
    males versus females,
      480-481
    traditional film
      cameras, 480-481
  movement
    architectural
      walkthroughs,
      488-489
    crane shots, 484
    digital effects, 61
    dolly shots, 483-484
    panning, 482-483
    tilting, 482-483
    tracking shots, 483-484
    traditional film
      cameras, 481-484
  MTV-style footage, 509
  optics, depth of fields,
    513-516
  "shaky-cam" technique,
    509-510
  shots, field of view, 478
  Video Post setup, 508
  virtual versus traditional
    film, 474-475
**camlock.max anima-
  tion, 285**
**candle.max anima-
  tion, 521**
candlelight
  adding
    secondary foreground
      light, 526-529
    tertiary foreground
      light, 526-529
  aesthetic elements,
    520-521
  animating, 535-544
    flames, 536-539

animation loop cycles,
  535-544
background lighting, 522
Bend modifiers, 535-544
candlestick material,
  creating, 534-535
creating primary fore-
  ground light, 523-529
elements, 521-529
flame material
  color settings, 530-535
  creating, 529-535
  opacity, 530-535
  shininess, 530-535
foreground lighting, 522
illumination intensity,
  animating, 540-543
multiplier animation,
  542-543
shadow-casting spotlight,
  animating, 539-540
tangent types, 542-543
Video Post rendering,
  532-535
**car-pedestrian accident
  scenario**
  car, positioning, 215-219
  forensic animation,
    creating, 212-219
  impact point, creating,
    216-219
  statistical details, 212
cartoon eyes
  animating, 455-457
  blinks, animating,
    456-457
  design samples, 455-457
**cartoon rendering, Sony
  Pictures Imageworks,
  21-23**
CD-ROM
  animated glows, 705
  bikefin.max anima-
    tion, 368
  biped03.max anima-
    tion, 342
  biped04.max anima-
    tion, 354

biped05.max animation, 359

bomber.avi animation, 108

bone-cyl.max animation, 383

bonehead.max animation, 452

bonepro.max animation, 392

camlock.max animation, 285

candle.max animation, 521

ch18e-1.avi animation, 657

ch20ex1.max animation, 702

clock.max animation, 762

Crepe project, 126-127

croach01.max file, 77-79

croach02.max file, 81-83

croach03.max file, 84-86

croach04.max file, 89-91

croach06.max file, 92-93

croach07.max file, 94-95

croach08.max file, 96-98

croach09.max file, 99-101

curling.avi animation, 642

dribble2.max animation, 364

duck_col.avi animation, 636

eyes.avi animation, 457

ffdbulge.max animation, 387

filling (Crepe project), 141-146

fmcstudio.avi animation, 229

fmtiming.avi animation, 219

fourskel.max animation, 313

fourwalk.avi animation, 316

hips-sho.max animation, 301

ik-skel.max animation, 281

leg1.max file, 71-74

legcyc2.max file, 74

mmdemo.max animation, 449

moonlit.max animation, 544

mouserun.avi animation, 650

mrejcct.avi animation, 662

muscles.avi animation, 402

noiseglw.avi animation, 710

pathwalk.max animation, 304

quake.avi animation, 513

roachwalk.avi animation, 320

snakeyes.avi animation, 630

splinehd.max animation, 441

storm.max animation, 552

toondog.max animation, 466

tv.max animation, 555-557

twister.max animation, 151-164

vertigo.avi animation, 487

walkcycle.max animation, 307

walktrax.avi animation, 248-249

wbootscomic.AVI, 191

whirl.max animation, 164

wpumped.avi animation, 182

xformhd.max animation, 442

Cebas' Real Lens Flare, 513

Center of Mass tool (Biped Utility), 334-335

ch18e-1.avi animation, 657

ch20ex1.max animation, 702

chains, terminating (inverse kinematics), 277-278

channels, mixing (weighted channel morphing), 449

character animation, camera placement

   close-up shots, 501-507

   long shots, 501-507

   medium shots, 501-507

Character Studio

   biped motion

     attributes, 219-230

     GravAccel spinner, 219-230

   features, 219-230

   forensic animation, importance of details, 230-231

   pedestrian-car accident scenario

     airborne pedestrian, 223-230

     implementing, 219-230

     post-impact creation, 220-230

   Sony Pictures Image-works, 21-23

characters

   tearing, polygon meshes, 257

   types

     hybrid, 261

     metaball, 260

     segmented, 254-256

     solid mesh, 256-259

chromakey process, 689-692

cladding points in objects

   HyperMatter, 618-620

   minimizing, 632-633

clock.max animation, 762

Clone Options dialog, 237

close-up shot
  camera placement, 501-507
  field of view, 478
closing shot
  creating architectural walkthroughs, 499-500
  design guidelines, 499-500
collide constraints
  curling game, 637-642
  one-way collisions (HyperMatter), 623-626
colors
  confetti, 569-572
  defining moonlight, 544
combining screen mapping (Shadow Matting), 686-687
Combustion objects, background cloud motion, 110-111
composited images
  bluescreening, 689-692
  shadows, 679
  viewing, 676-679
compositing
  advantages
    faster system performance, 666-667
    modular design approach, 667-668
  animations (Alpha Compositor), 668-669
  defined, 666
  images
    Alpha Compositor, 673-676
    defined, 666
    masking process, 687-689
    selection, 674-676
    shadows, 679
  modular design approach, 667-668
  multilayer, 677-679
  virtual memory, 666-667
compound target channel (MorphMagic), 448

computer games
  3D Studio MAX development, 24-27
  SoftImage development, 31-33
  Westwood Studios, 27
confetti
  coloring, 569-572
  creating snow particles, 567-572
configuring
  Audio Controller, 758-759
  dice, body dynamics, 625-626
  faces
    bones, 449-452
    eyes, 452-458
  Fractal Flow, 731-734
  image setup parameters (Alpha Compositor), 669
constraint points in HyperMatter objects, 618-620
contrasting lighting conditions, lightning storm effects, 552-554
control objects
  creating, 165-167
  defined, 163-164
  implementing expression controllers, 163-173
  parametric modifiers, 169-173
controllers
  Euler XYZ Rotation, 115-118
  Expression, 126-146
  List, 122-126
  Look-At, 119-121
  Noise, 122-126
  Path, 110-115
controlling
  crepe rolling, Bend (Main) modifier, 127-130
  facial muscles, 437
  free form deformation (FFDs), 386-387
  inverse kinematics, 275

  mesh behavior, 374-376
  whirl.max animation, vehicle rotation, 165-167
converting box bones to MAX bones, 265
Copy Posture tool (Biped Utility), 335
copying footsteps in bipeds, 342-344
corrupting virtual cameras
  depth of fields, 513-516
  perfect steadiness default, 510
courtrooms and forensic animation
  accuracy, 209-211
  admissibility, 208-209
  eyewitness testimony, 211-231
  importance of details, 230-231
  overview, 207-208
  timing, 212-219
creating
  3D animation, lens flares, 713
  alarm clock animation (Audio Controller), 762-766
  animated walk cycle, 298-301
  architectural walkthroughs
    closing shot, 499-500
    establishing shot, 489-492
    exterior detail shot, 492-494
    interior shot, 494-498
  background clouds (WWII Air Combat animation), 110-111
  Big Bang Theory (Bomb space warp), 610-614
  bipeds (Biped Utility), 330-331
  blurs, 722-727

bones
  *skeletal structure,
    266-267*
  skeletons, 263-264
bulges, 410-411
bulging muscles, free
  form deformations
  (FFDs), 387
candlelight
  *flame material,
    529-535*
  stick material, 534-535
car-pedestrian accident
  scenario, forensic
  animation, 212-219
control objects, 165-167
Cross Section Editor,
  bulges, 411-413
duck shoot
  (HyperMatter), 631-633
dynamic muscles
  (MetaReyes), 400-402
earthquake cam effect,
  510-513
faces
  *expressions library,
    458-459*
  radial, 438-441
footsteps, 336-338
ground surface for tires,
  601-605
gunfire from turrets,
  122-126
handles on skeletons,
  278-281
Image File List (IFL),
  672-676
image masking, 687-689
lightning storm effects,
  552-554
MAXTrax
  footprints, 239-249
  skid marks, 232-249
  tracks, 232-249
moonlight through
  window, 544-547
pedestrian-car accident
  scenario, impact point,
  216-219

primary foreground light
  for candlelight, 523-529
radial faces (Surface
  Tools), 438-441
robotic welder (Deflector),
  589-596
Roto-Rooter (Path Deform
  space warp), 605-610
shadows, 679-687
  *Camera mapping,
    683-684*
  *Shadow Matting,
    684-687*
"shaky-cam" techni-
  que, 510
simple walk in bipeds,
  338-339
six-legged creatures, walk
  expressions, 321-325
skeletons
  four-legged, 312-313
  *mesh deformation,
    262-265*
smoke effects with All
  Purpose Emitter (APE),
  573-578
snow particles, confetti,
  567-572
spheres, lightning arcs,
  203-204
spline patches (Surface
  Tools), 374-375
spray particles (Deflec-
  tor), 589-596
static muscles
  (MetaReyes), 399-400
sub-object solidification,
  645-650
Surface Tools, facial
  handle objects, 442-445
tendons (Physique),
  429-430
ticker tape parade,
  567-572
trains, smoke effects,
  573-578
tree shadows with
  moonlight, 548-551
"Vertigo" effect, 485-487

volumetric light, 555-557
walk cycles, 298-301
weld effects with particle
  collisions, 592-593
wind tunnel aerodynam-
  ics (Spray plug-in),
  582-588
Wireframe Express,
  vehicle models, 232
Crepe project
  Bend (Main) modifier, 127
  CD-ROM, 126-127
  filling preparation,
    140-146
  outer radius
    *Bend (Counter Offset)
      modifier, 138-140*
    *Bend (Offset) modifier,
      138-140*
    sizing, 138-140
  overview, 126-127
  rolling, 141-146
croach01.max file, 77-79
croach02.max file, 81-83
croach03.max file, 84-86
croach04.max file, 89-91
croach06.max file, 92-93
croach07.max file, 94-95
croach08.max file, 96-98
croach09.max file, 99-101
Cross Section Editor
  activating, 411-413
  bulge angles, creating,
    411-413
  bulges, creating, 411-413
  meshes, repairing,
    425-426
  tendons, creating,
    411-413
curling game
  animating (HyperMatter),
    636-642
  curling.avi anima-
    tion, 642
  stone
    *collide constraint,
      637-642*
    fix orientation, 637-642
    *friction parameters,
      637-642*

curling.avi anima-
    tion, 642
cycling glow effects
    (Animated Glow),
    704-705
cylinders, deforming
    Bones Pro, 383-384
    Linked XForms, 380-383
    Physique, 385

D

damping substance
    properties
    (HyperMatter), 620-621
DeBabelizer, file transla-
    tion programs, 62
deceleration, friction
    parameters, 640-642
Deflector
    bouncing particles,
        593-596
    creating collisions, weld
        effects, 592-593
    creating robotic welder,
        589-596
    Gravity space warp, weld
        effects, 594-596
    spray particles, creating,
        589-596
    weld effects
        emitter settings,
            589-591
        particle birth rate,
            590-596
deformation tools
    (meshes)
    Bones Pro, 383-384
        versus Physique, 386
    Linked XForms, 380-383
    MetaReyes, 396
    Physique, 385
deforming
    bodies (Bones Pro),
        392-396
    cylinders
        Bones Pro, 383-384
        Linked XForms,
            380-383
        Physique, 385

mesh overview, 373-374
objects, space warps,
    596-614
Roto-Rooter, linear tubes,
    606-610
tires, Displace space
    warp, 597-605
density
    setting in duck shoot,
        635-636
    substance properties
        (HyperMatter), 620-621
depth of fields
    animating, 514-516
    camera optics, 513-516
    corrupting virtual
        cameras, 513-516
    plug-ins
        Cebas' Real Lens
            Flare, 513
        Digimation LenzFX
            MAX, 513
designing
    architectural walk-
        throughs, 487-489
    glow effects
        animated para-
            meters, 710
        behind objects, 709-710
        location, 711-712
        text, 710-711
    internal eyes
        blinks, 453-470
        lid movements,
            453-470
    light guidelines, 103
Detailer, human
    models, 231
detailing
    joints, 376
    solid mesh characters,
        258-259
detonation parameters,
    setting for Big Bang
    Theory, 613-614
dialogs
    Add Image Input
        Event, 673
    Clone Options, 237
    Edit Stack, 177

Footstep Track, 349
Replace Controller, 152
Replace Rotation Control-
    ler, 267
Time Configuration, 299
dice
    body dynamics, configur-
        ing, 625-626
    face total, animating,
        628-630
    HyperMatter, throwing,
        627-630
    momentum, velocity
        constraint, 627-628
    rolling (HyperMatter),
        621-626
    snakeyes.avi anima-
        tion, 630
    velocity constraint,
        setting, 626-630
Diffuse Glow filter (Adobe
    Photoshop), 728-730
Digimation Clay Studio,
    metaball characters, 260
Digimation LenzFX
    MAX, 513
Digimation Sand Blaster
    particles
    assembling, 566-567
    disassembling, 566-567
    exploding, 578-581
    imploding, 578-581
digital effects
    2D compositing depart-
        ment, 46-49
    3D animation depart-
        ment, 46-49
    camera movement, 61
    image storage capacities,
        motion pictures, 50-52
    Silicon Graphics Render
        Servers, 51
    see also visual effects
Digital Phenomena,
    examples of visual
    effects, 36-38
digitizing sound, 742-743
direct animation in
    bipeds, 355-359

Displace modifier
animating Air Pump
project, 177-179
Decay slider, 178-179
Strength slider, 177-179
Displace space warp, 596
hose bulges, 189-191
mapping parameters
cylindrical, 601-605
planar, 601-605
shrink wrap, 601-605
spherical, 601-605
strength, modifying,
604-605
tires, applying, 597-605
**displaying metronome
(Track View), 757**
**dissimilar bipeds, splicing
motions, 369-370**
**distorting objects (XForm
modifiers), 91-93**
dolly shots
camera moves, 483-484
pedestrian gait speed, 484
**downloading Magpie
Sound Editor, 466-467**
DreamWorks Interactive
computer game develop-
ment, 24-27
current game develop-
ment, 24-27
exclusive tool, 24-27
Lost World animations,
25-27
**dribble2.max anima-
tion, 364**
dribbling
ball, 363-364
dribble2.max anima-
tion, 364
**DSP (Digital Signal
Processing) format, 747**
duck shoot
ball
*density settings,
635-636*
*gravity settings,
635-636*

collide constraints,
631-633
duck
*density settings,
635-636*
*gravity settings,
635-636*
duck_col.avi anima-
tion, 636
HyperMatter, creating,
631-633
**duck_col.avi anima-
tion, 636**
**duplicating walk cycle
(Track View), 308-309**
dynamic muscles
creating (MetaReyes),
400-402
defined, 400-402
Muscle Edit modifier, 404
**dynamics blend, setting
in bipeds, 346**

E

earthquake cam effect
creating, 510-513
Noise Position Controller,
510-513
quake.avi animation, 513
Edit Mesh modifier, 197
Edit Spline modifier, 185
Edit Stack dialog, 177
**editing animations,
694-697**
**elasticity, substance
properties (Hyper-
Matter), 620-621**
elliptical paths
locking ankles, 302-304
pathwalk.max anima-
tion, 304
emitters
patch in footprints,
240-249
setting particles, 568-569
smoke velocity, 575-578
**emotion in walking
mechanics, 295-296**

establishing shot
creating for architectural
walkthroughs, 489-492
purposes, 489-492
**Euler XYZ Rotation
controller (WWII Air
Combat animation)**
animating 115-118
bomber wobble, 116-118
**events, multilayer
compositing, 677-679**
exploding
objects (Bomb space
warp), 610-614
particles (Sand Blaster),
578-581
expression controllers
angle tracks, assigning,
130-137
animating (WWII Air
Combat animation),
126-146
braces/parentheses, 155
control objects, imple-
menting, 163-173
key information, overwriting, 152
mathematical syntax, 155
normalized time (NT),
153-154
open vectors, 155
overview, 150
parametric modifiers,
animating, 169-173
position expressions,
156-160
trajectories, 158-160
position type, 152-164
rotation type, 152-164
multiplier, 154
rotational expressions,
quaternions, 162-163
transform animation,
implementing, 151-163
upper limit tracks,
assigning, 130-137
use guidelines, 155
variable syntax, 155

expressions
creating six-legged
creatures, 321-325
defined, 321-325
library (faces), 458-459
**exterior detail shot,
creating for architec-
tural walkthroughs,
492-494**
**Exterminators animation
project**
cockroach run cycle, 83-86
demon shape change,
94-95
helper objects, 74-79
instance animation,
102-103
Linked XForm modifiers,
91-98
nested groups, 86-90
out-of-range type curves,
70-74
Pick Reference coordi-
nate, 99-101
script, 68-70
XForm modifiers, 91-98
**external eyes, modeling,
454-455**
**extreme close-up, field of
view, 478**
**extreme long shot, field of
view, 478**
eyes
cartoon, 455-457
configuring faces, 452-458
external, 454-455
eyebrows, animating,
457-458
internal, 453-470
lids
animating, 191-195
*Slice to/from values,
192-195*
'motion design, 452-458
eyes.avi animation, 457

F

faces
animation guidelines
spline details, 441
vertices, 441
animation tools (Surface
Tools), 438
bones
animating, 450-452
configuring, 449-452
*vertices assignments,
450-452*
expressions library,
creating, 458-459
eyebrows, animating,
457-458
eyes, configuring, 452-458
handle objects, creating,
442-445
modeling, 438
muscles
anatomy, 436
movements, 437
radial, creating, 438-441
**facial handle objects,
creating (Surface Tools),
442-445**
fade transitions, 479-480
**Falloff spinners (Bones
Pro), 390**
feet
attaching (Biped Utility),
362-363
walking mechanics,
290-292
**ffdbulge.max anima-
tion, 387**
field of view
calculating, 477-478
camera shots
close-up, 478
extreme close-up, 478
extreme long, 478
long, 478
medium, 478
defined, 476-478
focal length lenses,
476-478

Fields of Depth plug-in
Auto Focus, 723-726
Average Focus, 723-726
color settings, modifying,
725-726
launching, 723-726
Manual Focus, 723-726
Object Focus, 723-726
**fighter attack, animating
(WWII Air Combat
animation), 112-114**
file translation programs
DeBabelizer, 62
Missing Link, 62
filling (Crepe project)
CD-ROM, 141-146
preparing, 140-146
**Film Grain filter (Adobe
Photoshop), 728-730**
filters (Adobe Photoshop)
Diffuse Glow, 728
Film Grain, 728-730
Glass, 728-730
Ocean Ripple, 728-730
Paint Daubs, 728-730
Plastic Wrap, 728-730
Rough Pastels, 728-730
Smudge Stick, 728-730
Sponge, 728-730
Watercolor, 728-730
**fireworks, smoke effects,
574-578**
fitting meshes
bipeds, 417-419
skeletons, 377-378
**fix constraint (Hyper-
Matter), 633-636**
**fix orientation (Hyper-
Matter), 637-642**
Flame
features, 62
Silicon Graphics Irix
platform, 62
**flame material (candle-
light animation)**
color settings, 530-535
combustion, 529-535
creating, 529-535

opacity, 530-535
particles, 529-535
shininess, 530-535
**Flare module, RealLens-
Flare (RLF), 714-715**
**flickers, animating
volumetric light, 560**
Flics versus AVI files, 501
**flips, animating in bipeds,
355-359**
**FM (frequency modula-
tion) chips, 746**
versus Wavetable
synthesis, 746-747
**fmcstudio.avi anima-
tion, 229**
**fmtiming.avi anima-
tion, 219**
Follow constraint
HyperMatter
objects, 651-661
*rubber mouse testing,
658-661*
rubber mouse quality
(HyperMatter), 652-661
footprints
creating (MAXTrax),
239-249
emitter patch, 240-249
opacity maps, 240-249
patterns, 240-249
UV tiling, 240-249
**Footstep Track dialog,
349**
footsteps
activating, 338
bipeds
animating, 336
copying, 342-344
modifying, 340-342
pasting, 342-344
colored feet indicator
(Track View), 349-350
creating, 336-338
duration (Track View),
349-350
free-form animation,
360-361
jump option, 336-338

modifying (Track View),
349-350
run option, 336-338
stairs, planting, 352-354
states
lift, 351-354
move, 351-354
plant, 351-354
touch, 351-354
**foreground lighting in
candlelight, 522**
forensic animation
admissibility in court,
208-209
car-pedestrian accident
scenario, 212-219
Character Studio
features, 219-230
importance of details,
230-231
overview, 207-208
production guidelines,
208-211
accuracy, 209-211
*eyewitness testimony,
211-212*
timing, 212-219
skid marks, creating,
233-238
vehicle models, 232
walking speeds, 213-214
**forward kinematics,
animating**
legs, 302-306
segmented characters,
254-256
**four-leaved Rose curve,
159-160**
four-legged creatures
animating walk cycles,
315-316
fourwalk.avi anima-
tion, 316
walk analysis, 310-315
four-legged skeletons
creating, 312-313
fourskel.max anima-
tion, 313

**fourskel.max anima-
tion, 313**
**fourwalk.avi anima-
tion, 316**
Fractal Flow
configuring, 731-734
M channel, 733-734
panels
Control, 731-732
Distortion, 731-732
*Fractal Distortions,
731-732*
Ripples, 731-732
Waves, 731-732
Ripple tab, 733-734
settings, 731-734
Waves tab, 733-734
Y channel, 733-734
Fractal Fury
effects
*burning flames,
717-718*
electrical, 717-718
*glowing clouds,
717-718*
RealLensFlare, 717-718
frames
applying glow filters,
701-704
HyperMatter objects, 620
**free form deformations
(FFDs)**
bulging muscles,
creating, 387
controlling, 386-387
defined, 386-387
lattices, 386-387
free-form animation
overview, 359-361
with footsteps, 360-361
without footsteps, 360
friction parameters
deceleration, 640-642
stones in curling game,
637-642
substance properties
(HyperMatter), 620-621

fully deformable collision detection (Hyper-Matter), 631-633
fusion, metamuscles, 402-403

G

G-Buffer
3D geometric information, 671-672
defined, 671-672
Glass filter (Adobe Photoshop), 728-730
glow filters
color properties, 702-704
intensity, 702-704
objects, applying, 701-704
Glow module, RealLensFlare (RLF), 714-715
glow plug-ins
Animated Glow, 704-705
LensFX Glow, 709
Real Lens Glow, 708
RealLensFlare, 701
Super Glow, 707
Waveform Controller, 705-707
glows
CD-ROM contents, 705
design guidelines
animated para-meters, 710
behind objects, 709-710
location, 711-712
text, 710-711
effects, cycling, 704-705
noiseglw.avi animation, 710
GravAccel spinner (Character Studio), 219-230
gravitational acceleration
bipeds, setting, 346
duck shoot, 635-636
Gravity space warp, applying to weld effects, 594-596

green vertices, vertex assignments, 420
ground surface
tires, 601-605
walking, 309-310
grouped objects
croach03.max file, 84-86
transform animation, 79-86
transform type-in, 80-83
grouping metamuscles, 403-404
gunfire (WWII Air Combat animation)
animating, 122-126
creating turrets, 122-126
gymnastic flips
animating, 355-359
biped05.max anima-tion, 359

H

Halo space warp, All Purpose Emitter (APE), 573-578
handle objects
faces, creating, 442-445
skeletons, creating, 278-281
hands
animating, 284-285
arms, attaching, 283
attaching (Biped Utility), 362-363
camlock.max anima-tion, 285
skeletons, construct-ing, 282
head
inflating for Air Pump project, 182-184
movement, animating, 643-650
Roto-Rooter, rotating, 608-610
walking mechanics, 295

helper objects
croach01.max file, 77-79
movement axes, 74-79
Pick Reference coordi-nate, 98-101
pivot points, 74-79
RealLensFlares (RLFs), 715
transform animation, 74-79
hip-centric hierarchy, link methods, 272-273
hips
bone placement, 378
walking mechanics, 294-295
hips-sho.max anima-tion, 301
horizon tilting, camera angles, 480-481
horizontal bones, 266-267
hose (Air Pump project)
animating, 188-191
attaching, 184-188
bulges
Displace space warp, 189-191
strength, 188-191
smoke effects, 574-578
human models
Detailer features, 231
Poser 2 features, 231
hybrid characters, 261
HyperMatter
curling game, animating, 636-642
deceleration, friction parameters, 640-642
development by Second Nature Industries, 617-618
dice, rolling, 621-626
duck shoot
collide constraints, 631-633
creating, 631-633
density settings, 635-636
gravity settings, 635-636

Follow constraint, rubber mouse quality, 652-661
functional overview, 617-618
implementation guidelines, 620
objects
behavior, 618-620
calculating, 620
cladding, 618-620
constraint points, 618-620
fix constraint, 633-636
Follow constraint, 651-661
fully deformable collision detection, 631-633
guided by laws of physics, 618-620
keyframed momentum, 636-642
sub-object solidification, 643-650
"time-stepping", 620
one-way collisions
HyperMatter Walls, 623-626
setting, 623-626
running mouse
head movement, 643-650
sub-object solidification, 643-650
sub-object solidification
creating, 645-650
substance properties, 645-650
Substance Editor, 629-630
substance properties
damping, 620-621
density, 620-621
elasticity, 620-621
friction, 620-621
incompressibility, 620-621
throwing dice, 627-630

velocity constraint, setting, 626-630
HyperMatter Walls, one-way collisions, 623-626

I

ik-skel.max animation, 281
illumination
animating intensity of candlelight, 540-543
volumetric light, 555
Image File List (IFL)
creating, 672-676
defined, 672-676
slow network rendering, 672-673
images
composited, viewing, 676-679
compositing
Alpha Compositor, 673-676
bluescreening, 689-692
defined, 666
selecting, 674-676
digital effects, storage capacities, 50-52
G-Buffer information, 671-672
Image File List (IFL), 672-676
masking, 687-689
multilayer compositing, 677-679
RGBA channels (Virtual Frame Buffer), 670-671
screen mapping
applying, 680-683
shadows, 679-683
setup parameters
Alpha Compositor, 669
alpha data, 669
bits-per-pixel, 669
compression, 669
shadows, 679

implementing
expression controllers
control objects, 163-173
transform animation, 151-163
HyperMatter guidelines, 620
imploding particles (Sand Blaster), 578-581
incompressibility, substance properties (HyperMatter), 620-621
Industrial Light and Magic Company, 10
Influence Editor
bone & vertex exclusion button, 391-392
bones, selecting, 391
features, 390-392
tools, 390-392
vertices, selecting, 391
viewport (Bones Pro), 390-392
Visualize button, 391
instance animation, 102-103
Intel processors and 3D Studio MAX development, 12
interior shot, creating for architectural walkthroughs, 494-498
internal eyes
blinks, 453-470
lid movements, 453-470
inverse kinematics
animating
legs, 302-306
segmented characters, 254-256
bones, animating, 263-264
controlling, 275
dribbling ball, 363-364
riding bicycles, 364-368
terminating chains, 277-278

J - K

joints
bipeds
rotating, 333-334
translating, 333-334
detailing, 376
rotational limits,
setting, 276

**KA Share software
package, multiplatform
file translation, 61**
**keyframed momentum
(HyperMatter), 636-642**
**keyframes, setting,
179-180**
Kinetix web site, 485
AAPlay for Windows
Viewer, 500-501
knees
bending (Magnetic Boots
project), 197-204
skeletal bone place-
ment, 378
**Kodak Cineon digital
image format, 62**

L

**lap dissolves, camera
transitions, 479-480**
**lattices, free form defor-
mations (FFDs), 386-387**
launching
Biped Utility, 330-331
Blur (frame only) plug-in,
722-723
Fields of Depth plug-in,
723-726
layering
grouped objects (trans-
form animation), 79-86
nested objects (transform
animation), 86-90
**leaves, animating, tree
shadows, 548-551**
leg1.max file, 71-74
legcyc2.max file, 74

legs
animating, 302-306
ankle locking, 302-304
expressions
*creating for six-legged
creatures, 321-325*
mirrored, 324-325
walking mechanics,
290-292
lens flares
creating, 713
defined, 713
purpose, 713
tools
LensFX MAX, 718-720
*RealLensFlare (RLF),
714-715*
LensFX Focus module
blurs, 727
focal blur option, 727
radial blur option, 727
scene blur option, 727
LensFX Glow
color gradients, 709
glow transparencies, 709
LensFX MAX
Auto Secondaries, 720
glow plug-ins, 701
gradients, 720
LensFX Focus module,
727-728
modules
depth of field, 719-720
glow, 719-720
hilight, 719-720
lens flares, 719-720
source objects, 720
libraries
facial expressions,
building, 458-459
mouth/lip positions,
building, 460-462
**lighting design guide-
lines, 103**
**lightning arcs, creating
spheres, 203-204**
lightning storm effects
creating, 552-554
lighting condition,
contrasting, 552-554

sounds, 552-554
spikes, 552-554
water on window panes,
552-554
**linear tubes, deforming
(Roto-Rooter), 606-610**
Linked XForm modifiers
Air Pump project, 184-188
croach08.max file, 96-98
cylinders, deforming,
380-383
defined, 184-185
free form deformations
(FFDs), 386-387
lofted objects, modifying,
96-98
mesh deformation tools,
380-383
organic models, 96-98
linking
bones
*broken hierarchy,
274-275*
*hip-centric hierarchy,
272-273*
metamuscles, 402-403
**lip positions, animating,
460-462**
loading
biped motions, 368-370
sound, 463-464
**lofted objects, modifying,
96-98**
long shots
character animation,
camera placement,
501-507
field of view, 478
**Look-At controller,
animating (WWII Air
Combat animation),
119-121**
**looping animation, out-of-
range type curves, 70**
**lsphere.avi anima-
tion, 203**

M

Magnetic Boots project
Bend modifier, 197-204
Edit Mesh modifier,
197-204
eyelid reaction, animating, 191-195
knees, bending, 197-204
lsphere.avi animation, 203
mouth (Free Form
Deformation modifier),
194-195
Noise modifier, adding,
196-197
Skew modifier, adding,
200-204
wbootscomic.avi animation, 191
wobbling effects, animating, 198-204
**Magpie Sound Editor,
downloading, 466-467**
manipulating
bipeds, 332-334
hands, 284-285
mapping
metaball characters, 260
particles (Sand Blaster),
579-581
masking
animations, transition
effects, 696-697
creating, 687-689
defined, 687-689
FLC wipes, 696-697
images, 687-689
transparency data,
687-689
**Master Frame spinner
(Bones Pro), 389**
Matador, 62
**materials, selecting (Sand
Blaster), 579-581**
MAX Bones, bone creation, 263-264

MAXTrax
footprints, creating,
239-249
reference objects versus
target objects, 233
skid marks, creating,
232-249
tracks, creating, 232-249
medium shots
character animation,
501-507
field of view, 478
Mesh Smooth tool, 382-383
meshes
behavior, controlling,
374-376
Character Studio
Physique, 374
deformation
*creating skeletons,
262-265*
overview, 373-374
deformation tools,
373-374
Bones Pro, 383-384
*Bones Pro versus
Physique, 386*
*Linked XForms,
380-383*
MetaReyes, 396
Physique, 385
detailing joints, 376
Digimation Bones
Pro, 374
fitting bipeds, 417-419
outstretched arms,
building, 375
Physique, testing, 420
repairing (Cross Section
Editor), 425-426
skeletons, fitting, 377-378
smoothing Mesh Smooth
tool, 382-383
spline patches versus
polygon patches,
374-375
tendons, working,
428-429

vertices
modifying, 422-424
reassigning, 420-427
vertices assigments, 409
metaball characters, 260
defined, 396-397
mapping, 260
plug-ins
*Digimation Clay
Studio, 260*
MetaReyes, 260
metamuscles
control points, 398-399
fusion, 402-403
grouping, 403-404
linking, 402-403
radii, 398-399
types
dynamic, 400-402
static, 399-400
MetaReyes, 260, 396
dynamic muscles,
creating, 400-402
grouping metamuscles,
403-404
metaballs, defined, 260,
396-397
metamuscles
categories, 398-399
components, 398-399
Muscle Edit modifier,
dynamic muscle
options, 404
static muscles, creating,
399-400
**metronome, displaying
(Track View), 757**
**minimizing cladding
points in objects, 632-633**
mirrored expressions
legs, 324-325
tick offsets, 324-325
Missing Link, file translation program, 62
**Mixer Control (Windows
NT)**
CD audio, 753-755
line-in, 753-755
recording input, 753-755

synthesizer, 753-755
volume control, 753-755
Wave output, 753-755
mmdemo.max animation, 449
modeling
external eyes, 454-455
faces
animation tools, 438
radial, 438-441
modifiers
animating objects, 176
Bend, 127-144, 197-204
Displace, 177-179
Edit Mesh, 197
Edit Spline, 185
Free Form Deformation, 194-195
Linked XForm, 184-188
Noise, 196-197
prioritizing objects, 603-604
Ripple, 204
Skew, 200-204
spinning frequency, 200-204
modifying
Displace space warp, strength, 604-605
Fields of Depth plug-in, color settings, 725-726
footsteps in bipeds, 340-342
lofted objects, 96-98
primary foreground light parameters, 523-529
RealLensFlares (RLFs) settings, 715
strength keys for Air Pump project, 183-184
tendons, 432
Track View footsteps, 349-350
vertices, 422-424
modular systems, compositing, 667-668
Molasses space warp, All Purpose Emitter (APE), 573-578

moonlight
casting tree shadows, 548-551
colors, defining, 544
targeting, 544-547
windows effects, light project options, 546-547
moonlit.max animation, 544
morph target channel (MorphMagic), 448
morphing
Compund Objects Creation panel, 445-447
multiple target, 447
also known as shape animation, 445
single targeting, 445-447
weighted channel, 449
MorphMagic, 445-447
channels
compound target, 448
morph target, 448
selected vertices, 448
multiple target morphing, 447
motion dynamics in bipeds
balance factor, 347-348
ballistic tension, 347
dynamics blend, 346
gravitational acceleration, 346
overview, 344-345
motion pictures
3D animation development, 10-12
35 mm Anamorphic Wide Screen Format, 59-60
Blur Studio, 33-36
digital effects, image storage capacities, 50-52
Digital Phenomena, 36-38
Pyros Pictures, 39-42
role of service bureaus, 64
Silicon Graphics Render Servers, 51
SoftImage versus 3D Studio MAX, 28-33

Sony Pictures Imageworks, 20-23
visual effects, 33-38
motions
bipeds
loading, 368-370
saving, 368-370
dissimilar bipeds, splicing, 369-370
Motor Vehicle Regulation Directorate of Canada, vehicle specifications, 216-217
mouserun.avi animation, 650
mouths
Free Form Deformation modifier, 194-195
positions, animating, 460-462
moving
ground, 309-310
objects along surface, 101
mreject.avi animation, 661
MTV-style footage, camera technique, 509
multilayer compositing, images, 677-679
multiple platforms, KA Share software package, 61
multiple target morphing, 447
Channel Control menu, 447
maximum number of shapes, 447
multiplier, rotation type, 154
Muscle Edit modifier (MetaReyes), 404
muscles (facial)
anatomy, 436
movements, 437
muscles.avi animation, 402

N

naming bones, 268-272
National Advisory Committee on Uniform Traffic Control Devices, 213-214
Negative plug-in, Video Post filter, 734
nested groups (Exterminators animation project), 86-90
nested objects
    croach04.max file, 89-91
    transform animation, 86-90
New Riders Publishing web site, 86
Noise controller, animating (WWII Air Combat animation), 122-126
Noise modifier
    adding, 196-197
    alarm clock animation, 766
    frequency adjustments, 196-197
Noise Position Controller, earthquake cam effect, 510-513
noiseglw.avi animation, 710
non-amplified PC speakers, 749
normalized time (NT) in expression controllers, 153-154

O

object level animation, segmented characters, 254-256
objects
    applying
        glow filters, 701-704
        Path Deform space warp, 605-610
    behavior (HyperMatter), 618-620

calculating (HyperMatter), 620
cladding (HyperMatter), 618-620
constraint points (HyperMatter), 618-620
deforming space warps, 596-614
designing glow effects, 709-710
distorting with XForm modifiers, 91-93
exploding (Bomb space warp), 610-614
fix constraint (HyperMatter), 633-636
Follow constraint (HyperMatter), 651-661
fully deformable collision detection (HyperMatter), 631-633
guided by laws of physics (HyperMatter), 618-620
keyframed momentum (HyperMatter), 636-642
metaballs, 396-397
minimizing cladding points, 632-633
modifiers
    animating, 176
    prioritizing, 603-604
multiple instances, animating, 102-103
particles, defined, 565-566
space warps, defined, 565-566
spline path (Path Deform space warp), 605-610
sub-object solidification (HyperMatter), 643-650
surface, moving, 101
obtaining vehicle specifications, Motor Vehicle Regulation Directorate of Canada, 216
Ocean Ripple filter (Adobe Photoshop), 728-730

one-way collisions (HyperMatter)
    collide constraint, 623-626
    setting, 623-626
opacity channels, smoke effects, 577-578
opacity maps, footprints, 240-249
Opposite Tricks tool (Biped Utility), 335
out-of-range curve types, transform animation, 70-74
Outline plug-in, Video Post filter, 735
oversampling spinner, toondog.max animation, 466
overwriting key information in expression controllers, 152

P

Paint Daubs filter (Adobe Photoshop), 728-730
panes, window lighting effects, 546-547
panning
    speeds, frames per second, 482-483
    strobing effect, 482-483
parametric modifiers
    animating expression controllers, 169-173
    control objects, 169-173
particle emission, setting for wind tunnel aerodynamics, 582-588
particles
    All Purpose Emitter (APE), 566-567
    Halo space warp, 573-578
    Molasses space warp, 573-578
    Phasor space warp, 573-578

binding space warps, 570-572

bouncing in weld effects, 593-596

creating
   collisions for weld effects, 592-593
   confetti, 567-572
   ticker tape parade, 567-572

defined, 565-566

Deflector, 589-596

emitters, setting, 568-569

exploding (Sand Blaster), 578-581

imploding (Sand Blaster), 578-581

mapping selection (Sand Blaster), 579-581

material selection (Sand Blaster), 579-581

snow systems, 566-567
   overview, 567-572
   speed, 568-572
   tumble rates, 569-572

Spray plug-in, 582-588

systems
   3D Max Spray and Snow module, 715-716
   binding, 715-716
   Digimation Sand Blaster, 715-716
   Sisyphus All Purpose Particles, 715-716

timing (Sand Blaster), 580-581

Wind space warp, 582-588

Paste Posture Opposite tool (Biped Utility), 335

Paste Posture tool (Biped Utility), 335

Path controller (WWII Air Combat animation)

animating, 110-115

fighter attack, 112-114

relative velocities, 114-115

Path Deform space warp, 596

creating Roto-Rooter effect, 605-610

objects, spline path, 605-610

Roto-Rooter, rotating head, 608-610

pathwalk.max animation, 304

patterns in footprints, 240-249

PC speakers

amplified
   balance, 749-750
   bass control, 749-750
   treble control, 749-750

non-amplified, 749

satellite/subwoofer combination, 750

selecting, 747

pedestrian-car accident scenario (Character Studio)

airborne pedestrian, 223-230

fmtiming.avi animation, 219

forensic animation, creating, 212-219

impact point, creating, 216-219

post-impact creation, 220-230

statistical details, 212

Phasor space warp, All Purpose Emitter (APE), 573-578

Photron web site, 690

Primatte plug-in, 690-692

Physique

attaching tendons, 430

bipeds, applying, 419

blue vertices, vertex assignments, 420

creating
   bones, 263-264
   bulges, 410-411
   tendons, 429-430

Cross Section Editor functions, 411-413

cylinders, deforming, 385

faces, bone configurations, 449-452

Figure mode, 417

green vertices, vertex assignments, 420

mesh deformation tools, 385

modifying vertices, 422-424

muscle bulges, creating, 411-413

overview, 407-408

red vertices, vertex assignments, 420

skin
   bend parameters, 413
   scale parameters, 414-416
   tension parameters, 413
   twist parameters, 414

solid mesh characters, 256-259

sub-objects
   Link, 408-409
   Vertex, 408-409

tendons
   pinch, 430-432
   pull, 430-432
   radial distance, 430-432
   stretch, 430-432

testing meshes, 420

versus
   Biped Utility, 407-408
   Bones Pro, 386

vertex assignments, 409

Pick Reference coordinate

axes, transforming, 98-101

croach09.max file, 99-101

moving objects on surfaces, 101

transform animation, 98-101

pipes (Roto-Rooter)
deforming, 606-610
rotating head, 608-610
pixels, compositing process (Pseudo Alpha), 693
placing handles on skeletons, 278-281
planting footsteps on stairs, 352-354
Plastic Wrap filter (Adobe Photoshop), 728-730
playing sound (Track View), 463-464
plug-ins
blurs
Blur (frame only), 722-723
Fields of Depth, 723-726
glow, *see* glow plug-ins
MorphMagic, 445-447
Video Post filter
Negative, 734
Outline, 735
Stamper, 735
Starfield Generator, 736-738
polygon meshes
building solid mesh characters, 257
character tearing, 257
speed disadvantages, 257
polygon patches versus spline patches, 374-375
Poser 2, human models, 231
position effects
animating twister.max animation, 156-160
trajectories, expression controllers, 158-160
positioning
bones in skeletons, 268-272
car in car-pedestrian accident scenario, 215-219

preventing strobing effect, 483
previewing animations (AAPlay for Windows), 500-501
primary foreground light
candlelight, creating, 523-529
parameters, modifying, 523-529
Primatte plug-in, chromakey operations, 690-692
procuring source images, 58-60
production (animation)
deadlines and work environment, 57
division of labor with studios, 49-52
producer responsibilities, 58
scheduling charts, 60
Pseudo Alpha
3D Studio MAX compositing tools, 693
pixels, compositing process, 693
pumping keys, adding (Air Pump project), 180-181
Pyros Pictures
3D Studio MAX, motion picture effects, 39-41
examples of visual effects, 39-42

Q - R

quake.avi animation, 513
quaternions
defined, 162-163
interpolation schemes, 162-163
use in rotational controllers, 162-163

Real Lens Glow
density, 708
luminance, 708

RealLensFlares (RLFs)
alpha channel blur, 716-717
Automatic Analytical Binding System (AABS), 715
Distance Blur module, 726
fog, 716-717
Fractal Fury, 717-718
glow edges, 716-717
gradients, 716-717
GUIs, 715
helper objects, 715
modules
Depth of Field, 714-715
Flare, 714-715
Glow, 714-715
Starfilter, 714-715
particle systems, binding, 715-716
settings, modifying, 715
reassigning vertices in meshes, 420-427
red, green, blue, and alpha, *see* RGBA
red vertices, vertex assignments, 420
reference objects versus target objects (MAX-Trax), 233
relative velocities, WWII Air Combat project, 114-115
rendering
candlelight (Video Post), 532-535
file output, 50-52
Renderman Pro
.RIB format, 50-52
motion picture visual effects, 50-52
versus 3D Studio Max, 50-52
repairing mesh (Cross Section Editor), 425-426
Replace Controller dialog, 152
Replace Rotation Controller dialog, 267

RGBA (red, green, blue, and alpha) channels, images, 670-671

Ripple modifier and banners, 204

roachwalk.avi animation, 320

robotic welder, creating (Deflector), 589-596

rolling dice (HyperMatter), 621-626

rotating
dummy object (Air Pump project), 187-188
head (Roto-Rooter), 608-610
joints in bipeds, 333-334

rotation transformation, leg1.max file, 72

rotational limits, setting in bones, 276

Roto-Rooter
linear tubes, deforming, 606-610
Path Deform space warp, creating, 605-610
rotating head, 608-610

Rough Pastels filter (Adobe Photoshop), 728-730

rubber mouse
ch18e-1.avi animation, 657
material quality, testing, 651-661
mreject.avi animation, 662
substance parameters
setting, 652-653
testing, 651-661

running mouse
head movement
animating, 643-650
substance parameters, 647-650
mouserun.avi animation, 650

S

sampling rates
quality ranges, 743
sound, 743

Sand Blaster
exploding particles, 578-581
imploding particles, 578-581
particles
assembling, 566-567
disassembling, 566-567
mapping selection, 579-581
material selection, 579-581
timing, 580-581

satellite/subwoofer PC speakers, 750

saving motions of bipeds, 368-370

scale parameters of skin (Physique), 414-417

scanning source images, 58-60

screen mapping
applying, 680-683
combining with Shadow Matting, 686-687
defined, 679-683
shadows, 679-683

Second Nature Industries, HyperMatter development, 617-618

secondary foreground light, adding for candlelight, 526-529

segmented characters, 254-256
forward kinematics, animating, 254-256
inverse kinematics, animating, 254-256

selected vertices channel (MorphMagic), 448

selecting
bones (Influence Editor), 391
images, compositing, 674-676
PC speakers, 747
star settings (Starfield Generator), 736-738
vertices (Influence Editor), 391

service bureaus, 64

setting
balance factor in bipeds, 347-348
ballistic tension in bipeds, 347
Big Bang Theory, detonation parameters, 613-614
bones, rotational limits, 276
dynamics blend in bipeds, 346
gravitational acceleration in bipeds, 346
HyperMatter
one-way collisions, 623-626
velocity constraint, 626-630
particle emitters, 568-569
rubber mouse, substance parameters, 652-653
stomach pump, keyframes, 179-180
substance properties, sub-object solidification, 645-647
wind tunnel aerodynamics, particle emission, 582-588

Shadow Matting
creating shadows, 684-687
defined, 684-687
screen mapping, combining, 686-687

shadows
Camera mapping, 683-684
creating, 679-687
images, 679
screen mapping, 679-683
Shadow Matting, creating, 684-687
"shaky-cam" camera style, 509-510
shape animation, *see* **morphing**
shockwave, smoke effects, 574-578
shoulders
skeletal bone placement, 378
walking mechanics, 294-295
Silicon Graphics Irix, 62
Silicon Graphics Render Servers, 51
KA Share software package, 61
Simple Additive Compositor
compositing tool, 693
image transparency values, 693
single targeting morphing, 445-447
disadvantages, 445-447
polygonal models, 445-447
spline models, 445-447
Sisyphus All Purpose Emitter (APE), smoke effects, 566-567
Sisyphus All Purpose Particles, 715-716
sites (web)
3D Café, 707
Kinetix, 485
New Riders Publishing, 86
Photron, 690
Trinity Enterprises, 688
six-legged creatures
animating walk, 316-317
body movement, walk cycling, 317-318

front legs, animating, 318-319
rear legs, animating, 320
roachwalk.avi animation, 320
walk cycles, tick offsets, 325
walk expressions, creating, 321-325
skeletons
arranging bones, 268-272
bone placement
elbows, 378
hips, 378
knees, 378
shoulders, 378
bones
broken hierarchy, 274-275
hip-centric hierarchy, 272-273
constructing hands, 282
creating
bones, 263-267
handles, 278-281
fitting meshes, 377-378
four-legged, creating, 312-313
hands
animating, 284-285
arm attachment, 283
ik-skel.max animation, 281
inverse kinematic chains, terminating, 277-278
mesh deformation, creating, 262-265
rotational limits, 276
testing, 281
Skew modifier
adding (Magnetic Boots project), 200-204
spinning frequency, 200-204
skid marks, creating (MAXTrax), 232-249
skin (Physique)
bend parameters, 413
fitting on bipeds, 417-419

scale parameters, 414-416
tendons, working, 428-429
tension parameters, 413
twist parameters, 414
Slice to/from values, eyelid reaction, 192-195
smoke effects
All Purpose Emitter (APE), 573-578
bubbles, 574-578
creating for trains, 573-578
emitter velocity, 575-578
fireworks, 574-578
hose, 574-578
opacity channels, 577-578
shapes
cubes, 576-578
face mapping, 576-578
square planes, 576-578
shockwave, 574-578
trail, 574-578
weldsparks, 574-578
smoothing meshes (MeshSmooth tool), 382-383
Smudge Stick filter (Adobe Photoshop), 728-730
snakeyes.avi animation, 630
snow particles
binding space warps, 570-572
confetti
coloring, 569-572
creating, 567-572
emission speed, 568-572
overview, 567-572
tumble rates, 569-572
SoftImage
.DXF files, 63
computer game market, 31-33
features, 63
inverse kinematics, 63
product development, 28
product examples, 28

spline-based modeling, 63
versus 3D Studio MAX,
28-33
**solid mesh characters,
256-259**
placement of detail,
258-259
polygon meshes, 257
spline patches, building,
257-258
**Sony Pictures
Imageworks**
16-bit linear colorspace,
21-23
application development,
20-23
cartoon rendering, 21-23
Character Studio, 21-23
IK blending, 21-23
pre-visualization
methods, 20-23
stereoscopic titles, 21-23
title design, 20-23
sound
automatic lip synching,
464-466
bit depths, 744-745
cards
requirements, 745
Volume Control
(Windows NT), 753
digitizing, 742-743
DSP format, 747
FM (frequency modula-
tion) chips, 746
versus Wavetable
synthesis, 746-747
frame lengths, 467-470
loading, 463-464
MIDI format versus WAV
format, 745-746
oversampling spinner,
464-466
sampling rates, 743
third-party editors,
466-467
Track View, playing,
463-464
WAV files, playing, 755

source images
bluescreen spill, 58-60
procuring, 58-60
production quality, 58-60
scanning, 58-60
squeezed, 58-60
unsqueezed, 58-60
space warps
applying to wind tunnel
aerodynamics, 584-588
defined, 565-566
Displace modifier for
tires, 597-605
objects, deforming,
596-614
particle systems, binding,
570-572
Path Deform, 605-610
types
Bomb, 596
Displace, 596
Path Deform, 596
speakers
3D sound, 751
Surround Sound (Dolby
Pro-Logic), 751-752
see also PC speakers
special effects
glow plug-ins, 700-712
glow tools
Animated Glow,
704-705
Fractal Fury, 717-718
LensFX, 718-720
LensFX Glow, 709
Real Lens Glow, 708
RealLensFlare (RLF),
714-715
Super Glow, 707
Waveform Controller,
705-707
**speech, tongue anima-
tion, 458**
**spheres, lightning arcs,
creating, 203-204**
**spines, walking mechan-
ics, 294-295**
**splicing motions in
dissimilar bipeds,
369-370**

**spline patches (Surface
Tools)**
creating, 257-258,
374-375
Digimation Surface Tools,
257-258
versus polygon patches,
374-375
**splinehd.max anima-
tion, 441**
**Sponge filter (Adobe
Photoshop), 728-730**
**spray particles, creating
robotic welder (Deflec-
tor), 589-596**
**Spray plug-in, wind
tunnel aerodynamics,
582-588**
**squeezed source images,
58-60**
**Stamper plug-in, Video
Post filter, 735**
Starfield Generator
star settings, selecting,
736-738
Video Post filter, 736-738
**Starfilter module,
RealLensFlare (RLF),
714-715**
static muscles
creating (MetaReyes),
399-400
defined, 398-399
**step files (.STP), Biped
Utility, 368-369**
**stomach pump (Air Pump
project)**
animating, 179-184
keyframes, setting,
179-180
stones (curling game)
collide constraint,
637-642
fix orientation, 637-642
friction parameter,
637-642
storm.max animation, 552

storyboards
    interpretation of, 53-54
    visual effects, genesis to
        final product, 53-54
Strength slider (Displace
    modifier), 177-179
Strength spinners (Bones
    Pro), 390
stride length, calculating
    for walking, 308
strobing effect
    panning, 482-483
    preventing, 483
sub-object solidification
    creating, 645-650
    HyperMatter objects,
        643-650
    substance properties,
        setting, 645-647
Substance Editor
    (HyperMatter), 629-630
substance parameters
    HyperMatter properties,
        620-621
    setting
        rubber mouse, 652-653
        sub-object solidifica-
            tion, 645-647
    testing rubber mouse,
        651-661
Super Glow
    core glow, 707
    glow falloff, 707
Surface Tools
    facial handle objects,
        creating, 442-445
    features, 438
    modifiers
        Cross Section, 438
        Surface, 438
    radial faces, creating,
        438-441
Surround Sound (Dolby
    Pro-Logic) speakers
    adapting to PC usage,
        751-752
    matrix technology,
        751-752
    sound decoding process,
        751-752

swish pans, transitions,
    480-481
Symmetrical Tricks tool
    (Biped Utility), 334-335

T

target objects versus
    reference objects
    (MAXTrax), 233
targeting moonlight,
    544-547
tendons
    components
        attach points, 426-427
        base, 426-427
        cross sections, 426-427
    meshes, 428-429
    modifying, 432
    Physique
        attaching, 430
        creating, 429-430
    pinch, 430-432
    pull, 430-432
    radial distance, 430-432
    stretch, 430-432
terminating chains
    (inverse kinematics),
    277-278
tertiary foreground light,
    adding to candlelight,
    526-529
testing
    meshes (Physique), 420
    rubber mouse, substance
        parameters, 651-661
    skeletons, 281
text, glow effects, 710-711
The Yost Group, 3D
    Studio MAX develop-
    ment, 13-19
third-party sound editors
    (Magpie), 466-467
throwing dice
    (HyperMatter), 627-630
tick offsets, mirrored
    expressions, adding,
    324-325

ticker tape parade
    coloring confetti, 569-572
    particle systems, creating,
        567-572
Time Configuration
    dialog, 299
"timestepping"
    (HyperMatter), 620
timing
    forensic animation,
        accident re-creations,
        212-219
    particles (Sand Blaster),
        580-581
tires
    Displace space warp
        applying, 597-605
        mapping parameters,
            601-605
    ground surface, creating,
        601-605
tongues
    animating speech, 458
    bumps, 458
    textures, 458
toondog.max anima-
    tion, 466
torus, lightning arcs,
    creating, 203-204
Track View
    adding WAV files,
        755-757
    animating bipeds,
        348-354
    footsteps
        colored feet indicator,
            349-350
        duration, 349-350
        modifying, 349-350
    metronome, 757
    playing sound, 463-464
    walk cycle, duplicating,
        308-309
    waveforms, viewing,
        755-757
tracking shots
    camera moves, 483-484
    pedestrian gait speed, 484

traditional film cameras
elements
camera angle, 480-481
camera movement, 481-484
field of view, 476-478
transitions, 479-480
zoom lenses, 485
lens flares, 713
versus virtual cameras, 474-475
"Vertigo" effect, 485-487
trails
creating (MAXTrax), 232-249
smoke effects, 574-578
trains, smoke effects
All Purpose Emitter (APE), 573-578
creating, 573-578
transform animation
croach02.max file, 81-83
Exterminators animation project
cockroach run cycle, 83-86
script, 68-70
grouped objects, 79-86
transform type-in, 80-83
helper objects, 74-79
croach01.max file, 77-79
implementing expression controllers, 151-163
layering
grouped objects, 79-86
nested objects, 86-90
leg1.max file, 71-74
Linked XForm modifiers, 91-98
nested objects, 86-90
out-of-range curve types, 70-74
Pick Reference coordinate, 98-101
rotation transformation, leg1.max file, 72

twister.max animation, 151-164
XForm modifiers, 91-98
transforming Pick Reference coordinate axes, 98-101
transitions
dissolves, 479-480
effects
arranging, 694-696
FLC files, 694
masks, 696-697
exterior detail shot, 492-494
fades, 479-480
straight cuts, 479-480
swish pans, 480
wipes, 480
translating joints in bipeds, 333-334
transparency images (Simple Additive Compositor), 693
tree shadows
leaves, 548-551
moonlight, casting, 548-551
trials (forensic animation)
accuracy, 209-211
admissibility, 208-209
eyewitness testimony, 211-231
importance of details, 230-231
overview, 207-208
timing, 212-219
Trinity Enterprises web site, 688
troubleshooting meshes (Cross Section Editor), 425-426
tumble rates in particles, 569-572
turrets (WWII Air Combat animation)
gunfire, creating, 122-126
rotating, 120-121
tracking, 119-121

tv.max animation
CD-ROM, 555-557
flickers, animating, 560
twist parameters for skin (Physique), 414
twister.max animation, 151-164
expression controllers
position type, 152-164
rotation type, 152-164
position, 156-160
rotation, 152-154
teetering effect, 160-163
wobble, 160-163

U - V

Unit Setup command (View menu), 213
unsqueezed source images, 58-60
upper limit tracks, assigning, 130-137
UV tiling, footprints, 240-249

vehicles
creating (Wireframe Express), 232
forensic animation, 232
rotation, controlling, 165-167
skid marks, creating, 233-238
specifications, obtaining, 216-217
velocity constraint (HyperMatter)
dice momentum, 627-628
setting, 626-630
vertical bones, 266-267
vertices
animating (XForm modifiers), 94-95
assignments
blue, 420
bones, 389-392
green, 420
Physique, 409
red, 420

excluding bones, 391-392
modifying, 422-424
reassigning meshes,
  420-427
selecting (Influence
  Editor), 391
"Vertigo" effect
creating, 485-487
defined, 485-487
obtaining upgrade,
  485-487
vertigo.avi animation, 487
Video Post
animating depth of field,
  514-516
animations
  masks, 696-697
  transition effects,
    694-696
camera setup, 508
editing animations,
  694-697
filters
  Negative plug-in, 734
  Outline plug-in, 735
  Stamper plug-in, 735
  Starfield Generator
    plug-in, 736-738
image compositing, 666
rendering candlelight,
  532-535
special effects
  glow plug-ins, 700-701
  glows, 700-701
viewing
images, composited,
  676-679
Track View waveform,
  755-757
virtual cameras
perfect steadiness
  default, 510
unlimited depth of fields,
  513-516
versus traditional film
  cameras, 474-475

Virtual Frame Buffer
defined, 670-671
images (RGBA channels),
  670-671
virtual memory, 667
visual effects
3D Studio MAX, motion
  pictures, 33-38
Blur Studio, 33-36
camera movement, 61
concept to final product,
  53-54
Digital Phenomena, 36-38
genesis to final product,
  53-54
job completion, esti-
  mating, 54-56
production scheduling
  charts, 60
Pyros Pictures, 39-41
**Visualize button (Influ-
  ence Editor), 391**
**Volume Control, sound
  cards (Windows NT), 753**
**Volume Select modifier,
  glow effect, 711-712**
volumetric light
color settings, 557
creating, 555-557
defined, 555
elements, 555
flickers, animating, 560
fog color settings, 557
shadow parameters, 557
spotlight parameters, 557
**Vortex space warp, All
  Purpose Emitter (APE),
  573-578**

W

walk cycles
creating, 298-301
duplicating (Track View),
  308-309
four-legged, animating,
  315-316

ground movement,
  309-310
six-legged creatures, body
  movement, 317-318
stride length, calcula-
  ting, 308
tick offsets in six-legged
  creatures, 325
**walkcycle.max anima-
  tion, 307**
walking
animated cycles, creating,
  298-301
arm movement, 306-307
cycles, creating, 297-298
defined, 290
four-legged creatures
  analysis, 313-315
  overview, 310-311
mechanics, 290-298
  arms, 295
  body posture, 295-296
  emotion, 295-296
  feet, 290-292
  head, 295
  hips, 294-295
  legs, 290-292
  shoulders, 294-295
  spine, 294-295
six-legged creatures,
  animating, 316-317
speeds, 213-214
**walktrax.avi anima-
  tion, 248**
**Watercolor filter (Adobe
  Photoshop), 728-730**
WAV files
playing, 755
RAM consumption, 755
Track View, adding,
  755-757
**Waveform Controller,
  705-707**
waveforms
sound digitization,
  742-743
viewing Track View,
  755-757

Wavefront
features, 63
quad style polygonal
modeling, 63
Wavetable synthesis
processing overview,
746-747
versus FM (frequency
modulation) chips,
746-747
**wbootscomic.avi anima-
tion, 191**
web sites
3D Café, 707
Kinetix, 485
New Riders Publish-
ing, 86
Photron, 690
Trinity Enterprises, 688
**weighted channel
morphing, 449**
weld effects
emitter settings, 589-591
Gravity space warp,
applying, 594-596
particles
birth rate, 590-596
bouncing, 593-596
collisions, 592-593
smoke effects, 574-578
spray particles, creating,
589-596
**Westwood Studios,
computer games devel-
opment, 27**
**whirl.max anima-
tion, 164**
spins, animating, 167-168
vehicle rotation, controlling, 165-167
**wind tunnel aero-
dynamics**
creating, 582-588
particle emission, setting,
582-588
space warp effect,
applying, 584-588

window effects
moonlight, 544-547
light project options,
546-547
rain storm, 552-554
Windows NT
sound cards (Volume
Control), 753
Sound Mixer controls
CD audio, 753-755
line-in, 753-755
recording, 753-755
synthesizer, 753-755
volume, 753-755
Wave output, 753-755
wipe transitions, 480
**Wireframe Express,
vehicle models, 232**
wobble effect
Magnetic Boots project,
198-204
twister.max animation,
160-163
**wpumped.avi anima-
tion, 182**
**WWII Air Combat anima-
tion**
background clouds,
creating, 110-111
bomber wobble, 116-118
Euler XYZ Rotation
controllers, 115-118
Expression controller,
126-146
fighter attack, animating,
112-114
gunfire effects, 122-126
List controller, 122-126
Look-At controller,
119-121
Noise controller, 122-126
Path controller, 110-115
relative velocities,
114-115
turrets
rotating, 120-121
tracking, 119-121

X - Y - Z

XForm modifiers
croach06.max file, 92-93
croach07.max file, 94-95
squash animation, 91-93
stretch animation, 91-93
vertices, animating, 94-95
**xformhd.max anima-
tion, 442**

**Yost Group (The), 3D
Studio MAX develop-
ment**
future goals, 19
team members, 13-19

zoom lenses, 485